Introduction to

# CRIMINAL JUSTICE

*Second Edition*

# Introduction to

# CRIMINAL JUSTICE

*Second Edition*

**Joseph J. Senna, M.S.W.,J.D.**
*College of Criminal Justice*
*Northeastern University*

**Larry J. Siegel, Ph.D.**
*Department of Criminal Justice*
*University of Nebraska—Omaha*

## CRIMINAL JUSTICE SERIES

**West Publishing Company**
St. Paul    New York    Los Angeles    San Francisco

**Cover photos**

Photos courtesy Bob Gaylord.

**Photo credits**

2 Bob Gaylord. *36* Bob Gaylord. *110* Bob Gaylord. *182* Bob Gaylord. *222* Bob Gaylord. *264* Courtesy of Stock Boston, photographer Cary Wolinsky. *294* Bob Gaylord. *326* Bob Gaylord. *354* Courtesy of Jeroboam, Inc., photographer Peeter Vilms. *378* Bob Gaylord. *410* Bob Gaylord. *444* Ray Lustig. *476* Bob Gaylord. *504* Bob Gaylord. *532* Bob Gaylord. *562* Bob Gaylord. *588* Bill Powers, *Corrections Magazine*.

COPYRIGHT © 1981 By WEST PUBLISHING CO.
50 West Kellogg Boulevard
P.O. Box 3526
St. Paul, MN 55165

Library of Congress Cataloging in Publication Data

Senna, Joseph J.
  Introduction to criminal justice.

  (Criminal justice series)
  Bibliography: p.
  Includes index.
  1. Criminal justice, Administration of—United
States.  2. Criminal law—United
States.  3. Criminal procedure—United
States.  I. Siegel, Larry J., joint
author.  II. Title.  III. Series.

KF9223.S4      1981      345.73'05      80-27843

ISBN 0-8299-0409-3

2nd Reprint—1981

# Contents

# Preface

This book is about the American criminal justice system. It deals with the crime problem and with the agencies that try to prevent and control it. The book encompasses legal issues, sociological theories, legislative policy, and police, court, and correctional practices. Its emphasis is on the study of the contemporary criminal justice system.

As stated in the first edition, the purpose of this text is to set forth as clearly as possible the major components of the criminal justice system. It is intended primarily for use by junior college, community college, and university levels during their introductory study of criminal justice, criminology, or criminal law. Graduate level students may also find the text useful to them where the subject of criminal justice is a smaller portion of a more extensive course, or where they have had no contact with criminal justice as a field of study.

Interest in learning about criminal justice continues at an unprecedented level, particularly in the academic community, although there has been a leveling off in the growth of new programs and additional students in recent years. As a result, the authors believe, after a decade of teaching "Introduction to Criminal Justice" at the undergraduate and graduate level at Northeastern University in Boston, that students would profit greatly by reading a general comprehensive text about criminal justice before undertaking an in-depth analysis. This book is intended to serve that purpose. It meets the critical need for a comprehensive, well-organized, and objective analysis of the basic elements of the criminal justice process.

Since the publication of the first edition three years ago, numerous changes have occurred in the criminal justice field. Not only has crime and delinquency increased, but its prevention, deterrence, and control at all levels of society—from street violence to corporate crime—remain unreachable goals. The Carter administration has reorganized the Law Enforcement Assistance Administration and cut back on crime control funding. There is a growing shift from the rights of individuals, and concepts of treatment and rehabilitation, to punishment and the imposition of tough criminal penalties.

The second edition takes into account these changing philosophical approaches to crime control, while updating all aspects of the entire criminal justice system with new case decisions, current legislation, and important agency programs. The basic outline of the first edition remains the same but some significant adjustments have been made.

Part One details the framework of crime in America by examining the crime problem and criminal law, and presents an overview of the field of criminology. Included here is new material regarding victimization surveys, crime causation theories, including socio-biological and crime control concepts, and a greatly expanded section on criminal law, including the substantive crimes and criminal defenses.

Part Two describes the overview of the Criminal justice process, beginning with the police functions of arrest and investigation, and concluding with the correctional decision of release. A more detailed discussion of the relationship between criminal justice as a system and process is included here. In addition, Chapter Six, "Models of Justice" has been deleted in order to add additional information on police. This part also has a chapter on constitutional issues in criminal justice, with much updating of recent Supreme Court decisions, and new material on how a case gets to the United States Supreme Court.

In Part Three, the area of law enforcement and policing is discussed. A new chapter entitled "Issues in Policing" has been added to this part. It includes information on female and minority police officers, productivity in police work, police violence, and stress as a new dimension of police work. This part contains extensive amounts of information on the police in the criminal justice system as well as many references for the student who wishes to pursue this subject in greater detail.

Part Four is devoted to early court processing and covers such topics as the prosecution and defense attorney, pre-trial release and bail, the jury system, and diversion. New material has been added with regard to the role of the prosecutor and police officer, as well as the development of a major listing of United States Supreme Court Cases granting right to counsel throughout the pre-trial, trial, and post-trial stages of the criminal justice process. In addition, there is an expanded analysis of the concept of plea bargaining, using the latest supreme court decisions in that area, and a discussion of reform in the plea bargaining system.

Part Five is devoted to the court system, jury trial, sentencing, and probation. Chapter 13 on sentencing has been expanded, and contains new material on sentencing structures, particularly presumptive sentences. Included is a chart listing all of the various types of sentencing approaches and their characteristics. Also, there is an expanded analysis of capital punishment, and an update of United States Supreme Court decisions dealing with that problem. Lastly, this part incorporates the latest information on probation programs and concepts, with particular emphasis on recent empirical research on the effectiveness of probation in criminal justice.

Part Six focuses on post-trial procedures—corrections, parole, and prisoners rights. Current information on jails, the concept of community corrections, and restitution programs has been included here. In addition, there is a new section on prison violence, and new case decisions on prisoners rights. Finally, Part Seven, which explores juvenile justice in detail, reflects the changes underway in that system. Information about the juvenile justice standards project jointly sponsored by the Institute for Judicial Administration and the American Bar Association is used as an important source for changes in the juvenile justice system.

In addition to updating and improving the overall quality and quantity of the substantive material, some new features have been added to this addition which highlight the substantive practices in the criminal justice system. There is an increase in the number of illustrations and pictures used throughout the text which depict the criminal justice practice by police officers, prosecutors, judges, probation officers, and offenders. Each chapter is a self-contained integrated unit which has a chapter outline, key words, summary, questions for discussion, and application. The application in particular at the end of each chapter is designed to give the student an example of the programs and kinds of day to day activities that exist in the criminal justice system. This new edition also contains a current bibliography on criminal justice which allows the reader the opportunity to become familiar with additional learning resources. Both a new instructors manual by Gayle Shuman, Arizona State University, and student study guide by Ray Roberg, San Jose State University, have also been prepared.

The authors hope that this second edition will make teaching and learning about the criminal justice process more effective and enjoyable from the point of view of both students and teachers. It should continue to be particularly valuable to those students on an undergraduate and graduate level who may be coming into contact with the field of criminal justice for the first time. To further these goals, the innovative features of the first edition remain. First, both practical and conceptual material exists throughout the entire text; second, outside sources are used to supplement the authors writing; third, unique chapters on prisoners rights, juvenile justice, criminal law, and understanding crime and its causation have been included in this text. Hopefully these features, in addition to the wealth of material on the criminal justice process, will substantially contribute to the student's overall understanding of this discipline.

Special acknowledgement is in order for a number of people who helped in the construction of this text, most notably William Murphy for the glossary of terms, and Michael O'Neil, Charles MacLean and Shari Wittenberg. Also helping were Julie VanCamp, Susan Pease, Linda Bucci, Mike Myers, Steven Lagoy, and George Hayden. Special appreciation must go also to our typists, Patty Christo, Peggy Libby, and Shirley Davis.

We would like to thank the following colleagues who critiqued the first edition of Introduction to Criminal Justice. Their pertinent suggestions were most valuable in our development of this second edition: William Ashlen, Robert Culbertson, Earl Hamb, Donald Harrelson, William Hobbs, Michael Israel, Thomas McAninch, Robert Page, Rudy Sanfillippo, Gayle Shuman, Mark Tezak, and Howard Timm.

We are also indebted to the following sources for allowing us to reprint material: American Bar Association; National Institute of Mental Health; American Judicature Society; National Advisory Commission on Criminal

Justice Standards and Goals; Federal Probation; National Council on Crime and Delinquency; American Law Institute; President's Commission on Law Enforcement and the Administration of Justice; Scientific Methods Inc.; Warren, Gorham and Lamont Publishing; New England Law Review; Law Enforcement Assistance Administration; Federal Bureau of Investigation; Jail Administration Digest; Houghton-Mifflin Publishing Company; Gulf Publishing Company; American Bar Foundation; and Time Magazine.

The authors also wish to extend their appreciation to the staff of West Publishing who have been most helpful during this revision.

Last, but certainly not least, we wish to give our special thanks to our wives, Janet and Terry, for their patience and loyalty throughout the completion of this project.

Joseph J. Senna
Boston, Mass.


Larry J. Siegel
Omaha, Nebraska

# PART ONE

## Introduction

# Crime in America

CHAPTER OUTLINE

KEY TERMS

CRIME, A
NATIONAL
PHENOMENON

Crime has become a familiar and disturbing fact of life in America. The public has been confronted with daily newspaper stories, magazine articles, television series, and films depicting brutal murders, kidnapings, assault and terrorism. One commentator has frankly declared that "American justice is in turmoil,"[1] and his view is widely shared by government experts, members of the university community, and the general public alike. It is a sad but revealing commentary on the level of criminal activity in America when the National Advisory Commission on Criminal Justice Standards and Goals finds it necessary to promise citizens that *sometime in the near future* crime control efforts may reach a level of success whereby:

A couple can walk in the evening in their neighborhood without fear of assault and robbery.

A family can go away for the weekend without fear of returning to a home ransacked by burglars.

A woman can take a night job without fear of being raped on her way to or from work.

Every citizen can live without fear of being brutalized by unknown assailants.[2]

Fear of crime has been accentuated by a concomitant lack of faith in the government—especially in those agencies responsible for crime control. Almost daily, there are revelations of corruption and inefficiency in "high" places—Watergate, "Abscam," and the Burt Lance Case. Conditions like these present the average citizen with a pattern of crime and criminality that seems to pervade every aspect of American life and that so far appears immune to the law enforcement efforts designed to control it. Thus, one of the basic goals of our society is to develop an understanding of the causes of crime and to identify and implement plans for its elimination.

As the third century of our nation's existence begins, solutions to these goals seem a distant dream. Crime remains sadly commonplace and law enforcement officials seem incapable of dealing effectively with it. Yet America is now on the verge of entering into a new and innovative phase in the struggle against law violation: convicted offenders are no longer automatically treated as social degenerates or as dangerous "born criminals"; courts have attempted to institutionally protect the legal rights of citizens accused of crimes; and federal, state and local governments have made dramatic efforts to improve crime control by allocating funds for management and training in the criminal justice system.

In addition to these efforts, the university community has become increasingly involved in the study of crime. Academic programs in *Criminology*—the study of crime, its causes and control—and *Criminal Justice*—the study of how the American system of justice functions—have been developed. Just beginning to graduate from these programs is a new breed of better educated law enforcement officials who have skills at their disposal previously absent in the criminal justice system. The long-term effects of higher education in the field of criminal justice can only be guessed at, but at the least a more humane, intelligent, and flexible system of justice, should result.

While it is a distinct possibility that the justice system will change and improve, America is currently faced with a dilemma of staggering proportions. The police, court, and correctional systems are working under a terrific burden—dockets and treatment facilities are already filled to the breaking point. If the crime problem is actually met head-on, can our limited resources accommodate the potential influx of offenders? Wouldn't an increased and more efficient criminal justice system actually identify a greater number of criminal offenders, needing and expecting treatment, than society is aware exists today? The American citizen, though generally critical of the current state of affairs in the criminal justice system, may have second thoughts concerning its improvement if a substantial increase in the tax rate is needed to support it. Furthermore, some experts even question on theoretical grounds the efficacy of expanding and improving the criminal justice system. These scholars believe that a more efficient and effective system might actually work for its own detriment. They argue that by creating a new and increased supply of labeled offenders, the system would actually produce more career criminals "locked into" crime. There can be little hope that current ideas and programs can reconcile these conflicts and, at the same time, reassure (1) the citizen who lives in fear of crime, (2) the police officers uncertain of their current role and angry over the supposed advantages given to criminals, and (3) the victims of crime reluctant to step forward because they feel that nothing can be done.

Crime is, and will remain, a complex problem. Its control and elimination cannot be brought about without much sacrifice and understanding on the part of citizens. However, before we can even begin to effectively engage in crime control, much new knowledge must be accumulated. We are not even sure how much crime exists, although recent victimization surveys indicate that more crime occurs than is reported to police. In addition, the meaning of the term *crime* can vary. In one legal jurisdiction, for example, an act (e.g., possession of marijuana) may be punished by years in prison, while in another contiguous state the same act may be treated as a minor violation, punishable by a small fine or less. The debate over who should be punished, how and where punishment should be administered, and who is really at fault when a criminal act is committed is far from over. Crime has become a political issue, inspiring from time to time the slogan "law and order." Abraham Blumberg suggests that "law and order has become an ideology which serves to distort and disrupt relations between the middle class and the bottom, separating them into hostile enclaves which are in continuous confrontation."[3]

Whether it is a legal, social, political, or human issue—or a little bit of each—crime control continues to be a national concern and problem. Much to the chagrin and displeasure of the general public, crime is only efficiently handled by fictional characters on TV or in the movies; real solutions to the crime problem must remain a future aspiration of the American public.

## A DEFINITION OF CRIME

The average citizen who spends time thinking about crime is likely to conjure up familiar images such as a bank robbery, auto theft, assault, or burglary. But the term "crime" actually encompasses many more types of behavior than are commonly associated with it and can involve relatively simple, individual acts, complex group efforts, or even multinational plots. Crime can be as sophisticated as a scheme involving international payoffs to politicians, as secretive as a conspiracy to overthrow the existing governmental structure, or as seemingly innocent, simple, and commonplace as placing a 25¢ bet in the local football pool. For this reason, it has proven frustrating for students of criminal behavior patterns to adequately define what is actually meant by crime and to adequately identify the criminal.

A number of attempts have been made to create a concise, yet thorough and encompassing definition of crime. The eminent criminologists Edwin Sutherland and Donald Cressey have taken the popular stance of linking crime with the *criminal law*. They state:

> Criminal behavior is behavior in violation of the criminal law . . . it is not a crime unless it is prohibited by the criminal law . . . (which) is defined conventionally as a body of specific rules regarding human conduct which have been promulgated by political authority, which apply uniformly to all members of the classes to which the rules refer, and which are enforced by punishment administered by the state.[4]

This approach to crime implies that its definition is actually a function of the beliefs, morality, and direction of the existing legal power structure. Note also Sutherland and Cressey's statement that the definition of crime is applied "uniformly to all members of the classes to which the rules refer. . . ." In a statement such as this, the authors reveal their faith in the concept of an ideal legal system and its presumed capability to deal adequately with all classes and types of people. This view, however, may be received somewhat skeptically by critics who perceive class, racial, and sex bias in the way in which laws are upheld and managed. Former Attorney General Ramsey Clark has commented:

> Powerless people live by their wits. For them, rules of society are alien in spirit and in fact. The law is irrelevant except when it comes after them or their loved ones. The law and government pretend to give men rights. . . . The law protects citizens against assault and reveres the sanctity of property, but it works for the wealthy, not the poor.[5]

Of course, such sentiments mitigate the power—and the authority—of the legal code to define crime. Is it not conceivable that those who retain power to legally control the definition of crime might also use their control to legalize and justify their own behavior under the auspices of "good business sense," "justified campaign contribution," or "protective custody of dissidents," while outlawing behaviors which members of their economic class have little or no interest in engaging in (e.g., welfare fraud and street crime)? However, this distinction has not deterred experts from continuing to link crime with the existing criminal law. Yet another example of this link is found in Stephen Schafer and Richard Knudten's crime paradigm:

[A] crime is a conduct or an action that is defined and codified in law as a crime . . . The formal legal definition of crime upholds the principle that no crime exists unless it is so defined by the law (nullum crimen sine lege) . . . Crime, then, as defined in criminal law, involves disturbance of some legally protected interest. The disturbance of any interest not under the protection of criminal law by definition cannot be a crime.[6]

Recently, attention has been paid to the economic and political nature of the process by which acts are defined as crime and individuals as criminals. So-called radical criminologists have linked the definition of crime to the beliefs of the existing legal power structure, suggesting that an underlying feature of law is its maintenance of the status quo—letting those already in power remain there. Even such renowned criminologists as Richard Korn and Lloyd McCorkle have defined crime in this manner:

[A] person is assigned the status of a criminal when he is adjudged to be punishable by the authorities in continuous political control over the territory in which he is . . . a crime is an act or omission ascribed to a person when he is punished by the authorities in continuous political control over the territory in which he is.[7]

Notice how Korn and McCorkle shift the focus of their definition of crime away from elements of immoral behavior and law violation and into the realm of political power; they do not even insist that a law must be broken in order for a crime to occur. Thus, according to Korn and McCorkle, the criminal law depends on its function to define crime on the will of "authorities in continuous political control."

These sentiments are shared by Richard Quinney in his formulation of crime.[8] Even more radical in his views than Korn and McCorkle, Quinney has proposed a number of propositions expressing the sociopolitical influence which he believes functionally defines the social reality of crime. Three of Quinney's key propositions are:

1. Crime is a definition of human conduct that is created by authorized agents in a politically organized society.
2. Criminal definitions describe behaviors that conflict with the interests of segments of society that have the power to shape public policy.
3. Criminal definitions are applied by the segments of society that have the power to shape the enforcement and administration of criminal law.[9]

A critical element of Quinney's theory is that crime is neither naturally defined, nor is it a function of the moral values held by the common citizen. Crime is *created* by ruling authorities, it is *not* "inherent in behavior, but is a judgement made by some about the actions and characteristics of others."[10] The ability to confer criminal status is a privilege enjoyed by the propertied classes and suffered by the nonpropertied. The law, according to Quinney, is a function of political power which is held as a weapon over the heads of those unable or unwilling to enjoy or possess its resources.

Despite the obviously wide theoretical gulf separating these representative definitions of crime and criminality, they do in fact share some common ground: Crime is portrayed by each as a *violation of existing societal rules of behavior as interpreted and expressed by a criminal code which has been created by those holding political power, and those individuals who stand in violation of these rules are thereby subject to sanctions by state authority.* Thus, the law exists, regardless of the forces shaping and creating it, and violation of it becomes the subject of state interest. Yet, even if we accept this legally based definition of crime as a viable working model, it is important that we neither forget the constructs of radical criminologists nor ignore the fact that the criminal law upon which the definition of crime is based may have an *artificial political* basis. Thus, crime as it now exists is a political, social, and economic function of modern life.

## Crime and the Criminal
## Criminal Law

Our working definition of crime links criminal behavior to law violation and also to the beliefs and actions of political power groups. Later this book discusses the nature, properties, and extent of the criminal law. For now, it will suffice to say that the criminal law is a legal code which represents (in part) the influence of a number of sources—including traditionally proscribed types of behavior (common law), public opinion, the will and power of the state and its representatives, and the influence of pressure groups or lobbies, (e.g., pro- or anti-abortion lobbies), private enterprise, and the clergy—each attempting to control public behavior through control of the law. Most of the time, the criminal law is in accord with the attitudes of the majority of citizens. On other occasions, changes in lifestyles and attitudes are so rapid that the law seems out of step with the public's behavior. When a situation like this arises, change may be literally forced upon the legal system. For example, the near epidemic number of otherwise lawabiding youths who were arrested on drug charges has led some states to *decriminalize* minor drug violations, such as possession of small amounts of marijuana, which previously were serious offenses. Thus, a structural definition of crime with the criminal law as its source is liable to have different meanings, interpretations, and impacts at different times and in different jurisdictions. The flexibility built into the nature of the law does seem to move the concept of crime away from configurations of immorality and deviance and into the realm of public opinion and political policy. The status quo, the inability to quickly change legal definitions, and the maintenance of personal power all work to control the substance of the legal code and thus determine what constitutes crime and criminality. In this sense, crime is a constantly changing commodity, and behavior that is considered a breach of public morality in one generation may be found acceptable and commonplace in another.

HOW CRIME IS
MEASURED

Crime and its consequences are among the social problems most often discussed in the United States today. It is therefore ironic that no one is sure how much crime actually occurs, where and when it takes place, nor how many criminals and victims exist nationwide. The public is likely to get its information about these matters secondhand (e.g., from newspaper and television news); these sources often dwell on the sensational and lurid and are therefore inadequate for the serious student of criminal justice. The day-in, day-out varieties of criminal behavior well known to police and court personnel are usually hidden from the public view. Then how is it possible to discover the truth about the extent of the crime problem? Some tentative answers to these questions may be found in the statistical data currently being compiled by state and federal agencies concerned with accurately measuring criminal activity. These sources of statistics are by no means perfect; in fact, they have become a popular target for criticism by law enforcement experts who have raised questions about their validity. Despite the astuteness of these critics, official crime statistics do provide a valuable tool with which to estimate such information as the amount and type of current criminal behavior, the number of annual arrests, the number of incarcerated felons, and so on. Some of the major sources of crime statistics will now be discussed in this section.

## The Uniform Crime Reports (UCR)

Prepared by the Federal Bureau of Investigation (FBI), the *Uniform Crime Reports* (UCR) are the best known and most widely cited source of criminal statistics. The FBI receives and compiles reports from over 10,000 police departments serving a majority of the population of the United States. Its major unit of analysis is the *Index Crimes:* murder and nonnegligent manslaughter, forcible rape, robbery, aggravated assault, burglary, larceny, and auto theft.* The FBI tallies and annually publishes the number of reported offenses by city, county, standard metropolitan statistical area (SMSA) and by geographical divisions of the United States. In addition to these statistics, the UCR provides information on the number and characteristics of individuals who have been arrested and the number and location of assaults on police officers.

In the following sections we will review the methods the FBI uses to prepare the UCR, discuss some recent trends in crime statistics, and review criticism of the UCR.

---

* Arson will be included in the UCR starting in 1980.

**Reporting Procedures**
**Used in the Uniform**
**Crime Reports***

On a monthly basis, law enforcement agencies report the number of Crime Index offenses (murder and nonnegligent manslaughter, forcible rape, robbery, aggravated assault, burglary, larceny-theft, and motor vehicle theft) that become known to them. A count of these crimes, which are also known as Part I offenses, is taken from records of all complaints of crime received by law enforcement agencies from victims, officers who discovered the infractions, or other sources.

Whenever complaints of crime are determined through investigation to be unfounded or false, they are eliminated from the actual count. The number of "actual offenses known" in Part I is reported to the FBI whether anyone is arrested for the crime, the stolen property is recovered, or prosecution is undertaken. In addition, each month law enforcement agencies report the total number of these crimes cleared. Crimes are "cleared" in one of two ways: (1) at least one person is arrested, charged, and turned over to the court for prosecution; or (2) by exceptional means when some element beyond police control precludes the physical arrest of an offender. Data on the number of clearances involving only the arrest of offenders under the age of 18, the value of property stolen and recovered in connection with Part I offenses, and detailed information pertaining to criminal homicide are also reported.

Arrest data, which include the age, sex, and race of persons arrested, are reported monthly for both Part I and Part II offenses, by crime category. Part II offenses, while excluding traffic violations, include all other crimes except those classified as Part I.

Various data on law enforcement officers assaulted or killed are collected on a monthly basis. Other law enforcement employee data, specifically the number of full-time sworn officers and other personnel, are reported as of October 31 of each calendar year.

## TYPES AND TRENDS IN REPORTED CRIME

The United States is in the midst of a serious crime wave, and law enforcement agencies seem unable to alleviate the crime problem. Government agencies appear proud to announce success in their fight against crime, not only when there is a reduction in the crime rate but even when a relatively slight *increase* is recorded—a condition hardly reassuring to the average citizen.

Crime waves are not new to this century. Studies have indicated that a gradual increase in the crime rate, especially in the area of violent crime, occurred from 1830 to 1860. Following the Civil War, this rate increased significantly for about fifteen years. Then, from 1880 up to the time of the first World War, with the possible exception of the years immediately preceding and following the war, there was an actual decrease in the number of reported crimes. After a period of readjustment, the crime rate

---

* Source: Uniform Crime Reports, *Crime in the United States, 1978*, p. 2.

steadily declined until the depression (about 1930), whereupon another general increase or crime wave was recorded. Crime rates increased gradually following the 1930s until the 1960s, when the growth rate became much greater. The homicide rate, which had actually declined from the 1930s to the 1960s, also began a period of sharp increase.[11]

The upswing in crime seems to have continued through the end of the 1970s. The 1979 statistics indicate that reported crime rose 8% over the 1978 figure (11,141,434) to a total of more than 12 million serious criminal acts. Moreover, the FBI reported that the increase was shared by all city and county population groups, areas, and regions in the United States. This increase was the largest since an 18% increase in 1974 and a 10% increase in 1975. This result caused FBI director William Webster to exclaim:

The 1979 increase clearly indicates that crime remains one of our Nation's most serious problems . . . I am, of course, troubled by this trend. Every American should be troubled. Crime, after all, diminishes freedom; it casts an intimidating shadow across our free society. All of us—not just law enforcement—all of us should do what we can to reduce crime.[12]

These sentiments are borne out by the "Crime Clock," illustrated in Figure 1.1.

FIGURE 1.1

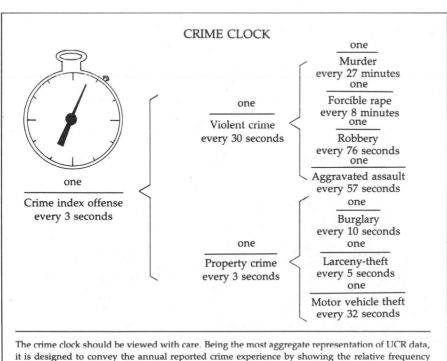

The crime clock should be viewed with care. Being the most aggregate representation of UCR data, it is designed to convey the annual reported crime experience by showing the relative frequency of occurrence of the Index Offenses. This mode of display should not be taken to imply a regularity in the commission of the Part I Offenses: rather it represents the annual ratio of crime to fixed time intervals.
*Source: UCR, Crime in The United States, 1978, p. 6.

The greatest increase for 1979 was experienced in cities outside metropolitan areas, where crime climbed 11%. Cities over 50,000 population registered an 8% upturn, while in both the suburban and rural areas, crime increased 9%.

Violent crimes as a group rose 11% over the 1978 total of 1,061,826. Forcible rape jumped 12% over the 1978 figure of 67,131, as did robbery (up 12%) over the 1978 figure, 417,036. Murder and aggravated assault each jumped 9% over the 1978 figure of 19,555 and 558,102, respectively. The only decrease in crime indicated in the 1979 statistics was a 2% decrease in murder in rural areas.

Property crime rose 8% over the 1978 total of 10,079,588. This included increases of 10% for motor vehicle theft (the 1978 figure was 991,611), 9% for larceny theft (5,983,401 in 1978), and 6% for burglary (3,104,496 in 1978).

Collectively, the property crimes rose 8% with increases of 10% for motor vehicle theft, 9% for larceny-theft, and 6% for burglary.

Geographically, all regions showed increases over 1978 figures. The South, the most populous region, experienced the greatest increase—10%. The Northeast, West, and North Central regions followed with rises of 9, 8, and 7%, respectively.

CRIME
PATTERNS

The individual crimes included in the UCR are discussed in some detail below.*

### Burglary

> DEFINITION
>
> The Uniform Crime Reporting Program defines burglary as the unlawful entry of a structure to commit a felony or theft. The use of force to gain entry is not required to classify an offense as burglary. Burglary in this Program is categorized into three subclassifications: forcible entry, unlawful entry where no force is used, and attempted forcible entry.

In 1979, burglary struck approximately 1,500 citizens in every 100,000. Most occur in private residences (65%) and the remainder (35%) in business establishments and other areas. In 1978, 73 percent involved forcible entry, 19% had no force, and 8% were attempts.

Burglary represents a substantial financial loss. In 1978, burglary victims suffered losses of 1.4 billion dollars, an average of $526 each. When this figure is added to the cost of police burglary units, insurance premium

---

*Figures used in this section are estimates based on reported 1979 percentage increases over 1978 figures. Final 1979 data was not available at the time of this writing.

increases due to theft losses, and costs of repairing damaged homes and other structures, the total cost of burglary is immense.

About 16% of the total burglary offenses were cleared by arrest. Persons under 25 years of age accounted for 84% of all arrests for burglary and 52% of those arrested were under 18. Of those arrested for burglary, 6% were female and 29 percent were black.

**Robbery**

---

DEFINITION

---

Robbery is the taking or attempting to take anything of value from the care, custody, or control of a person or persons by force or threat of force or violence and/or by putting the victim in fear.

---

Robbery is a frightening crime, one in which the victim's life may depend on the point of a knife or the touch of a trigger. This is borne out by the latest FBI figures showing that 41% of all reported robberies were committed using firearms, 37% using "strong-arm tactics," 13% with knives, and 1% by other means.

Latest government figures indicate that the average loss per robbery was $434 or a total of 181 million dollars. Law enforcement agents were successful in clearing 26% of robberies. Similar to burglary, robbery was a youth-oriented crime—56% of people arrested were under 21. Females made up 4% of those arrested and blacks, 59%.

John Conklin, an expert on robbery, has identified four distinct patterns which the crime of robbery takes:

1. *The Professional*—These robbers manifest a long-term commitment to crime as a source of their livelihood. They plan activities well in advance and often work with accomplices to promote their thefts.
2. *The Opportunist*—Lower-class youth who seize random opportunities to add to their cash supply. Their favorite victims are the elderly, especially women whose purses can be snatched, drunks, cab drivers and people walking alone at night. Often the opportunist is part of a teenage gang.
3. *The Addict Robber*—Steals solely to support the drug habit. The addict may turn to robbery as a last resort, often when they are suppressed in an act of simple theft.
4. *The Alcoholic Robber*—Alcoholic robbers do not rob for money, nor do they plan their crimes in advance. They get involved in crime usually as an afterthought, after their intoxication has led them to an ill-planned assault on an unsuspecting victim.[13]

Robbery is a crime often associated with teenage violence. It is rarely a crime involving skill or professionalism, but instead is a brutal attack by a street tough on a weak victim. Sometimes robbery is used as a means for a gang boy to prove his toughness or manhood. Consider this statement by a former teenage gang member:

I wanted everybody to know that I was one of the baddest guys that walked the street, so I walked around with my zip gun exposed or my switchblade knife in my hand. Then I started hanging out with a bunch and we wanted to be *something*, because everybody else, they weren't really doing nothing, they really wasn't makin' that money. So we started mugging.[14]

Fear of armed robbery and mugging has helped to change the patterns of American life. Suburban shopping centers have replaced inner-city stores in an effort to avoid the criminal element in urban areas, while parks and other city centers are no longer populated at night. If the trend to abandon the cities because of the fear of crime is to be halted, the stated objective of the National Advisory Commission on Criminal Justice Standards and Goals of reducing the robbery rate by 50% must be met or exceeded.

## Forcible Rape

---

### DEFINITION

Forcible rape, as defined in the Program, is the carnal knowledge of a female forcibly and against her will. Assaults or attempts to commit forcible rape by force or threat of force are also included; however, statutory rape (without force) and other sex offenses are not included in this category.

---

Reported acts of rape in the United States have steadily increased in number since the 1930s, with substantial increase in the 1960s.

During 1978 there was an estimated total of 67,131 forcible rapes, an increase of 6% over the preceding year; in 1979 the increase was another 12%, with a 30% total rate increase from 1974 to 1979. The FBI recognizes that rape is one of the most underreported of all crimes because of victims' fears of their assailants and their embarrassment over the incident. This may be because forcible rape is an extremely controversial, humiliating act, one in which the female victim is sometimes made to suffer much pain and embarrassment long after the actual crime is over. Since force and intent must be proven before an act of sexual relations is considered a rape, one common courtroom defense for a rapist is to claim that he was encouraged or even seduced by his victim(s). In many rape cases the female victim may find that she herself is on trial, and her character and behavior may be subject to humiliating scrutiny. A defense counsel's attempts to discredit the victim's testimony during the trial may actually be a more traumatic experience than the crime itself.

In a similar vein, there exists the stereotypical myth that women enjoy being dominated sexually and this well-enshrined belief accounts for the relatively high rape rate. Society's ambivalent attitudes toward the role of the victim in the crime of rape may also contribute to a victim's personal feelings of self-blame, fear, and shame. One middle-aged victim put it this way:

I'm convinced that talking about the experience so women will know what it's like is important. Holding it in is harmful. Women have been made made to feel guilty and ashamed about being raped, as though they were somehow to blame, or that they encouraged it. I feel sorry for women who don't have understanding husbands— as I did—or friends and relatives to talk to. I feel especially sorry for young women who have to convince everybody they didn't "ask" for it. No woman "asks" to be raped. No woman.[15]

Recently, there has been data accumulated suggesting that rape is more a crime of violence than a sexual assault. One research effort was conducted by psychologists A. Nicholas Groth and Ann Wolbert Burgess.[16] The fact that rape was not motivated predominantly by sexual desire became apparent to them from their work with rapists and victims of sexual assault. Data obtained on 133 offenders and 92 rape victims constituted the basis of the following findings:

**1.** In no case in the offender sample did the man have to rape for the purpose of sexual gratification.

**2.** The offenders did not appear to make any initial efforts to negotiate a consenting sexual relationship with their victims. Their approach, instead, was one of intimidation and assault.

**3.** The compulsive nature of rape behavior was reflected in the discovery that 53% of the 133 offenders had at least one previous conviction for rape.

**4.** A significant number of offenders (34%) reported experiencing some type of sexual problems at some point during the assault.

**5.** The offenses could be dichotomized into two categories on the basis of whether the predominant underlying psychological determinant was anger or power:

a. The anger rape (35%) is an expression of revenge and retaliation for what the offender perceived to be rejection and hurt inflicted on him by women in his life. Sexuality was clearly in the service of anger and aggression, with the purpose of the sexual assault being humiliation, abuse, and degradation of the victim. The rape experience for those who committed an anger rape was one of conscious anger or sadistic excitement. Older women or elderly women are a particular target victim for this type of rapist, although victims may be of any age.

b. The power rape (65%), in contrasts, is an expression of a sense of strength and power. Sexuality was clearly in the service of power and control, with the purpose of the sexual assault being the domination and conquest of his victim. The power rape is the way in which one type of offender asserts his identity, potency, mastery, strength, and dominance and denies his feelings of worthlessness, rejection, help-lessness, inadequacy, and vulnerability. The victim of this assault is typically within the same age group as the offender or younger.

About 50% of forcible rapes reported to police were cleared by arrest. Of those arrested for rape, 54% were males under 25. Blacks and whites were arrested an equal number of times (48%) and all other races comprised the remainder.

## Murder and Nonnegligent Manslaughter

### DEFINITION

Murder and nonnegligent manslaughter, as defined in the Uniform Crime Reporting Program, is the willful (nonnegligent) killing of one human being by another.

The classification of this offense, as in all other Crime Index offenses, is based solely on police investigation as opposed to the determination of a court, medical examiner, coroner, jury, or other judicial body. Not included in the count for this offense classification are deaths caused by negligence, suicide, or accident; justifiable homicides, which are the killings of felons by law enforcement officers in the line of duty or by private citizens; and attempts to murder or assaults to murder, which are scored as aggravated assaults.

Trends in the nation's murder rates have differed sharply from the patterns shown by the other major crime categories. Murder rates actually declined for the 30-year period 1933–1963 (except for a brief post-World War II upswing). The murder rate then rose sharply until 1974 when over 20,000 murders were recorded. Since then, the national murder rate has leveled off, and in 1978, there were approximately 19,555 murders, a rise of 2% over the preceding year; in 1979, the murder rate increased 12% to over 21,000.

Most murders are committed with a handgun (49%), about 19% of victims are cut or stabbed, 14% killed by rifle or shotgun, 6% beaten or kicked to death with hands or feet, and 12% killed by some other type of weapon, such as poison. Though most murders are committed with a gun or knife, the great majority of young children who are killed are victims of hands, fists, or feet; more than 50% of children under four (264 of 546) were found beaten to death. These figures probably represent a manifestation of the child abuse phenomenon, which only recently has come to receive national attention.

Murder is typically considered a crime of passion, often involving members of the same family. A study by Marvin Wolfgang found that homicide "usually involves intense personal interaction in which the victim's behavior is often an important factor."[17] The following characteristics were found by Wolfgang to be present in most cases of victim-precipitated murders:

1. Negro victims

2. Negro offenders

3. Male victims

4. Female offenders

5. Stabbings

6. Victim-offender relationship involving male victims of female offenders

7. Mate slayings

8. Husbands who are victims of mate slayings

9. Alcohol in the homicide situation

10. Alcohol in the victim

11. Victims with previous arrest records

12. Victims with previous arrest records of assault

Wolfgang's findings are supported by recent UCR data: in 1978 the majority of murder victims knew their assailants (at least 57%) and a disproportionate number (44%) were black; 49% of individuals arrested for murder were black.

In a recent analysis, sociologist Margaret Zahn found that homicide in the 1960s and 1970s, was primarily an intraracial (whites killing whites or blacks killing blacks) and intrasexual (males vs. males, females vs. females) phenomenon.[18] There was also an increase in "stranger" murders (and in cases where the offender simply remains unknown) although this increase was much more pronounced in northern cities. In southern or southwestern cities, domestic violence remains the most significant category, while in the North the stranger and the unknown assailant homicide is now a dominant (if not the dominant) murder relationship.[19]

Murder also seems to be a youthful pastime, though juveniles are less likely to be arrested for murder than they are for most other Index crimes: of the 19,980 persons arrested for murder in 1978, 43% were under 25 years old, but only 9% (1,735) were under 18.

## Aggravated Assault

> ### DEFINITION
>
> Aggravated assault is an unlawful attack by one person upon another for the purpose of inflicting severe or aggravated bodily injury. This type of assault is usually accompanied by the use of a weapon or by means likely to produce death or great bodily harm. Attempts are included since it is not necessary that an injury result when a gun, knife, or other weapon is used which could and probably would result in serious personal injury if the crime were successfully completed.

The number of aggravated assaults has increased steadily since the 1960s. Critics attribute this phenomenon to the civil disobedience, turmoil, and assassinations which occurred during the period. In the relatively tranquil 1970s, however, the trend did not subside; in 1979 approximately 600,000 assaults were reported to the police, about 280 per 100,000 population. Events such as the Miami riots of May, 1980 indicate that the assault rate may continue to increase through the 1980s.

About 62% of assaults were cleared by arrest. Of those arrested, 69% were over 21, 86% were males, and 58% were whites. Of assaults reported to police, 73% involved weapons, including 22% using knives.

Assaults often take place as a function of youthful gang behavior. In the Applications section of this chapter one young gang boy describes the violent nature of his activities.

## Motor Vehicle Theft

> ### DEFINITION
>
> In Uniform Crime Reporting, motor vehicle theft is defined as the theft or attempted theft of a motor vehicle. This definition excludes the taking of a motor vehicle for temporary use by those persons having lawful access.

Approximately 1,000,000 auto thefts occurred in 1979. The average cost of these offenses was $2,325 and only 15% (161,400) of reported offenses were eventually cleared by arrest.

Motor vehicle theft is another offense pattern especially prevalent among young offenders. The automobile has long served as an expression of adolescent freedom, and "joy-riding" in souped-up cars has always been—fuel shortages notwithstanding—a favorite pastime of rebellious adolescents. This phenomenon is reflected by the 1978 statistics: 70% of those arrested for motor vehicle theft were under 21 and those under 18 accounted for 51% of the total arrests (77,534).

## Larceny

> ### DEFINITION
>
> Larceny-theft is the unlawful taking, carrying, leading, or riding away of property from the possession or constructive possession of another. It includes crimes such as shoplifting, pocket-picking, purse-snatching, thefts from motor vehicles, thefts of motor vehicle parts and accessories, bicycle thefts, etc., in which no use of force, violence, or fraud occurs. In the Uniform Crime Reporting Program, this crime category does not include embezzlement, "con" games, forgery, and worthless checks. Motor vehicle theft is also excluded from this category for crime reporting purposes inasmuch as it is a separate Crime Index offense.

Larceny is by far the most common crime reported by the FBI; there were over 6 million larcenies recorded in 1979 alone.

Larceny is also a costly act—the latest figures estimate a per crime loss of $219 or a grand total of over one billion dollars. Moreover, only 20% of larcenies are ever cleared by arrest, so that the out-of-pocket loss to victims is rarely recovered.

Of those arrested, 42% are under 18, 32% female, and about 37% racial minorities.

There is no question that the FBI and many of its contributing law enforcement agencies have made a serious attempt to measure the incidence and amount of crime and delinquency in America. Nonetheless, there has been a great deal of criticism directed at the actual validity of the national crime statistics and official statistics in general. Methodological problems have compelled some experts to advocate the total abandonment of the use of official crime statistics in criminological research.

What issues most disturb critics? They may be categorized into two main divisions: (a) the fact that many citizens neglect or refuse to report delinquent and criminal acts to police; and (b) the problems caused by variations in law enforcement practices. Due to the importance of each of these issues, they will be discussed separately below.

ANALYSIS OF
THE UNIFORM
CRIME REPORTS

## Reporting Practices

American citizens are believed to report less than half of all criminal and delinquent acts to police. The reasons for this phenomenon are varied. Many individuals in lower class areas neglect to carry property insurance and therefore believe it is useless to report theft-related offenses to police since "nothing can be done." In other cases the victims may fail to notify police because they fear reprisals from friends or family members of the offenders.

A number of national surveys have attempted to uncover the factors that cause citizens to decide not to report delinquent or criminal acts to the police. In 1966 the President's Commission on Law Enforcement and the Administration of Justice sponsored one such effort.[20] Utilizing a nationally drawn sample of 10,000 citizens, the commission found that the most common citizen concerns were that the "police couldn't do anything about the matter," "it was a private—not criminal—affair," the person "was not sure if the real offenders would be caught," and the "police wouldn't want to be bothered."

In a more recent study conducted by the National Crime Survey (NCS),[21] a large nationally drawn sample of citizens was used to determine the factors which relate to the reporting or nonreporting of delinquent and criminal activity. (See the following section for a more detailed discussion of the NCS). The NCS data reveals that the reasons given for not reporting crime varied according to the type of criminal behavior examined. Rape and attempted rape victims said they did not report crime because it "was a private matter" (37%) and that they "feared reprisals" (21%). Assaults remained unreported because people felt "they were a private matter" (23%). However, for the most part, people did not report crimes such as robbery, burglary, and larceny because they believed "nothing could be done" and the "victimization was not important enough."

In an analysis of NCS data, Michael Hindelang and Michael Gottfredon found that for each category of personal, household, and business victimization, completed criminal acts were more often reported to police than attempted victimizations.[22] Similarly, the seriousness of delinquent or criminal activity influenced reporting; for example, the use of a weapon in the crime increased the likelihood that police would be notified. As the value of monetary loss increased, so did the probability that the act would be reported to police.

Hindelang and Gottfredson found that the personal characteristics of the victim also influenced reporting habits.[23] As a general rule, victim age was strongly related to failure to report crimes to police—victims under 35 were much less likely to report crimes than those over 35. Racial differences were found to be minor except among the youngest victims (12–19 years old), in which case whites were less likely to report crimes than blacks. Family income was found to be directly related to crime reporting— as income rose so too did the probability that citizens would contact police. However, whether the victim knew the criminal or whether they were strangers did not seem to effect the likelihood of the crime being reported.

### Law Enforcement Practices

The way police record and report criminal and delinquent activity also affects the validity of UCR statistics. For example, in New York City for the period of 1948 to 1952 burglaries rose from 2,726 to 42,491 and larcenies increased from 7,713 to 70,949. These significant increases were found to be related to the change from a precinct to a centralized reporting system for crime statistics.[24] A new central reporting system instituted in Philadelphia in 1952 resulted in a sharp rise in Index crimes from 16,773 in 1951 to 28,560 in 1953.[25]

Problems of a similar sort were encountered by Duncan Chappell, Gilbert Geis, Stephen Schafer, and Larry Siegel in their study of urban rape rates.[26] The initial purpose of their research was to discover the social factors which might account for the dramatic differences in the rape rates of two urban centers, Boston and Los Angeles (7.7 vs. 35.4 per 100,000, respectively). Careful examination of their data source—raw files submitted to the UCR—indicated that the most important factor differentiating the two cities was police discretion in reporting rapes. Los Angeles police were found to use extreme amounts of discretion and flexibility in their crime reporting; many alleged rapes occurring in Los Angeles in fact bore no resemblance to the UCR's definition of the deed. Chappell et al. were forced to observe:

The classification rules . . . are reasonably clear. It is another matter, however, to apply the rules carefully and uniformly around the nation, where the exigencies of daily police operations are not directed toward the niceties of classification, since such activities holds out little promise for easing the work burden. Nor, for that matter is the FBI able to exert any real suasion or provide much immediate guidance to an operating agency.[27]

Later, upon reflecting on the observed differences in police reporting styles, the authors concluded:

The need for standardized police reporting methods for the entire nation seems so obvious to us, particularly after our sessions with Boston and Los Angeles data, that the absence of such measures, given the nature of public and political concern about crime, appears almost incomprehensible.[28]

Of a more serious nature are the allegations that police officials may deliberately alter reported crimes in order to put their departments in a more favorable light with the public. David Seidman and Michael Couzens[29] suggest that police administrators interested in lowering the crime rate and thus improving their departments' images may falsify crime reporting, by deliberately undervaluing the cost of goods so that an index larceny will be relegated to a nonreportable offense category.

Beyond these immediate problems, it is also likely that police arrest and patrol practices vary significantly between neighborhoods within individual police jurisdictions, and also between the thousands of independent city police departments. Consequently, *any* crime reporting system may be inherently flawed and invalid. Police may release some suspects, especially juveniles, at the point of initial police contact since the arresting officer believes, often justifiably, that the delinquent activity in question is a matter best dealt with by the youth's own family. This practice may vary depending upon the recognition the family has in the community, its social standing or racial characteristics, the youth's attitude, arresting officer discretion, and so on. Therefore, any subsequent research efforts which make use of police arrest reports run the risk of being biased and misleading.

The above statement is especially important when we consider that, overall, only about 20% (1 in 5) reported index crimes are followed by an arrest of the culprit.[30] If the effect of citizen nonreporting is added in, it is likely that less than 10% (1 in 10) of Index crimes are cleared by an arrest. Thus, the use of official arrest records to gauge annual crime rates must be used with caution.

While improvement is obviously needed in the UCR, it remains a useful device for comparing long-term trends in crime rates and for establishing patterns and interrelationships between crime categories. The UCR may also serve as a helpful tool for determining the effectiveness of delinquency reduction programs by measuring *relative* changes in reported delinquency rates. A dramatic example of use of the UCR in this area may be found in the efforts of researchers to evaluate the deterrent effect of capital punishment by comparing crime rates before and after the death penalty was in effect, or by comparing homicide rates between jurisdictions which did and did not practice executions.[31] As an indicator of the absolute crime and delinquency rate, however, the UCR must be received somewhat skeptically. It remains a device which could dramatically improve in accuracy were more control exerted over its compilation and were serious attempts made to upgrade its components.

In light of these problems, it appears that the federal crime statistics function will soon be moved to a new Justice Department bureau, the Office of Justice Statistics. It is premature to speculate whether the move will improve our understanding of the current crime problem.

VICTIMIZATION
STUDIES

It has been estimated that fewer than one-half of all crimes are actually reported to police. For this reason, the criminal incidents reported by the FBI's UCR aggregate data do not tell a realistic or complete story of crime in America. To better understand the "dark figures" of crime, the federal government has sponsored a massive study of victimization in the United States, the National Crime Survey (NCS). Some preliminary data from this survey is now available, and it presents a dramatic picture of the role criminal activity plays in the United States.

The national victim survey is conducted by the Law Enforcement Assistance Administration in conjunction with the Census Bureau. Surveys have been ongoing in 26 major American cities; about 10,000 households and 2,000 businesses have been sampled in each metropolitan area. Respondents were asked about their victimization experiences during the preceeding 12 months. Household members 16 years or older were also asked about their perceptions of the crime problem, and attitudinal data was collected from about half of the total of over 500,000 subjects.[32]

The NCS data has been used to determine the nature and extent of crime in the United States. Survey data is subject to elaborate statistical analysis in order to estimate the amount of crime occurring in the nation as a whole. This procedure presents a picture of the crime problem without the methodological problems which plague the Uniform Crime Reports. In fact, NCS data indicates that only 46% of violent crimes, 25% of personal crimes of theft, and 38% of household crimes were brought to the attention of police. Many citizens reported that, among other reasons, they failed to contact police because they "felt nothing could be done" or that the criminal act "just wasn't important enough" to bother the authorities. Thus, NCS data accounts for many more criminal acts than those reported in the UCR. This is not to say that the NCS alone can be considered the "official" crime statistics. Victimization data is of course limited to crimes in which a "victim" actually exists, and cannot be used to measure such "victimless" crimes as drug use and gambling. Nor can NCS data accurately account for crimes, such as fraud, embezzlement, or tax violations, in which the respondents themselves may have participated. And, of course, national statistics are merely estimates of the crime problem, which may be subject to error and must therefore be interpreted accordingly.

Let us now review some of the more important findings of the NCS.

### Selected Findings

The most recent data from the National Crime Survey indicates that 40.3 million crimes, including both completed acts and attempts, occur annually.[33] This number is approximately four times as many as those reported by the UCR. Rape, personal robbery, and assault, as Figure 1.2 indicates, made up 15% of these crimes (about 6 million incidents), while larceny, probably the least serious crime, accounted for 65% of the total. Figure 1.3 illustrates the victimization rate per 1,000 population 12 and over: the "odds" of being a victim of a violent crime appears to be approximately 40:1,000; household larceny, 140:1,000; burglary, 90:1,000; and personal larceny, 100:1,000. These startling figures indicate the incredible severity and frequency of the crime problem.

### Victim Characteristics

The NCS also uncovered information about the background characteristics of crime victims. Men were found to be about twice as likely as women to have suffered a robbery and were more likely to be the victim of assault and personal larceny (without contact); as Figure 1.4 indicates men were also more prone to suffer violent attacks than women. On the other hand, between one and two women in every thousand was the victim of rape.

Age was also a factor in criminal victimizations. Individuals ages 12–24 sustained the highest victimization rates and, surprisingly, considering their physical weakness, elderly citizens had the lowest (see Figure 1.4). In fact, individuals under 25 were the victims of violent crime three times as often as those 25 and over.

FIGURE 1.2
Percent Distribution of
Victimizations, by
Sector and Type of
Crime, 1977

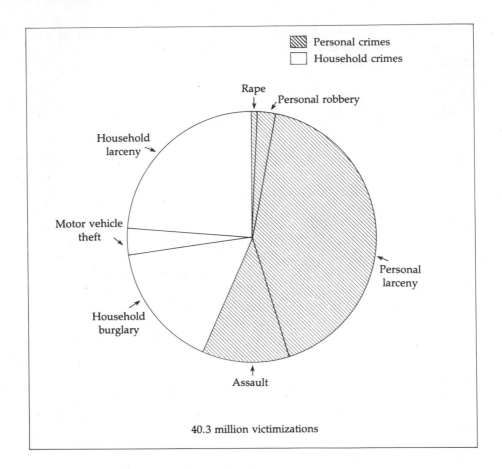

40.3 million victimizations

Racial characteristics also influenced a person's chances of being a victim of crime. Blacks experienced violent crimes at a somewhat higher rate than whites, a condition mostly attributable to the occurrence of robberies perpetrated against black male victims. Similarly, Hispanics as a group experienced higher victimization rates for violent crimes than citizens of other ethnic and racial backgrounds (see Figure 1.4).

The NCS data also shows that members of the lowest income categories (less than $3,000 per year) had the highest overall rate for violent crime. Low income homes had the lowest rates for theft-related crimes such as household larceny and auto theft, while conversely, they had the highest rate for household burglary and unlawful entries without force.

**Offense Characteristics**

The NCS data indicates some interesting characteristics of offenders and offenses.

Of offenses included in the survey, most occurred in the evening hours (6 p.m. to 6 a.m.); only personal larcenies with contact, such as purse snatching and pocket pickings, predominated during daytime hours. Crimes of violence occurred more often at night. Generally, the more serious forms of these crimes were more likely to take place after 6 p.m.;

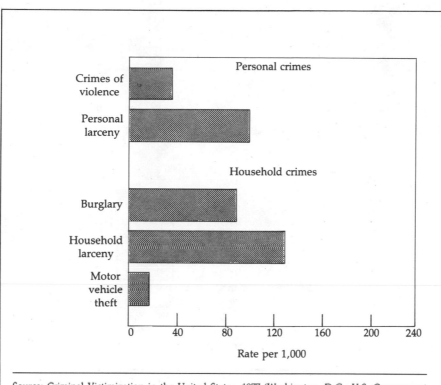

FIGURE 1.3
Victimization Rates,
1977

Source: Criminal Victimization in the United States, 1977 (Washington, D.C.: U.S. Government Printing Office, 1979), p. 5.
Source: Criminal Victimization in the United States, 1977 (Washington, D.C.: U.S. Government Printing Office, 1979), p. 5.

the less serious ones, before 6 p.m. Thus, greater proportions of aggravated assaults were concentrated at night while simple assaults occurred during the day. Larger numbers of robberies and assaults by armed offenders transpired during the evening or late night. "Stranger-to-stranger" robberies or assaults, generally conceded to be more threatening than the "nonstranger" forms, exhibited a similar pattern. For rape, however, there was no real difference between the proportions of "stranger" and "nonstranger" nighttime crime.[34]

The great majority of violent personal crimes were committed against lone victims; a large percentage of reported incidents (69%) involved single offenders. While rape and assaults were more likely to have beem committed by offenders acting alone, robberies tended to be committed by more than one offender. It was also found that for personal crimes of violence, weapons were used in 35% of reported incidents. Victims attacked by strangers were somewhat more likely to encounter weapons (38%) than those victimized by someone they knew (30%). Knives and firearms were used in 60% of armed incidents while clubs, sticks, stones, and other assorted weapons were used in the other 40%.

When attacked, victims of violence usually tried to protect themselves. Examination of race, sex, and age groups for differences in the proclivity

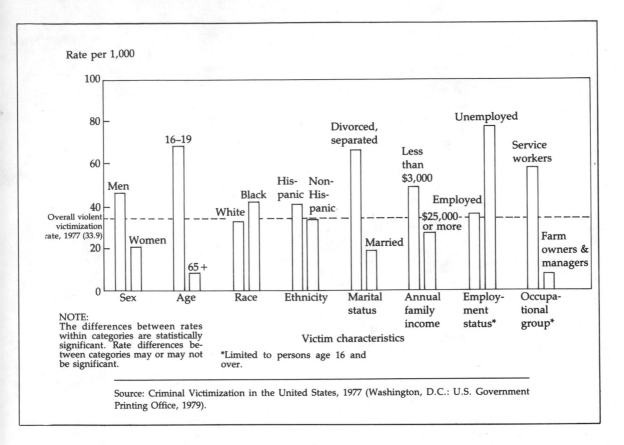

Rate per 1,000

NOTE:
The differences between rates within categories are statistically significant. Rate differences between categories may or may not be significant.

*Limited to persons age 16 and over.

Source: Criminal Victimization in the United States, 1977 (Washington, D.C.: U.S. Government Printing Office, 1979).

FIGURE 1.4
Crimes of Violence: Victimization Rates For Persons Age 12 and Over, by Selected Characteristics of Victims, 1977

to use self-protective measures revealed that for all violent crimes, persons in the eldest age category (65 and over) were the least prone to defend themselves, in comparison with individuals in the younger age groups. Blacks were less likely than whites to use self-defense against robbery, but more so than whites in cases of assault. For this latter crime only, males resorted to self-protective measures proportionally more often than females.

Physical force was the more frequently used form of self-protection followed by nonviolent resistance, threatening or reasoning with the offender, and trying to get help or frighten off the offender. Among victims in general, firearms or knives were used for self-defense relatively infrequently. Men invoked physical force proportionally more often than women, who were more apt to try to find help or to attempt evasion. Self-protective practices did not vary significantly by race.[35]

**Consequences of Crime**
Crime takes a terrific monetary and personal injury toll on American citizens. The NCS found that victims were physically harmed in 3 of every 10 personal robbery and assault incidents (all rape victims are, of course, "harmed"). There seemed to be no real difference between men and women, blacks and whites, or income groups in the probability of being

injured once attacked; however, the elderly were more injury prone than the young. Added to the physical costs were medical expenses which occurred in 6% of violent acts and the need for hospital treatment, occurring in 7% of these acts.

In addition to the costs of violent crimes, the NCS found that theft-related crime has an enormous impact on the American public. In 90% of household larcenies, 95% of personal larcenies and 67% of robberies, victims suffered losses. Most losses resulted from theft as opposed to damage to property. The costliest damage losses occurred in auto thefts, where more than 66% of the crimes involved a cost to the victim of more than $250. The majority of other crimes resulted in losses of $50 or less. Nonetheless, victim losses also involved other expenses, including work time lost due to personal injury or the unavailability of a motor vehicle.

### Offender Characteristics

The NCS data can be used to tell us something about the characteristics of people who commit crime. Of couse this information is only available about criminals who actually came in contact with the victim through such crimes as rape, assault, or robbery.

The survey found that strangers accounted for 63% of violent crimes; in the remaining 37%, the victim and criminal were acquainted with one another. As might be expected, criminal-victim acquaintance was most common in assaultive crime (41%) and least common in robberies (25%). Thus, someone you know is unlikely to steal from you, but is more likely to become involved in a fight with you.

The overwhelming number of criminals were perceived to be males. Moreover, the offender was perceived to have been over age 20 in most of the single-offender crimes, but crimes involving 2 or more law breakers were characterized by a much higher proportion of offenders under 21. This statistic may reflect the gang-related activity of American teenagers.

With respect to the racial identity of offenders, the data indicated that about 7 out of every 10 single-offender violent crimes were perceived to have been committed by whites, about 1 out of 4 by blacks, and the remainder, 5%, by members of other races. The largest proportion of rapes and assaults was committed by whites, who of course comprised a large majority of the national population. However, there was not a statistically significant difference between the relative number of personal robberies attributed to whites and blacks.[36] In addition, the great majority of offenses tended to be intraracial—that is, black offenders victimized blacks, and white criminals tended to victimize whites.

### Further Sources of Crime Data

Recently federal, state, and local crime agencies and the Academic Community have developed a number of new, innovative, and important data sources which hold great promise for future research. Among the most informative are:

*Uniform Parole Reports (UPRs).*[37] UPRs are a product of the National Council on Crime and Delinquency (NCCD). They contain information from almost all state and federal parole boards. UPR data provides information on the success or failure of the parole decision (that is, whether the former inmate made a successful adjustment in the community), the prior record and conviction status of the offender, and personal characteristics of the offender.

*National Jail Census; National Survey of Inmates of Local Jails.*[38] Conducted under the sponsorship of the United States Justice Department's Law Enforcement Assistance Administration (LEAA), the National Jail Census provides data on the number of jails in the country, the number and type of inmates, inmate-staff ratios, and educational and medical facilities in jails. In 1972, the LEAA contracted with the Census Bureau to conduct a survey of the personal characteristics of inmates in local jails (the National Survey of Inmates of Local Jails). Data included such variables as race, marital status, socioeconomic status, education, offense committed, and confinement status (convicted, awaiting trial, etc.). These two surveys seem to be valuable instruments for learning more about the characteristics of jailed inmates, of which previously very little was known.

*National Prisoner Statistics (NPS).*[39] The NPS entail a statistical profile of characteristics of adult inmates in the state and federal prisons, and include reports on inmate admissions and populations, as well as personal information such as an offender's race, sex, time served, and offense.

## FUTURE TRENDS IN CRIME STATISTICS

The few above-mentioned data sources provide an interesting first step in the collection and dissemination of relevant criminological statistics. What improvements does the future hold? One interesting source of statistics for the next decade is *transactional statistics,* otherwise referred to as *offender-based transactional statistics.* While not widely available at present, transactional statistics utilize the offender as the unit of analysis upon which data gathering is based. In collecting transactional statistics, the offender is followed from arrest through trial, confinement, and final release. The outcome of every criminal justice decision is then carefully recorded. Such comprehensive information should facilitate analysis of critical decision-making processes in criminal justice. It could enable researchers to determine whether the personal characteristics of offenders—race, sex, age, social status—influence the decision-making of criminal justice agents. The effects of legal counsel, bail, and other facets of the criminal justice system could also be determined. Offender-based data, which is now only beginning to be accumulated, seems to be an exciting future source of information about the criminal justice process.

FIGURE 1.5
Flow of California
Felony Offenders: Urban Areas[a]

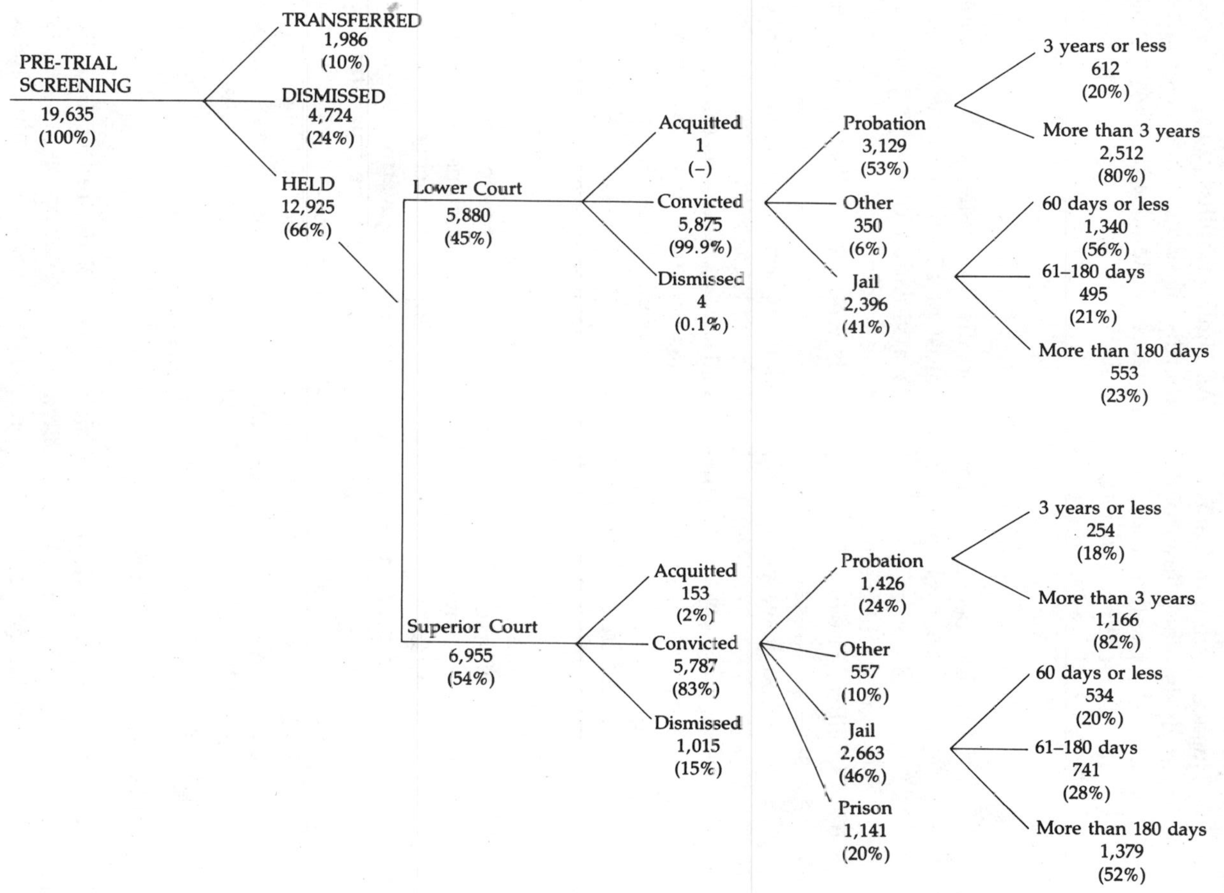

[a] The total number of cases at any one stage may not equal those of a preceding stage due to changes in the computation of the base rates. For example, while a probation disposition excludes those sentenced to both probation and jail, length of probation includes the latter category.

One example of the uses of offender-based statistics can be found in a recent Justice Department study of offender flow through the criminal justice system in California.[40] As Figure 1.5 illustrates, transactional data analysis may allow for the gathering of specific information on decision outcomes within the criminal justice system, such as the percentage of those actually convicted, how many defendants were incarcerated and for how long, and so on.

SUMMARY

Crime has become a familiar and disturbing fact of life in America. The country appears to be in the midst of a serious crime wave. When we speak about crime, we refer to a violation of existing societal rules of behavior which are expressed in the criminal code created by those holding political power. Those individuals who violate these rules are subject to state sanctions.

Today we get our information on crime from a number of different sources. One of the most important of these is the Uniform Crime Reports compiled by the FBI. This national survey of serious criminal acts reported to local police departments indicates that more than 12 million Index crimes (murder, rape, burglary, robbery, assault, larceny and motor vehicle theft) occurred in 1979. This figure represents an increase of 8% over 1978, and is even more troubling because violent acts rose 11% over the previous year.

Critics have questioned the validity of the UCR. They point out that many people fail to report crime to police due to fear, apathy, or lack of respect for law enforcement. In addition, questions have been raised about the accuracy of police records and reporting practices.

To remedy this situation, the federal government has sponsored a massive victim survey designed to uncover the true amount of annual crime. The National Crime Survey, or NCS, reveals that more than 40 million serious crimes are committed every year and that the great majority are not reported to police. Other forms of justice information include offender-based transactional statistics which follow an offender from first arrest to final disposition.

QUESTIONS FOR DISCUSSION

1. Discuss the degree to which crime statistics reflect the actual amount of crime committed in the United States. What problems are associated with reporting crime and recording crime? How can criminal justice personnel deal effectively with these problems?

2. What variables contribute to change in crime trends and types of crimes committed? Which crimes are reported more often than others? Why? Which crimes are underreported? Why?

3. In what ways does a democratic society contribute to the high incidence of crime?

**1.** Clarence Schrag, *Crime & Justice: American Style* (Washington, D.C.: U.S. Government Printing Office, 1971), p. 1.

**2.** National Advisory Commission on Criminal Justice Standards and Goals, *A National Strategy to Reduce Crime* (Washington, D.C.: U.S. Government Printing Office, 1974), p. 1.

**3.** Abraham Blumberg, "Law and Order: The Counterfeit Crusade," in *The Scales of Justice*, Abraham Blumberg, ed. (New Brunswick, N.J.: Transaction Books, 1973), p. 9.

**4.** E. Sutherland and D. Cressey, *Criminology* (Philadelphia: J.B. Lippincott Co., 1970), p. 4.

**5.** Ramsey Clark, *Crime in America* (New York: Simon & Schuster, 1970), p. 248.

**6.** S. Schafer and R. Knudten, *Juvenile Delinquency* (New York: Random House, 1970), p. 3.

**7.** R. Korn and L. McKorkle, *Criminology & Penology* (New York: Holt, Rinehart and Winston, 1965), p. 5.

**8.** Richard Quinney, *The Social Reality of Crime* (Boston: Little, Brown and Co., 1970).

**9.** Ibid., pp. 15–25.

**10.** Ibid., p. 16.

**11.** Schrag, *Crime & Justice: American Style*, p. 17.

**12.** FBI News Release, April 30, 1980.

**13.** John Conklin, *Robbery and the Criminal Justice System*, (Philadelphia: L. B. Lippincott, 1972).

**14.** Morton Hunt, *The Mugging* (New York Segment, 1972).

**15.** Nancy Glazer and Cathleen Schurr, *Sexual Assault: Confronting Rape in America* (New York: Grosset and Dunlap, 1976), p. 7.

**16.** A. Nicholas Groth and Ann Burgess, "Rape: A Pseudosexual Act," *International Journal of Women's Studies* 1:207–210 (1977); Groth and Burgess, "Rape: A Sexual Deviation," *American Journal of Orthopsychiatry*, 47:400–406 (1977), N. Groth, A. Burgess, and Lynda Holmstrom, "Rape: Power, Anger and Sexuality," *American Journal of Psychiatry* 134:1239–1243 (1977).

**17.** Marvin Wolfgang, *Patterns in Criminal Homicide* (New York: John Wiley and Sons, 1966).

**18.** Margaret Zahn, "Homicide in the Twentieth Century United States," unpublished manuscript, Temple University, 1980.

**19.** Ibid., p. 19.

**20.** Philip Ennes, *Criminal Victimization in the United States* (Field Survey II. A Report of a National Survey, President's Commission on Law Enforcement and Criminal Justice, Washington, D.C. 1967).

**21.** Nicolette Parisi, Michael Gottfredson, Michael Hendelang, Timothy Flanagan, *Sourcebook of Criminal Justice Statistics 1978* (Washington, D.C.: U.S. Government Printing Office, 1979) p. 362. Herein cited as *Sourcebook*.

**22.** Michael Hindelang and Michael Gottfredson, "The Victims Decision Not To Involve The Criminal Justice Process", in *Criminal Justice and the Victim*, William F. McDonald, ed. (Beverly Hills, CA: Sage Publication, 1976), pp. 57–74.

**23.** Ibid., pp. 71–73.

**24.** Paul Tappan, *Crime, Justice and Corrections* (New York: McGraw Hill, 1960).

**25.** Daniel Bell, *The End of Ideology* (New York: Free Press, 1967) p. 152.

**26.** Duncan Chappell, Gilbert Geis, Stephen Schafer and Larry Siegel, "Forcible Rape: A Comparative Study of Offenses Known to the Police in Boston and Los

Angeles", in *Studies in the Sociology of Sex*, James Henslin, ed. (New York: Appleton Century-Crofts, 1971), pp. 169–193.

27. Ibid., p. 180.

28. Ibid., p. 183.

29. David Seidman and Michael Couzens, "Getting The Crime Rate Down: Political Pressure and Crime Reporting", *Law and Society Review* 8:457 (1974).

30. Clearances are usually inversely proportional to the seriousness of a crime. Murder, rape, and assault are cleared much more often than larceny or motor vehicle theft.

31. See, for example, William Bowers, *Executions in America* (Lexington, Mass.: Lexington Books, 1974).

32. See James Garofalo, *Local Victim Surveys* (Washington, D.C.: U.S. Government Printing Office, 1977).

33. Information in this section comes from U.S. Department of Justice, *Criminal Victimization in the United States, 1977* (Washington, D.C.: U.S. Government Printing Office, 1979).

34. Ibid., p. 12.

35. Adapted from Ibid., p. 13.

36. Ibid., p. 11.

37. The following sources of statistics are explained in greater detail by Michael Hindelang and Carl Pope, "Sources of Research Data in Criminal Justice," in *Criminal Justice Research*, Emilio Viano, ed. (Lexington, Mass.: Lexington Books, 1975), pp. 135–144; *Uniform Parole Reports* may be obtained from the National Council on Crime and Delinquency, Hackensack, New Jersey.

38. Both available from the U.S. Department of Justice, Law Enforcement Assistance Administration, Washington, D.C.

39. Available from the U.S. Department of Justice, Law Enforcement Assistance Administration: Statistics Division, Washington, D.C.

40. Carl Pope, *Offender-Based Transaction Statistics: New Direction in Data Collection and Reporting*. Research Report No. 6, Utilization of Criminal Justice Statistics Project, Criminal Justice Research Center (Albany, New York).

# Manny A Criminal-Addict's Story

We used to have a lot of dances. That was during the time of Bill Haley and the Comets. Rock and roll was just starting to break through in the early fifties. We used to skip school and gather at people's houses. Their parents would be away working and we would throw big parties. But it was mostly dancing and fighting, with occasional making out. We'd drink a little, but there wasn't much booze around, and very little dope. We'd get all worked up dancing, and then it would feel good to go home and fight it out in the street with a rival gang member.

We used to have these dances in the school gym with four or five rival gangs. We're all supposed to go there; kind of a neighborhood integration thing. During the day we're trying to kill each other, but just 'cause it's nighttime we're supposed to be nice to each other? The chaperons would tell us that we couldn't wear sweaters to the dance. But we used to put our sweaters on under a white shirt and sport coat. So we had our front on until the shit started. At these dances there would always be an argument come up over something. There had to be arguments 'cause you had these rival gangs there. Anytime you got Young Stars and Hoods together, for example, you had an argument. It couldn't be any other way.

And pretty soon off the shirts would come and you'd see the different sweaters pop out. And we'd just get right down to the nitty-gritty right there. Kids would be busting heads; shivs would flash; tire irons and chains would start rapping. Before long there would be guys laying all over the dance floor bleeding. So they finally stopped having school dances trying to promote peace 'cause they just became another battlefield.

I remember, we used to roam the school halls looking for somebody to fight—anybody! I hear a lot of talk about race riots, and I know they are going on because I've been in a few; people getting killed for their color. But in those days it made no difference what color you were. If you were white, orange, blue, it made no difference. What mattered was the sweater you had on—what territory you were from—especially at night. And we never used to say that we were going out to fight all these "niggers," because a lot of gangs were made up of mixed groups. Even the Mau Maus over in Brooklyn were mixed, although they were mostly black guys. We used to ride the subways over into Nicky Cruz' area in Brooklyn. That was a bad thing to do, 'cause there were lots of warriors in the Mau Maus. All over the streets, and you could get caught short over in Brooklyn real easy. We just barely escaped with our lives once over there.

The gangs we used to rumble with mostly were the Hoods, of course, and then the Seven Crowns, the Scorpions, occasionally the Mau Maus, and then the Fordham Baldies. The Baldies were a group of guys made up of the sons of racketeers from the Fordham Road area. The Godfather up Fordham way used to be known as Baldie. So naturally the kids took the name. They were a pretty tough group so we mostly left them alone.

One all-black gang did emerge as a very powerful gang—like a couple that are going in LA right now. They must of had something like four thousand members. When they would get together they could down anybody. But we were in the upper Bronx and we had our territory. The Seven Crowns, the Mau Maus, and the Bishops were mostly from Brooklyn or Manhattan.

The Bishops used to have a guy called the Batman who walked around with a cape and all that regalia on all the time. He was a stone-cold killer. Everybody was scared shitless of the Batman. I mean, he was fourteen years old and he would kill just for the hell of it. One time Batman walked into a candy store over on Forty-fifth and sat down kind of behind some display cases. In walks this dude that had been making noises like he was looking to get the Batman. So, the Batman just takes this 12-gauge piece out from under his cape and blows the dude away. Killed him deader than a mackerel. He just walked up next to the guy, stuck the shotgun in his guts, pulled the trigger, and walked away. Just like that, no pain, no strain. The dude was dead before he hit the floor, and you know what? The Batman didn't give a shit. He just walked away.

Kids used to give the Batman contracts on other kids. For a few lousy bucks Batman would wipe out anybody. He threw a guy off the Third Avenue El one time for ten bucks. Just threw him off and killed him. They finally give him the electric chair. I don't know how many people Batman killed before that. But nobody thought much about it. That was the thing to do, in a way, for most of us. If you didn't like somebody, if they got in your way, kill them. So, in a sense we were all Batman. And the same way with appearance. We didn't look like most people think a "gang fighter" looks. If you'd have looked at Batman, you'd have never thought he was a stone-cold killer. I mean, he was really small and kind of pale looking. Always reading comic books. You guessed it; he was especially fond of Batman comics. That was his trip. Batman was the only dude I ever met who I was really scared of.

# WANTED BY THE FBI

## INTERSTATE FLIGHT - MURDER

# RONALD TURNEY WILLIAMS

## DESCRIPTION

Born April 4, 1943, Keystone, West Virginia; Height, 5'11"; Weight, 165 to 170 pounds; Build, medium; Hair, dark brown; Eyes, hazel/blue;Complexion, fair; Race, white; Nationality, American; Occupations, laborer, painter, salesman, welder; Scars and marks, mole below left ear, two small scars on forehead, small scars on lower left arm; Social Security Numbers used, 233-66-3731; 070-62-1084; Remarks, wears glasses.

## CAUTION

WILLIAMS, WHO WAS SERVING A LIFE TERM FOR THE MURDER OF A POLICE OFFICER, IS WANTED IN CONNECTION WITH A MASS PRISON ESCAPE IN WHICH GUARDS WERE OVER—POWERED AND A POLICE OFFICER WAS SLAIN. WILLIAMS, WHO IS BELIEVED TO ALWAYS BE ARMED SHOULD BE CONSIDERED ARMED, EXTREMELY DANGEROUS AND AN ESCAPE RISK.

# Understanding Crime and Its Causes

KEY TERMS

**Criminology**
**Survey Research**
**Life Histories**
**Cesare Lombroso**
**Sigmund Freud**
**Sociobiology**
**Emile Durkheim**
**Anomie**
**Subcultures**
**Edwin Sutherland**

**Albert Cohen**
**Travis Hirschi**
**Lloyd Ohlin**
**Richard Cloward**
**Walter Miller**
**Neutralization**
**Differential Association**
**Gangs**
**Focal Concerns**
**Labeling**

A DEFINITION OF
CRIMINOLOGY

✶ Criminology is the study of the causes of crime, the characteristics of criminals, and the prevention and cure of criminality. It is an international science which applies the scientific method of inquiry to the questions of law, morality, deviance, and illegal behavior which have long perplexed legal scholars, law enforcement officials, social scientists, and reformers.

Experts in criminology have observed and contemplated the causes of crime from a number of different perspectives: law, sociology, psychology, economics, political science, and history. Criminology utilizes the skills of experts from several different scholarly disciplines to better understand the crime problem, and many universities house academies exclusively devoted to the study of crime.

In recent years, criminologists have taken new and innovative approaches to the study of crime. For example, Stephen Schafer, among others, has introduced the study of *victimology*; in this branch of criminology, inquiry focuses on the victims of crimes as well as on the criminals, and examines, among other areas, the victim's need for injury compensation, the relationship between victim and criminal, and the possibility that the victim may have actually precipitated the crime he or she was involved in. ✶ Another recent trend or school in criminology is called *New* or *Critical Criminology*. This area of study focuses on the historical, economic, and political factors which influence crime, and interprets crime from a Marxist perspective.[2] These movements and others within the field indicate the dynamic nature of criminology and illustrate how its focus has shifted in recent years.

CRIMINOLOGICAL
METHODS

Criminologists have developed a set of technical procedures for data gathering and analysis. Some methods are unique to the field while others are similar to the research tools employed in areas such as sociology, psychology, and economics. A few of the more important methods are discussed below in detail.

### ✛ Survey Research

Survey research uses information obtained from probability samples drawn from populations (all those individuals who share at least one similar trait—for example, rapists, school teachers, and so on). A probability sample is one in which a limited number of subjects from the larger population is randomly selected; ideally, every individual in the population has an equal chance of being selected for the study. For example, the Nielsen survey, which evaluates American television viewing habits, involves a relatively small group of people who are randomly drawn from the millions of television watchers in the United States. Probability sampling assumes that the characteristics of the small, select sample group mirror or are similar to those of the larger population from which the sample group is drawn; thus, the criminologist who utilizes statistics gathered in probability sampling can generalize information collected from a few people and apply it to the behavior of millions.

Criminological surveys have been directed at such diverse issues as victimization, police and community relations, and beliefs about corrections and the penal system; anonymous self-report surveys have been conducted with high school students to determine their undetected participation in delinquent activity and the factors which influence it; and prison inmates have been surveyed in order to discover their attitudes, personalities, values, and so on.[3]

Surveys are usually conducted by means of mailed or personally distributed questionnaires which participants are asked to complete and return. Sometimes, surveyors also interview subjects about their attitudes and behavior; occasionally, both questionnaires and interviews are used. Periodically subjects are selected randomly from the telephone book and interviewed over the phone. While this latter method is quite inexpensive compared to most others, phone interviews are not as effective as might be wished, since no face-to-face relationship can exist between interviewer and subject and the interviewer is unable to show credentials which could help to build a sense of trust in participants.

### Observation Studies

The systematic observation, recording, and deciphering of types of behavior within a sample or population is another popularly used method of criminological research. Some observation studies are conducted in the field, where the researcher observes subjects in their normal environments; other observations take place in a contrived, artificial setting or laboratory. Still another type of observation study is called *participant observation*. In this type of research, the criminologist joins the group being studied and behaves as a member of the group. It is believed that participation enables the scientist to better understand the motives subjects may have for their behavior and attitudes. Participation also helps the researcher to develop a frame of reference similar to that of the subjects and allows the researcher to better understand how the subjects interact with the rest of the world. Well-known participant observation studies have been conducted by William F. White on the lives of young lower class youth (*Street Corner Society*) and Laud Humpherys on homosexual behavior in public places (*Tea Room Trade*).[4] Observation is a time-consuming way to conduct research, and occasionally contains some ethical risks; for example, Laud Humpherys engaged in what some construe as deviant behavior during the data-gathering stage of his research. Participant observation studies, however, do allow the researcher to gain insights into behavior that might never be available otherwise. In addition, since observation studies depend more on actual behavior than on surveyed opinions, the researcher can be fairly sure of the validity of the information because it will be more difficult for subjects to give false impressions or responses. It is hard if not impossible to standardize the conditions or replicate the results of observation studies;

thus, they usually stand as unique and valuable contributions of concerned scientists and scholars.

## Life Histories

Another fascinating technique of criminological research is the life history. This method utilizes personal accounts of individuals who have had experience in crime, deviance, law enforcement, and other related areas. Diaries or autobiographies can be used; sometimes, an account is given to an interested second party to record "as told to." Autobiographical accounts include Claude Brown's story of teenage crime, *Manchild in the Promised Land*, and Piri Thomas's *Down These Mean Streets*.[5] "As told to" accounts include *Box Man* by Harry King and Bill Chambliss, and *The Vice Lords: Warriors of the Street* by R. Lincoln Keiser.[6]

Life histories provide insights into the human condition that other less personal research methods cannot hope to duplicate. They are sometimes moving, often revealing individual testimonies of the feelings, beliefs, values, and attitudes of convicts, delinquents, and criminals. Of course life histories do not represent the average criminal. Most life histories are provided by talented, artistic individuals who eventually successfully readjust to society. Nonetheless, their stories often illustrate the conditions they had to overcome and the strengths they had to call upon in order to reenter society. Sometimes of course, the author of a life history does not draw the kinds of conclusions in his or her book that society would approve; in *The Box Man*, Harry King explains:

I've met some real wonderful people since I started to go straight . . . though I tell you. But I just can't accept this society. My parole officer beats on my head and the judge beats on my head: 'You are a member of society now.' And I don't feel any different about it than I ever did. I don't know.[7]

## Record Studies

A significant proportion of criminological research involves the compilation and evaluation of official records. The records may be acquired from a variety of sources including schools, courts, police agencies, social service centers, prisons, and jails. Some studies utilize the national data sources discussed in Chapter 1, such as crime statistics, jail and prison surveys.

Records can be used for a number of purposes. Prisoners' files can be analyzed in an effort to determine what types of inmates can adjust to prison, and what types tend to be disciplinary problems or suicidal. Parole department records are evaluated to determine the characteristics of inmates who successfully adjust to the outside and the characteristics of those who fail. Educational records are important indicators of IQ, academic achievement, school behavior, and other information which can be related to delinquent behavior patterns.

Analyses of official records are useful in a number of ways. They can help to determine trends in the crime rate or in crime patterns, or they can be used to uncover discriminatory practices in the criminal justice system. For example, are minorities given harsher sentences than others for similar crimes? Or are police arrests made in a fashion favoring one group over another? One interesting aspect of record studies focuses on the changes in the operating procedures of the criminal justice system which are brought about by the influence of an outside source or event such as a court decision, political change, or technological innovation. David Duffee and Larry Siegel, for example, studied how the Supreme Court's decision requiring the State to provide lawyers for juveniles might affect the outcome of delinquency hearings.[8] After analyzing the court records of juveniles who were not represented by counsel and comparing them to the records of those who were, they concluded that requiring legal counsel might actually result in harsher, more lengthy dispositions being handed out to juvenile offenders. In this instance, analysis of records provided information on the results of a new legal mandate which had not been anticipated prior to the passing of the mandate.

Remarkable progress has been made in the field of criminology within the last twenty years. Sponsored and unsponsored research efforts alike have provided tentative answers to some of the most puzzling criminological questions, while academic programs devoted to the study of crime have flourished. Despite these advances, problems and controversies continue to plague the field. Both supporters and critics of criminology have raised ethical questions. One in particular involves the general direction the field has taken. For quite some time, most criminological research has concentrated on the issue of lower-class urban crime. The inner city ghetto was a prime research area since, in fact, it was a major crime center. But other factors may have also been responsible for the fact that crime in the ghetto has been so thoroughly studied. Many large universities and research centers are located in the cities which house urban ghettos, making research within them an obvious and easy choice; in addition, law enforcement is practiced much more comprehensively in these areas and a ready-made sample of police-identified criminal subjects is accessible to the researcher. The ghetto was also an attractive area to study because crime there seems simpler to understand than crime in middle-class areas. The reasons why a poor inner-city dropout turns to crime seem obvious; the middle-class criminal who has all the benefits of education and wealth is a different matter entirely. Finally, solving ghetto crime became a politically attractive cause and a top government priority, and research funds for that purpose were readily available.

A period of concentration on urban—particularly Black—crime culminated in a number of reports and books which incensed critics. Some, such as Edward Banfield's *The Unheavenly City* or Daniel Moynihan's *Beyond the Melting Pot*, were interpreted as even suggesting that crime is a char-

**PROBLEMS OF CRIMINOLOGY**

acteristic of race or class.[9] Subsequent harsh reactions and demonstrations against these findings barred much criminological research from inner-city institutions. Schools which normally allowed researchers to study pupils and their records closed their doors to university scholars, and critics suggested that researchers spend equal time studying middle-class white-collar crime. Ethical questions remain valid today. Should participants be told of the true nature and use of the information they contribute to a research study? Should a particular group, race, or class be studied and then compared to another without first asking permission of the subjects? How far can researchers mislead subjects to obtain workable results? For example, can a researcher pose as a customer in order to study drug sales, prostitution, or gambling? Finally, how responsible should criminologists be for uncovering crimes in all walks of life—i.e., white-collar crime—in addition to studying street and property crime?

Another problem in the field of criminology is due to its relationship with government agencies. Much inquiry is sponsored and funded by the Justice Department, the National Science Foundation, the National Institute of Mental Health, and other agencies. How, then, critics ask, can criminologists be unbiased observers of governmental inefficiency and its role in the crime problem? In addition, criminologists often act as consultants to government agencies, evaluating their effectiveness, efficiency, and fairness. Is it possible for these observers to remain truly impartial while being financially supported by the agencies and foundations of which they are supposed to be objectively critical? Even though these questions are grave ones, the cost of conducting research without institutional support remains so prohibitive that the relationship between researchers and agencies must continue, at least into the near future. Criminologists, though, are cautioned to carefully consider their role, how it is influenced by outside support, and how it can be made immune from the possibility— a necessity—of compromise.

## THEORIES OF CRIMINOLOGY

It has proven difficult to pinpoint or even suggest the underlying causes of crime. Early scholars attempted to identify singular factors whose presence or absence would predispose individuals toward criminality. Physical factors such as body build and psychological, genetic, social, political, and economic influences were each at one time or another thought to be the single most important cause of crime. Almost unanimously, early crime experts believed that one fundamental factor could be identified as the primary underlying determinant of criminal behavior. Unfortunately, the single controlling cause of criminality remains as far beyond the grasp of criminologists as the Fountain of Youth did for the early explorer. There are too many different, complex individuals committing too many crimes for far too many reasons to allow for a single element to be responsible for them all.

Many competing single-factor theories flourished simultaneously, each theorist contradicting the others. As soon as one theory of the cause of crime appeared on the scene, it was almost inevitable that another criminologist would refute and replace it. Theoretical models were criticized as being too broad or too narrow, overly simplistic or too complex.

Today, the single-factor approach to the cause of crime has been rejected in favor of less dogmatic multiple-cause theories. These models portray individual crime patterns (e.g., lower-class gang delinquency) as products of a variety of independent or related influences. While the effects of any single factor are not considered sufficient to account for crime as a whole, a number of these individual influences working together are believed significant enough to cause criminal behavior. Today, each individual criminal act is seen as a function of a varied number of social, psychological, or environmental factors, with no two sets of factors necessarily being exactly alike.

Unfortunately, multiple-cause theories are beset by some of the same problems which plague single-cause approaches. Regardless of how broad a theory's explanation of criminality is meant to be, critics can always identify some criminal types whose behavior patterns seem to fall outside the theory's suggested framework. Broadening a theory's scope to accommodate these deviant cases often causes it to become overly complex and burdensome.

As a result of the problems inherent in both the single- and multiple-cause approaches, some researchers have abandoned the search for the causes of crime and have begun instead to explore *process models*. The process approach, already practiced in criminal justice research, entails the observing, recording, and understanding of the interpersonal reactions and transactions which occur when a criminal deals with peers and society and its official institutions. Process research examines such areas as police encounters with citizens and general decision making in the criminal justice system. Process models also critically regard the criminal's interactions with peers, community, and family. Proponents of this approach are less concerned with the causes of crime than they are with its consequences in the lives of criminals, victims, and society.

The historical foundations of criminological theory can be traced to early social reformers such as Phillipe Pinel (1745–1840) and Dorothea Dix (1802–1887). These humanitarians suggested that mentally ill persons or criminals were not "touched by the devil," as some believed, need not be chained or whipped, and in fact might someday be rehabilitated. Until these reformers spoke out, law violators were confined to dungeons, banished, mutilated, branded, publicly humiliated, tortured, or summarily and brutally executed. Stocks or pillories were a favorite means of public punishment. Criminals were forced to place their heads and arms through holes between two boards which were then clamped shut, after which townspeople would throw stones or refuse at the unfortunates, sometimes causing permanent disfigurement or even death. The stocks were used for minor crimes such as breaking the peace, drunkenness, or scolding

INDIVIDUALISTIC
THEORIES OF
CRIMINAL
BEHAVIOR

(women were more frequently accused of this crime than were men). For thieves, murderers, and others who committed serious crimes, punishment was brutal and final.

Another of the early advocates of prison reform, Cesare Beccaria (1738–1794), an Italian scholar, also helped improve the quality of justice by helping to revise the criminal law. Beccaria espoused a philosophy called *utilitarianism*—he believed that laws should serve the people, protect them from governmental interference, and improve their lives. He was one of the first to argue for democratic laws which would bring justice to all equally; his works are believed to have influenced many great scholars of his time, including Jefferson and Voltaire.

The origins of modern criminological thought are found in the biophysical theories of Cesare Lombroso (1835–1909). Lombroso was an Italian army physician fascinated by human anatomy who became interested in finding out what motivated criminals to commit crimes. He physically examined hundreds of prison inmates and other criminals in order to discover any similarities between them. On the basis of his research, Lombroso proposed that criminals manifest atavistic or degenerate anomalies; in other words, the active criminal is a physical and biological throwback to early stages of human evolution who adjusts poorly to modern society and is thrust into criminal activities. Frustrated by incompetence in relating to society and stung by subsequent societal rejection, the atavistic individual reacts with criminal or violent outbursts. Careful physical measurement of hundreds of convicted criminals led Lombroso to catalogue the following attributes as denoting criminality; an assymetric face or excessive jaw, eye defects, large eyes, a receding forehead, prominent cheekbones, long arms, a twisted nose, and swollen lips.[10]

Today, Lombroso's work is viewed more as a historical curiosity than a serious scientific explanation of criminal behavior. However, his pioneering efforts have not been completely forgotten, and his influence can be seen in the more recent efforts of the Gluecks, for example, who attempted to find a biological basis for crime.[11]

Another branch of early criminological theory to emerge was the psychobiological school of thought. Rather than studying physical characteristics, members of the psychobiological school believed that inherited traits resulted in the deficiencies which characterize the "born criminal." One of the earliest advocates of the psychobiological theory, Henry Maudsly (1835–1918), a British psychotherapist, believed that criminals were *morally insane*, and that moral insanity was an inherited quality; his theoretical statements implied that criminals are "born and not made." According to Maudsly, crime was a way in which the criminal could express or alleviate the pathological urges which were inherited from mentally or morally deficient ancestors.

Advocates of the psychobiological or inheritance theory also studied the family trees of criminal offenders. This type of research utilizes historical documents and other data sources to trace the activities of several generations of families believed to have an especially large number of criminal members. The most famous of these studies involved the Jukes and Kallikaks. Richard Dugdale's book, *Crime, Pauperism, Disease and Heredity* (1895), and Arthur Estabrook's later work, *The Jukes in 1915,* traced the history of the Jukes, a family believed to have been responsible for a disporportionate amount of crime. Dugdale concentrated his efforts on one branch of the family tree, the offspring of Ada Jukes, whom he labeled the "mother of criminals." Dugdale succeeded in locating over 1,000 of her descendents and found that among them were included 280 paupers, 60 thieves, 7 murderers, 140 criminals, 40 persons with venereal diseases, 50 prostitutes, and other assorted deviants and undesirables. Estabrook studied the Jukes family even more closely and accumulated data on 2,000 members. He found an additional 170 paupers, 118 criminals, 378 prostitutes, and assorted other deviants. In an associated study, Goddard studied the offspring of Martin Kallikak, who lived during the time of the American Revolution. Kallikak first had an illegitimate son by a woman of "low-born" family, and then married into a "good" family. Goddard located 480 relations of the illegitimate offspring and 496 descendants of Kallikak's marriage—the former group was found to contain substantially more deviant and criminal members than the latter "normal" group. The immediate implication of these studies was that undesirable hereditary characteristics, even in distant relatives, were enough to condemn succeeding generations of a family to a life of criminal degeneracy. Again, criminals were seen as being "born and not made."[12]

Studies such as these were taken quite seriously during their time; of course, the writings of the psychobiological school are no longer considered reputable. Even if more families like the Jukes or Kallikaks were located, this alone would not prove that psychodegeneracy is a cause of criminality. Considering the thousands of family bloodlines within the United States, it would be expected that a few would produce a disproportionate number of deviants. Furthermore, many of the "best" families have produced murderers and thieves. Finally, these theories provide no explanation as to why many members of psychodegenerate families live perfectly normal lives and become productive members of their communities.

### Psychological Theory

The psychobiological school was soon supplanted by theories of individual psychological abnormalities. Advocates of this approach were spurred by the development of psychoanalysis under the leadership of Sigmund Freud (1856–1939). Criminal behavior began to be viewed in light of discoveries about the human mind, different personality types, stresses, sexual yearnings, and the relationship of all these psychological factors to crime.

Currently, psychological explanations of criminal behavior seem to be divided into two main branches: the *clinical-psychoanalytic approach* and the *behavioral-developmental* approach. The former position holds that most criminal acts are actually caused by unconscious personality disturbances or problems, marked by such abnormal mental conditions as psychoses, neuroticism, depression, schizophrenia, and so on. Crime, according to the clinical-psychoanalytic approach, can be eliminated by treating the symptoms of these abnormal psychological conditions. Leading names in the clinical-psychoanalytic approach to crime causation include among others Hans Eysenck, R. Starke Hathaway, and Elio Monachesi.[13]

Proponents of the *behavioral-developmental* school, including psychologists Jean Piaget, Erik Erikson, and Lawrence Kohlberg, suggest that behavior is learned. Learning occurs when a person goes through a series of life stages or cycles during which infants, children, young adults, and adults must learn to successfully cope with changing life situations. Improper socialization can lead to the adaptation of inappropriate, deviant or antisocial behaviors.[14]

Of course there are differing views on the level of control learning has on human behavior. Some psychologists would suggest that learned behavior has strict control over behavioral choices and that people retain little freedom in deciding what course of action to take. Others would maintain that, despite a person's developmental history, freedom of choice is still a prerogative. In either case, advocates of this approach would maintain that criminals can be treated by providing behavior therapy and behavior modification techniques to help them learn new ways of adapting to varying life situations.

Theories of psychological abnormality have not fared well under empirical testing. A review of relevant psychological studies by Gordon Waldo and Simon Dinitz, found that few measurable differences exist between the personalities of offenders and non-offenders.[15] Moreover, a psychological explanation of criminality ignores what are called "normal" crimes—crimes that are common and regularly committed by a significant portion of the population. Emile Durkheim, the eminent French sociologist, believed that crime is actually normal because a society without it is inconceivable. Durkheim suggested that criminal acts are a necessary part of every healthy society. This is not to say that all criminals are "normal"; Durkheim believed that an excessive rise in the crime rate indicates "abnormality." The mere occurrence of crime cannot automatically be considered as evidence of psychopathology, however; nor can a criminal "be considered psychologically unbalanced simply because he/she committed and was apprehended for an illegal behavior."[16]

## Sociobiology

The most recent development in criminological theory is *Sociobiology*. Sociobiologists view all human behavior as a function of a person's (a) biological makeup (including body chemistry, and genetic makeup), (b) the *environment* in which the person lives, and (c) individual *learning* potential and experiences. A combination of these three factors are believed to control individual behavior.[17] However, sociobiologists hold that no one factor absolutely controls behavior and a deficiency in one area can possibly be made up by increased efforts in another. For example, a youth with a learning deficiency can be given special corrective care to compensate for the learning problems; or a youth whose violent acts are attributable to a chemical imbalance may be put on a drug program (or even vitamins) to correct biological deficiencies.

Criminologists using a sociobiological approach have examined many different biological functions to determine whether they are predictive of criminal behavior. A recent publication lists the following sociobiological issues, many of which seem complex and technical, as having received research attention:

Influence of various epileptic disorders, as they relate to criminal behavior . . . studies of electroencephalogram abnormalities. Learning disabilities, minimal brain dysfunctions, and visual problems among delinquents have also recently been examined. Neurological abnormalities, disorders of the brain or disturbances in its chemical balance, such as hyperkinesis, may influence criminality. Genetic research concerning chromosomal abnormalities, such as 47, XXY (Klinefelter's syndrome) producing extreme tallness and distinct EEG pattern, examines the possibility of inheritable aspects of criminality. The work of K.O. Christiansen and his cohort studies of Danish twins is a prime example of the research on genetic influences. Disorders in the endocrine system, the system of glands regulating internal functions, have been associated with criminal behavior, often with regard to sexual offenders. Limbic system disorders, affected by sugar diabetes and hypoglycemia (low blood sugar), have been associated with violent, sometimes criminal, behavior. Psychophysiological indices related to emotional response may also play a role. Galvanic skin response may be indicative of the aptitude for learning inhibiting behavior; biochemical balances, such as levels of adrenaline and noradrenaline, are associated with aggression.[18]

In addition to the above, the biological basis for psychological disorders such as schizophrenia have been extensively studied, and the relationship between intelligence (I.Q.) and crime has received research attention.[19] Recent evidence suggests that delinquents have substantially lower IQs than nondelinquents and that their diminished intellectual ability may be somehow linked to their criminal acts.[20] This finding is highly controversial because by implication it suggests that hard-core delinquents are unlikely to be "reformed" by any known rehabilitation technique using social or psychological support mechanisms.

Sociobiology itself is extremely controversial. Critics charge that it is racist, class-biased, and antihuman since it may be interpreted as suggesting that criminality-producing traits are biologically inherent in a person. By implication, sociobiologists seem to be suggesting that a person who once engages in antisocial behavior is unlikely to conform to social rules. Charges of racism stem from the disproportionate number of blacks represented in arrest statistics and the prison population. In light of this fact, sociobiology might be interpreted as suggesting that there is a link between racial background, biological makeup, and criminal behavior. Numerous books and articles using a sociobiological perspective have been published, however there is inconclusive evidence that the position is valid,[21] and critics are more than likely to challenge any research finding.

SOCIALLY
BASED
THEORIES OF
CRIME

Modern criminological theory can be said to have originated in the works of early European social thinkers such as Aldophe Quetelet (1796–1874) and, later, Emile Durkheim (1858–1917). Quetelet, supported by statistics gathered in France and Belgium, discovered that many social phenomena such as marriage, divorce, suicide, birth, and crime were not purely individually controlled, and that the study of crime in the mass (i.e., criminal statistics) could lead to the development of social laws to explain the occurrence of crime. The best-known of his studies concluded that the volume and kind of criminal behavior in a particular area or country are constant, and that any fluctuations which may occur over a period of time are comparatively insignificant provided that the basic circumstances—economic, political, and social—do not substantially change.[22] Quetelet believed in a statistical probability that a certain small percentage of a given number of individuals in a certain country and at a certain time would "have" to commit crimes.

Durkheim also viewed crime as a social phenomenon.[23] In his formulation of the Theory of Anomie and his analysis of the division of labor, Durkheim concluded that crime is an intrinsic part of society and a function of its internal conflict. As he used the term, *Anomie* means the absence or weakness of rules and social norms in any person or group; the lack of these rules or norms may lead an individual to lose the ability to distinguish between right and wrong. Social strictures ordinarily limit individual desires and aspirations and maintain the structure and integrity of the group as a whole; if these restraints are removed—as they are in times of strife or famine, for example—individual security is not only jeopardized, but the boundaries of individual freedom become less certain. When the familiar balance between cultural expectations and social aspirations is destroyed, deviant, criminal, or suicidal behavior may develop.

Quetelet, Durkheim, and other early theorists who linked crime to social phenomena moved the study of criminology out of the individual, personal, psychological, or moral spheres into a collective social one. Equating the cause of criminal behavior with socially derived pressures or other societal factors was instrumental in the development of treatment-oriented crime prevention techniques. For if, in fact, criminals are "made and not born"—if they are forged in the crucible of societal action—then it logically follows that crime can be eradicated by the treatment and eventual elimination of the responsible social elements. The focus of crime prevention consequently shifted from the individual to the social forces causing criminal behavior. Reformers asked, "How can we blame an individual for committing a crime when society was the cause of the deviance in the first place?" Thus was born the conflict between those advocating treatment and rehabilitation and those who view punishment as the only way to control crime.

We now turn to some of the most important recent criminological theories. Rather than attempting to mention or classify all relevant theoretical formulations, we will discuss a few of the most important ones in some detail. The theories chosen for inclusion in this text apply to both adult crime and juvenile delinquency. The reader is cautioned to remember that no clear-cut link has been established between these two independent types of criminality, and that theories explaining one need not represent the other. Nonetheless, some of the theoretical models presented—*e.g.*, Labeling, Differential Association, and Anomie—may in fact adequately explain the etiology or cause for both adult and juvenile crime, and should be interpreted accordingly.

SOCIOCULTURAL
THEORIES

Sociocultural theories link the cause of crime and delinquency to the frustrations, problems, and values which abound in lower-class culture and inner-city poverty areas. Since reported crime rates are highest in these areas, it is alleged that citizens who dwell within them are more susceptible to the temptations of gaining material goods through theft, or venting their frustrations through violence. Moreover, some sociocultural theorists suggest that lower-class citizens form a separate "subculture" which maintains a unique set of values in opposition to those held by the middle class.

In this section, we will examine the most prominent sociocultural theories of crime.

### Anomie

Robert Merton's Theory of Anomie is an extension of and elaboration on Durkheim's original concept of the anomic or normless condition.[24] Merton argues that societies are not monolithic wholes, but instead are made up of individual substrata or subcultures. Often, these mini-groups have their own particular sets of values, goals, and rules or norms, which may be in conflict with those held by members of their society's predominant culture. In American society, for example, teen-age gangs, political subgroups like the Ku Klux Klan, or even cohesive racial or religious groups such as Catholics, Jews, or Blacks might be considered subcultures.

Compounding the problem of adjusting to a pluralistic society such as ours is the fact that people are often members of a number of subgroups, and their multigroup memberships may force them to adhere to conflicting sets of values and rules. A youth's membership in a gang may conflict with the demands of his religious beliefs, his family, or his school. Consequently, each individual is faced with the dilemma of knowing that the behavior demanded by one membership group (sometimes called a *reference group*) may conflict with the demands of another. Often the pattern of social norms shifts and changes so rapidly that people are not even quite sure what the rules are; this condition is traditionally called Anomie, or normlessness.

When faced with a dilemma of such overwhelming proportions, the anomic person may wish to substitute illegitimate means or goals for acceptable ones. For example, the lower-class, inner-city youth may overwhelmingly believe that his only hope for achieving personal success is through illegitimate means; thus, he must steal a car to obtain one. Meanwhile, the wealthy suburban youth may perceive a much more readily available supply of legitimate means: he can ask his parents to buy him a car. Or, goals may be differently perceived within the same subgroup— while one girl strives to be street-wise and tough, another yearns to get into Harvard.

The various relationships between goals and means in our society appear in Merton's Table 2.1.

TABLE 2.1.
Merton's Model of
Goals and Means

| Goals | Means | Resulting Behavior |
|-------|-------|--------------------|
| + | + | Conformity |
| + | − | Innovation |
| − | + | Ritualism |
| − | − | Retreatism |
| ± | ± | Rebellion |

*Conformity* occurs when a person perceives goals and means to be complementary. This position is exemplified by the so-called average citizen.

*Innovation* results when a person adheres to the prescribed goals of society—such as, wealth, power, and prestige—but does not have access to legitimate means for achieving them. Innovation dictates the use of new, innovative, illegitimate, or criminal means for attaining goals.

*Ritualism* involves the maintenance of traditional means or lifestyle without any particular purpose or goal. The British foreign service officer formally dressing to dine alone in the tropics is the classic example of ritualism.

*Retreatism* occurs when a person rejects both goals and means. Merton ascribes this orientation to the drug addict, skid row bum or alcoholic who has retreated from modern society into a private world.

An individual with a *rebellion* orientation has rejected conventional societal goals and means and substituted alternatives to them. In a capitalist society, rebels may plot the violent overthrow of the government and plan to substitute a Marxist regime in its place. In a Marxist society, a similar rebel group may plot a republican or fascist alternative to the government.

Adherence to one of these deviant orientations (retreatism, ritualism, rebellion, or innovation) may force an individual to enter into a subculture (or counterculture) of like-minded people who join together to reject conventional norms and practices. As involvement in the proscribed group is solidified by negative societal reactions, the deviant may eschew other group memberships which tend to promote conventional society and openly espouse the outlaw orientation. Sometimes, this conversion is a slow process, marked by a series of social acceptances and rejections; on other occasions, the conversion is rapid, brought about or abetted by some outside influence, such as an arrest or public exposure.

Merton's Theory of Anomie can be criticized on the grounds that it does not explain why certain goals are conventional and accepted while others are forbidden and sanctioned. Nor does it explain why one individual perceives an absence of legitimate means (or goals) while another in close and intimate contact with the first is able to conform to society. Anomie theory may also be criticized in that it may not be appropriate to assume that an individual adheres solely to *only* deviant solutions, but may instead vary goals and means depending on the particular social situation. In the 1960s, for example, "weekend hippies" found it possible to wear love-beads on the weekends and return to more conventional lifestyles during working hours.

### Theory of Delinquent Gangs

Following Merton's lead, sociologists have developed theorectical models which seek to explain the disproportionate amount of crime and delinquency found in lower-class inner-city neighborhoods. As a group, they suggest that lower-class areas develop "subcultures" of delinquency with a unique set of values and attitudes. The most prominent of these theories are discussed below.

Sociologist Albert Cohen's Theory of Delinquent Gangs is a significant example of a subcultural theory that seeks to explain the disproportionate amount of crime and delinquency found in lower-class areas.[25] Cohen argues that most lower-class youths are unable to cope with the pressures exerted by middle-class society. Their learning, home life, mannerisms, and interests render them incapable of legitimately succeeding in a world controlled by middle-class values. Their first failures come at the hands of teachers and other school officials who use what Cohen labels "middle-class measuring rods," to evaluate them. This means that teachers expect these youth to be attentive, use proper grammar, show respect for authority; they are quick to brand lower-class youths as "bad" or "stupid" for the slightest failure.

Lower-class youth adapt to this predicament by assuming one of several identities: "the college boy" attempts to implement middle-class behaviors and strives (usually vainly) for legitimate success; the "corner boy" is happy to "hang out" with his peers, engage in mildly antisocial activity such as drinking and gambling, and then eventually marry and hold a marginal job; the "delinquent boy" engages in various criminal activities, which Cohen characterizes as malicious, destructive, and negativistic. The delinquent boy is the most likely to join a teenage gang and evolve into a criminal as an adult.

Thus, Cohen views the *cause* of serious crime as a product of culture conflict in which the cards are stacked against lower-class boys. This portrayal is not too dissimilar from the one illustrated in the popular film "Saturday Night Fever" in which the central character, Tony, lives an unhappy existence (corner boy) in a lower-class area of New York. The ritual of his boring, marginal job is relieved by "hanging out" with his friends, seeking danger and excitement, and—most important—going out on the town on Saturday night. By the end of the film, Tony realizes that the only way to break out of this pattern is to leave the neighborhood and his "hanging-out" group behind him. Therefore, he goes to seek his success by planning to reside in a wealthier area of town where he will exploit his talent as a dancer. Cohen would argue that his chances for "making it" are quite slim.

Criticisms of Cohen's theory have centered upon its failure to distinguish between types of crime: why does one youth steal, another commit arson, another engage in violence, and so on. Nor does it explain criminal activity that is productive and beneficial to the people who engage in it. It seems likely that many youthful and adult criminals steal for profit and luxury and not merely to be "negativistic" or "destructive." Thus, Cohen's portrayal of the delinquent boy as purely antisocial and destructive ignores all the "benefits" of criminal activity. Similarly, Cohen ignores the existence of middle-class crime, and also fails to explain why lower-class youths eventually quit gangs for other careers.

**Opportunity Theory**
In the spirit of Cohen's subcultural approach, Richard Cloward and Lloyd Ohlin presented a somewhat more sophisticated rendition of social-class–based theory of criminal behavior in their 1960 book *Delinquency and Opportunity*.[26] Opportunity theory can be differentiated from both Merton's and Cohen's earlier works because it maintains that not only are legitimate opportunities unavailable to many people, but even opportunities for criminal gain are closed or "blocked" to many citizens.

As Cloward and Ohlin see it, middle- and upper-class youths (and adults) are usually able to forego serious criminal behavior because they have the *opportunity* by means of their wealth, good education, professional jobs, or other advantages to become successful within the boundaries of the law.

In stable lower-class areas, this pattern simply does not exist. In such neighborhoods, people are blocked from attaining legitimate opportunities, and are able to profit by engaging in a variety of illegal acts. They can join preexisting *criminal gangs* which specialize in sophisticated theft-related behavior, resulting in highly profitable, though illegal, rewards. Criminal gangs thrive in areas in which adult thieves and racketeers provide deviant role models and help youths "learn the ropes" of organized criminal activity.

However, according to Cloward and Ohlin, in highly depressed and unstable slum areas, where adult role models are absent, even criminal activity is blocked to most youths. In slum areas, *conflict gangs* form. These cohesive youth groups engage in "warfare" to protect their "turf" and provide a sense of support for their alienated members. Youths whose path to success in both the "legitimate world" and in criminal gangs is "blocked" because of their racial and/or economic background, can instead become a "success" as a gang leader.

Finally, Cloward and Ohlin suggest that there are youth who physically or emotionally are incapable of joining either criminal or violent gangs.

They instead may join *retreatist gangs* which use alcohol and drugs—especially heroin, marijuana, cocaine, or amphetamines—in order to withdraw from society. Thus, Cloward and Ohlin view the cause of delinquency as a function of social stratification and the lack of opportunities available to lower-class youth. Because these youth want a share in the American dream but lack the capability of getting it, they resort to theft, violence or drug-related acts.

Criticism of Opportunity Theory centers on its failure to explain why more than one type of gang may flourish in a similar neighborhood and why some youths are able to avoid memberships in either of the three gang types. Nor does it explain the existence of middle-class crime or white-collar crime. Finally, Cloward and Ohlin do not seem to adequately explain why many youthful gang members eventually become law-abiding adults—the "aging out process." Nonetheless, Opportunity Theory has been a very powerful influence on delinquency control policy. Development of "war on poverty" social and economic improvement projects in the 1960s and 1970s, such as the preschool "Head Start" program and the Job Corp vocational training program, may be traced to the huge impact Cloward and Ohlin had on crime prevention planning.[27]

### Theory of Lower-Class Culture

Another theory in the subcultural tradition is sociologist Walter Miller's Theory of Lower-Class Culture. Miller maintains that criminal activity is common in working class ghetto areas because of the unique value structure that prevails there. According to Miller's widely read work, there exists a unique group of value-like "focal concerns" in lower-class neighborhoods which dominate life among adolescent boys.[28] The most important of these concerns include:

—— *Trouble*—involves such behavior as fighting, gambling, sex, drinking, and similar escapades;

—— *Toughness*—involves the desire to prove masculinity, athletic skill, bravery, "macho," fearlessness, and so on;

—— *Smartness*—being street-wise, cool, displaying the wise-guy or con-man image;

—— *Excitement*—the search for fun, excitement, activity action;

—— *Autonomy*—the desire to be free, uncontrolled, and in charge of one's own life.

Miller's view is that by adhering to the demands of lower-class focal concerns, youths in ghetto areas are likely to run afoul of the law (which is actually based on a middle-class value structure). What appears to be purposive criminal activity is actually a consequence of living in a culture which values toughness, getting into and out of trouble, sexual prowess, and freedom over hard work, saving money, marriage, and obeying law.

Finally, Miller sees the lower-class neighborhood as being dominated by single-sex teen gangs which provide a powerful lure to youth who often come from fatherless homes. In lower-class areas, to resist the gangs is to admit you are a coward, without "heart" and someone who leaves himself open to be victimized by other gang boys. This incentive is too much for most youths and they fall prey to gang membership.

Miller's work has been criticized because he fails to provide specific instances where this so-called lower-class culture exists. Moreover, he ignores what influence middle-class goals and values may actually have on the feelings and actions of the lower-class citizens. While Miller's focal concerns may be elements of lower class culture, it is difficult to imagine they are the only interests of residents. Finally, Miller's work, similar to previously mentioned subcultural theories, does little to explain middle-class youth crime, the aging out process, and the variety of delinquent acts (why are some youth violent, others thieves, and others vandals?).

SOCIAL
PROCESS
THEORIES

Social process theories view criminal behavior as a function of a person's life experiences and the accompanying social processes. This approach may be contrasted with the previously discussed sociocultural theories which view criminal behavior as a function of social class conflicts.

Social process theories are sensitive to the fact that citizens in all walks of life commit crime. Thus, social process theorists suggest that some undefined element of socialization, learning experiences, relationships with others, interaction with social control agents, or peer relations may be the true "cause" of criminal behavior. Let us review the most important of these theoretical models:

**Differential Association**
Edwin Sutherland's Theory of Differential Association is the best-known American theory of adult criminality (it may also be applied to juvenile crime). Primarily a learning theory, its major premises have been concisely defined by Clarence Schrag as follows.[29]

1. Criminal behavior is learned. In this respect crime is similar to all other forms of social behavior. Crime is neither inherited nor is it invented by unsophisticated persons.
2. Criminal behavior is learned as a result of the communication that occurs in social interaction, and this communication is most effective in primary groups that are characterized by intimacy, consensus, and shared understandings. Impersonal communications, in general, are less effective.
3. When criminal behavior is learned, the learning includes both the techniques that are necessary in order to commit the crime and the motives, rationalizations, and social definitions that enable an individual to utilize his criminal skills. In some

situations (societies, neighborhoods, families, groups, etc.) an individual is surrounded by people who almost invariably define the laws as rules to be observed, while in other situations the individual encounters many persons whose definitions are favorable to law violations. Although the relative numbers of people who endorse criminal and noncriminal definitions may vary in time, place, and other circumstances, it seems almost inevitable that there will be some conflict over the efficacy and the morality of legal codes, especially in pluralistic societies.

4. More specifically, criminal behavior is learned when an individual encounters an excess of definitions favoring law violations over those that support conformity. This is the basic principle of differential association. It refers to the counteracting influences of both criminal and noncriminal contacts, and it maintains that the probability of criminal behavior varies directly with the number of criminal definitions. Hence the generic formula for criminal behavior may be written as follows:

$$\text{Probability of crime} = \frac{\text{Definitions favorable to violations}}{\text{Definitions opposed to violations}}$$

5. Differential association with criminal and noncriminal behavior patterns may vary in frequency, duration, priority, and intensity. Frequency refers to the number of contacts during a given interval of time. Duration indicates the length of time during which a pattern of contacts is maintained. Priority designates an individual's age at the time of establishing contact with distinctive behavior patterns or developing certain modes of response. Intensity is not precisely defined but deals with things such as the prestige of the carriers of social norms or the affective attachments that may be generated among individuals involved in certain contact patterns.

As is the case with many well-known theories, Differential Association has been subject to close scrutiny by members of the scientific community, and critics have questioned its validity. Donald Cressy, who has continued Sutherland's work, acknowledges the presence of what he considers to be widespread misconceptions about the theory.[30] One of the most serious misinterpretations of the theory, according to Cressy, is the belief that Differential Association is based on the idea that contacts with criminal elements will result in criminal behavior. If this were true, police officers, lawyers, judges, and criminologists might eventually turn to crime. Cressy interprets the theory to mean that an overabundance of criminal definitions and a lack of noncriminal ones, and not simply contact with criminals alone, cause criminal behavior to occur. Thus, while policemen, lawyers, and others involved in the criminal justice system may come into contact with criminals, they have more than enough relationships with legitimate society to cancel out the effects of criminal definitions. Cressy also contends that the Theory of Differential Association does not apply only when an individual is in contact with criminal persons; it is enough to have associated at some time in the past with any person or element utilizing criminal definitions. Thus, the law-abiding mother of a boy who pushes him to get ahead at any cost may be influencing his subsequent criminality.

As Stephen Schafer points out, however, some criticisms of the theory are more difficult to explain away, especially those which point to the "disregard of the role of freedom of the will, the neglect of the biological factors, the dynamics of crime that demand the consideration of the victim's role in the law-breaking, the lack of concern for personality traits . . . , the oversimplification of the otherwise complex learning processes, and especially the absence of an explanation for the origin of crime."[31] As Schafer rightly contends, Differential Association explains only how the second criminal came into being—not how the role model was originally created.

### Neutralization Theory

Neutralization Theory resulted from the work of criminologists David Matza and Gresham Sykes,[32] who suggest that the common portrayal of criminals and delinquents as belonging to unique subcultures or counter-cultures and adhering to separate sets of norms and values is spurious and misleading. Their argument is based on observations of a number of character traits and behavior types of delinquent youth.

First, Sykes and Matza found that delinquents experience a sense of guilt due to their involvement in illegal activities. If, in fact, juvenile delinquents reject conventional norms and values and substitute illegal ones for them, it does not follow that they should feel guilty or remorseful. Second, the researchers found that young criminals actively respect leaders of the legitimate social order—such as parents, teachers, actors, sports figures, and clergy. Again, they reason that these articulated feelings may be a sign that delinquents have not forsaken all conventional ties. Another conflicting behavior pattern Sykes and Matza observed is that delinquents draw a line between those who can be victimized and those who can't. For example, the may choose not to harm their own kind. Such discretion implies that delinquents appreciate the wrongfulness of their actions. Juveniles were also found to actively participate in normative roles, their delinquency appearing to be an episodic rather than a committed experience. Finally, the great numbers of undetected middle-class crimes indicate that delinquency is not solely a lower-class phenomenon or a product of a lower-class subculture.

These observations led Sykes and Matza to suggest that delinquents are neither committed to their deviant roles nor are they necessarily members of delinquent subcultures. Instead, delinquents adhere to conventional values while "drifting" into episodic instances of illegal behavior. In order to drift, the delinquent must first neutralize legal and moral constraints and values. Neutralization is accomplished through the following specific techniques.

1. Denial of Responsibility—the delinquent claims that environmental, peer, or other pressures led to the committing of crime.

2. Denial of Victim—the delinquent claims that the victim "had it coming." The store flaunted its wares; the assaulted youth was boasting too much.

3. Denial of Injury—the delinquent claims not to have done anything wrong. "I just gave him a shove"; "they could afford it."

**4.** Condemnation of Condemners—the delinquent wonders why every-one is picking on him/her. "I'm no worse than anyone else"; "cops are on the take"; "judges take bribes."

**5.** Appeal to Higher Loyalties—the delinquent didn't want to do it but had to protect his/her buddies or go along with crowd.

Sykes and Matza suggest that psychological adherence to one or more of these five orientations insulates a youth from the constraints of conventional values and precipitates the drift into delinquency.

Critics have questioned the limited research the authors conducted before formulating their ideas. There also seems to be a dilemma in the theory—might it not be the case that people who participate in deviant acts would then also be likely to neutralize (rationalize) their deviant modes of adaptation? The time sequence during which neutralization takes place must also be considered—does neutralization precede commission of a delinquent act, or does it come after the act has been committed? In addition, empirical testing of Neutralization Theory has not provided clearcut authentication of its major principles. For example, in one study by Siegel et al., it was found that delinquents shared some conventional attitudes but also differed significantly from a nondelinquent control group in their attitudes toward such concepts as the law, crime, and the police.[33] Thus, Neutralization Theory has received mixed support and its validity is still in question.

### Control Theory

Travis Hirschi's Control Theory is a significant development in the social process view of crime and delinquency.[34]

According to Hirschi, most individuals have the potential for committing crime, but are kept in check by their equally potent commitment to the rules, controls, values, and conditions of the society in which they live. However, when their "bond" to society becomes weakened or broken, they are free to engage in deviant acts which otherwise would be avoided.

Hirschi postulates that a person's bond to society is predicated on a number of different elements:

—— *Attachment*—means caring for and valuing relationships with others, including parents, friends, teachers, and so on. A person with a strong sense of attachment will seek out the advice of teachers, associate with friends and maintain strong ties with family members; these activities are believed to shield a person from criminal temptations.

—— *Commitment*—involves the time, energy, and effort expended in the pursuit of conventional lines of action. Commitments may embrace such activities as spending time in school or working to save money for the future. The more commitment one has, the less chance there is of engaging in criminal activity.

—— *Involvement*—means an individual's participation in conventional activities such as school, recreation, church, family or hobbies. The youth who is always active will not have time for delinquent acts.

—— *Belief*—reflects a person's sharing commonly held moral values such as sharing, sensitivity to others, obeying the law, refraining from hurting others, and so on.

Hirschi maintains that people who share the character traits listed above are unlikely to engage in criminal misconduct because they have a strong stake in society. Those, however, who find their social bond weakened, are much more likely to succumb to the temptations of criminal activity. After all, crime does have rewards such as excitement, action, material goods, and pleasures. While Hirschi does not give a definitive reason for what causes a person's social bond to weaken, it seems likely that the process has two main sources: disrupted home life, and poor school ability (leading to subsequent school failure and dislike of school).

Though Hirschi's work appears extremely sound, he does not precisely define why one person's bond becomes weakened while another's stays strong; nor does he discuss whether once weakened, a social bond can be strengthened later (that is, can the criminal be "reattached" to society). Nonetheless, Control Theory is one of the more important theoretical statements of the past two decades.

**SOCIAL REACTION THEORIES**

Social Reaction Theories view criminal behavior as a result of the reaction society has to the activities of certain of its members. By trying to control, punish, and stigmatize the less powerful members of society, social control agencies actually encourage criminality. Below, two of the more prominent Social Reaction Theories are discussed:

### Labeling Theory

Labeling Theory attempts to explain both adult and juvenile crime by linking the causes of deviance to the label-producing agencies operating within American society.[35] Labeling Theory is a reaction theory; instead of concentrating on the causes or etiology, of individual criminal or delinquent acts, its major objective is to characterize the relationships between criminals and society which result in the bestowal of negative social labels (e.g., ex-con, queer, or thief).

The labeling approach does not portray the deviant as psychologically unbalanced, as adhering to a separate set of norms and values, or as anomic. Rather, it views society as creating deviance through a system of social control agencies, such as courts and prisons, which is designed to designate certain individuals as deviants. Given the self-sustaining, indelible nature of labels, the stigmatized individual is thrust outside the normal social order and is made to feel like an outsider. In time, the deviant begins to believe that the label is accurate, assumes it as a personal identity, and eventually enters into a deviant or criminal career.

Labeling Theory portrays criminality as a political rather than a moral function. Acts are not intrinsically bad but are so defined by the criminal law, which in fact is an instrument of power groups within society. Thus, a person does not become a criminal merely by engaging in deviant behavior, but is actually designated a criminal by the reactions of societal sanctioning bodies which have the power to place an individual in an outcast position.

Accompanying the criminal label are a variety of degrading social and physical restraints—handcuffs, incarceration, a criminal record, bars, cells, and so on—which leave an everlasting impression on the accused. Moreover, labels and sanctions work to define the whole person—meaning that a label evokes stereotypical conceptions of the criminal which carry over to other aspects of character. Thus, the negatively labeled person may be portrayed as evil, cruel, or untrustworthy and prevented from reentering the legitimate social order.

Faced with such condemnation, the negatively labeled person may join with society and use the label to define a personal role. The labeled offender may find no alternative but to seek others who are similarly stigmatized who can afford him or her equal status, thus promoting other deviant acts. If apprehended again and subjected to even more severe negative labels, the offender may be transformed into a "real" deviant—one whose view of self is in direct opposition to conventional society. The deviant label may become a more comfortable and personally acceptable social status than any other, and the individual whose original crime may have been a relatively harmless act may be transformed by societal action into a career deviant. The principles of Labeling Theory are listed below in greater detail.[36]

1. No act is intrinsically criminal. It is the law that makes an act a crime. Crimes therefore are defined by organized groups having sufficient political power to influence the legislative process. Many acts that are socially harmful and morally indefensible fall outside the purview of the criminal law, and some acts defined as crimes are of little social consequence.

2. Criminal definitions are enforced in the interest of powerful groups by their official representatives, including the police, courts, correctional institutions, and other administrative bodies. While the law provides detailed guidelines in its substantive definitions and rules of procedure, the way the law is implemented may be determined by the decisions of local officials who depend upon political and social leaders for financial support and other resources.

3. A person does not become a criminal by violating the law. Instead, he is designated a criminal by the reactions of authorities who confer upon him the status of an outcast and divest him of some of his social and political privileges. Although the degree of deprivation may vary by offense, victim, time, place, and other circumstances, the identification of a person as a criminal always justifies his being consigned to a deprived status.

4. The practice of dichotomizing people into criminal and noncriminal categories is contrary to common sense and empirical evidence. According to self-reports and other unofficial sources, most of the acts committed by criminals are in conformity with the law, while some of the actions of so-called conformists are

in violation of the law. The criminal label therefore designates a person's legal status, not his behavior.

5.  Only a few persons are caught in violation of the law though many may be equally guilty. The ones who are caught may be singled out for specialized treatment. Their arrest precipitates a sequence of experiences which most others do not share. There suddenly appear the police, the jail, the criminals and misfits found in the jail, the court with its retinue of lawyers, judges, witnesses, and other personnel. There are handcuffs, cells, bars, uniformed guards. There are investigations, examinations, tests, questions, allegations, accusations, verdicts and judgments over which the offender has little control. Although the accused person may be no different from the rest of his group, he suddenly becomes the central character in a drama that can have one of two endings: acquittal or conviction. If he is acquitted, the curtain is soon raised again with someone else in the major role; if convicted, he is condemned not only for what he has done but for all evils attributed to criminals in general. By being labeled a criminal he becomes one of the few that many can blame for the ills of all. He becomes a scapegoat.

6.  While the sanctions used in law enforcement are directed against the total person and not only the criminal act, the penalties vary according to the characteristics of the offender. It may be true that the law is no respecter of persons and that technically a previous criminal record is not relevant in determining the validity of charges against an individual. But it is also true that recidivists are ordinarily treated more harshly than first offenders. Usually, the more serious the prior record the greater the penalty for the instant offense. Thus, the decisions of many authorities seem to reflect the belief that, "Once a criminal always a criminal; but some are more criminal than others."

7.  Criminal sanctions also vary according to other characteristics of the offender, and for any given offense they tend to be most frequent and most severe among males, the young (excepting juveniles handled in civil courts), the unemployed or underemployed, the poorly educated, members of the lower classes, members of minority groups, transients, and residents of deteriorated urban areas. These are precisely the population segments that continue to have the highest rates for most criminal offenses. The greater the punishment the greater the crime rate.

8.  Criminal justice is founded on a stereotyped conception of the criminal as a pariah—a willfull wrongdoer who is morally bad and deserving of the community's condemnation. Condemnation is achieved by means of status-degradation ceremonies, such as the criminal trial, which strip the offender of his former identity and commit him to the new and inferior status of an evil person. Further stripping occurs if the offender is sent to prison, where he is deprived of personal possessions, assigned a number, and cloaked in a uniform symbolizing his outcast position. After discharge from the institution, he is shunned by respectable people, prevented from voting in elections or holding office, handicapped in finding employment or other legitimate pursuits, and deprived in many other ways. He cannot leave the community, change his residence, buy a car, get married, or enter into other contractual agreements without the approval of his parole officer.

 It is true that the offender's skills may be developed and his attitudes modified by correctional treatment. But these are relatively unimportant if they do not alter his position in the community or the public's attitudes towards him. And the community's attitudes are not likely to change, for the system of justiced dramatizes evil men rather than evil acts and evil practices. The criminal label alerts citizens to the presence of an evil person in their midst, and this designation, once given, is likely to be held regardless of the offender's present or future behavior. If he continues his criminal activities, this merely confirms the community's previous verdict; if he mends his ways, he may encounter doubt and suspicion, and his efforts may be viewed as a devious device for concealing his criminalistic inclinations. The public's reluctance in accepting evidence of the criminal's rehabilitation is regarded as one of the reasons for our high recidivism rates and for the limited success of our correctional programs, especially our efforts at treatment and therapy.

9. Confronted by public condemnation and the label of an evil person, it may be difficult for an offender to maintain a favorable image of himself. Initially, he may blame his low status on bad luck, lack of opportunity, discrimination, or other things beyond his control, and in this manner he may resist people's opinions of him. In rejecting these opinions, however, he is inclined also to reject the persons holding them—just as he has been rejected as a person on the basis of his criminal act. He may therefore develop an antagonism towards the community, especially its officials, and this is likely to increase the probability of further offenses.

Further offenses tend to elicit more strenuous countermeasures on the part of the authorities, thereby escalating the negative actions and reactions in a manner that hardens and crystallizes the antagonistic attitudes of actor and reactor alike. Eventually the offender comes to see himself as an enemy of society engaged in war in which right is more on his side than on society's. He acquires the traits first imputed to him and becomes the evil person he was labeled to be. In some cases beginning with an isolated and perhaps innocuous violation, an offender may be propelled by the criminalization process into careers of crime as a way of life.

Despite its widespread initial acceptance, Labeling Theory has also received quite a bit of scholarly criticism. Among its alleged failures is its inability to precisely distinguish between deviance and legitimate behavior—that is, to specify the conditions which must occur before an act or individual is to be considered deviant. Another criticism is leveled at the jurisdictional relativism of labeling. In the American justice system, rules and laws are applied within narrow boundaries dependant on community attitudes, the discretion of social control agents, public opinion, and other factors. Thus, what is labeled deviant behavior in one area may be considered generally acceptable in another.

Labeling Theory has also been criticized because it fails to consider what might have motivated someone to commit the initial deviant act, knowing full well that such behavior is subject to sanctions and labels. Ronald Akers has stated, "One sometimes gets the impression from reading the literature that people go about minding their business and then 'Wham'—bad society comes along and slaps them with a stigmatized label."[37]

The lack of attention given to those labeled offenders who *don't* go on to become career criminals after their initial labeling experience is another source of critical concern. Why one person is able to disregard a label while another succumbs to it has not been adequately explained by labeling theorists. David Bordua suggests that until this point is cleared up the theory will "be extremely weak if not positively misleading."[38]

Despite these and other criticisms, the labeling approach has been instrumental in dictating criminal justice policies in the 1970s. For example, a concerted effort has been made to limit the stigma suffered by apprehended adult and juvenile offenders. The system has been sensitized to the possible damaging power of negative labels, and programs designed to eliminate labels have flourished (see Chapter 10).

### Critical Criminology

While not a formal theory, Critical Criminology, also referred to as Radical or Marxist Criminology, is a perspective on the cause of crime which has found many adherents among scholars concerned with the politics of criminal behavior.[39]

Critical criminologists look to the state as the primary source of criminality. As articulated by Gresham Sykes, Critical Criminology views the criminal law and criminal justice system as vehicles for controlling the poor, have-not members of society. The criminal justice system is believed to help the powerful and rich to:

1. Impose their particular morality and standards of good behavior on the entire society.

2. Protect their property and physical safety from the depredations of the have-nots, even though the cost may be the loss of the legal rights of those it perceives as a threat.

3. Extend the definition of illegal or criminal behavior to encompass those who might threaten the status quo.

Sykes further asserts that the ruling elite draws the middle classes into this pattern of control because they are led to believe they too have a stake in maintaining the status quo, and they are made a part of social control agencies and the rewards of organizational careers provide inducements for keeping the poor in their place.[40]

The poor, according to Critical Criminology, may or may not commit more crimes than the rich, but they certainly are arrested more often. Sykes argues that the poor are driven to crime for the following reasons:

1. The rules imposed from above have little relationship to the dictates of their cultural norms.

2. A natural frustration exists in a society where affluence is well-publicized but unattainable.

3. There is a deep-rooted hostility generated among members of the lower class toward the social order which they are not allowed to shape or participate in.

Eugene Doleschal and Nora Klapmuts have termed Critical Criminology the *New Criminology*. According to them, the new criminologist disdains looking for the causes of crime and considers crime control a waste of time:

Official crime and the detected criminal are produced and maintained by social forces that have little or nothing to do with the harmfulness of actual behavior. The most successful criminals . . . are rarely caught, rarely prosecuted, and rarely punished. . . . These are persons with power or access to power, the rich and the intelligent. The less successful criminals are more likely to be . . . punished. . . . They are the powerless, the poor, the unintelligent.[41]

Whether it is termed Critical or New, Radical, Conflict, or Marxist, this branch of criminology seeks to redefine our current notions of crime and criminality. Instead of dwelling on theft, violence, and other street crimes, critical criminologists are more concerned with government-inspired crimes—imperialism, sexism, and racism—or crimes of the wealthy classes—fraud, greed, price fixing, and tax evasion. While, as Sykes admits, Critical Criminology cannot be tested empirically, it is an important perspective and one which every student of criminology should understand.

No discussion of criminal behavior theories would be complete without mention of female criminality. While some of the previously mentioned theories can be applied to women and girls, it is probably true that the majority of criminological theories are directed toward males. Therefore, the role of woman in crime is a unique and independent topic.

THE FEMALE
CRIMINAL

Criminologists have traditionally devoted little time or effort to studying the female's role in the crime problem. Since the percentage of crimes women engaged in seemed so minimal, studies focusing on the female criminal were often relegated to the back burner of criminological inquiry. Even less appealing to the concerned criminologist were the types of crimes women were believed to commit; unlike their male counterparts, women tended to forego major criminal acts and concentrated instead on crimes involving minor theft (e.g., shoplifting or passing bad checks) or offenses against public morality (e.g., prostitution). Crimes against public morality were especially prevalent among female juvenile delinquents. Young girls were often arrested and incarcerated for such "offenses" as immoral behavior, pregnancy, or running away. Law enforcement officials were quick to clamp down on the delinquent girl whenever they felt she was heading into a life of dissolution. As Cavan comments:

The offense of girls is almost always normal heterosexual relations carried out under conditions that seem to threaten the girl's reputation or future personal development[42]

Modern criminologists have begun to consider the female criminal with renewed and greater interest. On the one hand, the rise of feminine consciousness has caused social scientists to grant more significance to the role of women in society, and criminal activity is an aspect of that role which is of particular importance. On the other hand, women are simply committing more crimes and the rise in their arrest and incarceration rates justifies greater social concern.[43]

These criminal behavior patterns have not always been as prevalent or extensive as they are today. At one time the female criminal was regarded as an oddity. Pioneer criminologists such as Cesare Lombroso made note of the physiobiological differences between men and women and suggested that they were responsible for woman's passive, law-abiding nature.[44] Women were believed less "primitive" than men and thus less likely to be violent or offensive. The rare woman who did commit criminal acts was viewed as being more masculine in personality and demeanor than her law-abiding sisters, or she was considered sexually maladjusted or otherwise psychologically unfit. Explanations of feminine crime by criminologists such as Pollak were often based on the widely held belief that women engaged in crimes that were amoral or sexual in nature rather than violent or motivated by profit.[45]

Current theory concerning feminine crime has probably not progressed as far past the formulations of these early experts as might be desired. Two theoretical strains prevail today, one stressing psychosocial disturbance and the other focusing on sociopolitical factors.

The psychosocial disturbance school may best be illustrated in the works of Gisela Konopka, who suggests that the conflict found in the role of today's female—her need for emotional support and understanding and the consequent frustrations when these needs are not met—is a cause of crime.[46] Often, when support from her family, loved ones, or society is not forthcoming, the troubled female suffers from a low self-image and depression, resulting in criminal behavior or sexual promiscuity. Sources of conflict include overpowering or absent parents, lack of outlets for frustration (boys can fight or play football while girls can't), and the persistent double standard which labels women and girls deviant if they engage in or submit to sexual activity outside the realm of marriage, while this sort of behavior is acceptable among males.

Advocates of a sociopolitical view of female criminality suggest that the emancipation of women has appreciably affected their crime rate. Women have emerged as an identifiable, cohesive group ready to take their rightful place in the economic and social spheres of American society. As a result, the social forces which for decades played a strategic role in the life struggles of the American male are believed to have begun to have similar effects on his female counterpart. The female offender is no longer classified solely by the stereotype of sexual deviant, and is believed to commit many crimes which heretofore have fallen within the exclusive domain of the male. In commenting on the "new" female (with regard to youth crime), Freda Adler stated:

The emancipation of women appears to be having a two-fold influence on female juvenile crimes. Girls are involved in more drinking, stealing, gang activity and fighting—behavior in keeping with their adoption of male roles.

We also find increases in the total number of female deviancies. The departure from the safety of traditional female roles and the testing of uncertain alternative roles coincide with the turmoil of adolescence creating crimogenic risk factors which are found to create this increase.[47]

Adler substantiates her claims by noting that while the arrest rate for male delinquents rose 82% between 1960 and 1972, it rose 306% for female delinquents. Certainly, this dramatic increase suggests that female delinquents and criminals are rapidly intensifying their overall participation in the American crime scene.

Further evidence that sociopolitical factors affect feminine criminality is provided by recent FBI data which indicates a remarkable increase in the number of women arrested for white-collar crimes such as embezzlement, larceny, and forgery. Not surprisingly, the arrest rate for morals offenses seems to be stable (or even declining). Thus, women more frequently appear to be committing crimes which closely resemble those of their male counterparts—more serious and consequently more severely punished crimes. Simon has commented on this trend, stating that woman's new-found freedom—including emerging economic and legal rights such as simplified divorce, and abortion, and a new sense of group identification via the women's movement—mean that she will be less likely to be "victimized, dependent, and oppressed" by the men in her life.[48] As a consequence, the liberated woman may also be less likely to engage in violence (hence the trend toward maintenance of arrest rates in that crime classification) and more likely to become involved in business-related crimes.

Of course, these theoretical positions cannot be accepted without question. The rise in female property-related crime may merely reflect an adjustment in law enforcement practices toward an already existing phenomenon. As women begin to draw attention toward their new-found socioeconomic power and receive legal protection via affirmative action programs, the historically protective attitude shown them by police may be changing. Current statistics on the female crime rate may merely be more objective than those of the past, rather than indicating a real increase in criminal activity. Some support for this position comes from Schafer's analysis of crime data from thirty-one countries concerning women's participation in various offenses.[49] He found evidence that female criminality actually *increases* after marriage, a finding that contradicts assertions that the independent, single woman forced into the labor force is responsible for the upsurge in feminine crime.

Despite all the evidence that female criminal activity is increasing, relatively little empirical research has been conducted in this area. Many crime patterns still need to be investigated. These include patterns of the violence-prone mother (the battered child syndrome), the woman who commits family-centered homicide, the female white-collar criminal, and others. It is unfortunate that we know so little more today about the causes of female criminality than Lombroso did almost eighty years ago.

The *Applications* section of this chapter includes cases histories illustrating the variety of types of female crime and delinquency.

THE JUVENILE
DELINQUENT

The term *juvenile delinquency* refers to participation in law violation, deviant behavior, immoral conduct, and the like by youths within a statutory age limit (usually under 18 years of age). These types of behavior can be mild (e.g., public drinking or breaking a window) or they can be serious (e.g., juvenile homicide or rape). In 1975, the FBI recorded over 1,700 youthful arrests for murder and over 4,500 for rape, and the trend has been for these figures to increase rather than decrease. In the past, juvenile delinquency was portrayed as a lower-class, inner-city phenomenon. Theorists such as Thrasher[50] and the Gleucks[51] believed that delinquency was inspired by the forces and pressures confronting youth who dwelled in the slums and ghettos of our cities. Parental neglect, absent fathers, working mothers, peer pressure, and the need to substitute the success of illegal activities for unattainable lawful goals were all seen as contributing to delinquent behavior. Initially, the public responded to these portrayals of ill-treated and misunderstood youth with an outburst of charitable concern; the early juvenile court movement, and the development of social-work oriented community centers designed to get young people off the streets and into solid middle-class environments, were examples of the public's benevolent response to delinquency.[52]

Unfortunately, this spirit of public charity was somewhat dampened by the celebrated outbreak of juvenile gang violence in the 1950s. Post-war youth, experiencing a new sense of personal freedom, began to scorn the traditional values of their parents, which centered on moderation and delayed gratification. Lower-class youth—especially newly emigrated minorities—were able to glimpse American wealth and luxury from afar but were prevented from attaining a fair share of it. Poor educational environments, ethnocentrism, racism, and the culture of poverty of which they were a part helped to alienate many youths from the mainstream of American life. Many lower-class youth turned to gang membership as an alternative lifestyle. This meant pledging allegiance to a neighborhood gang which met together regularly to socialize, protect its territory, and engage in criminal activity. The fighting gangs into which they evolved provided a sense of achievement and community which could not be obtained elsewhere. The gang became a feared menace repeatedly portrayed in films and popular books. Walter Miller comments on this phenomenon and its consequences:

Close to the core of the public imagery of violence is the urban street gang. The imagery evokes tableaux of sinister adolescent wolf packs prowling the darkened streets of the city intent on evil-doing, of grinning gangs of teen-agers tormenting old ladies in wheelchairs and ganging up on hated and envied honor students, and of brutal bands of black-jacketed motorcyclists sweeping through quiet towns in orgies of terror and destruction. The substance of this image and its basic components of human cruelty, brutal sadism, and a delight in violence for its own sake have become conventionalized within the subculture of professional writers. The tradition received strong impetus in the public entertainment of the early 1950's with Marlon Brando and his black-jacketed motorcycle thugs, gathered momentum with the insolent and sadistic high-schoolers of *The Blackboard Jungle*, and achieved the status of an established ingredient of American folklore with the Sharks and Jets of the *West Side Story*.[53]

Today, the menace of the "Bopping-Gang" appears, with a few exceptions, to have somewhat abated. The detached street worker program of the 1960s which assigned sympathetic social workers to individual gangs is believed to have had marked success in the control of delinquency.[54] Yet, the problem of juvenile crime did not end here. Taking the place of the gang rumble was the heroin plague of the 1960s; instead of preying upon one another, youthful criminals began searching out middle-class victims to support their drug habits. At the same time, the incidence of suburban or middle-class crime increased dramatically. In the newly created suburbs, a development of the post-war housing shortage and industrial upswing, the baby boom of the late 1940s produced a great number of children who reached their teens in the early 1960s. Many were materially pampered and supplied with cars, allowances, and clothes. All too often, they could not communicate with and lacked the support of their parents, who were either busy earning enough to support their lifestyle or were themselves engaging in the varied social outlets the suburbs provided. Vandalism, shoplifting, and auto theft rapidly increased in these areas. Even more frightening was the increased use of soft (e.g., marijuana), hard, and hallucinogenic drugs, which were readily available and eagerly sought. Criminologists began to suspect that the vast differences in the arrest rates in lower-class and suburban environments was more a function of police policy and practice than a reflection of the actual crime rate.[55] Researchers such as the Meyerhoffs accompanied and observed middle-class delinquents and found that:

The adolescent in our culture, it is suggested, may be viewed as an aristocrat, a gentleman of leisure who, for a time, is not required to work but is allowed to play, explore, test limits, indulge his pleasures, and little else besides.[56]

Idleness, the availability of a car and other easily obtained luxuries all contributed to the suburban youth's crime pattern of drugs, vandalism, and motor vehicle crime. The shopping center, another post-war development which rapidly spread to the suburbs, displayed goods openly and curtailed the deployment of sales personnel; shoplifting became a favorite suburban teen-age pastime. Compounding these problems was the immunity the middle-class delinquent seemed to have from prosecution. Intensive law enforcement campaigns were generally absent from affluent suburban communities and, where present, were designed to keep troublemakers out and not to overtly bother residents. Above all, reputations of families and youths in the community had to be maintained. It appeared that police were as interested in protecting the middle-class offenders and the families involved as they were in making an arrest or helping a victim.

Today, delinquent behavior is unfortunately a phenomenon found in all types of communities and neighborhoods. It is believed that nearly every youngster engages in some behavior which, if caught, would make the offender legally eligible for an arrest, court appearance, and delinquency label. However, it is estimated that only 3% or less of court-eligible youth are actually contacted by police. In a study entitled *Delinquent Behavior in an American City*, Gold cites evidence which corroborates this contention: only a small percentage (15%) of the *most* delinquent youth in his sample were ever arrested, and of these only 11% went to court.[57] Thus, juvenile delinquency remains largely undetected and, though it is certainly prevalent, no one really knows how much actually exists.

Today, much of what is known of the extent of juvenile delinquency comes from *self-report studies*. This type of research employs anonymous survey questionnaires which are handed out to students in high schools, community centers, and the like. Youths participating in these surveys are presented with a list of crimes and asked to indicate how many times in the past year or during their lives they have engaged in each of the delinquent types of behavior noted. Self-reported delinquent behavior can later be compared to police records to help determine the amount of hidden delinquency in a community. In addition, the personalities, attitudes, and behavior of delinquent youths can be compared to those of nondelinquents through additional substantive questions on particular topics of interest.

Table 2.2 shows the results of one such high school study conducted by the authors in an upper middle class suburb in the northeastern United States. Though the official crime rate in this town was quite low, it is evident that its teenage population engaged in serious and widespread delinquency:

As Table 2.2 indicates, a significant proportion of surveyed youths reported having engaged in drinking, drug use, theft, and property damage. It becomes clear from this data that delinquent behavior is commonplace even among the wealthier young members of our society.

To combat the excesses of juvenile delinquency, federal, state, and local governments have poured millions of dollars into prevention programs, treatment facilities, and correctional programs designed to steer youth away from delinquent modes of behavior. These efforts include after-school activities, drug crisis intervention hot lines, and innovative treatment methods such as group therapy. However, any initial optimism that these programs would successfully eliminate juvenile crime has waned as the delinquency rate continues to rise. One result of this program failure is that experts have pointed accusative fingers at the justice system itself and suggested that it is actually responsible for much of the delinquent activity that exists in the United States.

On what do they base this accusation? Scholars who collectively comprise the "Labeling School"[58] suggest that processing a youth through the juvenile justice system automatically confers a negative social label which remains long after a specific legal experience has ended. Labels such as

| Delinquent Act | Males % | Females % | Total % |
|---|---|---|---|
| Theft under $10 | 62.2 | 43.6 | 52.9 |
| Theft over $10 | 28.3 | 12.5 | 20.4 |
| Sniffed heroin | 3.4 | 3.1 | 3.3 |
| Shot up heroin | 2.7 | 1.1 | 1.9 |
| Used uppers | 9.9 | 8.1 | 9.0 |
| Shot up uppers | 3.5 | 2.4 | 3.0 |
| Drank beer | 68.5 | 58.0 | 63.3 |
| Drank liquor | 52.5 | 50.7 | 51.6 |
| Drank wine | 35.3 | 38.3 | 36.8 |
| Used marijuana | 52.0 | 47.0 | 49.5 |
| Used downers | 8.0 | 10.3 | 9.2 |
| Used LSD | 11.9 | 9.1 | 10.5 |
| Used cocaine | 7.1 | 2.4 | 4.8 |
| Engaged in fist fighting | 65.7 | 20.3 | 43.0 |
| Carried weapon | 38.2 | 8.2 | 23.2 |
| Fought with weapon | 12.5 | 2.6 | 7.6 |
| Stole car | 9.4 | 1.9 | 5.7 |
| Used force to steal | 6.9 | 1.7 | 4.3 |
| Engaged in forcible sex | 6.6 | — | — |
| Engaged in drunk driving | 22.1 | 13.6 | 17.9 |
| Destroyed property | 41.8 | 12.1 | 27.0 |
| (N) | (786) | (883) | (1669) |

TABLE 2.2. Percent of Respondents Admitting to One or More Acts During Past Twelve Months.

"troublemaker," "delinquent," and "hoodlum" identify youths as potential or actual social misfits, and help to permanently remove labeled offenders from the legitimate social order. More important, it is believed that delinquent labels help to change the self-image of the youth—a transformation which results in the delinquent actually using that label as a personal identity and coming to believe in the validity of the label. If in fact recognition by official law enforcement agencies results in a permanent negative label being bestowed upon a youth, then it follows that any treatment, no matter how benevolently conceived, may actually be harmful.

This dilemma has resulted in the "Diversion Movement," which seeks to eliminate as much contact as possible between the juvenile justice system and young offenders (see Chapter 10). Thus, the trend in the 1970s was to curtail or eliminate rather than improve treatment for delinquents. Later in the text, more detailed accounts will be made of the history of the juvenile justice system and of juvenile law (Chapter 19).

The control or elimination of crime and delinquency are among the most frequently stated goals of the American criminal justice system. Crime control actually involves a very complex set of behavior types and the term entails a number of unique, independent processes.

CAN CRIME BE PREVENTED?

The all-inclusive category of crime prevention includes, for one, the *general prevention* concept. Proponents of this idea maintain that crime can be gradually eliminated by identifying its causes and substituting alternatives to them.[59] The community center, after-school programs, and Boys and Girls Clubs are examples of programs designed for delinquency prevention, while job training, welfare, and mental health clinics are intended to lessen the incidence of adult crime.

*General deterrence* is another type of crime prevention, one which requires powerful laws and efficient law enforcement agencies to administer them. It is believed that this approach frightens the potential criminal into not committing crimes. Drug laws with severe mandatory sentences are an example of general deterrence. *Special prevention* entails the rehabilitation of the known criminal through treatment programs based in prisons, community centers, and other locations. Special prevention programs include vocational counseling of ex-offenders and group therapy. Finally, crime prevention also involves *special deterrence*. This approach aims at eliminating recidivism (repetition of crime) by punishing individual offenders severely and threatening even stronger punishments if they commit further crimes. Mandatory life sentences for three-time felons would be an example of special deterrence.

## General and Special Deterrence

Today, crime prevention primarily relies on the general deterrence concept. In our society, general deterrence refers to the power of the criminal law to prevent crime through its explicit, well-publicized system of punishments. At first glance, the deterrent power of punishment seems straightforward. Harsh legal and social penalties accompanying convictions for law violations should deter the potential criminal from committing crime and, therefore, eventually eliminate any thoughts or desires of citizens to break the law. Penalties may include the loss of liberty through imprisonment or other modes of incarceration, loss of social status through the shame and stigma accompanying conviction, and loss of privileges such as a driver's license; of course, the most extreme penalty is death.

Regardless of what form punishment takes, it connotes a sense of disapproval by the community and casts the convicted offender outside the boundaries of social acceptability. It exposes to all members of society the fact that this person is reprehensible in the eyes of peers. This social penalty may actually constitute the primary deterrent power of the law.

Unfortunately, the deterrent power of the criminal law appears to be somewhat illusory; even the harshest penalty, the death sentence, has had relatively little effect on the violent crime rate.[60] And though there is no absolutely valid way to determine the deterrent effect of the law, a constantly rising crime rate does little to allay our fears over its ineffectuality.

What, then, are the problems that diminish the criminal law's deterrent effect? While the old adage says "crime does not pay," the truth of the matter may be somewhat different. Individuals are often made aware at an early age that it is fairly easy to get away with crime. These perceptions transcend class boundaries; upper-class youth may hear and observe their elders openly discussing illegal business practices, such as income tax evasion and employee pilferage, while lower-class youth may discover that the wealthiest citizens in their cultures have successfully managed illegal careers—in these neighborhoods, the bookie, pimp, or drug dealer is usually identified by an expensive car, well-tailored clothes, and fine jewelry. In this climate, it is difficult for the law to have a real deterrent effect.

Another factor inhibiting the deterrent power of the law is its *fundamental fairness*. For years, judges and legislators have built into the American legal system a series of checks and balances, procedures and philosophies expressly designed to protect the rights of the accused. Each step in the criminal justice process may be challenged in a court of law if the standards promised the accused individual have not been precisely met. Included within this policy of fairness is the notion that a person accused of crime is innocent until proven guilty, and this concept remains one of the cornerstones of our legal system. Upholding it places the burden of proof (that is, the need to prove absolutely that an individual has committed a crime) squarely on the shoulders of the state's legal authorities. Furthermore, the Supreme Court of the United States, the nation's highest legal tribunal, has set up a strict code of conduct for law enforcement agents which protects the rights of persons accused of crimes. Consequently, the legal maze through which a person must travel before conviction has become so lengthy and complex that many persons guilty of crimes go free due to legal technicalities and, when punishment is leveled, it is often years after the crime has been committed. Such procedural roadblocks do little to heighten the deterrent power of the law. At the same time, of course, legal checks and balances protect the rights of innocent persons accused of crimes; regardless of how many legal snarls these guarantees create, they are an essential feature of American democracy.

Other stumbling blocks facing the general deterrence concept are the biased fashion in which the criminal law is applied in America and the consequences of this bias. It is no coincidence that a disproportionate number of minority group members are found in courts, jails, and prisons, or have faced execution.[61] Discrimination by agents of the criminal justice system serves to diminish respect for the law and creates barriers between the criminal justice system and large segments of the population. Compounding the problem is the widespread belief that wealthier members of society are merely given slaps on the wrist for their white-collar infractions while lower-class offenders are punished more severely for comparable crimes. In a climate of anger and mistrust, the inconsistent application of the law may frustrate and alienate people and turn them toward criminal solutions to their problems.

The concept of special deterrence relates directly to the punishment and control of convicted criminals. In this type of crime prevention, those convicted of criminal acts are subjected to sanctioning so severe that future criminal behavior is psychologically no longer viable. The special deterrence concept contains a number of different features. One aspect is containment of crime through the incapacitation of offenders. Obviously, criminals who are locked up do not constitute a threat to society or its institutions. Even when an offender is released on parole or subjected to other means of community supervision, the threat of immediate punishment if established rules are violated acts as a special deterrent to crime. The severity of punishment, the inhuman qualities of prisons, and the threat of future sanctions and degradations supposedly impress the criminal with the senselessness of future law violations. These combined factors are all intended to divert the motivation the convicted criminal has to commit additional crimes. Advocates of special deterrence assume that a rational choice is made to commit a crime and that society can inhibit and neutralize that choice by making its consequences all too real and unpleasant. What, then, are the problems associated with this approach?

First of all, the efficiency of special deterrence may be criticized on the grounds that it does not effectively perform its specific function and that it is applied in an unfair and biased manner. Often, the best candidates for deterrence are never apprehended and go free even if they are caught. It may not be far from the truth to argue that only the poorest, clumsiest criminals wind up in prison while their wealthier, more capable peers go free. Thus, special deterrence is particularly lacking in social responsibility.

The effectiveness of special deterrence can also be challenged on the grounds that it is a low-efficiency, high-cost system of crime prevention. Incarcerating individuals for many years may cost the taxpayer far more than the amount of money involved in the original crime. It has been estimated that it costs $10,000 to build facilities to keep one offender in a state prison.[62] The costs of guards, buildings, grounds, food, and other essentials are prohibitive. At the same time, a prisoners' family often survives on public subsidy (welfare) until the wage earner is released. Finally, potential taxpayers become unwilling wards of the state, diminishing rather than increasing the public revenue.

When considering the future consequences of special deterrence, many critics are apprehensive of the stigma and public shame experienced by those punished by society. There are those who suggest that crime deterrence is specious since the officially sanctioned never outlive their criminal records, are shunned by normal society, and are mistrusted by potential employers. What can they do but turn back to the criminal activities which put them in prison in the first place? This argument is supported by the high recidivism rates which are the norm in most correctional systems.

"Let the punishment fit the crime" was the policy of the Lord High Executioner,[63] but special deterrence often ignores this homily. Thus, it may be difficult for criminals to link the effects of their crimes to subsequent punishments when there is no logical connection between them. An individual convicted of violent crime in our society is often subjected to the same type of punishment as is the thief, though their crimes are committed for different reasons and involve different actions. While blanket punishments seem inadequate, alternatives to them have not been forthcoming.

In ancient days, more effort was made to link the punishment with the crime—for example, a thief's hand was cut off. The Code of Hammurabi, the legal system of the Babylonia in the eighteenth century B.C., advocated an "eye for an eye" and consisted of an explicit set of rules matching specific crimes and punishments. The American criminal justice system has rejected the brutality and motives of revenge inherent in such a legal code, but the current practice of similar universal punishments has done little to improve the special deterrence feature of the legal system.

Finally, both special and general deterrence assume *rationality* on the part of the criminal. It is expected that the individual will think before acting and contemplate the possible sanctions, weigh the consequences, and remember previous punishments. Yet there is no real evidence that this thought process actually occurs before a crime is committed. Some crimes, especially those involving violence, may be immediate, explosive responses to stimuli and may not involve any rational thought at all. Property crimes, on the other hand, may result from societal pressures which are so powerful that the offender is incapable of reflecting upon the consequences of committing such a crime. The spontaneity of criminal behavior is a special problem and threat to the deterrence concept, and so far has proven an almost insurmountable barrier to its effectiveness.

### General and Special Prevention

General prevention is based on the assumption that some classes of criminal and delinquent activity may be functionally eliminated by the presence of treatment alternatives. Prevention advocates believe that the commission of crime is a rational human response to the realities of life, based on such motives as need, anger, revenge, and frustration. General prevention programs hope to relieve the root causes of crime by providing such services as financial aid for the needy, mental hygiene for the angry and depressed, and social outlets for the alienated and lonely. Such community-based programs as Head Start, the Job Corps, and Upward Bound have attempted to lower crime rates by providing educational and job-related opportunities.

There are many problems associated with general prevention. Probably the greatest dilemma is that of resource allocation. A true prevention effort applied on a national level would cost billions of dollars, since each offender, crime, and personal situation is unique and must be treated as such. Compounding the problem is the fact that crime prevention funds often find their way into the pockets of middle-class treatment personnel and thus are taken out of the community in which they would do the most good.

Also associated with general prevention are the twin problems of labeling and stigma. Some experts believe that any sort of treatment for crime may actually contribute to its eventual commission by alerting the world to the potential deviant nature of the treated individual. Prevention programs may also help to stigmatize or label criminals. Sociologists call this phenomenon the "self-fulfilling prophecy." For example, a teacher may consider a student to be a potential delinquent though he has never actually engaged in delinquent behavior. Sending him to special classes or counseling to prevent his future delinquency alerts his peers, other school officials, and the boy himself to his supposedly deviant nature. The resulting social consequences may frustrate, anger, and alienate the youth and finally propel him into delinquency. Without the initial societal recognition, the boy might never engage in deviant behavior.

Special prevention, on the other hand, requires rehabilitation facilities—prisons, jails, halfway houses or in the community—for those already convicted of crimes. Some programs are job-oriented, others involve mental hygiene, and still others deal with counseling families and individuals; special facilities can help to alleviate some of these pressures (see Chapter 16).

Special prevention programs suffer from the same set of problems as do general prevention programs, with one unfortunate addition. Critics of special prevention argue that convicted criminals should not receive a substantial share of the nation's resources; they do not deserve it, nor should it be siphoned away from other needy law-abiding citizens. This principle is known as "less eligibility." Furthermore, critics argue that special prevention programs coddle the criminal and encourage rather than discourage crime.

Both special and general prevention programs suffer from the lack of specific knowledge of the causes of crime; unless the factors which precipitate crime are known, it is difficult to design programs that can eliminate it. Studies that have attempted to isolate or identify the most beneficial prevention programs have concluded that no single type of prevention is superior to the others and not one has shown any lasting benefits.[64]

SUMMARY

Criminology is the study of the cause of crime, the nature of criminals, and the prevention of illegal activity. Criminologists use many different techniques in order to study crime, including survey research, observation, life histories, and record studies.

A number of different groupings of criminological theory have been formulated over the years. One position holds that the cause of crime is individualistic in nature and results from some weakness or fault in the crime-prone person. Individual problems may have genetic, psychological, biological, or other sources.

Another prominent view suggests that there are sociological reasons for the development of criminal behavior patterns. On the one hand, the frustrations caused by maintaining a lower-class status are viewed as turning youths into delinquents, then adult criminals. On the other hand, the process of living in society, including learning, social experiences, school, and family, are viewed as contributing to criminal careers. Finally, the activities of social control agencies are believed to encourage rather than discourage delinquent and criminal activities.

Criminologists are also concerned with the control of criminal behavior, and have therefore developed models to prevent crime by providing criminals with *legitimate* behavioral alternatives, or to deter it by making potential criminals afraid of the power of the law and punishment.

QUESTIONS FOR
DISCUSSION

**1.** What factors interfere with the deterrent power of the criminal law? What can be done to improve crime prevention methods in your community?

**2.** How might crime on college campuses be studied? Would it be ethical to study crime without telling the subjects what you were doing?

**3.** Do most theories of crime and delinquency seem to discriminate against the poor? Which theories account for "white-collar" or middle-class crime?

NOTES

**1.** For a discussion of the victim-criminal relationship and its implications, see Stephen Schafer, *Compensation & Restitution to Victims of Crime* (Montclair, N.J.: Patterson Smith, 1970).

**2.** See, for example, Gresham Sykes, "The Rise of Critical Criminology," *Journal of Criminal Law and Criminology* 65:206 (June 1974); Ian Taylor et al., *The New Criminology—For a Social Theory of Deviance* (New York: Harper & Row, 1973).

**3.** For an important discussion of how survey techniques are used (and abused) in criminological research, see Travis Hirschi and Hannon Selvin, *Principles of Survey Analysis* (New York: Free Press, 1973); See also Earl Babbie, *Survey Research Methods* (Belmont, Cal.: Wadsworth Publishing Co., 1973).

**4.** William F. Whyte, *Street Corner Society: The Social Structure of an Italian Slum* (Chicago: University of Chicago Press, 1955); Laud Humpherys, *Tea Room Trade: Impersonal Sex in Public Places* (Chicago: Aldine Publishing Co., 1975), revised edition.

**5.** Claude Brown, *Manchild in The Promised Land* (New York: Macmillan, 1965). Piri Thomas, *Down These Mean Streets* (New York: Alfred A. Knopf, 1967).

**6.** Harry King and William Chambliss, *Box Man: A Professional Thief's Journey* (New York: Harper & Row, 1972); R. Lincoln Keiser, *The Vice Lords: Warriors of the Street* (New York: Holt, Rinehart and Winston, 1969).

**7.** King and Chambliss, *Box Man*, p. 24.

**8.** David Duffee and Larry Siegel, "Organization Man: Legal Counsel in Juvenile Court," *Criminal Law Bulletin* 7:544 (July/August 1971).

**9.** Edward Banfield, *The Unheavenly City* (Boston: Little, Brown and Co., 1968); Nathan Glazer and Daniel Moynihan, *Beyond the Melting Pot* (Cambridge, Mass.: M.I.T. Press, 1963).

**10.** Quoted in Stephen Schafer, *Introduction to Criminology* (Reston, Virginia: Reston Publishing Co., 1976), p. 43.

**11.** William Sheldon and Eleanor Glueck, *Physique & Delinquency* (New York: Harper & Brothers, 1956); see also William Sheldon et al., *Varieties of Human Physique* (New York: Harper & Row, 1940).

**12.** The above-mentioned studies are quoted and discussed in Schafer, *Introduction to Criminology*, pp. 60–61.

**13.** See for example, H.J. Eysenck, *The*

*Biological Basis of Personality* (Springfield, Ill.: Charles Thomas, 1967); *Crime and Personality* (London: Routledge, 1964); S.R. Hathaway and E.D. Monachesi, "The M.M.P.I. in the Study of Juvenile Delinquents," in A.M. Rose, ed., *Mental Health and Mental Disorder* (London: Routledge, 1956).

**14.** For a general review of this approach, see M. Phillip Feldman, *Criminal Behavior: A Psychological Analysis* (New York: John Wiley, 1977).

**15.** G. Waldo and S. Dinitz "Personality Attributes of The Criminal: An Analysis of Research Studies, 1950–65," *Journal of Research in Crime & Delinquency* 4:185 (1967).

**16.** Emile Durkheim, *Suicide: A Study In Sociology*, John Spaulding and George Simpson, trans. (Glencoe, Ill.: Free Press, 1951).

**17.** For a general view, see Leonard Hippchen, *Ecologic-Biological Approaches to Treatment of Delinquents and Criminals* (New York: Van Nostrand Reinhold, 1978).

**18.** James Brantley and Marjorie Kravitz, *The Etiology of Criminality: Nonbehavioral Science Perspectives* (Washington, D.C.: U.S. Government Printing Office, 1979), p. vi.

**19.** For a general review, see Travis Hirschi and Michael Hindelang, "Intelligence and Delinquency: A Revisionist Review," *American Sociological Review* 42:571–585 (1977).

**20.** Ibid.

**21.** For an anthology of relevant studies, see S.A. Mednick and K.O. Christiansen, *eds.*, *Biosocial Bases of Criminal Behavior* (New York: Gardner Press, 1977).

**22.** Quoted in Hermann Mannheim, *Comparative Criminology* (Boston: Houghton Mifflin Co., 1965), p. 96.

**23.** Emile Durkheim, *Suicide: A Study in Sociology*.

**24.** Robert K. Merton, "Social Structure and Anomie," in *Social Theory and Social Structure* (Glencoe, Ill.: Free Press, 1957).

**25.** Albert Cohen, *Delinquent Boys: The Culture of the Gang* (Glencoe, Ill.: Free Press, 1955).

**26.** Richard Cloward and Lloyd Ohlin, *Delinquency and Opportunity: A Theory of Delinquent Gangs* (Glencoe, Ill.: Free Press, 1960.

**27.** See Paul Lerman, *Delinquency and Social Policy* (New York: Praeger Publishers, 1970).

**28.** Walter Miller, "Lower-Class Culture as a Generating Milieu of Gang Delinquency," *Journal of Social Issues* 14:5 (1958).

**29.** This section has been taken from Clarence Schrag, *Crime & Justice American Style*, pp. 46–47.

**30.** Edwin Sutherland and Donald Cressy, *Criminology* (Philadelphia: J.B. Lippincott Co., 1970), pp. 71–91.

**31.** Stephen Schafer, *Introduction to Criminology*, p. 71.

**32.** Gresham Sykes and David Matza, "Techniques of Neutralization: A Theory of Delinquency." *American Sociological Review* 22; 664 (December 1957); See also David Matza, *Delinquency & Drift* (New York: John Wiley & Sons, 1964).

**33.** Larry Siegel, et al. "Values & Delinquent Youth: An Empirical Reexamination of Theories of Delinquency," *British Journal of Criminology* 237 (July 1973).

**34.** Travis Hirschi, *Causes of Delinquency* (Berkeley, Cal.: University of California Press, 1969).

**35.** For an extensive overview of labeling theory, see ·Edwin Schur, *Labeling Deviant Behavior*.

**36.** The principles listed below are adapted from Clarence Schrag, *Crime & Justice: American Style*, pp. 89–91.

**37.** Ronald Akers, "Problems in the Sociology of Deviance: Social Definitions

& Behavior," *Social Forces* 46:463 (Spring 1968).

**38.** David Brodua, "On Deviance," *Annals* 111:121 (1967).

**39.** Gresham Sykes, "The Rise of Critical Criminology."

**40.** Ibid.

**41.** E. Doleschal and N. Klapmuts, "Toward a New Criminology," *Crime & Delinquency* 5:607 (December 1973).

**42.** Ruth Cavan and Theodore Ferdinand, *Juvenile Delinquency* (Philadelphia: J.B. Lippincott Co., 1975), pp. 217–230.

**43.** For further data, see Federal Bureau of Investigation, *Uniform Crime Report 1978* (Washington, D.C.: U.S. Government Printing Office, 1975).

**44.** Caesar Lombroso and William Ferrero, *The Female Offender*, (New York: D. Appleton & Co., 1899).

**45.** Otto Pollak, *The Criminality of Women* (New York: A.S. Barnes & Co., 1950).
**46.** Gisela Konopka, *The Adolescent Girl In Conflict* (Englewood Cliffs, N.J.: Prentice-Hall, 1966).

**47.** Freda Adler, *Sisters in Crime: The Rise of the Female Criminal* (New York: McGraw-Hill Book Co. 1975), p. 95.

**48.** Rita Simon, "Women & Crime Revisited," *Social Science Quarterly* 56:658 (March 1976).

**49.** Stephen Schafer, "Criminality of Women," *Journal of Criminal Law, Criminology & Police Science* 39:77 (May/June 1948).

**50.** Fredric Thrasher, *The Gang* (Chicago: University of Chicago Press, 1927).

**51.** Sheldon and Eleanor Glueck, *One Thousand Juvenile Delinquents* (Cambridge, Mass.: Harvard University Press, 1934).

**52.** Anthony Platt, *The Child Savers* (Chicago: University of Chicago Press, 1969).

**53.** Walter Miller, "Violent Crime and City Gangs," in *Delinquency, Crime & So-cial Process*, Cressey and Ward, Eds. (New York: Harper & Row, 1969), p. 689.

**54.** See Irving Spergel, *Street Gang Work: Theory & Practice* (Reading, Mass.: Addison-Wesley Publishing Co., 1966).

**55.** See, for example, Edmund Vaz, "Middle Class Adolescents: Self-Reported Delinquency and Youth Crime Activities," *The Canadian Review of Sociology & Anthropology* 2:52 (February 1965).

**56.** Howard and Barbara Meyerhoff, "Middle-Class Gangs," in *The Sociology of Crime & Delinquency*, Marvin Wolfgang et al., ed. (New York: John Wiley & Sons, 1970), p. 470.

**57.** Martin Gold, *Delinquent Behavior in an American City* (Belmont, Cal.: Brooks/Cole Publishing Co., 1970), pp. 102–104.

**58.** See, for example, Edwin Schur, *Labeling Deviant Behavior* (New York: Harper & Row, 1971).

**59.** For examples of prevention programs, see S. Kobrin, "The Chicago Area Project—A 25-year Assessment," *Annals* 322:22 (March 1959); G. Robin, "Anti-Poverty Programs & Delinquency," *J. Criminal Law, Criminology and Police Science* 60:327 (1969); H.L. Witmer and E. Tufts, *The Effectiveness of Delinquency Prevention Programs* (Washington, D.C.: U.S. Government Printing Office, 1954), Children's Bureau Publication No. 350.

**60.** The most important studies in the area of deterrence are situated in the area of capital punishment. For a discussion, see Chapter 13.

**61.** See, for example, William Bowers, *Executions in America* (Lexington, Mass.: Lexington Books, 1974).

**62.** Mark Richmond, "Measuring The Cost of Correctional Services," *Crime and Delinquency* 245 (July 1972).

**63.** See Gilbert and Sullivan, The Mikado.

**64.** Robert Martinson, "What Works? Questions & Answers About Prison Reform," *The Public Interest* 35:22 (Spring 1974).

# The Female Delinquent—3 Portraits*

## CASE HISTORY 1—
## BARBARA

Barbara is a 14 year old black female, who has spent the last 18 months in a training school. She is an epileptic who has had a history of assaults. Prior to placement, she had been involved in a street gang that was responsible for several robberies and assaults on the elderly. She is an out-of-wedlock child residing intermittently between her mother and her grandmother. She scores below average on the I.Q. tests—but she reads on a ninth grade level.

Physically, Barbara is very small. She has lost several front teeth in fights but has never been to a dentist. Her moods range from a personality that is utterly charming to one that "tunes out" when she no longer wants to deal with the realities of a situation. She has learned that feigning epileptic attacks provides her with attention that she craves, but has also had several real attacks that have scared her.

Barbara's mother has four other children, each with different fathers, residing with her in a three-room apartment. She is employed as a domestic full time and also works as a waitress in an all-night eatery. There is little, if any, supervision for Barbara or the other children in the home. The grandmother lives in the same town and is a welfare recipient. Barbara has never met her father.

Because of her violent history, Barbara cannot be placed in any of the smaller community-based group homes. She insists that the only acceptable place for her is home. She will probably be in the training school until she is 18 years old.

## CASE HISTORY 2—
## MELISSA

Melissa was 15 when she was first arrested. She was living with her parents and her two sisters. Her father supported the family on his $7,000 annual salary. Melissa is an attractive young woman and, until the time of her first arrest, was doing well in school. According to school officials she is intelligent, made excellent grades and had a good attitude about school.

Within a month's time Melissa was arrested twice. The first time her mother called the police requesting that they pick Melissa up because she refused to go to school, and because lately

---

*Source: Excerpted from *Little Sisters and the Law*, U.S. Department of Justice, Office of Juvenile Justice and Delinquency Prevention (Washington, D.C., Government Printing Office, 1977).

she had been "getting upset too easily and having lots of emotional scenes." When the police arrived Melissa had left the house. They found her a few minutes later walking in the rain a short distance away. She was arrested and charged with running away. Melissa explained to the police that she did not want to return home because she and her mother were not getting along and because her father beat her. She asked the police if she could go to live with an aunt. However, her mother would not give her approval because "it wouldn't look right." Melissa then spent eight days in detention before she was returned to her parents' home. A few days later the police received a call from Melissa asking that they please come get her because she had just had an "argument" with her father and she was afraid he would hurt her. When the police arrived, they arrested Melissa at her request and again charged her with running away.

This time Melissa waited in detention for two weeks until she was placed with a foster family and ordered to attend a day school for troubled girls where she could receive counseling. Melissa was unhappy at the new school and eventually was dismissed for fighting with other girls. A few days later she was asked to leave her foster home for "abusing the telephone" and having a "belligerent and nonconforming attitude," according to her foster parents.

Melissa was then placed at St. Ann's, a residential parochial school for "difficult" boys and girls. After a month and a half she ran away from there. While on the street she tried unsuccessfully to find a new foster home so she would not be returned to St. Ann's. Apprehended by the police, she refused to go back to St. Ann's and was placed in detention where she remained for two weeks.

She was then placed in a community residential program but was soon dismissed for leaving without permission to attend a local fair and for spending time with an unknown young man. She was returned to the detention center for four months before being committed to the state training school for girls.

## CASE HISTORY 3— SALLY

Sally is 17 years old, white, and has spent the last two and a half years in a state training school. She was sent to the institution because of a long history of running away and truancy. She also allegedly had been involved in prostitution since age 13, although this was never proven in court.

Sally lived in the suburbs of a major metropolitan area with her mother and maternal grandmother. Her mother, divorced since Sally was 12, is unskilled and has been living on welfare for the past five years.

Sally's problems began soon after her father left home. She began to stay out of school and ran away from home frequently. Her mother turned to alcohol as an escape and soon became so unable to cope with Sally that she asked her mother to come and live in their home to help raise Sally. The school finally turned Sally's case over to the county probation department. After extensive testing, the department recommended that Sally be placed out of the home. Although an institutional setting was not recommended for Sally, other alternatives, including foster care, had a three-month waiting list for girls. Because there were no appropriate community-based residential programs for young women in Sally's community, she was sent to a state institution.

After she was released, she immediately started her pattern of running away again. She was eventually transferred to a secure institution, but her behavior did not improve. After spending eight months in a secure setting, Sally was paroled to her own home. This decision was made solely because the facility in which she was confined was being converted to a program for difficult boys.

Sally was seen once by an aftercare counselor after returning home. During that visit, the counselor explained the rules of parole, but made no effort to help her enroll in school or in a vocational or job training program. Sally stayed at home for two weeks. She disappeared one evening and has not been heard from since.

# 3

# Criminal Law

## CHAPTER OUTLINE

## KEY TERMS

**Law of Precedent**
**Substantial Capacity**
**Procedural Law**
**Substantive Law**
**Model Penal Code**
**Durham Rule**
**M'Naghten**
**Insanity**
**Intent**

**Misdemeanor**
**Mens Rea**
**Felony**
**Tort**
**Common Law**
**Crime**
**Actus Reus**
**Self-Defense**
**Civil Law**

AN
INTRODUCTION
TO CRIMINAL
LAW

In the preceding two chapters, we have examined the nature and extent of crime and the theories which seek to explain criminal behavior. Mention was made of how crime is defined as a function of our social, political, and legal systems. In this chapter, we discuss the basic principles of the criminal law and how it regulates conduct in our society.

The legal system of the United States is based upon the British structure of jurisprudence. Prior to the writing of the Constitution and state legal codes, formal law in the original colonies was adopted from English law. The principles of English law, derived from various cases and decisions handed down by judges in Great Britain, remain the basis for much of the philosophy of the American legal system. British law was the basis for what is known today as the *common law*. The common law developed when English judges actually "created" many crimes by ruling certain actions to be crimes. Thus, most serious crimes such as murder, rape, arson, and burglary were originally *judge-created* offenses, and were not determined by existing criminal statutes or a sense of moral outrage. The original colonists abided by these various common-law rulings and adapted them to fit their needs, making extensive changes in them when necessary. Most state legislatures have taken the common law and standardized it in statutory form, while some states have abolished common-law crimes by passing comprehensive penal codes. Other states have retained the common law by reference, or by incorporating it into their penal codes.[1] Today, it is unlikely that an offender will be charged with a common-law crime because most such crimes are covered by state statutes or decisions. On a federal level there are no common-law crimes since the British common law did not serve as the basis for the creation of federal law. What constitutes a crime in the federal level has been determined by the United States Congress through the enactment of a federal criminal statute.

One virtue of the common law is that it is related to the *law of precedent*. Once a decision has been made by a court, that judicial decision is generally binding on the courts in subsequent applicable cases. Since the common law represents decisions handed down by judges, as distinguished from those determined by statutes, it follows the rule of precedent. This legal principle, known as *stare decisis*, originated in England and is used as the basis for deciding future legal decisions.[2] The courts are generally bound to follow the common law as it has been judicially determined in prior cases. The principle is also used in interpreting evidence given in trials and in determining trial outcomes. The advantage of this legal doctrine is that it promotes trial outcomes. The advantage of this legal doctrine is that it promotes stability and certainty in the process of making legal decisions. However, where sufficient reason exists for varying from precedent, the court need not follow previous decisions. For example, when the United States Supreme Court decided the landmark decision of *Gideon v. Wainwright* in 1963,[3] it overruled the law established in the case of *Betts v. Brady* in 1942[4] by granting that a criminal defendant has a constitutional right to counsel in a state felony prosecution. Thus, changing social conditions occasionally make it necessary for higher courts to adopt new laws.

In order to further understand the law, it is necessary to study its primary sources. The foundations of law generally can be found in case decisions and legislation. Legal cases, such as those decided by American courts, constitute judge-made decisions. Law in the form of public acts passed by legislative bodies, such as the United States Congress or state legislatures, constitutes the statutory or legislative law. To be aware of what the law is on a given subject requires that one examine both the existing case decisions and statutes. Furthermore, legislative law is also determined by the United States Constitution and state constitutions. In addition, governmental rules and regulations exist which have the force of law. The President of the United States or the governor of a state can issue an executive order, or a police or corrections department can issue regulations pertinent to a legislative delegation of authority. For example, in 1966 President Johnson issued an executive order creating the President's Crime Commission.[5] Similarly, the Massachusetts Department of Corrections developed rules and regulations for a work furlough program after its passage by state legislation.[6] These rules, along with local and municipal ordinances, constitute the major sources of all fields of law. A comprehensive listing of the various sources of law appears in Table 3.1.

Sometimes, conflicts in legal interpretation arise between these various sources of the law, forcing an eventual reinterpretation of a law's meaning. For example, a state legislature might pass a statute banning the possession of unlicensed handguns. A provision in the United States Constitution, however, reaffirms the right of all citizens to bear arms. Thus, these two legal sources apparently conflict. To settle the issue, a citizen may bring suit in a court of law questioning the legality of the statute. This third source of law, the court, will interpret both legal documents in order to first decide whether they are in conflict and then work out an equitable solution. In this case, the court might decree that the Constitution actually refers to firearms, such as rifles, and not to concealed weapons, such as handguns; or it might suggest that requiring a license does not impede the right to bear arms; or it might conclude that the statute was actually unconstitutional and should be abolished. In any event, one source of the law can conflict with another and may then be modified or changed by a third source via a legislative or court-made decision. Finally, it is important to remember that the nation's law, regardless of its source, must always

TABLE 3.1
Major Sources of Law

1. United States Constitution.
2. State constitutions.
3. Federal and state court decisions.
4. Common law.
5. Federal and state legislation.
6. Federal, state, and local agency rules and regulations.
7. Local ordinances and town bylaws.

stand before the test of constitutionality; that is, a law—whether statutory or case law—must not violate the rights of citizens as guaranteed by the United States Constitution. The United States Supreme Court has the final say on whether a judicial, agency, or statutory law violates the Constitution.

## THE NATURE OF CRIMINAL LAW

Cases and legal decisions are important components of the criminal law. Beyond that, the criminal law has its own distinguishing features.

It can, for instance, be categorized as *substantive* or *procedural*. The substantive part of the criminal law is concerned with the rules of conduct imposed by our society to control antisocial behavior. The objectives of the substantive criminal law are specifically set out in the American Law Institute's Model Penal Code, Section 1.02, which states:

(1) The general purposes of the provisions governing the definition of offenses are:
  (a) to forbid and prevent conduct that unjustifiably and inexcusably inflicts or threatens substanial harm to individual or public interests;
  (b) to subject to the public control persons whose conduct indicates that they are disposed to commit crimes;
  (c) to safeguard conduct that is without fault from condemnation as criminal;
  (d) to give fair warning of the nature of the conduct declared to constitute an offense;
  (e) to differentiate on reasonable grounds between serious and minor offenses.

(2) The general purposes of the provisions governing the sentencing and treatment of offenders are:
  (a) to prevent the commission of offenses;
  (b) to promote the correction and rehabilitation of offenders;
  (c) to safeguard offenders against excessive, disproportionate, or arbitrary punishment;
  (d) to give fair warning of the nature of the sentences that many be imposed on conviction of an offense;
  (e) to differentiate among offenders with a view to a just individualization in their treatment;
  (f) to define, coordinate and harmonize the powers, duties, and functions of the courts and of administrative officers and agencies responsible for dealing with offenders;
  (g) to advance the use of generally accepted scientific methods and knowledge in the sentencing and treatment of offenders;
  (h) to integrate responsibility for the administration of the correctional system in a State Department of Correction [or other single department or agency.] [7]

The substantive criminal law defines what types of conduct are criminal and prescribes the penalties to be imposed engaging in criminal conduct. The following definition of the crime of burglary as stated in the Massachusetts General Laws, Chapter 266, number 14, is a specific example of the substantive criminal law:

Whoever breaks and enters a dwelling house in the nighttime, with intent to commit a felony, or whoever, after having entered with such intent, breaks such dwelling house in the nighttime, any person being lawfully therein, and the offender being armed with a dangerous weapon at the time of such breaking or entry, or so arming himself in such house or making an actual assault on a person lawfully therein, [commits the crime of burglary].[8]

The elements of the crime are:

1. Nighttime.

2. Breaking and entering, or breaking or entering.

3. A dwelling house.

4. Being armed, or arming the self after entering or committing an actual assault on a person lawfully therein; and

5. Intent to commit a felony.

✳The procedural law involves the use of rules designed to implement the substantive law. It is concerned with the criminal process—the legal steps through which an offender passes—commencing with the initial criminal investigation and concluding with release of the offender. Some elements of procedural criminal law include the rules of evidence, the law of arrest, the law of search and seizure, questions of appeal, and the right to counsel. Many of the criminal rights which have been granted to offenders over the past two decades lie within the field of procedural law.

## THE LEGAL DEFINITION OF CRIME

There is no single universally accepted legal definition of crime. Since the determination of what constitutes a crime rests with the individual jurisdiction in which a crime is committed, the federal government and each state has its own body of criminal law. However, most general legal definitions of a crime are basically similar in nature. A crime can be defined as follows:

It is an act that is in violation of the criminal code of a given jurisdiction.

A more comprehensive legal definition of a crime would be:

A crime is (1) a legal wrong (2) prohibited by the criminal law (3) prosecuted by the state (4) in a formal court proceeding (5) in which a criminal sanction or sentence may be imposed.

As determined by most legal systems, crime can result from the commission in violation of the law or from the omission of a required legal act. For example, a crime can be a positive act of intentionally striking another person or of stealing someone else's property. On the other hand, a crime can also involve the failure of a person to act, such as the failure to file an income tax return, a parent's failure to care for a child, the failure to report a crime, or the failure to report an automobile accident.

Another important way of understanding what constitutes a crime is by distinguishing the criminal law from the civil law. In the criminal law, the major objective is to protect the public against harm by preventing the commission of criminal offenses. In the civil law—for example, in the area of private wrongs or *torts*—the major concern is that the injured party be compensated for any harm done. This usually requires that the aggrieved person initiate proceedings to recover monetary damages. In contrast, when a crime is committed, the state initiates the legal process and imposes a punishment in the form of a criminal sanction. Furthermore, in criminal law the emphasis is on the *intent* of the individual committing the crime; in civil law, primary attention is given to negotiating a suitable settlement among the conflicting parties.

In spite of these major differences, similarities do exist between criminal and civil law—both areas of the law seek to control people's behavior by preventing them from acting in an undesirable manner, and both impose sanctions upon those who commit violations of the law. The payment of a fine in a tort case, for example, is not much different than the payment of a fine in a criminal case. The criminal law sentences offenders to prison, while the civil law also imposes confinement on such individuals as the mentally ill, alcoholic, and mentally defective. In addition, many actions such as assault and battery, various forms of larceny, and negligence are the basis for criminal as well as civil actions. A summary of the similarities and differences between the criminal law and tort law is presented in Table 3.2.

TABLE 3.2
Similarities and
Differences Between
Criminal and Tort Law

| *Similarities* | |
|---|---|
| 1. Both areas of law seek to control behavior. | |
| 2. Sanctions are imposed in both criminal and tort law. | |
| 3. Similar areas of legal action exist. | |
| *Differences* | |
| *Criminal Law* | *Tort Law* |
| 1. Crime is a public offense. | 1. Tort is a civil or private wrong. |
| 2. The purpose of criminal law is punishment. | 2. The purpose of tort is to seek monetary damages. |
| 3. The right of enforcement of crime is in the state. | 3. In tort, the individual brings action. |
| 4. The goverment ordinarily does not appeal. | 4. Both parties can appeal. |
| 5. The sentence of fine goes to the state. | 5. The individual receives damages as compensation for harm done. |

In summary, the criminal law usually applies in an action taken by the local, state, or federal government against an individual who has been accused of committing a crime, while the civil law comes into effect when an individual or group seeks monetary recompense for harmful actions committed by another individual or group.

HOW CRIMES
ARE CLASSIFIED

The decision of how a crime is to be classified rests with the individual jurisdiction. Each state has developed its own body of criminal law, and consequently determines its own penalties for the different crimes. Thus, the criminal law of a given state defines and grades offenses, sets levels of punishment, and classifies crimes into different categories. Over the years, crimes have been grouped into the following classifications: (1) *mala in se* and *mala prohibitum* offenses, (2) felony and misdemeanor offenses, and (3) other statutory classifications.

### Mala In Se And Mala Prohibitum

*Mala in se* crimes are those which appear inherently wrong or evil by their nature. Crimes involving moral turpitude or depravity—such as murder, armed robbery, kidnaping and rape—are all essentially evil and are considered mala in se offenses. The common-law crimes are generally considered to be mala in se because the common law concerned itself with actions wrong in themselves, and not with crimes forbidden by statutory law.

*Mala prohibitum* offenses are those that are sanctioned because they are prohibited by statute. These offenses generally belong to the large group of crimes which are expressly violations of laws because they have been defined as crimes by the penal code. The question of moral turpitude does not exist in mala prohibitum crimes since these crimes are created by legislative enactment for the well-being of society. Such crimes include speeding, driving under the influence of alcohol, going through a red light, vagrancy, disorderly conduct, and other similar breaches of the public peace.

The *mala in se* and *mala prohibitum* classifications for crimes can be traced back to early English history. The use of this classification is mentioned in a 1496 case dealing with the king's power to grant permission to disobey a criminal statute if the crime is mala prohibitum and not mala in se.[9]

A leading case that defines these two terms is the case of *State v. Horton* (1905):[10]

An offense mala in se is properly defined as one which is naturally evil as adjudged by the sense of a civilized community, whereas an act mala prohibitum is wrong only because made so by statute.[11]

In *Horton*, the court released a defendant charged with manslaughter because the accidental killing occurred in the commission of a misdemeanor, which was mala prohibitum, rather than in connection with a crime defined as mala in se. Thus, the distinction is important when considering criminal intent and liability.

## Felonies and
## Misdemeanors

Another classification of crime, and the one that is the most common in the United States, is the felony-misdemeanor classification. This distinction is based primarily on the degree of seriousness of the crime.

The general way to distinguish between a felony and a misdemeanor is usually ambiguous and ill-defined. We might simply say that a felony is a serious offense and a misdemeanor a less serious one.

Black's Law Dictionary defines the two terms as follows:[12]

A felony is a crime of a graver or more atrocious nature than those designated as misdemeanors. Generally it is an offense punishable by death or imprisonment in a penitentiary. A misdemeanor is lower than a felony and generally punishable by fine or imprisonment otherwise than in a penitentiary.

Each jurisdiction in this country determines by statute what types of conduct constitute felonies or misdemeanors. The most common definition of a felony is that it is a crime punishable in the statute by death or imprisonment in a state prison. In Massachusetts, for example, any crime that a statute punishes by imprisonment in the state prison system is considered a felony, and all other crimes are misdemeanors.[13] Another way of determining what category an offense falls into is by providing in the statute that a felony is any crime punishable by imprisonment for more than one year. In the former method, the place of imprisonment is critical; in the latter, the length of the prison sentence distinguishes a felony from a misdemeanor.

In the United States today, felonies include serious crimes against the person such as criminal homicide, robbery, and rape, or crimes against property such as burglary and larceny. Misdemeanors include petit, or petty, larceny, assault and battery, and the unlawful possession of marijuana. The least serious, or petty, offenses, often involving criminal traffic violations, are called "infractions."

The felony-misdemeanor classification has a direct effect on the offender charged with the crime. A person convicted of a felony may be barred from certain fields of employment or from entering some professional fields of study, such as law or medicine. A felony offender's status as an alien in the United States might also be affected, or the offender might be denied the right to hold public office, vote, or serve on a jury.[14] These and other civil liabilities exist only when a person is convicted of a felony offense, not a misdemeanor.

Whether one is charged with a felony also makes a difference at the time of arrest. Normally, the law of arrest requires that if the crime is a misdemeanor and has not been committed in the presence of a police officer, the officer cannot make an arrest. This is known as the *in-presence requirement*. However, the police officer does have the legal authority to arrest a suspect for a misdemeanor at a subsequent time by the use of a validly obtained arrest warrant. An arrest for a felony, on the other hand, may be made regardless of whether the crime was committed in the officers' presence, as long as the officer has reasonable grounds to believe that the person has committed the felony.

Another important effect of this classification is that a court's jurisdiction often depends upon whether a crime is considered a felony or a misdemeanor. A person charged with a felony must be tried by a court which has jurisdiction over the type of offense. Similarly, some states prosecute felonies only upon grand jury indictment (see Chapter 10); in other states, conviction of more than one felony offense may cause the defendant to be classified as a habitual offender as well as increase the criminal sanction that may be imposed by the court (see Chapter 13).

### Other Classifications

In addition to the mala in se–mala prohibitum and felony-misdemeanor classifications, crimes may be classified by the nature of the actions involved. All states, for example, have juvenile delinquency statutes which classify children under a certain age as juvenile delinquents if they commit acts which would constitute crimes if committed by adults. Some states have special statutory classifications for sex offenders, multiple offenders, youthful offenders, and first offenders. Generally, no special statutory classification exists, for such actions as white-collar crimes, which usually involve nonviolent conduct like embezzlement, fraud, and income tax violation. Nor is there a specific statute for organized crime. However, there are criminal statutes which specifically deal with gambling, extortion, drug offenses, and other organized crime activities.

In addition, some jurisdictions have created categories for crimes less serious than misdemeanors, which are known as violations or offenses. These generally include violations of town and municipal ordinances such as common traffic violations, minor destruction of public property, burning rubbish without a permit, or using alcoholic beverages on Sunday.

Certain basic elements are required in order for an act to be considered a crime. These elements form what is known as the *corpus delecti,* or "body of the crime." Often, the term corpus delecti is misunderstood. Some people, for instance, wrongly believe that it refers to the body of the deceased in a homicide. The term corpus delecti is used to describe all of the elements which together constitute a crime, and includes the following: (1) the *actus reus,* (2) the *mens rea,* and (3) the combination of actus reus and mens rea.

The terms actus reus, which literally translates as "guilty act," refers to the forbidden act itself and is used in the criminal law to describe the

**THE BASIC ELEMENTS OF A CRIME**

physical crime and/or the commission of the criminal act (or omission of the lawful act). In their *Treatise on Criminal Law*, Lafave and Scott state:

Bad thought alone cannot constitute a crime, there must be an act, or an omission to act where there is a legal duty to act. Thus, the criminal law crimes are defined in terms of act or omission to act and statutory crimes are unconstitutional unless so defined. A bodily movement, to qualify as an act forming the basis of criminal liability, must be voluntary.[15]

The physical act in violation of the criminal statute is usually clearly defined within each offense. For example, in the crime of manslaughter, the unlawful killing of a human being is the physical act prohibited by statute; in burglary, it is the actual breaking and entering into a dwelling house for the purpose of theft. Regarding an omission to act, many jurisdictions hold a person accountable if a legal duty exists and the offender avoids it. For example, the law recognizes that a parent has a legal duty to a child. Where a parent refuses to obtain medical attention for the child and the child dies, the parent's actions constitute an omission to act and that omission may be considered unlawful.

The second element basic to the commission of any crime is the establishment of the mens rea, literally translated as "guilty mind." Mens rea is that element of the crime that deals with the defendant's intent to commit the act. A person ordinarily cannot be convicted of a crime unless it is proven that he or she intentionally, knowingly, or willingly committed the criminal act.

The following case illustrates the absence of mens rea. A student at a university took home some books, believing them to be her own, and subsequently found that the books belonged to her classmate. When she realized that the books did not belong to her, she returned them to their proper owner. The student could not be prosecuted for theft since she did not intend to steal the books in the first place.

Another case that illustrates a lack of criminal intent, but one in which actual harm occurs, is that in which a pedestrian is accidentally killed in an automobile accident. At the time of the accident, the driver is operating the motor vehicle legally and with appropriate care, but the victim steps out in front of the car and is struck and killed. The driver cannot be found guilty of manslaughter unless evidence can be found that some intent or gross criminal negligence existed at the time of the accident. This situation would be legally considered in a completely different light if it could be proved that the driver actually intended to hit the pedestrian, or had been driving the car in a willful and reckless manner indicating criminal negligence.

Thus, in order for an individual to be found guilty of committing most crimes, it must be proved that he committed the physical act itself and that he intended to do so with full awareness of the consequences of the act.

Other variations on the concept of criminal intent exist. Different degrees of intent are used to determine the mental state needed in order for an individual to commit a particular crime. Where a criminal homicide occurs, it may be necessary to prove that a mental state of premeditation and malice existed in the accused before a judgment of first degree murder can be reached; for a judgment of second degree murder, it may be necessary to prove malice; and for a judgment of third degree murder, it may be necessary to prove guilty knowledge or criminal negligence.

Mens rea conditions also differ among the types of crime when considering whether a *general* or *specific intent* to commit the crime exists. For most crimes, a general intent on the part of the accused to act purposefully or to accomplish a criminal result must be proved. A specific intent requires that the actor intended to accomplish a specific purpose as an element of the crime. Burglary, for example, involves more than the general intent of breaking and entering into a dwelling house; it usually also involves the specific intent of committing a felony, such as stealing money or jewels. Many other crimes such as robbery, larceny, assault with intent to kill, false pretense, and even kidnaping may require a specific intent.

The third element needed to prove the corpus delecti of a crime is the relationship of the act to the criminal intent or result. The law requires that the offender's conduct must be the approximate cause of any injury resulting from the criminal act. If, for example, a man chases a victim into the street intending to assault him, and the victim is struck and killed by a car, the accused could be convicted of murder if the court felt that his actions made him responsible for the victim's death. On the other hand, if a victim dies from a completely unrelated illness after being assaulted, the court has to determine whether the death was a probable consequence of the defendant's illegal conduct or whether it may have resulted even if the assault had not occurred.

In another case, if a person intends to kill or harm another and then decides against such action, the person cannot be found guilty of a crime if the victim is accidently harmed by him at a later date. Criminal liability, as previously explained, cannot be imposed for simply having had bad thoughts about the victim at a previous time. Thus, a concurrence of act and intent—actus reus and mens rea—must be present if a crime is to occur. However, cases do exist where one person intends criminal action against another but harms a third party instead; for example, the accused intends to shoot one person but misses and shoots another. In this instance, the law transfers the original criminal intent to the innocent bystander. Under the legal doctrine of *transferred intent*, the accused would be considered criminally responsible for transferring wrongful intent to the other person.

It has been stated that both existence of a criminal intent and a wrongful act must be proved before an individual can be found guilty of committing a crime. However, certain statutory offenses exist in which mens rea is not essential. These offenses fall within a category known as public welfare, or strict liability crimes. A person can be held responsible for such a violation independent of the existence of intent to commit the offense. Strict liability criminal statutes generally include narcotics control laws, traffic laws, health and safety regulations, sanitation laws, and other regulatory statutes. The general purpose of such laws is to protect the public and to provide the prosecution with an opportunity to convict offenders of crimes that would ordinarily be difficult to prove in court. Over the years, most legal commentators have been critical of strict liability offenses because it seems unfair to punish a person without referring to that person's state of mind when committing the crime.[16] However, these statutes still remain part of the legal codes in many jurisdictions.

Table 3.3 presents some categories of major substantive crimes common to all states. The basic elements of each crime are contained within the definitions.

TABLE 3.3
Some Common
Categories of Major
Substantive Crimes

I. *Crimes Against Government*
  1. Treason — a crime involving giving aid and comfort to the enemy of a country.
  2. Official Misconduct — unlawful behavior by a public official in the performance of his duties.
  3. Terrorism — use of terror or violence by agents of revolutionary government against people for political gain.

II. *Crimes Against Person*
  1. Murder — criminal homicide involving the killing of one human being by another, committed with malice.
  2. Assault & Battery — actions threatening harm to a victim and putting him in fear, or the unlawful touching of another with the intent to inflict injury.
  3. Rape — unlawful carnal knowledge of a woman by a man against her will.

III. *Crimes Against Property*
  1. Arson — malicious and intentional burning of any building or its contents.
  2. Burglary — breaking and entering a dwelling house in the nighttime with the intent to commit a felony.
  3. Larceny — wrongful taking of personal property from the possession of another, with the intent to take the property permanently.

IV. *Crimes Against Public Order*
  1. Disorderly Conduct — actions causing public inconvenience by engaging in fighting or threatening or in violent behavior, or creating a physically dangerous condition to the public.
  2. Contempt — refusal to obey court orders is civil contempt; disobedience and disrespect to a court is criminal contempt.

(Table 3.3—
continued)

| | |
|---|---|
| 3. Riot | –groups of people acting against the public peace by using force to threaten or harm others and their property. |
| V. *Victimless Crimes* | |
| 1. Use and Sale of Unlawful Drugs | –knowingly and intentionally possessing and distributing controlled substances without valid prescription. |
| 2. Prostitution | –offering or permitting sexual intercourse or engaging generally in sexual activities with person of opposite sex for compensation or other consideration. |
| 3. Gambling | –illicit betting in racing, lotteries, cards, dice, and casino style gambling in violation of state or federal law regulating such actions. |
| VI. *Inchoate (Incomplete) Offenses* | |
| 1. Attempt | –behavior by individuals who attempt to commit a crime by doing acts that are intended to accomplish the crime. |
| 2. Conspiracy | –voluntary agreement between two or more people where such agreement is forbidden by law and has as its purpose an unlawful end. |
| 3. Solicitation | –efforts by one person to encourage another to commit or attempt to commit a crime. |

CRIMINAL
RESPONSIBILITY

The idea of criminal responsibility is also essential to any discussion of criminal law. Certain conditions regarding mental state might excuse an individual from acts which the criminal justice system would otherwise consider criminal. These factors have been used in establishing legal defenses during trial which are necessary to negate the intent required for the commission of a crime. For example, a person who kills another and is insane while committing the crime may argue in court against responsibility for criminal conduct. Similarly, a child who violates the law may not be treated as an adult offender. Three major types of criminal defenses are explained below in some detail.

### Insanity

Criminal insanity is a legal defense involving the use of rules and standards to determine if a person's state of mental balance negates criminal responsibility. Over the years, the law has been struggling to define the rules relating to the use of insanity as a defense in a criminal trial. Before examining these, it is important to realize that a person who is sane while committing an offense cannot be excused at a later time from criminal responsibility. Furthermore, if a person becomes insane at the time of trial, the trial is held in abeyance until the accused regains sanity; after a proper hearing, a defendant who is declared incompetent to stand trial may be committed to a hospital until judged sane.

The different tests for criminal responsibility involving insanity followed by the American courts are: (1) the *M'Naghten Rule;* (2) the *Irresistible Impulse* test; (3) the *Durham Rule;* (4) and the *Substantial Capacity* test suggested in the Model Penal Code.

The M'Naghten Rule, or the right-wrong test, is based on the early English decision made in the *M'Naghten* case.[17] In 1843, Daniel M'Naghten shot and killed Edward Drummond, believing Drummond to be Sir Robert Peel, the Prime Minister of Great Britain. M'Naghten was prosecuted for murder and, at his trial, claimed that he was not criminally responsible for his actions because he suffered from delusions at the time of the killing. M'Naghten was found not guilty by reason of insanity. Because of the importance of the case and the unpopularity of the decision, the House of Lords of the British Parliament reviewed the decision and asked the court to define what the law was with respect to crimes committed by persons suffering from insane delusions. The court's answer became known as the M'Naghten Rule and has subsequently become the primary test for criminal responsibility in the United States. The M'Naghten Rule can be stated as follows:

A defendant may be excused from criminal responsibility, if at the time of the commission of the crime, the person was under such defect of reason from a disease of the mind, as not to know the nature and quality of the act he was doing; or if he did understand what he was doing, he lacked the capacity to know the difference between right and wrong.

Thus, according to *M'Naghten,* a person is basically insane if he is unable to distinguish between right and wrong as a result of some mental disability.

Over the years, the courts have become critical of the M'Naghten Rule. For example, many individuals who are insane are able to distinguish between right and wrong. Also, a clear determination by the courts of the meaning of the M'Naghten rule which adequately explains such terms as "disease of the mind," "know," and "the nature and quality of the act" has never been made. As a result, many jurisdictions which follow M'Naghten have supplemented it with the Irresistible Impulse test. This rule excuses from criminal responsibility a person whose mental disease makes it impossible to control personal conduct. The criminal may be able to distinguish between right and wrong, but may be unable to exercise self-control due to a disabling mental condition. Approximately fifteen states use a combined M'Naghten–Irresistible Impulse test.

Another rule for determining criminal insanity, used only in about three states and the District of Columbia, is the Durham Rule. Originally created in New Hampshire in 1871, the Durham Rule was reviewed and subsequently adopted by the Court of Appeals for the District of Columbia in 1954 in the case of *Durham v. United States.*[18] In that opinion, Judge

David Bazelon rejected the M'Naghten formula and stated that *an accused is not criminally responsible if his unlawful act was the product of mental disease or defect*. This rule, also known as the Product Test, is based upon the contention that insanity represents many personality factors, all of which may not be present in every case. It leaves the question of deciding whether a defendant is insane in the hands of jurors. The Durham Rule has been viewed with considerable skepticism primarily because the problem of defining "mental disease or defect" and "product" does not give the jury a reliable standard by which to make its judgment.

Another test for criminal insanity, and one which is becoming increasingly popular with many courts, is the Substantial Capacity test. In summary, this test as presented in Section 4.01 of the American Law Institute's Model Penal Code states:

A person is not responsible for criminal conduct if at the time of such conduct as a result of mental disease or defect he lacks substantial capacity whether to appreciate his criminality (wrongfulness) of his conduct or to conform his conduct to the requirements of law.[19]

This rule is basically a broader restatement of the M'Naghten-Irresistible Impulse test. It rejects the Durham Rule because of its lack of standards and its inability to define the term "product." The most significant feature about this test is that it requires only a lack of "substantial capacity" rather than complete impairment in the defendant's ability to know and understand the difference between right and wrong.

These, then, are the various rules for determining criminal insanity. In reality, only a small number of offenders actually utilize the insanity defense. This is due to the fact that many cases involving insane offenders are processed through civil commitment proceedings; in addition, a large majority of offenders tend to plead guilty as a result of plea bargaining. The Application, at the end of this chapter, entitled the "Return of Dr. Jekyll", is an example of how difficult it is to assess criminal responsibility regarding insanity.

### Intoxication

As a general legal rule, intoxication, which may include drunkenness or the taking of drugs, is not considered a defense. However, a defendant who becomes involuntarily intoxicated under duress or by mistake may be excused for crimes committed. Voluntary intoxication may also lessen the degree of a crime—for example, a judgment may be decreased—from first to second degree murder because the defendant may use intoxication to prove the lack of the required element of intent.

### Age

The law holds that a child is not criminally responsible for actions committed at an age that precludes a full realization of the gravity of certain types of behavior. At common law, there is generally a conclusive pre-sumption of incapacity for a child under seven; a reliable presumption for a child between seven and fourteen; and no presumption for a child over fourteen. This means that a child under seven years of age who commits a crime will not be held criminally responsible for these actions; that a child between seven and fourteen may be held responsible; and that a child fourteen and over will be held responsible. These common-law rules have been changed by statute in many states. Today the maximum age of criminal responsibility for children may range from fourteen to seventeen, while the minimum age may be set by statute at seven or under fourteen.[20] In addition, every state has established a juvenile court system to deal with juvenile offenders and children in need of supervision, so that the criminal responsibility of youth is actually a moot, or legally insignificant, issue. The juvenile court system is discussed in detail in Chapter 19.

## CRIMINAL DEFENSES

In the previous section, we discussed the law regarding the capacity to commit a crime. This concept is often referred to as criminal responsibility. When a crime is committed, certain conditions in a defendant's capacity might mitigate or relieve the accused of criminal responsibility. If these conditions exist, such as insanity or infancy, they can relieve the defendant of responsibility under the criminal law. Consequently these defenses gen-erally negate the voluntary nature of the criminal act and the defendant's ability to have the requisite mental intent to commit a crime.

On the other hand, there are criminal defenses not necessarily based on criminal responsibility, but on the concept of justification or excuse. In other words, there are certain defenses that allow for the commission of a crime to be justified or excused based upon grounds of fairness and public policy. In these instances, the defendant normally acknowledges that the act was committed, but claims that he can't be prosecuted for it because he was justified in doing the act. The following four major types of criminal defenses regarding justification or excuse are explained below in some detail: (1) Consent, (2) Self-defense, (3) Entrapment, and (4) Double jeopardy.

### Consent

As a general legal rule, the consent of a victim to a crime does not justify or excuse the defendant who commits the action. The nature of the type of crime involved generally determines the validity of consent as an ap-propriate legal defense. Crimes such as common law rape and larceny require the lack of consent on the part of the victim. In other words, a rape does not occur if consent to sexual relations exists. In the same way, a larceny cannot occur if the owner voluntarily consents to the taking of the property. Consequently, in such crimes, consent is an essential element of the crime, and it is a valid defense where it can be proven or shown that it existed at the time the crime was committed. In statutory rape, on the other hand, consent is not an element of the crime, and is considered irrelevant, because the state presumes that young people are not capable of providing consent.

Consent is also not an appropriate defense in cases involving assaults and batteries, mayhems, homicide, or in any injury involving a person-oriented crime where serious harm can come to a person. In addition, regardless of whether both parties give consent to a fight, if there is a likelihood of serious bodily injury, mutual consent is not a valid defense.

There are certain situations in which a crime does not exist even when the victim consents to the action. For instance, players who participate in sports, such as football or hockey engage in hitting each other and no crime is usually committed. However, if they engage in a fight which causes serious harm during a game, or after a sports activity, the party may be guilty of a serious crime. Sports players often give implied consent to physical actions against them which are a normal activity of the physical sport.

In addition, if the legal defense of consent is to be effective, it cannot be caused by duress on the victim. Threats of bodily harm which produce fear cannot be used to force a person to give consent to a given action. The validity of any defense in the criminal law must be based on voluntariness.

### Self-Defense

In certain instances, the defendant who admits to the acts which constitute a crime may claim to be not guilty because of an affirmative self-defense. In order to set out the necessary elements to constitute a self-defense, the defendant needs to act under a reasonable belief that he or she was in danger of death or great harm and had no means of escape from the assailant. As a general legal rule, however, a person defending himself may use only such force as is reasonably necessary to prevent personal harm. A person who is assaulted by another with no weapon is ordinarily not justified in hitting the assailant with a baseball bat. A person threatened by another is not justified in striking the other party. If a woman hits a larger man, generally speaking, the man would not be justified in striking the woman and causing her physical harm. In other words, in order to exercise the self-defense privilege, the danger to the defendant must be immediate. In addition, the defendant is obligated to look for alternative means of avoiding the danger, such as escape or retreat, or looking for assistance from others.[21]

The characteristics described above concerning self-defense are also applicable to the defense of another and to the defense of one's property. The right to defend another is based on the responsibility of a citizen to use force to exercise a citizen arrest, and to defend members of a family group. The right to defend one's property is dependent on the exercise of reasonable force to retain property, remove a trespasser, or protect one's property. Most jurisdictions use the "reasonableness" test determined by the facts of the action to decide an appropriate defense of property. In some other jurisdictions, force has been accepted as a reasonable way to prevent a burglary. Generally speaking, however, force to protect property is ordinarily considered by the court acceptable only as a last resort when the police are unavailable, or when reasonable requests to control trespass or unlawful action are ignored.[22]

### Entrapment

The term entrapment is an affirmative defense in the criminal law which excuses a defendant from criminal liability when law enforcement agents use traps, decoys, and deception to induce criminal action. It is generally legitimate for law enforcement officers to set traps for criminals by getting information about crimes from informers, undercover agents, and codefendants. Police officers are allowed to use ordinary opportunities for defendants to commit crime, and create these opportunities without excessive inducement and solicitation to commit and involve a defendant in a crime. However, when the police instigate the crime, implant criminal ideas, and coerce individuals into bringing about a crime, defendants have the defense of entrapment available to them.

Entrapment is not a constitutional defense but has been created by court decision and statute in most jurisdictions.

The degree of governmental involvement in a criminal act leading to the entrapment defense has been defined in a number of U.S. Supreme Court decisions beginning in 1932. The majority view of what constitutes entrapment is seen in the 1932 case of *Sorrells v. U.S.*[23] During prohibition, a federal officer passed himself off as a tourist while gaining the defendant's confidence by talking about previous war experiences. The federal agent asked and was refused, but eventually did entice the defendant to go out and buy illegal liquor for the officer. He was then arrested and prosecuted for violating the National Prohibition Act. The Court held that the officer used improper inducements which amounted to entrapment. In deciding this case, the Court settled on the "subjective" view of entrapment, which means that the predisposition of the defendant to commit the offense is the determining factor in entrapment. Following the Sorrells case, the U.S. Supreme Court handed down a decision in *Sherman v. U.S.* in 1958.[24] In the Sherman case, the defendant was enticed to supply a narcotics agent with drugs. In reversing the conviction of the defendant, the Court stated that the function of law enforcement is the prevention of crime and the apprehension of criminals, and not to implant a criminal design which originates with the officials of the government in the mind of an innocent person.

In 1973, the U.S. Supreme Court ruled on the entrapment case of the *U.S. v. Russell*.[25] In this case, an agent of the Federal Bureau of Narcotics offered to supply defendants with essential ingredients necessary to manufacture speed. The agent was shown the laboratory where the speed was produced and eventually obtained a search warrant and arrested the defendants for the unlawful manufacture, sale, and delivery of drugs. Defendant Russell raised the defense of entrapment in his criminal trial. The Court ruled that the participation of the narcotics agent was not entrapment in this case and rejected the "objective" test of entrapment, which looks solely to the police conduct to determine if a law-abiding citizen has been persuaded to commit crime. Consequently, the major legal rule today considers entrapment primarily in light of the defendant's predisposition to commit a crime.

## Double Jeopardy

By virtue of the Fifth Amendment of the U.S. Constitution, no person shall be subject for the same offense to be twice put in jeopardy of life or limb.[26] The objective of this constitutional protection is to prohibit the reprosecution of a defendant for the same offense by the same jurisdiction. Thus, a person who has been charged and convicted of armed robbery in the State of Massachusetts by a judge or jury may not be tried again in that state for the same offense.

A review of the double jeopardy question involves a number of issues: (1) Does prosecution for the same or similar offenses by the state and federal government constitute double jeopardy? (2) When does double jeopardy attach in a criminal prosecution? (3) What effect does the double jeopardy clause have on sentencing provisions.

The issue of federal versus state prosecutions arises from the existence of offenses that are crimes against the state as well as against the federal government. The U.S. Supreme Court has held, in the case of *Bartkus v. Illinois* and in numerous other cases, that both state and federal prosecutions against a defendant for the same crime are not in violation of the Fifth Amendment.[27] The Court has reasoned that every citizen is a citizen of the United States and of a state. Consequently, either or both jurisdictions can try and seek to punish an offender.

On the other hand, a state or its local jurisdiction is able to try an accused only once. The state has the responsibility of seeking to legally convict the defendant and/or have the defendant obtain an acquittal of all charges. The Fifth Amendment prohibits a second prosecution, unless there has been an appeal by the defendant. The state may obtain a second trial in cases involving a mistrial, a hung jury, or some other trial defect.

With regard to when double jeopardy attaches, the general rule is that the Fifth Amendment applies when a criminal trial begins before a judge or jury. In the case of *Benton v. Maryland,* the U.S. Supreme Court held the double jeopardy provisions of the Fifth Amendment applicable to the states.[28] The accused has the right to be tried until a final determination of the case is made. Jeopardy may exist when a jury is selected and sworn or even when a defendant is indicted for a crime. However, in the case of *Illinois v. Somerville,* the double jeopardy clause did not bar the retrial of a defendant where a mistrial was caused because of a fatal defect in the government's indictment.[29] Also, a dismissal which occurs prior to jeopardy attaching does not prohibit a second prosecution under the Fifth Amendment.

When dealing with the sentence itself, the double jeopardy clause does not restrict the court's decision with regard to length of the sentence imposed on a defendant in a second trial. However, the court is required to sentence fairly in accordance with due process of law. Vindictiveness or harshness against a defendant for being successful in overturning the first conviction is not appropriate grounds for imposing a sentence in the second trial. Thus, although, the double jeopardy clause does not prevent or restrict harsh sentences on retrial, the case of *North Carolina v. Pierce* makes clear that sentences upon retrial must be realistic and in accordance with fair principles of law and procedure.[30]

Pearce was convicted of assault with intent to commit rape in North Carolina. He was sentenced to 12 to 15 years in prison. After a reversal of his conviction, Pearce was retried, convicted, and sentenced to a term which amounted to a longer sentence than was originally imposed. The court made clear that, although the double jeopardy clause is not an absolute bar to a more severe sentence, vindictiveness against a defendant can play no part in the new sentence.

The above defenses primarily refer to situations where the defendant admits that he did commit the act but claims that he cannot be punished for it because of such affirmative defenses. Such is the case when a person exercises proper self-defense, when the police deliberately entice a defendant to commit a crime, or when someone is tried twice for the same offense. In addition to these defenses, the criminal defendant has various procedural guarantees by virtue of constitutional mandate, including the right to counsel, freedom from unreasonable search and seizure, and the right to a speedy trial. These defenses are discussed primarily in Chapter 5 dealing with "The Constitutional Rights of the Accused," and Chapter 12, "The Criminal Trial."

## REFORM OF CRIMINAL LAW

In addition to having some understanding of the law, the definition of crime, various legal classifications, and criminal responsibility, it is also important to recognize the need for criminal law reform.

In recent years many states and the federal government have been examining and revising their substantive and procedural criminal codes. The law reflects the state of public opinion regarding various forms of behavior. What was a crime forty years ago—such as the use of alcoholic beverages—may no longer be a crime today. Many experts believe that offenses like drunkenness, disorderly conduct, vagrancy, gambling, and minor sexual violations are essentially violations of moral norms and should not be considered crimes. The Model Penal Code of the American Law Institute offers a comprehensive model of the substantive criminal law which serves as a sound guide to the elimination of outdated laws. The United States Supreme Court, particularly during the 1960s, revised the laws of criminal procedure by providing defendants with basic constitutional rights under the fourth, fifth, sixth, and fourteenth Amendments, and these have curtailed unwarranted and arbitrary practices by criminal justice agencies.[31] Criminal law and procedure change slowly, but nevertheless it is necessary to constantly weigh the kinds of actions that should be defined as criminal while simultaneously insuring that persons accused of crime are treated fairly.

One of the most serious and difficult areas of criminal law reform has been the effort to revise the federal Criminal Code. For the past 20 years, Congress has been dealing with this matter in earnest. The proposed federal legislation would restructure and modernize the entire 3,000 or so criminal acts in the present penal law. At present, the current federal laws, organized into Title 18 of the U.S. Code, are a patchwork of ill-defined, loosely organized, and often outdated provisions. There are, for example, over 200 offenses in the present code dealing with theft, forgery, and counterfeiting. Criminal liability of a corporation, as well as computer crime, are not even mentioned in the code. Outdated statutes, such as engaging in piracy, and violations of selective service laws, remain in the present code.

But the most serious problem appears to be the inconsistency of criminal sanctions attached to crimes. Federal judges are presently given broad discretion over the length and type of sentence. After a criminal sentence is imposed, the Federal Parole Board reviews the sentence and often lowers the prison term. Because of these problems, the federal Congress has grappled with criminal code reform without success for over two decades.

The present proposed act seeks to streamline the code, standardize sentences, trim the discretionary power of judges and parole boards, and incorporate new laws on civil rights, criminal acts by corporations, and consolidate person and property-oriented offenses.[32] Without question, its most important provisions are in the sentencing area. Here, it would eliminate indeterminate sentences, generally phase out parole, and make sentencing fairer and more certain. A sentencing commission would be established to determine sentencing guidelines. This guidelines approach is designed to reduce the problem of sentencing disparity by reducing judicial discretion.

Although controversial, because of such provisions as governmental appeal, pre-trial detention restrictions, and laws limiting civil rights and civil liberties, particularly for protestors, the proposed bill would be a great improvement over present federal criminal code regulations.

Despite our present problems with the criminal justice system, much progress has been made in the field of criminal law and procedure over the past 25 years.[33] And although there has been a lack of systematic attention paid to substantive criminal law in particular, and a rejection and apathy for crime control efforts, certain genuine advances have occurred. The American Law Institute's Model Penal Code was formulated in 1964. Comprehensive revisions of criminal legislation has been enacted in numerous states throughout the country since the establishment of the Model Penal Code. In the area of constitutional criminal procedures, the U.S. Supreme Court has exercised its supervision over criminal justice systems, particularly during the Warren era with great intensity. In addition, American legislatures have passed laws involving political crimes, morality offenses, and regulatory crimes concerned with economic control and general public welfare. This type of legislation is often controversial because it seeks to punish behavior that is not generally condemned by everyone in the community. The enforcement of this type of legislation is often difficult and discretionary in nature.

The future direction of the criminal law in America remains unclear. More attention probably will be paid to the substantive nature of criminal law, particularly because we realize its importance in the preservation of our society. We can also anticipate both the expansion and the contraction of the criminal law itself. Certain actions will be adopted as criminal and given more attention, such as white-collar crime, juvenile delinquency, crimes by corporations, and political corruption. Other offenses, such as habitual drunkenness, traffic violations, use of drugs, and petty criminal offenses may be reduced in importance or removed entirely from the criminal law system. In addition, efforts will probably be made to develop a system of judicially fixed sentences, possibly abolish parole, and seek to make criminal sentencing fairer and more certain for the justice system, the public, and the offender.

## SUMMARY

The criminal justice system is basically a legal system. Underlying its foundation is the criminal law, which is concerned with people's conduct. Its purpose is to regulate behavior and maintain order in society. What constitutes a crime is defined primarily by state and federal legislatures and reviewed by the courts.

What is considered to be criminal conduct changes from one period of time to another. Social norms, values, and community beliefs play major roles in determining what conduct is antisocial. Crimes are generally classified as felonies or misdemeanors, depending upon their seriousness. Since a crime is a public wrong against the state, the criminal law imposes sanctions in the form of fines, probation, or imprisonment on a guilty defendant.

Under the criminal law, all adults are presumed to intend the consequences of their actions, but the law does not hold an individual blameworthy unless that person is capable of intending to commit the crime as accused. Such factors as insanity, a mental defect, or age mitigate a person's criminal responsibility. States periodically revise and update the substantive criminal law and the procedural laws in their penal codes which deal with the rules for processing the offender from arrest through trial, sentencing, and release.

## QUESTIONS FOR DISCUSSION

1. What are the specific aims and purposes of the criminal law? To what extent does the criminal law control behavior?

2. What kinds of activities should be labeled criminal in our contemporary society? Why?

**3.** What is a criminal act? What is a criminal state of mind? When are individuals liable for their actions?

**4.** Discuss the various kinds of crime classifications. To what extent or degree are they distinguishable?

**5.** In recent years, numerous state have revised their penal codes. What are some of the major categories of substantive crimes you think should be revised?

**6.** Entrapment is a defense when the defendant was entrapped into committing the crime. To what extent should law enforcement personnel induce the commission of an offense?

**7.** What legal principles exist for self-defense? Are they sound when we seek to prevent crime, and not promote it?

NOTES

**1.** See generally Wayne R. LaFave and Austin W. Scott Jr., *Criminal Law* (St. Paul, Minn.: West Publishing Co., 1972), Chapter 2.

**2.** *Stare decisis* is a legal principle expressed in Latin referring to the court's policy to stand by prior cases and not disturb settled law.

**3.** 372 U.S. 335, 83 S.Ct. 792, 9 L.Ed.2d 799 (1963).

**4.** 316 U.S. 455, 62 S.Ct. 1252, 86 L.Ed. 1595 (1942).

**5.** See Executive Order No. 11236, July 25, 1965.

**6.** See Massachusetts General Laws, Chapter 124, Sec. 1, as amended by Chapter 777 of Acts of 1972.

**7.** Model Penal Code, § 1.02. Copyright 1962 by the American Law Institute. Reprinted with the permission of the American Law Institute.

**8.** See Massachusetts General Laws Ann., Chap. 266 § 14.

**9.** See Holdsworth, *History of English Law* (1927), pp. 218–219.

**10.** 139 N.C. 588, 51 S.E. 945 (1905).

**11.** Ibid.

**12.** Black's Law Dictionary, Revised Fourth Edition (St. Paul, Minn.: West Publishing Co., 1967), pp. 744 and 1150.

**13.** See Massachusetts General Laws Ann., Chap. 274 § 1.

**14.** See generally Hazel B. Kerper and Janeen Kerper, *Legal Rights of the Convicted* (St. Paul, Minn.: West Publishing Co., 1974).

**15.** See LaFave and Scott, *Criminal Law*, p. 177.

**16.** See Henry Hart, "The Aims of the Criminal Law," *Law and Contemporary Problems* 23, 401 (1956).

**17.** 8 *Eng. Rep.* 718 (1843).

**18.** 94 U.S. App.D.C. 228, 214 F.2d 862 (1954).

**19.** Model Penal Code, § 4.01. Copyright 1962 by the American Law Institute. Reprinted with the permission of the American Law Institute.

**20.** Samual M. Davis, *Rights of Juveniles, The Juvenile Justice System* (New York: Clark Boardman Co., 1974), Chapter 2.

**21.** See Thomas Gardner and Victor Manian, *Criminal Law—Principles, Cases and Readings* (St. Paul, Minn.: West Publishing Co., 1975), p. 144.

**22.** Ibid.

**23.** 287 U.S. 435, 53 S.Ct. 210, 77 L.Ed. 413 (1932).

**24.** 356 U.S. 369, 78 S.Ct. 819, 2 L.Ed.2d 848 (1958).

**25.** 411 U.S. 423, 93 S.Ct. 1637, 36 L.Ed.2d 366 (1973).

**26.** See U.S. Constitution, Fifth Amendment, 1791.

**27.** 359 U.S. 121, 79 S.Ct. 676, 3 L.Ed.2d 684 (1959).

**28.** 395 U.S. 784, 89 S.Ct. 2056, 23 L.Ed. 707 (1969).

**29.** 410 U.S. 458, 93 S.Ct. 1066, 35 L.Ed.2d 425 (1973).

**30.** 395 U.S. 711, 89 S.Ct. 2072, 23 L.Ed.2d 656 (1969).

**31.** John D. Weaver, *Warren, The Man, The Court, The Era* (Boston: Little, Brown and Co., 1967), Chapter 15.

**32.** See 96th Congress, H.R. 6233, S. 1722 (1979–1980); Also *The Christian Science Monitor*, Series on U.S. Criminal Code, Feb. 4, 5, 6, 1980.

**33.** Francis A. Allen, *The Borderlane of Criminal Justice* (Chicago: University of Chicago Press, 1974), p. 123.

APPLICATION

# Return of Dr. Jekyll

*The following application is an example of the insanity defense as one issue in this chapter dealing primarily with the substantive criminal law. The "Return of Dr. Jekyll" shows how understanding human behavior is one of the most complex areas of the criminal law.*

The hijacker boarded the Los Angeles-to-New York airliner with an automatic pistol concealed inside a fake plaster arm cast. Once he had seized control in the cockpit, he started making a wild series of demands over the radiotelephone. He wanted to talk to President Nixon; he wanted the release of Angela Davis; he wanted a ransom payment of exactly $306,800. Eight hours after the hijacker struck, two FBI agents disguised as crew members boarded the plane at John F. Kennedy Airport, shot the hijacker in the hand and captured him.

There was no doubt about his identity. He was Garrett Brock Trapnell, 34, a dark-haired man with piercing eyes and a long record of bank robberies. Trapnell himself did not deny the hijacking, but he claimed it had been done by his wicked alter ego, Gregg Ross. He was a Jekyll-Hyde personality, he said. Appearing in Brooklyn's U.S. District Court last month, he pleaded not guilty.

If Trapnell was indeed insane, he had a background that provided quite a few explanations. His father was an Annapolis graduate who rose to be a commander in the Navy but whose private life was less than stable. He had five wives, one of whom was a heavy-drinking Boston Brahmin, Trapnell's mother. They divorced when Trapnell was four, and he moved form home to home, including a stay in Panama, where he says his father, the commander, moonlighted by running a brothel.

Trapnell's criminal record began when he was 15—an arrest for petty theft. Then came a hitch in the Army (terminated by an early discharge); a reported stint of gunrunning to Fidel Castro; and finally a series of armed robberies in New Mexico, Iowa and Maryland. After he was caught, he later recalled in an unpublished 1971 interview with Freelance Writer Cy Berlowitz, "A lawyer came to me and said, 'Trap, you are going to prison for 20 years, or you can go to the state hospital.' So I went to the state hospital and I dug the whole action. I read more damned books on psychiatry and psychology than probably any psychology student will in any school in the world."

Trapnell spent a year in a mental hospital and then began a bizarre series of crime and nonpunishment. Throughout the '60s, he staged robberies whenever he needed money—at one point he and a partner flew to Canada and robbed a bank once a month for seven months (total take: $130,000). Along the way he lived in bank-robber style: a Mercedes-Benz, a private plane, $40-a-day hotel rooms in Miami, a Las Vegas trip with a go-go dancer. Whenever he was caught, he would bring out his insanity defense, get committed to a hospital, then escape. "Psychiatry as a science," he observed, "is the only science in the world that deals with extreme intangibles. I probably know more about psychiatry than your average resident psychiatrist."

At his latest trial the interview with Berlowitz was placed in evidence to show that Trapnell was faking. Assistant U.S. Attorney Peter Schlam also brought in two psychiatrists to testify that, in their opinion, Trapnell was perfectly sane (he has an IQ of 130). The prosecution had not discovered, however, that one juror, Gertrude Hass, had worked for 30 years as a psychiatric social worker. To Miss Hass's professional eye, apparently, Trapnell's account of how he had faked insanity was itself further evidence of his actual insanity.

Last week, after a five-week trial, the jury deliberated the case and found to its dismay that it was divided 11 to 1. The eleven argued with Miss Hass, but she remained adamant; when the arguing grew louder, she sent a message to Federal District Judge George Rosling saying that she was being pressured. At that point, Judge Rosling had to discharge the jury—not without some pressure of his own. "She may expect some visits from Government agencies," he said, "to find out if this was the performance of her jury function or some other function."

The threat was instantly challenged by the American Civil Liberties Union, and Rosling duly retracted his accusations, setting a new trial for March 5. Trapnell is quite prepared. "I have committed all these crimes and have never gotten a number for any of them," he had said to his interviewer. "If Gregg Ross committs a crime, then Gary Trapnell is not responsible. It's the fallacy of your legal system."

# PART TWO

## The Structure
## of Criminal
## Justice

# An Overview of Criminal Justice

THE STUDY OF
CRIMINAL
JUSTICE

In July of 1965, the President's Commission on Law Enforcement and Administration of Justice was created to study crime and the criminal justice system in the United States.[1] Since that time, other national groups and agencies, including the American Bar Association and the National Advisory Commission on Criminal Justice Standards and Goals, have also explored the American criminal justice system in depth.[2] Many of their major recommendations have been implemented. For example, in 1968 Congress passed the Safe Streets and Crime Control Act providing for the expenditure of federal funds for state and local crime control efforts.[3] On the state level, numerous jurisdictions have reformed their criminal codes. In addition, hundreds of new crime control programs have been adopted by police, courts, and correctional agencies. And, while considerable disagreement exists over the effectiveness of such programs, it is generally agreed that significant emphasis should continue to be given to the problems of the criminal justice system.

As a result, a "field" of criminal justice has come into being. An area of knowledge and work based on controlling crime through the administration of criminal justice services now exists. The term "criminal justice" encompasses many different things, including a variety of crime control organizations and institutions and their processes and interactions. Nearly every federal, state, and local crime control program uses the term in one way or another. One of the most conspicuous applications of the term has been by academic institutions in the development of departments or colleges of criminal justice. Academic institutions have become a major resource for those trying to find solutions to our crime problem; university involvement in problems of criminal justice has given much impetus and authenticity to this new field.

Unfortunately, few experts in criminal justice administration have concentrated on developing an all-encompassing definition of criminal justice or exploring its relationship to other disciplines. Authors in many fields such as law, criminology, and social work discuss problems of crime control primarily from their own perspectives. Each contributes knowledge to the development of the criminal justice field, but no one group has been responsive to all facets of the criminal justice process. Consequently, a new field of study which attempts to bring together the knowledge from various disciplines has emerged. Information is gathered about the criminal justice practices of police, courts, and correctional agencies, and the contributions of such major disciplines as criminology, sociology, psychology, social work, and law are sought. Criminal justice practitioners, for instance, emphasize the practical considerations of processing large groups of offenders through an inadequate system with limited resources. Criminologists concentrate on such issues as defining what constitutes a crime, who the criminal is, what causes crime, and how crime can be prevented. Sociologists tend to theorize that family, community, and environment contribute to the offender's deviant behavior, and generally have only a peripheral interest in criminal justice itself. Psychologists and social workers usually favor an individual treatment philosophy; they believe that the offender's criminal behavior is symptomatic of some emotional or mental health problem. Treatment personnel have generally ignored the organizational and institutional frameworks of criminal justice to concentrate instead on their own specialties.

The legal profession, on the other hand, uses the legal process to maintain social control. The field of criminal justice is very much a legal system where criminal conduct and many criminal justice agencies are controlled by the legal process. As a result, the law is the formal means of preventing illegal conduct through its control of the detection, apprehension, trial, and punishment of the offender. In the past, the legal profession directed its attention solely to legal issues without showing much concern for the nature of the criminal justice process. Only in recent years have lawyers become active participants in seeking to improve the entire system.[4]

The field of criminal justice is also aided by a variety of other disciplines. Political scientists explore the role of federal and state governments in relation to urban problems, deal with political parties and pressure groups, examine legislation, and study how civil liberties are affected by United States Supreme Court decisions. Economists, who have largely ignored the crime problem for many years, have recently entered the field by seeking to apply economic theory to an analysis of crime and suggesting, for instance, that the crime problem cannot be solved until fundamental changes are made in the distribution of economic power. The field of public administration has also been helpful in its analysis of crime and criminal justice theories of administration, organization, and management. Other fields such as medicine, the physical sciences (particularly forensic chemistry), and urban and social planning are also contributing new ideas to the body of knowledge relating to crime and criminal justice.

What exists, then, is a great deal of information taken from various disciplines and consolidated to serve as the knowledge base for this new area of study. Understanding what knowledge is represented in this field helps us to reach a working definition of criminal justice. The world *criminal*, for instance, relates to the nature of an illegal act or to a person guilty of committing such an act,[5] while the term *justice* refers to the use of authority to uphold what is right, and reflects how the law is applied in society and how offenders are processed when in violation of the law.[6] Thus, a literal definition of criminal justice would seem to be as follows:

Criminal justice is a field of study that deals with the nature of crime in society, as well as analyzing the formal processes and social agencies that have been established for crime control.

Before describing the criminal justice system and its component parts, it is essential to establish an understanding of how our governmental structure operates. The basic framework of the American criminal justice system is found in the legislative, judicial, and executive branches of the government. Legal authority to establish crime control programs rests initially within this governmental structure. The legislature defines the law by

GOVERNMENTAL
STRUCTURE AND
CRIMINAL
JUSTICE

determining what conduct is criminal and establishes criminal penalties; the appellate courts interpret the law and make sure it is constitutionally sound; and the executive branch plans programs, appoints personnel, and exercises administrative responsibility for criminal justice agencies. In addition, public agencies such as police departments, parole boards, and correctional programs also function as parts of the government and are created to implement particular legislation.

The legislature is often seen as having the most important role among the three branches of government because it defines criminal behavior, while the judicial and executive branches appear to be secondary sources of crime control authority. This perception of the criminal justice power structure is not entirely correct. All three branches and the governmental bureaucracy generally work together to influence the operation of the criminal justice system. The legislature is not totally independent of the executive branch, nor is the judiciary independent of the other two branches of government. For example, when the legislature passes a criminal statute making conviction for possession of a handgun a one-year mandatory sentence, both the judicial and executive branches share in its implementation and effect on the criminal justice system. Such a law may have been a product of the executive branch, requiring legislative approval and judicial review. The trend toward court intervention in the operational procedures of police agencies (cf. the *Miranda* decision as discussed in Chapter 8) is another example of the interrelationship of the legislative, judicial, and executive functions, as are the constitutional safeguards established by the courts. Similarly, the sentencing process is based on the operations and functions of the three branches of government. Thus, in order to recognize how criminal justice works, one must examine the legislative, judicial, and executive systems as well as the administrative agencies, which are often collectively referred to as the fourth branch of government.

### Legislature

Federal and state constitutions grant authority for legislatures to pass laws. The primary responsibility of legislatures as related to the justice system is to define criminal behavior and establish criminal penalties. Legislatures throughout the country consider thousands of bills each year, many involving the criminal justice system. Only a small number of bills, however, actually become laws. This lawmaking function involves not only passing bills, but modifying and rejecting them as well. The U.S. Congress has debated, modified, and to this date rejected a major bill which would have overhauled the entire federal penal code. When a criminal statute is passed, the courts require that it be sufficiently definite and clear. Vague laws, such as those relating to disorderly conduct, juvenile delinquency, and morality crimes involving drunkenness, gambling, obscenity, and sexual misconduct create uncertainty in police and judicial enforcement practices. Thus, laws prescribing substantive crimes must be clearly stated.

In addition to establishing definitions of crimes, legislatures also pass laws involving criminal procedures. These include rules and regulations involving the laws of arrest, search warrants, bail, trial court proceedings, and sentencing. And, although much criminal procedure in recent years has resulted from leading constitutional cases (i.e., Miranda v. Arizona) relating to the investigation and prosecution of crime, such rules are often enacted into statutory form. Framing the substantive criminal law, however, rather than establishing procedural requirements, is the more basic function of the legislative system.

The initiative to pass a law may come from a legislator, criminal justice agency, public official, or a group of citizens. In criminal justice, the legislature may be considering a new capital punishment bill. The issue is first studied by a legislative committee. Lobbyists and outside interest groups add their influence and knowledge to the proposed bill. The respective legislative bodies are subsequently given the bill for a vote. If the legislation is not originally passed in its initial form, it is given to a joint legislative committee of the House of Representatives and Senate. A compromise bill is eventually voted on by both bodies. When the bill has been passed, it is given to the Chief Executive Officer for his signature. If signed, the bill becomes a law. If vetoed the bill may be dropped or referred back to the legislature for reconsideration. This process represents how statutes are passed by legislatures which govern the day-to-day operations of criminal justice agencies.

Besides defining crimes and fixing sentences, the legislature also provides financial support for crime control programs. Whether funds for such programs are available remains one of the major concerns of the criminal justice system. Criminal justice agencies often lack financial support for facilities, adequate staff, and new programs. In many cases, police courts and correctional agencies compete with each other for the same tax dollar. For the past decade, much monetary support for improvements in state criminal justice systems has come from the Federal Law Enforcement Assistance Administration. Other important functions of the legislature include: acting as a forum for the public expression of views on criminal justice issues; investigating potential criminal activity, as exemplified by the action of the Senate Watergate Committee in 1973; and working with the executive branch to develop and pass improved legislation.

### Judiciary

Although the legislature enacts laws, most criminal procedures are established by the appellate courts. As described in Chapter 12, America has a dual system of courts. Each state has a court system which deals with the enforcement of its laws, while the federal judiciary enforces federal laws. Within each system are both trial and appellate courts. Trial courts handle criminal trials and impose sentences on guilty offenders, while appellate courts interpret the law in light of constitutional standards. These courts, the most important of which is the U.S. Supreme Court, write legal

This chart seeks to present a simple yet comprehensive view of the movement of cases through the criminal justice system. Procedures in individual jurisdictions may vary from the pattern shown here. The differing weights of line indicate the relative volumes of cases disposed of at various points in the system, but this is only suggestive since no nationwide data of this sort exists.

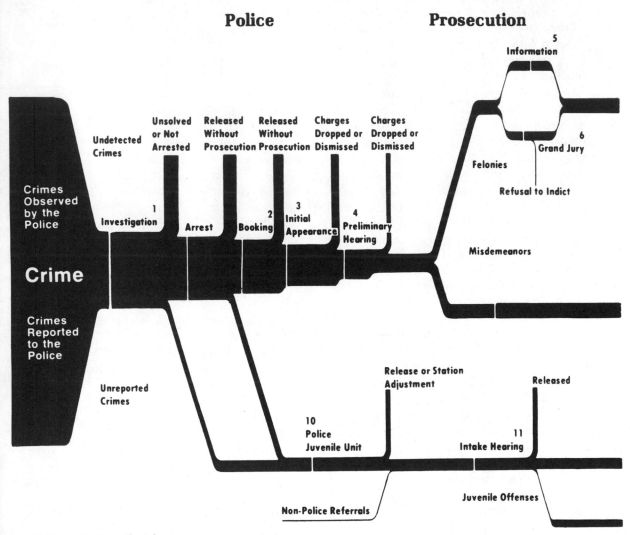

1. May continue until trial.

2. Administrative record of arrest. First step at which temporary release on bail may be available.

3. Before magistrate, commissioner, or justice of peace. Formal notice of charge, advice of rights. Bail set. Summary trials for petty offenses usually conducted here without further processing.

4. Preliminary testing of evidence against defendant. Charge may be reduced. No separate preliminary hearing for misdemeanors in some systems.

5. Charge filed by prosecutor on basis of information submitted by police or citizens. Alternative to grand jury indictment; often used in felonies, almost always in misdemeanors.

6. Reviews whether Government evidence sufficient to justify trial. Some States have no grand jury system; others seldom use it.

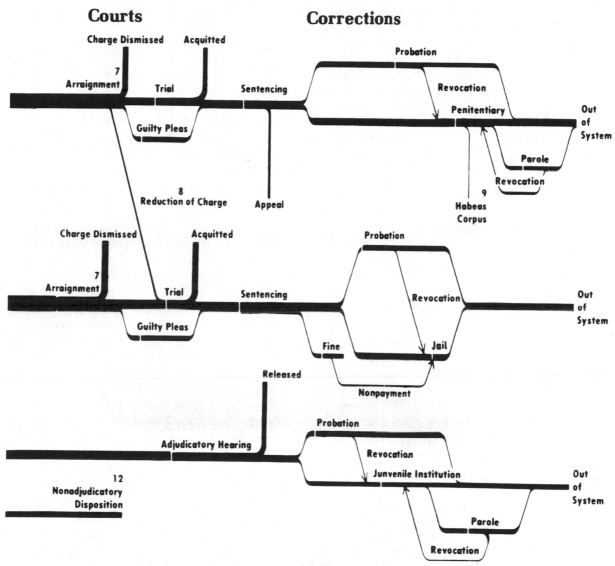

**Courts** **Corrections**

7. Appearance for plea; defendant elects trial by judge or jury (if available); counsel for indigent usually appointed here in felonies. Often not at all in other cases.

8. Charge may be reduced at any time prior to trial in return for plea of guilty or for other reasons.

9. Challenge on constitutional grounds to legality of detention. May be sought at any point in process.

10. Police often hold informal hearings, dismiss or adjust many cases without further processing.

11. Probation officer decides desirability of further court action.

12. Welfare agency, social services, counseling, medical care, etc., for cases where adjudicatory handling not needed.

decisions about how laws should be applied. The Warren Court, for example, exercised a great deal of judicial leadership by deciding many criminal cases involving the expansion of individual rights. Were it not for the power of judicial review, established within the federal system in the case of Marbury v. Madison (1 Cranch 137, 1803), the courts would exert only limited influence in the criminal process. In addition, the supremacy clause of the U.S. Constitution has allowed the Supreme Court to declare state and local laws unconstitutional. Over the years, the principle of judicial review has been applied both actively and with restraint. Those in favor of judicial activism argue that it is the responsibility of the courts to monitor and control governmental infringement on our civil rights. On the other hand, advocates of judicial restraint suggest that laws should be upheld by the courts unless they clearly violate constitutional provisions. Further discussion of this issue is found under "Due Process, Crime Control, and the U.S. Supreme Court" in this chapter.

### Executive

The third major governmental authority with functions related to criminal justice is the executive branch. Executive power is vested in such public officials as president, governors, and mayors. Today's officials are often actively involved in criminal justice issues. Many have extensive powers of appointment; they appoint judges and heads of administrative agencies such as police chiefs, commissioners of corrections, and executive directors of criminal justice planning agencies. They also have the authority to remove administrative personnel. Another important executive function involves the power to grant pardons for crimes. President Ford's pardon of Richard Nixon's involvement in the Watergate scandal is a controversial example of this power.

The elected official also plays a very important leadership role in criminal justice matters. Through the submission of legislative programs, executive persuasion, and party politics, a governor can influence others to follow his or her suggestions. A governor also has a veto power to nullify any legislation, and thus maintains a system of checks and balances within our governmental structure. In addition, each chief executive has a staff to develop programs and at least theoretically direct the operations of the various criminal justice departments and agencies. Thus a president, governor, or mayor is both a chief executive and the administrative head of a segment of the governmental bureaucracy.

No discussion of the functions of the legislative, judicial, and executive branches is complete without mention of the major criminal justice agencies. Police departments, trial courts, and correctional programs have a tremendous impact on the authority of the criminal justice system. Offenders are affected more directly by these administrative agencies than by the legislative or appellate processes.

Criminal justice agencies are often created by legislative acts, by executive orders, or by constitutional requirements. The authority of an administrative organization is set by its legislature and by agency discretion.

Traditional agencies, such as corrections departments or parole boards, often have broad discretion and delegated authority to provide services for convicted offenders. Law enforcement groups and trial courts, on the other hand, are generally given more legislative direction. Nonetheless, all criminal justice agencies directly affect the rights of citizens. They have the authority to investigate criminal behavior, develop rules and regulations with regard to their operational policies, enforce the law, and adjudicate, or decide by judicial procedure, guilt or innocence. Even though criminal justice agencies have a great amount of delegated authority and discretion, there are ways of controlling this power. For instance, the legislature can pass a new law restricting the activities of a particular agency. In addition, the judicial system retains the authority to review the actions of administrative agencies.

With this general understanding of our governmental structure, we can begin to examine the criminal justice system.

THE CRIMINAL JUSTICE SYSTEM

The contemporary criminal justice system within the United States is monumental in size. It consists of over 60,000 public agencies, a total annual budget of over $10 billion, and a staff of almost 12 million people.[7] There are approximately 20,000 police agencies, nearly 17,000 courts, over 8,000 prosecutorial agencies, about 4,600 correctional institutions, and over 3,200 probation and parole departments,[8] and the numbers of people processed through the system annually are enormous. During 1976 the police made over 9,600,000 arrests and the courts prosecuted more than 2,000,000 offenders.[9] In addition, over 1 million juveniles were processed by the juvenile courts.[10] The average daily population of correctional institutions is approximately ½ million inmates, while over 1 million offenders are thought to be under probation supervision and about 150,000 are on parole.[11] The magnitude and complexity of agency services in crime control has led to the development of what experts term the "criminal justice system."

The idea that the agencies of justice actually form a system has become increasingly popular among practitioners, academicians, and other professionals who deal with crime. Theoretically, the term refers to the interrelationship among all those agencies concerned with the prevention of crime in our society. The systems approach to criminal justice sees a change in one part of the system as effecting change in the others. It implies that a closely knit coordinated structure of organizations exists among the various components of the system. Unfortunately, this approach exists more in theory than in practice. The various elements of the criminal justice system—such as police, courts, and corrections—are all related, but only to a degree that they are influenced by the others' policies and practices; they have not yet become so well coordinated that they can be described as operating in unison. "Fragmented," "divided," and "splintered" continue to be the adjectives most commonly used to describe the American system of criminal justice.[12]

COMPONENTS
OF CRIMINAL
JUSTICE

Crime control in the United States today is not a system as such but rather a group of agencies organized around the following major components:

1. The police.

2. The courts, including the prosecution and the defense.

3. Corrections, including probation, institutionalization, and parole.

### The Police

Law enforcement officers are basically concerned with maintaining order and enforcing the criminal law. The system and process of criminal justice depends on effective and efficient police work, particularly when it comes to preventing and detecting crime, and apprehending and arresting probable criminal offenders. As our society becomes more complex, new and additional functions are required of the police officer. Today, police work actively with the community to prevent criminal behavior: they divert juveniles, alcoholics, and drug addicts from the criminal justice system; they participate in specialized units such as the Juvenile Aid Bureau; they work with public prosecutors, court officials, correctional authorities, and criminal justice research and planning agencies; they resolve family conflicts; they facilitate the movement of people and vehicles; and they provide other services, such as preserving civil order on an emergency basis.[13]

Because of these expanded responsibilities, the role of the police officer has become a more professional one. The officer must not only be technically competent to investigate crimes, but must also be aware of the rules and procedures associated with arrest, apprehension, and investigation of criminal activity. The police officer must be aware of the factors involved in the causes of crime in order to screen and divert those offenders who might be better handled by other more appropriate agencies.

The police officer's role is established by the boundaries of the criminal law. While the officer sets the criminal justice system in motion by the authority to arrest, and this authority is vested in the law, it is neither final nor absolute. The police officer's duty requires discretion on numerous matters dealing with a variety of situations, victims, criminals, and citizens. The officer must determine when an argument becomes disorderly conduct or a criminal assault; whether it is appropriate to arrest a juvenile or refer him or her to a social agency; or when to assume that probable cause exists to arrest a suspect for a crime. Chief Justice Warren Burger stressed the importance of individual decision making and discretion when he stated:

The policeman [or woman] on the beat, or in the patrol car, makes more decisions and exercises broader discretion affecting the daily lives of people every day and to a greater extent, in many respects, than a judge will ordinarily exercise in a week.[14]

Thus, police officers today are required to exercise a great deal of individual discretion in deciding whether to arrest, or refer, or to simply investigate a situation further; their actions represent the exercise of discretionary justice.[15] A more detailed analysis of police discretion is found in Chapter 7.

## The Courts

The criminal court is considered by many to be the core element in the administration of criminal justice. As the President's Crime Commission has stated:

It is [the] part of the system that is the most venerable, the most formally organized, and the most elaborately circumscribed by law and tradition. It is the institution around which the rest of the system has developed and to which the rest of the system is in large measure responsible. It regulates the flow of the criminal process under governance of the law. . . . It is expected to articulate the community's most deeply held, most cherished views about the relationship of individual and society.[16]

The criminal court is responsible for determining the guilt or innocence of those offenders brought before it. Ideally, it is expected to convict and sentence those found guilty of crimes while insuring that the innocent are freed without any consequence or burden. The court system is formally required to seek the truth and to obtain justice for the individual brought before its tribunals, and also to maintain the integrity of the government's rule of law.

Once the truth has been determined, and in the event the defendant is found guilty, the criminal court is responsible for sentencing the offender. Whatever sentence is ordered by the court may serve not only to rehabilitate the offender, but also to deter others from crime. Once sentencing is accomplished, the corrections component of the criminal justice system beings to function.

The entire criminal court process is undertaken with the recognition that the rights of the individual should be protected at all times. These rights, determined by federal and state constitutional mandates, statutes, and case laws, form the foundation for individual protection of the accused. They include such basic concepts as the right to an attorney, the right to a jury trial, and the right to a speedy trial. A defendant also has the right to be given due process, or to be treated with fundamental fairness. This includes the right to be present at trial, to be notified of the charge(s), to have an opportunity to confront hostile witnesses, and to have favorable witnesses appear. Such practices are an integral part of a system and process that seeks to balance the interests of both the individual and the state.

The court system administering the criminal process includes lower criminal courts, superior courts, and supreme courts. Each state and the federal government has its own independent court structure unique to that particular jurisdiction. Where a crime is a violation of state law, it is ordinarily prosecuted in the state court, while offenses against federal laws are generally handled by the federal court system.

The lower criminal courts of any state, variously called police courts, district courts, or recorders courts, deal with the largest number of criminal offenses. Referred to as the people's courts, they are scattered throughout the state by county, town, or geographic district. They daily handle a large volume of criminal offenses, including crimes such as assault and battery, disorderly conduct, breaking and entering, possession of drugs, petty larceny, traffic violations, and juvenile offenses. Many cases are disposed of without trial, either because the defendant pleads guilty or because the circumstances of the offense do not warrant further court action. Where a trial is required in the lower courts, it often occurs before a judge rather than before a jury because the defendant often waives the constitutional right to a jury trial. Lower criminal courts, although primarily responsible for misdemeanor offenses, also process the first stage of felony offenses by holding preliminary hearings, making bail decisions, and conducting trials of certain felonies where they have jurisdiction as defined by statute.

In sum, the lower criminal courts often dispense routine and repetitious justice, and are burdened with a heavy responsibility they are not generally equipped to fulfill. Characterized by cramped courtrooms and limited personnel, they remain a critical problem area in criminal justice administration.

The superior courts, or major trial courts, have general jurisdiction over all criminal offenses but ordinarily concentrate on felony offenses. They conduct jury trials with much formality and strict adherence to the defendant's constitutional rights. In addition to conducting trials, these courts accept guilty pleas, generally give offenders longer sentences due to the more serious nature of their crimes, and in certain instances review sentences originally imposed by lower courts.

The highest state court is a supreme or appeals court, whose functions are similar to those of the United States Supreme Court in the federal judicial system. State supreme courts are primarily appellate courts which do not conduct criminal trials. They receive and act upon appeals from the lower courts and settle controversies arising from such lower-court trials. Appellate courts deal with procedural errors arising in the lower courts, such as the use of illegal evidence, the applicability of statutes, or possibly erroneous technical motions. Questions of fact which were decided in the original trial are not ordinarily reviewed in the appellate process. The appellate court has the authority to affirm, modify, or reverse decisions of the lower criminal court.

### The Prosecutor and Defense Attorney

The prosecutor and the defense attorney are the opponents in that aspect of the administration of criminal justice known as the adversary system. The two parties oppose each other in a contest—namely, the criminal trial—in accordance with rules of law and procedure. In every criminal case, the state acts against the defendant before an impartial judge or jury, with each side trying to bring evidence and arguments forward to advance its case. Theoretically, the ultimate objective of the adversary system is to seek the truth, in this way determining the guilt or innocence of the defendant from the formal evidence presented at the trial. The adversary system insures that the defendant is given a fair trial, that the relevant facts of a given case emerge, and that an impartial decision is reached.

The prosecutor is the public official who represents the government and presents its case against the defendant who is charged with a violation of the criminal law. Traditionally, the prosecutor is a local attorney whose area of jurisdictional responsibility is limited to a particular county or city. The prosecutor is known variously as a district attorney or a prosecuting attorney, and is either an elected or appointed official. On a state level, the prosecutor may be referred to as the attorney general, while in the federal jurisdiction the title is United States Attorney. The prosecutor not only is responsible for charging the defendant with the crime, but also for bringing the case to trial and to a final conclusion. The prosecutor's authority ranges from determining the nature of the charge to reducing the charge by negotiation or recommending that the complaint be dismissed. The prosecutor also participates in bail hearings, presents cases before a grand jury, and appears for the state at arraignments. In sum, the prosecutor is responsible for presenting the state's case from the time of the defendant's arrest through conviction and sentencing in the criminal court.

The prosecutor, like the police officer, exercises a great deal of discretion; he or she can decide initially whether to file a criminal charge, determine what charge to bring, or explore the availability of noncriminal dispositions. Prosecutorial discretion would not be as important as it is were it desirable to prosecute all violations of the law. However, full enforcement of every law is not practical since most police officers and prosecutors ordinarily lack sufficient resources, staff, and support services to carry out that goal. Therefore, it makes sense to screen out cases where the accused is obviously innocent, where the evidence is negligible, or where criminal sanctions may seem inappropriate. Thus, instead of total or automatic law enforcement, a process of selective or discretionary law enforcement exists; as a result, the prosecutor must make many decisions which significantly influence police operations and control the actual number of cases processed through the court and correctional systems.

The defense attorney, on the other hand, is responsible for providing legal defense representation to the defendant. This role involves two major functions:

1. Protecting the constitutional rights of the accused.

2. Presenting the best possible legal defense for the defendant.

The defense attorney represents a client from initial arrest through the trial stage and during the sentencing hearing and, if needed, through the process of appeal. The defense attorney is also expected to enter into plea negotiations and obtain for the defendant the most suitable bargain regarding type and length of sentence.

Any person accused of a crime who is able to afford private counsel can obtain any attorney desired. One of the most critical questions in the criminal justice system has been whether an indigent (poor) defendant has the right to counsel. The federal court system has long provided counsel to the indigent on the basis of the Sixth Amendment, which allows the accused the right to have the assistance of a defense counsel. Through a series of landmark United States Supreme Court decisions beginning with *Powell v. Alabama* in 1932 and continuing with *Gideon v. Wainwright* in 1962 and *Argersinger v. Hamlin* in 1972, the right of a criminal defendant to have counsel has become fundamental to our system of criminal justice.[17] Today, state courts must provide counsel to indigent defendants who are charged with criminal offenses where the possibility of incarceration exists. A detailed discussion of the criminal defendant's right to counsel is continued in Chapter 12.

### Sentencing and Corrections

Following a criminal trial resulting in conviction and sentencing, the offender enters the correctional system. Of the three major components of the criminal justice system, corrections has received the most attention in recent years. Public interest has become widespread as a result of well-publicized prison riots, such as occurred in Attica in 1971, and the alleged inability of the system to rehabilitate offenders.

In the broadest sense, corrections involve probation, various types of incarceration (including jails, houses of correction, and state prisons), and parole programs for both juvenile and adult offenders. Corrections ordinarily represent the post-adjudicatory care given to offenders when a sentence is imposed by the court and the offender is placed in the hands of the correctional agency.

The American system of corrections is massive. In 1967, the President's Crime Commission stated that:

The American Correctional System . . . handles nearly 1.3 million offenders on an average day. It has 2.5 million admissions in the course of a year . . . One third of all offenders (426,000) were in institutions; the remaining two thirds (857,000) were under supervision in the community. The cost of corrections is estimated at over 1 billion dollars a year.[18]

Complicating this system is the expected dramatic population explosion in prisons. A study by the University of Wisconsin predicted that the prison population of the nation will continue to increase until 1985 and may not level off until the end of the century.[19]

Despite its tremendous size and cost, the correctional system suffers from an extremely poor performance record. It has not been able to offer public protection, nor does it effectively rehabilitate criminal offenders. It is often plagued with high recidivism rates (many offenders return to crime shortly after incarceration). Furthermore, there is reason to believe that methods used by corrections, particularly incarceration, contribute to the number of offenders who return to criminal activity upon release. High recidivism rates are believed to result from the lack of effective treatment and training programs within incarceration facilities, poor physical environments and health conditions, and the fact that offender populations in many institutions are generally unstable and mixed. It seems apparent why the correctional system has failed to correct or alleviate the crime problem.

Despite these problems, corrections nevertheless play a critical role in the criminal justice system. By exercising control over those sentenced by the courts to incarceration or community supervision, the system acts as the major sanctioning force of the criminal law. As a result, the system of corrections has many responsibilities, among them protecting society, deterring crime, and—equally important—rehabilitating offenders. The achievement of both proper restraint and the effective reform of the offender is the system's most frustrating yet awesome goal. Below, some of the major components of correction are discussed.

**Probation.** Probation is a judicial action or legal disposition which allows the offender to remain in the community subject to conditions imposed by court order under the supervision of a probation officer. It allows the offender to continue working and providing for his or her family and avoid the debilitating effects of incarceration.

At the same time, social services are provided to help the offender adjust in the community; counseling, assistance from social workers, and group treatment, as well as the use of community resources to obtain employment, welfare, and housing, are offered to the offender while on probation. In providing these services, probation officers perform the dual functions of preparing pre-sentencing reports for the court and supervising probationers in the community.

The origins of probation can be found in English common law, where such devices as benefit of clergy, judicial reprieve, and recognizance were used to mitigate harsh sentences and avoid capital punishment.[20] Subsequently, probation practices were established in the state of Massachusetts in 1841 by John Augustus, who is considered the father of probation in this country.[21] His efforts resulted in the enactment of the first statutory probation program in Massachusetts in 1878.[22] Since that time, probation as a court action and as a method of social service has been introduced into all the states and the federal government. Most experts believe that community treatment programs such as probation are of great significance in rehabilitating offenders and reducing recidivism rates.

**Confinement.** In the narrow sense, the system of corrections represents the institutional care of offenders brought into the criminal justice system.

A person given a sentence by the court involving incarceration ordinarily is confined to a correctional institution for a specified period of time. Different types of institutions are used to hold offenders. First, the jail holds offenders awaiting trial, or those involved in other proceedings such as grand jury deliberations, arraignments, or preliminary hearings. The jail is ordinarily operated by local government and is referred to as a detention facility. Jails are often considered to be the worst of all penal institutions because of their poor physical conditions, lack of adequate staff, and custodial philosophy. The "Tombs" in New York City, as well as the Suffolk County or "Charles Street" jail in Boston, are examples of facilities which have become notorious in recent years due to their inability to conform to adequate institutional detention standards. The Federal District Court of Boston ordered that the Charles Street Jail be closed as of June 30, 1976 because of its physical conditions, which were found to be so poor that they violated an offender's constitutional right under the Eighth Amendment to be free from cruel and unusual punishment.[23]

A second type of institution is ordinarily known as a house of correction. This type of facility holds sentenced prisoners who commit less serious offenses. Normally, the misdemeanant, or minor offender, is incarcerated in the house of correction for two years or less. Because the distinction between serious and less serious offenses is not always easy to establish, however, some jurisdictions admit felons as well as misdemeanants to houses of correction. Many of these short-term institutions are administered by local county governments, as are jails, and suffer from the same shortcomings. Little is done in the way of inmate treatment, principally because the personnel and institutions lack the qualifications, services, and resources.

The third type of correctional institution is that group of state-operated facilities which receive felony offenders sentenced by the criminal courts. These institutions are variously called prisons or penitentiaries, and include reformatories, forestry camps, and so on. They are often divided into minimum, medium, and maximum security institutions. Prison facilities vary throughout the country; some have high walls, cells, and large heterogeneous inmate populations, while others offer inmates much freedom, good correctional programs, and have small, homogeneous populations.

When an offender is sentenced by the court to a period of confinement, responsibility for custody and rehabilitation is transferred from the court to a correctional agency. A separate department of corrections, which is in the executive branch of a state's government, ordinarily administers all the correctional institutions within a state. Each institution is under the general supervision of a prison warden or superintendent.

Most new inmates are first sent to a reception and classification center, where each is given a diagnostic evaluation and assigned to an institution which meets individual needs as much as possible within the system's resources. The diagnostic process in the reception center may range from a physical examination and a single interview to an extensive series of psychiatric tests, orientation sessions, and numerous personal interviews.

Classification is a way of evaluating inmates and assigning them to appropriate placements and activities within the state institutional system.

When entering the assigned institution, the offender is placed in available programs in accordance with the diagnostic evaluation. Most institutions offer varying degrees of programs and services which include the following:

1. Health and medical care.

2. Counseling.

3. Academic education.

4. Recreation.

5. Vocational training.

6. Religious study.

7. Visiting privileges and many other special interest activities.

These programs and services combine to form the treatment component of institutional confinement. Although most programs look good on paper, they generally serve only a small proportion of inmates; other programs are ineffective, and some do not exist at all. Thus, the philosophy and process of rehabilitation and treatment upon which these programs are based are often more rhetoric than reality.

Some progress has been made, however, in those jurisdictions which have instituted a fourth type of confinement—community-based correctional institutions. The current trend is to deemphasize the use of large prisons and use smaller, community-based facilities as well as halfway houses, pre-release centers, and work-release and home-furlough programs. This movement is a result of the fact that experts believe that only a small percentage of prison inmates require maximum security and that most can be more effectively rehabilitated in community-based facilities. Rather than totally confining the offender to an impersonal and harsh prison experience, such programs offer the opportunity to maintain normal family and social relationships while giving access to rehabilitative services and resources at lower cost to the taxpayer.

**Parole.** More than 70% of all offenders released from correctional institutions reenter the community via the parole system. Parole is a process whereby an inmate is selected for early release and serves the remainder of a sentence in the community under the supervision of a parole officer. It is the predominant form of release for prison inmates and exists in all states and in the federal government.[24] Other ways in which an offender may be released from an institution include mandatory release upon the completion of a sentence and pardon, a form of executive clemency.

The main purpose of parole is to help the ex-inmate bridge the gap between institutional confinement and a positive adjustment within the community. It is often confused with probation; although the two are different in some respects, they are also similar in some very important ways. In both cases, evaluation data about the offender is gathered after the person is placed in the community. If the offender violates conditions of community supervision, probation or parole may be revoked. In that event, the probationer is returned to the court for further sentencing while the parolee may be sent back to the correctional institution. Parole and probation also use similar techniques of counseling and supervision to help offenders avoid further criminal behavior.

One of the major differences between parole and probation is that parole is part of the administrative structure of the government, while the granting of probation is a judicial function. When an offender may be released from an institution, what parole conditions will be fixed, and when a parole should be revoked are all decisions which rest with an agency known as the parole board, often located in the executive branch of government. Decisions regarding probation, however, are the court's responsibility. Parole and probation also differ significantly in that parole is awarded after a period of incarceration while probation is usually granted prior to or instead of confinement.

The future of parole is undecided. Changes are being made in sentencing provisions throughout the country, and some thought is being given to eliminating parole altogether. The state of Maine recently implemented fixed sentencing statutes requiring offenders to serve their entire sentences in confinement. If this type of movement expands, the future of parole in the criminal justice system will be in dispute.[25]

THE CRIMINAL
JUSTICE
PROCESS

It is important to realize that criminal justice refers to a process as well as to a system of agencies and organizations. This process is reasonably well-defined in that it takes an offender through a series of steps beginning with arrest and concluding with the offender's reentry into society. The emphasis throughout the process is on the offender and the various sequential stages that person passes through. When criminal justice is viewed as a system, the various crime control organizations are the major concern; the process model approach concentrates instead on the movement of individual cases through the criminal justice system. A comprehensive view of this process would normally include the following ten critical points:

1. Investigation.

2. Arrest and booking.

3. Custody.

4. Formal complaint.

5. Initial court appearance—preliminary hearing.

6. Arraignment.

7. Bail-detention.

8. Adjudication.

9. Disposition (sentencing).

10. Appeal.

These steps are the most apparent ones in the criminal process, although procedures may vary from one jurisdiction to another. Herbert Packer describes the process:

The image that comes to mind is an assembly line conveyor belt down which moves an endless stream of cases, never stopping, carrying them to workers who stand at fixed stations and who perform on each case as it comes by the same small but essential operation that brings it one step closer to being a finished product, or to exchange the metaphor for the reality, a closed file. The criminal process is seen as a screening process in which each successive stage—pre-arrest investigation, arrest, post-arrest investigation, preparation for trial, trial or entry of plea, conviction, disposition—involves a series of routinized operations whose success is gauged primarily by their tendency to pass the case along to a successful conclusion.[26]

The criminal justice process normally proceeds in a step-by-step fashion. When a criminal statute has been violated, a police officer first seeks to locate the possible offender. The officer, if successful, then arrests the offender, files a criminal complaint, and has the offender brought before a judge or magistrate as quickly as possible. If the offense is relatively minor, the judge may dispose of the case immediately; if the crime is more serious, the judge formally acquaints the defendant with the charge, seeks to have counsel provided, and takes possible action on bail. The public prosecutor is then notified of the case and, if the defendant pleads not guilty to the charge, the case goes to trial. The facts and evidence of the case are then developed by the prosecution on behalf of the government and by the defense attorney for the defendant. A trial on the merits is then held either before a judge alone or before a jury under the direction of a judge to determine the guilt or innocence of the defendant. The defendant, if found guilty, is then sentenced by the judge to a period of incarceration or directed to remain in the community under the supervision and control of probation authorities.

Many cases are disposed of in this way, while others may be dealt with through more informal procedures, such as the use of diversion programs, withholding prosecution, or dropping the charges. Figure 4.1 illustrates how offenders are removed from the criminal justice system. Theoretically, nearly every part of the process requires that individual cases be disposed of as quickly as possible. However, the criminal justice process is a slower and more tedious one than could be desired due to congestion, inadequate facilities, limited resources, lack of knowledge, and the nature of governmental bureaucracy. When defendants are not processed smoothly, often because of large caseloads and inadequate facilities,

FIGURE 4.1.
Funneling Effect from
Reported Crimes
Through Prison
Sentence

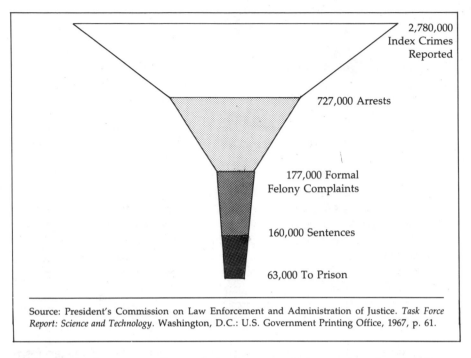

2,780,000
Index Crimes
Reported

727,000 Arrests

177,000 Formal
Felony Complaints

160,000 Sentences

63,000 To Prison

Source: President's Commission on Law Enforcement and Administration of Justice. *Task Force Report: Science and Technology.* Washington, D.C.: U.S. Government Printing Office, 1967, p. 61.

such as exist in many urban criminal courts, the procedure breaks down, the process within the system fails, and the ultimate goal of crime control in society is not achieved. Table 4.1 represents the interrelationship between the criminal justice system and the criminal justice process.

TABLE 4.1
The Interralationship of
the Criminal Justice
System and the
Criminal Justice
Process

| *The System: Agencies of Crime Control* | *The Process* |
|---|---|
| 1. Police | 1. Investigation |
| | 2. Arrest |
| | 3. Custody |
| 2. Prosecution and defense | 4. Complaint |
| | 5. Initial appearance—preliminary hearing |
| | 6. Arraignment |
| | 7. Bail—detention |
| | 8. Plea bargaining |
| 3. Court | 9. Adjudication |
| | 10. Disposition |
| | 11. Post-conviction remedies |
| 4. Corrections | 12. Community supervision |
| | 13. Incarceration |
| | 14. Release |
| | 15. Restoration of rights |

Criminal justice has thus far been described as a field of study, an inter-related system of agencies, and a process that involves moving offenders from the initial stage of arrest to eventual release from the correctional system. Regardless of what seems the best definition, experts agree that the criminal justice system is an extremely complex set of institutions.

One of the most important reasons why it is difficult to comprehend, merge, and reform the system is that its basic goals and objectives are unclear. Criminal justice has neither a commonly agreed-upon philosophy nor an accepted statement of goals. In a discussion of the problem of multiple goals for criminal justice, Donald Newman points out that neither the total system nor any single process or agency within the system has just one objective. He adds:

The multiplicty of purposes, and of hopes, not only makes the system controversial, but often adds a dimension of confusion to any attempt to assess or evaluate it.[27]

What exactly are the various goals of criminal justice? Experts today continue to debate whether one goal should take precedence, whether the system should have multiple goals or which goals if any should be most emphasized. Some individuals, such as those in law enforcement, might claim that crime control efforts are best served by the goal of deterrence. Others in corrections might argue that rehabilitation is most significant. Still others might spend considerable time talking of crime prevention.

It appears that two major categories of goals exist for the criminal justice system. They are: (1) theoretical or abstract goals, which include retribution, deterrence, incapacitation, and rehabilitation; and (2) prag-matic goals such as crime prevention, diversion of offenders from the criminal justice system, fairness in procedures for handling the offender, efficiency in criminal justice operations, and evaluation.

Concerning theoretical goals, Herbert Packer maintains that retribu-tion, deterrence, incapacitation, and rehabilitation are not only goals but the justifications for criminal punishment.[28] Retribution or revenge rests on the idea that it is right for the offender to be punished. This view holds that each person is responsible for individual actions and deserves to be punished for breaking societal norms. This is what Packer describes as the nonutilitarian view of retribution, as distinguished from the utilitarian justification which rests on the assumption that any punishment used be linked to crime control. The utilitarian rationale is the underlying basis for the goals of deterrence, incapacitation, and rehabilitation. As disucssed in Chapter 1, deterrence holds that the threat of punishment will discourage others from committing crimes; Packer calls this concept one of general deterrence. The threat of capital punishment in past years is believed by some to deter potential offenders from committing certain offenses for which it is the legislative penalty. General deterrence is to be distinguished from what Packer describes as special deterrence, an approach in which individuals who have committed crimes are punished to dissuade them from committing future crimes. Due to high recidivism rates, it might safety be said that special deterrence does not work.

Another goal of criminal justice involves the use of physical restraint or incapacitation. This goal presumes that a person with a tendency to keep committing crimes will be unable to do so if kept in prison. From a historical perspective, incapacitation became a major criminal sanction following the decline of corporal punishment in the nineteenth and early twentieth centuries. Today, all American criminal courts are authorized to pronounce sentences involving terms of imprisonment.

The idea of incapacitation is often associated with the goal of rehabilitation, since placing a person in prison is often seen as a means of rehabilitation. Packer claims that rehabilitation is a justification of punishment. While punishment often emphasizes that a person has been found guilty of criminal conduct, rehabilitation focuses instead on the offender as an individual in need of treatment. One of the major objections to rehabilitation has been the question of whether we actually know how to accomplish this goal. This raises such questions as: What is rehabilitation? What causes criminal behavior? Do we have the resources to effectively treat large groups of diverse offenders?

In addition to these abstract goals, other more practical goals have been suggested. In its summary report, *A National Strategy to Reduce Crime* (January 1973), the National Advisory Commission on Criminal Justice Standards and Goals identifies the reduction in the rates of five major crimes—homicide, forcible rape, aggravated assault, robbery, and burglary—as a major goal of the criminal justice system. The Commission further provides four priorities for reducing such offenses:

Preventing juvenile delinquency
Improving delivery of social services
Reducing delays in the criminal justice process
Securing more citizen participation in the criminal justice system.[29]

In recent years, other organizations such as the various state planning agencies established as a result of the Safe Streets and Crime Control Act of 1968 have adapted such goals as:

1. The prevention of criminal behavior.

2. The diversion of offenders and potential offenders from the criminal justice system.

3. Fairness in procedures for those within the system.

4. Efficiency in organization and management of criminal justice agencies.

5. The study and evaluation of the system and process as well as its strategies and programs.

These goals reflect a desire to improve all segments of the operating criminal justice system. Let us look at each individually.

## Prevention

Prevention is a means of control which seeks to divert an individual away from criminal behavior during the early stages of life. Building stronger family units, providing counseling in schools, and developing better environmental conditions are all examples of prevention.

By participating in prevention, support services can play a significant role in achieving crime control, but prevention is not limited to support services alone. It also entails discouraging and thwarting criminal behavior even after it has occurred. If, for example, the police allocated more personnel to street work, the increased police presence might serve to discourage further crime. The corrections process could also prevent crime if its programs could obtain some semblance of a valid capacity for rehabilitation.

## Diversion

In the area of diversion, criminal justice agents have often exercised discretion in excluding individuals from the system. An individual may be diverted from the justice system at any stage of the process. Basically, diversion has focused on certain groups of offenders, such as minor noncriminal delinquents and adult offenders who might be more appropriately handled by social agencies.

## Fairness

The goal of fairness seeks to insure that all persons processed through the criminal justice system will be treated fairly and humanely. No distinctions should be made between criminal offenders in minority groups or the lower classes and those in the middle and upper classes. Proper procedures representing due process safeguards should be present in all aspects of the criminal justice system. Therefore, the methods and techniques implemented in the areas of arrest, sentencing, and incarceration must be consistent with our democratic ideals and frame of government.

## Efficiency

Efficiency as a goal requires that proper organization and management exist in criminal justice agencies. Effectiveness suffers if law enforcement, courts, and correctional agencies are not organized and managed in such a way as to insure optimum utilization of personnel and resources. Efficient operations require qualified personnel, adequate organizational framework, sound fiscal planning, and the development of successful programs of crime control.

### Evaluation

Last, the goal of evaluation is vital to criminal justice administration. Without constantly evaluating the crime problem, those in the criminal justice field would be incapable of developing realistic and effective programs and services. Examples of programs which have been effectively evaluated include the methadone program and the classification and community treatment of youthful offenders. Conducting evaluative research throughout the entire criminal justice system is one way in which the system can be changed for the better.

Thus, criminal justice and its components—police, courts, and corrections—work in an atmosphere involving diverse goals and objectives. And, while it might be possible to say which goals are more popular than others, it remains for further research to determine which goals are achievable and which will have the most significant impact on crime control.

## CRITICAL ISSUES IN CRIMINAL JUSTICE

The criminal justice system is confronted with a variety of problems and issues. The most obvious problem is its apparent inability to prevent and control crime. Over the years, few significant steps have been taken to effectively lower the volume of crime committed in America. The failure may be understandable in light of our country's heterogeneous culture, mixed political system, the conflict over what really causes crime, and the kinds of societal values held within our industrial system. Nonetheless, the public remains interested in learning how to reduce the incidence of crime. Citizens and criminal justice scholars alike recognize the destructive effects crime has on all of our lives. As a result, we continue to commit enormous amounts of time and money to crime control—nevertheless, there appear to be no real solutions to the problem.

We have, however, seen the development of many programs, innovative ideas, and legal decisions which have affected the practices of police, judicial, and correctional agencies. Some of these activities put into effect theories which have existed over the past decade, while others are emerging issues that can influence future criminal justice operations. Since it is impossible to identify all of the changes taking place within the criminal justice system, attention is given here to a few major issues.

### Due Process, Crime Control, and the United States Supreme Court

A major problem within the criminal justice system is caused by the need to balance the individual rights of offenders with effective law enforcement. Too much due process of law can hamper crime control efforts, while arbitrary police and correctional practices can infringe on human and constitutional rights.

The United States Supreme Court has been particularly active in seeking to establish the proper balance between due process of law and the enforcement of criminal justice. Five amendments to the United States Constitution have direct bearing on this issue. They include the Fourth Amendment (search and seizure); the Fifth Amendment (double jeopardy, self-incrimination, and due process clause); the Sixth Amendment (speedy and public trial, right of confrontation and cross-examination, and right to counsel); the Eighth Amendment (bail and cruel and unusual punishments); and the Fourteenth Amendment (due process of law). Through the continual constitutional application and interpretation of these amendments, the courts have set guidelines for balancing the interests of both the individual and the state in the criminal justice system.

At issue is whether the Supreme Court has weakened criminal justice efforts to control crime by broadening the base of individual rights. The Warren Court in the early 1960s greatly expanded constitutional liberties within the criminal justice system.[30] The Supreme Court ruled that procedural due process protection must be given to all accused offenders in the police, judicial, and correctional systems. Other rights for law-abiding citizens, such as the freedom of religious choice, the freedom of the press, and the right to free speech, were also protected and expanded. The Warren Court evinced a willingness to accept criminal cases for review and to vindicate the rights of accused individuals and minorities mistreated by the criminal process and society. In many respects, the Supreme Court decisions of the Warren era established a constitutional code of criminal procedure; as a result, many changes were made in the ways in which states and the federal system process criminal offenders.

Many legal scholars believe, however, that the Supreme Court's expansion of constitutional liberties has slowed considerably since 1969—the year following Richard Nixon's election to the Presidency. Today's Supreme Court, with its four Nixon appointees—Chief Justice Burger and Justices Blackmun, Powell, and Rehnquist—seems less sympathetic to the plight of the accused and more receptive to prosecutional arguments. During the 1975–1976 term, the Court upheld capital punishment as a penalty for murder, cut back on Fourth Amendment protections against unreasonable searches and seizures, and made it more difficult for persons claiming violations of their constitutional rights to have their cases heard in the federal court system.

Thus, while the Warren Court was the champion of the underdog, the Burger Court has been more conservative and has interpreted the Constitution more strictly and specifically. As criminal justice issues reach the Supreme Court in the future, it may be that the legacy of the Warren Court will be forgotten.

The trend toward judicial activism, however, is far from over. In recent years, federal courts have ordered busing in order to integrate public schools, have ruled that city jails be closed in violation of the Eighth Amendment, have declared criminal abortion statutes unconstitutional, and have imposed new procedural rules on a host of human service agencies. It seems as if no other major country gives its judiciary as much power as does America; perhaps, then, the question is not one of loose vs. strict constitutional construction, but one of whether the judicial system will continue to play an activist role in our society.

## Decriminalization vs. Overcriminalization

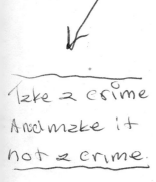

Take a crime
And make it
not a crime.

For the past few years, many experts in criminal justice, law, and the social sciences have suggested that certain offenses be removed from the criminal statutes. These include public drunkenness, vagrancy, minor traffic violations, gambling, the use of marijuana, prostitution, sexual acts between consenting adults in private, and juvenile delinquency. The elimination of such offenses from the criminal law embodies the theory of *decriminalization* while *overcriminalization* involves the misuse of the criminal sanction.[31] Advocates of the decriminalization approach suggest that the criminal law is overextended when it invokes criminal sanctions in regard to social and moral problems; they believe that the primary purpose of criminal law should be to control serious crimes affecting persons and property. As a result, it is argued that these "victimless" crimes, as they are often called, should not be the responsibility of the criminal justice system but of other social service-type agencies.

Decriminalization is seen as a sound approach to the crime problem for the following reasons: (1) it is felt that the criminal law must reflect current societal values and attitudes; (2) decriminalization would relieve the overburdened criminal justice system and free the police and courts to concentrate on more serious criminal offenses; and (3) many of the statutes controlling victimless crimes are vague and thus subject to constitutional challenge.

On the other hand, there are those who contend that these borderline crimes remain within the reach of the criminal law, and that even victimless crimes should be deterred by the threat of criminal punishment or rehabilitation. Between these two extreme positions, however, is the necessity for each state to review its criminal statutes so that they reflect the values of society and the resources of the criminal justice system.

The general reform view today appears to favor implementing the decriminalization process by legislative change. For example, a number of states have eliminated public drunkness as a crime. This movement was influenced by (1) two federal court decisions, *Easter v. District of Columbia* [32] and *Driver v. Hinnant*,[33] which declared that a chronic alcoholic could not be found guilty of the crime of public intoxication; by (2) the findings of the President's Crime Commission, which estimated that over two million arrests were being made each year for drunkenness; and by (3) the 1968 United States Supreme Court decision of *Powell v. Texas* [34] which, although it did not declare alcoholism a disease, recognized the lack within the criminal justice system of rehabilitation services for the alcoholic.

In addition to decriminalizing public intoxication, a number of states have passed legislation facilitating the noncriminal treatment of drug addicts. This was made possible after the United States Supreme Court case of *Robinson v. California* [35] in 1962 declared that an addict was actually a sick person and could not as a result be prosecuted for the crime of being a drug addict. Today, large numbers of offenders who would ordinarily be charged with crimes are treated instead of being criminally prosecuted.

Other examples of the movement toward decriminalization exist, particularly with regard to minor traffic offense, disorderly conduct, and statutes dealing with wayward and stubborn children. It is important to keep this trend in mind when viewing the purposes as well as the effectiveness of the criminal justice system. Much more research, however, is needed to determine what crimes should be decriminalized and how such actions could affect the criminal justice process and society as a whole.

## Standard Setting

Criminal justice agencies have traditionally exercised broad discretion when processing offenders charged with crimes. Such decisions as how to treat a suspect who is arrested, how to handle a parolee who wants to leave the jurisdiction, or how to deal with an inmate requesting transfer to another institution were often made without the benefit of clearly-defined agency procedures. Court decisions have provided some procedural protections, but there has also been a need to encourage administrative agencies and legislative bodies to establish guidelines in the field of criminal justice.

In recent years, such groups as the American Bar Association (ABA), the National Council on Crime and Delinquency (NCCD), and the National Advisory Commission on Criminal Justice Standards and Goals have developed detailed standards in an effort to help states improve their criminal justice systems.[36] These organizations have attempted to provide guidelines to govern the processing of both criminal and delinquent offenders from the time of the initial complaint through their eventual release from the system. For example, the *Standards on Criminal Justice* of the American Bar Association consist of seventeen separate guidelines and cover each stage of the adult criminal process, beginning with the police function and concluding with post-conviction proceedings. All were prepared by leading lawyers, judges, and academicians in the field of criminal justice administration. The ABA *Standards,* as well as those of the National Advisory Commission and the NCCD, were designed to reform the criminal justice system by prompting effective law enforcement and to safeguard the constitutional rights of those accused of crimes. In addition, the American Bar Association, in conjunction with the Institute of Judicial Administration, has compiled a comprehensive set of standards for juvenile justice.[37]

Serious efforts to implement such standards have been made during the past few years. Although no jurisdiction is required to adopt any of these standards, they do serve as reference points for states that wish to completely remodel or even modify their current criminal justice practices and procedures. Today, most states and the federal government as well are active in implementing many of the various standards proposed by these different organizations. The decision whether to implement a particular standard involves a consideration of such factors as (1) the administrative and judicial organization of the state; (2) the availability of resources such as financial assistance and personnel; and (3) the political climate as well as geographic structure of a given jurisdiction. Present unworkable practices can be changed and new standards implemented by such measures as legislation, court rulings or administrative orders. For example, Florida has become the first state to implement almost all of the seventeen ABA *Standards* by formal court rulings.[38]

The ultimate goal of standard setting is the reform of the criminal justice system. Standards represent the comprehensive collection and progressive discussion of current information in the field of criminal justice. As the National Advisory Commission has stated:

The Commission hopes that its standards and recommendations will influence the shape of the criminal justice system in this nation for many years to come. And it believes that adoption of these standards will contribute to a measurable reduction of the amount of crime in America.[39]

### Financial Support for Criminal Justice Reform

Whether federal funding should be used to update America's criminal justice system has been a major issue since the mid-1960s. Prior to then, most crime control agencies operated under the traditional dual philosophy of state independence and local control; however, this left many states with fragmented and uncoordinated criminal justice systems. In addition, the major components of the system—police, courts, and corrections— were sorely understaffed, ill-equipped, and financially unable to cope with the escalating crime problem.

In 1967, the President's Commission on Law Enforcement and Criminal Justice acknowledged these problems by recommending the development of a federal assistance program to improve the nation's crime control efforts. Congress responded in 1968 by creating the Law Enforcement Assistance Administration (LEAA) within the Department of Justice, under Title I of the Omnibus Crime Control and Safe Streets Act.[40]

The LEAA is the agency which provides the majority of federal funds to states in the area of criminal justice. In order for a state to be eligible for federal assistance, it must have a State Criminal Justice Planning Agency (SPA), as required by the Safe Streets Act, for the purpose of developing an annual comprehensive criminal justice plan. Upon approval of a state's plan by the LEAA, a block grant or lump sum based on population is awarded to the state for law enforcement purposes. Program development is the responsibility of the SPA. In addition, the LEAA supports discretionary grants for special programs, educational grants, and special research efforts. In its first seven years of operation, the LEAA allocated approximately $4.2 billion in federal funds for state crime control programs.[41]

The structure of the LEAA has been altered to some extent since its adoption under the original Safe Streets Act of 1968. In 1970, the Congress amended Title I and revised the agency's administrative structure by establishing regional offices and providing special funds for corrections facilities and programs. Another amendment in 1973 revised the block grant program, expanded the role of the National Institute of Law Enforcement (the research center of the LEAA), and added security and privacy guidelines to safeguard criminal history information. The Juvenile Justice and Delinquency Act of 1974 established an office of juvenile justice within the LEAA to provide funds for the control of juvenile crime. Finally, a 1976 amendment to the Safe Streets Act extended the life of the LEAA through 1979. With these changes, however, the LEAA's purposes remain the same: (1) to reduce the incidence of crime in America, and (2) to improve the overall efficiency and effectiveness of the criminal justice process.

Whether these goals are being achieved remains unclear. Over the past eight years, the LEAA—and the entire concept of federal funding for state and local criminal justice programs—have received widespread and valid criticism. Initially, many experts argued that the level of LEAA expenditures was not sufficient to have a substantial impact on rising crime rates. Others, particularly those in the correctional field, complained that police agencies were getting the largest share of the funds. Recently, state criminal justice personnel, legislatures, and lawyers have directed their attacks at the overall operations and administrative practices of the LEAA. Many recipients of the funds, for example, object to the increasing role of the LEAA in attaching special conditions and controls to major grants. In addition, the LEAA is a federal agency and, as such, is subject to the political pressures of the White House and Congress. High staff turnover, lack of leadership, and shifting priorities have also contributed to negative public opinion about the LEAA.

On the other hand, when this federal-state-local partnership was originally formed, everyone recognized that the job of controlling crime even with financial assistance would not be easy. LEAA funds support many worthwhile criminal justice programs which otherwise would not exist. In Massachusetts the LEAA made possible the experimental closing of juvenile institutions and their replacement with community-based facilities. In addition it has created exemplary projects—such as probation counselor, public defender, and police management programs—and has financed the work of the National Commission on Criminal Justice Standards and Goals. The LEAA's real success has been in developing and financing programs to improve the effectiveness and efficiency of criminal justice agencies, rather than in achieving a significant reduction in the crime problem. As previously mentioned, Congress extended the LEAA to 1979 with yearly appropriations of over $800 million during that time. Program emphasis in these three years was on community crime prevention projects, court improvement programs, civil rights enforcement, and juvenile delinquency control.

Then, in 1980, Congress passed into law the Justice System Improvement Act, significantly changing the way the federal government provides financial aid to state and local jurisdictions to fight crime and improve the criminal justice system.[42] This act creates an Office of Justice Assistance, Research and Statistics (OJARS), the Law Enforcement Assistance Administration (LEAA), the National Institute of Justice (NIJ), and the Bureau of Justice Statistics (BJS). The act authorizes federal support for criminal justice assistance programs through 1983, with maximum authorized appro-

*OJARS — no longer provide money*

priations of up to $750 million, but funding for LEAA remains uncertain at this time under the Reagan administration.

Under the new legislation, OJARS is authorized to coordinate the activities of the above three agencies. LEAA will continue to distribute grants to the states. NIJ will support basic and applied research into criminal justice issues. BJS will provide a variety of statistical services and help state and local governments develop a data base to improve the effectiveness of the criminal justice system. The application section provides a detailed description of LEAA's accomplishments over the past decade.

## Unification of the Criminal Justice System

*Need more coordination—*

Another major issue in criminal justice has been the inability of the various crime control agencies to work together effectively. This problem exists primarily because these agencies—law enforcement, courts, and corrections—generally operate independently of one another. Their different legal, budgetary, and personnel requirements increase the sense of isolation and conflict between them; as a result, the level of cooperation and coordination needed to effectively and efficiently manage the crime control system is markedly reduced.

In an article on "the criminal justice non-system" Daniel Skoler cites the following as causing the system's fragmentation: (1) the constitutional separation of powers between the executive, legislative, and judicial branches of government; (2) the predominently local character of police and prosecutional agencies; (3) the elective nature of the attorney general's office in most jurisdictions; (4) the desire of the different components of the criminal justice system to enjoy cabinet-level status with one another; and (5) the tendency states have to group adult and juvenile services into human service rather than public service agencies.[43]

As previously noted, the three principal components of criminal justice are law enforcement, the judicial system, and corrections. The police are probably least receptive to the idea of a unified system; first, because law enforcement has traditionally been carried out by local branches of government; second, because most people are skeptical about the creation of state-level police agencies, believing that they would represent the first step toward the creation of a police state; and third, because the large size of many police departments discourages their working together as a system. A survey conducted in 1976 by the National Institute of Law Enforcement and Criminal Justice confirmed the belief that the police are generally uninterested in the possibility of unified departments.[44]

On the other hand, the judicial system has generally experienced some success in its efforts to consolidate components of the criminal justice system, particularly in unifying the trial courts into a central administrative structure. This central authority is the unified court system's most important feature in that it permits uniform court procedures and allows for relocation of judicial personnel to meet changing workloads. The National

Advisory Commission on Criminal Justice Standards and Goals advocates the creation of unified judicial systems, and many states have already made substantial progress in this area of court reform.[45]

The system of corrections is equally as fragmented as the police and judicial systems. This often impedes court processing and divides responsibility for convicted offenders among many overlapping agencies. The situation in America is in sharp contrast to correctional systems in Western Europe, where corrections generally are the responsibility of the central government.

Unification of correctional agencies, however, is a highly controversial subject. Although adult and juvenile institutional care, probation, and parole are all parts of the same process, each agency has its own vested interests. Many jurisdictions have at least partially unified these services, while an equal number have been consistently opposed to complete state control. The principle controversy concerning parole continues to be one of whether it should be administered by a department of corrections or by an independent parole board. In probation, the debate centers around whether probation services should be placed in the executive branch of government or should remain a function of the court. In corrections, the issue is generally one of whether a state corrections program should be responsible for county and municipal institutional services. These kinds of organizational problems illustrate the need to coordinate many aspects of our correctional system.

Over the past decade, some efforts have been made to bring these various agencies of criminal justice closer together. The comprehensive criminal justice planning requirements of the Safe Streets and Crime Control Act of 1968 is a good example of one such approach. Each state receiving federal funds under this legislation is required to develop annual comprehensive criminal justice plans and these plans serve as blueprints for action programs used to improve the quality of the criminal justice system. This planning approach is intended to facilitate increased coordination between the various agencies, as well as to create a more unified system.

In addition, many police, courts, and correctional agencies are studying their own functions and interrelationships from a systems perspective. This has encouraged such efforts as (1) the thrust of higher education into criminal justice academic programs; (2) the development by law enforcement agencies of shared information systems on local, state, and federal levels; the establishment of joint training activities; (3) the promulgation of criminal justice standards; and (4) the creation of metropolitan planning units to improve the overall operation of local criminal justice agencies.

Skoler has proposed the formation of a "superagency" to administer the criminal justice system.[46] Such an approach would provide more efficient services to local agencies while simultaneously encouraging efforts at regionalization and coordination. The state police, the prosecutor's office, adult corrections, and the state public defender's office would each be a part of this superagency. Along these lines, Alaska has a unified criminal justice system in which all of its crime control agencies, excepting municipal law enforcement, are under the authority of the state government.

All of the above approaches seek to improve the criminal justice system through organizational change. Although it is probably unrealistic to expect that states will build totally unified systems, even an attempt at unification could heighten efficiency in criminal justice operations by encouraging mutual planning, the sharing of resources, and increased cooperation between existing criminal justice institutions.

## MODELS IN CRIMINAL JUSTICE

Finally, there are certain theories and concepts of justice that characterize the criminal justice system, and these are discussed below.

In recent years, such groups as the President's Crime Commission, the American Bar Association, and the National Advisory Commission on Criminal Justice Standards and Goals have proposed numerous and detailed recommendations for improving the administration of criminal justice in America.*[47]

Underlying the many changes initiated within the last decade are the concepts and principles upon which criminal justice administration is based. These models, or "schools of thought," are often the foundation for programs of crime control, and for progress or lack of it in the criminal justice system. Such models may be thought of as existing on three conceptual levels: (1) those which refer to criminal justice as a system; (2) those which refer to criminal justice as a process; and (3) those which are concerned with theories of organization.[48] The models discussed here are not the only ones in existence, nor does any one represent the ideal model. They are all merely distillations of current thinking about the conceptual framework of criminal justice.

Increased knowledge of present-day models of criminal justice administration is essential to the development of more sensible and effective crime control programs because such models significantly influence the operations of the criminal justice system. In addition, they provide a theoretical basis for knowledge and growth.

### Systems Models

It is currently popular to view the administration of criminal justice as a system of crime control organizations. Three components—police, courts and corrections—comprise this system. This model describes the administration of criminal justice as an interrelated system of agencies, beginning with arrest and concluding with the eventual release of the offender. According to this model, changes in any one part of the system affect the

---

*Some of the material contained in this section originally appeared in, Joseph J. Senna, "Models in Criminal Justice: Building Blocks for Change," *Judicature* 59, no. 1 (June/July 1975): 34–40.

other parts. Increasing the capability of the police to arrest possible offenders adds to the burden of the courts; changing sentencing procedures
affects prison population; and revising the criminal code increases or
decreases the overall number of offenders coming into contact with the
system. Proponents of this model emphasize systems planning, mutual
goal-setting, the sharing of resources, and increased coordination and cooperation between existing criminal justice institutions.

Recognizing these agencies as a system is one thing; realizing it in fact
is another. The President's Crime Commission, the American Bar Association Survey, and the National Advisory Commission on Criminal Justice
Standards and Goals agree that the system remains basically a loose fed-
eration of agencies having some mutual concerns, but in many cases operating independently of one another.[49] Thus far, efforts to bring criminal
justice organizations together have been hampered by the multiplicity of
their goals, as well as by problems of agency isolation, conflict, and independence.

While various components of a private enterprise system share common objectives—production, sales, and profit—the objectives of the criminal justice agencies often differ. Where the police may take a hard-line
approach to crime prevention, the probation department may suggest therapeutic methods of crime control. While private enterprise systems seek
to achieve operating efficiency, the criminal justice system establishes policies based on constitutional guarantees and individuals' rights to due
process which can restrict efficiency. These difficulties limit close coordination and cooperation between agencies, resulting in what may be more
aptly described as a "non-system" of criminal justice.

Nonetheless, the police, judiciary, and correctional agencies do work
together and, as a system, influence criminal justice programs. The systems
model has demonstrated the need for overall penal reform and a reeval-
uation of what kinds of actions constitute criminal behavior. Also, the
police, courts, and correctional agencies are studying their own functions
and interrelationships from a systems perspective, which tends to improve
their overall effectiveness. Furthermore, this model has given impetus to
the recent thrust of higher education into criminal justice academic programs. In addition, the systems model has brought about greater cooperation between various criminal justice agencies. Programs involving
shared information systems, joint training efforts, and technical assistance
are examples of this trend. Yet, even the combination of these many
achievements, at least for the moment, does not embody the theoretical
model which requires that all components of the system work as a coordinated unit toward the general goal of protecting society and insuring
justice.[50]

Richard Danzig suggests that the systems perspective is applicable to
a decentralized system of criminal justice.[51] Danzig proposes the development of neighborhood criminal justice cabinets which would operate
concurrently with municipal and state systems. This idea seeks to achieve
greater efficiency in criminal justice operations on a local level. Essentially,
this approach has led to the establishment of metropolitan planning units

through which local communities can improve their criminal justice operations without being hampered by the need to plan for the entire state. However, even here, the systems model—relating independent organizations to each other—remains the central issue.

### Process Models

Other observers, among them many criminal lawyers and judges, do not perceive criminal justice as a system, but rather as a process or series of decision-making points. The emphasis of the process model is on the offender and the various sequential stages through which he or she passes, beginning with arrest and ending with reentry into society.

A number of ideological approaches rely heavily upon the process concept. In 1964, Herbert Packer described two models which illustrate the problems of ideology in criminal justice and criminal procedure: the "crime control" model and the "due process" model.[52]

The crime control model is based on the theory that the repression of criminal conduct is by far the most important function to be performed by the criminal process. Criminal conduct must be kept under tight control to preserve public order, and the process must maintain a high rate of apprehension and conviction and place a premium on speed and finality. Such an approach naturally leads to emphasis on effective law enforcement and formal control by law. It has the effect of maintaining broad definitions of criminal and juvenile law, expanding lawful arrest provisions, attempting to amend the exclusionary rule, and increasing the use of detention and incarceration facilities. Programs of preventive detention, statutes lengthening sentencing provisions and the acquisition of more efficient police equipment are examples of the effect of the crime control model.

On the other hand, Packer's due process model is based upon the concept of the primacy of the individual and the complementary concept of limitation of official power. This model builds protections for the accused at every step of the criminal process. The main characteristics of such a model are: the concept of legal guilt and the presumption of innocence; the conception of the criminal process as an appropriate forum for the correction of its own abuses; and the insistence upon the state's duty to ensure that an accused is not deprived by poverty of the capacity to effectively invoke the protections which the process must afford.

The due process model has affected the trial stage of the criminal process by demanding defense counsel, jury trials, and other procedural safeguards. Furthermore, this model tends to restrict the legal definition of criminal behavior by removing offenses, such as victimless crimes, juvenile delinquency, traffic offenses, and certain drug violations from the criminal statutes. It has resulted in the elimination of a variety of vague laws, such as overly broad juvenile delinquency, abortion, vagrancy, and disorderly conduct statutes. Beyond this, the due process model has resulted in the establishment of a variety of procedures to cover the ways in which criminal justice agencies operate, particularly with regard to their discretionary power.

Both process models influence the values, structure, and practices of the criminal justice system. And although the models may seem to polarize the system, they actually help to achieve a meaningful balance between community protection and individual rights.

Other authors have also commented on theoretical models of the criminal process. John Griffiths suggests that Packer's two models are not really opposites, but rather represent a union known as the "battle" model.[53] Griffiths' conception of the nature of the criminal process begins with an assumption of mutually supportive interests. In Griffiths' "family" model, the interests of society and the offender need not be incompatible. Offenders are not a special group of people with a unique relationship to the state, but simply persons who have failed to exercise self-control. Under this model, the state consistently acts in the best interests of the offender. The juvenile and family court system is a reasonably close approximation of Griffiths' family model in operation. Here, theoretically, the best interests of the juvenile are paramount, while such matters as the trial and the roles of the participants are based on the mutual concerns of all the parties. In reality, this model doesn't apply to the criminal process, nor does it exist in the juvenile court because of recent procedural protections given to juveniles by such cases as *Kent v. United States* (1966), *In re Gault* (1967), and *In re Winship* (1970). Basic changes in society's attitudes about criminal behavior are necessary before the criminal process will be affected by the family model.

Walter Miller describes the criminal process as falling basically into two divergent ideological patterns: "right" and "left."[54] He believes that criminal justice agencies and their personnel adhere to one approach or the other. Miller seems to indicate that the majority of working police professionals subscribe to the ideological premise which he designates as "rightist," while those in the courts as well as treatment workers tend to fall into a "leftist" category. Miller's analytic approach seems to parallel Packer's crime control and due process models, and results in similar program recommendations.

Frank J. Remington identifies five basic perspectives from which to examine the criminal justice process; evidence sufficiency; consent; fairness and propriety of procedures; effectiveness and efficiency of criminal justice practices; and discretion.[55] These perspectives are used not so much as models but as a pragmatic framework for analysis of the principle steps of the process. This approach has the major advantage of studying issues that cut across the entire criminal justice system.

According to A. Goldstein, due process represents "inquisitorial" themes of criminal procedure with both "adversary" and "accusatorial" models.[56] The main characteristics of the inquisitorial model are: an affirmative obligation by the state to carry out policies of criminal procedure; an emphasis on publication of written materials compiled through the trial process, by an investigating magistrate; a procedure wherein control is entirely under the judicial officer who, rather than being neutral, takes the initiative in the investigation; and a concern with enforcing the law by treating the accused as the primary source of evidence. This approach represents the English system of criminal procedure more than the

American. Yet it is a model of some significance because, according to Goldstein, inquisitorial themes are emerging in our criminal process. This is evident particularly in the more active role played by judges in guilty pleas, applications for warrants and grand jury proceedings. Judge John Sirica's handling of the Watergate trials is a good example of such judicial activism.

The adversary and accusatorial models represent the resolution of conflict between the state and defendant through the traditional contested trial. In the adversary model, the prosecutor and defense attorney present evidence to the court while the judge supervises the trial. The accusatorial model not only takes the adversary process into account, but also places great emphasis on the degree of evidence needed for guilt, beginning with the issuance of a complaint and continuing through to the trial and eventual disposition of the case. The arrest, search and seizure, and interrogation procedures of the police, the formal rules of evidence used in trials, and the sentencing policies of judges all reflect the adversary and accusatorial nature of the criminal process.

### Organizational Models

A third kind of model-building is represented by theories of organization and management, which are also applicable to criminal justice administration. The Organization for Social and Technical Innovation has identified three models or schools of thought on how those in criminal justice perceive the nature of crime and delinquency. These are: the "regulatory" model, which is legalistic and based on the process of the arrest, trial, and sentencing of the offender; the "patient" model, which rests on the work of treatment specialists who view the offender in terms of personal pathology; and the "community disintegration" model, where criminal justice is viewed within the context of the social community.[57]

The regulatory model is intended to provide community protection by imposing greater physical restraints on offenders such as higher bail, tough plea negotiation, lengthy sentencing, and limited parole. The patient model sees the offender as a client in need of services and follows incarceration with programs of classification and treatment as well as educational and vocational training. The community disintegration model, on the other hand, tries to help the offender adjust or reintegrate within the community. This model suggests programs of community crime prevention and control, alternatives to incarceration, and greater use of community resources in rehabilitating offenders.

Another organizational approach, oriented towards corrections and developed by D. Duffee and V. O'Leary, uses models of "correctional policies."[58] Four models are identified: "reform," "rehabilitation," "restraint," and "reintegration." The reform model is concerned with community protection through effective programs such as education and training for inmates; the rehabilitation model represents efforts to change the personality of the offender; the restraint model deals with steps to contain the offender; and the reintegration model stresses the use of community resources.

Another approach, the "management" model of criminal justice, emphasizes roles, functions, skills, programming, budget control, and other managerial considerations.[59] This model argues for a clear definition of managerial roles in criminal justice. Great significance is placed on achieving effectiveness and efficiency, with decisions based on obtaining necessary information, proper planning, budget control, and program review. This model demonstrates the importance of studying the internal operations of criminal justice agencies, and has led to the reorganization of many such agencies by administrative action as well as reform legislation and to the professionalization of their personnel. The difficulty with most management models is that they deal with one component of the system at a time and lose the opportunity to study and influence the entire criminal process.

However, Donald Newman has recently suggested a model entitled "functional analysis," which would provide a method for reviewing the entire structure of the criminal justice system.[60] "Functional analysis" emphasizes the decision-making and flow of the criminal process. It considers the critical functions of police, courts, and correctional personnel not singly but in unison. According to Newman, the flow of persons both through the system and away from it measures its parameters and provides the most comprehensive way of dealing with the system in a total context. Although Newman's approach seems to represent an organizational model because of its emphasis on functional analysis and decision making, it can also be viewed as a systems model.

## Implications

Implicit in model building is the realization that changes in the criminal justice system are based on such models. They can serve as valuable techniques of scientific inquiry upon which to test new ideas. It is necessary for all those involved with change to recognize the existence of the various models and to understand how they affect actual practice. All professionals working in criminal justice are generally limited by their own expertise. Thus, models are often related to the values and knowledge of a particular group only. This makes it all the more urgent to publicize models of criminal justice so that all those working in the field can evaluate the entire conceptual system.

Model building directly affects the goals of criminal justice administration. The different models embody philosophies that are inherent and often controversial parts of the system. The systems model, for instance, seeks to accomplish a variety of criminal justice objectives. These objectives include crime prevention, deterrence, rehabilitation, reintegration, and even punishment. As a result, systems analysis can deal with conflicting and controversial agency practices. Interagency training programs between police officers and social workers, or correctional officers and treatment specialists, are often instances where conflict can be viewed.

The process model generally reflects concern over both deterrence and restraint while emphasizing the concept of fairness and strict procedural safeguards for the criminal offender. Organizational models tend to avoid the moral dilemma posed by the imposition of criminal sanctions by seeking goals involving efficiency and effectiveness. What is important in the consideration of any model is that the goals of each model be kept in mind as well as the overall goals of the system and individual agencies.

Finally, model building relates itself to research in criminal justice administration. The basic question is one of whether the models can be tested in the "real world." For instance, Remington's perspectives provide a good basis for analyzing the system. The question here is one of how criminal justice measures up to such a model. The process model allows the researcher to examine the movement of offenders through the system; organizational models help to identify the best ways to manage the system. The results of the implementation of various models may support new ways to improve the system.

The work of model building is just beginning. The core problems—such as implementing criminal justice standards, dealing with the meaning of the different ideologies, and testing the success or failure of the different models—still remain. A need exists to recognize and build upon present thought and expand into new areas or perception. The utility of models for criminal justice is found in their ability to help all those both within and outside the system to study its total structure—both ideological and operational—from different perspectives. Failure to see the importance of such models is to continue to look at criminal justice administration from one perspective only.

SUMMARY

The term "criminal justice" became prominent around 1967 when the President's Commission on Law Enforcement and Administration of Justice began a nationwide study of America's crime problem. Since then, a field of study has emerged which uses knowledge from various disciplines in an attempt to understand what causes people to commit crimes and how to deal with the crime problem. Criminal justice, then, consists of the study of crime and of the agencies concerned with its prevention and control.

Criminal justice is both a system and a process. As a system it ideally functions as a cooperative effort among the primary agencies—police, courts, and corrections; at least, this is how we would like it to function. The process, on the other hand, consists of the actual steps the offender takes from the initial investigation through trial, sentencing, and appeal.

How criminal justice deals with the offender is determined by the multiple goals of the system and its individual agencies. Criminal justice as a system is so complex that the frequently stated goals of prevention, deterrence, or fairness may be unrelated to its operational aspects. Its laws and policies, however, are directly influenced by such issues as due process, federal funding, and agency isolation.

**1.** What is the criminal justice "system?" How does it differ from the criminal justice "process?"

**2.** Considering the criminal justice system as a method of social control, what goals should the system seek to achieve? Have we been successful in reaching any particular goals? Why or why not, and if so, how?

**3.** Discuss some of the major issues confronting the field of criminal justice today. Which of these issues do you believe will have a significant impact on crime control?

**1.** President's Commission of Law Enforcement and Administration of Justice, *The Challenge of Crime in a Free Society* (Washington, D.C.: U.S. Government Printing Office, 1967).

**2.** See American Bar Association, *Project on Standards for Criminal Justice* (New York: Institute of Judicial Administration, 1968–1973); National Advisory Commission on Criminal Justice Standards and Goals, *A National Strategy to Reduce Crime* (Washington, D.C.: U.S. Government Printing Office, 1973).

**3.** See Public Law 90–351, Title I—Omnibus Crime Control and Safe Streets Act of 1968, 90th Congress, June 19, 1968.

**4.** *Time*, June 30, 1975, p. 10.

**5.** See Black's Law Dictionary, Revised Fourth Edition (St. Paul, Minn.: West Publishing Co., 1967).

**6.** Ibid., p. 1002.

**7.** See generally Michael J. Hindelang, et al., U.S. Department of Justice, Law Enforcement Assistance Administration, National Criminal Justice Information and Statistics Service, *Sourcebook of Criminal Justice Statistics* (Washington, D.C.: U.S. Government Printing Office, 1978).

**8.** Ibid.

**9.** Ibid., pp. 477–478.

**10.** Ibid., p. 522.

**11.** Ibid., p. 594.

**12.** National Advisory Commission on Criminal Justice Standards and Goals, *A National Strategy to Reduce Crime*, p. 41.

**13.** American Bar Association, *Standards Relating to Urban Police Function*, (New York: Institute of Judicial Administration, 1973), Standard 2.2, p. 9.

**14.** From an address by Chief Justice Warren T. Burger, U.S. Supreme Court, as reported in *Criminal Law Reporter* (1972), p. 3059.

**15.** For an excellent text on the general issue of discretion, see Kenneth C. Davis, *Discretionary Justice: A Preliminary Inquiry* (Baton Rouge: Louisiana State University Press, 1969); also, Kenneth C. Davis, *Police Discretion* (St. Paul, Minn.: West Publishing Co., 1975).

**16.** President's Crime Commission, *The Challenge of Crime in a Free Society*, p. 125.

**17.** Powell v. Alabama 287 U.S. 45, 53 S.Ct. 55, 77 L.Ed. 158 (1932); Gideon v. Wainwright, 372 U.S. 335, 83 S.Ct. 792,

9 L.Ed. 2nd 799 (1963); Argersinger v. Hamlin, 407 U.S. 25, 92 S.Ct. 2006, 32 L.Ed. 2nd 530 (1972).

18. President's Commission on Law Enforcement and Administration of Justice, *The Challenge of Crime in a Free Society*, p. 159.

19. See J. F. Lanagan, "Imminent Crisis in Prison Populations," *American Journal of Corrections* 20 (1975); also Norman Carlson, "Corrections in the United States Today," *The American Criminal Law Review* 13: 615 (1976).

20. "The Legal Origins of Probation," Probation and Related Measures (New York: Department of Social Affairs, United Nations, E/CN/.5/230, 1951).

21. See Charles L. Chute and Marjorie Bell, *Crime, Courts and Probation* (New York: Macmillan, 1956).

22. Edwin Powers, *The Basic Structure of the Administration of Criminal Justice in Massachusetts* (Boston: Massachusetts Correctional Association, 1973), Chapter 6.

23. Inmates of Suffolk County Jail v. Eisenstadt, *Prison Law Reporter 2*, no. 8 (July 1973): 389–431.

24. National Advisory Commission on Criminal Justice Standards and Goals, *Corrections* (Washington, D.C.: U.S. Government Printing Office, 1973), p. 389.

25. Maine Revised Statistics Ann., Title 17-A, S 1201.

26. Herbert L. Packer, *The Limits of the Criminal Sanction* (Stanford, Cal.: Stanford University Press, 1968), p. 159.

27. Donald J. Newman, *Introduction to Criminal Justice* (New York: J. B. Lippincott Co., 1975), p. 21.

28. Herbert Packer, *Limits of the Criminal Sanction*, pp. 35–61.

29. The National Advisory Commission on Criminal Justice Standards and Goals, *A National Strategy to Reduce Crime*, pp. 34–40.

30. Bureau of National Affairs, *The Criminal Law Revolution and Its Aftermath 1960–1971* (Washington, D.C.: Bureau of National Affairs, 1972).

31. See Norval Morris and Gordon Hawkins, *The Honest Politician's Guide to Crime Control* (Chicago: University of Chicago Press, 1970).

32. 361 F.2d 50 (D.C. Cir. 1966).

33. 356 F.2d 761 (4th Cir. 1966).

34. 392 U.S. 514, 88 S.Ct. 2145, 20 L.Ed. 2nd 1254 (1968).

35. 370 U.S. 660, 82 S.Ct. 1417, 8 L.Ed. 2nd 758 (1962).

36. American Bar Association, *Project on Standards for Criminal Justice*, (New York: Institute of Judicial Administration, 1968–1973); National Council on Crime and Delinquency, *Model Acts*, (Hackensack, New Jersey); National Advisory Commission on Criminal Justice Standards and Goals (Washington, D.C.: U.S. Government Printing Office, 1973).

37. Irving R. Kaufman, "Juvenile Justice System," *American Bar Association Journal* 62:730 (1975).

38. See generally, "A Symposium on the American Bar Association Standards," *The American Criminal Law Review* 12:493 (1975).

39. National Advisory Commission on Criminal Justice Standards and Goals, *A National Strategy to Reduce Crime*, Foreward.

40. Public Law 90–351, 90th Congress, June 19, 1968..

41. United States Department of Justice, Law Enforcement Assistance Administration, *A Partnership for Crime Control* (Washington, D.C.: U.S. Government Printing Office, 1976).

42. U.S. Department of Justice, Justice

Assistance News, Vol. 1, February 1980, p. 1.; also P.L. 96–157, Dec. 1979.

**43.** Daniel Skoler, "Antidote for the Non System, State Criminal Justice Superagencies," *State Government* 46:2 (Winter 1976).

**44.** United States Department of Justice, Law Enforcement Assistance Administration, National Institute of Law Enforcement, *Recent Criminal Justice Unification, Consolidation and Coordination Efforts: An Exploratory National Survey* (Washington, D.C.: U.S. Government Printing Office, 1976).

**45.** National Advisory Commission on Criminal Justice Standards and Goals, *Report on Courts,* Standard 8.1, p. 164.

**46.** Skoler, "Antidote for the Non System, State Criminal Justice Superagencies," p. 2.

**47.** See *The Challenge of Crime in a Free Society,* A Report by the President's Crime Commission on Law Enforcement and Administration of Justice, U.S. Government Printing Office, 1967; *American Bar Association Standards on Criminal Justice,* 18 Volumes, and particularly Vol. 18, *A National Strategy to Reduce Crime,* A Report by the National Advisory Commission on Criminal Justice Standards and Goals and Related Reports, U.S. Government Printing Office, 1973.

**48.** For a good recent review regarding different models of criminal justice, see L. Wollan, Jr., "Models of Criminal Justice" *Law in American Society* 3:26 (November 1974).

**49.** See President's Crime Commission, supra n. 1 at 7; The National Advisory Commission, supra n. 1 at 41; and Geoffrey Hazard, Jr., "Epilogue to the Criminal Justice Survey," *American Bar Association Journal* 55:1048 (November 1969). The entire American Bar Foundation Survey on the Administration of Criminal Justice consists of the following five-volume series of books: La Fave, *Arrest: The Decision to Take a Suspect into Custody* (1965); Newman, *Conviction: The Determination of Guilt or Innocence Without Trial* (1966); Tiffany, McIntyre, and Rottenberg, *Detection of Crime: Stopping and Questioning, Search and Seizure, Encouragement and Entrapment* (1967); and Dawson, *Sentencing: The Decision as to Type, Length and Conditions of Sentence* (1969). All were published by Little, Brown and Co., Boston, MA.

**50.** Donald M. McIntyre, Herman Goldstein, and Daniel L. Skoler, *Criminal Justice in the United States,* American Bar Foundation, 1974 at 50.

**51.** See Richard Danzig, "Toward the Creation of a Complementary, Decentralized System of Criminal Justice," *Stanford Law Review* 26:1–54 (November 1973).

**52.** See Herbert Packer, "Two Models of the Criminal Process," *University of Pennsylvania Law Review* 113:1–68 (November 1964); this essay appears in Part II of his book, *The Limits of the Criminal Sanction* (Stanford, Cal.: Stanford University Press, 1968).

**53.** See John Griffiths, "Ideology in Criminal Procedure or a Third Model of the Criminal Process," *Yale Law Journal* 79:359–417 (January 1970).

**54.** See Walter Miller, "Ideology and Criminal Justice Policy: Some Current Issues," *Journal of Criminal Law and Criminology* 64:142–162 (June 1973).

**55.** See Frank J. Remington et al., *Criminal Justice Administration,* Bobbs-Merrill, 1969, Chapter 1, pp. 30–44.

**56.** A. Goldstein, "Reflections on Two Models: Inquisitional Themes in American Criminal Procedure," *Stanford L. Review* 26:1009–1025 (May 1974).

**57.** The Organization for Social and Technical Innovation (OSTI), Implementation Report Submitted to President's Commission on Law Enforcement and Administration of Justice, 1967, at 8.

58. See D. Duffee and V. O'Leary, "Models of Correction: An Entry in the Packer—Griffiths Debate," *Criminal Law Bulletin* 7:329–351 (May 1971).

59. For an excellent recent text on management approaches to the criminal justice system, see A. Caffey, *Administration of Criminal Justice—A Management Systems Approach*, Prentice-Hall, 1974.

60. Donald J. Newman, *Introduction to Criminal Justice*, J. B. Lippincott Co., Philadelphia, PA. 1975 at 6.

# LEAA: More Than A Decade of Criminal Justice Assistance

" . . . To prevent crime and to insure the greater safety of the people, law enforcement efforts must be better coordinated, intensified, and made more effective."—Omnibus Crime Control and Safe Streets Act of 1968.

With these words, Congress launched an unprecedented partnership among federal, state, and local governments to control crime and improve the American criminal justice system. The Omnibus Crime Control and Safe Streets Act created the Law Enforcement Assistance Administration to carry out this mandate.

During the past 11 years, LEAA financial and technical assistance has helped states, counties, and cities set in motion far-reaching reforms and modernization of their criminal justice systems. Under LEAA sponsorship and encouragement, thousands of anti-crime programs tailored to meet local needs and problems have been carried out.

With the birth of OJARS, the federal commitment to improving the criminal justice system continues and a new LEAA takes up the fight.

But, before we start this new decade of commitment, let us reflect on the decade plus one year of LEAA.

**1968–1969**
—LEAA, the first comprehensive crime control program enacted by Congress, formally began operations on October 21, 1968. Acting Administrator Patrick V. Murphy took office the same day.
—By the end of 1969, plans for criminal justice reforms had been submitted by 50 states, Washington, D.C., Puerto Rico, the Virgin Islands, and Guam. All states had established state planning agencies.

**1970**
—Congress amended LEAA's enabling legislation, expanding corrections improvement programs and approving the financing of construction projects.
—The National Institute of Law Enforcement and Criminal Justice established a Pilot Cities Program to test the impact of across-the-board criminal justice improvements.

From: Justice Assistance News, U.S. Department of Justice. February 1980, Vol. 1.

—Project SEARCH (System for Electronic Analysis and Retrieval of Criminal Histories) began. It was a 10-state project for sharing computerized criminal justice records between jurisdictions.
—LEAA established seven regional offices around the country to "provide expert assistance closer to state planning agencies."

**1971**
—LEAA issued regulations forbidding discrimination in employment by state and local governmental agencies receiving crime control funds.
—First census of the nation's jails was released. It contained data on jail population, overcrowding, facilities, and operating costs.
—Number of regional offices increased to 10 by LEAA Administrator Jerris Leonard.
—National Advisory Commission on Criminal Justice Standards and Goals established to set priorities for improvement in the nation's criminal justice system.
—National Center for State Courts, National Crime Prevention Institute, the Law Enforcement Standards Laboratory, and the National Clearinghouse for Criminal Justice Planning and Architecture were created with LEAA seed money.

**1972**
—National crime victimization surveys began.
—High Impact Anti-Crime Program, designed to reduce street crime and burglary in eight major cities, was announced by Vice-President Spiro Agnew. LEAA spent $160 million over two years to support the project.
—"Brandy," a bomb-sniffing German shepherd trained under an LEAA grant, sniffed out a plastic bomb at New York City's Kennedy Airport just minutes before it was set to explode.

—LEAA launched $12 million Comprehensive Data Systems Program to develop comprehensive criminal justice statistics programs in all 50 states.

**1973**
—The National Advisory Commission on Criminal Justice Standards Goals issued its far-ranging report containing hundreds of recommendations for states and localities to reduce crime.
—LEAA's Private Security Advisory Council began developing recommendations for a model code—covering licensing, personnel training, and firearms control—for the nation's private security industry.
—The National Sheriffs' Association and LEAA launched the National Neighborhood Watch Program with the slogan, "Never Give A Burglar An Even Break!"
—The National Institute established an Exemplary Projects Program to focus national attention on outstanding criminal justice efforts. The first award was to an innovative court services program in Polk County, Iowa.
—Testing of a computerized 911 emergency telephone dialing system began.

**1974**
—The Juvenile Justice and Delinquency Prevention Act placed all federal juvenile justice programs under LEAA.
—President Gerald R. Ford announced $3 million LEAA program to speed prosecution of career criminals.
—LEAA developed new programs for involving citizens in the criminal justice system and for making the system more responsive to citizen needs.
—An LEAA study of jury operations found that the size of criminal court pools could be reduced by 20 to 25 percent yet still provide adequate number of jurors for trials.

**1975**
—LEAA earmarked $8.5 million to support programs to keep juvenile status offenders—truants, runaways, and incorrigibles—out of detention and correctional facilities.
—Police in 15 cities donned LEAA-funded bullet resistant vests to test the vest's effectiveness under actual working conditions.
—Portland, Oregon, was selected as the first site to test the effectiveness of LEAA's Crime Prevention Through Environmental Design Program. The program featured innovative architectural design concepts in a high-crime commercial area.
—A study of Operation Identification—a system in which householders engrave property with an identifying number and register the number with police—reported use of the system significantly reduced burglary rates.

**1976**
—Crime Control Act established within LEAA an Office of Community Anti-Crime to support grassroots crime prevention projects.
—First "Sting" anti-fencing operations took place in Washington, D.C. LEAA "buy" money underwrote the two operations which recovered more than $3.5 million in stolen goods.
—Kentucky became the first state to adopt a model procurement code developed by the American Bar Association under an LEAA grant.
—A forensic scientist working under an LEAA grant developed a method to determine the sex of a person from a dried bloodstain.
—A 15-member National Minority Advisory Council on Criminal Justice was created to advise LEAA on ways to resolve problems of minorities and women in dealing with the criminal justice system.

**1977**
—LEAA earmarked $1 million for programs dealing with family violence, including the problems of battered women and child abuse.
—A $2 million program to implement and evaluate restitution as a viable means of rehabilitation began in seven states.
—LEAA's 10 regional offices closed.
—The American Medical Association and LEAA started implementing standards for inmate health care in the nation's prisons.
—One Day/One Trial jury experiment began in Wayne County, Michigan, with LEAA financing.
—Office of Juvenile Justice and Delinquency Prevention announced a $2.8 million program to combat school crime.

**1978**
—President Jimmy Carter unveiled a legislative package for submission to Congress that would create a Justice System Improvement Act to restructure the LEAA program.
—Neighborhood Justice Centers for citizen dispute resolution opened in three cities.
—Community corrections agencies in four cities received the first nationally-recognized professional accreditations ever awarded American correctional programs. The accreditation standards were developed by the American Correctional Association and LEAA.
—Juvenile Justice programs focused on the International Year of the Child.
—LEAA-funded study showed police patrolwomen perform just as effectively as patrolmen.

**1979**
—President Carter signed the Justice System Improvement Act which created an Office of Justice Assistance, Research, and Statistics to coordinate the efforts of a new LEAA, a National Institute of Justice, and a Bureau of Justice Statistics. Henry S. Dogin and Homer F. Broome, Jr., named acting heads of the new agencies.

—Vice President Walter Mondale announced a national strategy to combat arson. LEAA grants totaling $9 million were awarded to support the effort.
—LEAA sponsored development of accreditation standards for law enforcement officers.
—LEAA begins developing national model to prevent government fraud and abuse.

# We the People

of the United States, in Order to form a more perfect Union, establish Justice, insure domestic Tranquility, provide for the common defence, promote the general Welfare, and secure the Blessings of Liberty to ourselves and our Posterity, do ordain and establish this Constitution for the United States of America.

## Article. I.

Section. 1. All legislative Powers herein granted shall be vested in a Congress of the United States, which shall consist of a Senate and House of Representatives.

Section. 2. The House of Representatives shall be composed of Members chosen every second Year by the People of the several States, and the Electors in each State shall have the Qualifications requisite for Electors of the most numerous Branch of the State Legislature.

No Person shall be a Representative who shall not have attained to the Age of twenty five Years, and been seven Years a Citizen of the United States, and who shall not, when elected, be an Inhabitant of that State in which he shall be chosen.

Representatives and direct Taxes shall be apportioned among the several States which may be included within this Union, according to their respective Numbers, which shall be determined by adding to the whole Number of free Persons, including those bound to Service for a Term of Years, and excluding Indians not taxed, three fifths of all other Persons. The actual Enumeration shall be made within three Years after the first Meeting of the Congress of the United States, and within every subsequent Term of ten Years, in such Manner as they shall by Law direct. The Number of Representatives shall not exceed one for every thirty Thousand, but each State shall have at Least one Representative; and until such enumeration shall be made, the State of New Hampshire shall be entitled to chuse three, Massachusetts eight, Rhode Island and Providence Plantations one, Connecticut five, New York six, New Jersey four, Pennsylvania eight, Delaware one, Maryland six, Virginia ten, North Carolina five, South Carolina five, and Georgia three.

When vacancies happen in the Representation from any State, the Executive Authority thereof shall issue Writs of Election to fill such Vacancies.

The House of Representatives shall chuse their Speaker and other Officers; and shall have the sole Power of Impeachment.

Section. 3. The Senate of the United States shall be composed of two Senators from each State, chosen by the Legislature thereof, for six Years; and each Senator shall have one Vote.

Immediately after they shall be assembled in Consequence of the first Election, they shall be divided as equally as may be into three Classes. The Seats of the Senators of the first Class shall be vacated at the Expiration of the second Year, of the second Class at the Expiration of the fourth Year, and of the third Class at the Expiration of the sixth Year, so that one third may be chosen every second Year; and if Vacancies happen by Resignation, or otherwise, during the Recess of the Legislature of any State, the Executive thereof may make temporary Appointments until the next Meeting of the Legislature, which shall then fill such Vacancies.

No Person shall be a Senator who shall not have attained to the Age of thirty Years, and been nine Years a Citizen of the United States, and who shall not, when elected, be an Inhabitant of that State for which he shall be chosen.

The Vice President of the United States shall be President of the Senate, but shall have no Vote, unless they be equally divided.

The Senate shall chuse their other Officers, and also a President pro tempore, in the Absence of the Vice President, or when he shall exercise the Office of President of the United States.

The Senate shall have the sole Power to try all Impeachments. When sitting for that Purpose, they shall be on Oath or Affirmation. When the President of the United States is tried, the Chief Justice shall preside: And no Person shall be convicted without the Concurrence of two thirds of the Members present.

Judgment in Cases of Impeachment shall not extend further than to removal from Office, and disqualification to hold and enjoy any Office of honor, Trust or Profit under the United States: but the Party convicted shall nevertheless be liable and subject to Indictment, Trial, Judgment and Punishment, according to Law.

Section. 4. The Times, Places and Manner of holding Elections for Senators and Representatives, shall be prescribed in each State by the Legislature thereof; but the Congress may at any time by Law make or alter such Regulations, except as to the Places of chusing Senators.

The Congress shall assemble at least once in every Year, and such Meeting shall be on the first Monday in December, unless they shall by Law appoint a different Day.

Section. 5. Each House shall be the Judge of the Elections, Returns and Qualifications of its own Members, and a Majority of each shall constitute a Quorum to do Business; but a smaller Number may adjourn from day to day, and may be authorized to compel the Attendance of absent Members, in such Manner, and under such Penalties as each House may provide.

Each House may determine the Rules of its Proceedings, punish its Members for disorderly Behaviour, and, with the Concurrence of two thirds, expel a Member.

Each House shall keep a Journal of its Proceedings, and from time to time publish the same, excepting such Parts as may in their Judgment require Secrecy; and the Yeas and Nays of the Members of either House on any question shall, at the Desire of one fifth of those Present, be entered on the Journal.

Neither House, during the Session of Congress, shall, without the Consent of the other, adjourn for more than three days, nor to any other Place than that in which the two Houses shall be sitting.

Section. 6. The Senators and Representatives shall receive a Compensation for their Services, to be ascertained by Law, and paid out of the Treasury of the United States. They shall in all Cases, except Treason, Felony and Breach of the Peace, be privileged from Arrest during their Attendance at the Session of their respective Houses, and in going to and returning from the same; and for any Speech or Debate in either House, they shall not be questioned in any other Place.

No Senator or Representative shall, during the Time for which he was elected, be appointed to any civil Office under the Authority of the United States, which shall have been created, or the Emoluments whereof shall have been encreased during such time; and no Person holding any Office under the United States, shall be a Member of either House during his Continuance in Office.

Section. 7. All Bills for raising Revenue shall originate in the House of Representatives; but the Senate may propose or concur with Amendments as on other Bills.

Every Bill which shall have passed the House of Representatives and the Senate, shall, before it become a Law, be presented to the President of the

# The Constitutional Rights of the Accused

THE UNITED
STATES
CONSTITUTION
AND THE BILL
OF RIGHTS

The United States Constitution plays a critical role in the criminal justice system. In recent years, the Supreme Court's interpretation of the Constitution has served as the basis for the development of the legal rights of the accused. In this chapter, the origins of the Constitution and its applicability to the criminal process will be reviewed.

The Articles of Confederation, adopted by the Continental Congress in 1781, was the forerunner of our present federal Constitution. The Articles, however, were found to be generally inadequate as the foundation for effective government because they did not create a proper balance of power between the states and the central government. As a result, the Continental Congress in 1787 adopted a resolution calling for a convention of delegates from the original states to be held in Philadelphia for the express purpose of revising the Articles of Confederation. The work of that convention culminated in the development of our Constitution, its ratification by the states in 1788, and its acceptance in 1789.

In its original form, the Constitution consisted of a preamble and seven articles. The basic structure of the Constitution divided the powers of government into three independent but equal parts: the executive, the legislative, and the judicial branches. The purpose of the separation of powers was to ensure that no single branch of the government could usurp power for itself and institute a dictatorship. The measures and procedures initiated by the Founding Fathers have developed over time into the present form of government with which we are familiar.

How does the Constitution, with its formal set of rights and privileges, affect the operations of the criminal justice system? One way in which it does is to guarantee that no one branch of government can in and of itself determine the fate of those accused of crimes. This is shown by the workings of the criminal justice process itself. A police officer, who represents the executive branch of government, makes an arrest on the basis of laws passed by the legislative branch, and the accused is subsequently tried by the judiciary. In this way, offenders are protected from the arbitrary abuse of power by any single element of the law.

In addition to providing protection by ensuring a separation of powers within the government, the Constitution also controls the operations of the criminal justice system by guaranteeing individual freedoms in the ten amendments added to it in 1791, which are collectively known as the Bill of Rights.

The Bill of Rights was added to the Constitution to prevent any future government from usurping the personal freedoms of citizens. The original form of the Constitution was somewhat lax in specifying individual rights, and the Founding Fathers, aware of the past abuses perpetrated by the British government, wanted to ensure that the rights of citizens of the United States would be safe in the future. The Bill of Rights was adopted only to protect individual liberties from being abused by the national government, however, and did *not* apply to the actions of state or local officials. This oversight resulted in abuses which have been rectified only with great difficulty, and remain even today the subject of court action.

Because certain amendments in the Bill of Rights—namely the First, Fourth, Fifth, Sixth, and Eighth—are especially important to the criminal justice process, they are discussed below.

### The First Amendment

"Congress shall make no law respecting an establishment of religion, or prohibiting the free exercise thereof; or abridging the freedom of speech, or of the press; or the right of the people peaceably to assemble, and to petition the Government for a redress of grievances."

Events over the years have caused much attention to be focused on the First Amendment. The United States Supreme Court has consistently litigated (heard and decided) cases dealing with the separation of church and state regarding such matters as financial aid to private schools, the introduction of prayers in school systems, and student liberties. The right of free speech, the freedom of the press, and the right to assemble are generally thought to be absolute rights, but they are often limited by state legislation in such areas as obscenity, pornography, and unlawful assembly.

Recently, one of the most controversial issues involving the First Amendment has been the apparent conflict between the constitutional guarantees of fair trial and freedom of the press. With wide pretrial publicity given to such cases as the Chicago Seven trial, the Manson murder case, the Watergate trials, and others, whether an accused can have a fair trial as guaranteed by the Sixth Amendment has been a matter of great concern. Judges involved in newsworthy criminal cases have moved to place restraints on press coverage to preserve the defendant's right to a fair trial; at the same time, it was believed that the press had a constitutional legal right to provide news coverage. In the 1975–76 term of the United States Supreme Court, it finally handed down a long-awaited decision on the fair trial-free press issue in the case of *Nebraska Press Association v. Stuart*.[1] The Court ruled unconstitutional an order by a trial judge in a well-publicized murder case prohibiting the press from reporting the confessions of the defendant which implicated him in the crime. The Court's decision was based primarily on the fact that "prior restraints on speech and publication are the most serious and least tolerable infringement on First Amendment rights."[2]

But in 1979, U.S. Supreme Court ruled in the case of *Gannett Co. Inc. v. DePasquale* that the Constitution does not give the press an affirmative right of access to pre-trial proceedings.[3] The legal problem in this case was whether members of the public and press have an independent constitutional right to insist upon access to pre-trial judicial proceedings, even though the accused, prosecutor, and trial judge all agreed to the need to close the court to assure a fair trial. The Court decided (1) that the constitutional guarantee of a public trial is for the defendant; and (2) that there is no right in members of the public or press to insist upon a public trial.

Consequently, this case raises some question about whether the courts are moving towards curbing access to judicial proceedings by the press and other members of the general public.

Standards have been developed by bar and press groups in an attempt to find an acceptable middle ground between First and Sixth Amendment rights concerning public trial.[4]

## The Fourth Amendment

"The right of the people to be secure in their persons, houses, papers, and effects, against unreasonable searches and seizures, shall not be violated, and no warrants shall issue, but upon probable cause, supported by Oath or affirmation, and particularly describing the place to be searched, and the persons or things to be seized."

The Fourth Amendment is designed to protect the individual's right to privacy. This means that a police officer cannot indiscriminately use police authority to investigate a possible crime or arrest a suspect unless either or both actions are justified by the law and the facts of the case. Stopping, questioning, or searching an individual without legal justification represents a serious violation of the Fourth Amendment right to personal privacy.

The right to privacy becomes secondary, however, when properly balanced against the need for public protection. The police can search and seize evidence under certain circumstances with a properly authorized search warrant, or when probable cause exists in their minds to reasonably believe that a crime has been committed. Because the police are constantly involved in street encounters with suspects, issues involving the Fourth Amendment are always before the courts. For example, a person accused of a crime who believes that an illegal search was conducted can have an attorney file a motion before the court to suppress any evidence obtained during that search. Evidence seized under such circumstances may not be used against the defendant in a trial. A large body of complex legal decisions, often referred to as *the law of search and seizure,* deals with rights protected by the Fourth Amendment; these will be discussed in more detail in Chapter 8.

In addition, the U.S. Supreme Court has extended Fourth Amendment privacy protections to such diverse areas as wiretapping and issues involving criminal abortion statutes. For example, the constitutionally derived right to privacy was recently made explicit by the Supreme Court in *Roe v. Wade,*[5] where the Court declared unconstitutional a Texas statute which made it a crime to procure an abortion. The Court argued in this case that a person's body is private and therefore the government cannot make laws to control it.

## The Fifth Amendment

"No person shall be held to answer for a capital, or otherwise infamous crime, unless on a presentment or indictment of a Grand Jury, except in cases arising in the land or naval forces, or in the Militia, when in actual service in time of War or public danger; nor shall any person be subject for the same offense to be twice put in jeopardy of life or limb; nor shall be compelled in any criminal case to be a witness against himself, nor be deprived of life, liberty, or property, without due process of law; nor shall private property be taken for public use, without just compensation."

One of the primary purposes of the Fifth Amendment is to provide that no person shall be compelled to be a witness against him or herself. There are two separate parts to this protection. First, the witness has the right not to answer questions in any proceeding which would tend to be self-incriminating. A witness can claim the Fifth Amendment right against self-incrimination in a congressional investigation, grand jury proceeding, or criminal trial. This privilege normally extends to all kinds of proceedings, including those of civil as well as criminal nature. Second, the Fifth Amendment provides the defendant with the right not to take the stand in a criminal trial. If the defendant decides not to testify, the prosecution cannot comment on the silence or infer in any way that failure to testify is evidence of guilt.

The Fifth Amendment has had a tremendous impact on the American criminal justice system. In 1966, for instance, the U.S. Supreme Court held in the landmark case of *Miranda v. Arizona* [6] that a person accused of a crime has the right to refuse to answer questions when placed in custody. The *Miranda* case, which will be discussesd in detail in Chapter 8, resulted in the Supreme Court's development of a set of rules with which the police must comply when questioning a suspect prior to trial. Law enforcement officers throughout the country have generally been disturbed by the *Miranda* decision, believing that it will seriously hamper their efforts to obtain evidence and virtually nullify their ability to elicit confessions and other self-incriminating statements from defendants. However, what research has been done on the impact of *Miranda* indicates that the decision has had little or no effect on the number of confessions obtained by the police, nor has it affected the rate of convictions.[7]

It is also important to realize that the Fifth Amendment right against self-incrimination does not stand alone but is often interrelated with the Fourth Amendment protections against unreasonable searches and seizures. Thus, when the police investigate a crime and make an arrest, or when they question a suspect to obtain a confession or admission, they may also search the defendant in an effort to obtain incriminating evidence. In each step of the criminal justice process, the police must respect the rights accorded to every individual under the law. Constitutional violations against both amendments are often present in the same case and represent a dual constitutional protection against governmental intrusions.

## The Sixth Amendment

"In all criminal prosecutions, the accused shall enjoy the right to a speedy and public trial, by an impartial jury of the State and district wherein the crime shall have been committed, which district shall have been previously ascertained by law, and to be informed of the nature and cause of the accusation; to be confronted with the witnesses against him; to have compulsory process for obtaining the witnesses in his favor, and to have the assistance of counsel for his defense."

The Sixth Amendment guarantees the defendant the right to a speedy and public trial by an impartial jury, the right to be informed of the nature of the charges, and the right to confront any prosecution witnesses. This amendment has had a profound effect upon how a person is treated when accused of a crime and has been the basis for numerous significant Supreme Court decisions which have increased the rights of criminal defendants. Regarding the right to a speedy trial, the Sixth Amendment demands that a defendant be brought to trial within a reasonable amount of time following accusation without undue delay by the prosecution. The Sixth Amendment has also been interpreted to mean that a defendant must be given a trial by a jury of peers in all criminal cases where imprisonment for more than six months may be authorized. The right to a trial by an impartial jury means that the jury must be free from any prejudice, bias, or preconceived notions of the defendant's guilt. The defendant's right to a public trial protects from a secret or closed trial by making such trials unconstitutional.

Many Supreme Court decisions regarding the Sixth Amendment have concerned the individual's right to counsel. The right of the individual to be represented by an attorney has been extended to numerous stages of the criminal justice process, including pretrial custody, identification and lineup procedures, the preliminary hearing, the submission of a guilty plea, the trial, sentencing, and post-conviction appeal. In other sections throughout the text, the right to counsel will be examined in greater detail.

### The Eighth Amendment

"Excessive bail shall not be required, nor excessive fines imposed, nor cruel and unusual punishment inflicted."

Bail is a money bond put up by the accused in order to attain freedom between arrest and trial. Bail is meant to insure a trial appearance, since the bail money is forfeited if the defendant misses the trial date.

The Eighth Amendment does not guarantee a constitutional right to bail but rather prohibits the exactment of excessive bail. Nonetheless, since many state statutes place no precise limit on the amount of bail a judge may impose, many defendants who cannot make bail are often placed in detention while awaiting trial. It has become apparent over the years that the bail system is discriminatory in that a defendant who is financially well-off is more likely to be released on bail than one who is poor. In addition, placing a person in jail results in serious financial burdens to local and state governments—and, in turn, taxpayers—who must pay for the cost of confinement. These factors have given rise to bail reform programs which depend on the defendant's personal promise to appear in court for trial (recognizance) rather than on the financial ability to meet bail (see Chapter 10).

The Eighth Amendment restriction on excessive bail may also be interpreted to mean that the sole purpose of bail is to insure that the defendant return for trial; bail may not be used as a form of punishment, nor may it be used to coerce or threaten a defendant.

The second section of this amendment, which forbids cruel and unusual punishment, has also become quite significant in recent years. It has affected the imposition of the death penalty and other criminal dispositions, and has become a guarantee which serves to protect the accused and convicted offender from actions regarded as unacceptable by a civilized society. Many prison reforms—such as those moderating prison discipline, isolation, and segregation, and allowing the prisoner to express grievances—have resulted from litigation based on the cruel and unusual punishment prohibition.

## The Fourteenth Amendment

All of the above amendments came into being in 1791. However, as the years passed and the new Republic grew, it became apparent that in spite of the Bill of Rights many oppressive conditions remained. Slavery existed in many states, while some men were forced into military service and others worked for the state without pay. Land and property were confiscated by the state, and those rights guaranteed by the Bill of Rights were frequently denied individuals and their families.

At the conclusion of the Civil War, the Thirteenth Amendment abolishing slavery was added to the Constitution. Because other substantial infringements of individual rights continued to exist, the Fourteenth Amendment was adopted in 1868. This amendment states: "All persons born or naturalized in the United States, and subject to the jurisdiction thereof, are citizens of the United States and of the State where they reside. No state shall make or enforce any law which shall abridge the privileges or immunities of citizens of the United States; nor shall any State deprive any person of life, liberty, or property without due process of law; nor deny any person within its jurisdiction the equal protection of the law."

The most important aspect of this amendment is the clause which provides that "No State shall . . . deprive any person of life, liberty, or property without due process of law." This meant that the same general constitutional restrictions previously applicable to the federal government were to be imposed on the states. It is essential to keep the following constitutional principles in mind while examining the amendment:

**1.** The first ten amendments, ordinarily referred to as the Bill of Rights of the United States Constitution, originally applied only to the federal government. They were designed to protect the citizens against injustices enacted by federal authorities. The Bill of Rights restricts the actions of the federal government and does not apply to the states.

**2.** The Fourteenth Amendment's due process clause applies to state government. It has been used to provide individuals in all states with the basic liberties guaranteed by the Bill of Rights.

**3.** The United States Supreme Court has expanded the right of defendants in the criminal justice system by interpreting the due process clause to mean that the states must be held to similar standards applicable to the federal government in the Bill of Rights.

For over a century, the Supreme Court has been struggling with the meaning and significance of the concept "due process of law," particularly in terms of how the Bill of Rights applies to the separate states. From its inception and until about the middle of the twentieth century, the Bill of Rights had little bearing on the state criminal justice process. Individuals charged with federal crimes would be guaranteed rights under the Fourth, Fifth, and Sixth Amendments, but defendants charged with criminal acts in state cases were denied similar treatment. The fact that the Bill of Rights was originally designed to refer to the relationship between the individual and the federal government was pointed out by Chief Justice John Marshall in the case of *Barron v. Baltimore* [8] in 1833. In *Barron,* Justice Marshall rejected the claim that the Fifth Amendment was applicable to the states and held that the Constitution was binding on the federal government alone. The question of whether the Bill of Rights was applicable to the states was further explored by the U.S. Supreme Court in 1884 in the case of *Hurtado v. California.*[9] This case dealt with an interpretation of whether the due process clause of the Fourteenth Amendment contained the liberties expressed in the Bill of Rights. The Court claimed that the writers of the Constitution did not intend that all of the provisions of the Bill of Rights be binding on the states through the Fourteenth Amendment.

Gradually, however, through a long process of case decisions, the Supreme Court has held that all of the guarantees of the original ten amendments apply to state as well as federal law. The movement to make the Bill of Rights applicable to the states has gained impetus during the latter half of this century. It is based upon a number of legal theories which describe the relationship of the Bill of Rights to the Fourteenth Amendment. The first theory is referred to as *The Incorporation Theory,* and states that all the provisions of the Bill of Rights are incorporated into the Fourteenth Amendment's due process clause. Thus, such fundamental rights as freedom from unreasonable search and seizure, the right to jury trial, and the right to counsel are all considered binding on the states through the Fourteenth Amendment. However, the idea of total incorporation has never received majority support in any Supreme Court decision nor has it been accepted in any substantial way by legal scholars or historians. Those supporting total incorporation argue that an individual is a citizen of both the federal government and state government and should receive similar protections from each, while those arguing against this position suggest that states should be allowed to develop their own criminal procedures.

The most widely recognized theory of constitutional responsibility is called the *Theory of Selective Incorporation*, which states that the Bill of Rights applies to the states through the due process clause of the Fourteenth Amendment but must be considered only on a case-by-case basis. Advocates of this theory believe that some of the provisions of the Bill of Rights may be binding on the states—such as the right to a jury trial or the right to be free from self-incrimination—but that these should apply only after a careful consideration of the facts, or merits, of each case.

One way of determining which federal rights must be incorporated into the states' criminal justice systems was set forth in the case of *Palko v. Connecticut* [10] in 1937. That case questioned whether the defendant's second trial for a state crime constituted double jeopardy and violated the due process clause of the Fourteenth Amendment. The Supreme Court decided that the defendant's due process rights were not violated because the Fourteenth Amendment applied to the states only those aspects of the Bill of Rights "which are the very essence of a scheme of ordered liberty."[11] Double jeopardy was considered "fundamental" or "so rooted in the traditions and conscience of our people" that it should apply to the states as well as to the federal government. Thus, what evolved from the U.S. Supreme Court was a new legal theory called *Fundamental Fairness*; if the Supreme Court decided that a particular guarantee in the Bill of Rights was *fundamental* to and *implicit* in the American system of justice, it would hold that right applicable to the states. This became the method by which states could be held to the same standards of criminal due process as the federal government.

Based on the formula derived from the *Palko* case, the incorporation of the provisions of the Bill of Rights into the Fourteenth Amendment moved forward slowly on a case-by-case basis, intensifying in 1953 when Earl Warren became the Chief Justice of the U.S. Supreme Court. Under this leadership, the due process movement reached its peak. Numerous landmark cases focusing on the rights of the accused were decided, resulting in a revolution in the area of constitutional criminal procedure. The Warren court granted many new rights to those accused of crimes and went so far as to impose specific guidelines on the policies of police, courts, and correctional services which insured that due process of law would be maintained.

Today, the Fourteenth Amendment's due process clause has been interpreted by the Supreme Court to mean that an accused in a state criminal case is entitled to the same protections available under the federal Bill of Rights. Some of the major Supreme Court decisions making the Bill of Rights applicable to the states have been *Mapp v. Ohio* (1961), which guaranteed the right of an individual to be free from unreasonable searches and seizures and to exclude the illegally seized evidence from criminal trials; *Malloy v. Hogan* (1964), which guaranteed the right of an individual to be free from forced self-incrimination; *Gideon v. Wainwright* (1963), which guaranteed the right to counsel; *Klopfer v. North Carolina* (1967), which guaranteed the right to speedy trial; *Pointer v. Texas* (1965), which guaranteed the right to confront witnesses; and *Benton v. Maryland* (1969), which guaranteed the right to be free from double jeopardy. These, then, are some of the pertinent decisions which grant similar rights to an accused person on both state and federal levels. A schematic diagram of the relationship between the Bill of Rights and Fourteenth Amendment is presented in Figure 5.1.

## DUE PROCESS OF LAW

We have examined the term *due process* as a basis for incorporating the Bill of Rights into the Fourteenth Amendment. Due process has also been used to evaluate the constitutionality of legal statutes and to set standards and guidelines for fair procedures in the criminal justice system.

Due process has often been divided into both substantive and procedural areas. The substantive aspects of due process are generally used to determine whether a statute is a fair, reasonable, and appropriate use of the legal power of the legislature. The concept of substantive due process was used extensively in the 1930s and 1940s to invalidate minimum wage standards, price fixing, and employment restriction statutes. Today, substantive due process is used relativey sparingly; for example, it can be employed to hold that a criminal statute—such as disorderly conduct,

FIGURE 5.1
Relationship of Bill of Rights and Fourteenth Amendment to Constitutional Rights of Accused

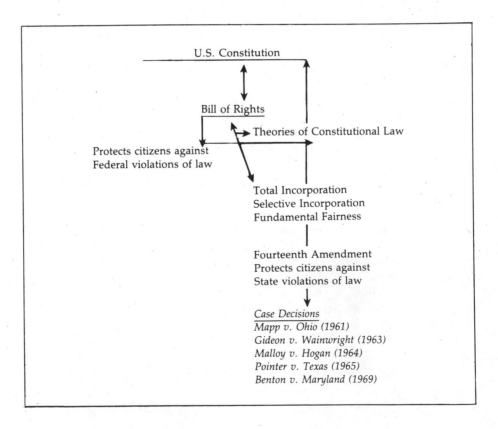

capital punishment, or a ban on pornography—may be unconstitutional because it is arbitrary or unreasonable.

Much more important today are the procedural aspects of due process of law. In seeking to define the meaning of the term, most legal experts believe that it refers to the essential elements of fairness under law.[12] An elaborate and rather complex definition of due process is found in *Black's Law Dictionary:*

Due process of law in each particular case means such an exercise of the powers of government as the settled maxims of law permit and sanction, and under such safeguards for the protection of individual rights as those maxims prescribe for the class of cases to which the one in question belongs.[13]

This definition basically refers to the need for rules and procedures in our legal system which protect individual rights. The actual objectives of due process help to define the term even more explicitly. Due process seeks to insure that no person be deprived of life, liberty, or property without notice of charges, assistance from legal counsel, a hearing, and an opportunity to confront those making the accusations. Basically, due process is intended to guarantee that fundamental fairness exists in each individual case. This doctrine of fairness as expressed in due process of law is guaranteed under both the Fifth and Fourteenth Amendments.[14]

Abstract definitions are only one aspect of due process. Much more significant are the procedures which give meaning to due process in the everyday practices of the criminal justice system. In this regard, due process provides numerous procedural safeguards for the offender. They include:

1. Notice of charges.

2. A formal hearing.

3. The right to counsel or some other representation.

4. The opportunity to respond to charges.

5. The opportunity to confront and cross-examine witnesses and accusers.

6. The privilege to be free from self-incrimination.

7. The opportunity to present one's own witnesses.

8. A decision made on the basis of substantial evidence and facts produced at the hearing.

9. A written statement of the reasons for the decision.

10. An appellate review procedure.

Exactly what constitutes due process in a specific case depends on the facts of the case, the federal and state constitutional and statutory provisions, previous court decisions, and the ideas and principles that society considers important at a given time and in a given place.[15] The late Justice Felix Frankfurter emphasized this latter point in *Rochin v. California* (1952) when he wrote:

Due process of law requires an evaluation based on a disinterested inquiry pursued in the spirit of science on a balanced order of facts, exactly and clearly stated, on the detached consideration of conflicting claims . . . on a judgment not ad hoc and episodic but duly mindful of reconciling the needs both of continuity and of change in a progressive society.[16]

The nature of due process is examined in the application section where the Rochin case is set out in detail.

Both the elements and the definition of due process seem to be flexible and constantly changing. For example, the concept of due process at one time did not require a formal hearing for parole revocation, but does today. Prior to 1968, juvenile offenders did not have the right to an attorney at their adjudication; counsel is now required in the juvenile court system. Thus, the interpretations of due process of law are not fixed but rather reflect what society deems fair and just at a particular time and in a particular place. The degree of loss suffered by the individual (victim or offender) balanced against the state's interest also determines which and how many due process requirements are ordinarily applied. Where a person's freedom is at stake in the criminal justice system, all applicable due process rights are usually granted the accused; in other cases, due process may be modified.

Due process has been increasingly applied to protect individual rights when the government seeks to deprive a person of life, liberty, or property. The trend toward a wider use of procedural safeguards to prevent abuses of power has spread to many fields including criminal justice, public welfare, mental health, and juvenile delinquency. More than ever before, due process of law based on the Fifth and Fourteenth Amendments is used to challenge various types of arbitrary actions, such as the termination of aid by welfare officials or the imposition of punishment on prison inmates. Consistent judicial intervention has made these and other fields more responsive to reform through the application of constitutional rights.

HOW A CASE
GETS TO THE
U.S. SUPREME
COURT

Since many of the basic due process rights of the accused have resulted from the application of constitutional principles, it is important for the student to understand how a legal case reaches the U.S. Supreme Court. No court is as unique and different as this nation's highest court. First of all, it is the only court established by constitutional mandate rather than federal legislation. Second, it decides basic social and political issues of grave consequence and importance to the country. Third, the Court's nine Justices shape the future meaning of the American Constitution. Their decisions identify the rights and liberties of citizens throughout the entire country.

Not every legal problem, however, comes to the U.S. Supreme Court. The jurisdiction of the Court, as discussed in detail in Chapter 11, is defined by Article 3 of the Constitution and by the Court's previous decisions. The important clauses in Article 3 indicate that the Federal Courts have jurisdiction under the Constitution, the laws of the United States and treaties, and cases involving admiralty and maritime jurisdiction, as well as controversies between two or more states and citizens of different states.[17] This complex language generally means that unless an offender violates a federal criminal statute or is involved in a civil suit between citizens of different states, the state normally has jurisdiction over the majority of cases tried each day in local jurisdictions. The U.S. Supreme Court has jurisdiction when there are violations and questions of federal or constitutional law. For example, an accused might be charged with a felony such as kidnapping under a federal statute. On the other hand, there might be a constitutional question, such as whether an accused can be convicted of a crime in violation of due process of law.

When our country was first established, the Supreme Court did not review state court decisions involving issues of federal law. Even though the federal Congress had given the Supreme Court jurisdiction to review state decision, there was still much resistance and controversy surrounding the relationship between the states and the federal government. However, in a famous decision called *Martin v. Hunter's Lessee*, the U.S. Supreme Court reaffirmed the legitimacy of the Supreme Court's jurisdiction over state court decisions when such courts handled issues of federal or constitutional law.[18] This Court decision allowed the U.S. Supreme Court to actively review actions by states and their courts and reinforce the Court's power as making the supreme law of the land. Since that time, when a defendant who indicates that governmental action—whether state or federal—violates constitutional law, the person is in a position to have the U.S. Supreme Court review such action.

In order for the Court to carry out its responsibilities, it had to develop a method to deal with a large volume of cases coming from the state and federal courts for final review. In the early years of its history, the Court sought to review every case brought before it. However, since the middle of the twentieth century, the Court has used a technical device known as a writ of certiorari to decide what cases should be heard by the Court. Certiorari is an old Latin term which means "to bring the record of a case from a lower court up to a higher court for immediate review." When applied, it means that an accused in a criminal case is requesting the U.S. Supreme Court to hear the case. The other method of having a case reach the U.S. Supreme Court is through an absolute right to appeal. More than 90% of the cases heard in the U.S. Supreme Court are brought by petition for a writ of certiorari. Under this procedure, the Court and its Justices have discretion to select cases that they will review for a decision. Each year, in the past decade or so, of the thousands of cases filed before the Court, only two to three hundred cases are heard. Four of the nine Justices sitting on the U.S. Supreme Court must vote to hear a case brought by a writ of certiorari for review. Generally, these votes are cast in a secret meeting attended only by the Justices.

After the Court has decided to hear a case, written and oral arguments are provided for review before the Court. The written materials are referred to as legal briefs and oral arguments are normally presented to the Justices at the U.S. Supreme Court in Washington, D.C.

After the material is reviewed and the oral arguments heard, the Justices of the Court normally meet in what is known as a "case conference." This case conference is a meeting to discuss the case and vote to reach a decision. The cases voted on by the Court generally come from the judicial systems of the various states, or from the U.S. courts of appeals, and represent the entire spectrum of law.

In reaching a decision, the Supreme Court reevaluates and reinterprets states statutes, the U.S. Constitution, and previous case decisions. On the basis of a review of the case, the decision of the lower court is either affirmed or reversed. When a decision is reached by the Justices, the Chief Justice of the Court assigns someone of the majority group to write the opinion. In addition, a Justice normally writes a dissent or minority opinion. In the final analysis, the Justices join with the majority or dissenting opinion. When the case is finished, it is submitted to the public and becomes the law of the land. The decision represents the legal precedents which add to the existing body of law on a given subject, change it, and guide its future development.

In the area of criminal justice, the decisions of the U.S. Supreme Court have had the broadest impact in reforming the system. Its action is the final step in settling constitutional criminal disputes throughout the country. By discretionary review through a petition for certiorari, the U.S. Supreme Court requires state courts to accept its interpretation of the federal Constitution.[19] In doing so, the Court has changed the day-by-day operations of the criminal justice process.

THE
EXCLUSIONARY
RULE

No review of constitutional principles is complete without a discussion of the *Exclusionary Rule*. As previously mentioned, the Fourth Amendment guarantees the rights of individuals to be secure in their persons, homes, places, and effects against unreasonable searches and seizures. The exclusionary rule provides that all evidence obtained by illegal searches and seizures is inadmissible in criminal trials.

It has often been the case that evidence obtained by law enforcement officers has been gathered in violation of constitutional protections. For many years, however, evidence obtained by unreasonable search and seizure that should have consequently been considered illegal was made inadmissible by State and Federal governments in criminal trials. The only criteria for admissibility were whether the evidence was incriminating, and whether it would assist the judge or jury in ascertaining the innocence or guilt of the defendant. How evidence was obtained was unimportant; its relevance to the criminal case was what determined its admissibility.

However, in 1914, a direction regarding the admissibility of evidence was adopted when the U.S. Supreme Court decided the case of *Weeks v.*

*United States.*[20] The defendant, Freemont Weeks, was accused by federal law enforcement authorities of using the mails for illegal purposes. After his arrest, the home in which Weeks was staying was searched without a valid search warrant. Evidence in the form of letters and other materials was found in his room and admitted at the trial. Weeks was then convicted of the federal offense based on incriminating evidence. On appeal, the Supreme Court held that evidence obtained by unreasonable search and seizure must be excluded in a federal criminal trial. The Court in *Weeks* stated:

If letters and private documents can thus be seized and held and used in evidence against a citizen accused of an offense, the protection of the Fourth Amendment declaring his right to be secure against such searches and seizures is of no value, and, so far as those thus placed are concerned, might as well be stricken from the Constitution. The efforts of the courts and their officials to bring the guilty to punishment, praiseworthy as they are, are not to be aided by the sacrifice of those great principles established by years of endeavor and suffering which have resulted in their embodiment in the fundamental law of the land.[21]

Thus, for the first time, the Court held that the Fourth Amendment barred the use in a federal prosecution of evidence obtained through illegal search and seizure. With this ruling the Court established the exclusionary rule. The rule was not based on legislation, but rather on judicial decision making.

Over the years, subsequent federal and state court decisions have gradually applied the exclusionary rule to state court systems. These decisions have not always been consistent, however. For instance, in 1949, the states received notice that the U.S. Supreme Court was considering making the *Weeks* doctrine binding upon state courts in the case of *Wolf v. Colorado.*[22] Wolf was charged in a Colorado state court with conspiring to perform abortions. Evidence in the form of patient's names was secured by a sheriff from a physician's office without a valid search warrant. The patients were subsequently questioned and the evidence used at Wolf's trial. The case was appealed and the Supreme Court was asked to decide the question: "Does a conviction by a state court for a state offense deny the defendant due process of law because evidence admitted at the trial was obtained under circumstances which would have rendered it inadmissible in a federal trial?"[23] In a six to three decision, the Court decided that the evidence was admissible and not in violation of the Fourteenth Amendment. The Court recognized that the Fourth Amendment forbade the admissibility of illegally seized evidence, but did not see fit to impose federal standards of criminal procedure on the states. One important fact the court considered in reaching its decision on *Wolf* was that only 16 states were in agreement with the exclusionary rule, while 31 states had rejected it by 1949.

However, many states changed their positions and, by 1961, approximately half had adopted the exclusionary rule. In that same year, the U.S.

Supreme Court, despite past decisions, reversed itself and made the exclusionary rule applicable to state courts in the landmark decision of *Mapp v. Ohio.*[24] Because of the importance of the *Mapp* case, it is discussed in some detail below.

Apart from its legal development, the exclusionary rule had been a controversial subject in the administration of criminal justice. It was originally conceived to control illegitimate police practices, and that remains its primary purpose today. It is justified on the basis that it is a deterrent to illegal searches and seizures. Yet, most experts believe that no impartial data exists to prove that the rule has an impact on police behavior. This is by far the most significant criticism of the rule. The rule more directly affects the criminal trial by excluding evidence than it does the police officer on the street. Furthermore, the rule is powerless when the police have no interest in prosecuting the accused or in obtaining a conviction. In addition, it does not control the wholesale harassment of individuals by law enforcement officials bent on disregarding constitutional rights.

The most popular criticism of the exclusionary rule, however, is that it allows guilty defendants to go free. Because courts decide frequently in many types of crimes (particularly in victimless offenses such as gambling

## MAPP V. OHIO

**Facts:** On May 23, 1957, three police officers arrived at Dolree Mapp's residence pursuant to information that "a person (was) hiding out in the home, who was wanted for questioning in connection with a recent bombing, and that there was a large amount of police paraphernalia being hidden in the home." Mapp and her daughter by a former marriage lived on the top floor of the two-family dwelling. Upon their arrival at the house, the officers knocked on the door and demanded entrance but Mapp, after telephoning her attorney, refused to admit them without a search warrant.

The officers again sought entrance three hours later when four or more additional officers arrived on the scene. When Mapp did not immediately come to the door, the police forcibly opened one of the doors to the house and gained admittance. Meanwhile, Mapp's attorney arrived, but the officers would not permit him to see Mapp or to enter the house. Mapp was halfway down the stairs from the upper floor to the front door when the officers

broke into the hall. She demanded to see the search warrant. A paper, claimed to be a search warrant, was held up by one of the officers. She grabbed the "warrant" and placed it in her bosom. A struggle ensued in which the officers recovered the piece of paper and handcuffed Mapp because she had ostensibly been belligerent.

Mapp was then forcibly taken upstairs to her bedroom, where the officials searched a dresser, a chest of drawers, a closet, and some suitcases. They also looked into a photo album and through personal papers belonging to her. The search spread to the rest of the second floor, including the child's bedroom, the living room, the kitchen, and the dinette. In the course of the search, the police officers found pornographic literature. Mapp was arrested and subsequently convicted in a Ohio court of possessing obscene materials.

**Decision:** The question in the *Mapp* case was whether the illegally seized evidence was in and drug use) that certain evidence should be excluded, enactment of the rule is believed to result in excessive court delays and to negatively affect plea bargaining negotiations.[26]

Because the exclusionary rule may not deter illegal police action, and because its use results in many guilty offenders escaping conviction, proposals for modifying the rule have been suggested. In recent years, recommendations have stemmed from the fact that the rule is a single inflexible requirement which holds regardless of the nature of the offense or the type of police misconduct. Chief Justice Burger, for example, in his dissent in the case of *Bevnis v. Six Unknown Named Agents of Federal Bureau of Narcotics*,[27] has stated that honest police mistakes should not be equated with intentional police misconduct. In line with this problem, and after more than a decade of work, the American Law Institute has given final approval to a Model Code of Pre-Arraignment Procedure, which limits the use of the exclusionary rule to substantial violations by law enforcement officials. This means that evidence should be suppressed only if the court finds that the constitutional violations are substantial. The code does not precisely define the term *substantial* but enumerates six criteria for determining substantial violation. They are:

violation of the search and seizure provisions of the Fourth Amendment and therefore inadmissible in the state trial, which resulted in an obscenity conviction. The Supreme Court of Ohio found the conviction valid. However, the U.S. Supreme Court overturned it, stating that the Fourth Amendment's prohibition against unreasonable searches and seizures, enforcible against the states through the due process clause, had been violated by the police. Justice Thomas Clark, in delivering the majority opinion of the Court, made clear the importance of this constitutional right in the administration of criminal justice when he stated:

There are those who say, as did Justice (then Judge) Cardozo, that under our constitutional exclusionary doctrine "[t]he criminal is to go free because the constable has blundered." In some cases this will undoubtedly be the result. But . . . there is another consideration— the imperative of judicial integrity. . . . The criminal goes free, if he must, but it is the law that sets him free. Nothing can destroy a

government more quickly than its failure to observe its own laws, or worse, its disregard of the charter of its own existence.[25]

**Significance of the Case:** In previous decisions, the U.S. Supreme Court had refused to exclude evidence in state court proceedings based upon Fourth Amendment violations of search and seizure. The *Mapp* case overruled such decisions, including that of *Wolf v. Colorado*, and held that evidence gathered in violation of the Fourth Amendment would be inadmissible in a state prosecution. For the first time, the Court imposed federal constitutional standards on state law enforcement personnel. In addition, the Court reemphasized the point that a relationship exists between the Fourth and Fifth Amendments which forms a constitutional basis requiring the use of the exclusionary rule.

1. [The] extent of deviation from lawful conduct;
2. [The] extent to which [the] violation was willful;
3. [The] extent to which privacy was invaded;
4. [The] extent to which exclusion will tend to prevent violations of this Code;
5. [W]hether, but for the violation, the things seized would have been discovered; [and]
6. [The] extent to which the violation prejudiced the moving party's ability to support his motion, or to defend himself in the proceedings in which the things seized are sought to be offered in evidence against him.[28]

Although the Code is only a proposed model, its modification of the exclusionary rule would seem to offer some relief from the problem of having to free guilty criminals due to minor Fourth Amendment violations by police officials.

Other suggested approaches to dealing with violations of the exclusionary rule include (1) criminal prosecution against police officers who violate constitutional rights; (2) internal police control; (3) a civil lawsuit against a state or municipal police officer; and (4) a federal lawsuit against the government under the Federal Tort Claims Act. An individual using any of these alternatives, however, would be faced with such obstacles as the cost of bringing a lawsuit, the difficulty of proving damages, and the problems of dealing with a bureaucratic law enforcement system.

In conclusion, it appears that many legal experts are included toward modifying the exclusionary rule in some manner. The rule's inflexibility and questionable deterrent value suggest the need for possible reform. There are indications that even the U.S. Supreme Court is looking critically at the deterrent value of the rule and no doubt will devote much attention in the future to the exclusionary rule. For example, in *U.S. v. Calandra* in 1974, the Court held that the exclusionary rule does not apply at grand jury proceedings.[29] In 1976 the court continued to express a narrow view of the scope of the rule by holding the rule inapplicable to civil tax proceedings in *U.S. v. Janis*.[30] But more important, the Court ruled in *Stone v. Powell*, also in 1976, that a prisoner could not present his search and seizure claims to a federal court if he had been given a fair chance to litigate them in a state forum.[31] Whether federal and state lawmakers will adopt any changes in the rule, however, will depend primarily upon the ability of experts to create and promote alternative solutions to controlling unlawful police misconduct.

SUMMARY

The Bill of Rights was established as a limitation upon the federal government's powers to usurp the personal liberties of citizens. In 1868, the Fourteenth Amendment extended this protection to citizens in their relationships with state governments by providing that no state may "deprive any person of life, liberty and property without due process of law." Of the first ten amendments, the Fourth, Fifth, Sixth, and Eighth Amendments encompass many of the rights guaranteed to individuals accused of crimes.

Over the years, the United States Supreme Court has advanced three major theories to justify the application of the Bill of Rights to the states. These include: (1) the belief that the Fourteenth Amendment includes the idea of fundamental fairness and due process; (2) the view that the Fourteenth Amendment totally incorporates the Bill of Rights; and (3) the theory that not all rights in the Bill of Rights are fundamental, but that each right should be viewed on a selective incorporation or case-by-case basis. In reality, during the past two decades, nearly every provision in the Bill of Rights which deals with the criminal offender has been held applicable to the states through the due process clause of the Fourteenth Amendment.

Probably the most controversial Supreme Court decisions of the past two decades have been those placing restrictions on law enforcement practices, such as interrogation, searches, wiretapping, and lineup procedures. The exclusionary rule, which precludes the use of illegally obtained evidence, is an example of a federal rule being made binding on the states.

1. Discuss the relationship between the United States Constitution and the Bill of Rights. What particular provisions of each protect individuals as state and federal citizens?

**QUESTIONS FOR DISCUSSION**

2. What is the meaning of the term "due process of law"? Explain why and how due process has had an impact on the criminal justice system.

3. What is the exclusionary rule? What United States Supreme Court cases have established this rule? How does it protect the rights of the accused?

4. By what process does a legal case reach the United States Supreme Court?

5. What effect do decisions of the United States Supreme Court have on the local criminal justice system? On the accused? On the police officer?

**NOTES**

1. 423 U.S. 1319, 96 S.Ct. 237, 49 L.Ed.2d 24 (1975).

2. Ibid.

3. 435 U.S. 1006, 99 S.Ct. 2898 (1979).

4. See American Bar Association, *Standards Relating to Fair Trial and Free Press* (New York: Institute of Judicial Administration, Tentative Draft, 1966).

5. 410 U.S. 113, 93 S.Ct. 705, 35 L.Ed.2d 147 (1973).

6. 384 U.S. 436, 86 S.Ct. 1602, 16 L.Ed.2d 694 (1966).

7. Michael Wald et al., "Interrogations in New Haven: The Impact of Miranda," *Yale Law Journal* 76:1519 (1967).

8. 32 U.S., 7 Peters 243, 8 L.Ed. 672 (1833).

9. 110 U.S. 516, 4 S.Ct. 111, 28 L.Ed. 232 (1884).

10. 302 U.S. 319, 58 S.Ct. 149, 82 L.Ed. 288 (1937).

11. Ibid. at 325.

12. See *Time*, February 26, 1973, p. 95.

13. Black's Law Dictionary, Revised Fourth Edition (St. Paul, Minn.: West Publishing Co., 1967), p. 590.

14. See generally Joseph J. Senna, "Changes in Due Process of Law," *Social Work* 19:319 (1974).

15. 370 U.S. 660, 82 S.Ct. 1417, 8 L.Ed.2d 758 (1962).

16. Ibid. at 172.

17. See U.S. Constitution, Article 3, Sec. I & II (1789).

18. I. Wherton 304, 4 L.Ed. 97 (1816).

19. See generally, Bob Woodward and Scott Armstrong, *The Brethren—Inside the Supreme Court* (New York: Simon and Schuster, 1979).

20. 232 U.S. 383, 34 S.Ct. 341, 58 L.Ed. 652 (1914).

21. Ibid. at 393.

22. 338 U.S. 25, 69 S.Ct. 1359, 93 L.Ed. 1782 (1949).

23. Ibid. at 25, 26.

24. 367 U.S. 643, 81 S.Ct. 1684, 6 L.Ed.2d 1081 (1961).

25. Ibid. at 659.

26. See generally Arnold Enker, "Perspectives on Plea Bargaining" in President's Commission on Law Enforcement and Administration of Justice, *Task Force Report: The Courts* (Washington, D.C.: U.S. Government Printing Office, 1967), pp. 109–119.

27. 403 U.S. 388, 91 S.Ct. 1999, 29 L.Ed.2d 619 (1971).

28. American Law Institute, *A Model Code of Pre-Arraignment Procedure* (Washington D.C.: American Law Institute 1975), Article 290 and 290.2(4).

29. 414 U.S. 338, 94 S.Ct. 613 (1974).

30. 428 U.S. 433, 96 S.Ct. 3021 (1976).

31. 428 U.S. 465, 96 S.Ct. 3037 (1976).

# Nature of Due Process: Rochin v. California,

## FACTS

Having some information that the defendant, Rochin, was selling narcotics, three deputy sheriffs of the Los Angeles Sheriffs Department, went to the two-story dwelling house in which Rochin lived with his mother, wife, brothers, and sisters. Finding the door open, they entered the house, and then forced open the door to Rochins apartment. Inside, they found Rochin sitting partly dressed on the bed, where his wife was lying. The deputies saw two capsules on a nightstand beside the bed. When Rochin was asked what they were, Rochin seized the capsules and put them in his mouth. The deputies jumped on Rochin and attempted to extract the capsules, but were unsuccessful. He was handcuffed and taken to a hospital. At the direction of one of the officers, a doctor forced an emetic solution through a tube into Rochins stomach against his will. The stomach pumping produced vomiting. In the vomit matter were found two capsules which proved to contain morphine. Rochin was tried and convicted of possessing morphine and sentenced to 60 days imprisonment. The two capsules were the primary evidence used against him at his trial.

## DECISION

The legal problem in this case was whether the shocking methods used by the deputies to obtain the evidence, including extracting it from Rochin at the hospital violated the due process clause of the Fourteenth Amendment. In our federal system, the administration of criminal justice is predominantly committed to the care of the states. Nonetheless, the U.S. Supreme Court has as its responsibility to determine if actions by state police personnel offend the canons of decency and fairness. The court indicated that due process of law is "a summarized constitutional guarantee of respect for those personal immunities which, as Judge Cardoza stated, are so rooted in the traditions and conscience of our people as to be ranked as fundamental, or are implicit in the concept of ordered liberty." Applying this principle to the Rochin case, the Court found the actions of the police to be conduct that shocks the conscience. Illegally breaking into the privacy of the petitioner, the struggle to open his mouth, the forceable extraction of the contents of his stomach—all are found to offend even hardened sensitivities. They are methods too close to the rack and screw to permit constitutional differentiation. Consequently, the Court concluded that the conviction of Rochin was obtained by methods that offend the due process clause.

## SIGNIFICANCE OF CASE

The decision established the basis for court review of extreme police practices on the admissibility of evidence. The majority opinion stated that a conviction resting on real evidence obtained from the body of a defendant is as invalid as involuntary verbal confessions. Both are inadmissible under the Due Process Clause. Whereas coerced confessions offend the community's sense of fair play and decency, so does brutal physical conduct need to be condemned by the court. Thus, the Court found no valid ground for distinguishing between verbal confessions and evidence obtained from a defendant's body by physical abuse.

# PART THREE

## Law
## Enforcement

# The Police in Society

CHAPTER OUTLINE

KEY TERMS

POLICE ROLES:
INTRODUCTION

The following three chapters contain a detailed analysis of the police component of the criminal justice system. The police play a significant role in crime control by virtue of their investigatory, arrest, and law enforcement powers. In addition, they have many important community service functions, such as directing the flow of traffic and enforcing motor vehicle regulations, as well as controlling crowds, giving emergency medical care, and enforcing curfews.

Police are probably the most controversial elements of the criminal justice system. They are the most numerous and visible agencies of justice. People who never come into contact with judges, prosecutors, wardens, or prison guards are daily affected by police activities. When police pursue their job too vigorously, citizens are quick to cry out against a "police-state" atmosphere. If police fail to control crime effectively, these same citizens will decry the "fear stalking the city" and call for increased police protection. The "damned if you do, damned if you don't" attitudes of many citizens and public officials has caused a concomitant sense of dissatisfaction among police officers; job stress is a major issue in police forces today.

In this and the following two chapters, we will evaluate the history, role, organization issues, and procedures of police agents and agencies.

HISTORY OF THE
POLICE

The face of America has changed since colonial days from a collection of predominantly rural and independent jurisdictions to an industrialized urban nation.* Yet in several respects law enforcement has not kept pace with this change. As America has grown and policing has become correspondingly complex, the existing law enforcement system has not always been altered to meet the needs of a mechanized and metropolitan society.

Over the years, the proliferation of independent and, for the most part, local policing units has led to an overlapping of responsibilities and a duplication of effort, causing problems in police administration and in the coordination of efforts to apprehend criminals. America is a nation of small, decentralized police forces.

Other problems have plagued the police over the years. Forces have lacked an adequate number of sufficiently qualified personnel. Unattractive salaries and working conditions, and a general lack of public support have hindered police development. And the need for harmonious police-community relations has been a persistent problem, one which, unfortunately, has not been widely recognized until recently. Community relations problems are nothing new; they have existed since American cities were divided into subsocieties by virtue of different ensuing waves of immigrants from western, and later eastern Europe, who started settling in urban centers before the turn of this century.

To understand better the prevailing problems that police agencies face today, it is helpful to examine their development in England as well as in the United States;

---

*From The President's Commission on Law Enforcement and Administration of Justice, *Task Force Report: The Police*, Washington: U.S. Government Printing Office, 1967, pp. 3–7.

there are many weaknesses in the existing system that stem from practices developed in the rural colonies and from the colonial philosophy of law enforcement.

## The Early History of
## English Law Enforcement

France and other continental countries maintained professional police forces of a sort as early as the seventeenth century. But England, fearing the oppression these forces had brought about in many of the continental countries, did not begin to create police organizations until the nineteenth century. Moreover, England, in its early history, did not maintain a permanent army of paid soldiers that could enforce criminal laws when not engaged in guarding the country's borders against invaders. The cost of developing a force specifically for peace-keeping duties was believed to be too high for the royal purse. Private citizens could do the job cheaper, if given a few shillings reward for arrests. This simple law enforcement expedient, which had begun with Alfred the Great (870–901), can be recognized as the forerunner of American police agencies.

Primarily, the system encouraged mutual responsibility among local citizens' associations, which were pledged to maintain law and order;[1] it was called the "mutual pledge" system. Every man was responsible not only for his own actions but also for those of his neighbors. It was each citizen's duty to raise the "hue and cry" when a crime was committed, to collect his neighbors, and to pursue a criminal who fled from the district. If such a group failed to apprehend a lawbreaker, all were fined by the Crown.

The Crown placed this mutual responsibility for group police action upon 10-family groups. Each of these was known as a "tithing." From the tithing, there subsequently developed the "hundred" comprised of 10 tithings. From this developed the first real police officer—the constable.[2] He was appointed by a local nobleman and placed in charge of the weapons and equipment of each hundred.

Soon, the "hundreds" were grouped to form a "shire," a geographical area equivalent to a county.[3] A "shire-reeve"—lineal antecedent of tens of thousands of sheriffs to come—thus came into being, appointed by the Crown to supervise each county. The constable's breadth of authority remained limited to his original "hundred." The shire-reeve was responsible to the local nobleman in ensuring that the citizens enforced the law effectively. From his original supervisory post, the sheriff soon branched out to take part in the pursuit and apprehension of lawbreakers.

It was during the reign of Edward 1 (1272–1307), that the first official police forces were created in the large towns of England. These were called the "watch and ward," and were responsible for protecting property against fire, guarding the gates, and arresting those who committed offenses between sunset and daybreak. At the same time the constable became the primary law enforcement officer in all towns throughout England.

In 1326, to supplement the "shire-reeve" mutual pledge system, Edward II created the office of justice of the peace. The justices, originally noblemen, were appointed by the Crown to assist the sheriff in policing the county. This led in time to their taking on local judicial functions, in line with the primary duty of keeping the peace in their separate jurisdictions.

The constable, who retained the responsibility of serving as a major official within the pledge system, meanwhile gained in importance. He became an assistant to the justice, responsible for supervising the night watchmen, inquiring into offenses, serving summonses, executing warrants, and taking charge of prisoners.[4] It was here that the formal separation between judge and police officer developed.

As law enforcement increasingly became the responsibility of the central government in fourteenth century England, the justice, as the appointee of the King, exercised a greater degree of control over the locally appointed constables. By the end of the century the constable no longer functioned independently as an official of the pledge system. Rather, he was obliged to serve the justice. This essentially set the justice-constable patterns for the next 500 years. The "justice (remained) the superior, the constable the inferior, conservator of the peace"[5] until the second quarter of the nineteenth century.

Meanwhile, over these years, the local pledge system continued to decline. Community support languished. And with considerable reason.[6]

What was everybody's business became nobody's duty and the citizens who were bound by law to take their turn at police work gradually evaded personal police service by paying others to do the work for them. In theory constables were appointed annually, but in fact their work was done by deputies or substitutes who so acted year after year, being paid to do so by the constables. These early paid police officers did not rank high in popular estimation as indicated in contemporary references. They were usually ill-paid and ignorant men, often too old to be in any sense efficient.

But as the local pledge system was declining, innovations in policing were cropping up in the emerging cities of the seventeenth and eighteenth centuries. Those first law enforcement officers were increasingly assisted by a paid nightwatch force. Although these nominally were responsible for guarding the cities against thieves and vandals, apparently they were not effective. Reportedly they did little more than roam the streets at night, periodically calling out the condition of the weather, the hour, and the fact that "all was well."

## Industrialization in England

While England remained essentially a rural country, the dominance of the justice of the peace in law enforcement machinery aroused little formal opposition. But with the advent of the Industrial Revolution at the end of the 1700s, families by the thousands began traveling to factory towns to find work. Inevitably, as the cities grew, established patterns of life changed and unprecedented social disorder resulted. Law enforcement became a much more complex enterprise.

Government and citizens alike responded to this need for better law enforcement. A number of fragmented civic associations, such as the Bow Street Horse and Foot Patrol, were formed to police the streets and highways leading out of London and the Government passed statutes creating public offices, later to be known as police offices. Each of these housed three paid justices of the peace, who were authorized to employ six paid constables. These new posts thus helped to centralize law enforcement operations within a small area.

By the beginning of the nineteenth century, nine police offices had been established within the metropolitan area of London, but there was little apparent effort to coordinate their independent law enforcement activities. This was reportedly due to the fact that each office refused to communicate with another for fear that the other might take credit for detecting and apprehending an offender.

In London especially, these weaknesses combined to make the police forces seemingly powerless to combat crime. Highwaymen on the road, thieves lurking in the cities, daily bank robberies, juvenile delinquency—all presented major law enforcement problems.[7] However, out of this difficult situation emerged a unique remedy to discourage thieves from attacking citizens; in the early 1800s, gaslights were introduced on the streets of London.

Many of the experiments in law enforcement before 1820 failed "because no scheme could reconcile the freedom of action of individuals with the security of person and property."[8] In 1822, Sir Robert Peel, England's new Home Secretary, contended that, while better policing could not eliminate crime, the poor quality of police contributed to social disorder. Seven years later he introduced and guided through Parliament an "Act for Improving the Police In and Near the Metropolis." This led to the first organized British metropolitan police force. Structured along the lines of a military unit, the force of 1,000 was the first one to wear a definite uniform. The men were commanded by two magistrates, later called commissioners, who were given administrative but not judicial duties. Ultimately, the responsibility for equipping, paying, maintaining, and to a certain degree supervising the "bobbies," as they later became known, was vested in the Home Secretary. Because he was made accountable to the Parliament "for the exercise of his authority over the Metropolitan police, it could (thus) be said that the new force was under the ultimate control of a democratically elected Parliament."[9]

Availability of competent manpower, then as today, became an immediate problem. It was difficult to recruit suitable men to serve in the "new police," for the salaries were poor and the commissioners selective. And there were other harassments. Parliament objected to appropriating government funds to maintain a police force. The radicals were afraid of tyranny. The aristocracy, though willing to accept the protection of such a force, was disgruntled because the commissioners refused to abide by the traditional rules of patronage in making appointments.

Nevertheless, the London metropolitan police proved so effective in suppressing crime and apprehending criminals that within five years the provinces, which were experiencing increasing crime problems and violent riots, asked London for policing help.[10] Shortly after, Parliament enacted a series of police reform bills. Among them, one empowered justices of the peace in 1839 to establish police forces in the counties; and in 1856 another required every borough and county to have a police force.

As regular police forces developed, the justices of the peace voluntarily relinquished their law enforcement duties and confined themselves to deciding questions of law. Before this change occurred, the police had served as the agents of the powerful justices and had consequently used the justices' authority to carry on investigation of those in custody. When the justices relinquished their law enforcement powers, the legislature gave no consideration as to what, if any, investigative responsibilities should be transferred to the police. As a result, the statutes for law enforcement officers that remain on the books today contain little recognition of the broad discretion that police continue to exercise.[11]

## Law Enforcement in the American Colonies

American colonists in the seventeenth and eighteenth centuries naturally brought to America the law enforcement structure with which they were familiar in England. The transfer of the offices of constable and sheriff to rural American areas—which included most colonial territory—was accomplished with little change in structure of the offices. Drawing upon the pattern of the mutual pledge system, the constable was made responsible for law enforcement in towns, while the sheriff took charge of policing the counties. The crown-appointed governors bestowed these offices on large land-owners who were loyal to the king. After the revolution, sheriffs and constables tended to be selected by popular elections, patronage then being on the wane.

In many colonial cities the colonists adopted the British constabulary-nightwatch system. As early as 1636 Boston had nightwatchmen, in addition to a military guard. New York and Philadelphia soon developed a similar nightwatch system. The New York nightwatchmen were known as the "rattlewatch," because they carried rattles on their rounds to remind those who needed reminding of their watchful presense.

## Urbanization in the United States

As American towns grew in size and population during the first half of the nineteenth century, the constable was unable to cope with the increasing disorder. As in England years before, lawlessness became more prevalent.[12]

*New York City was alleged to be the most crime-ridden city in the world, with Philadelphia, Baltimore and Cincinnati not far behind. . . . Gangs of youthful rowdies in the larger cities . . . threatened to destroy the American reputation for respect for law. . . . Before their boisterous demonstrations the crude police forces of the day were often helpless.*

Again, as in England, many American cities began to develop organized metropolitan police forces of their own. Philadelphia was one of the first. In 1833 a wealthy philanthropist left a will that provided for the financing of a competent police force in Philadelphia. Stimulated by this contribution, the city government passed an ordinance providing for a 24-man police force to work by day and 120 night-watchmen. The force was unfortunately shortlived, for the ordinance was repealed less than 2 years later.

In 1838, Boston created a day police force to supplement the nightwatch, and other cities soon followed its lead. Crime, cities were finding, was no respecter of daylight. There were certain inherent difficulties, however, in these early two-shift police systems. Keen rivalries existed between the day and night shifts, and separate administrations supervised each shift. Recognizing the evils of separate police forces, the New York Legislature passed a law in 1844 that authorized creating the first unified day and night police, thus abolishing its nightwatch system. Ten years later Boston consolidated its nightwatch with the day police.

Following the New York model, other cities developed their own unified police forces during the next decade. By the 1870s the nation's largest cities had full-time police forces. And by the early 1900s there were few cities of consequence without such unified forces. These forces gradually came under the control of a chief or commissioner, often appointed by the mayor, sometimes with the consent of the city council and sometimes elected by the people.

These first formal police forces in American cities were faced with many of the problems that police continue to confront today. Police officers became the objects of disrespect. The need for larger staffs required the police to compromise personnel standards in order to fill the ranks. And police salaries were among the lowest in local government service, a factor which precluded attracting sufficient numbers of high standard candidates. It is small wonder that the police were not respected, were not notably successful, and were not known for their vitality and progressiveness. Moreover, the police mission in the mid-1800s precluded any brilliance.[13]

*The aim of the police departments was merely to keep everything quiet that (was) likely to arouse public (ire).*

Many of the problems that troubled these first organized metropolitan police forces can perhaps be traced to a single root—political control. As one authority has explained:[14]

*Rotation in office enjoyed so much popular favor that police posts of both high and low degree were constantly changing hands, with political fixers determining the price and conditions of each change . . . The whole police question simply churned about in the public mind and eventually became identified with the corruption and degradation of the city politics and local governments of the period.*

In an attempt to alleviate these problems, responsible leaders created police administrative boards to replace the control exercised over police affairs by mayors or city councils. These boards were given the responsibility of appointing police administrators and managing police affairs. Unfortunately, this attempt to cure political meddling was unsuccessful perhaps because the judges, lawyers, and local businessmen who comprised the administrative boards were inexpert in dealing with the broad problems of the police.

Another attempt was made at police reform during the close of the nineteenth century. Noting that poor policing tended to occur mainly in urban areas, the State legislatures, which were dominated by rural legislators, required that police administrators be appointed by authority of the state. Thus state control became an alternative to local control of law enforcement. This move brought little success, for many problems had not been anticipated:[15]

*For one thing, the theory of state control . . . was not uniformly applied. It was primarily directed at the larger cities, by legislatures seeking to (perpetuate) rural domination in public affairs.*

In spite of increased state control, the large city continued to pay for its police service, and police costs rose. One reason was that police boards were not even indirectly responsible to the local taxpaying public which they served. In cases where the state and city governments were not allied politically, friction increased. It increased further when the state-appointed administrator instituted policy out of harmony with the views of the majority of the city population. It was not until the first decades of the twentieth century that cities regained control of police forces in all but a few cases.[16]

After these sincere attempts at reform during the last half of the nineteenth century, police forces grew in size and expanded in function. However, there was very little analysis of the changes in society that made expansion necessary, nor of the effect such changes would work upon the role of the police. Civil service proved helpful, spreading to local police agencies and alleviating some of the more serious problems of political interference. The concept of merit employment, which some reformers had been proposing, was embraced by some forces.

One of the most notable police advancements of the 1900s was the advent of police training schools, even though on a somewhat modest basis. In the early 1900s the new policeman learned chiefly in the school of experience:[17]

*Thus, for the most part the average American city depends almost entirely for the training of its police recruits upon such casual instruction as older officials may be able and willing to give.*

In numerous areas, however, it was not until the 1940s and notably in the 1950s that police departments established and, in many cases, greatly expanded their recruit training programs.

### State and Federal Law Enforcement Agencies

Although a state police force, known as the "Texas Rangers," was organized in 1835 to supplement Texas' military forces, modern state police organizations did not emerge until the turn of the century. In 1905, the Governor of Pennsylvania, in the absence of an effective sheriff-constable system, created the first state force. Its initial purpose was to cope with a public dispute between labor and management. Soon such continuing factors as the inadequacy of local policing by constables and sheriffs and the inability or unwillingness of city police forces to pursue lawbreakers beyond their jurisdictional limits convinced state legislatures of the need for state-wide police forces.[18]

The majority of state departments were established shortly after World War I to deal with the increasing problem of auto traffic and the accompanying wave of car thefts. Today all states except Hawaii have some form of state law enforcement body. While some state agencies are restricted to the functions of enforcing traffic laws and protecting life and property on the highways, others have been given general policing authority in criminal matters throughout the state.

The role of the federal government in law enforcement has developed in a sporadic and highly specialized manner. Federal law enforcement actually started in 1789, when the Revenue Cutter Service was established to help prevent smuggling. In 1836, Congress authorized the Postmaster General to pay salaries to agents who would investigate infringements involving postal matters. Among the more important law enforcement responsibilities later recognized by Congress were internal revenue investigation and narcotics control. Congress authorized a force of 25 detectives in 1868 and increased the number in 1915. In 1924, J. Edgar Hoover organized the Federal Bureau of Investigation in the Justice Department.[19]

With the expansion of interstate movement of people and goods, and federal involvement in all aspects of life, the responsibilities of federal agencies have increased significantly within the last few years. These federal agencies are responsible to departments of the national government. For example, the Treasury Department's Secret Service charged with the protection of the President and with investigating counterfeiting and forgery of federal documents. Civilian departmental agencies, with the sole exception of the FBI, function under civil service regulations.[20]

The manpower and jurisdiction of the FBI have increased greatly since its establishment. Some of the statutes that have been responsible for this expansion are the National Stolen Property Act, the Federal Kidnapping Act, the Hobbs Act (extortion), the Fugitive Felon Act, the White Slave Act, the National Bank Robbery Act, federal interstate gambling laws, and the Dyer Act. The last brings within the FBI's jurisdiction automobiles stolen and taken across the border of a state. Recent passage of strong federal legislation has enhanced the FBI's role in the enforcement of civil rights.

## Modernization

Serious study of police reform in America began in 1919. The problems exposed then and those faced by police agencies today are similar in many respects. For example, in 1931 the Wickersham Commission noted that the average police chief's term of office was too short, and that his responsibility to political officials made his position insecure. The Commission also felt that there was a lack of competent, efficient, and honest patrolmen. It said that no intensive effort was being made to educate, train, and discipline prospective officers, or to eliminate those shown to be incompetent. The Wickersham Commission found that with perhaps two exceptions, police forces in cities above 300,000 population had neither an adequate communications system nor the equipment necessary to enforce the law effectively. It said that the police task was made much more difficult by the excessively rapid growth of our cities in the past half century, and by the tendency of different ethnic groups to retain their language and customs in large cities. Finally, the Commission said there were too many duties cast upon each officer and patrolman.[21] The Missouri Crime Commission reported that in a typical American city the police were expected to be familiar with and enforce 30,000 federal, state, or local enactments![22]

Despite the complexity of these problems, many hopeful improvements have occurred in the past few decades. Some cities, counties, and states have taken great strides in streamlining their operations through reorganization and increased use of technology and the use of modern techniques to detect and apprehend criminal offenders. Others are on the threshold of modernization. But many departments remain static. And it is these that obviously constitute a burden on the machinery of justice, and are detrimental to the process of achieving a truly professional police service.

LOCAL, STATE, AND FEDERAL LAW ENFORCEMENT AGENCIES

The President's Commission on Law Enforcement and the Administration of Justice estimated that around 40,000 independent law enforcement agencies exist in the United States though the true figure is probably only about 20,000.[23] The majority are local law enforcement agencies situated within the county, city, town, or village level of jurisdiction. In addition, about 200 state level and 50 federal police agencies are in existence. In total, the FBI estimates that these agencies employ over 400,000 full-time law enforcement personnel, or about 2 per 1000 people. In this section, the organization and duties of some representative examples of these diverse police agencies are discussed.

### Metropolitan Police

City police comprise the majority of the nation's authorized law enforcement personnel. Metropolitan police departments range in size from the New York City police department with its 30,000 employees, and the Los Angeles police department with 10,000, to police departments in Harpersville, Alabama and Hastings, Florida which each maintain a staff of one police officer.[24]

Regardless of how large or small an individual metropolitan police department is, almost all such departments perform the same standard set of functions and tasks and provide similar services to the community. These include the apprehension and conviction of law violators, the arbitration of neighborhood and family disputes, patroling the area, the enforcement of traffic laws, and the recovery of stolen property, among other duties. Municipal police departments also provide such personal services as giving directions and tourist information, providing crowd control at public events, and issuing licenses and permits. Larger police departments often maintain specialized services such as vice control divisions, detective bureaus, juvenile squads, and tactical patrol forces. These will be discussed in more detail in a later section.

While many municipal police departments maintain jurisdiction over law enforcement matters in their home districts, they are often assisted by a number of local auxiliary agencies. The Boston police department is a good example of this type of arrangement. In addition to maintaining the normal compliment of internal bureaus, agencies, and services, the department is aided in the municipal police role by a number of independent agencies. The Capitol police, a force of 75 officers, have special police powers and are charged with protecting the grounds and persons of the Massachusetts state government on Capitol Hill in Boston. This group is similar to the White House police and other police agencies around the country.

The transit system in Boston is policed by its own force of more than 60 full-time officers. Similar to various railroad police agencies and the New York City Transit Authority force, the Massachusetts Bay Transit Authority (MBTA) police have special police powers which allow them to provide services at stations and along the railway.

The parks, beaches, and parkways in the city of Boston and its environs are patrolled by the Metropolitan District Commission (MDC) police, whose duties are similar to those of city park police in New York, Washington, D.C. and other cities. The MDC is responsible for protecting persons visiting public park facilities, maintaining public property, and overseeing private businesses and homes in the vicinity of the parks.

The Boston police are also assisted by the Massachusetts state police in carrying out traffic duties on expressways and state roads leading into and out of the city. Finally, colleges and universities in the area maintain private police forces which patrol and supervise activities at local institutions and have the power of arrest.

These are only a few examples of the multiplicity of police agencies which exist today in some of the larger urban areas around the country. Often, jurisdictional dilemmas arise between these agencies, and information and duties which should rightfully be shared among them are not. Whether unification of smaller police agencies into "super-agencies" would improve services is an often debated topic among police experts. Smaller municipal agencies can provide important specialized services which might have to be relinquished were these agencies combined and incorporated into larger departments.

### County Law Enforcement

The county police department is an independent agency whose senior officer, the sheriff, is usually an elected political official. The county sheriff's role has evolved from that of the early English Sheriff, whose main duty was to assist the royal judges in trying prisoners and enforcing sentences. During the time of America's westward expansion and until municipal departments were developed, the sheriff often acted as the sole legal authority over vast territories.

The duties of a county sheriff's department vary according to the size and degree of development of the county in which it is located. Officials within the department may serve as coroners, tax assessors, tax collectors, overseers of highways and bridges, custodians of the county treasury, keepers of the county jail, court attendants, and executors of criminal and civil processes; in years past, the sheriffs' offices also conducted executions. However, many of the Sheriff's law enforcement functions today are restricted to incorporate areas within a county and are called upon only when city department requests aid in such matters as patrol or investigation.

In the past, the sheriff's salaries were almost always based upon the fees they received for the performance of official acts. They received fees for every summons, warrant, subpoena, writ, or other process they served; they were also compensated for summoning juries or locking prisoners in cells.[25] Today, many sheriffs are salaried in order to avoid conflict of interest charges.

The sheriff's office is also usually assigned the task of caring for and feeding local prisoners. The pay scale for these services is fixed by statute or local ordinance, although a sheriff may be allowed to keep money left over from providing such services. This practice has encouraged some sheriffs to sell special articles of food, tobacco, and other luxury items to prisoners in order to supplement their own incomes.

Probably the most extensive sheriff's department is located in Los Angeles county. This department provides services to over one million people and has service contracts with thirty-two cities.[26] It maintains a modern communication system, and a police laboratory as well as performing standard enforcement functions.

## State Police

Police departments organized on state levels are found today in all states except Hawaii. Unlike municipal police departments which developed through historical necessity, state police were legislatively created to deal with the growing incidence of crime in nonurban areas, a consequence of the increase in population mobility and the advent of personalized mass transportation in the form of the automobile. County sheriffs—elected officials with occasionally corrupt or questionable motives—had proven to be ineffective in dealing with the wide-ranging criminal activities which developed during the latter half of the nineteenth century. In addition, most local police agencies were unable to effectively prevent criminal activity engaged in by highly mobile lawbreakers who randomly struck at cities and towns throughout a state. In response to citizens' demands for effective and efficient law enforcement, state governors began to develop plans for police agencies which would be responsible to the state instead of being tied to local politics and corruption.

The Texas Rangers, created in 1835, were one of the first state police agencies to be formed. Essentially a military outfit which patrolled the Mexican border, they were followed by the Massachusetts state constables in 1865 and the Arizona Rangers in 1901.[27]

Today, most state police agencies have the same general police powers as do municipal police, and are territorially limited in their exercise of law enforcement regulations only by the state's boundaries. In some jurisdictions, state police are also given special police powers. New York, Pennsylvania, and West Virginia employ their state police as fire, fish, and game wardens. In Michigan, state police may be required to execute civil process in actions to which the state is a party, while in Connecticut and Pennsylvania they conduct road tests for those desiring motor vehicle licenses.

Other states have formed statewide agencies for the primary purpose of highway patrol and traffic law enforcement. Some state police, such as those in California, specialize in the protection of the motorist and direct most of their attention to the enforcement of traffic laws.

Most state police organizations are restricted by legislation from becoming involved in the enforcement of certain areas of the law. In Connecticut, Pennsylvania, New York, and New Hampshire, for example, state police are prohibited from entering incorporated areas to suppress riots or civil disorders except when directed by the governor, or by a mayor with the governor's approval. In some states, such as Massachusetts and Mississippi, state police are prohibited from becoming involved in strikes or other labor disputes unless violence erupts.

Today, according to the Uniform Crime Report, there are over 45,000 full-time state police officers. These men and women are not only involved in law enforcement and highway safety, but also carry out a variety of multiservice functions for local police agencies. In Iowa, for example, state police maintain a training academy for both state and municipal law enforcement officers. A crime laboratory helps local departments in investigating crime scenes and analyzing evidence. The Iowa state police also provide special services and technical expertise in such areas as bomb site analysis and homicide investigation. Other state police departments, such as California's, are involved in highly sophisticated traffic and highway safety programs, including the use of helicopters for patrol and rescue, the testing of safety devices for cars, and the conducting of postmortem examinations to determine the causes of fatal accidents.

## Federal Law Enforcement Agencies

The federal government has within its jurisdiction a number of law enforcement agencies designed to protect the rights and privileges of U.S. citizens; no single agency has unlimited jurisdiction, and each has been purposefully created to enforce specific laws and cope with particular situations. Federal police agencies have no particular rank order or hierarchy of command or responsibility, and each reports to the specific department or bureau to which it is responsible. The most important of these include the following:

*The Department of Justice.* The Department of Justice is the legal arm of the United States Government. Headed by the Attorney General, it is empowered to (1) enforce all Federal laws, (2) represent the United States when it is party to court action, and (3) conduct independent investigations through its law enforcement services. The branches and responsibilities of the Department of Justice are included below:

*Legal Divisions.* The department maintains several separate bureaus which are responsible for enforcing federal laws and protecting United States citizens. The *Civil Rights Division* proceeds legally against violations of federal civil rights laws which protect citizens from discrimination on the basis of their race, creed, ethnic background, or sex. Areas of greatest concern include discrimination in education (e.g., the bussing controversy), fair housing laws and job discrimination, including affirmative action cases. The *Tax Division* brings legal actions against tax violators. The *Criminal Division* prosecutes violations of the Federal Criminal Code. Their responsibility includes enforcing statutes relating to bank robbery (since bank deposits are federally insured), kidnapping, mail fraud, interstate transportation of stolen vehicles, narcotics and drug trafficking, and so on.

The Justice Department also contains the Law Enforcement Assistance Administration whose function was described in Chapter 4. In addition, the Justice Department maintains administrative control over a number of independent investigative and enforcement branches which are described below:

*The Federal Bureau of Investigation (FBI).* In 1870, the U.S. Department of Justice became involved in actual policing when the Attorney General hired investigators to enforce the Mann Act (White Slavery). These investigators were formalized in 1908 into a distinct branch of the government, the Bureau of Investigation; in the 1930s, the agency was reorganized into the Federal Bureau of Investigation (FBI) under the direction of J. Edgar Hoover.

Today's FBI is not a police agency but an investigative one, with jurisdiction over all matters in which the United States is, or may be, an interested party. It limits its jurisdiction, however, to federal laws including all federal statutes not specifically assigned to other agencies.[28] These include: espionage, sabotage, treason, civil rights violations, the murder and assault of federal officers, mail fraud, robbery and burglary of federally insured (FDIC) banks, kidnapping, interstate transportation of stolen vehicles and property.

The FBI has probably been our most glamorous and widely publicized law enforcement agency. In the 1920s and 1930s they pursued gangsters such as Dillinger, Mad Dog Coll, Bonnie and Clyde, Machine-Gun Kelly, and Pretty Boy Floyd. During World War II they hunted Nazi agents and prevented any major sabotage from occurring on American military bases. After the war they conducted a crusade against Russian KGB agents and investigated organized crime figures. They have been instrumental in cracking tough criminal cases, which brings the FBI enormous public respect. For example, when heiress Barbara Jane Mackle was kidnapped and buried in an underground chamber with a temporary supply of air and water, it was the FBI who cracked the case before the kidnappers' demands were met or the woman was left to die.

The FBI offers a number of important services to local law enforcement agencies. Their identification division, established in 1924, collects and maintains a vast fingerprint file which can be used for identification purposes by local police agencies. Their sophisticated crime laboratory, established in 1932, aids local police in testing and identifying evidence such as hairs, fibers, blood, tire tracks, and drugs. The Uniform Crime Reports is another service of the FBI. As discussed in Chapter 1, the UCR has been an annual compilation which includes crimes reported to local police agencies, arrests, police killed or wounded in action, and other information. Finally, The National Crime Information Center (NCIC) is a computerized network linked to local police departments by terminals. Information on stolen vehicles, wanted persons, stolen guns, and so on is made readily available to local law enforcement agencies.

*Drug Enforcement Administration (DEA).* Government interest in drug trafficking can be traced back to 1914 when the Harrison Act established Federal jurisdiction over the supply and use of narcotics. A number of drug enforcement units, including the Bureau of Narcotics and Dangerous Drugs, were originally charged with enforcing drug laws. However, in 1973, these agencies were combined to form the Drug Enforcement Administration (DEA). Agents of the DEA assist local and state authorities in their investigation of illegal drug use, and carry out independent surveillance and enforcement activities to control the importation of narcotics.

For example, DEA agents will work with foreign governments in cooperative efforts aimed at destroying opium and marijuana crops at their source—hard-to-find fields tucked away in the interiors of Latin America, Asia, Europe, and Africa. Undercover DEA agents will infiltrate drug rings and simulate narcotics buying in order to arrest drug dealers.

The DEA maintains regional laboratories which are essential to testing seized drugs so that accurate records and measures can be presented at the trial of drug offenders. The DEA also has an Office of Intelligence which coordinates information and enforcement activities with local, state, and foreign governments.

*Other Department of Justice Agencies.* Other federal law enforcement agencies under the direction of the Justice Department include: the U.S. Marshals, the Immigration and Naturalization Service, and the Organized Crime and Racketeering Unit. The U.S. Marshals are court officers who help implement federal court rulings, transport prisoners, and enforce court orders. The Immigration and Naturalization Service is responsible for administration, exclusion, and deportation of illegal aliens and the naturalization of aliens lawfully present in the United States. This service also maintains border patrols to prevent illegal aliens from entering the United States. The Organized Crime and Racketeering Unit, under the direction of the U.S. Attorney General, has coordinated federal efforts to curtail organized crime and to contain members of the (alleged) national criminal syndicate.[29]

**Treasury Department.** The Treasury Department maintains the following enforcement branches:

*Alcohol, Tobacco, Firearms Bureau (ATF)\*.* Tucked away in the hill country of Alabama, moonshiners are preparing their famous home brew for sale to anxious patrons. Suddenly, federal agents swoop down, confiscating

---

\*Adapted from Bureau Publications, 1979.

the still and arresting the culprits. Though glamorized in films such as Burt Reynolds' "White Lightnin'," the unlicensed manufacture of liquor is illegal. Stopping this illicit manufacture of alcohol is the work of the Alcohol, Tobacco and Firearms division of the Treasury Department.

ATF concentrates its anticrime efforts on preventing and investigating the criminal misuse of firearms, ammunition and explosives. Special agents are the backbone of ATF's Office of Criminal Enforcement which deals with violations of the Gun Control Act of 1968 and other federal firearms laws. The goal is to keep firearms out of the hands of criminals.

Since 1863, special agents traditionally have uncovered and destroyed illegal whiskey distilleries. The work of these ATF "Revenooers" has contributed to a significant decrease in moonshining.

Through the Gun Control Act of 1968 and the Organized Crime Control Act of 1970, ATF has jurisdiction in several types of explosives crimes. ATF investigates about 70% of all explosives incidents reported to it.

ATF assists any state and local law enforcement agency upon request. This assistance ranges from joint criminal investigations to training classes concerning firearms, explosives, and police methods. State and local law enforcement agencies throughout the United States use ATF services to help solve many crimes. ATF provides operations, technical, and scientific assistance.

ATF is the central agency for all gun tracing. Approximately half of all ATF gun traces are for local law enforcement agencies. The ATF tracer tracks the gun from manufacturer to the first retail purchaser. The .44 caliber "Bulldog" revolver used in "Son-of-Sam" murders in New York was traced in minutes from the manufacturer to the man who purchased it from a pawnshop in Houston, Texas.

ATF lab scientists were pioneers in many forensic techniques—ink analysis, atomic absorption, and neutron activation analysis to detect gunshot residue and other important evidence.


*Other Department of the Treasury Enforcement Agencies.* The Internal Revenue Service, established in 1862, enforces violations of income, excise, stamp, and other tax laws. Their Intelligence Division actively pursues gamblers, narcotics dealers, and other violators who do not report their illegal financial gains as taxable income. For example, the career of Scarface Al Capone, the famous 1920s gangster, was brought to an end by the efforts of IRS agents.

The Customs Bureau guards points of entry into the United States and prevents smuggling of contraband into (or out of) the country. They insure that taxes and tariffs are paid on imported goods and help control the flow of narcotics into the country.

The Secret Service is an arm of the U.S. Treasury Department and was originally charged with enforcing laws against counterfeiting. Today, of course, the Secret Service is also accountable for the protection of the President and the Vice President and their families, presidential candidates, and former presidents. The Secret Service maintains the White

House Police Force, which is responsible for the protection of the executive mansion, and the Treasury Guard, which protects the mint.

*Other Federal Law Enforcement Agencies.* Many other special law enforcement agencies exist within federal jurisdiction. Post Office Inspectors investigate and enforce postal laws and regulations. Their efforts are directed at schemes to defraud, extortion cases, mail losses through robbery and thefts, and related offenses. The Department of the Interior has four units charged with the investigation and enforcement of federal laws: the Fish and Wildlife Service enforces laws involving migratory game birds, fish and wildlife restoration acts, and agreements of interstate transportation of wildlife; the Bureau of Indian Affairs maintains order on Indian reservations and suppresses illegal liquor and drug traffic in these areas; the Bureau of Mines investigates and enforces regulations concerning mine accidents, explosions, and fires; and the National Park Service maintains a staff of park rangers who perform police services in the national parks.

In addition, the Department of Health and Welfare maintains quasi-police agencies for enforcement in areas such as purity and standards of food, drugs, and cosmetics, and standard labeling laws. The Department of Agriculture enforces more than fifty laws that protect the farmer and the consumer. It is also responsible for setting national standards for weights and measures in cooperation with local and state agencies.[30] Finally, the U.S. Coast Guard operates as a division of the Department of Transportation. The Coast Guard enforces or assists in the curtailment of criminal activity on the sea and the importation of illegal aliens and contraband.

Most American municipal police departments are independent agencies, operating without specific administrative control from any higher governmental authority. On occasion, police agencies will cooperate and participate in mutually beneficial enterprises, such as sharing information on known criminals, or they may help federal agencies engage in interstate or intrastate criminal investigations. These cooperative efforts aside, police departments tend to be functionally independent organizations having unique sets of rules, policies, procedures, norms, budgets, and so on.

Most larger urban police agencies are organized in a military-like, hierarchical manner as illustrated in Figure 6.1.

Within this organizational model, the senior decision-makers—the chief and the deputies—are functionally removed from the bulk of their subordinates; personnel decision making and interagency feedback tend to be stifled rather than fortified. In addition, each element of the department normally has its own chain of command. For example, in a large municipal department, the Detective Bureau might have a captain as director of a particular division (e.g., homicide) while a lieutenant oversees individual cases and acts as liaison with other police agencies, and sergeants and inspectors carry out the actual field work. Smaller departments

THE
ORGANIZATION
AND FUNCTION
OF MUNICIPAL
POLICE

FIGURE 7.1.
Organization of a
Metropolitan Police
Department*

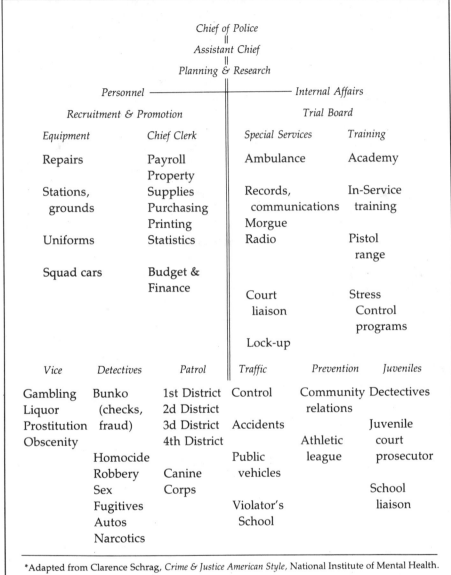

*Adapted from Clarence Schrag, *Crime & Justice American Style*, National Institute of Mental Health.

may have a captain as head of all detectives while lieutenants supervise individual subsystems (e.g., robbery or homicide). Many departments also follow a military-like system in promoting personnel within the ranks; at an appropriate time a promotion test may be given and, based on scores and other recommendations, an officer may be advanced in rank. This organizational style frustrates many police officers from futhering their education, since a college or advanced degree may have little direct impact on their promotion or responsibilities. Furthermore, some otherwise competent police officers are unable to increase their rank due to their inability to take tests.

A number of additional problems are associated with the typical police department's organizational structure. First, the overlapping assignments between the top administrators (chief and assistant or deputy chief) make it difficult for citizens to determine who is actually responsible for the department's policies and operations. Second, the large number of operating divisions and the lack of any clear relationship among them almost guarantees that the decision-making practices of one branch will be unknown to another; two divisions may actually unknowingly compete with each other over jurisdiction on a particular case. Even where cooperation is assured, the absence of a close working relationship between the various divisions of a department often causes inefficiency in the allocation and use of resources.[31]

The organizational structure of most municipal police agencies also makes it difficult for community leaders or other concerned individuals to monitor police activities. Avenues for internal investigations are restricted, and public complaints or community involvement is directed away from the individuals with whom the public is most often in direct contact—e.g., detectives or patrol officers.

### Police Function and Services

As Figure 6.1 indicates, large metropolitan police departments carry out a wide variety of tasks, and maintain a number of highly specialized units. Below the most important of these are discussed in some detail.

*Patrol Functions. It's 8 A.M., and officers Bill O'Connel and Gene Simmons begin their routine patrol over a three-mile area in downtown Eastern City. On the way to their first stop, a store whose owner has filed a complaint about loitering youths, they spot a man running down an alley with a woman's purse tucked under his arm. Hearing screams, they stop their cruiser; O'Connel pursues the fleeing suspect, while Simmons calls for back-up from the station, then goes to find the possible victim. Moments later, suspect in hand, they conduct a field identification in which the victim positively "ID's" the suspected purse snatcher. When other patrol cars arrive, they turn over their prisoner to a second team of officers and proceed to the store beseiged by loitering teens.*

So begins the day of many metropolitan patrol officers.

Patrol officers are the backbone of the police department. In fact, they are the most highly visible components of the entire criminal justice system. They are charged with patrolling specific areas of their jurisdiction, called "beats," on foot, in a patrol car, or by motorcycle, horse, helicopter, or even boat. Each beat has different shifts so that the area is covered 24 hours a day. The major purpose of patrol is to (1) deter crime by maintaining a visible police presence, (2) maintain public order (order maintenance or "peace keeping") within the patrol area and (3) enable the police department to respond quickly to law violations or other emergencies.

Patrol officers' responsibilities are immense: they may suddenly be faced with an angry mob, an armed felon, or a suicidal teenager, and be forced to make split-second decisions on what action to take. At the same time, they must be sensitive to the needs of citizens living in their jurisdiction who are often of diverse racial and ethnic backgrounds.

The basic duties of the patrol officer are quite varied. Some of these have been described by the American Bar Association:

*Major Current Responsibilities of Police.* In assessing appropriate objectives and priorities for police service, local communities should initially recognize that most police agencies are currently given responsibility, by design or default:

(i) to identify criminal offenders and criminal activity and, where appropriate, to apprehend offenders and participate in subsequent court proceedings;

(ii) to reduce the opportunities for the commission of some crimes through preventive patrol and other measures;

(iii) to aid individuals who are in danger of physical harm;

(iv) to protect constitutional guarantees;

(v) to facilitate the movement of people and vehicles;

(vi) to assist those who cannot care for themselves;

(vii) to resolve conflict;

(viii) to identify problems that are potentially serious law enforcement or governmental problems;

(ix) to create and maintain a feeling of security in the community;

(x) to promote and preserve civil order; and

(xi) to provide other services on an emergency basis.[32]

When patrol officers take inappropriate action, or if their behavior results in violence or death, they are subject to intense scrutiny by public agencies and may be subject to disciplinary measures from the police departments' Internal Affairs Division. Thus, patrol officers are expected to make mature and reasoned decisions while facing a constant flow of people in emotional crises.

A patrol officer's job is therefore extremely demanding and often unrewarding and unappreciated. It is not surprising that the attitudes of police officers toward the public have been characterized by ambivalence, cynicism, and tension.[33]

The consequent development of a negativistic "police personality" and its influence on patrol work will be discussed in the following chapter.

*Effectiveness of Patrol.* For many years, preventive police patrol has been considered one of the greatest deterrents of criminal behavior. The visible presence of patrol cars on the street and the rapid deployment of police officers to the scene of a crime were viewed as a particularly effective law enforcement technique. However, recent research efforts have questioned the basic assumptions. The most widely heralded attempt at measuring patrol effectiveness was undertaken in Kansas City, Missouri under sponsorship of the Police Foundation.[34]

To evaluate the effectiveness of patrol, 15 independent police beats or districts were divided into three groups: one group retained normal police patrol; the second ("proactive") set of districts were supplied with two to three times the normal amount of patrol forces; the third ("reactive") group had its preventive patrol entirely eliminated and police officers responded only when summoned by citizens to the scene of a particular crime.

Surprisingly, data from the Kansas City study indicated that these variations in patrol techniques had little effect on the crime patterns in the 15 separate locales. The presence or absence of patrol did not seem to affect residential or business burglaries, auto thefts, larcenies involving auto accessories, robberies, vandalism, or other criminal behavior.[35]

Moreover, variations in police patrol techniques appeared to have little effect on citizen attitudes toward the police, their satisfaction with police, or their fear of future criminal behavior.[36]

It is difficult to assess the implications of the Kansas City Project since it was carried out in a single police jurisdiction under a controlled set of circumstances. However, as police experts Robert Sheehan and Gary Cordner maintain:

These findings, although highly controversial, will undoubtedly spur further research into the effectiveness of police patrol as we know it and could result in a rethinking about the patrol function.[37]

Today, police departments using computer-based technology are constantly searching for ways to make patrol a more effective and reliable deterrent of criminal behavior.[38] Areas of particular concern are response time, the optimum number of police officers who should be on patrol at any one time, and what the duties of patrol officers should be (for example, should they aid citizens engaged in domestic disputes?).

*Investigation Function.* Since the first independent detective bureau was established by the London Metropolitan Police in 1841 [39] criminal investigators have been romantic figures vividly portrayed in novels such as Agatha Christie's Hercule Poirot series, motion pictures including "Madigan" and "Dirty Harry," and television shows such as "Columbo" and "Kojak." The fictional police detective is usually depicted as a loner, willing to break departmental rules, perhaps even violate the law himself (or herself as in the case of the "Policewoman" television series) in order to capture the suspect. The average fictional detective views departmental policies and United States Supreme Court decisions (which guarantee civil liberties to citizens) as unfortunate roadblocks to police efficiency. Civil rights are either ignored or actively scorned.[40]

Though it is likely that there exist in every police department a few "hell-bent for leather" detectives who take matters into their own hands at the expense of citizens' rights, a more accurate picture of the modern criminal investigator is an experienced civil servant, trained in investigatory techniques, knowledgeable about legal rules of evidence and procedure, and who is at least somewhat cautious about the legal and departmental consequences of his or her actions.[41] Though detectives are often handicapped by time, money, and resources,[42] they are certainly aware of how their actions will one day be interpreted in a court of law. Police investigators are therefore more concerned with the most recent court cases regarding search and seizure and in custody interrogation than they are with engaging in "shoot-outs" with suspected felons.[43] Detectives, in fact, are probably the elite of the police force: they are usually paid more than patrol officers, engage in interesting tasks, wear "civilian clothes" and are subject to a less stringent departmental control than patrolmen.[44]

Detectives investigate the causes of crime and attempt to identify the individuals or groups responsible for committing particular offenses. They may enter a case subsequent to an initial contact by patrol officers, as when a patrol car interrupts a crime in progress and the offenders flee before they can be apprehended, they can investigate a case entirely on their own, sometimes by following up on leads provided by informants.

Detective divisions are typically organized into sections or bureaus such as homicide, robbery, or rape. Some jurisdictions maintain morals or vice squads, which are usually staffed by plainclothes officers and/or detectives specializing in victimless crimes such as prostitution or gambling. In this latter capacity, vice squad officers may set themselves up as customers for illicit activities in order to make arrests. For example, undercover detectives may frequent public men's rooms and make advances toward entering men; those who respond are arrested for homosexual soliciting. In other instances, female police officers may pose as prostitutes. These covert police activities have often been criticized as violating the personal rights of citizens, and their appropriateness and fairness have been questioned.

In a recent book, James Q. Wilson described the function of investigation as containing four separate types of action:

In the first, a suspect has been apprehended, or a subject placed under control and there is adequate information about the person's behavior.

In the second case, there is reliable information that a crime has been committed, but the suspect has not been identified, or if identified, not apprehended . . . This is the classic problem of *detection*: to discover reliable information that will permit the identification and arrest of a perpetrator.

In the third case, a suspect or subject may be known or even under continuous observation or control, but there is no reliable or adequate information about this person's past behavior, present connections, or future intentions. . . . This case is to be distinguished from the preceding one by noting that the investigators are not reacting to the fact that a crime has been committed but are hoping to discover a crime that can implicate a targeted individual or his confederates.

The final case involves the absence of both an identified subject and adequate information. Nonetheless, there are reasons, ranging from a hunch to the tips of untested informants to the implications of other investigative reports that "something may be up" or something bears watching.[45]

Within the framework described above, the detective branch maintains discretion over the amount and intensity of effort to put into each case. Recently, a great deal of criticism has been leveled at the nation's detective forces for being "bogged-down" in paperwork and at the same time being relatively inefficient at clearing cases.[46] In 1975, a study conducted by the Rand Corporation of 153 detective bureaus found that a great deal of a detective's time was spent in nonproductive work and that investigative expertise did little to solve cases; the Rand researchers estimated that one half of all detectives could be replaced without negatively influencing crime clearance rates.[47] A number of efforts have been made to revamp investigation procedures. One practice has been for patrol officers to be given greater responsibilities to conduct preliminary investigations at the scene of the crime. In addition, the "old-fashioned" precinct detective is being replaced by specialized units, such as homicide or burglary squads, which operate over larger areas and can bring specific expertise to bear on a particular case.

Another trend has been the development of regional squads of local, state, and federal officers who concentrate on major crimes such as narcotics and organized crime (called Regional Strike Forces) and use their wider jurisdiction and multiple expertise to provide services beyond the capability of a metropolitan police department.[48] Thus, the coming years may witness major changes in the organization and function of detective forces.

*Traffic Function.* Another important public contact police task is traffic control. This involves such activities as intersection control (directing traffic), traffic law enforcement, radar operations, parking law enforcement, and accident investigations.[49]

Traffic control is a complex daily task involving thousands, or even millions of motor vehicles within a single police jurisdiction. Consequently, police departments use *selective enforcement* in their maintenance of traffic laws. Police departments neither expect nor wish to punish all traffic law violators. A department may set up a traffic control unit only at particular intersections, though its traffic coordinators know that many other areas of the city are experiencing violations. Manpower may be allocated to traffic details based on accident or violation expectancy rates, determined by analysis of previous patterns and incidents.

Some officers will use wide discretion when enforcing the traffic laws, allowing many violations to go unchecked or merely issuing violators a warning, while giving citations to others who commit similar violations. Other officers "play it by the book" and sanction by citation or arrest all traffic law violations. Almost every citizen who drives has turned an anxious, sorrowful face to a stern police officer while the latter decides whether to "write them up" or to give them a break. The latter action always seems to elicit feelings that police are really doing a good job and are a fair bunch.

How and why traffic laws are enforced can have a serious effect on the way citizens view police work, and may even influence more important police-citizen contacts, such as reporting crime to police, aiding police in trouble, or stepping forth as witnesses.[50]

*Support Function.* As the model of a typical police department in Figure 6.1 indicates, not all members of a police department engage in what the general public regards as "real police work"—patrol, detection, and traffic control. A large part of police resources is actually devoted to support and administrative functions.

On an administrative and operational level, a large portion of police resources is devoted to the maintenance and control of police services. While there exist too many tasks to mention all in detail, a few of the most important include:

*Personnel.* Many police departments maintain their own personnel service which controls such activities as recruitment of new police recruits, creating police exams to choose the most qualified applicants, design and implementation of promotions and transfers. Later in this chapter we will discuss in more detail the specific problems and issues associated with the rather complex task of creating adequate entrance exams.

*Internal Affairs.* Larger police departments often maintain an internal affairs branch which is charged with "policing the police." Internal affairs officers process citizen complaints of police corruption, investigate what may be the unnecessary use of force by police officers, or even investigate police participation in actual criminal activity, such as burglaries or narcotics violations. In addition, internal affairs bureaus may assist police management personnel when disciplinary action is brought against individual subordinate officers.

Internal affairs is a controversial function since investigators are feared and mistrusted by fellow police officers. Nonetheless, rigorous self-scrutiny is the only way police departments can earn the respect of citizens within their jurisdiction.

*Budget and Finance.* Many police departments take responsibility for the administration and control of departmental budgets and financial management. This task includes payroll, purchasing equipment and services, planning budgets for future expenditures, and auditing departmental financial records.

Smaller police departments have been plagued by the fact that police chiefs and other officers in charge of budgetary considerations often lack the requisite skill to accurately and effectively manage police finances. In recent years police managers seeking to maximize the growth and efficiency of their departments have turned to a Planning-Programming Budgeting System, or PPBS, to improve their financial operations. This new method requires police administrators to identify goals and objectives of their departments and then to achieve these goals by systematically allotting available funding to them.[51] Use of PPBS and similar modern management techniques may significantly improve police operations during the coming decade.

*Records and Communication.* Police departments maintain separate units which are charged with maintaining and disseminating information on wanted offenders, stolen merchandise, traffic violators, and so on. Modern data management systems enable police to use their records in a highly sophisticated fashion. For example, a patrol car which spots a suspicious looking vehicle can instantly receive a computer-based rundown on whether it has been stolen; or if property is recovered during an arrest, police can determine who reported the loss of similar merchandise and arrange for its return.

Another important function of police communication is the effective and efficient dispatching of police patrol cars. Again, modern computer technologies have been used to maximize the benefits of available resources. For example, the computer-assisted "911" emergency number has been instituted in many large cities.[52]

*Training.* In many departments, training is carried out on a continuous basis throughout an officer's career. Training usually begins at a pre-service police academy, which may be run exclusively for single, larger departments or be part of a regional training center servicing smaller and varied governmental units.

After assuming their police duties, new recruits are assigned to field training officers who break them in on the job. However, training does not stop here. On-the-job training is a continuous process in the modern police department and includes such areas as weapons skills, first aid, crowd control, and community relations. Some departments use *roll-call training* in which superior officers or outside experts address police officers at the beginning of the work day. Other departments allow police officers time off to attend annual training sessions to sharpen their skills and learn new policing techniques.

*Stress Training.* One area in which training has been of great help to police is stress reduction. It has been alleged that police undergo tremendous stress, a factor that leads to alcoholism, divorce, depression, and even suicide. As one commentator suggests:

It would be difficult to find an occupation that is subject to more consistent and persistent tension, strain, confrontations and nerve wracking than that of the uniform patrolman.[53]

The results of efforts to study job-related stress and its effects on police performance have led researchers to conclude that stress is one of the most significant problems affecting job performance.[54] "Stressors" influencing police performance include frustration, poor pay, poor supervision, marital strain, fear and danger, and lack of self-confidence.[55]

Today, stress training includes information on diet, biofeedback, relaxation and meditation, and exercise. Keeping this in mind, the Dallas, Texas Police Department has studied the effects of physical fitness on overall officer performance and has subsequently instituted an exercise program and developed fitness standards to insure higher performance levels.[56]

Attacking the stress problem from another perspective, the Kansas City, Missouri Police Department has implemented the Marriage Partner Program, designed to involve police wives in the effort to reduce stress.[57] In Minnesota, the Couple Communications Program works with officers and their wives to identify issues present in their relationship which might produce on-the-job stress.[58]

Thus, stress-control training has begun to make an important contribution to effective police administration.

*Additional Police Services.* In addition to the above-mentioned activities, modern police departments also maintain such varied and comprehensive services as:

*Community Relations.* Police departments provide emergency aid to the ill, counsel youngsters, speak to schools and community agencies on safety and drug abuse, and provide countless other services designed to improve the climate of citizen-police interactions. (The police-community relations issue will be discussed more fully in the following chapter.)

*Crime Prevention.* Larger police departments maintain specialized units which aid citizens to protect themselves from criminal activity. For example, they advise citizens on effective home security techniques or conduct "Project ID" campaigns—engraving valuables with an identifying number so that they can be returned if recovered after a burglary.

*Laboratory.* Police agencies maintain (or have access to) forensic laboratories which enable them to identify substances to be used as evidence, aid in investigations, classify fingerprints, and so on.

*Planning and Research.* Design new programs to increase police efficiency, develop strategies to test program effectiveness. Police planners monitor recent technological developments and institute programs to adapt them to ongoing police services.

✷*Property*. Police handle evidence such as weapons and narcotics seized during investigations; hold stolen property recovered by investigators; maintain prisoners' personal effects, lost property, abandoned or towed motor vehicles; and so on.

↰*Detention*. Police stations maintain detention facilities for the temporary custody of suspects after their arrest.

The operation of a large urban police department is an exceedingly difficult and complex task. Police personnel management has long been an area of special interest and concern; police officials and other law enforcement managers have determinedly sought to improve their departments' abilities to attract qualified candidates, create efficient promotional procedures, and produce effective leaders. While an entire text could be devoted to the subject of police personnel administration and the management of a modern department, this section will focus on only a few of the more important issues in this area.[59]

ISSUES IN
POLICE
ADMINISTRATION

**Police Leadership
Training**

Police departments cannot operate to their fullest potential without effective leadership at all administrative levels. It is evident, however, that the police chief is the individual whose leadership is of greatest importance in most police departments. In the past, police chiefs were charismatic figures who maintained political power and connections. Their control of departmental operations and policies were often absolute and since they directed the appointments of subordinates and advisors, their authority was seldom questioned. Today, the role of police chief is a changing one. Police benevolent organizations and unions are able to exert some control over departmental policy and decision making; in addition, citizens' concern about police behavior has resulted in departmental leadership being more sensitive to the needs of the public.

To improve and promote leadership qualities in chiefs and other police managers, national, state, and local agencies have developed both in-service and pre-service training programs. The FBI provides training at the National Police Academy in Quantico, Virginia. Though this program is primarily intended to teach the fundamentals of police work, it also can prove beneficial by helping trainees to develop the confidence necessary for effective leadership. Other national agencies interested in promoting police leadership are the Law Enforcement Assistance Administration (LEAA) and the International Association of Chiefs of Police (IACP). On a local level, colleges and universities have sponsored training courses in police executive development. One example is the Southern Police Institute at the University of Louisville, which offers a fourteen-week course directed at improving police executive qualities and features classroom sessions, seminars, and small group interaction. On a state level, training academies—some run under the auspices of civil service and others controlled by the state police—provide regular career development sessions for improving police leadership skills.

These leadership training efforts are directed at stressing many qualities including the ability to effectively communicate with subordinates and understand their needs; the ability to organize and manage tasks of great complexity; and the capacity to analyze situations and make intelligent rational decisions. Often, leadership training stresses techniques borrowed from the business world; tomorrow's police executives may be quite similar to their corporate counterparts.

## Recruitment and Selection

Another important area of police personnel management and administration is the recruitment and selection of new police officers. If police departments are to substantially improve their performance, they must be able to attract a qualified body of young men and women whose backgrounds, intelligence, and capabilities give them the potential to be effective law enforcement agents.

In recent years, a number of political and social factors have resulted in better and more effective police recruitment. The depressed labor market and the scarcity of good jobs have made the security of a police career seem particularly inviting; the end of the military draft has increased the pool of eligible candidates; and the growing numbers of criminal justice programs in colleges have attracted a pool of educated young people seeking law enforcement degrees. Equally important has been the development of a competitive salary structure in larger communities which, with the addition of educational pay incentives, have provided patrol officers with annual salaries in the neighborhood of $19,000.

Despite these improved recruiting conditions, police administrators still have difficulty obtaining qualified personnel in certain areas, particuarly in minority recruitment and selection. Police have traditionally been the target of minority resentment and qualified minority candidates have been skeptical of joining an organization resented by their peers; some police admissions tests are believed to effectively screen out minority candidates; height and weight requirements work against certain nationalities; and the minority candidate who may qualify for police work is often sought by other employers who pay higher wages.

As a result, modern police administration has resorted to an active recruitment campaign to lure qualified candidates. One aspect of this campaign has been the creation of minimum educational standards which heighten the attraction of a law enforcement career. As Baker and Danielson have found:

The relatively few police agencies that have adopted educational standards above the high school level have in almost every case been able to attract men and women to law enforcement who otherwise would never have applied.[60]

In addition, police recruiters have adopted campaigns to promote public awareness of the responsiveness and professionalism of their departments, conducted "ride-along" programs, and sent recruiters to college career days.

The most significant changes have taken place in the areas of testing and selecting of minority candidates who have been recruited or who have shown interest in police work. Most police departments employ all or some of the following criteria for selecting interested police candidates: written tests, oral interviews, psychiatric/psychological appraisals, polygraphs, background investigations, biographical data, and medical exams. Many metropolitan police departments place heavy emphasis on written examinations which are created and administered by the departments themselves or by state civil service commissions. In recent years, minority group leaders have charged that these tests are designed in such a fashion as to be discriminatory and biased. Model tests have been created which contain culturally equivalent terms comparable to those found on standardized tests; when administered to groups of black and white police officers, blacks performed better by as much as 30%. Those questioning the validity of written police tests also point to the findings of studies which show that they do not actually predict effective police performance in the field. To find a middleground in the testing controversy, some departments have attempted to gear entrance exams away from the standard IQ—intelligence test format. Experts have created job-related examinations which measure a candidate's ability to take quick and reasonable action in stress situations. The New York State Police, for example, have created a Job Analysis branch with the express purpose of creating job-oriented entrance exams. A sample question of this type might read as follows:

*While on patrol, you find a panicked group of people standing at the shore of a frozen lake, staring helplessly at a youth, 15 feet off shore, who has fallen through the ice. You would:*
*A. Dash across the ice to rescue the boy;*
*B. Radio headquarters for help and wait by lake;*
*C. Try to form a "human chain" to attempt rescue;*
*D. Proceed with patrol since this is not a criminal matter.*

The candidate is then asked to rank the answers according to their accuracy. The "correct" answers in this type of test are determined by analyzing responses made by experienced, qualified police officers.

Another innovative selection technique has been used by the St. Louis (Missouri) Metropolitan Police Department. The test contains sections with items on:

1. Portrait Identification. Candidates are shown 24 portraits before the test booklets are distributed. After the portraits are placed out of view, candidates must choose which one out of a set of four pictures corresponds to one of the portraits they saw.

2. License Plate Identification. Candidates view 30 pairs of license plates and must indicate which are not identical.

3. Name Identification. Candidates view 30 pairs of names and must indicate which are identical.

4. Recall of Details. Candidates are given two minutes to study photographs of auto accidents. After the photographs are placed out of view, candidates must answer questions which test their recall of details.

5. Altered Portrait Identification. Candidates view a series of pictures where the subjects have conventional hairstyles. Applicants are given four pictures of bald subjects and must choose which depicts a person who appeared in the original series.[61]

It is believed that these questions measure the ability to identify suspects, to be able to quickly and accurately recall names, license numbers, and accident scene details.

Other departments have employed both individual or group simulation models. The former tests provide candidates with materials familiar to police agencies (police blotters, logs, memoranda, etc.) and ask them to make mock decisions on the basis of what they have been provided. Group simulation allows candidates to interact with one another in a problem-solving situation. Verbal skills, interpersonal relations, sensitivity, and other qualities can all be assessed using this method.[62]

Another way in which the obstacles presented by written test biases could be overcome would be by lowering the passing grade, allowing many more applicants to pass, and then using oral interviews or other screening mechanisms as the primary selection devices. A department could then encourage or select those candidates bearing desired educational or racial backgrounds in order to meet departmental needs and standards.

Improvement of recruitment and selection procedures has resulted in greater numbers of minorities and women being added to urban police forces. Minority police officers are employed in such specialized tasks as community relations, undercover detective work, and in quelling disturbances in inner-city areas. Women officers are making an important contribution to policing. By serving as plain-clothes officers, they have helped to decoy and capture muggers and rapists. In addition, they are being assigned to rape squads in numerous jurisdictions, where they help victims cope with the trauma produced by their experience.

### Promotion

Most large police departments use somewhat similar techniques for assessing promotional qualities. However, no single method is universally used, nor is there agreement over which method may be superior to the rest. The most commonly used device in most police departments is the written examination. Tests may be devised by local civil service agencies, by experts from the local university, or by consultants to the field. Departments using written tests may promote those individuals who receive the highest scores, or may present the top few candidates to the chief for selection. Often, these tests attempt to evaluate the candidate's familiarity with the components of the job desired; for example, a sergeant's test may contain questions on patrol techniques, supervision, and legal rules.

Some police agencies have developed other methods for determining promotional eligibility; usually, these are used in conjunction with written examinations. For example, a survey conducted by the International Association of Chiefs of Police in 1973 found that 35% of the responding police agencies had seniority requirements for promotion.[63] In about 20%, points toward promotion were granted for length of service, and the same number used seniority to rank candidates. However, no general rule applied to the way in which seniority influences promotion, and it is generally believed to have relatively little effect on the selection process itself.

The IACP survey also found that about 30% of police departments used performance evaluations in their promotional decision making. Approximately 15% allowed points toward promotion on the basis of superior officers' ratings; again, this method did not seem to carry much weight in the larger jurisdictions.

The survey also found that many jurisdictions (35%) used oral interviews, during which a candidate was confronted by a panel of superior officers who attempt to assess that person's suitability for advancement. In some departments, such as Los Angeles, the oral test counts heavily toward promotion.

One of the more controversial promotional criteria has been that of educational achievement. There are many arguments both for and against continuing education for police officers. Those who argue for the granting of education credits suggest that a college-trained supervisory staff is more professional and promotes human understanding, better judgment, and overall sophistication on the part of police officers. Those who argue against the idea maintain that a college degree does little to help a police officer understand the community, other officers, or the general tasks of police work. The IACP found that opponents of education are still in the majority; only 10% of the departments surveyed grant extra credit for education and, where credit is given, it is minimal.

In summary, most departments grant promotions based on a number of criteria, the most important of which is a written test, followed in importance by oral interviews, seniority, and education. Candidates are awarded points on the basis of one or more of these factors, and those who score most highly are promoted.

One of the most important goals of American law enforcement agencies has been to incorporate major technological advances into standard operating procedures.* In recent years, technology has come to mean the use of computers and other complex electronic equipment; in past years, however, police technology was more simple.

**TECHNOLOGY AND POLICE WORK**

---

*Adapted from Law Enforcement Assistance Administration, *Two Hundred Years of American Criminal Justice* (Washington, D.C.: U.S. Government Printing Office, 1976).

The first technological breakthroughs in police operations came in the area of communications. In 1867, the first telegraph police boxes were installed; an officer could turn a key in a box and his location and number would automatically register at headquarters. Some boxes contained special keys to call for the police wagon or for emergency assistance. In some cities, the police gave cooperative citizens keys to police boxes to use in case of emergency.

By 1880, police had begun to replace their telegraph boxes with the newly invented telephone. This latter development had a major impact on police patrol and investigations. Emergency calls could be quickly made, calls for help were more easily responded to, and descriptions of suspects could be telephoned rapidly to all precincts in a city.

After World War I, further technological advancements improved police performance. One major advance was the teletype printer, which transmitted photos of criminals along telegraph wires from one city to another. In 1926 the first radios which were able to receive transmissions from headquarters were installed in police cars in Berkeley, California. By 1935, two-way radios were being installed in patrol cars in many cities.

Additional technological advances were made in the area of transportation. The Detroit police department outfitted some of their patrol officers with bicycles in 1897. By 1913, the motorcycle was being employed by departments in the eastern part of the country. The first police car was used in Akron, Ohio in 1910, and the police wagon became popular in Cincinnati, Ohio in 1912.

Laboratory techniques also improved at the turn of the century. In 1894, a process was developed to enable officers to identify typewriter faces and thus determine the source of letters or notes. In 1910, Albert Gross developed a system to authenticate questioned documents. The Henry System of fingerprint classification was developed by Scotland Yard in 1901 and, over the next decade, became standard in most American jurisdictions. Finally, the polygraph, or lie-detector, was developed by John Larson in 1921 for the Berkeley Police Department.

In recent years, the use of technology in police work has markedly increased, prompted in part by World War II breakthroughs and discoveries and the infusion of federal support into scientific inquiry in the law enforcement field. In no area have these changes been more apparent than in electronic data processing. In 1964, for example, only one city, St. Louis, had a police computer system; by 1968, ten states and fifty cities had state-level criminal justice information systems. One example of computer use is the Police Information Network (PIN), which electronically links the ninety-three independent law enforcement agencies in the San Francisco area in order to share criminal justice information. On a broader jurisdictional level, the FBI implemented the National Crime Information Center (NCIC) in 1967. This sytem makes possible the rapid collection and retrieval of data about persons wanted for crimes anywhere in the 50 states. In all, it is estimated that over 400 criminal justice computerized information systems are operational in the U.S.; of these, 41% serve the needs of police agencies on both local and state levels.

How are the police relating to the increased number of computer-controlled operations? A LEAA survey in 1972 identified 39 different police functions which were significantly aided by computers. These tasks include administrative functions such as personnel and budget management, and operational functions such as keeping track of missing persons, criminal histories, stolen cars, and burglaries. The computer's effect on the area of administration is aptly illustrated by the Tulsa, Oklahoma police department, which estimated that it saved $180,000 during the first year that computers were used by the department in managerial functions.

On the operational level, the computer's benefit can be seen in the Philadelphia police department's development of a computer model that reports the numbers and kinds of crimes committed according to certain classifications: the particular times at which they were committed, the weather conditions, the months of the year, and the neighborhoods. When used with current socioeconomic data on specific neighborhoods (e.g., the percent of the population that is unemployed), this tool can produce highly detailed, historically accurate statistics which can be used to predict the incidence of crime for sections of the city at any given time. Given this information, the police can deploy their forces where they are most needed and predict where increased forces will do the most good at a particular time and location.

Computers are not the only technological advances currently in use. Lightweight two-way radios have been developed to link the patrolling officer to the rest of the force, and armor made of lightweight synthetics has also been developed in hopes of decreasing the number of police on-the-job fatalities.

The fields of biology, chemistry, and physics have also been tapped to provide law enforcement agencies with up-to-date crime lab capabilities. At centers such as Northeastern University's Forensic Science Institute, researchers are developing advanced techniques for identifying the sources of physical evidence such as hair, blood, or other bodily substances. Highly sophisticated tools—including emission spectrographs, microprobes, and radioisotopes—which were originally developed for the natural sciences are now being used in crime labs.

As technology improves, the police may find that courts are more willing to accept scientifically prepared evidence during trial. For example, the development of spectrographic analysis to identify the voice of a criminal making a threat or phoning in an extortionary demand may someday be recognized in courts as admissible evidence. In addition, it is not far-fetched to believe that someday every patrol car will have a direct link-up to a central computer bank and be able to get an instant readout on the record of a suspect or the status of a stopped vehicle. Also feasible is the future advent of computers into such diverse areas as promotion, budgeting, beat assignment, and investigation activity. The future police chief may not want to make a move without first consulting an electronic assistant for advice.

The applications section of this chapter shows how the use of technology to combat crime was implemented in Seattle, Washington.

SUMMARY

Present-day police departments have evolved out of early European and American crime-control forces. Today, most police agencies operate in a military-like fashion; policy generally emanates from the top of the hierarchy, and it is difficult for both police officers and the public to understand or identify the source of orders and directives. Most police officers therefore use a great deal of discretion when making daily on-the-job decisions.

There are many different types of organizations which are involved in law enforcement activities; these agencies are organized on the local, state and federal levels of government. The most visible law enforcement agents, however, are local police departments which conduct patrol, investigative and traffic functions, as well as conducting many different support activities. Police departments have also been concerned with developing proper techniques for training their leaders, recruiting new officers, promoting deserving veterans, and developing technical expertise.

QUESTIONS FOR
DISCUSSION

**1.** Does having many different police organizations help or hinder law enforcement efficiency?

**2.** Should police departments be charged with so many non-law enforcement activities?

**3.** Should police departments select recruits on the basis of written tests? What other mechanism might be used for personnel selection?

**4.** How can the public contribute to the effective management of police behavior?

NOTES

**1.** Daniel Devlin, *Police Procedure, Administration and Organization* (London: Butterworth & Co., 1966), p. 3.

**2.** A. C. Germann, Frank D. Day, and Robert R. J. Gallati, *Introduction to Law Enforcement* (Springfield: Charles C. Thomas, 1966), p. 32.

**3.** Ibid.

**4.** Devlin, *Police Procedure, Administration and Organization*, p. 5.

**5.** Royal Commission on the Police. *Royal Commission on the Police 1962, Final Report* (London: Her Majesty's Stationery Office), p. 12.

**6.** Devlin, *Police Procedure, Administration and Organization*, p. 7.

**7.** Germann, Day, and Gallati, *Introduction to Law Enforcement*, p. 59.

**8.** Devlin, *Police Procedure, Administration and Organization*, p. 10.

**9.** Ibid., p. 16.

**10.** Christopher Hibbert, *The Roots of Evil* (London: Weidenfield and Nicolson, 1963), pp. 125–128.

**11.** Edward J. Barrett, Jr., "Police Practices and the Law—From Arrest to Release or Charge," *California Law Review* 50:17–18 (March 1962).

**12.** Arthur Charles Cole, *The Irrepressible Conflict, 1859–1865*, A History of American Life in 12 Volumes, vol. VIII, Arthur M. Schlesinger, Sr., and Dixon Ryan Fox, ed. (New York: Macmillan, 1934), pp. 154–155.

**13.** Arthur M. Schlesinger, Sr., *The Rise of the City, 1878–1898*. A History of American Life in 12 Volumes, vol. X,

Arthur M. Schlesinger, Sr., and Dixon Ryan Fox, ed. (New York, Macmillan, 1934) p. 115.

**14.** Bruce Smith, Sr., *Police Systems in the United States*, Revised Second Edition (New York: Harper and Bros., 1960), pp. 105–106.

**15.** Ibid., p. 186.

**16.** Ibid., pp. 186–187. State control of urban police continues to exist in certain cities in Missouri, Maryland, Massachusetts, Maine, and New Hampshire.

**17.** Elmer D. Graper, *American Police Administration* (New York: Macmillan, 1921), pp. 109–110.

**18.** Smith, *Police Systems in the United States*, pp. 147–150.

**19.** Germann, Day, and Gallati, *Introduction to Law Enforcement*, pp. 67–68.

**20.** John Coatman, *Police* (London: Oxford University Press, 1959), p. 50.

**21.** National Commission on Law Observance and Enforcement, *Report on the Police* (Washington: U.S. Government Printing Office, 1931), pp. 5–7.

**22.** Preston William Slossom, *The Great Crusade and After, 1914–1929*. A History of American Life in 12 Volumes, vol. XII, Arthur M. Schlesinger, Sr., and Dixon Ryan Fox, ed. (New York: Macmillan, 1931), p. 102.

**23.** The President's Commission on Law Enforcement and the Administration of Justice, *Task Force Report: The Police* (Washington, D.C.: U.S. Government Printing Office, 1967), pp. 1–9; the information in the following sections is derived from a number of sources, with special emphasis on Thomas Adams, *Law Enforcement* (Englewood Cliffs, New Jersey: Prentice-Hall, 1968); A. C. Germann, et al., *Introduction to Law Enforcement and Criminal Justice* (Springfield, Ill.: Charles C. Thomas, 1968) pp. 64–72, 135–155; Bruce Smith, *Police Systems in the United States* (New York: Harper & Row, 1960), pp. 66–81; John Sullivan,

*Introduction to Police Science* (New York: McGraw-Hill Book Co., 1968), pp. 17–38.

**24.** A. C. Germann, et. al., *Introduction to Law Enforcement and Criminal Justice*, p. 126.

**25.** Bruce Smith, *Police Systems in the United States*, p. 72.

**26.** John Sullivan, *Introduction to Police Science*, p. 24.

**27.** Bruce Smith, *Police Systems in the United States*, p. 13.

**28.** Thomas Adams, *Law Enforcement*, p. 99.

**29.** A. C. Germann, et. al., *Introduction to Law Enforcement and Criminal Justice*, p. 147.

**30.** The above mentioned are cited in Thomas Adams, *Law Enforcement*, p. 100.

**31.** Clarence Schrag, *Crime & Justice: American Style* (Washington, D.C.: U.S. Government Printing Office, 1971), pp. 142–150.

**32.** American Bar Association, *Standards Relating to Urban Police Function*, (New York: Institute of Judicial Administration, 1974) Standard 2.2. Reprinted with the permission of the American Bar Association which authored these standards and which holds the copyright.

**33.** See Harlan Hahn, "A Profile of Urban Police," in A. Niederhoffer and A. Blumberg, eds. *The Ambivalent Force* (Hinsdale, Ill.: Dryden Press, 1976) p. 59.

**34.** George Kelling, Tony Pate, Duane Dieckman and Charles Brown, *The Kansas City Preventive Patrol Experiment: A Summary Report* (Washington, D.C.; Police Foundation, 1974).

**35.** Ibid., pp. 3–4.

**36.** Ibid.

**37.** Robert Sheehan and Gary Cordner, *Introduction to Police Administration* (Reading, Mass.: Addison-Wesley, 1979).

**38.** For an up-to-date analysis of modern police patrol allocation techniques, see Richard Larson, ed. *Police Deployment* (Lexington, Mass.; D.C. Heath, 1978).

**39.** See Belton Cobb, *The First Detectives* (London; Faber and Faber Ltd., 1957).

**40.** See, for example, James Q. Wilson "Movie Cops—Romantic vs. Real," *New York Magazine,* August 19, 1968, pp. 39–41.

**41.** For a view of the modern detective, see William Sanders, *Detective Work: A Study of Criminal Investigations* (New York, Free Press, 1977.)

**42.** James Ahern, *Police in Trouble* (New York: Hawthorn Books, 1972) pp. 83–85.

**43.** For a discussion of the concerns of a police officer, see George Kirkham, "From Professor to Patrolman," *Journal of Police Science and Administration,* 2:127–137 (1974).

**44.** The comradery of detectives is described in Arthur Niederhoffer, *Behind the Shield* (New York: Doubleday, 1967) pp. 77–81.

**45.** James Q. Wilson, *The Investigators: Managing FBI and Narcotics Agents* (New York: Basic Books, 1978) pp. 21–23.

**46.** See, for example, P. Greenwood and J. Petersilia, *The Criminal Investigation Process, Volume I: Summary & Policy Implications* (Santa Monica, Cal.: Rand Corp., 1975)

**47.** P. Greenwood et al., *The Criminal Investigation Process, Vol. III, Observations Analysis* (Santa Monica, Cal.: Rand Corp., 1975)

**48.** Thomas Reppetto, "The Uneasy Milieu of the Detective," in Niederhoffer and Blumberg, eds., *The Ambivalent Force,* pp. 133–135.

**49.** Sheehan & Cordner, *Introduction to Police Administration,* p. 63.

**50.** For a more complete discussion of the traffic function, see Paul Weston, *The Police Traffic Control Function* (Springfield, Ill.: Charles C. Thomas, 1978).

**51.** Sheehan & Cordner, *Introduction to Police Administration,* p. 91.

**52.** See, for example, Richard Larson, *Urban Police Patrol Analysis* (Cambridge, Mass.: MIT Press, 1972).

**53.** Clement Milanovich, "The Blue Pressure Cooker," *The Police Chief* 47:20 (1980).

**54.** Charles Gruber, "The Relationship of Stress to the Practice of Police Work," *The Police Chief* 47:16–19 (1980).

**55.** John Stratton, "Police Stress, an Overview," *The Police Chief* 45:58–62 (1978).

**56.** Ibid., pp. 58–62.

**57.** Marshall Saper, "Police Wives: The Hidden Pressure," *The Police Chief* 47:28–29 (1980).

**58.** Ibid., pp. 28–29.

**59.** The material in this section was adapted and aided in part from Stahl and Staufenberg, *Police Personnel Administration* (North Scituate, Mass.: Duxbury Press, 1974).

**60.** Ibid., at 65.

**61.** Described in Hindy Lamer Schactter, "Job Related Examinations for Police: Two Developments," *Journal of Police Science and Administration,* 7:87 (1979).

**62.** Ibid.

**63.** *Survey of Police Personnel Practices in State and Local Courts,* International Association of Chiefs of Police and Police Foundation, 1973.

# Hidden Cameras Project, Seattle, Washington

Like many urban areas, Seattle recorded a dramatic increase in robbery during the last decade. Between 1966 and 1975, the number of reported robberies jumped from 650 to more than 2,000—a 224% increase. At the same time, clearance rates remained consistently low—approximately 25%. Because robbery often results in injury as well as financial loss to the victim, the city made it a priority "target crime."

The Seattle Law and Justice Planning Office decided to focus on commercial robbery for three reasons: First, potential targets could be readily identified through police crime reports. Second, commercial robbers were believed to be repeat offenders, so that any arrests would have a telling effect on robbery rates. Third, since commercial robberies were widely publicized, they engendered a disproportionate amount of fear among the public.

In 1975 the Seattle Police Department installed cameras in 75 commercial establishments that had been identified as high risk robbery locations. The cameras were hidden in stereo speaker boxes and activated by removing a dollar "trip" bill from the cash drawer. The project director, who is on call 24 hours a day, 7 days a week, immediately retrieves the film, develops prints, and distributes them to police within hours to aid in the identification, apprehension and prosecution of robbery suspects.

The city's Law and Justice Planning Office conducted a rigorously controlled experiment to measure the project's impact on arrests, convictions, and the overall commercial robbery rate in Seattle. The results are compelling:

—The overall clearance rate for robberies of businesses equipped with hidden cameras was 68%, compared to a 34% clearance rate for the control group of businesses without the hidden cameras.

—Fifty-five% of all hidden camera cases were cleared by arrest, compared to only 25% of control group cases.

—Forty-eight% of the robbers at hidden camera sites were eventually identified, arrested, and convicted, compared to only 19% of control group robbers.

*From Law Enforcement Assistance Administration, *Exemplary Projects*, 1980.

—Commercial robbery in Seattle declined by 38% in the one-year period following project onset; noncommercial robberies increased by 6.7% in that same period.

—Case processing time from arrest to conviction was approximately one month shorter for hidden camera cases than for control group cases.

The Seattle project is relatively simple, straightforward and inexpensive, requiring only one staff member. It requires technical skills which are widely available or easily learned. As an even greater plus, it is likely to be greeted warmly by local merchants in any community. Seattle plans to make the camera project a permanent part of the City's anti-crime program.

# Issues In Policing

CHAPTER OUTLINE

KEY TERMS

POLICING IN
AMERICA

For the past 20 years, a great deal of attention has been given to the police role in society; interestingly, the focus of public concern has changed considerably during the course of this period. In the late 1960s and early 1970s, great issue was taken with the existing political and social role of the police. Critics viewed police agencies as racially biased organizations which harassed minority citizens, controlled political dissidents, and which generally seemed out of touch with the changing times.[1] The major issue of the day appeared to be controlling the abuse of police power and making police agencies more responsible to public control.

During this period, police review boards, which investigated citizen complaints against police officers, were developed in most major cities (examples include Philadelphia's Police Advisory Board and the short-lived New York City Civilian Complaint Review Board). In addition, serious charges of police corruption were raised against officers in major departments. For example, in New York City, the Knapp Commission found that some plain clothes officers collected regular weekly (or monthly) payoffs of up to $3,500 from gambling establishments, while narcotics officers received single payments of up to $80,000 from drug traffickers.[2] It is safe to conclude that this time period was marked by public mistrust of police agencies, and concomitantly, police agency defensiveness about their actual or perceived role in society.

Since the midpoint of the 1970s, there seems to have occurred significant change in the climate of police-citizen interaction. The resolution of the war in Vietnam and the "cooling-off" of unrest in urban ghettos have signalled a diminution of the highly publicized police involvement in controlling social and political behavior. Moreover, police departments have begun to include stress reduction techniques in their recruit training and have made a significant effort to teach both recruits and experienced officers how to deal effectively with the public. New innovations, such as neighborhood team policing units and stress management efforts, have been used to bring the police and public close together.

During the late 1970s and into the 1980s, therefore, public interest in police work has been directed at issues other than controlling the abuse of police power. It appears that people are more than ever concerned with increasing police effectiveness—the public wants its police agencies to control the law-violating members of society. Consequently, questions are being asked about the type of officer employed in American police agencies. Is a college education necessary? Should the hiring of minorities and women be a top priority? Other important questions have been raised about what police officers actually do. Are they spending their time productively? How do they make decisions? How do they treat citizens? Another concern is police officer personality and style. Is there a "cop personality," and if so does it influence the way police officers carry out their daily activities? Thus, while areas of concern have changed somewhat, interest in policing has not abated.

This chapter discusses these critical issues in some detail. The first area of interest will be the police personality and its effect on job performance and style.

It has become commonplace to argue that a majority of American police officers maintain a unique set of personality traits which place them apart from the "average" citizen. The typical police personality is thought to include: authoritarianism, suspicion, racism, hostility, insecurity, conservatism, and cynicism.[3] Maintenance of these negative values and attitudes is believed to cause police officers to be secretive and isolated from the rest of society, producing what has been described by William Westly as the "blue curtain":

Policemen are under explicit orders not to talk about police work with anyone outside the department; there is much in the nature of a secret society about the police; and past experience has indicated that to talk is to invite trouble from the press, the public, the administration, and their colleagues.[4]

There are two opposing viewpoints on the cause of this phenomenon: one position holds that police departments attract recruits who are by nature cynical, authoritarian, secretive, and so on; in opposition to this view, other experts maintain that socialization and experience on the police force itself causes these character traits to subsequently develop in police officers.[5] Since research evidence supportive of both viewpoints has been produced, no one position dominates on the issue of how the police personality develops, or even if one actually exists.

A number of research studies have attempted to describe the development of the police personality. One of the most influential authorities in this area is social psychologist Milton Rokeach. In comparing the values of police officers in Lansing, Michigan with those of a national sample of private citizens, Rokeach and his associates found some significant differences: police officers seemed more oriented toward self-control and obedience than the average citizen; in addition, police were more interested in personal goals, such as "an exciting life" and less interested in social goals such as "a world at peace."[6] When comparing the values of veteran officers with those of recruits, Rokech and his associates found evidence that police officers' on-the-job experience did not significantly influence their personalities, and that most police officers probably had a unique value orientation and personality when they first embarked upon their career in the police force.

In a similar study, James Teevan and Bernard Dolnick compared the value orientations of officers in the Cook County, Illinois Sheriff Department with those Rokeach had encountered in Lansing, Michigan.[7] The results of the Teevan-Dolnick study suggest that the values of police in a large urban department are also far removed from those of the general public. Teevan and Dolnick propose four reasons for this generalized value gap: (1) the police officers are overworked, their tasks too broad, and they suffer from a lack of departmental guidelines and control; (2) police officers are isolated because of the public's view of them as adversaries; (3) police suffer because of their need to enforce unpopular laws, such as those banning gambling, drinking, or prostitution; (4) police officers view themselves as defenders of an idealized middle-class morality and therefore may tend to unconsciously separate themselves from its other members.[8]

Probably the most well-known study of police personality, Arthur Niederhoffer's *Behind the Shield*, takes an opposite viewpoint.[9] Niederhoffer examines the assumption first popularized by William Westly that most policemen develop into cynics as a function of their daily duties.[10] Westly had earlier maintained that being constantly faced with keeping people in line and believing that most people are out to break the law or harm a police officer caused police officers to learn to mistrust the citizens they protect. Niederhoffer tested Westly's assumption by distributing a survey measuring attitudes and values to 220 New York City police officers. Among his most important findings were that police cynicism did increase with length of service, that patrol officers with college educations become quite cynical if they were denied promotion, and that military-like police academy training caused new recruits to quickly become cynical about themselves, the department, and the community. For example, Niederhoffer found that nearly 80% of first-day recruits believed that the police department was an "efficient, smoothly operating organization"; two months later, less than a third professed that belief. Similarly, half the new recruits believed that a police superior was "very interested in the welfare of his subordinates"; two months later, that number declined to 13%.[11]

## Consequences of Police Personality Characteristics

The development and maintenance of negative attitudes and values by police officers may have an extremely detrimental effect on their job performance. In a recent review of police literature, Robert Regoli and Eric Poole found evidence that a police officer's feelings of cynicism intensifies the need to maintain respect, and increases the desire to exert authority over others.[12] Unfortunately, as police escalate the use of authority, citizens learn to mistrust and fear them. These feelings of hostility and anger in turn create feelings of potential danger among police officers, resulting in "police paranoia."[13] Regoli and Poole also find that by maintaining negative attitudes, police tend to be very conservative and resistant to change, factors that interfere with the efficiency of police work.[14]

It has also been charged that the unique police personality causes most officers to band together in a "police subculture," characterized by clannishness, secrecy, and insulation from others in society. Police officers tend to socialize together and believe their occupation cuts them off from relationships with civilians. Joining the "police subculture" means having to always stick up for fellow officers against outsiders, maintaining a tough "macho" exterior personality, and being mistrustful of the motives and behavior of outsiders to the police field.[15]

Despite this evidence, there is by no means certainty that a unique (and negative) police personality exists. Sociologist Robert Balch claims:

It looks like policemen may be rather ordinary people, not greatly unlike other middle-Americans. We cannot be sure there is such a thing as a police personality, however loosely we define it.[16]

Larry Tifft also dismisses the idea that a typical police personality exists. He finds:

Task related values, attitudes, and behavior are occupationally derived or created out of specialized roles rather than being primarily due to the selection factors of background or personality.[17]

Though Tifft's research leads him to speculate that police officers' attitudes are influenced by their duties, he rejects the notion that police officers maintain uniform personality traits developed either through socialization or predisposition.

In the following sections, we will explore more fully the idea that police officers maintain different working personalities or "styles" and find out how they affect individual beliefs and job performance.

Many patrol cars bear the inscription "to serve and protect"; these words sum up the ideal role of the police officer.* However, police business entails many more routine duties than the devotees of crime shows realize. The police officer is an enforcer of the law, an arbitrator of disputes, a mover of traffic, and a single-handed rescue team, to name just a few.

Regardless of how explicitly policy is stated, it is often subject to interpretation by individual law enforcement agents. As police officers become more experienced, they often develop a personal style which they maintain in their everyday operations. Police style affects the way in which departmental rules are interpreted and consequently affects relationships with the public. When using discretion in handling a case, the police officer may fall back on personal style as a determining factor in decision making.

Several studies have attempted to define and classify police styles into behavioral clusters. These classifications, called typologies, attempt to categorize law enforcement agents by groups, each of which has a unique approach to police work. The purpose of such classifications is to demonstrate that the police are not a cohesive, homogeneous group as many believe, but rather are individuals with differing approaches to their work. Police administrators and other individuals who wish to modify or improve police performance should be aware of the nature and extent of these stylistic undercurrents. Do all officers within their jurisdiction operate with similar, unique, or conflicting styles? Is one style more effective than another? Does the existence of numerous styles within a single jurisdiction detract from good police work?

An examination of the recent literature suggests that the following four styles of police work seem to fit the current behavior patterns of most

STYLES OF
POLICE WORK

---

*The material in this section was prepared with the assistance of Michael W. O'Neill. For a more comprehensive examination see, Michael W. O'Neill, *The Role of the Police: Normative Role Expectation in a Metropolitan Police Department* (unpublished doctoral dissertation, State University of New York at Albany, 1974).

police agents: the crime fighter, the social agent, the law enforcer, and the watchman. These four types are discussed in detail below.

## ✳ The Crime Fighter

To the Crime Fighter, the most important police work consists of investigating serious crimes and prosecuting criminals. This type of police officer believes that murder, rape, and other major personal crimes should be the major concerns of police agencies. Property crimes are considered less significant, while matters such as misdemeanors, traffic control, and social service functions would be better handled by other agencies of government. This type of police officer believes that the ability to investigate criminal behavior which poses a serious threat to life and safety, combined with the power to arrest criminals, separates a police department from other municipal agencies. To dilute these functions with minor social service and nonenforcement duties is seen as harmful to police efforts to create a secure society.

The Crime Fighter is primarily interested in dealing with hard crimes; on patrol, the senses are attuned to assaults, rapes, burglaries, and the like and situations are interpreted by their relative importance to these crimes. Some occurrences considered by others as appropriate occasions for police intervention (such as minor traffic violations or requests for enforcement of nonemergency situations) may be ignored or brushed off by the Crime Fighter on the grounds that they are relatively unimportant and undeserving of the police officer's attention and time. In other situations, particularly those in which the officer feels forced to intervene, he or she may find a link to serious crime that most people would fail to recognize and approach the problem from a crime-fighting standpoint. Thus, the Crime Fighter treats domestic disputes as actual or potential felonious assaults, and approaches erratic drivers with a bias for suspecting drunkenness.

## ✳ The Social Agent

Strongly opposed to the Crime Fighter is the sort of police officer one can describe as the Social Agent. Defenders of this type of officer note that police departments are merely part of a larger organization of several government agencies, and feel that officers are responsible for a wide range of duties other than crime fighting. They argue that police could better spend their time trying to do well those things that have to be done rather than conceiving of worlds where most police contacts are crime related. Proponents of the Social Agent approach argue that establishing new governmental agencies or modifying existing ones to perform the duties relinquished by the Crime Fighter would create an exorbitant drain on municipal resources.

The Social Agent believes that police should get involved in a wide range of activities, without regard for their connection to law enforcement.

The Social Agent does not believe enforcement to be the essence of policing, and may point out that the word police is commonly used (e.g., in such phrases as "the state's police powers" and "police the parade grounds") in contexts that have at best only a tenuous relation to law enforcement. The Social Agent who is well versed in the history of the American police will note, for example, that the Boston Police Department developed in the early nineteenth century as much in response to a health and sanitary crisis as to criminal apprehension needs.

Rather than viewing themselves as criminal-catchers, Social Agents consider themselves problem-solvers. They are troubleshooters who keep busy patching holes that appear where the social fabric wears thin. If someone is victimized by crime, the Social Agent will investigate and initiate the machinery of justice; if a citizen is in danger of personal injury, the Social Agent will attempt to ameliorate the situation. Likewise, if a husband and wife or two neighbors engage in excessive disputes, this type of police officer will help them find ways to solve their problems, or refer them to social agency counselors; if juveniles band together and disturb the peace at night, the Social Agent will find or originate less disruptive activities for them.

### The Law Enforcer

Like the Crime Fighter, the police officer embodied in this third typology tends to emphasize the detection and apprehension aspects of police work. Unlike the Crime Fighter, the Law Enforcer does not distinguish between major and minor crimes. Although a Law Enforcer may prefer working on serious crimes—they're more intriguing and rewarding in terms of achievement, prestige, and status—he or she sees the police role as one of enforcing all statutes and ordinances. According to this officer's view, duty is clearly set out in law and the Law Enforcer stresses "playing it by the book"; since the police are specifically charged with apprehending all types of lawbreakers, they are viewed in this typology as generalized law enforcement agents. They do not perceive themselves as lawmakers or as judges of whether existing laws are fair; quite simply, legislators legislate, courts judge, and police officers perform the functions of detecting violations, identifying culprits, and taking the lawbreakers before a court.

The Law Enforcer's quarrel with the Crime Fighter is that the latter, by choosing to deal only with the most serious forms of criminal behavior, illegitimately seeks to restrict the police role. To be sure, police work would be more exciting and glamorous were it not necessary to enforce a miscellaneous hodgepodge of minor legislation; the law, however, clearly sets out the police mission as one of impartially enforcing all law, and the Law Enforcer takes this role quite seriously.

This type of officer takes a more militant stance toward advocates of the Social Agent position. The Law Enforcer frequently points out that police are not social workers, and views the Social Agent's nonlegal (or extralegal) modes of dealing with offenders as too lenient. The Law Enforcer has faith in the basic soundness of punishment as a deterrent and, while cynical about the rehabilitative success of the criminal justice system, this officer sees the system's failure as resulting from plea-bargaining prosecutors, soft judges, and bleeding heart correctional personnel.

## ✗ The Watchman

James Q. Wilson's study of interdepartmental differences in police orientations provides the fourth major typology.[18] In Wilson's analysis, three general departmental styles were observed and related to different demographic characteristcs of American cities. One of the styles Wilson noted, the service type, was similar to the Social Agent, while a second, the Legalist, seemed to resemble parts of the Crime Fighter and the Law Enforcer. A third orientation, which Wilson called the Watchman style, was characterized by an emphasis on the maintenance of public order as the police goal rather than on law enforcement or general service. Police in Watchman-type departments chose to ignore many infractions and requests for service unless they believe that the social or political order is being jeopardized:

Juveniles are "expected" to misbehave, and thus infractions among this group— unless they are serious or committed by a "wise guy"—are best ignored or treated informally. . . . Motorists . . . will often be left alone if their driving does not endanger or annoy others. . . . Vice and gambling are . . . problems only when the currently accepted standards of public order are violated. . . . Private disputes—assaults among friends or family—are treated informally or ignored unless the circumstances . . . require an arrest. . . . The police are watchmanlike not simply in emphasizing order over law enforcement but also in judging the seriousness of infractions less by what the law says about them than by their immediate and personal consequences. . . . In all cases, circumstances of person and condition are taken seriously into account.[19]

One can construct an accurate account of a Watchman's view of the police role. A Watchman would argue that the police cannot be effective as agents of social control when their power is used for nonessential behavioral regulations. Community norms and values are more effective in regulating conduct regarding most small infractions than are police, and the strict enforcement of laws which go counter to local customs and morality can breed disrespect for police officers and contempt for their authority. The best strategy is thus to maintain a low profile and to intervene only where there is a clear indication of public danger or disorder. At these times, police may use any reasonable method available to restore order.

Since the Watchman role appeared from Wilson's study to be frequently enacted by police officers, and since a simple, logical and persuasive rationale could be constructed to support it, this role has been generally accepted as one of the elements of style displayed by American police officers.

**An Analysis of Police Styles**

No one of the above four idealized police styles best describes the activities of most American law enforcement agents. Every police officer may be— or show characteristics of—in turn, a Crime Fighter, a Law Enforcer, a Social Agent, or a Watchman.

This view of police performance as a combination of many styles has been somewhat substantiated by the findings of some recent studies designed to find out what police really do. One survey of 700,000 calls received by the police department in Baltimore, Maryland obtained the following results:[20]

| Type of Call | Percent of Total Calls |
|---|---|
| Index crimes | 10.7% |
| Other crimes | 8.4% |
| Other calls (including sick persons, dog bites, sanitation complaints, and the like) | 63.0% |
| Accidents involving vehicles and/or pedestrians | 5.0% |
| Duplicate calls (more than one person calling to report the same incident) | 6.8% |
| Unfounded calls (like a false alarm of fire, an officer had to respond) | 6.1% |
| Total | 100.0% |

TABLE 7.1
Analysis of Police Calls
in Baltimore

If this data from Baltimore can be said to support any one of the four styles, it is probably that of the Social Agent since almost two-thirds of the calls surveyed were for noncriminal matters such as medical or sanitation emergencies.

Similar results were obtained in a study by Webster who found that police apportioned their time as follows:[21]

| Activity | Percent of Time Spent |
|---|---|
| Social service | 14% |
| Criminal investigation | 18% |
| Travel and surveillance | 18% |
| Administration | 50% |
| Total | 100% |

TABLE 7.2.
Time Spent on Police
Activities

Webster found that police spend about half their time in such activities as preparing and writing reports, attending court, participating in community relations, doing errands, and carrying out other administrative duties.

Though these duties represent operations in only two police departments, they can be seen as providing a fairly accurate picture of the average police officer's daily activities. It is apparent that very little of a police officer's time is spent in chasing "real" criminals; it is likely, however, that a police officer's role orientation or style affects the amount of time spent on each task. An officer who adheres to the Crime Fighter style will probably spend more time actively pursuing criminals, or at least attempting to, than will the Watchman or the Social Agent. The Crime Fighter might put in for duty in the high crime areas of a city or ask for an evening shift in a crime-prone neighborhood. The Social Agent, on the other hand, might pursue an opportunity to speak at the local high school, work with minority groups, counsel juveniles, and become involved in interagency cooperation. The data in Tables 7.1 and 7.2 does suggest, however, that the Crime Fighter will by necessity occasionally engage in social services as will the Law Enforcer and the Watchman, while a Social Agent may be thrust into crime fighting duties.

## POLICE DISCRETION

Police discretion is defined as the selective enforcement of the law by duly authorized police agents. It is one of the most controversial and important of all police practices since it often results in the law being applied differently in varying situations. Examples of police discretion at work could be: two drivers are caught speeding and only one is given a citation while the other is let off with a warning; two youths are drunk and disorderly and one is sent home to his parents while the other is booked and sent to juvenile court; or two persons are found to be operating an after-hours establishment and only one is fined and has his license suspended.

Regardless of the enforcement style employed, every police officer maintains a high degree of personal discretion in carrying out daily tasks. Jerome Skolnick has termed the exercise of police discretion a prime example of low visibility decision making in criminal justice.[22] This statement suggests that, unlike members of almost every other criminal justice agency, police are neither regulated in their daily procedures by administrative scrutiny nor are they subject to judicial review (except when their behavior clearly violates an offender's constitutional rights). As a result, the exercise of discretion may sometimes deteriorate into discrimination, violence, and other abusive practices on the part of police.[23]

### Environment and Discretion

The extent of police discretion an officer will exercise is at least partially defined by the living and working environment. Police officers may work or dwell within a community culture that either tolerates eccentricities and personal freedoms, or expects extremely conservative, professional, no-

nonsense behavior on the part of its civil servants. The police officer who resides in a liberal or conservative environment is probably strongly influenced by and shares a large part of the community's beliefs and values, and is likely to be sensitive to and respect the wishes of neighbors, friends, and relatives. Conflict may arise, however, when the police officer commutes to an assigned area of jurisdiction, as is often the case in the urban inner-city precincts. The officer who holds personal values in opposition to community attitudes can exercise discretion in such a way as to conflict with the community and result in ineffective law enforcement.

The policies, practices, and customs of the local police department provide a second source of environmental influence. These conditions, discussed more fully in the following section, vary from department to department and strongly depend on the judgment of the chief and others in the organizational hierarchy. For example, patrol officers will be pressured to issue more tickets and make more arrests, or to refrain from arresting under certain circumstances. Occasionally, a directive will instruct officers to be particularly alert for certain types of violations or to make some sort of interagency referral when specific events occur. These factors affect the decision of the police officer who has to produce appropriate performance statistics by the end of the month or be prepared to offer justification for following a course of action other than that officially prescribed.

Another source of influence, which is similar to departmental policies and customs, although its effects are not as uniform, is the pressure exerted by individual supervisors on the patrol officers in their charge. The sergeant, for example, not only serves to relay orders issued from above, but also acts to initiate additional directives and restrictions. Unless special mention is made of the source of an order, the patrol officer seldom knows whether instructions were formulated by the sergeant or by the chief; if they are delivered in the same manner by the same supervisor, they receive the same weight. Thus, if the sergeant personally believes that liquor is the root of crime and directs subordinate officers to exercise vigilance in uncovering tavern violations, the patrol officer must follow this order as though it were official departmental policy.

Another influence on police discretion is exerted by other officers. As William Westley noted, police are particularly subject to peer pressure.[24] They suffer a degree of social isolation on the one hand because the job itself involves such strange working conditions and hours and demands that the officer be subject to 24 hour call, and on the other hand because their authority and responsibility to enforce the law cause embarrassment during social encounters. At the same time, officers must deal with irregular and emotionally demanding encounters dealing with the most personal and private aspects of people's lives. As a result, police officers turn to their peers for both on-the-job advice and off-the-job companionship, essentially forming a subculture to provide a source of status, prestige, and reward.

The peer group affects how police officers exercise discretion on two distinct levels. In an obvious, direct manner, other police officers dictate acceptable responses to street-level problems by displaying or withholding approval in office discussions. The officer who takes the job seriously and desires the respect and friendship of others will take their advice and abide by their norms, and will seek out the most experienced and most influential patrol officers on the force and follow their behavior models.

A final environmental factor affecting the police officer's performance is his or her perception of community alternatives to police intervention or processing. A police officer may exercise discretion to arrest an individual in a particular circumstance if it seems that nothing else can be done even if the officer doesn't believe that an arrest is the best possible example of good police work. In an environment where a proliferation of social agencies exists—detoxification units, drug control centers, and child care services, for example—a police officer will obviously have more alternatives to choose from in the decision-making process. In fact, referring cases to these alternative agencies saves the officer both time and effort—records do not have to be made out, and court appearances can be avoided. Thus, social agencies provide for greater latitude in police decision making.

## Situational Influences on Discretion

The situational factors attached to a particular crime provide another extremely important influence on police actions and behavior. Regardless of departmental or community influences, the officer's immediate interaction with a criminal act, offender, citizen, or victim will weigh heavily on the use of discretionary powers.

While it is difficult to catalogue every situational factor influencing police discretion, a few do stand out as having major significance. Studies have found that police officers rely heavily on demeanor (the attitude and appearance of the offender) and political factors in making decisions. For example, in a study of the decision-making practices of police with juveniles, Nathan Goldman discovered that community attitudes, political pressures, and the bias of the individual police officer may influence the decision to arrest, take into custody, or release an offender.[25] Factors related to the suspect's perceived needs or the seriousness of the crime often play only a small part in the officer's decision whether to take a suspect into custody. In a similar study, Aaron Cicourel found that the decision to arrest is often based on information regarding the offender's demeanor, dress, and attitude.[26]

While observing a metropolitan police department, Irving Piliavin and Scott Briar found that the offender's demeanor had a significant influence on police decision making and discretion.[27] Specifically, their findings suggest that the offender's perceived attitudes toward police, the law, and his or her own behavior were seen as the most important factor when deciding whether to process an offender through the criminal justice system.

A majority of empirical studies indicate that police discretion works against the young, the poor, and minority group members, and may often favor the wealthy, the politically connected, and the majority group members. Some crimes are more strictly enforced than others; some police officers will go by the book, while others will essentially write their own laws.

A final set of situational influences on police discretion concerns the manner in which a crime or situation is encountered. If, for example, a police officer stumbles on an altercation or break-in, the discretionary response may be quite different than if the officer is summoned by police radio. If official police recognition has been given to an act, police action must be taken or an explanation made as to why it was not. Or, if a matter is brought to an officer's attention by a citizen observer, the officer can ignore the request and risk a complaint or take discretionary action. When an officer chooses to become involved in a situation, without benefit of a summons or complaint, maximum discretion can be used. Even in this circumstance, however, the presence of a crowd or of witnesses may contribute to the officer's decision making.

And, of course, the officer who acts alone is affected by personal matters—physical condition, mental state, police style, whether there are other duties to perform, and so on.

Police discretion is one of the most often debated issues in criminal justice. On its face, the unequal enforcement of the law smacks of unfairness and violates the Constitution's doctrines of due process and equal protection. Yet, were some discretion not exercised, police would be forced to function as automatons merely following the book. Administrators have sought to control discretion so that its exercise may be both beneficial to citizens and nondiscriminatory. In the following section, some of the management techniques used by police supervisors to limit discretion are discussed.

### Controlling Police Discretion

The management of police behavior and discretion is one of the most difficult tasks facing law enforcement administrators. The chief and other police managers must ensure that the officers under their command do not arrest the wrong people for the wrong reasons or practice racial, sex or class discrimination. At the same time, the administrator must inspire the officers' interest in community affairs and encourage them to maintain their vigilance against actually dangerous crimes. These combined tasks have proven to be complex ones and do not involve merely stating the rules or telling subordinates to play it by the book lest they face departmental punishment or sanctions. The police administrator must create a climate which both inspires patrol officers and encourages them to exercise their discretion properly.

One suggested approach to managing police behavior is by obedience to a formal set of policies or guidelines which can ensure the just administration of the law. The National Advisory Commission on Criminal Justice Standards and Goals provides an extensive set of guidelines for administrators wishing to effectively manage police discretion.[28] And, of course, there are certain areas in which stated or written policies can be helpful.

When laws are unclearly written or police officers are unfamiliar with the application of some statute, guidelines provided by police legal counsel can be useful. When the effect of policy is to inform officers of a new legal tool to use in disposing of cases (e.g., the "Miranda Warning"), written guidelines may publicize the availability and utility of the device. When the objective is to limit a particular tactic or use of discretion in the field, however, formal policies have proved less successful.

Since policies limiting police discretion are usually formal statements, they fall prey to the same inherent difficulties as does the criminal law when used to define the differences between acceptable and unacceptable behavior. For example, it is difficult to define when a friendly, boisterous street gathering becomes disorderly conduct. Police policy developers have also found that the individual circumstances of an event are so varied that the laws and policies governing it must be extremely broad in order to delineate its acceptable (or unacceptable) boundaries. Formal policies can do little to make such limits exact, and informal guidelines can do little except in gross and obvious examples of misuse.

Another type of problem arises when policy makers attempt to limit police discretion in the use of a particular legal tool. If, for example, patrol officers are intervening more formally than desired (utilizing arrest func-tion) in domestic disturbances, the development of a general policy curbing their behavior may not produce constructive results. The officers may feel deprived of one of their favorite tactics for restoring public order and informally decide to significantly curtail their intervention in similar cases. A domestic disturbance call might be checked into, be classified as a civil disturbance, and be ignored. A full-fledged assault and battery might be necessary before police actually intervene. While formal departmental reg-ulation may direct officers to intervene in problem areas without making arrests, it becomes particularly troublesome to uphold this regulation since police have been charged with the upholding of the law as their most important duty, and arrest is certainly a viable part of this duty. Thus, those wishing to manage police discretion may find that their efforts are in direct conflict with existing statutory doctrine.

Despite these stated difficulties, a number of internal techniques have proved to be of some value to the police administrator in managing the behavior of officers; one such technique is the development of interagency cooperation. In their study of the operations of a rape squad, Jerome Skolnick and Richard Woodworth found that pressure for formal prose-cution of statutory rape cases (sex with minors) which were compounded with nonsupport for resulting offspring was much stronger in precincts where the rape victim applied for financial assistance with the local welfare department than where such support was not needed.[29] Pressure from the welfare authorities in this instance helped to escalate police activity; one conclusion that can be drawn from this study is that a resourceful police administration may use cooperation with social and government agencies such as welfare, the district attorney, or probation to reduce or increase police discretion and activities.

An administrator may also be able to increase or limit police discretion through organizational changes within the department itself. By creating a specialized detail for vice, traffic, or rape, an administrator may shift the department's focus and the type of services provided to the community. On the other hand, the elimination or curtailment of a unit might be used to diminish interest in a particular area of policing. Such measures usually depend on high morale and cooperation from within the department if they are to be effective.

Another administrative technique the police supervisor may use to successfully direct police behavior is the establishment of departmental norms—known sometimes as "the numbers game"—for arrests, tickets, and other activities. These quotas, which may be interpreted as criteria for promotion or other forms of approval within the department, have been found by John Gardiner to actually affect police practices without the necessity of creating a specialized unit.[30] However, limiting police discretion by creating departmental norms seems more attuned to increasing the number of formal procedures than decreasing them. The alternative of creating departmental maximums—for example, forcibly limiting the number of arrests or summonses—would obviously be an impossible doctrine to manage. Administrators might, however, attempt to accurately define for officers what constitutes acceptable boundaries of police efficiency and suggest that any behavior in excess of these limits will not be tolerated within the department. Types of behavior to be limited might include number of permissible citizen complaints per officer, arrests involving physical violence, and arrests not prosecuted due to illegal evidence or searches. Limiting discretion in this fashion may, of course, negatively affect departmental morale; for this reason, police managers have not actively pursued the technique of creating maximums.

Today, no clear answer to the management of police discretion exists. Advocates of specialized units, policy statements, legal mandates, and other approaches can only assume that the officer in the field will comply with the intent and spirit of the administrator's desire. Little knowledge is currently available concerning the specific influence any particular legal or administrative measure will have on police discretion, whether it will affect all officers equally, or why some officers will be affected one way and others will respond in an opposite fashion. It is not known what police officers are really like, how they differ from or resemble one other, or how they react to pressures from above.

Despite criticisms leveled at police by the media, studies suggest that most citizens have a high opinion of the police and their activities. However, this is not to suggest that all citizens share these feelings. Whites have been found to hold somewhat more positive attitudes about police then nonwhites. There seems to be considerable disparity in the attitudes black and white Americans have with regard to police effectiveness, police courtesy, honesty, and conduct. Consequently, some citizens are less likely to go to police for help, report crimes, step forward as witnesses, or cooperate and aid police.

The police response has been to improve police-community relations through efforts at the station house and departmental levels designed to

## POLICE AND THE COMMUNITY

make citizens more aware of police activities, alert them to methods of self-protection, and improve general attitudes toward policing. Some departments have instituted specialized Police-Community Relations (PCR) sections to actively pursue the improvement of community attitudes toward police. The San Francisco Police instituted such a division for the purpose of bringing together citizens of diverse socioeconomic and ethnic backgrounds.

Other departments have instituted specialized programs to improve PCR. Some cooperate in Neighborhood Watch Programs, which aid citizens by instructing them in home security measures and enlist their assistance in watching their neighbor's homes. Another national program first implemented in Monterey Park, California in 1963 is Operation ID. Police provide engraving tools with which citizen participants mark their valuables so that they may be easily identified if stolen. Police also donate to citizens tags for their homes which alert potential thieves that valuables have been marked. Preliminary results suggest that Operation ID has dramatically improved burglary protection. Still other jurisdictions have undertaken Crime Prevention Clinics, Citizen's Police Alert Programs, and similar efforts to help citizens and police in identifying suspicious characters in their neighborhoods.

While all of these programs are interesting first steps, they have not proved to be the cure for what ails the relationship between the police establishment and various societal subgroups. Though there has been a gradual reduction in recent years of violent confrontations and riots involving police, (the recent Miami riot, notwithstanding) many citizens still resent the police role, and skepticism still exists concerning the actual effectiveness of systematic police efforts to promote citizen involvement and better community relations. Commenting on the dilemma confronting the police in dealing with minority citizens, James Q. Wilson has stated:

The chief policy implication of this argument is that police-community relations cannot be substantially improved by programs designed to deal with the citizen in settings other than encounters with patrolmen; evening meetings, discussion groups, block clubs, police-community councils, and the like will be seen by both officer and citizen as tangential to their central relationship. Nor can the behavior of patrolmen be modified other than by providing him with incentives and instructions relevant to his central task; lecturing him on good behavior, sending him to one-week human relations training institutes, or providing him with materials designed to make him think of blacks as just like everybody else will be ignored and even scorned by him.[31]

The key to improving police-community relations, according to many experts both within and outside the police establishment, may lie in improving the sensitivity and performance of every police officer and not in creating specialized PCR units. Some of the measures advocated include improving the education and training of the average patrol officer and detective, using promotional criteria to encourage sensitivity to citizens' needs, and creating decentralized citizen-controlled police departments.

With regard to the latter principle, some communities such as Holyoke, Massachusetts have experimented with the team-policing approach. This concept relies on neighborhood-based, decentralized teams of police which have primary responsibility over independent geographical areas within the jurisdiction. Such programs are designed to maximize citizen contact with police and strengthen their accessibility to and control over police operations. Evaluation of team-policing projects, however, have indicated they do not provide clear-cut evidence of improvement in citizen attitudes toward police.

During the 1970s, the number of in-service police officers attaining a college education increased markedly. This development is not to be unexpected considering that higher education for police officers has been recommended by national commissions on policing since 1931.[32] Though the great majority of American police departments do not require a college education of their recruits, the trend for police officers to desire post-high school training has been spurred on by the development of law enforcement and criminal justice academic programs and the availability of federal and state scholarship aid to offset their tuition costs.[33]

Despite the growth of educational opportunities for police, the issue of higher education for police officers is not a simple one. Those in favor of educating the police suggest that exposure to a college curriculum will significantly add to police professionalism, aid police in becoming more sensitive to the needs of the diverse ethnic groups within their jurisdictions, make them better equipped to understand their police role and duties, and help them to communicate better. Criminologist Peter Lejins suggests circumstances within which university level education could aid police officers to more effectively perform their assigned duties:

1. Among the frequent disturbances to which a policeman is called are family conflicts, which often reach the level of disturbances of the peace, fights, assault and manslaughter. It stands to reason that an officer who has been exposed to some educational experience in the area of family relationships, the types of family conflict and the way they run their course, would approach this type of disturbance with a much broader and sounder perspective than someone equipped with many conventional folklore stereotypes permeated by punitive, disciplinary or ridiculing impulses. . . .

2. An even more obvious example is a disturbance anchored in the area of ethnic relations and ethnic tensions. Exposure to the university-level study of ethnic relations, contributing an historical and broader perspective . . . again suggests itself, and again one would expect that such study would tend to diminish the effect of prejudice, racial and ethnic stereotypes, erroneous and often exaggerated, rumors, etc. . . .

3. Still another example is the handling of disturbances for which mentally abnormal people are responsible. The use of conventional and straight-forward evaluations of behavior as being or not being a violation of law, and the use of conventional law enforcement steps to arrest the ongoing violation and secure the violator for

HIGHER
EDUCATION AND
THE POLICE

action of the criminal justice system, would often cause unnecessary harm to the perpetrator, who is viewed by contemporary society as a sick person, and to the community itself, by injecting what basically amounts to an improper solution of the problem. . . .

4. Whatever has been said with regard to the above three categories of disturbances could be properly restated with regard to the handling of drunks and drug addicts. . . .

5. And finally, let us take the so-called area of civil rights and contemporary struggles for them, which often express themselves in disturbances and so-called riots. Here again the quick and sharp discernment between permissible actions in terms of freedom of speech, and freedom of demonstration, and actions that violate the individual rights of others and have all the characteristics of plain criminal acts, presupposes alert and sophisticated individuals. Persons without any higher education, acquired either in their college-age period or subsequently by means of adult education and in-service training, can hardly be cast in the role of the wise law enforcement officer who manages to lessen the tensions between ideologically antagonistic mobs, protects the rights of innocent bystanders and would-be victims, and contains the amount of violence. . . .[34]

It is also likely that requiring a college education will help attract better-qualified personnel to the law-enforcement profession and upgrade the image of police departments.

However, there are those who suggest that a college education can do little to help the "average" police officer perform daily activities.[35] The diversity of the police role, the need for split-second decision making, and the often boring and mundane tasks police are required to do, are all considered reasons why formal education for police officers may be a waste of time.[36]

Compounding these problems is the fact that the most appropriate type and structure of educational programs for police officers is still at issue. Many police officers attend broad-based liberal arts programs which they believe will sharpen their skills in human relations and help them to better understand the many social problems they commonly confront. Another approach to police education is through criminal justice programs which stress a varied curriculum including law, justice, social policy, and criminology. Still another popular type of police education involves technical training in police science and administration, report writing and patrol techniques.

Not surprisingly, there has not been agreement on which education model is the most effective one for training the modern police officer. For example, liberal arts may be too general, criminal justice too focussed, and law enforcement too technical, to be of use to the "street" cop. This important issue has been addressed by a recent report of the National Advisory Commission on Higher Education for Police Officers (commonly called the Sherman Report).[37] The Sherman Report examined the findings of a national study of existing college curriculum and educational delivery systems for police education in America. Generally critical of current police education techniques, the Sherman Report recommends that a number of basic changes be made: it calls for a halt to federal tuition assistance for programs with narrow curriculum and unqualified faculty. The report is especially critical of police educational programs with limited academic orientations. The Sherman Report instead advocates a limit to the amount of criminal justice courses that can be allowed in any in-service or pre-service student's program. It also calls for discontinuing the practice of granting academic credit for in-service training programs such as those conducted by various state police academies.

Another problem the Report found was the requirement that the faculty in some criminal justice programs have practical field experience before they can be hired; this practice is believed to limit academically trained people from acquiring teaching jobs in law enforcement programs. Finally, the Report stresses that criminal justice courses and course material should emphasize ethical considerations and moral values in law enforcement, not the "nuts and bolts" of police procedures.

The findings of the Sherman Report are considered highly controversial in many quarters of law enforcement education. Nonetheless, it raises important issues which must be addressed in the years to come.

While the jury is still out on the value of police education, there is some indication that it does have a beneficial influence on police performance. Studies have shown that college-educated police officers receive fewer citizen complaints and have better behavioral and performance characteristics than their less-educated peers.[38] R. P. Witte compared police performance in two similar districts, one manned by college graduates and another staffed by officers with only a high school education. He found that after six months, the crime rate remained the same in each district, but that the district manned by college trained officers showed a higher rate of morale, fewer complaints, and a quicker response to calls.[39]

Findings of a similar nature were indicated by Wayne Cascio in an analysis of the effect formal education had on police officer performance.[40] Cascio found that higher levels of education were associated with fewer on-the-job injuries, fewer injuries by assault and battery, fewer disciplinary actions from accidents, fewer sick times per year, and fewer physical force allegations.[41]

Despite these early indications of success, the value of police education is still being debated and further research is needed to test its true merit.[42]

During the end of the 1970s and into the 1980s, American citizens have actively participated in what is commonly known as the "great taxpayer's rebellion." Government spending cutbacks forced by inflation and legislative tax-cutting measures such as California's Proposition 13, have prompted belt-tightening in many areas of public service. Police departments have not been spared the budgetary pinch caused by decreased governmental spending. To combat the probable damage that would be caused by police service cutbacks, police administrators have sought to increase the productivity of their line, support, and adminstrative staff.

POLICE
PRODUCTIVITY

As used today, the term *police productivity* refers to the amount of actual order, maintenance, crime control, and other law enforcement activities provided by individual police officers, and concomitantly, by police departments as a whole. By improving police productivity, a department could keep the peace, deter crime, apprehend criminals, and provide useful public services without necessarily increasing its costs. This goal is accomplished by having each police officer operate with greater efficiency, thus using less resources to achieve greater effectiveness.

Confounding the situation, and heightening its importance, has been the dramatic increase in the cost of maintaining police personnel, including such items as salaries, fringe benefits, and retirement plans. Moreover, the modern police department depends on expensive electronic gear, communications systems, computers, weapons, and transportation; and the cost of basic supplies from gasoline to paper is constantly increasing. It has been estimated that the cost of running American police departments has increased to over $10 billion annually.[43]

Despite the oft-stated desire to increase police effectiveness, there have been serious questions raised about how the police accomplish their assigned tasks. In a now-famous Rand Corporation study of police detective services, the productivity of investigators was strongly assailed.[44] This nationwide study found that police investigators give only limited attention to about half the serious cases reported to them. Even cases in which the suspect was caught immediately required more time for paperwork and administrative tasks than was devoted to identifying the criminal. The study also found that a patrol officer's gathering information at the site of the crime was more important to its solution than the subsequent efforts of the detective force.

Patrol forces have also been concerned about their productivity. One basic complaint has been that the average patrolman spends relatively little time on what is considered "real" police work.[45] More often than not, highly skilled police officers can be found writing reports, waiting in court corridors, getting involved in domestic disputes, and handling what are generally characterized as "miscellaneous noncriminal matters."[46] In a recent study of the Newport, Kentucky Police Department, J. Robert Lilly found the following types of calls were made to police during a four-month period (out of a total of over 18,000 calls):[47]

1. Calls requesting information, 59.98%;

2. Calls about traffic, 12.9%;

3. Calls regarding juvenile problems, 5.38%;

4. Calls relating to protection and assistance, 3.9%;

5. Calls of a nuisance nature, 3.72%;

6. Calls about violence, 2.78%;

7. Calls relating to family trouble, 2.75%;

8. Calls about health services, 2.35%;

**9.** Calls about prowlers, 2.33%;

**10.** Calls about thefts, juvenile and adult, 1.87%;

**11.** Calls which are unclassifiable, 1.04%;

**12.** Calls regarding missing persons, .93%; and

**13.** Calls about vice, .12%.

Lilly's study indicates that the overwhelming number of police calls are for such matters as information and traffic news. It is evident that if we view productivity as a function of enforcing laws and keeping the peace, many police departments are not very effective.

How have police administrators responded to the challenge of improving police productivity? As mentioned previously, applying modern technology to information, communication, and record-keeping systems has helped police improve their ability to respond to calls in a more effective fashion. For example, the "911" emergency code has been used in many cities to improve police response time.

Another productivity improvement measure has been to simply ask individual police officers to shoulder a greater work load. Some jurisdictions have decreased the number of officers in patrol cars from two to one, saving approximately $80,000 per beat annually (since three shifts are assigned to each patrol area).[48]

Another move to increase police efficiency has come in the area of consolidating police services. This means combining small departments (usually with under ten employees) in adjoining areas into a super-agency which services the previously fragmented jurisdictions. Consolidation has the benefit of creating departments large enough to utilize expanded services such as crime labs, training centers, communications centers, and emergency units, which are not cost-effective in smaller departments. Of course, this procedure is controversial, since it demands that existing lines of political and administrative authority be drastically changed. Nonetheless, consolidation of departments or special services (such as a regional computer center) has been attempted in California (L.A. Sheriff's department), Massachusetts, New York, and elsewhere.

Below are some of the popular police department consolidation techniques:[49]

*Increase Productivity*

**1.** *Informal arrangements* are unwritten cooperative agreements between localities to collectively perform a task that would be mutually beneficial (i.e., the monitoring of neighboring radio frequencies so that needed backup can be provided).

**2.** *Sharing* is the provision or reception of services which aid in the execution of a law enforcement function (i.e., the sharing of a communications system by several local agencies).

**3.** *Pooling* is the combination of resources by two or more agencies to perform a specified function under a predetermined, often formalized, arrangement with direct involvement by all parties (i.e., the use of a city-county law enforcement building or training academy, or the establishment of a crime task force such as those used in St. Louis, Kansas City, Topeka, Tuscaloosa, and Des Moines).

✱4. *Contracting* is a limited and voluntary approach in which one government enters into a formal, binding agreement to provide all or certain specified law enforcement services (i.e., communications, patrol service, etc.) to another government for an established fee. Many communities which contract for full law enforcement service do so at the time they incorporate to avoid the costs of establishing their own police capability.

✱5. *Police service districts* law enforcement service districts are areas, usually within an individual county, where a special level of service is provided and which is financed through a special tax or assessment. In California, residents of an unincorporated portion of a county may petition to form such a district to provide more intensive patrol coverage than is available through existing systems. Such service may be provided by a sheriff, another police department or a private person or agency. This system is used in Contra Costa and San Mateo Counties in California and Suffolk and Nassau County in New York State.

Another practice used to increase police productivity is the employment of civilians in administrative support or even in some line activities. Their duties have included operating communication gear; performing clerical work, planning, and research; and staffing traffic control ("meter maids"). The use of civilian employees can be a considerable savings to taxpayers since their salaries are considerably lower than regular police officers. In addition, they allow trained, experienced officers to spend more time on direct crime control and enforcement activities. It is not surprising that the FBI estimates that today almost 20% of police employees are civilians.[50]

There are several other avenues being explored to improve police effectiveness. Experts Wesley Skogan and George Antunes have outlined several strategies to significantly increase productivity.[51] They suggest that a strong effort should be made to include citizens in the crime control process. Citizens must be made aware, as the Kansas City experiments suggest, that the police acting on their own have a limited impact on crime control. If witnesses (or victims) could significantly increase their crime reporting response, then the arrest rate would also increase dramatically.

Skogan and Antunes also suggest that police must increase the amount and quality of information available to them, preserve it more carefully, and make more efficient use of it. They cite a study done in Rochester, New York which found that lack of cooperation and information sharing between patrol officers and detectives seriously impedes the probability that a case will ever be solved.[52] While Skogan and Antunes view computer applications, such as computerized "MO" (modus operandi or method of operation), fingerprint, and mugshot files as important future considerations, they find that police departments can significantly increase their potential with techniques currently on hand.[53]

In summary, given current conditions, there exists an important need to identify avenues for increasing police productivity and to actively pursue them.

For the past decade, American police departments have made a concerted effort to attract women and minority police officers. The latter group includes blacks, Orientals, Hispanics, native Americans, and members of other racial minorities. The reasons for minority and female recruitment are varied. Viewed in its most positive light, police departments recruit women and minority citizens to field a more balanced force which truly represents the community it serves. A heterogeneous police force can be instrumental in gaining the public's confidence by helping to dispel the view that police departments are generally bigoted or biased organizations. Furthermore, women and minority police officers possess special qualities which can serve to improve police performance. For example, Spanish-speaking officers are essential in hispanic neighborhoods, and women officers can be especially effective in rape control details.

Another important reason for recruiting women and minority police officers may be attributed to the need to comply with the various federal guidelines on employee hiring illustrated in Figure 7.1. A series of legal actions brought by minority representatives have resulted in local, state, and federal courts ordering police departments to either create hiring quotas to increase minority representation, or to rewrite entrance exams and

WOMEN AND
MINORITY
POLICE
OFFICERS

FIGURE 7.1
Equal Employment
and Hiring Orders

---

1. **The Equal Employment Opportunity Act of 1972,** amending Title VII of the Civil Rights Act of 1964.

    This basic law regulates employment in respect to race, color, religion, sex, or national origin and applies to:

    - All private firms employing 15 or more persons
    - All educational institutions, both public and private, state and local governments and their agencies
    - Public and private employment agencies
    - Labor unions with 15 or more members
    - Joint labor-management committees for apprenticeship and training

    Under this act, the Equal Employment Opportunity Commission (EEOC) was established to initiate and investigate cases of discrimination.

2. **The 1973 Amendment to the Omnibus Crime Control and Safe Streets Act**

    This act distinctly prohibits discrimination in police departments, courts, juvenile agencies, correctional institutions, and drug treatment programs. At the same time Equal Employment Opportunity Program Guidelines were issued for Law Enforcement Assistance Administration grantees.

---

*SOURCE: *General Recruitment Strategies for Criminal Justice Agencies,* National Institute of Law Enforcement and Criminal Justice, 1980.

(Figure 7.1
continued)

**3. Executive Orders 11246 and 11375 and Revised Orders 4 and 14**

These Presidential orders affect all organizations holding government contracts. The Office of Federal Contract Compliance Programs of the Department of Labor adminsters these orders that prohibit employment discrimination and require organizations to develop and implement affirmative action.

**4. Equal Pay Act of 1963**

This act requires all employers to provide equal pay for both men and women performing similar work. Wage and Hour Division of the Department of Labor administers the law.

**5.  The Age Discrimination in Employment Act of 1967 and the Revision of 1977**

The Wage and Hour Division also administers this act which prohibits discrimination in employment against people between the ages of 40 and 70.

**6. The Rehabilitation Act of 1973 as Amended**

Section 503 and 504 require organizations with government contracts over $50,000 to provide employment opportunities for handicapped individuals. Part of the affirmative action plan of the contractors should provide for reasonable accommodations to meet physical and mental handicaps.

**7. The Vietnam Era Veterans' Readjustment Assistance Act of 1974**

Section 402 requires organizations with Federal contracts over $10,000 to provide employment opportunities for disabled veterans and veterans from the Vietnam war.

**8. The Crime Control Act of 1976**

Because ambiguities over the administration of the civil rights provision of the Onmibus Crime Control and Safe Streets Act were frequently voiced, Representative Barbara Jordan sponsored an amendment (the Jordan Amendment) directed to this difficulty. This legislation includes the phrase "or denied employment" to the prohibitions of discrimination and provides "triggers" that automatically initiate administrative procedures for the cutoff of funding. In 1976 Revenue Sharing legislation was also amended to provide the same triggers for the aged and handicapped.

requirements in order to encourage minority employment.[54] One example of litigation brought to force change in police hiring practices occurred in Bridgeport, Connecticut. A suit brought against the city's Civil Service Commission charged that while 25% of Bridgeport was composed of black and Spanish-speaking minorities, only 17 members (3.6%) of the 469-man police department was black or Puerto Rican.[55] The court found that the city's police entrance examination discriminated against minorities since 58% of white applicants and only 17% of minorities were successful in passing it. Consequently, the federal district court set up stringent quotas for appointing minority officers. In this case as in others, the court found that the Civil Service Commission's discrimination, though unintentional, nonetheless prevented minorities from having an equal chance at being hired. The result has been the attempted creation of a job-oriented nondiscriminating police entrance exam similar to those described in the previous chapter.

Regardless of the reason, during the late 1970s and into the 1980s, police departments have made an intensive effort to recruit minority and women officers. Some departments have changed minimum entrance requirements, such as height and weight levels, in order to accommodate women. Others have set up elaborate recruiting campaigns to encourage talented women and minorities to choose a law enforcement career. Educational institutions specializing in criminal justice education, such as State University of New York at Albany's School of Criminal Justice, have established minority scholarship programs to create a pool of highly educated minorities who can fill positions in the law enforcement field.

Despite these efforts, minorities and women continue to be underrepresented in police departments. Since 1967, only Atlanta, Washington D.C., and Detroit have registered substantial gains in the number of minority policemen. Between 1967 and 1974, the percentage of nonwhite police officers increased from 21 to 40% in Washington, 10 to 22% in Atlanta, and from 5 to 17% in Detroit.[56] However, such representation is unusual: the Equal Employment Opportunity Commission reports that only 3.8% of professional employees in state and local police departments were black,[57] and the Federal Bureau of Investigation found that slightly over 3% of the nation's police officers were women.[58] If police departments are to be truly representative, even greater efforts are obviously needed to recruit women and minority officers.

### Women Police Officers

Women have proven to be highly successful police officers. In an important study of recruits in the Metropolitan Police Department of Washington, D.C., conducted by the Police Foundation, policewomen were found to exhibit extremely satisfactory work performances.[59] When compared to male officers, women were found to respond to similar types of calls, and the arrests they made were as likely to result in conviction. Women were more likely than their male colleagues to receive support from the community and were less likely to be charged with improper police conduct. However, women officers received somewhat lower supervisory ratings than males and made fewer felony and misdemeanor arrests.[60]

In a recent study of policewoman performance conducted in New York City, the results prove equally favorable to women patrol officers. Based on 3,625 hours of observation of patrol, including 2,400 police-civilian encounters, the study found that women police officers were perceived by civilians as being more competent, pleasant and respectful; the research team also found that the female's performance seemed to create a better civilian regard for police. The study also found that women officers performed better when serving with other women. Females paired with male companions seemed to be intimidated by their partners and were less likely to be assertive and self-sufficient.[61] These generally positive results are not dissimilar from findings accumulated in other studies conducted in major American cities.[62]

Despite their apparent merit, policewomen have not always been fully accepted by their peers or the public. The major bone of contention has been the policewoman's ability to perform in situations involving violence, and the consequent need for their having physical strength and dexterity. For example, in a survey conducted by Kenneth Kerber, Steven Andes, and Michelle Mittler, citizens in Illinois were asked to share their perceptions of policewomen's competence.[63] In most instances, the citizens respondents found male and female police officers about equal (in such areas as "apprehending shoplifters," "settling family disputes," "dealing with traffic accidents"). In some areas, female officers were preferred over males—"problems with children under 13," "dealing with a rape victim." However, in action-oriented activities such as "patrol in a squad car" and "stopping a fist fight," male officers were clearly viewed as more competent and more highly preferred. The authors reached the rather negative conclusion:

. . . if a police administrator were concerned about satisfying the sex preferences of the largest number of citizens contacted by the police and about having the largest number of citizens feel they are receiving the highest quality service possible, then there might be some argument for not hiring a large number of female police officers and for assigning those who are hired to only certain types of calls.[64]

Given the sometimes hostile reception afforded them by their male peers and the general public, policewomen have been forced to perform their jobs under extreme pressure. This condition is bound to affect their performance. Sociologist Susan Martin describes the roles female police officers take as a consequence of this pressure as falling somewhere in a continuum between two idealized professional identities: the *police*woman and police*woman*. The *police*woman gains her peer's acceptance by trying to closely adhere to the norms of behavior governing police in general, and exhibits a strong law enforcement orientation.[65] She tries to be more loyal, professional, hardworking, and tough than women are generally expected to be. *Police*women are neither afraid to engage in physical action or take punishment. She quotes one *police*woman as stating:

You have to fight the way the people fight out here. . . . You fight to win. . . . You have to be physical. Hit, kick, do what you can . . . and the person who doesn't do that should be disciplined. Often, it's the women, and they are said not to know any better. But they've been trained; they *do* know better. Generally, the women aren't aggressive enough, but once you've been punched a couple of times, you learn to get the punch in first.[66]

On the other end of the spectrum are police*women* who behave in a "traditionally feminine manner." They make few arrests, rarely attempt to engage in hazardous physical activity and put emphasis on "being a lady." Police*women* feel comfortable in the role of being of secondary importance in a police agency. Martin's interviews with 32 female officers reveal 7 could be classified as typical police*women*, 8 *police*women with the remaining subjects falling in between.

As the numbers of female police officers increase in the years ahead, it can be expected their role dilemmas will ease. In the future, the gulf between males and females in police work should narrow substantially.

### Minority Police Officers

Aided by the impetus of court ordered hiring quotas, the number of racial minorities in American police agencies is gradually increasing. Nonetheless, their police experience can often be a difficult one. As Nicholas Alex points out, black police officers suffer "double marginality."[67] On the one hand, the black officer must deal with the expectation that he will give members of his own race "a break." On the other hand, the black officer often experiences overt racism from his police colleagues. Alex found that black officer's adaptation to these pressures range from denying that blacks should be treated differently than whites to one of treating black offenders more harshly than white offenders to prove their lack of bias. Alex offers a number of reasons why some black police officers are tougher on black offenders: They desire acceptance from their white colleagues; they are particularly sensitive to any disrespect given them by black teenagers; they view themselves as the protectors of the black community.[68]

Minority police officers have also been the victim of intentional and sometimes unintentional departmental discrimination. For example, some departments in an effort to provide representative coverage to minority areas of the city assign all their black, hispanic, or oriental officers to a single patrol area or beat. In one Florida city, an inner-city patrol zone was manned entirely by black officers and all the department's black officers were assigned to this one zone.[69] The U.S. 5th Circuit Court labeled this practice discriminatory and ordered a halt to its use. Nonetheless, this practice is not unusual and minority police officers have resorted to court suits to seek relief from what they consider to be discriminatory or demeaning activity.[70]

Another problem faced by minority officers is resentment from their white colleagues. One of the dangers of court-ordered hiring is that "white back-lash" may occur. As sociologists James Jacobs and Jay Cohen point out, white police officers view affirmative action hiring and promotion programs as a threat to their job security.[71] They note that in Chicago, white officers intervened on the side of the city when a black police officer organization filed suit to change promotional criteria.[72] They further cite the case of the Detroit Police Officers' Association which filed suit to prevent the police department from setting up a quota plan for hiring black police sergeants. In the latter case, the court upheld the white officers' claim and struck down the promotional scheme. The court stated:

Inevitably race quotas do not accomplish the result of equal employment opportunity. The polarization of races that quotas exhibit creates a divided police department—

instead of unifying and strengthening it, the quota underscores differences and sows seeds of internal hatred.[73]

Jacobs and Cohen conclude:

So far documentation of intradepartmental race relations has been limited. Clearly, intensified racial conflict within the police poses enormous challenges for law enforcement administration. If intradepartmental race relations deteriorate, the solidarity which has always undergirded the social organization of the urban police may be seriously eroded. In that case, the very capacity of the urban police to carry out their basic law enforcement goals is at issue.[74]

**POLICE VIOLENCE AND THE COMMUNITY**

It is evident that minorities will continue to increase their presence on American police forces, especially if the recruitment mechanisms ordered by courts are followed. It will be a challenge to police administrators to maximize the important contribution they can make to effective law enforcement while at the same time easing morale problems presented by court interference in police hiring, promotion, and administration.

An issue of growing concern to criminal justice experts has been the use of excessive force and violence by the nation's patrolmen and detectives. It is alleged that the use of force by police has reached epidemic proportions and that an alarming percentage of people who meet violent deaths each year do so at the hands of police officers.[75] Moreover, the suggestion has been made that the use of police force is most often directed at blacks and other racial minorities.[76] So strong is the evidence that it has caused one critic to claim in a recent federal government publication:

The news gets around the community when someone is killed by police. It is part of a history—a very long history of extralegal justice that included whippings and lynching. But let us explore the statistics a bit further. Take the age group where 'desperate' criminals are much less likely to be found, the very young, ages 10 to 14, and the very old, those 65 years of age and older. In proportion to population, black youngsters and old men have been killed by the police at a rate 15 to 30 times greater than that of whites of the same age. It is the actual experiences behind statistics like these which suggest that police have one trigger finger for whites and another for blacks.[77]

The question of police use of force has two main areas of concern: (1) Are the average police officers generally brutal, violent, and disrespectful to the citizens they come into daily contact with? (2) Are the police overzealous and discriminatory in their use of *deadly force* when apprehending suspected felons? Let us examine each of these issues separately.

**Police Brutality**

Charges of generalized "police brutality" were common between the 1940s and 1960s. Surveys undertaken by the President's Commission on Law Enforcement and the Administration of Justice and various other national commissions found that many citizens believed that police discriminated against minorities when they used excessive force in handling suspects, displayed disrespect to innocent bystanders, and so on.[78] However, by 1967, the President's Commission concluded that the police use of physical brutality had somewhat abated:

The Commission believes that physical abuse is not as serious a problem as it was in the past. The few statistics which do exist suggest small numbers of cases involving excessive use of force. Although the relatively small number of reported complaints cannot be considered an accurate measure of the total problem, most persons, including civil rights leaders, believe that verbal abuse and harassment, not excessive use of force, is the major police-community relations problem today.[79]

While charges of police brutality continue to be made in many jurisdictions, the evidence suggests that actual instances of physical abuse of citizens by police officers is less frequent than commonly imagined. In a well-known study, Albert Reiss employed 36 college students to observe police-citizen interactions in high-crime areas in Washington, D.C., Chicago, and Boston.[80] Reiss found that while verbal abuse of citizens was quite common, the excessive use of physical force was relatively rare. In only 37 cases out of the 5,360 observations made by Reiss's researchers did police seem to employ excessive or unreasonable force. Moreover, there appeared to be little difference in the way police treated blacks and whites; when force was used, it was against more selective groups—those who showed disrespect or disregard for police authority once they were arrested. Thus, while not perfect, police officers do seem to have improved their relationships when interacting with citizens of all races.[81]

### Deadly Force

A more recent area of concern has been the police use of *deadly force* in apprehending fleeing or violent offenders. As commonly used, the term *deadly force* refers to the actions of a police officer who shoots and kills a suspect who is either fleeing from arrest, assaulting a victim, or attacking the police officer.[82] In most state jurisdictions, police officers may use deadly force against any fleeing felon though their life or the safety of others is not in apparent jeopardy.[83]

The justification for the use of deadly force can be traced to English Common Law in which almost every criminal offense merited a felony status and subsequent death penalty. Thus, execution while effecting the arrest of a felon was considered expedient, saving the state from the burden of trial.[84]

Today, there appears to be great variation in the police use of deadly force. Richard Kania and Wade Mackey found that statewide rates of persons killed by police range from a low of 2.97 in New Hampshire to a high of 37.97 in Georgia (per 100,000 population during the period 1961–1970).[85]

The factors which cause (or are associated with) police violence have been the subject of a recent research effort conducted by police expert

James Fyfe. Dr. Fyfe discovered that the following factors have been related to police violence rates:[86]

**1.** *Exposure to threat and stress*—areas with an unusually high incidence of violent crime are likely to experience police shootings.

**2.** *Police workload*—violence corresponds to the number of police on the street, the number of calls for service, the number and nature of police dispatches, and the number of arrests made in a given jurisdiction.

**3.** *Firearm availability*—cities which experience a large number of crimes committed with firearms are also likely to have high police violence rates. Houston, which ranks first in firearm availability, had 21.5 police shooting per 1000 violent crime arrests, while San Francisco, which ranks tenth, had only 1.5 shootings per 1000 violent crime arrests.[87]

**4.** *Population type and density*—jurisdictions which are swollen by large numbers of transients or nonresidents are generally not as heavily populated as the surrounding areas. Research findings suggest that many individuals shot by police are nonresidents caught at or near the scenes of robberies or burglaries of commercial establishments.[88]

**5.** *Racial variations*—it is alleged that blacks and other racial minorities are killed at a significantly higher rate than whites. Catherine Milton and her associates found that 79% of those shot by police in the seven cities they studied were black (blacks made up 39% of the population of the cities). In a similar study, Betty Jenkins and Adrienne Faisson found that 52% of those killed by police in 1970–1973 were black and 21% Hispanic.[89] It is common to focus on the racial factor as the primary predictive factor in police violence.[90]

Despite the evidence indicating that police shootings are motivated by racial bias, research conducted by Fyfe himself reveals some contradictory results. In a study of New York City shootings occurring over a five-year period (1971–1975), Fyfe found that police officers are most likely to shoot suspects when they attack police officers (Table 7.3), that many shootings stem from incidents in which police officers themselves were injured or killed (Table 7.4), and that minorities are more likely to be involved in weapon assaults on police officers than whites (37% of events involving white citizens were gun incidents while the black and hispanic percentages were 58 and 56% respectively).[91]

Fyfe's data reveals that minority police officers are responsible for a disportionate amount of police shootings.[92] Fyfe found that minority officers are often assigned to inner-city ghetto areas in which violence against police is common, and it is therefore not surprising that minority officers' use of violence is relatively more frequent. Thus, Fyfe's research *does not* support the widely held contention that white police officers have little regard for the lives of minority citizens, and instead suggests that police use of deadly force is situationally motivated and often justified under the circumstances.

## Controlling Deadly Force

Efforts to control deadly force have been neither uniform, nor as we have seen, entirely successful. Seven states including Colorado, Iowa, Kentucky, and Nebraska, have adopted as law the Model Penal Code policy on use of deadly force, which states in part:

| Incident Type | Opponent Injury | | | |
| --- | --- | --- | --- | --- |
| | None | Injured | Killed | Unknown |
| Physical Assault on Lone Officer | 67.3% (37) | 12.7% (7) | 0.0% (0) | 20.0% (11) |
| Gun Assault on Lone Officer | 47.2% (267) | 15.9% (90) | 8.7% (49) | 28.3% (160) |
| Knife Assault on Lone Officer | 49.7% (97) | 28.2% (55) | 10.8% (21) | 11.3% (22) |
| Vehicle Assault on Lone Officer | 57.1% (36) | 12.7% (8) | 0.0% (0) | 30.2% (19) |
| Other Assault on Lone Officer | 48.2% (53) | 28.2% (32) | 5.5% (6) | 18.2% (20) |
| Physical Assault on Two or More Officers | 68.9% (144) | 17.2% (36) | 5.7% (12) | 8.1% (17) |
| Gun Assault on Two or More Officers | 57.3% (754) | 18.9% (248) | 10.0% (132) | 13.8% (181) |
| Knife Assault on Two or More Officers | 45.5% (122) | 30.2% (81) | 18.7% (50) | 5.6% (15) |
| Vehicle Assault on Two or More Officers | 62.7% (163) | 10.4% (27) | 1.9% (5) | 25.0% (65) |
| Other Assault on Two or More Officers | 66.1% (109) | 13.3% (22) | 7.3% (12) | 13.3% (22) |
| No Assault, Intentional Shooting | 76.6% (357) | 11.4% (53) | 3.0% (14) | 9.0% (42) |
| Totals | 58.3% (2139) | 17.9% (658) | 8.2% (301) | 15.6% (574) |

TABLE 7.3 New York City Police Shooting Incident Type by Opponent Injury,[a] January 1, 1971–December 31, 1975

[a]Includes data for up to three opponents per incident; does not include opponent suicides (n = 3).

Source: data provided by James Fyfe, American University, Washington, D.C., with permission of author

TABLE 7.4
New York City Police
Shooting Types of
Officer Injury

| Shooting Type | N | Officers Injured/ Killed |
|---|---|---|
| Gun Assault on Lone Officer | 322 | 15.8% |
| Gun Assault on Two or More Officers | 777 | 10.2% |
| Knife Assault on Lone Officer | 119 | 23.5% |
| Knife Assault on Two or More Officers | 194 | 15.5% |
| Other Assault[a] on Lone Officer | 64 | 32.8% |
| Other Assault on Two or More Officers | 119 | 20.2% |
| Vehicle Assault on Lone Officer | 41 | 9.8% |
| Vehicle Assault on Two or More Officers | 150 | 24.0% |
| Physical Assault[b] on Lone Officer | 64 | 37.8% |
| Physical Assault[b] on Two or More Officers | 119 | 20.2% |
| Non-Assaultive | 308 | 1.6% |

[a]Includes assaults with chains, clubs, bats, etc.
[b]Includes assaults with fists and feet, biting, etc.

Source, James Fyfe, American University, Washington, D.C. with permission of author

Model Penal Code Section § 307(2)(B)

The use of deadly force is not justifiable under this Section unless; (i) the arrest is for a felony; and (ii) the person effecting the arrest is authorized to act as a peace officer or is assisting a person whom he believes to be authorized to act as a peace officer; and (iii) the actor believes that the force employed creates no substantial risk of injury to innocent persons; and (iv) the actor believes that: (1) the crime for which the arrest is made involved conduct including the use of threatened use of deadly force; or (2) there is a substantial risk that the person to be arrested will cause death or serious bodily harm if his apprehension is delayed.

The Model Penal Code rule forces the police to evaluate the danger to the suspect, the officer, and society as a whole before any action can be taken. In another seven states, only felonies involving force and violence justify the use of violence by police. However, 24 states adhere to the Common Law rule of allowing police to shoot fleeing felons who do not absolutely provide a clear and present danger to them, while 12 states have no state statutes concerning this matter at all.[93]

Another method of controlling police use of deadly force is through court action. The federal courts, however, have given mixed messages on

*I. Policy*

The Police Department is given special powers to use force by physical means and by firearms and other weapons. With the rapid growth of the country's cities, private citizens have increasingly entrusted to law enforcement agencies their rights to use violent force. Not to have done so would have continued and perhaps made worse the lawlessness and general violence which was common before the appearance and growth of metropolitan police departments.

The stakes for the proper execution of the responsibility to hold weapons and use them only with restraint and when necessary are very high. Abuse by police officers of the use of force violates the trust the public has given to the police and leads citizens injured or offended by such abuse to revoke that trust. Once this happens, people increasingly take matters into their own hands and dispense force and violence themselves. Such a situation has disastrous consequences for the peace of any modern, civilized community.

No other area of police work is so sensitive as this or as important to the implementation of the Department's peace keeping mission. In no other area is the exercise of sound judgment by the individual police officer and conformity to departmental policies and procedures more necessary.

*II. Guidelines and Procedures*

    A. Firearms

        1. Use of firearms in particular situations—a police officer is to:

           a. Use only the minimum amount of force which is consistent with the accomplishment of his duties, and exhaust every other reasonable means of apprehension or defense before resorting to the use of firearms.

           b. Never discharge a firearm in the performance of his duties except under the following circumstances:

               1. To defend himself or another from attack which the officer has reasonable cause to believe could result in death or serious physical injury.

               2. To apprehend one who has committed or attempted to commit a felony in the officer's presence, providing that the felony involved an actual or threatened attack which the officer has reasonable cause to believe could result in death or serious bodily injury.

               (Note: If the felony described above is not committed in the officer's presence, he is to have sufficient information to know as a virtual certainty that the suspect has committed the felony.)

               3. To kill a dangerous animal, or an animal that is so badly injured that humanity requires its removal from further suffering.

           c. Never use firearms to fire a warning shot, or in cases involving only misdemeanors.

        2. Reports

           a. Whenever he discharges a firearm, except when practicing with it, submit as soon as possible afterwards a written report on a 650 to his commanding officer.

           b. Include in the report:

               (1) The names of the officer and other persons concerned.

               (2) The circumstances under which the firearm was used.

               (3) The nature of the injury inflicted, if any.

FIGURE 7.2
Cambridge, Massachusetts Police Policy: Use of Weapons

the validity and constitutionality of statutes allowing the police to shoot fleeing felons. In *Mattis vs. Schnarr*,[94] one of the few cases in which a court overruled a police shooting policy, the Eighth Circuit Court of Appeals recommended that force could only be used:

. . . where the officer has a warrant or probable cause to arrest the felon where the felon could not be otherwise apprehended and where the felon had used deadly force in the commission of the felony, or the officer reasonably believed the felon would use deadly force against the officer or others if not immediately apprehended.[95]

Despite *Schnarr's* clear-cut limitation on police power, other state and federal courts have seen fit to allow a police officer all necessary means (including shooting) to arrest any fleeing felon.[96] Thus, judicial control over police use of force seems at this writing extremely cloudy.

Another method of controlling police shootings is through internal review and policy making by police departments themselves. For example, following the imposition of a Firearms Discharge Review Board in New York City, incidents of police shootings of suspects who did not physically assault an officer declined 75%.[97] Still another method of internal police control is to create explicit standards of police conduct which must be followed by officers lest they risk departmental review and discipline. Figure 7.2 sets out one such policy designed by the Cambridge, Massachusetts Police Department to control police shootings.

Despite such efforts, police violence against citizens continues to be an issue which erodes confidence in the police and the criminal justice system in general.

SUMMARY

Police officers today are faced with many critical problems, including the proper use of discretion, the assimilation of minority and women officers into police roles, and the development of an understanding of the police personality and how it affects job performance. Still another critical issue concerns police use of force and whether it discriminates against minority citizens.

It is evident considering these various key issues that much effort is needed to study the police role and to determine whether a generalized understanding of police behavior can be achieved. The benefit of such an accomplishment has been outlined by sociologist Lawrence Sherman:

There is no reason to assume that the causes of police behavior need necessarily be the same as the causes of judicial behavior or of the behavior of other service organizations. A substantive theory of police behavior would be valuable as an intermediate step in building up to more general theories, rather than working down. It would also provide more immediately useful implications for policy issues. The problem is to develop a theory that not only explains variance, but also offers the symmetry, coherence, and elegance of formal theories. Whether such a theory is possible remains to be seen.[98]

QUESTIONS FOR DISCUSSIONS

1. Should police be allowed to use "deadly force" at any time other than when their own or a victim's life is in danger?

2. Define police discretion, and identify its positive and negative aspects.

3. Is it possible for a college education to actually harm a police officer?

**1.** See, for example, Seymour Martin Lipset, "Why Cops Hate Liberals and Vice Versa," *The Atlantic* 223:76–83 (1969); Hubert Klein, *The Police: Damned If They Do, Damned If They Don't* (New York: Crown Publishers, 1969).

**2.** The Knapp Commission Report on Police Corruption (New York: Braziller, 1972) p. 1; see Laurence Sherman, *Police Corruption: A Sociological Perspective* (Garden City, New York: Doubleday/Anchor Books, 1974).

**3.** Richard Lundman, *Police and Policing* (New York: Holt, Rinehart, and Winston, 1980); see also, Jerome Skolnick, *Justice Without Trial* (New York: Wiley, 1966).

**4.** Cited in Arthur Niederhoffer, *Behind the Shield: The Police in Urban Society* (Garden City, New York: Doubleday, 1967), p. 65.

**5.** See, for example, Richard Bennett and Theodore Greenstein, "The Police Personality: A Test of the Predispositional Model," *Journal of Police Science and Administration* 3:439–445 (1975).

**6.** Milton Rokeach, Martin Miller, and John Snyder, "The Value Gap Between Police and Policed," *Journal of Social Issues* 27:155–171 (1971).

**7.** James Teevan and Bernard Dolnick, "The Values of the Police: A Reconsideration and Interpretation," *Journal of Police Science and Administration* 1:366–369 (1973).

**8.** Ibid., p. 366.

**9.** Arthur Niederhoffer, *Behind the Shield: The Police In Urban Society* (Garden City, New York: Doubleday, 1967).

**10.** William Westly, *Violence and the Police: A Sociological Study of Law, Custom,* and Morality (Cambridge, Mass.: The MIT Press, 1970); W. Westly, "Violence and the Police," *American Journal of Sociology* 49:34–41 (1953).

**11.** A. Niederhoffer, *Behind the Shield*, pp. 216–220.

**12.** Robert Regoli and Eric Poole, "Measurement of Police Cynicism: A Factor Scaling Approach," *Journal of Criminal Justice* 7:37–52 (1979).

**13.** Ibid., p. 43.

**14.** Ibid., p. 44.

**15.** See, for example, Richard Harris, *The Police Academy: An Inside View* (New York: Wiley, 1973); John Van Maanen, "Observations on the Making of Policemen," *Human Organization* 32:407–418 (1973); Jonathan Rubenstein, *City Police* (New York: Ballantine, 1973); John Broderick, *Police in a Time of Change* (Morristown, N.J.: General Learning Press, 1977).

**16.** Robert Balch, "The Police Personality: Fact or Fiction?" *Journal of Criminal Law, Criminology and Police Science* 63:117 (1972).

**17.** Larry Tifft, "The 'Cop Personality,' Reconsidered," *Journal of Police Science and Administration* 2:268 (1974).

**18.** James Q. Wilson, *Varieties of Police Behavior* (Cambridge, Mass.: Harvard University Press, 1968), Chapter 7.

**19.** Ibid., p. 141.

**20.** See Franklin Ashburn, "Changing the Rhetoric of Professionalism" in Law Enforcement Assistance Administration, *Innovation in Law Enforcement* (Washington, D.C.: U.S. Government Printing Office, 1973), p. 6.

**21.** Cited by Schrag, *Crime and Justice: American Style*, p. 147.

22. Jerome Skolnick, *Justice Without Trial*, (New York: John Wiley & Sons, 1966).

23. Clarence Schrag, *Crime & Justice: American Style*, p. 148.

24. William Westley, *Violence and The Police* (Cambridge, Mass.: Massachusetts Institute of Technology Press, 1970).

25. Nathan Goldman, *The Differential Selection of Juvenile Offenders For Court Appearance* (New York: National Council on Crime & Delinquency, 1963).

26. Aaron Cicourel, *The Social Organization of Juvenile Justice* (New York: John Wiley & Sons, 1968).

27. Irving Piliavin and Scott Briar, "Police Encounters with Juveniles," *American Journal of Sociology* 70:206 (1964).

28. National Advisory Council on Criminal Justice Standards and Goals, *Police*, pp. 21–22.

29. Jerome Skolnick and J. Richard Woodworth, "Bureaucracy, Information & Social Control: A Study of a Morals Detail" in *The Police, Six Sociological Essays*, David Bordua, ed. (New York: John Wiley & Sons, 1960).

30. John Gardiner, *Traffic & The Police: Variations in Law Enforcement Policy* (Cambridge, Mass.: Harvard University Press, 1969).

31. James Q. Wilson, "The Police in the Ghetto" in *The Police and the Community*, Robert F. Steadman, ed. (Baltimore: Johns Hopkins University Press, 1972), p. 68.

32. See, for example, National Commission on Law Observance and Enforcement, *Report on Police* (Washington, D.C., 1931) p. 70. Similar views have been expressed by *The President's Commission of Law Enforcement and the Administration of Justice* (1967) and the *National Advisory Commission on Criminal Justice Standards and Goals*.

33. See, Larry Hoover, *Police Educational Characteristics and Curricula* (Washington, D.C.: U.S. Government Printing Office, 1975).

34. Peter P. Lejins, *Introducing a Law Enforcement Curriculum at a State University*, a report of the National Institute of Law Enforcement and Criminal Justice (Washington, D.C.: Government Printing Office, 1970), pp. 13–16.

35. See, for example, James Erickson and Mathew Neary, "Criminal Justice Education: Is It Criminal?" *The Police Chief* 42:38 (1975).

36. See Lawrence Sherman and Warren Bennis, "Higher Education for Police Officers: The Central Issues," *The Police Chief* 44:32 (1977).

37. Lawrence Sherman, Warren Bennis, Tom Bradley, Lee Brown, Hugo Masini, Stephen May, Norval Morris, Patrick Murphy, Robert O'Neil, and Charles Saunders, *The Quality of Police Education* (San Francisco: Josey-Bass, 1978).

38. See, for example, B. E. Sanderson, "Police Officers: The Relationship of College Education to Job Performance," *The Police Chief* 44:62 (1977); James Finnegan, "A Study of Relationships Between College Education and Police Performance in Baltimore, Maryland," *The Police Chief* 43:50 (1976); R. Trojanowicz and Thomas Nicholson, "A Comparison of Behavioral Styles of College Graduate Police Officers vs. Non-College Going Police Officers," *The Police Chief* 43:57 (1976).

39. R. P. Witte, "The Dumb Cop," *The Police Chief* 36:38 (1969).

40. Wayne Cascio, "Formal Education and Police Officer Performance," *Journal of Police Science and Administration* 5:89 (1977).

41. Ibid., p. 90.

42. Charles Swanson, "An Uneasy Look at College Education and the Police Organization," *Journal of Criminal Justice* 5:311–320 (1977).

**43.** U.S. Commerce Department, Economic Indicators in Government Services (mimeo) (Washington, D.C.: U.S. Department of Commerce, 1978).

**44.** P. Greenwood and J. Petersilia, *The Criminal Investigation Process, Volume I: Summary and Policy Implications;* and P. Greenwood, J. Chaiken, J. Petersilia, and L. Prusoff, *The Criminal Investigation Process, Volume III: Observations and Analysis* (Santa Monica, Cal.: Rand Corporation, 1975).

**45.** G. Douglas Gourley, "Police-Public Relations," *Annals of the American Academy of Police and Social Science* 291: 136 (1954).

**46.** Raymond Parnas, "The Police Responses to Domestic Disturbance," *Wisconsin Law Review* 914–960 (1967).

**47.** J. Robert Lilly, "What Are The Police Now Doing," *Journal of Police Science and Administration* 6:51 (1978).

**48.** See, for example, "One-Man Patrol Cars," *Police Chief* 18–24 (1963).

**49.** Adapted from Terry Koepsell and Charles Gerard, *Small Police Agency Consolidation: Suggested Approaches* (Washington, D.C.: U.S. Government Printing Office, 1979).

**50.** FBI, *Uniform Crime Reports, 1978,* p. 234.

**51.** Wesley Skogan and George Antunes, "Information, Apprehension, and Deterrence: Exploring the Limits of Police Productivity," *Journal of Criminal Justice* 7:217–241 (1979).

**52.** P. B. Block and J. Bell, *Managing Investigations: The Rochester System* (Washington, D.C.: The Police Foundation, 1976).

**53.** Ibid., p. 236.

**54.** See, for example, Arnold v. Ballard, 390 F.Supp. 723 (1955). (Evidence showed that between 1965 and 1971 only 10 blacks and 277 whites had been appointed to the Akron, Ohio Police Department.) Similar cases have been decided in many major American cities.

**55.** Bridgeport Guardians, Inc., v. Bridgeport Civil Service Commission, 354 F.Supp. 778 (1973); 482 F.2d 1333 (2nd Cir., 1973); 497 F.2d 1113 (2nd Cir., 1974).

**56.** Cited in James Jacobs and Jay Cohen, "The Impact of Racial Integration on the Police," *Journal of Police Science and Administration* 6:175 (1978).

**57.** Reported in *LEAA Newsletter,* Vol. 7, No. 2, p. 7 (1978). Different figures on minority police officers which indicate that their total amount is uncertain are reported by B. Regoli and D. Jerome, "The Recruitment and Promotion of a Minority Group in an Establishment Institution: The Police," *Journal of Police Science and Administration* 3:412 (1975).

**58.** Federal Bureau of Investigation, *Crime in the United States, 1978* (Washington, D.C.: U.S. Government Printing Office, 1978), p. 234.

**59.** Peter Bloch and Deborah Anderson, *Policewomen on Patrol: Final Report* (Washington, D.C.: Police Foundation, 1974).

**60.** Ibid., pp. 1–7.

**61.** Joyce Sichel, Lucy Friedman, Janet Quint, Micall Smith, *Women on Patrol. A Pilot Study of Police Performance in New York City* (Washington, D.C.: National Criminal Justice Reference Service, 1978).

**62.** See, for example, William Weldy, "Women in Policing: A Positive Step Toward Increased Police Enthusiasm," *Police Chief* 43:47 (1976).

**63.** K. Kerber, S. Andes, and M. Mittler, "Citizen Attitudes Regarding the Competence of Female Police Officers," *Journal of Police Science and Administration* 5:337–346 (1977).

**64.** Ibid., p. 346.

**65.** Susan Martin, *"Police*women and Police*women*: Occupational Role Dilemmas and Choices of Female Officers, *Journal of Police Science and Administration* 7:314 (1979).

**66.** Ibid., pp. 317–318.

**67.** Nicholas Alex, *Black in Blue: A Study of the Negro Policeman* (New York; Appleton-Century Crofts, 1969).

**68.** Ibid., pp. 154–155.

**69.** Baker v. City of St. Petersburg, 400 F.2d 294 (5th Cir., 1968).

**70.** See, for example, Allen v. City of Mobile, 331 F.Supp. 1134 (1971). Affirmed 466 F.2d 122 (5th Cir., 1972).

**71.** James Jacobs and Jay Cohen, "The Impact of Racial Integration on the Police," *Journal of Police Science and Administration* 6:182 (1978).

**72.** See Afro-American Patrolmen's League v. Duck, 366 F.Supp. 1095 (1973); 503 F.2d 294 (6th Cir. 1974); 538 F.2d 328, (6th Cir., 1976).

**73.** Detroit Police Officers Association v. Young, 46 U.S. Law Week 2463 (E.D. Mich. 1978).

**74.** Jacobs and Cohen, "The Impact of Racial Integration on the Police," p. 183.

**75.** See, for example, John Goldkamp, "Minorities as Victims of Police Shootings: Interpretations of Racial Disproportionality and Police Use of Deadly Force," *Justice System Journal* 2:169–183 (1976).

**76.** See Paul Takagi, "Death by Police Intervention," in R. N. Brenner and M. Kravitz, *A Community Concern: Police Use of Deadly Force*, (National Criminal Justice Research Service) (Washington, D.C.: U.S. Government Printing Office, 1979), pp. 31–38.

**77.** Ibid., p. 34.

**78.** See, for example, President's Commission on Law Enforcement and the Administration of Justice, *Task Force Report: The Police* (Washington, D.C.: U.S. Government and Printing Office, 1967) pp. 181–182; Report of the National Advisory Commission on Civil Disorders, "Police and the Community," (Washington, D.C.: U.S. Government Printing Office, 1968) pp. 158–159.

**79.** President's Commission on Law Enforcement and the Administration of Justice, *Task Force Report: The Police*, pp. 181–182.

**80.** Albert Reiss, *The Police and the Public* (New Haven, Conn.: Yale University Press, 1972).

**81.** Lawrence Sherman, "Causes of Police Behavior, The Current State of Quantitative Research," *Journal of Research in Crime and Delinquency* 17:80–81 (1980).

**82.** Larry Sherman and Robert Langworthy, "Measuring Homicide by Police Officers," *Journal of Criminal Law and Criminology* 4:546–560 (1979).

**83.** See Karen Popek, "The Unconstitutional Use of Deadly Force by the Police," *Chicago-Kent Law Review* 55:541 (1979).

**84.** Ibid.

**85.** Richard Kania and Wade Mackey, "Police Violence as a Function of Community Characteristics," *Criminology* 15:27–48 (1977).

**86.** James Fyfe, "Toward a Typology of Police Shootings," paper presented at the Academy of Criminal Justice Science meeting, Oklahoma City, March 1980 (mimeo).

**87.** See Steven Brill, *Firearm Abuse: A Research and Policy Report* (Washington, D.C.: Police Foundation, 1977).

**88.** Sherman and Langworthy, "Measuring Homicide by Police Officers," p. 554.

**89.** Catherine Milton, Jeanne Halleck, James Lardner, and Gary Abrecht, *Police*

*Use of Deadly Force* (Washington, D.C.: Police Foundation, 1977); Betty Jenkins and Adrienne Faison, *An Analysis of 248 Persons Killed by New York City Policemen* (New York: Metropolitan Applied Research Center, Inc., 1974), see also Paul Takagi, "Death by Police Intervention."

**90.** See P. Takagi, "Death by Police Intervention."

**91.** James Fyfe, *Shots Fired: An Examination of New York City Police Firearms Discharges*, Ph.D. Dissertation, SUNY-Albany. (Ann Arbor, Mich.: University Microfilms, 1978).

**92.** James Fyfe, "Officer Race and Police Shooting," paper presented at American Society of Criminology, (Philadelphia, Penn. 1979), p. 5.

**93.** Ozell Sutton, "Police Use of Excessive Force: A Community Relations Concern," *A Community Concern: Police Use of Deadly Force*, (Washington, D.C.: U.S. Government Printing Office, 1979), pp. 27–30.

**94.** 547 F.2d 1007 (9th Cir. 1976); vacated as moot, *Asheroff v. Mattis* 431 U.S. 171 (1977).

**95.** *Mattis v. Schnarr*, p. 1020.

**96.** See, for example, *Cunningham v. Ellington*, 323 F.Supp. 1072 (W. D.Tenn. 1971); *Wiley v. Memphis Police Department*, 548 F.2d 1247 (6th Cir.) (1977).

**97.** See James Fyfe, "Administrative Interventions on Police Shooting Discretion: An Empirical Examination," *Journal of Criminal Justice* 7:313–325 (1979).

**98.** L. Sherman, "Causes of Police Behavior: The Current State of Quantitative Behavior," p. 94.

# 'Walking In A Cop's Shoes . . .': The Experiences of Prof. George Kirkham

What might happen to an academician turned police officer, particularly a criminology professor who had always been critical of the police role in our society? What changes might occur in his attitudes toward the law or his feelings about crime, its victims and perpetrators?

In 1973, challenged by a number of my undergraduate criminology students who either were or had been police officers and who disagreed with many of my classroom statements about the police, I decided to become a policeman for several months in order to examine empirically the accuracy of some of the things I had been saying and writing about the police and crime in modern society.

## ATTITUDES CHANGED

Because I wanted to experience the strains and pressures of today's urban patrolman, I selected a large and rather typically metropolitan area within which to conduct this unorthodox "experiment" (Jacksonville, Fla.;

population 500,000). I further requested one of the high-crime, inner-city beats on the evening watch and assignment to the same duties as any other uniformed patrolman.

After completing Florida's mandatory police training curriculum as a balding, 31-year-old recruit, background investigations, polygraphs, physical exams and the like, I found myself standing on the steps of the Jacksonville Police Station feeling incredibly awkward in the creaking leather and crisp new uniform of a new police officer.

That was how it all began—an experience that was to profoundly change my life, both as a criminologist and a human being.

While working as an urban patrolman did not transform me into either a John Bircher or a flaming right-wing apologist for the police, it did leave me with a dramatically changed view of the modern law enforcement officer and the magnitude of problems confronting him or her. Moreover, the experience profoundly changed my thinking about such subjects as crime, offenders, victims, and the criminal justice system itself.

Source: *LEAA Newsletter*, Vol. 6, No. 10, 1977, p. 11.

In retrospect, victims of crime had been largely abstractions to me until I became a policeman. For most criminology professors, a victim is a relatively inconsequential bit of ink on a page, a number on a chart to be coldly and methodically examined in an effort to understand the cause of crime. Robbery, rape, murder—it makes no difference really—all are remote, impersonal phenomena to the average criminology professor.

## WITNESSED SUFFERING

Much the same perspective characterizes the viewpoints of many judges, criminal lawyers, jurors, probation officers, and others connected with our criminal justice system. They all enjoy the luxury of confronting the victims of crime retrospectively, in a highly antiseptic and safe environment.

I found during those months in Jacksonville than to a police officer—even the most callous of them—the victims of crime become something inescapably personal. My horror at witnessing their suffering firsthand, of literally picking up the pieces of shattered lives, permanently altered the meaning of the word "victim" in my vocabulary.

One night early in my new career I knelt on a wet sidewalk beside an old man who was dying from a bullet wound in the chest. He had been robbed on the street by a youth gang and then shot in anger because he had only three dollars. The memory of that incident—and too many others like it—is forever etched in my mind.

Such things began to change my thinking in ways that only personal exposure to human tragedy can. To my university colleagues who are appalled to discover that I now advocate capital punishment for felony murder, I can only say that personally seeing one innocent shopkeeper who has been calmly executed with a shot in the back of the head has infinitely more impact on one's thinking than all the books and articles that have ever been written about capital punishment!

## HUMBLED BY EXPERIENCE

As a policeman, I found myself forced to make the gravest of decisions about other people's lives and futures in a matter of minutes, sometimes seconds—always with the nagging certainty that if I was in error, I would be judged by people like by former self, people who enjoy the luxury of great amounts of time in which to act and think.

I learned so many things about myself on the streets of that police beat—learned that I had a limit to the frustration and disrespect I could endure, learned that I got tired of handling other people's troubles night after night, learned that I sometimes made mistakes under pressure.

The experience of walking even a few miles in a cop's shoes was a humbling one. Above all, it brought me to the very personal realization that true knowledge about any subject has an applied and practical—as well as an abstract and theoretical—dimension.

# The Police Process

## CHAPTER OUTLINE

## KEY TERMS

CRIME
DETECTION

In the preceding chapter, the history and role of the police in society, police structure and organization, and other operational aspects of the field of law enforcement were discussed. This chapter focuses on the methods and scope of authority available to the police when they investigate a crime and arrest a suspect. Particular emphasis is placed on the legal standards as well as the rules and procedures required of the police in accomplishing their tasks.

The police are generally the first agency in the criminal justice system to deal with the commission of a crime. They generally become aware of the crime in one of three ways: through a reported complaint initiated by a witness, through a complaint from a victim, or through personal investigation. Victim-reported crime may involve the woman who complains to the police officer on patrol that her pocketbook was stolen; the man who goes to the local police station and claims that he is being threatened by a neighbor, or the woman who calls the police to inform them that she was assaulted by her boyfriend. Witness-reported crimes may involve the neighbor who has observed someone unfamiliar breaking into a home, the passerby who sees a woman molested by a youthful offender, or the woman who observes a teenager stealing a pair of pants from a local clothing shop. Where the victim or witness seems to be telling the truth, the police will usually proceed to investigate the crime, obtain information about the suspect, and seek to apprehend the offender.

In some instances, the police themselves discover the crime. During patrol activities, police often witness crimes and may seek to arrest a suspect at the scene. For example, the police officer on patrol at night may observe a youth breaking into a gas station; or the traffic officer on the highway may stop a suspicious automobile, find out that it has been stolen, and arrest the driver for larceny. Police also investigate individuals and situations because they are linked in some way to criminal activity; for instance, the police chief may ask an officer to talk with a pharmacist about local drug traffic to learn where juveniles are obtaining unauthorized drugs without prescriptions. On a more intensive level, a police department may assign detectives to investigate a vice, gambling, or narcotics ring that is flourishing in a community. This approach to crime detection may often take months, since the police must not only obtain evidence for criminal prosecution, but must do so within strict legal boundaries. In deciding to proceed with this type of investigation, the police are often influenced by the availability of their own resources, the seriousness of the crime, community attitudes, and societal pressures relating to certain types of criminal activities perceived as being more harmful than others.

In many situations where criminal acts occur, no one is arrested at the scene. For example, the police may be informed that a cab driver has been killed in an attempted robbery and that his body has been found in the cab at a particular location, or that a woman has been raped and her attacker has escaped. These types of criminal cases are often referred to the police agency's detective bureau. The investigating detectives may then question everyone remotely connected with the crime and examine the crime scene for evidence. People in the general area of the scene will usually be interviewed for information, witnesses will be questioned, skilled crime scene technicians will gather physical evidence, and other officers will generally search the area for clues to the identification of the offender.

Generally, because these investigative steps are so time-consuming and involved, they are taken in only a few of the criminal acts encountered by police. Obviously, serious crimes such as those mentioned above will require many investigative tools; on the other hand, minor offenses, such as the theft of a television set or stereo, do not require a serious police investigative response. Since few formal rules and no uniformity exists regarding procedures used in police investigation, the degree to which a crime is investigated often depends on the overall resources of a given police department.

Often, police are not the only criminal justice agency which initially comes into contact with criminal activity. The district attorney's office, for instance, is frequently involved in special kinds of criminal investigations and in enforcing particular statutes dealing with such activities as organized crime, white-collar crime, and political corruption. During the Watergate investigation, the Special Prosecutor's Office established by the President and staffed with lawyers, police personnel, accountants, and other professionals investigated serious criminal activity even though it was not a police agency per se. Congress has made subsequent efforts to create a permanent federal prosecutor's office, but so far such legal legislation has not been successful.[1]

Other nonpolice investigative agencies include grand juries and legislative committees. The primary responsibility of a grand jury is to hear evidence presented by the prosecutor and determine if a person should be charged with a crime. It ordinarily has the statutory power to compel witnesses to appear before it, to examine the witnesses, and to inquire into matters related to a specific crime or a broader area of criminal activity such as political corruption. A congressional legislative committee, consisting of selected members of a legislature and staff, can also hold hearings to investigate and identify criminal activity. Information about crimes can then be brought to the attention of the police and prosecutorial agencies for appropriate action. Legislative criminal investigation is exemplified by the work of the Senate Watergate Committee and the House Judiciary Committee of the federal congress in exposing the alleged political crimes of the Nixon administration.

**POLICE INVESTIGATION**

Once a crime has been committed and the purpose of the investigation has been determined, the police may use various means to collect the evidence needed for criminal prosecution. In each crime, police must decide how to proceed with the primary focus of the investigation. Should surveillance techniques be employed to secure information? Is there reasonable suspicion to justify stopping and frisking a suspect? Has the investigation shifted from a general inquiry and begun to focus on a particular suspect so that the police can initiate a legally appropriate interrogation procedure? In certain circumstances, one investigative technique may be more appropriate than another. The American Bar Association's *Standards Relating to the Urban Police Function* identify many of the methods currently employed by the police in responding to situations involving both criminal and noncriminal activity:[2]

1. Resolving conflict (e.g., as applied to disputes between individuals such as husbands and wives, landlords and their tenants, neighbors, businessmen and their customers; and as applied to disputes between groups, such as protesters and an agency of government, one religious sect and another, one racial group and another, labor and management, etc.)

2. Ordering people to move away from a particular site (e.g., as applied to the spectators or bystanders at the scene of an accident, crime, fire, or conflict; the persons involved in a conflict that erupts or threatens to erupt in one of the situations described in method 1 above; or at the scene of a parade, speech, or an informal gathering).

3. Stopping and questioning people (e.g., on suspicion of criminal activity, with regard to the criminal activity of others, or merely to acquire information with which to carry out any of the wide variety of activities for which the police are responsible).

4. Taking or sending a person to a location where he can get immediate help or shelter (e.g., such as his own residence; a hotel or residence of a friend or relative; or a hospital, mental institution, detoxification center, or temporary shelter for the young or the aged).

5. Finding a caretaker for a person unable to take care of himself (e.g., spouse, parent or other relative; friend or neighbor).

6. Referring matters to court for private prosecution (e.g., informing parties to a dispute that they may seek to initiate a prosecution on their own by filing a complaint with a court which, if approved, will result in the issuance of a warrant or a summons).

7. Referring matters to an agency or individual in a position to provide assistance (e.g., such as some other governmental agency, a private social agency, a minister, a health service, or a lawyer).

8. Issuing warnings (with or without threat of subsequent surveillance) (e.g., putting a person on notice not to do a certain act; not to omit doing a certain act; not to repeat an action or to continue to fail to act; to stay away from an area or to get out of a certain area).

9. Threatening to report (e.g., issuance of instructions to correct a condition or to cease from engaging in a specific form of activity with the threat that a continuance will result in a report being made to, for example, a governmental agency, parents, school officials, an employer, a spouse, etc.).

10. Engaging in surveillance (e.g., keeping a situation under observation—overtly or covertly—with the objective of acquiring additional information or evidence, with the objective of providing a sense of security, or with the objective of discouraging certain forms of activity).

11. Frisking and searching of persons and searching of vehicles and premises (e.g., in connection with an arrest or, independent of an arrest, as a means of protecting the officer, acquiring evidence of a crime, acquiring information generally, or simply making the presence of the police known).

12. Confiscating illegal objects (e.g., drugs, guns, gambling devices, paraphernalia or money—either in connection with an arrest or simply as a means of removing such items from use and circulation).

13. Trading immunity from enforcement for information or cooperation (e.g., in allowing a narcotics user, a petty gambler, or a prostitute to continue to operate despite evidence of a violation of the law in exchange for their providing information leading to the identity and prosecution of those engaged in more serious forms of behavior).

14. Detaining persons temporarily (e.g., the use of arrest and subsequent detention for purposes other than prosecution, such as further investigation, safekeeping, or simply harassment).[3]

Criminal detection, apprehension, and arrest are the primary investigative functions performed by law enforcement officers. Proper police investigations involve collecting facts and information that will lead to the identification, arrest, and conviction of the criminal defendant. Many investigative methods are informal—such as referring an alcoholic to a hospital or resolving a family dispute—and are based upon agency policy or police discretion. On the other hand, the primary techniques of investigation—such as stopping and questioning people or interrogating a suspect—are controlled by statute and constitutional case law, and are subject to review by the courts. The following methods of police investigation are discussed in this chapter: (1) search and seizure, (2) warrantless searches, (3) arrest, (4) custodial interrogation, and (5) lineups.

Evidence collected by the police is governed by the search and seizure requirements of the Fourth Amendment of the United States Constitution as interpreted by the United States Supreme Court (see Chapter 5). The Fourth Amendment protects the defendant against any unreasonable searches and seizures resulting from unlawful activities. The general rule regarding the application of the Fourth Amendment, although there are exceptions, is that any search or seizure undertaken without a validly obtained search warrant is unlawful. Furthermore, it provides that no warrant shall be issued unless there is probable cause to believe that an offense has been or is being committed. A police officer concerned with investigating a crime can undertake a proper search and seizure if a valid search warrant has been obtained from the court, or if the officer is functioning under one of the many exceptions to the search warrant requirement.

A search warrant is an order from a court authorizing and directing the police to search a designated place for property stated in the order and to bring that property to court. The order must be based on the sworn testimony of the police officer that the facts upon which the request for the search warrant is made are trustworthy. Examples of an affidavit for a search warrant and the search warrant itself are found in Figure 8.1 and Figure 8.2.

Three critical concepts in the Fourth Amendment are directly related to the search warrant: _unreasonableness_, _probable cause_, and _particularity_.

**WARRANTLESS SEARCHES**

FIGURE 8.1
Search
Warrant

```
ACODC NO. 30            Commonwealth of Massachusetts

Middlesex              , ss.              Concord District
                                                     Court
                         (Search Warrant)
TO THE SHERIFFS OF OUR SEVERAL COUNTIES, OR THEIR DEPUTIES, ANY STATE POLICE
OFFICER, OR ANY CONSTABLE OR POLICE OFFICER OF ANY CITY OR TOWN, WITHIN OUR
SAID COMMONWEALTH:

Proof by affidavit having been made this day before  Special Justice J.Q. Jones
                                                     (Name of person issuing warrant)
by    Police Chief Sam Buckley
                   (Name of person or persons signing affidavit)
*that there is probable cause for believing that certain property has been stolen, embezzled, or obtained by false
pretences — certain property is intended for use or has been used as the means of committing a crime — certain
property has been concealed to prevent a crime from being discovered — certain property is unlawfully
possessed or kept or concealed for an unlawful purpose.

    WE THEREFORE COMMAND YOU in the daytime (or at any time of the day or night) to make an
immediate search of    123 Smith Street, Concord
                                (Identify premises)
(occupied by   Francine Taggart                                 ) and of the person of
                      (Name of occupant)
                                                   , and of any person present who may
                  (Name of person)
be found to have such property in his possession or under his control or to whom such property may have been
delivered, for the following property:

                              (Description of property)


    One small brown suitcase believed to contain heroin.


and if you find any such property or any part thereof to bring it and the persons in whose possession it is found
before the   Concord District Court
                              (Name of Court)
at    Concord, Massachusetts
                              (Court location)
in said County and Commonwealth, as soon as it has been served and in any event not later than seven days of
issuance thereof. (Officer to make return on reverse side)

       Witness                         , Esquire, Justice, at   Concord          ,

                              aforesaid, this  21  day of  June
in the year of our Lord one thousand nine hundred and  80

*Strike inapplicable clauses          Justice
                                       Clerk
                                       Assistant Clerk
G.L. c. 276, ss. 1 to 7; St. 1964, c. 557
              APPROVED BY THE CHIEF JUSTICE OF THE DISTRICT COURTS
```

Unreasonableness in searches and seizures generally refers to whether an officer exceeds the scope of police authority. Most unreasonable actions are those in which the police officer did not have sufficient information to justify the search. In discussing probable cause, the Fourth Amendment provides clearly that no warrants shall issue unless probable cause is supported by oath or affirmation; in other words, a search warrant can only be obtained if the request for it is supported by facts which would convince the court that a crime has been or is being committed. Particularity generally refers to the search warrant itself; the Fourth Amendment requires that a search warrant specify the place to be searched and the reasons for searching it. When the police request a search warrant, the warrant must

ACODC NO. 29

## Commonwealth of Massachusetts

Middlesex _____, ss.                                    _____ Concord District Court _____
                                                                          Court

### AFFIDAVIT IN SUPPORT OF APPLICATION FOR SEARCH WARRANT*
G.L. c. 276, ss. 1 to 7; St. 1964, c. 557 As Amended

I, __Sam Buckley__ _____, being duly sworn, depose and say: _____21__June__, 19_80_.
Name of applicant

1. I am __Police Chief of Concord, Massachusetts__ _____
(Describe position, assignment, office, etc.)

2. I have information based upon (describe sources, facts indicating reliability of source and nature of information; if based on personal knowledge and belief, so state) (If space is insufficient, attach affidavit or affidavits hereto)

Based on information from a Federal Drug Enforcement Officer, the above has reason to believe at 123 Smith Street, one-story red brick house, with garage, 2 bedrooms, kitchen, living room, and bathroom, there is a small brown suitcase containing a controlled substance believed to be heroin.

*3. Based upon the foregoing reliable information — and upon my personal knowledge and belief — and ~~attached affidavits~~ — there is probable cause to believe that the property hereinafter described — ~~has been stolen~~ — or is being concealed, etc.

and may be found in the possession of __Miss Francine Taggart__ _____
Name of person or persons

at premises _____123 Smith Street, Concord _____
(Identify number, street, place, etc.)

4. The property for which I seek the issuance of a search warrant is the following (here describe the property as particularly as possible).

One small brown suitcase taken from a station locker by Francine Taggart on June 19, 1980, containing heroin.

WHEREFORE, I respectfully request that the court issue a warrant and order of seizure, authorizing the search of (identify premises and the person or persons to be searched)

and directing that if such property or evidence or any part thereof be found that it be seized and brought before the court; together with such other and further relief that the court may deem proper.

_Police Chief Sam Buckley_
Signature of Applicant

Then personally appeared the above named _Chief Buckley_
and made oath that the foregoing affidavit by him subscribed is true.
Before me this ___21___ day of __June__, 19_80_

_J. C. Jones - Special Justice_
Justice or Special Justice
Clerk or Assistant Clerk of the Municipal District Court.

* Strike inapplicable clauses

REVISED JULY 1965          APPROVED BY THE CHIEF JUSTICE OF THE DISTRICT COURTS

FIGURE 8.2
Affidavit
in Support
of a Search
Warrant

identify the premises and the personal property to be seized and it must be signed under oath by the officer requesting it. The essential facts and information justifying the need for the search warrant are set out in an affidavit requesting the warrant.

In a practical sense, law enforcement officers do not often rely on the use of search warrants for entering a home or searching a person. In certain kinds of cases—such as organized crime investigation, gambling and drug offenses, and pornography cases—search warrants are particularly useful.

They are also often requested in other offenses when the police can be reasonably sure that the evidence sought cannot be removed from the premises, destroyed, or damaged by the suspect. The police are generally reluctant to seek a warrant, however, because of the stringent evidentiary standards courts require for obtaining the warrant and the availability of search and seizure alternatives.

The United States Supreme Court has played an active role in interpreting the legal requirements of a search warrant. One of the major issues litigated by the Court has been the reliability of the evidence contained in the affidavit. In many instances, the evidence used by the police in requesting a search warrant originates with a police informer rather than the police officer. This kind of information is normally referred to as hearsay evidence. The Supreme Court has determined that such evidence must be corroborated to serve as a basis for probable cause and thereby justify the issuance of a warrant. In the case of *Spinelli v. United States* (1964),[4] the Supreme Court held that statements by an informer that he had personal knowledge of the facts about the crime and had supplied prior truthful information was sufficient corroboration. The case of *Aguilar v. Texas* (1964)[5] provided a two-part credibility test of hearsay evidence obtained from an informant in cases of arrest or search with or without a warrant: (1) the police must show why they believe the informant; and (2) the circumstances as to how the informant acquired personal knowledge of the crime must be explored.

In summary, the procedural requirements for obtaining a search warrant are: (1) the police officer must request the warrant from the court; (2) the officer must submit an affidavit establishing the proper grounds for the warrant; and (3) the affidavit must state the place to be searched and the property to be seized. Whether the affidavit contains sufficient information to justify the issuance of the warrant itself is the aspect which determines the validity of the warrant once issued.

WARRANTLESS
SEARCHES

There are some exceptions to the search warrant requirement of the Fourth Amendment. Significant exceptions include: (1) warrantless searches incident to a lawful arrest, (2) field interrogation, (3) consent searches, and (4) automobile searches.

### Searches Incident to a Lawful Arrest

Traditionally a search without a search warrant is allowable if it is made incident to a lawful arrest. For example, if shortly after the armed robbery of a grocery store officers arrest a suspect with a briefcase hiding in the basement, a search of the suspect's person and of the briefcase would be a proper search incident to a lawful arrest and without a warrant. The legality of this type of search depends almost entirely on the lawfulness of the arrest. The arrest will be upheld if the police officer observed the crime being committed or had probable cause to believe that the suspect committed the offense. If the arrest is found to have been invalid, then any warrantless search made incident to the arrest would be considered illegal.

The police officer who searches a suspect incident to a lawful arrest must generally observe two rules. First, it is important that the police officer search the suspect at the time of or immediately subsequent to the arrest. Second, the police may search only the suspect and the area within the suspect's immediate control; that is, when a police officer searches a person incident to a lawful arrest, such a search may not legally go beyond the area where the person can reach for a weapon or destroy any evidence. The United States Supreme Court dealt with the problem of the permissible scope of a search incident to a lawful arrest in the case of *Chimel v. California,*[6] which is summarized in this chapter.

There are exceptions to the *Chimel* ruling on the scope of the permissible search. For example, when a person is arrested for an offense, such

## CHIMEL V. CALIFORNIA

**Facts:** On the afternoon of September 13, 1965, three police officers arrived at the Santa Ana, California home of Ted Chimel with a warrant authorizing his arrest for the burglary of a coin shop. The officers knocked on the door, identified themselves to Chimel's wife, and asked if they could come inside. She admitted the officers into the house, where they waited ten or fifteen minutes until Chimel returned home from work. When he entered the house, one of the officers handed him the arrest warrant and asked for permission to look around. Chimel objected, but was advised that the officers could conduct a search on the basis of the lawful arrest. No search warrant had been issued.

Accompanied by Chimel's wife, the officers then looked through the entire three-bedroom house. The officers told Chimel's wife to open drawers in the master bedroom and sewing room and "to physically move contents of the drawers from side to side so that (they) might view any items that would have come from (the) burglary." After completing the search, the officers seized numerous items, including some coins. The entire search took between forty-five minutes and an hour.

At the defendant's subsequent state trial on two charges of burglary, the coins taken from his house were admitted into evidence against him over his objection that they had been unconstitutionally seized. He was convicted and the judgment was affirmed by the California Supreme Court.

**Decision:** The United States Supreme Court decided that the search of Chimel's home went far beyond any area where he might conceivably have obtained a weapon or destroyed any evidence, and that no constitutional basis existed for extending the search to all areas of the house. The Court concluded that the scope of the search was unreasonable under the Fourth Amendment as applied through the Fourteenth Amendment, and Chimel's conviction was overturned.

**Significance of the Case:** The *Chimel* case changed the policy with regard to the scope of a search made by an officer incident to a lawful arrest. In the past, a police officer was permitted to search all areas under the control of the defendant. The Court's ruling on the Chimel case allows the officer to search only the defendant and the immediate physical surroundings under the defendant's control, generally interpreted as an arm's-length distance around the defendant. No longer can a police officer who arrests a person in that person's home search the entire house without a valid search warrant.

as a traffic violation, a full search is often conducted even when the officer has no reason to believe that the suspect is concealing a weapon or evidence. The United States Supreme Court has concluded that such an arrest is lawful, even though it may only be for a traffic offense, and a full search under these circumstances is acceptable. In the case of *United States v. Robinson* (1973)[7] for example, Robinson was arrested for operating a motor vehicle after revocation of his operator's license. While conducting a full search, the police obtained a cigarette pack containing heroin. When Robinson was arrested and convicted of possession of heroin he appealed the conviction, claiming that the evidence obtained from the search violated his rights under the Fourth Amendment. The United States Supreme Court denied the defendant's appeal, stating that the search had been lawful as incident to a valid arrest for the traffic violation.

### Field Interrogation—Stop and Frisk

Another important exception to the rule requiring a search warrant is the *threshold inquiry,* or the *stop and frisk* procedure. Police examination of a suspect on the street does not always occur during or after arrest; officers frequently stop persons who appear to be behaving in a suspicious manner or about whom complaints are made. Ordinarily, police are not required to have sufficient evidence to make an arrest in order to stop a person for brief questioning. If the only way in which the police could stop a person was by making an arrest, they would be prevented from investigating many potentially criminal situations. For this reason, the courts have given the police the authority to stop a person, ask questions and search the person in a limited way, such as frisking for a concealed weapon. The courts have concluded that it is unreasonable to expect a police officer to immediately decide whether to arrest a suspect. With a limited power to stop and frisk, the police officer is able to investigate suspicious persons and situations without having to meet the probable cause standard for arrest. If the police officer did not have this authority, many innocent individuals would probably be arrested.

The threshold inquiry or stop and frisk exception applies to an important point of contact between the police officer and the citizen—the street encounter. Stopping a suspect provides for the brief questioning of a person, while frisking affords the officer an opportunity to avoid the possibility of attack. For instance, if a police officer patrolling a high-crime area observes two young men loitering outside a liquor store after dark who confer several times and stop to talk to a third person who pulls up alongside the curb in an automobile, the officer may conclude that the men are casing the store for a possible burglary. He can then stop the suspects and ask for some identification and an explanation of their conduct. If, after questioning the suspects, the officer has further reason to believe that they were planning to engage in criminal activity, and that they are a threat to his safety, the officer can conduct a proper frisk or carefully limited search of the suspects' outer clothing. In the case of *Terry v. Ohio*, (1968),[8] the Supreme Court upheld the right of the police to conduct brief threshold inquiries of suspicious persons when there is reason to believe that such persons may be armed and dangerous to the police or others. The Court's intent was to allow the officer, who interacts with members of the community many times each day, to conduct proper investigations where necessary, while at the same time keeping invasions of personal rights to a minimum and protecting the officer from harm. The case of *Terry v. Ohio*, which the Supreme Court utilized to create the stop and frisk exception to the search warrant requirements, is discussed below.

The field interrogation process is based primarily on the ability of the police officer to determine whether suspicious conduct exists which gives the officer reason to believe that a crime is about to be committed. This standard has been established in some jurisdictions through legislation authorizing the stop and frisk procedure, thus codifying the *Terry v. Ohio* case. Courts have ruled that frisking must be limited to a determination by the police officer of whether his or her safety or that of others is at stake. The stop and frisk exception cannot be used, however, to harass citizens or conduct exploratory searches.

The Supreme Court has continued to interpret the *Terry v. Ohio* case as an exception to the general rule requiring probable cause for arrest. In 1979, the Court decided the *Dunaway v. New York* case in which it limited the scope of *Terry v. Ohio* to stop and frisk actions.[10] In this case, the police obtained information from an informant that the accused was implicated in a murder-robbery. The defendant was taken into custody, although not placed under arrest. He was questioned and eventually made statements incriminating him in the crime. The Court raised the question of the legality of the custodial questioning on less than probable cause for a full arrest. It concluded that such police action violated the defendant's Fourth and Fourteenth Amendment rights. Because the Terry case departed from the general requirements of probable cause for arrest and search and seizures, the Court has been careful to maintain its narrow scope.

### Consent Searches

Warrantless searches may also be undertaken by police officers when the person in control of the area or object voluntarily consents to the search. Those who give their consent to search essentially waive their constitutional rights under the Fourth Amendment. Ordinarily, courts are reluctant to accept such waivers and require the state to prove that the consent was voluntarily given. In addition, the consent must be given intelligently and, in some jurisdictions, consent searches are valid only after the suspect is informed of the option to refuse consent.

The major legal issue in most consent searches is whether the police can prove that consent was voluntarily given. For example, in the case of *Bumper v. North Carolina*, 1968,[11] police officers searched the home of an elderly woman after informing her that they possessed a search warrant.

## TERRY V. OHIO

**Facts:** A Cleveland detective, Martin McFadden, was patrolling a downtown beat where he had been working for many years when he observed two strangers, Terry and Richard Chilton, on a street corner. He saw them proceed alternately back and forth along an identical route about twenty-four times, pausing each time to stare in the same store window. Each completion of the route was followed by a conference between the two on a corner. During one conversation, they were joined by a third man, Katz, who left swiftly. Suspecting the two men of casing the store for a burglary, the officer followed them and saw them rejoin the third man a couple of blocks away in front of another store.

The officer approached the three, identified himself as a policeman, and asked their names. The men mumbled something, whereupon McFadden spun Terry around, patted down his outside clothing, and found a pistol in his overcoat pocket but was unable to remove it. The officer ordered the three into the store. He removed Terry's overcoat, removed the revolver, and ordered the three to face the wall with their hands raised. He patted down the outer clothing of Chilton and Katz and seized a revolver from Chilton's outside overcoat pocket. McFadden did not put his hands under Katz's outer garments since he discovered nothing during the frisking which might have been a weapon, nor did he put his hands under Terry's or Chilton's outer garments until he felt the guns. The three were taken to the police station.

Terry and Chilton were charged with concealing weapons. The defense moved to suppress the evidence of the weapons. Though the trial court rejected the prosecution's theory that the guns had been seized during a search incident to a lawful arrest, the court denied the motion to suppress the illegally seized evidence and admitted the weapons into evidence on the grounds that the officer had cause to believe that Terry and Chilton were acting suspiciously, that their interrogation was warranted, and that the officer for his own protection had the right to pat down their outer clothing because he had reasonable cause to believe that they might be armed. The court distinguished between an investigatory stop and an arrest, and between a frisk of the outer clothing for weapons and a thorough search for evidence of crime. Terry and Chilton were found guilty and the case was subsequently appealed to the United States Supreme Court.

**Decision:** The Court affirmed the conviction of the defendant, stating that "where a reasonably prudent officer is warranted in the circumstances of a given case in believing that his safety or that of others is endangered, he may make a reasonable search for weapons of the person believed by him to be armed and dangerous regardless of whether he has probable cause to arrest that individual for crime or the absolute certainty that the individual is armed."[9] Though it is important for the police to obtain a warrant whenever possible before undertaking a search and seizure, the warrant requirement obviously cannot be followed where immediate action based on street observations is required. Thus, the revolver seized from Terry was properly admitted into evidence, since the search which led to the seizure of the gun was reasonable under the Fourth Amendment.

**Significance of the Case:** *Terry v. Ohio* established the constitutional rule that an officer who does not have authority to arrest may stop a person and make a pat-down search of the individual if the officer reasonably believes there is a threat to safety. The Court agreed that stopping a suspicious person or investigating questionable conduct was a legitimate police function and would aid in the prevention and control of crime, while at the same time protecting the police officer from the danger of an unexpected armed attack. The court emphasized, however, that the officer's search was confined to what was minimally necessary to determine whether the suspects were armed, and the intrusion, which was made for the sole purpose of protecting the officer and others nearby, was confined to ascertaining the presence of weapons.

At the trial, the prosecutor informed the court that the search was valid because the woman gave her consent. The United States Supreme Court declared that the consent had been illegally obtained by the false claim of the police that they had a search warrant. When the government was unable to produce the warrant, the court decided that the search was invalid because the woman's consent was not voluntarily given.

In most consent searches, however, voluntariness is a question of fact to be determined from all the circumstances of the case. Furthermore, the police are usually under no obligation to inform a suspect of the right to refuse consent. Failure to tell a suspect of this right does not make the search illegal, but it may be a factor used by courts to decide if the suspect gave consent voluntarily. The decision whether to inform a defendant of the right of refusal is not equivalent to other enforceable constitutional safeguards. Under the *Miranda* decision, for instance, where the United States Supreme Court held that a defendant has a right to counsel and a right to be free from self-incrimination, the defendant must be informed of these rights before being able to waive them.

## Warrantless Searches of Automobiles

The United States Supreme Court has established that situations exist which justify the warrantless search of an automobile on a public street or highway. For example, evidence can be seized from an automobile when a suspect is taken into custody subject to a lawful arrest. After analyzing the law, courts have decided that distinctions should be made between searches of automobiles, persons, and homes, and have also concluded that a warrantless search of an automobile is valid if the police have probable cause to believe that the car contains evidence they are seeking.[12]

The law of search and seizure regarding automobiles remains unclear. In the case of *Chambers v. Maroney* (1970),[13] the United States Supreme Court held that a warrantless search of an automobile conducted at the station house hours after the arrests of the suspects which resulted in the seizure of weapons and other evidence was lawful. On the other hand, in the case of *Coolidge v. New Hampshire* (1971),[14] where the police were involved in the investigation of a murder of a young girl, the court held that a search warrant was required to search the car related to the crime, which had been in police custody for a long period of time. The Supreme Court seems to be saying that a warrantless search of an automobile on the highway is justified where there is probable cause to believe it was involved in a crime because the car is a moving object and the evidence may be lost. In situations where the police know that an automobile is involved in a crime, and where the evidence in the car will not be taken away or destroyed, the court is more likely to require a search warrant.

In sum, the most important requirement for a warrantless search of an automobile is that it must be based on the legal standard of probable cause that a crime related to the automobile has been or is being committed. Police who undertake the search of a car must have reason to believe that it contains evidence pertaining to the crime.

## Other Exceptions

Other exceptions to the search warrant requirement exist. Until quite recently, those mentioned above received the most attention. Lately, however, the United States Supreme Court has carefully examined cases involving warrantless searches made in hot pursuit, border searches, searches made in emergency situations, and administrative searches such as those of passengers at airline terminals and searches involving electronic surveillance.

The use of wiretapping to intercept conversations between parties has significantly affected police investigative procedures. Electronic devices have been created that allow us to listen and record the private conversations of parties over telephones, through walls and windows, and even over long distances. Police using these devices are able to secretly intercept communications and obtain information related to criminal activity. Electronic eavesdropping by law enforcement personnel, however, represents an invasion of a citizen's right to privacy unless a court gives prior permission to intercept conversations in this manner. Police can obtain criminal evidence by eavesdropping only if such activities are controlled under rigid guidelines relating to the Fourth Amendment, and they must normally request a court order based upon probable cause before using electronic eavesdropping equipment.

Many citizens believe that electronic eavesdropping through hidden microphones, radio transmitters, and telephone taps and bugs represents a grave threat to personal privacy.[15] Although the application of such devices in the field of criminal justice is a controversial subject, the police are generally convinced of their value in investigating criminal activity. Others, however, believe that these techniques are often used beyond their lawful intent to monitor political figures, harass suspects, or investigate cases involving questionable issues of national security. In response to concerns about invasions of privacy, the United States Supreme Court has increasingly limited the use of electronic eavesdropping in the criminal justice system. The case of *Katz v.United States* (1967),[16] summarized below, is one example in which the government failed to meet the necessary requirements to justify electronic surveillance.

As a result of the controversy surrounding the use of electronic eavesdropping, Congress in 1968 enacted the Omnibus Crime Control Act which provides legislative controls over the interception of oral communications.[18] In addition, the American Bar Association has promulgated standards relating to the use of electronic eavesdropping in the criminal justice system.[19]

## ARREST

Once a crime has been committed and the person responsible is identified by the police, an arrest can be made. The arrest power of the police involves taking a person into custody in accordance with lawful authority and holding the person to answer for a violation of the criminal law. For all practical purposes, the authority of the police to arrest a suspect is the basis for crime control; without such authority, the police would be powerless to implement the criminal law.

## KATZ V. UNITED STATES

**Facts:** Katz was convicted of transmitting wagering information by telephone in violation of a federal statute. At his trial, the government was permitted to introduce evidence of Katz's end of the telephone conversations, which had been overheard by FBI agents who had attached an electronic listening and recording device to monitor the outgoing calls. Katz appealed, claiming that the actions of the FBI violated his search and seizure rights under the Fourth Amendment.

**Decision:** Justice Stewart of the United States Supreme Court, speaking for the majority, reversed the conviction, holding that the interception and recordings of Katz's telephone conversations represented unreasonable searches and seizures of the conversations in violation of the Fourth Amendment. Stewart said, "The government agents here ignored 'the procedure of antecedent justification . . . that is central to the Fourth Amendment,' a procedure that we hold to be a constitutional precondition of the kind of electronic surveillance involved in this case. Because surveillance here failed to meet that condition, and because it led to the petitioner's conviction, the judgment must be reversed."[17]

**Significance of the Case:** In *Katz*, the court declared that the Fourth Amendment was not to apply solely to protected places involving privacy, but that such protections also relate to the privacy of individuals. Thus, the Supreme Court abandoned the emphasis or definition of a search based on property and concluded that a search results whenever police violate a person's privacy.

People in telephone booths, offices, apartments, rooms, and taxicabs, stated the court, should be able to rely on the safeguards of the Fourth Amendment. The right of privacy protects the person anywhere and is not restricted to certain physical places.

The method of arrest is primarily used by law enforcement officers. Generally, law enforcement personnel are employed by public police agencies, derive their authority from statutory laws, and take an oath to uphold the laws of their jurisdiction. Most police officers have complete law enforcement responsibility and unrestricted powers of arrest in their jurisdictions; they carry firearms, and they give evidence in criminal trials. In America, private citizens also have the right to make an arrest, generally when a crime is committed in their presence. For the most part though, private citizens rarely exercise their power of arrest, except when they apprehend offenders who have committed crimes against them.

An *arrest*, the first formal police procedure in the criminal process, occurs when a police officer takes a person into custody or deprives a person of freedom for having allegedly committed a criminal offense. Since the police stop unlimited numbers of citizens each day for a variety of reasons, when an arrest actually occurs may be confusing. Some persons are stopped for short periods of questioning, others are informally detained and released, and still others are formally placed under arrest. An actual arrest occurs when the following conditions exist: (1) the police officer believes that sufficient legal evidence exists that a crime is being or has been committed, and intends to restrain the suspect; (2) the police officer deprives the individual of freedom; and (3) the suspect believes that he or she is in the custody of the police officer and cannot voluntarily leave. The police officer is not required to use the term *arrest* or some similar word in order to initiate an arrest, nor does the officer first have to bring the suspect to the station house. For all practical purposes, a person who has been deprived of liberty is under arrest.

Arrests can be initiated with or without an arrest warrant and must be based on probable cause. The arrest warrant, an order issued by the court, determines that an arrest should be made and directs the police to bring the named person before the court. An arrest warrant must be based upon probable cause that the person to be arrested has committed or is attempting to commit a crime. The police wil ordinarily obtain a warrant where no danger exists that the suspect will leave the area. For example, where a long-term investigation of organized crime is taking place, where probable cause exists to arrest suspects, and where there is no danger of their immediate flight, it would be appropriate for police to go before a judge and obtain an arrest warrant. Figure 8.3 shows an example of an arrest warrant.

Most arrests are made without a warrant, however. The decision to arrest is often made by the police officer during contact with the suspect. An arrest may be made without a warrant.

**1.** Only where the arresting officer is able to establish probable cause that a crime has been committed and that the defendant is the person who committed it.

**2.** Where the law of a given jurisdiction allows for arrest without a warrant.

In the case of a felony, most jurisdictions provide that a police officer may arrest a suspect without a warrant where probable cause exists, even though the officer was not present when the offense was committed. In the case of a misdemeanor, probable cause as well as the officer's presence at the time of the offense are required. When there is some question as to the legality of an arrest, it usually involves whether the police officer has probable cause or a reasonable belief based on reliable evidence that the suspect has committed a crime. This issue is reviewed by the judge when the suspect is brought before the court for a hearing.

**Police Discretion to
Arrest**

In Chapter 7, the issue of discretion was discussed in general terms of how decisions are made in police operations. Discretion is an especially critical issue in the authority of the police to make legal arrests. Although millions of arrests occur annually, police exercise much discretion in deciding whether to invoke their arrest power. This decision to arrest or not is an extremely difficult one because (1) the police are required to exercise numerous laws in a manner that is fair to all citizens; (2) police officials rarely outline through departmental policy when arrest is proper, when it is improper, what criteria should be used for arrest, and what other alternatives exist other than arrest; and (3) the probable cause standard for

FIGURE 8.3
Warrant for Arrest

WARRANT FOR ARREST

## THE COMMONWEALTH OF MASSACHUSETTS.

MIDDLESEX, ss.

FOURTH DISTRICT COURT OF EASTERN MIDDLESEX.        *To any Officer qualified to serve criminal*

*process throughout the Commonwealth,*        GREETING:

WE COMMAND you in the name of the Commonwealth of Massachusetts, forthwith to apprehend

John Williams

of        Concord        in the County of Middlesex,        if    he    be

found in your precinct, and bring    him        before the Justice of the Fourth District Court

of Eastern Middlesex within and for our County of Middlesex, to answer to the said Common-

wealth on complaint of   Officer Smith        of Concord Police Department

in the County of Middlesex        this day made on oath before our said Court,

wherein said Officer Smith complains that the said   John Williams

of First Street    at    Concord        in the County of Middlesex, on the

15th        day of    June        in the year of our Lord

one thousand nine hundred and  80.

Violated Massachusetts General Laws, Chapter 276, § 14
(assault and battery on a police officer).

against the peace of said Commonwealth

and the form of the statute in such case made and provided.

Hereof fail not at your peril.

Witness, FRANCIS P. CULLEN, Esquire, at Woburn, the   20        day of  June

in the year of our Lord one thousand nine hundred and    80

Clerk.  *J. S. Salvatore*

arrest, although used throughout this country, is so broad and indefinite that its use often raises questions about the validity of an arrest in a given situation. Richard Donnelly described the plight of the police officer in regard to police discretion:

The policeman's lot is indeed a difficult one. He is charged with applying or enforcing a multitude of laws or ordinances in a degree or proportion and in a manner that maintains a delicate balance between the liberty of the individual and a high degree of social protection. His task requires a sensitive and wise discretion in deciding whether or not to invoke the criminal process. He must not only know whether certain behavior violates the law but also whether there is probable cause to believe that the law has been violated. He must enforce the law, yet he must determine whether a particular violation should be handled by warning or arrest. . . . He is not expected to arrest every violator. Some laws were never intended by the enactors to be enforced, and others condemn behavior that is not contrary to significant moral values. If he arrested all violators, the courts would find it impossible to do their work, and he would be in court so frequently that he could not perform his other professional duties. Consequently, the policeman must judge and informally settle more cases than he takes to court.[20]

In 1967, the President's Crime Commission observed that the patrol officer, the lowest-ranking officer within a police department, is responsible for making some of the most complex and difficult decisions in our society.[21] Kenneth Davis points out the uniqueness of having subordinates make so many policy decisions:

No other federal, state, or local agency, so far as I know, delegates so much power to subordinates. No other agency, so far as I know, does so little supervising of vital policy determinations which directly involve justice or injustice to individuals.[22]

Whether initiation of criminal prosecution against a citizen should occur is usually a matter of an individual police officer's judgment. While in theory this judgment is based upon the legal definition of each crime, in practice there are many situations in which police do not exercise their arrest authority. Some common offenses where police exercise great latitude in arresting offenders include gambling, family assaults, juvenile offenses, prostitution, and disorderly conduct.

Recognizing that police officers need guidance in deciding when to arrest, the President's Commission made the following recommendations:

Police departments should develop and enunciate policies that give police personnel specific guidance for the common situations requiring exercise of police discretion. Policies should cover such matters, among others, as the issuance of order to citizens regarding their movements and activities, the handling of minor disputes, and safeguarding of the rights of free speech and free assembly, the selection and use of investigative methods, and the decision whether or not to arrest in specific situations involving specific crimes.[23]

Yet, in spite of this and other recommendations made by the American Bar Association's *Standards on the Urban Police Function* and the National Advisory Commission on Criminal Justice Standards, the arrest process continues to be based to a large degree on the individual judgment of the police officer.[24]

A suspect who comes under police custody at the time of arrest—either on the street, in a police car, or in the police station—must be warned of the right under the Fifth Amendment to be free from self-incrimination prior to any questioning by the police. In the landmark case of *Miranda v. Arizona* (1966),[25] the United States Supreme Court decided that the police must give the *Miranda* warning to the person in custody before questioning begins. Suspects in custody must be told that:

*✳ Miranda Warning ✳*

**1.** They have the right to remain silent.

**2.** If they decide to make a statement, the statement can and will be used against them.

**3.** They have the right to have an attorney present at the time of the interrogation, or they will have an opportunity to consult with an attorney.

**4.** If they cannot afford an attorney, one will be appointed by the state.

This case has had a historic impact on police interrogation practices at the arrest stage of the criminal justice process. Prior to *Miranda*, the police often obtained confessions through questioning methods which violated the constitutional privilege to protect one's self against self-incrimination. The principal test for the admissibility of a defendant's confession or admission was whether the statements were made voluntarily, based on a review of all the circumstances involved in obtaining the statements. The police often used such techniques as coercive interrogation, force, trapping a suspect in an explanation, and inducing the suspect to admit guilt to relieve a guilty conscience. However, in 1964, the Supreme Court held in the case of *Escobedo v. Illinois* [26] that a confession taken from a defendant in custody was inadmissible because the defendant, Danny Escobedo, requested and was denied an opportunity to consult his lawyer and was not warned of his right to remain silent. This case was significant because the Court rejected for the first time the idea that voluntariness of a confession was based on a totality of the circumstances. Rather, it was to be only one factor in whether a defendant was voluntarily giving information to the police. Then, in 1966, the Supreme Court went beyond *Escobedo* and declared in the *Miranda* case that the police had a duty to warn defendants of their rights. The court declared that certain specific procedures (i.e., the *Miranda* warning) must be followed or any statements by a defendant would be excluded from the evidence. The purpose of the warning was to implement the basic Fifth Amendment right of a citizen to be free from self-incrimination.

As a result, the interrogation process is protected by the Fifth Amendment and, if the accused is not given the *Miranda* warning, any evidence obtained during interrogation is not admissible to prove the state's case. It is important to note, however, that the *Miranda* decision does not deny the police the opportunity to generally question a suspect as a witness at the scene of an unsolved crime as long as the person is not in custody and the questioning is of an investigative and nonaccusatory nature. In addition, a suspect can still offer a voluntary confession after the *Miranda* rights have been stated.

Because of the historic impact of *Miranda*, a summary of the case follows.

When *Miranda* was decided, many people became concerned that the Supreme Court under Chief Justice Warren had gone too far in providing procedural protections to the defendant. Some nationally prominent persons, including Richard Nixon and Senators John McClellan, and Strom Thurmond, expressed opinions which made it seem as if the Supreme Court were emptying the prisons of criminals and that law enforcement would never again be effective. They believed that the police were failing in their efforts to control crime in part due to Supreme Court decisions such as *Miranda*. Since *Miranda*, however, little empirical evidence has

## MIRANDA V. ARIZONA

**Facts:** Ernesto Miranda, a 25-year-old mentally retarded young man, was arrested in Phoenix, Arizona and charged with kidnapping and rape. Miranda was taken from his home to a police station where he was identified by a complaining witness. He was then interrogated and, after about two hours, signed a written confession. Miranda was subsequently convicted and sentenced to twenty to thirty years in prison. His conviction was affirmed by the Arizona Supreme Court and he appealed to the United States Supreme Court, claiming that he had not been warned that any statement he made would be used against him, and that he was not advised of any right to have counsel present at his interrogation.

The *Miranda* case was one of four cases heard simultaneously by the Supreme Court which dealt with the legality of confessions obtained by the police from a suspect in custody. In *Vignera v. New York* (1966),[27] the defendant was arrested in connection with a robbery and taken to two different detective headquarters, where he was interrogated and subsequently confessed after eight hours in custody. In *Westover v. United States* (1966),[28] the suspect was arrested by the Kansas City police, placed in a lineup, and booked on a felony charge. He was interrogated by the police during the evening and in the morning, and by the FBI in the afternoon when he signed two confessions. And in *California v.*

*Stewart*,[29] the defendant was arrested at his home for being involved in a robbery. He was taken to a police station and placed in a cell where, over a period of five days, he was interrogated nine times. The Supreme Court in *Miranda* described the common characteristics of these four cases by stating:

> In each, the defendant was questioned by the police in a room in which he was cut off from the outside world. In none of these cases was the defendant given a full and effective warning of his rights at the outset of the interrogation process. In all the cases, the questioning elicited oral admissions, and in three of them, signed statements as well which were admitted at their trials. They all thus share salient features—incommunicado interrogation of individuals in a police-dominated atmosphere, resulting in self-incriminating statements without full warnings of constitutional rights.[30]

**Decision:** The major constitutional issue in *Miranda*, as in the other three cases, was the admissibility of statements obtained from a defendant questioned while in custody or while otherwise deprived of his freedom. The Fifth Amendment provides that no person shall be "compelled" to be a witness against himself. This means that a defendant cannot be required to testify at his trial and that a suspect who is questioned before trial cannot be subjected to any physical or psychological pressure to confess.

been found to prove that the decision has had a detrimental impact on law enforcement efforts. Instead, it became apparent that the police relied too heavily on confessions to prove a defendant's guilt. Other forms of evidence, such as the use of witnesses, physical evidence, and expert testimony, have proved more than adequate to win the prosecution's case.

Despite its apparent clarity, the *Miranda* decision has been followed by a series of litigations. One of the central issues of the *Miranda* case concerns a need to define the specific instances in which the *Miranda* warning must be given. Questions here, for example, involve ascertaining what custodial interrogation is, who the interrogator is, and whether damaging statements result from a specific interrogation. Other problems generally raised by a defendant focus on whether the *Miranda* warning was properly given. Different issues in this regard include whether the warning

In the opinion of Chief Justice Warren in the *Miranda* case, "the third degree method was still 'sufficiently widespread to be the object of concern.'"[31] Of greater concern, he believed, was the increased use of sophisticated psychological pressures on suspects during interrogation. Thus, in a five to four decision, Miranda's conviction was overturned and the court established specific procedural guidelines for police to follow before eliciting statements from persons in police custody.

The Court's own summary of its decision is stated as follows:

Our holding will be spelled out with some specificity in the pages which follow but briefly it is this: the prosecution may not use statements, whether exculpatory or inculpatory, stemming from custodial interrogation of the defendant unless it demonstrates the use of procedural safeguards effective to secure the privilege against self-incrimination. By custodial interrogation, we mean questioning initiated by law enforcement officers after a person has been taken into custody or otherwise deprived of his freedom of action in any significant way. As for the procedural safeguards to be employed, unless other fully effective means are devised to inform accused persons of their right of silence and to assure a continuous opportunity to exercise it, the following measures are required. Prior to any questioning, the person must be warned that he has a right to remain silent, that any statement he does make may be used as evidence against him, and that he has a right to the presence of an attorney, either retained or appointed. The defendant may waive effectuation of these rights, provided the waiver is made voluntarily, knowingly and intelligently. If, however, he indicates in any manner and at any stage of the process that he wishes to consult with an attorney before speaking there can be no questioning. Likewise, if the individual is alone and indicates in any manner that he does not wish to be interrogated, the police may not question him. The mere fact that he may have answered some questions or volunteered some statements on his own does not deprive him of the right to refrain from answering any further inquiries until he has consulted with an attorney and thereafter consents to be questioned.[32]

**Significance of the Case:** The *Miranda* decision established that the Fifth Amendment privilege against self-incrimination requires that a criminal suspect in custody or in any other manner deprived of freedom must be informed of his or her rights. If the suspect is not warned, then any evidence given is not admissible by the government to prove its case.

was adequate, whether the defendant waived his rights, or whether statements made after the initial interrogation require the repetition of the *Miranda* rules.

Since the *Miranda* decision in 1966, the United States Supreme Court has, on a number of occasions, been asked to consider different aspects of this controversial ruling. For instance, in the case of *Harris v. New York* [33] in 1971, the court agreed that evidence obtained in violation of the *Miranda* warning could be used by the government to impeach a defendant's testimony during trial. In *Michigan v. Tucker* [34] in 1974, the court allowed the testimony of a witness whose identity was revealed by the suspect even though a violation of the *Miranda* rule occurred. And, in the case of *Michigan v. Mosley*,[35] in 1975, the court upheld the renewed questioning of a suspect who had already been given the *Miranda* warning and had refused to answer any questions.

Thus, it appears that the Supreme Court has somewhat weakened the *Miranda* ruling in recent years, holding that statements made in violation of this ruling can be used for limited trial purposes.

During the 1976–77 term, the United States Supreme Court considered for the first time whether to override the *Miranda* decision in the case *Brewer v. Williams*.[36] Robert Williams was convicted of the sex slaying of a 10-year-old girl on December 26, 1968 and sentenced to life in prison. The Iowa Supreme Court upheld the decision, but the United States Circuit Court of Appeals overturned his conviction because remarks made to him by a policeman while the two were in an automobile without the presence of counsel led Williams to show the officers where the girl was buried. State officials in Iowa asked the Court to rule that the only test for the admissibility of William's statements as evidence should be whether or not they were given voluntarily. However, the United States Supreme Court upheld the *Miranda* decision by ruling that the right to counsel is indispensable to the administration of our adversary system.

In his dissent, Chief Justice Burger expressed the opinion that Williams received the assistance of counsel, did waive his right under the Sixth and Fourteenth Amendments, and that the police properly interrogated him in the absence of counsel. The following statement of the Chief Justice summarizes the minority view of the Court:

The result reached by the Court in this case ought to be intolerable in any society which purports to call itself an organized society. It continues the court—by the narrowest margin—on the much criticized course of punishing the public for the mistakes and misdeeds of law enforcement officers, instead of punishing the officer directly, if in fact he is guilty of wrongdoing. It mechanically and blindly keeps reliable evidence from juries whether the claimed constitutional violation involves gross police misconduct or honest human error. Williams is guilty of the savage murder of a small child; no Member of the Court contends he is not. While in custody, and after no fewer than *five* warnings of his rights to silence and to counsel, he led police to the place where he had buried the body of his victim. The Court now holds the jury must not be told how the police found the body.[37]

After arrest, the accused is ordinarily brought to the police station where the police list the possible criminal charges, while at the same time obtaining other information, such as a description of the offender and circumstances of the offense, for booking purposes. The booking process is generally a police administrative procedure consisting of recording the date and time of the arrest; making arrangements for station-house bail, detention, or removal to court; and obtaining other information for identification purposes. The defendant may be fingerprinted and photographed and may be required to participate in a lineup. The lineup is basically a pre-trial identification procedure where a suspect is placed in a group for the purpose of being viewed by a witness. In accordance with the United States Supreme Court cases of *United States v. Wade*[38] and *Kirby v. Illinois*,[39] the accused has the right to have counsel present at what is known as the post-indictment lineup or identification procedure.

THE LINEUP

In the *Wade* case, the court held that a defendant has a right to counsel if the lineup takes place after the suspect has been formally charged with a crime. This decision was based on the Supreme Court's belief that the post-indictment lineup procedure is a critical stage of the criminal justice process. On the other hand, the suspect does not have a comparable right to counsel at a pre-trial lineup where a complaint or indictment has not been issued. When the right to counsel is violated, the evidence of any pre-trial identification must be excluded from the trial.

When the offense involved is a minor misdemeanor, the suspect may be released from the police station to answer the criminal charge before the court at a later time. A suspect arrested on a serious misdemeanor or a felony charge is usually detained by the police to be taken before a judge for consideration of bail. Since the length of station-house detention is strictly limited by law, the police are required to bring the accused before the court as quickly as possible. This means that the suspect must be brought to the next immediate court sitting; in certain urban areas, where arrests are constantly being made, 24-hour courts have been established to handle immediate appearances of criminal defendants. Once the defendant is released from police custody and placed in the hands of the court, further decisions, such as pre-trial release, determination of a plea, and preparation for trial, will be made during the criminal court process.

Law enforcement officers use many different investigatory techniques to detect and apprehend criminal offenders. These include searches, electronic eavesdropping, interrogation, the use of informants, surveillance, and witness identification procedures. Over the past two decades, serious constitutional limitations have been placed upon the pre-trial process, with primary emphasis being placed on United States Supreme Court decisions. In the area of the Fourth Amendment, for example, the police are required to use search warrants or conduct searches only under clearly defined exceptions to this rule. Evidence obtained in violation of the Fourth Amendment can be excluded under the *Mapp v. Ohio* case. When efforts

SUMMARY

are made to exclude evidence from a trial, a motion to suppress the evidence is heard at a preliminary hearing. The application section of this chapter contains a memorandum in support of a defendant's efforts to exclude tainted evidence.

Police interrogation procedures have also been reviewed extensively. The *Miranda* rule shows how the Supreme Court established an affirmative procedure as a requirement for all custodial interrogations. Many issues concerning *Miranda* continue to be litigated. Lineups and other police practices, such as taking blood samples and fingerprinting, have also been subject to court review. To what degree a defendant's rights should be protected at the pre-trial stage while maintaining the government's interest in crime control remains a source of constant debate in the present criminal justice system.

QUESTIONS FOR DISCUSSION

1. Discuss some of the major methods the police use to investigate a crime. Why have the courts established guidelines for police investigations?

2. What is the *Miranda* rule? Is *Miranda* the result of a proper judicial function or a legislative responsibility?

3. Discuss the nature of the rights of the accused during the pre-trial stage of the criminal process.

NOTES

1. See Note, "The Special Prosecutor in the Federal System: A Proposal," *American Criminal Law Review* 11:577 (Spring 1973).

2. See generally American Bar Association, *Standards Relating to the Urban Police Function* (New York: Institute of Judicial Administration, 1973).

3. American Bar Association, *Standards Relating to Urban Police Function*, pp. 91–93. Reprinted with the permission of the American Bar Association which authored these standards and which holds the copyright.

4. 393 U.S. 410, 89 S.Ct. 584, 21 L.Ed.2d 637 (1969).

5. 378 U.S. 108, 84 S.Ct. 1509, 12 L.Ed.2d 723 (1964).

6. 395 U.S. 752, 89 S.Ct. 2034, 23 L.Ed.2d 685 (1969).

7. 414 U.S. 218, 94 S.Ct. 467, 36 L.Ed.2d 177 (1973).

8. 392 U.S. 1, 88 S.Ct. 1868, 20 L.Ed.2d 889 (1968).

9. Ibid. at 20–27.

10. 99 S.Ct. 2248, (1979).

11. 391 U.S. 543, 88 S.Ct. 1788, 20 L.Ed.2d 797 (1968).

12. See Carroll v. United States, 267 U.S. 132, 45 S.Ct. 280, 69 L.Ed. 543 (1925).

13. 399 U.S. 42, 90 S.Ct. 1975, 26 L.Ed.2d 419 (1970).

14. 403 U.S. 443, 91 S.Ct. 2022, 29 L.Ed.2d 564 (1971).

15. See generally P. Allan Dionesopoulos and Craig R. Ducat, *The Right to Privacy, Essays and Cases* (St. Paul, Minn.: West Publishing Co., 1976).

16. 389 U.S. 347, 88 S.Ct. 507, 19 L.Ed.2d 576 (1967).

17. Ibid. at 359.

**18.** 18 U.S.C. Chap. 119 enacted by The Omnibus Crime Control and Safe Streets Act of 1968, 802.

**19.** American Bar Association, *Standards Relating to Electronic Surveillance* (New York: Institute of Judicial Administration, Tentative Draft, 1968).

**20.** Richard C. Donnelly, "Police Authority and Practices," *The Annals of the American Academy of Political and Social Science* 339:91–92 (January 1962).

**21.** President's Commission on Law Enforcement and Administration of Justice, *The Challenge of Crime in a Free Society* (Washington, D.C.: U.S. Government Printing Office, 1967), p. 103.

**22.** Kenneth C. Davis, *Discretionary Justice—A Preliminary Inquiry,* (Baton Rouge, La.: Louisiana State University Press, 1969), p. 4.

**23.** President's Crime Commission, *The Challenge of Crime in a Free Society,* p. 103.

**24.** American Bar Association, *Standards Relating to the Urban Police Function,* (New York: Institute of Judicial Administration, Tentative Draft, 1972); also see National Advisory Commission on Criminal Justice Standards and Goals, *Police* (Washington, D.C.: U.S. Government Printing Office, 1973).

**25.** 384 U.S. 436, 86 S.Ct. 1602, 16 L.Ed.2d 694 (1966).

**26.** 378 U.S. 478, 84 S.Ct. 1758, 12 L.Ed.2d 977 (1964).

**27.** 384 U.S. 436, 86 S.Ct. 1602, 16 L.Ed.2d 694 (1966) (No. 760).

**28.** Ibid. at (No. 761).

**29.** Ibid. at (No. 584).

**30.** 384 U.S. at 445.

**31.** Ibid. at 436.

**32.** Ibid. at 436, 444.

**33.** 401 U.S. 222, 91 S.Ct. 644, 28 L.Ed.2d (1971).

**34.** 417 U.S. 433, 94 S.Ct. 2357, 41 L.Ed.2d 182 (1974).

**35.** 423 U.S. 96, 96 S.Ct. 321, 46 L.Ed.2d 313 (1975).

**36.** 430 U.S. 387, 97 S.Ct. 1232, 51 L.Ed.2a 424 (1977).

**37.** 430 U.S. at 394.

**38.** 388 U.S. 218, 87 S.Ct. 1926, 18 L.Ed.2d 1149 (1967).

**39.** 306 U.S. 682, 92 S.Ct. 1877, 32 L.Ed.2d 411 (1972).

# APPLICATION

---

MIDDLESEX, SS.      WALTHAM DISTRICT COURT
                              NO: 3325, 3309

COMMON-         )
WEALTH

                )   MEMORANDUM IN SUPPORT OF

VS.              )

                )   DEFENDANT'S MOTION TO SUPPRESS

RONALD F. JONES  )   ILLEGALLY SEIZED EVIDENCE

## I.  STATEMENT OF FACTS

On the morning of August 7, 1979 the defendant was driving a friend home in his truck. Defendant was stopped at a blinking red light when he saw a police cruiser with its lights blinking behind him.

A Waltham Police Officer approached the defendant, and concomitantly the defendant started to get out of his car. Before the defendant had fully emerged from his vehicle the Officer pulled the defendant out.

The Police Officer asked the defendant for his license and registration which he produced. The Officer then ran his flashlight over the defendant's truck and asked if he could inspect the vehicle for stolen hubcaps. The request to inspect was made four times, to all of which defendant's response was no.

The Officer then reached inside the defendant's pocket and removed a bag alleged to contain marijuana. Thereafter the defendant was placed under arrest, handcuffed and told by the Officer that the truck was going to be searched. The Officer broke the lock on the camper portion of the truck, searched inside and subsequently discovered three hubcaps lying under a blanket. The defendant was transported to the police station and his truck was towed away under the direction of the Police. The defendant was charged with possession of marijuana and also receiving stolen property.

## II.  ISSUES

1. Whether the evidence obtained on defendant's person was a product of an unreasonable search and seizure.
2. Whether the arrest subsequent to the search of the defendant's person was invalid.
3. Whether the evidence obtained in the motor vehicle was a product of an unreasonable search and seizure.

## III.  STATEMENT OF PREVAILING LAW

A stop and frisk is a search and seizure within the meaning of the Fourth Amendment. *Terry v. Ohio, 392 US 1, 88 S.Ct. 1868 (1968)*

In stop and frisk cases the inquiry is two-fold: first, whether the initiation of the investigation by the police was permissible in the circumstances and second, whether the scope of the search was justified by the circumstances. *Commonwealth v. Silva, 366 Mass. 402, 318 N.E.2d 895 (1974)*

In a threshold inquiry the search must be confined to a pat-down of the outer clothing of the suspect. Only after the pat-down gives indication that a weapon is present do the police have the privilege to search further. *Commonwealth v. McGrath, 365 Mass. 631, 310 N.E.2d 601 (1974); Commonwealth v. Silva, 366 Mass. 402, 318 N.E.2d 895 (1974)*

The Fourth Amendment of the Constitution of the United States protects persons from arbitrary and unreasonable search and seizure. A search without consent and without a warrant is unreasonable unless the search falls within certain, carefully delineated exceptions. *Katz v. United States, 389 U.S. 347, 88 S.Ct. 507 (1967)*

If the Constitutional requirements are not met, then the evidence must be suppressed. *Mapp v. Ohio, 367 U.S. 643, 81 S.Ct. 1684 (1961)*

The intrusion is the beginning of the search and if the search is illegal at the start, it is illegal, despite what is discovered during the search. Neither an arrest nor a search otherwise unlawful may be validated by what it produces. *Wong Sun v. United States, 371 U.S. 471, 83 S.Ct. 407 (1963)*

There is no constitutional justification, in the absence of a search warrant, for extending a search incident to arrest beyond the area of the arrestee's immediate control. *Chimel v. California, 395 U.S. 752, 89 S.Ct. 2034 (1969)*

A search conducted incident to an arrest may be made only for the purpose of seizing fruits, instrumentalities, contraband and other evidence of the crime for which the arrest has been made, in order to prevent its destruciton or concealment; and removing any weapons that the arrestee might use to resist arrest or effect his escape. Property seized as a result of a search in violation of the provisions of this paragraph shall not be admissible in evidence in criminal proceedings. *Massachusetts General Laws Annotated, Chapter 276, Section 1 as amended*

An arrest made without probable cause is illegal and subsequent search is invalid. *Commonwealth v. Rossetti, 349 Mass. 626, 211 N.E.2d 658 (1965)*

A warrantless search of an automobile may be reasonable only if based upon probable cause and if exigent circumstances exist. *Carroll v. United States, 267 U.S. 132, 45 S.Ct. 280 (1925); Coolidge v. New Hampshire, 403 U.S. 443, 91 S.Ct. 2022; Commonwealth v. Antobenedetto, 366 Mass. 51, 315 N.E.2d 530 (1974).*

It has been held that exceptions to the warrant requirement are:
1. A search incident to a lawful arrest;
2. Exigent circumstances in which seizure would be impossible if warrant had to be obtained;
3. Consent.

## IV.  ARGUMENT

In this case the defendant was stopped in a motor vehicle on a public way in early morning by the Police Officers. At no time was he ever accused of or charged with any motor vehicle or traffic violation. The Police Officer did not have probable cause to arrest prior to the search of defendant's person. Therefore, the Police Officer's actions amounted to a stop and frisk, which was without reason and went beyond a search for weapons. In this case the search consisted of reaching into the defendant's pocket even though there was no indication that a weapon was present.

The search cannot be justified as incident to a lawful arrest. To be so justified the search must follow a lawful arrest. In this case the search of defendant was initiated and carried out prior to the arrest. The arrest, being predicated upon the results of the search, was therefore unlawful. Prior to the search there was no probable cause nor other justification either to stop the defendant or to arrest him. The evidence found on defendant's person was not in plain view but rather was found inside defendant's pocket.

Even assuming arguendo, that the search of defendant's person and that the arrest were justified, the search of defendant's automobile did not fall within the exceptions to warrantless searches. First, in a search incident to arrest the only area that can be searched is that which is in the immediate control of the arrestee. In this case the defendant was outside the motor vehicle standing several feet from the locked camper. He had been found to be unarmed and was not in any manner threatening to the Officer.

Second, neither probable cause nor exigent circumstances existed to justify a warrantless search of the motor vehicle. In this case the motor vehicle was towed away at the direction of the Police Officers, thus indicating that the Officers were not faced with the possibility of losing control of the vehicle. However, even assuming arguendo the existence of exigent circumstances, the facts and circumstances known to the Officers were insufficient to give rise to a reasonable belief amounting to probable cause which would justify a warrantless search.

The evidence which was finally seized was not in plain view but rather found under a blanket within the vehicle. There was no consent to the search. The defendant was asked four times if the vehicle could be searched, and all four times the response was in the negative.

## V.  CONCLUSIONS

The warrantless search and seizure of defendant's person and motor vehicle conducted in this case was unreasonable and violated the defendant's right to be secure from unreasonable search and seizure. At the time the defendant was stopped he was not in violation of the law. The defendant's driver's license and registration were made available to the Officers. The search of the defendant was not incident to a lawful arrest. The evidence seized was not in plain view and the Officers had no right to conduct a more thorough search because probable cause was lacking and any further search violated the defendant's Fourth Amendment rights.

Because the arrest was unlawful, the search of the automobile was not a search incident to a lawful arrest. However, assuming the arrest was valid, the search went beyond the scope of reasonableness for a search incident to arrest. The search based on exigent circumstances alone was not justified because neither probable cause nor said circumstances existed at the time.

Therefore, it is respectfully submitted that the evidence seized should be suppressed and its introduction into evidence forbidden.

# PART FOUR

## Early Court Processing

## CHAPTER 9

# The Prosecution and the Defense

CHAPTER OUTLINE

**The Prosecutor**
**The Role of Prosecutor and Police Officer**
Types of prosecutors
**Prosecutorial Discretion**
**Alternatives to Prosecution**
**The Defense Attorney**
**Role of Criminal Defense**

**Attorney**
**The Lawyer as Professional Advocate**
**Right to Counsel**
**Public Defender Services**
**Summary**
**Questions For Discussion**
**Application**

KEY TERMS

**U.S. Attorney**
**District Attorney**
**Evidence**
**Charge**
**Pre-trial Motion**
**Indigency**
**Argersinger v. Hamlin**
**Preliminary Hearing**
**Public Defender**
**Sentence**

**Appeal**
**Interrogation**
**Sixth Amendment**
**Prejudice**
**Gideon v. Wainwright**
**Morrissey v. Brewer**
**Indictment**
**Admissibility**
**Assigned Counsel System**

## THE PROSECUTOR

Normally, the criminal trial process in the United States has three major participants: the judge, the counsel for the government (also known as the prosecutor), and the defense attorney. If any one of these three is missing, except where the defendant has decided to waive the right to an attorney, the criminal trial is incomplete. Through this tripartite relationship, the powers of government are applied to all persons accused of crimes who elect to go to trial.

Depending upon the level of government and jurisdiction in which he or she functions, the prosecutor may be known as a district attorney, a county attorney, a state's attorney, or a U.S. attorney. Whatever the precise title, the prosecutor is ordinarily a member of the practicing bar and has become a public prosecutor via political appointment or popular election.

Although the prosecutor participates with the judge and defense attorney in the adversary process, it is the prosecutor's responsibility to bring the state's case against the accused. The prosecutor focuses the power of the state on those who disobey the law by charging a person with a crime, releasing the individual from prosecution, or eventually bring the accused to trial.

While the prosecutor's primary duty is to enforce the criminal law, the fundamental obligation as an attorney is to seek justice as well as to convict those who are guilty. For example, if the prosecutor discovers facts suggesting that the accused is innocent, this information must be brought to the attention of the court. The American Bar Association's Code of Professional Responsibility Canon 7-103 deals with the ethical duties of the attorney as a public prosecutor in the following:

DR 7–103 Performing the Duty of Public Prosecutor or Other Government Lawyer.

(A) A public prosecutor or other government lawyer shall not institute or cause to be instituted criminal charges when he knows or it is obvious that the charges are not supported by probable cause.

(B) A public prosecutor or other government lawyer in criminal litigation shall make timely disclosure to counsel for the defendant, or to the defendant, if he has no counsel, of the existence of evidence, known to the prosecutor or other government lawyer, that tends to negate the guilt of the accused, mitigate the degree of the offense, or reduce the punishment.[1]

Many individual prosecutors are often caught between being compelled by their superiors to do everything possible to obtain a guilty verdict and acting as a concerned public official to insure that justice is done. A similar dilemma exists for the senior prosecutor who administers the office staff. The senior prosecutor must make policy decisions to exercise prosecutorial enforcement powers in a wide range of cases in criminal law, consumer protection, housing, and other areas. In so doing, the prosecutor determines, and ultimately shapes the manner in which justice is exercised in society. Justice Sutherland described the role of the prosecutor in the case of *Berger v. United States.*[2]

The United States Attorney is the representative not of an ordinary party to a controversy, but of a sovereignty whose obligation to govern impartially is as compelling as its obligation to govern at all; and whose interest, therefore, in a criminal prosecution is not that it shall win a case, but that Justice shall be done. As such, he is in a peculiar and very definite sense the servant of the law, the twofold aim of which is that guilt shall not escape or innocence suffer. He may prosecute with earnestness and vigor—indeed, he should do so. But while he may strike hard blows, he is not at liberty to strike foul ones. It is as much his duty to refrain from improper methods calculated to produce a wrongful conviction as it is to use every legitimate means to bring about a just one.[3]

In recent years, the prosecutor has received a great deal of attention in the media. Much of this publicity resulted from the Watergate scandals and other famous criminal trials of the late 1960s and 1970s, including the Charles Manson and Patty Hearst cases. Some prosecutors have even sought higher political office based on the publicity they received while participating in nationally publicized trials; former Chief Justice Earl Warren of the United States Supreme Court, former New York Governor Thomas Dewey, Robert Kennedy, and Illinois Governor James "Big Jim" Thompson are all national political leaders who at one time were prosecuting attorneys.

The prosecutor is either elected or appointed and is consequently a political figure in the criminal justice system. The prosecutor normally has a party affiliation, a constituency of voters and supporters, and a need to respond to community pressures and interest groups. In this regard. The American Bar Association's *Standards Relating to the Prosecution Function and Defense Function* states:

The political process has played a significant part in the shaping of the role of the American prosecutor. Experience as a prosecutor is a familiar stepping stone to higher political office. The "DA" has long been glamorized in fiction, films, radio, television, and other media. Many of our political leaders had their first exposure to public notice and political life in this office. A substantial number of executive and legislative officials as well as judges have served as prosecuting attorneys at some point in their careers. The political involvement of a prosecutor varies. In most jurisdictions he is required to run with a party designation. In some places prosecutors are elected on a nonpartisan basis. The powers of a prosecutor are formidable and he is an important personage in his community. If he is not truly independent and professional, his powers can be misused for political or other improper purposes. Perhaps even more than other American public officials, the prosecutor's activity is in large part open to public gaze—as it should be—and spotlighted by the press. The importance of his function is such that his least mistake is likely to be magnified, as are many of his successful exploits.[4]

The prosecutor is also the chief law enforcement officer of a particular jurisdiction. General duties of a prosecutor include: (1) enforcing the law, (2) representing the government, (3) maintaining proper standards of conduct as an attorney and court officer, (4) developing programs and legislation of law and criminal justice reform, and (5) being a public spokesperson for the field of law. Of these, representing the government while presenting the state's case to the court is the prosecutor's most frequent task. In this regard, the prosecutor does many of the following:

1. Investigates possible violations of the law.

2. Cooperates with police in investigating a crime.

3. Determines what the charge will be.

4. Interviews witnesses in criminal cases.

5. Reviews applications for arrest and search warrants.

6. Subpoenas witnesses.

7. Represents the government in pre-trial hearings and in motion procedures.

8. Enters into plea bargaining negotiations.

9. Tries criminal cases.

10. Recommends sentences to courts upon convictions.

11. Represents the government in appeals.

In addition, many jurisdictions have established special prosecution programs aimed at seeking indictments and convictions of those committing such crimes as major felonies, violent offenses, rapes, and white-collar crimes. The application section of this chapter contains an example of a prosecution program of this kind.

## THE ROLE OF THE PROSECUTOR AND POLICE OFFICER

Although the prosecutor has a variety of functions, one of the most important concerns the relationship between the prosecutor and the police officer. The prosecutor has broad discretion in decisions to charge the suspect with a crime and is generally the chief law enforcement official of his jurisdiction. When it comes to processing everyday offenses and minor fines, the prosecutor often relies on law enforcement officers to provide and initiate the formal complaint. In the area involving more serious offenses such as felonies, the prosecutor is involved in investigating criminal violations. Some offices of the district attorney are involved in special investigations concerning organized crime, corruption of public officials, corporate and white collar crime, as well as vice and drug investigations. Much of the staff and investigative work in such offices is handled by police personnel.

Police and prosecutorial relationships vary from one jurisdiction to another, and often depend on whether the police agency is supplying the charge, or the district attorney is investigating the matter. In either case, the prosecutor is required to maintain regular liaison with the police department in order to properly develop the criminal prosecution. Some of the areas where the police officer and prosecutor work together are as follows:

1. Police investigation report. This report is one of the most important documents in the prosecutor's case file. It is basically a statement of the details of the crime including all the evidence which is needed to support each element of the offense. Such a report is a critical first step in developing the government's case against a suspect.

2. Providing legal advice. Oftentimes the prosecutor advises the police officer about the legal issues in a given case. The prosecutor may also assist the officer in limiting unnecessary court appearances, informing police officers of the disposition of cases, and helping to prepare the police officer for pre-trial and trial appearances.

3. Prosecutorial training of police personnel. In many jurisdictions, prosecutors assist police departments in training police officers. Through such training programs, police officers are made more aware of what is involved in securing a warrant, making a legal arrest, interrogating a person in custody, and conducting legal lineups for the purposes of identification. Some police departments have police legal advisers who cooperate with the prosecutor in providing legal training for new and experienced police personnel.[5]

These, then, are some of the areas where police and prosecutor can work together and maximize coordination within the criminal justice system. There are, however, situations where the police and prosecutor because of their different roles function with minimal cooperation and even mistrust. Police and prosecutors often compete with each other in seeking credit for the successful arrest, prosecution and conviction of a particular defendant. In some cases, the prosecutor is insensitive to the problem of unnecessary court appearances by police officers. And in some jurisdictions, there might even be outright antagonism between police and prosecutors where there is little or no interchange of information about a particular case. Furthermore, the police department may be unwilling to understand the prosecutor's decision not to charge a suspect with a crime after much police work has gone into an investigation. The police may not agree with alternative procedures developed by the prosecutor and would prefer to press for full enforcement in the charging decision. In some cases, the prosecutor might not handle the witnesses or informants properly, which may place the police officer in an embarrassing position. These kinds of problems do exist between prosecutors and police officers and vary from one court to another.

The prosecutor, however, as the chief law enforcement official of a given jurisdiction, ordinarily is dependent on police and other investigative agencies for information regarding criminal violations. A large part of the prosecutor's work comes from complaints made by citizens or arrests made directly by police agencies. Consequently, the prosecutor needs the cooperation of the police in processing the case. Even in those cases in which the prosecutor investigates suspected criminal acts on his own initiative, the investigations are generally conducted by police personnel. Most professional prosecutors willingly cooperate with law enforcement personnel so as to have a greater impact and probability of successfully prosecuting their cases. Much of the conflict between the parties stems from the prosecutor's unlimited discretion in whether or not to proceed with an accusation; or the prosecutor may believe the police have legally bungled and mishandled evidence in a criminal investigation.

## Types of Prosecutors

In the federal system, prosecutors are known as United States attorneys and are appointed by the President. They are responsible for representing the government in federal district courts. The chief prosecutor is usually an administrator, while assistants normally handle the actual preparation and trial work. The federal prosecutors are professional civil service employees with reasonable salaries and job security.

On a state or county level, the attorney general and district attorney, respectively, are the chief prosecutorial officers. Again, the bulk of criminal prosecution and staff work is performed by scores of full-time and part-time attorneys, police investigators, and clerical personnel. Most attorneys who work for prosecutors on state and county levels are political appointees who earn low salaries, handle many cases, and in some jurisdictions maintain private law practices. Many young lawyers serve in this capacity in order to gain trial experience, and leave when they obtain better paying positions. In some state, county, and municipal jurisdictions, however, the office of the prosecutor can be described as having the highest standards of professional skill, personal integrity, and work conditions.

In urban settings, the structure of the district attorney's office is often specialized, having separate divisions for felonies, misdemeanors, and trial and appeal assignments. In rural offices, chief prosecutors will handle many of the criminal cases themselves. Where assistant prosecutors are employed, they often work part-time, have limited professional opportunities, and are dependent on the political patronage of chief prosecutors for their positions. The National Advisory Commission on Criminal Justice Standards and Goals has suggested the following personnel and organizational standards for prosecutors.[6]

***Professional Standards for Assistant Prosecutors.*** The primary basis for the selection and retention of assistant prosecutors should be demonstrated legal ability. Care should be taken to recruit lawyers from all segments of the population. The prosecutor should undertake programs, such as legal internships for law students, designed to attract able young lawyers to careers in prosecution.

The position of assistant prosecutor should be a full-time occupation, and assistant prosecutors should be prohibited from engaging in outside law practice. The starting salaries for assistant prosecutors should be no less than those paid by private law firms in the jurisdiction, and the prosecutor should have the authority to increase periodically the salaries for assistant prosecutors to a level that will encourage the retention of able and experienced prosecutors, subject to approval of the legislature, city or county council as appropriate. For the first 5 years of service, salaries of assistant prosecutors should be comparable to those of attorney associates in local private law firms.

The caseload for each assistant prosecutor should be limited to permit the proper preparation of cases at every level of the criminal proceedings. Assistant prosecutors should be assigned cases sufficiently in advance of the court date in order to enable them to interview every prosecution witness, and to conduct supplemental investigations when necessary.

The trial division of each prosecutor's office should have at least two attorneys for each trial judge conducting felony trials on a full-time basis or the equivalent of such a judge. Each office also should have a sufficient number of attorneys to perform the other functions of the office.

**Supporting Staff and Facilities.** The office of the prosecutor should have a supporting staff comparable to that of similar-size private law firms. Prosecutors whose offices serve metropolitan jurisdictions should appoint an office manager with the responsibility for program planning and budget management, procurement of equipment and supplies, and selection and supervision of nonlegal personnel. Paraprofessionals should be utilized for law-related tasks that do not require prosecutorial experience and training. There should be adequate secretarial help for all staff attorneys. Special efforts should be made to recruit members of the supporting staff from all segments of the community served by the office.

The office of the prosecutor should have physical facilities comparable to those of similar-size private law firms. There should be at least one conference room and one lounge for staff attorneys, and a public waiting area separate from the offices of the staff.

The prosecutor and his staff should have immediate access to a library sufficiently extensive to fulfill the research needs of the office. Staff attorneys should be supplied with personal copies of books, such as the State criminal code, needed for their day-to-day duties.

The basic library available to a prosecutor's office should include the following: the annotated laws of the State, the State code of criminal procedure, the municipal code, the United States code annotated, the State appellate reports, the U.S. Supreme Court reports, Federal courts of appeals and district court reports, citators covering all reports and statutes in the library, digests for State and Federal cases, a legal reference work digesting State law, a legal reference work digesting law in general, a form book of approved jury charges, legal treatises on evidence and criminal law, criminal law and U.S. Supreme Court case reporters published weekly, looseleaf services related to criminal law, and if available, an index to the State appellate brief bank.

Today, the personnel practices, organizational structures, and political atmospheres of many prosecutor's offices restrict the effectiveness of individual prosecutors to investigate and prosecute criminal offenses. The above standards suggest the need to improve public prosecution in all of these areas if the goal of efficient government representation in the criminal justice system is to be realized.

PROSECUTORIAL
DISCRETION

After the police arrest and bring a suspect to court, it might be expected that the entire criminal court process would be mobilized. This is not the case. For a variety of reasons, including insufficient evidence, unwilling witnesses, or because the evidence has been illegally seized, a substantial percentage of defendants are never brought to trial. In other cases, particularly where a conviction is likely, the government will invoke the full criminal process, including the imposition of criminal penalties.

The power to institute formal charges against the defendant is the key to the prosecutorial function. The ability to initiate or discontinue charges against a defendant represents the control and power the prosecutor has over an individual's liberty. The prosecutor has broad discretion in the exercise of his duties. It is the prosecutor's primary responsibility to institute criminal proceedings against the defendant; this discretionary decision is subject to few limitations, and often puts the prosecutor in the position of making difficult decisions without appropriate policies and guidelines. Over forty years ago, Newman Baker discussed the problems of prosecutorial decision making when he stated:

"To prosecute or not to prosecute?" is a question which comes to the mind of this official scores of times each day. A law has been contravened and the statute says he is bound to commence proceedings. His legal duty is clear. But, what will be the result? Will it be a waste of time? Will it be expensive to the state? Will it be unfair to the defendant (the prosecutor applying his own ideas of justice)? Will it serve any good purpose to society in general? Will it have good publicity value? Will it cause a political squabble? Will it prevent the prosecutor from carrying the offender's home precinct when he, the prosecutor, runs for Congress after his term as prosecutor? Was the law violated a foolish piece of legislation? If the offender is a friend, is it the square thing to do to reward friendship by initiating criminal proceedings? These and many similar considerations are bound to come to the mind of the man responsible for setting the wheels of criminal justice in motion.[7]

Once involved in a case, the prosecutor must also determine the formal charge. The decision to charge or not to charge a person with a crime is often not an easy one. Should a 17-year-old boy be charged with burglary, or handled as a juvenile offender in the juvenile court? Would it be more appropriate to reduce a drug charge from sale of marijuana to mere possession? What if the offense could be considered mayhem, battery, or simple assault?

In determining what course of action to take, the prosecutor has a significant effect on the criminal justice system. Initiating formal charges against all defendants arrested by the police would clog the courts with numerous petty crimes and prosecute many cases in which little chance of conviction exists. In addition, the prosecutor will waste time on minor cases that could have been better spent on the investigation and prosecution of more serious crimes. Effective screening by prosecutors can eliminate many cases from the judicial system in which convictions cannot reasonably be obtained or which may be inappropriate for criminal action, such as petty thefts, minor crimes by first offenders, and criminal acts involving offenders in need of special services (e.g., emotionally disturbed or mentally retarded offenders.) The prosecutor can then concentrate on bringing to trial offenders who commit serious personal and property crimes such as homicide, burglary, rape, and robbery.[8]

As the person ultimately responsible for deciding whether to prosecute, the prosecutor must be aware of the wide variety of circumstances that affect his decision. In *Prosecution: The Decision to Charge a Suspect With A Crime*, Frank Miller has identified a list of factors which affect discretion and the charging decision. Some of these include: (1) the attitude of the victim; (2) the cost of prosecution to the criminal justice system; (3) undue harm to the suspect; (4) the availability of alternative procedures; (5) the use of civil sanctions; and (6) the willingness of the suspect to cooperate with law enforcement authorities.[9]

Because of the very nature of prosecutorial discretion, its proper exercise can improve the criminal justice process. For example, its use can prevent the unnecessary rigid implementation of the criminal law. Discretion allows the prosecutor to consider alternative decisions and humanize the operation of the criminal justice system. If the prosecutor had little or no discretion, he would be forced to prosecute all cases brought to his attention. Judge Breital has stated that: "If every policeman, every prosecutor, every court, and every post sentence agency performed his or its responsibility in strict accordance with rules of law, precisely and narrowly laid down, the criminal law would be ordered but intolerable."[10]

On the other hand, too much discretion can lead to abuses which result in the abandonment of the law. One of America's most eminent legal scholars, Roscoe Pound, has defined discretion in the following way:

[Discretion is] an authority conferred by law to act in certain conditions or situations in accordance with an official's or an official agency's considered judgment and conscience. It is an idea of morals, belonging to the twilight zone between law and morals.[11]

In terms of prosecutorial practices, this definition of discretion implies the need to select and choose among alternative decisions—to remove cases from the criminal process, to modify criminal charges, or to prosecute to the fullest intent of legal authority. Because there is no easy way to make these decisions, it has been recommended that the prosecutor establish standards for evaluating whether criminal proceedings should be brought against an accused. The American Bar Association's *Standards Relating to the Prosecution and Defense Function* provide the following guidelines for prosecutorial discretion in the charging decision:

A. In addressing himself to the decision whether to charge, the prosecutor should first determine whether there is evidence which would support a conviction.

B. The prosecutor is not obliged to present all charges which the evidence might support. The prosecutor may in some circumstances and for good cause consistent with the public interest decline to prosecute, notwithstanding that evidence exists which would support a conviction. Illustrative of the factors which the prosecutor may properly consider in exercising his discretion are:

1. the prosecutor's reasonable doubt that the accused is in fact guilty;

2. the extent of the harm caused by the offense;

3. the disproportion of the authorized punishment in relation to the particular offense or the offender;

4. possible improper motives of a complainant;

5. prolonged nonenforcement of a statute, with community acquiescence;

6. reluctance of the victim to testify;

7. cooperation of the accused in the apprehension or conviction of others;

8. availability and likelihood of prosecution by another jurisdiction.

C. In making the decision to prosecute, the prosecutor should give no weight to the personal or political advantages or disadvantages which might be involved or to a desire to enhance his record of convictions.

D. In cases which involve a serious threat to the community, the prosecutor should not be deterred from prosecution by the fact that in his jurisdiction juries have tended to acquit persons accused of the particular kind of criminal act in question.

E. The prosecutor should not bring or seek charges greater in number or degree than he can reasonably support with evidence at trial.[12]

These standards are aimed at controlling and improving prosecutorial decisions regarding what cases should be prosecuted in the criminal process. Other methods of controlling prosecutorial decision making include: (1) identifying the reasons for charging decisions; (2) the publication of office policies; (3) review by nonprosecutorial groups; (4) charging conferences; and (5) the evaluation of charging policies and decisions and the development of screening, diversion, and plea negotiations procedures.[13]

Even in felony cases, the prosecutor ordinarily exercises much discretion in deciding whether to charge the accused with a crime. After a police investigation, the prosecutor may be asked to review the sufficiency of the evidence to determine if a criminal complaint should be filed. In some jurisdictions, this may involve presentation of the evidence at a preliminary hearing. In other cases, the prosecutor's recommendation may involve seeking a criminal complaint through the grand jury or other information procedure. These procedures, representing the formal methods of charging the accused with a felony offense, are discussed in Chapter 10.

The prosecutor may play a limited role in exercising discretion in minor offenses. It may consist of simply consulting with the police after their investigation results in a complaint being filed against the accused. In these instances, the decision to charge a person with a crime may be left primarily to the discretion of the law enforcement agency. The prosecutor may decide to enter this type of case after an arrest has been made and a complaint filed with the court, and subsequently determine whether to adjust the matter or proceed to trial. In some minor crimes, the prosecutor may not even appear until the trial stage of the process (or not at all); in some jurisdictions, the police officer handles the entire case, including its prosecution.

While determining which cases should be eliminated from the criminal process or brought to trial, the prosecutor has the opportunity to select alternative actions which may be more appropriate. Charging an accused with a misdemeanor or felony, or bringing a single complaint instead of multiple complaints, involves prosecutorial discretion in criminal matters. In addition, there are many situations in which the prosecutor must decide if noncriminal alternatives are more appropriate.

ALTERNATIVES
TO
PROSECUTION

The President's Commission on Law Enforcement and Administration of Justice *Task Force Report on The Courts* made the following statement on this issue:

Noncriminal Alternatives. When the prosecutor decides that a case should not be prosecuted criminally, a simple dismissal will often be appropriate: Investigation may reveal that the accused is not guilty of the offense for which he was arrested, or that although he is guilty, the offense is minor and there is no reason to believe he will commit such an offense again. But there are many cases where some followup should be provided: The offender may be an alcoholic or a narcotics addict; he may be mentally ill; he may have been led to crime by his family situation or by his inability to get a job. If he is not helped, he may well return to crime.

There are many cases in which minimal intrusions on the defendant's liberty would be all that seem necessary. Often it will be enough simply to refer the offender to the appropriate agency in the community, and hope that he will take advantage of the help offered. The prosecutor might, for example, be willing to drop charges if the defendant goes to an employment agency and makes a bona fide effort to get a job, or if he consults a family service agency, or if he resumes his education. The prosecutor retains legal power to file a charge until the period of limitations has run, but as a practical matter, unless the offense is repeated, it would be unusual for the initial charge to be revived.[14]

Today, particularly in those jurisdictions where alternative programs exist, prosecutors are identifying and diverting offenders to community agencies in cases where the full criminal process does not appear necessary. This may occur in certain juvenile cases, with alcoholic and drug offenders, and in nonsupport paternity, prostitution, and gambling offenses. The American Bar Association's *Standards on the Prosecution and Defense Function* recommend the utilization of social service programs as appropriate alternatives to prosecution:

DISCRETION AS TO NON-CRIMINAL DISPOSITION

A. The prosecutor should explore the availability of non-criminal disposition, including programs of rehabilitation, formal or informal, in deciding whether to press criminal charges; especially in the case of a first offender, the nature of the offense may warrant non-criminal disposition.

B. Prosecutors should be familiar with the resources of social agencies which can assist in the evaluation of cases for diversion from the criminal process.[15]

The opportunity to deal with the accused in a noncriminal fashion represents what has become known as pre-trial diversion, in which the prosecutor postpones or eliminates criminal prosecution in exchange for the alleged offender's participation in a rehabilitation program. Project Crossroads in Washington, D.C.; the Manhattan Court Employment Project in New York City; and the Boston Court Resources Project in Boston, Massachusetts are examples of employment-oriented diversion programs.[16] In recent years, the development and apparent success of such programs has made them an important factor in prosecutorial discretion and a major part of the criminal justice system. A more detailed discussion of pre-trial diversion is found in Chapter 10.

## THE DEFENSE ATTORNEY

The defense attorney is the counterpart of the prosecuting attorney in the criminal process. The accused has a constitutional right to counsel and, when the defendant cannot afford one, the state must provide the cost of a legal defense. The accused may obtain counsel from the private bar if he or she is in a financial position to do so; in the case of the indigent defendant, private counsel or a public defender may be assigned by the court.

For many years, the role of the criminal defense attorney and the practice of criminal law have generally been looked down upon by the legal profession and community. This attitude resulted from the kinds of legal work a defense attorney was forced to do—working with shady characters, negotiating for the release of known thugs and hoods, and often overzealously defending alleged criminals in the criminal trial. Lawyers have been reluctant to specialize in criminal law because the pay is relatively low and criminal lawyers often provide services without receiving any compensation. In addition, law schools in the past have failed to develop courses in the criminal law and trial practices beyond the one or two courses traditionally in their curricula.

In recent years, however, with the advent of constitutional requirements regarding the assistance of counsel, interest in the area of criminal law has grown. Almost all law schools today have clinical programs which employ students as voluntary defenders. They also offer courses in trial tactics, brief writing, and appellate procedures. In addition, legal organizations such as the American Bar Association, the National Legal Aid and Defenders Association, the National Association of Criminal Defense Lawyers, and others have assisted in recruiting able lawyers to participate in criminal defense work. As the American Bar Association has noted, "An almost indispensable condition to fundamental improvement of American criminal justice is the active and knowledgeable support of the bar as a whole."[17]

Today, the lawyer whose practice involves a substantial proportion of criminal cases is often considered a specialist in the field. Since most lawyers are not prepared in law school for criminal work, their skill often results from their experience in regularly defending the accused offender in the trial courts. Lawyers like F. Lee Bailey, Edward Bennett Williams, Percy Foreman, Melvin Belli, and William Kunstler are the elite of the private criminal bar; they are nationally known criminal defense attorneys who often represent defendants for large fees in celebrated and widely publicized cases. Attorneys like these are relatively few in number and do not regularly defend the ordinary criminal defendant.

In addition to this very limited group of well-known criminal lawyers, some lawyers and law firms serve as house counsel for such professional criminals as narcotics dealers, gamblers, prostitutes, and even big-time burglars. Because of their criminal law expertise, these lawyers are often involved in representing organized crime and syndicate members on a continuing basis. Well-known lawyers and proficient house counsel criminal lawyers, however, constitute a very small percentage of the private criminal bar.

A larger proportion of criminal defendants are represented by lawyers who often accept many cases for small fees and are frequent participants in the criminal court process. They may belong to small law firms or work alone, but a sizeable portion of their practice involves representing those accused of crime. There are also private practitioners who occasionally take on criminal matters as part of their general practice. Since most people accused of a crime cannot afford their own attorneys, however, most defense work is done by public defenders or by private attorneys appointed by the court at fixed fees paid by the county, state, or federal government. As these public defender services increase, it would appear that there would be less opportunity for the lawyer who infrequently represents a defendant to participate in the criminal process. This could result in more effective criminal representation, since the President's Crime Commission has pointed out:

Often the lawyer in general practice feels incapable of handling criminal matters skillfully. It is commonly known that criminal courts function under a system of rules and practices familiar only to insiders which in some cases supercedes the written codes of criminal procedure. The nonspecialist legitimately doubts his capabilities in the practice of criminal law, a field that received little attention in his formal legal education.[18]

On the other hand, the President's Crime Commission was concerned about the quality of legal service provided by the experienced attorney who regularly practices criminal law in the local courts. The Commission has said:

All but the most eminent criminal lawyers are bound to spend much of their working lives in overcrowded, physically unpleasant courts, dealing with people who have committed questionable acts, and attempting to put the best possible construction on those acts. It is not the sort of working environment that most people choose. Finally, the professional status of the criminal lawyer tends to be low. To some extent the criminal lawyer is identified unjustifiably in the public eye with the client he represents. Indeed some criminal lawyers are in fact house counsel for criminal groups engaged in gambling, prostitution, and narcotics. The reprehensible conduct of the few sometimes leads the public to see honest, competent practitioners as 'mouthpieces' also. Furthermore, in nearly every large city a private defense bar of low legal and dubious ethical quality can be found. Few in number, these lawyers typically carry large caseloads and in many cities dominate the practice in routine cases. They frequent courthouse corridors, bondsmen's offices, and police stations for clients, and rely not on legal knowledge but on their capacity to manipulate the system. Their low repute often accurately reflects the quality of the services they render. This public image of the criminal lawyer is a serious obstacle to the attraction of able young lawyers, and reputable and seasoned practitioners as well, to the criminal law.[19]

The problem of where to get enough good lawyers to represent the accused may be solved by the recent establishment of public defender programs. Often, however, the full-time salaried public defender is inexperienced, overworked, and unwilling to challenge the system.

The answer to fulfilling constitutional mandates regarding assistance of counsel remains unclear. Presently, not enough competent private lawyers or law firms are exclusively involved in criminal practice. The lawyer who is in the general practice of law ordinarily does not have enough expertise to handle all criminal matters well. The public defender system represents the most indigent defendants and normally works under the burden of large caseloads. Under these conditions, there continues to be an urgent need to recruit and train better criminal lawyers, particularly as the role of the attorney expands beyond the pre-trial and trial stages and enters into appeal and other proceedings.

## THE ROLE OF THE CRIMINAL DEFENSE ATTORNEY

The defense counsel is an attorney as well as being an officer of the court. As an attorney, the defense counsel is obligated to uphold the integrity of the legal profession and to observe the requirements of the Code of Professional Responsibility in the defense of a client. In this regard, the Code states the following regarding the duties of the lawyer to the adversary system of justice:

Our legal system provides for the adjudication of disputes governed by the rules of substantive, evidentiary, and procedural law. An adversary presentation counters the natural human tendency to judge too swiftly in terms of the familiar that which is not yet fully known; the advocate, by his zealous preparation of facts and law, enables the tribunal to come to the hearing with an open and neutral mind and to render impartial judgements. The duty of a lawyer to his client and his duty to the legal system are the same: To represent his client zealously within the boundaries of the law.[20]

As an officer of the court, along with the judge, prosecutors, and other trial participants, the defense attorney participates in a process of seeking to uncover the basic facts and elements of the criminal act. In this dual capacity of being both a defensive advocate and an officer of the court, the attorney is often confronted with conflicting obligations to client and profession. Monroe Freedman identifies three of the most difficult problems involving the professional responsibility of the criminal defense lawyer:

1. Is it proper to cross-examine for the purpose of discrediting the reliability or credibility of an adverse witness whom you know to be telling the truth?
2. Is it proper to put a witness on the stand when you know he will commit perjury?
3. Is is proper to give your client legal advice when you have reason to believe that the knowledge you give him will tempt him to commit perjury?[21]

These questions and others reveal serious difficulties with respect to a lawyer's ethical responsibilities.

There are other equally important issues. Suppose, for example, that a client confides that he is planning to commit a crime. What are the defense attorney's ethical responsibilities in this case? Obviously, the lawyer would have to counsel his client to obey the law; if he assisted his client in engaging in illegal behavior, it would subject him to charges of unprofessional conduct and even criminal liability. In another area, what is the duty of the defense attorney who is well aware that her client committed the act she is accused of, but is also aware that the police made a procedural error in the case and that the client could be let off on a technicality. The criminal lawyer needs to be aware of these troublesome situations in order to properly balance the duties of being an attorney with those of being an officer of the court.

The defense counsel performs many functions while representing the accused in the criminal process. These include, but are not limited to: (1) investigating the incident; (2) interviewing the client, police, and other witnesses; (3) discussing the matter with the prosecutor; (4) representing the defendant at the various prejudicial procedures, such as arrest, interrogation, lineup and arraignment; (5) entering into plea negotiations; (6) preparing the case for trial, including developing tactics and strategy to be used; (7) filing and arguing legal motions with the court; (8) representing the defendant at trial; (9) providing assistance at sentencing; and (10) determining the appropriate basis for appeal. These are some of the major duties of any defense attorney, whether privately employed by the accused, appointed by the court, or serving as a public defender.

**THE LAWYER AS PROFESSIONAL ADVOCATE**

The adversary system cannot operate without the services of highly trained advocates for each side as well as a judge skilled in advocacy.* Although our law

*From American Bar Association, *Standards Relating to Prosecution Function and Defense Function* (New York: Institute of Judicial Administration, 1971) pp. 145–151. Reprinted with the permission of the American Bar Association which authorized these standards and which holds the copyright.

recognizes the right of a defendant to defend himself without the assistance of counsel if he so chooses, judges, prosecutors and defense counsel are unanimous in the opinion that justice is undermined when any party proceeds without a professional advocate. The accused lacks the knowledge which would permit him to take full advantage of his legal rights and demonstrate his position if he elects a trial. It seems amply clear today that a professional advocate for the accused is indispensable to the system, but, curiously, recognition of this came relatively late in common law legal history.

The primary role of counsel is to act as champion for the client. In this capacity he is the equalizer, the one who places each litigant as nearly as possible on an equal footing under the substantive and procedural law under which he is tried. Of course, as a practical matter he does this not by formally educating the client on every legal aspect of the case, but by taking those procedural steps and recommending those courses of action which the client, were he an experienced advocate himself, might fairly and properly take. A lawyer cannot be timorous in his representation. Courage and zeal in the defense of his client's interest are qualities without which one cannot fully perform as an advocate. And, since the accused may well be the most despised of persons, this burden rests more heavily upon the defense lawyer. Against a "hostile world" the accused, called to the bar of justice by his government, finds in his counsel a single voice on which he must be able to rely with confidence that his interests will be protected to the fullest extent consistent with the rules of procedure and the standards of professional conduct.

The second role of counsel is as intermediary. This is not to say that the caricature, in which counsel becomes mere "mouthpiece" for or alter ego of his client, is a valid description of this role, any more than that it is part of counsel's function as champion to employ threats, force, falsehood or chicanery in defense of his client. From time to time over the past one hundred years or more, in both England and America, an occasional voice is raised advocating what has come to be known as the "alter ego" theory of advocacy. The thesis depicts defense counsel as an agent permitted, and perhaps even obliged, to do for the accused everything he would do for himself if only he possessed the necessary skills and training in the law; in short, that the lawyer is always to execute the directives of the client. This spurious view has been totally and unequivocally rejected for over one hundred years under canons governing English barristers and is similarly rejected by canons of the American Bar Association and other reputable professional organizations. It would be difficult to imagine anything which would more gravely demean the advocate or undermine the integrity of our system of justice than the idea that a defense lawyer should be simply a conduit for his client's desires. As intermediary, counsel expresses to the court objectively, in measured words and forceful tone, what a particular defendant may be incapable of expressing himself simply because he lacks the education and training. The defendant must not be judged on his own forensic skill or lack of it.

Compensating for the client's inarticulateness is only part of the purpose of introducing an intermediary into the process. As in other contexts of human endeavor, the intermediary brings to the controversy an emotional detachment which permits him to make a more dispassionate appraisal. He translates the desired course of action into those steps which the form and procedure of the system permit and professional judgment dictates. He channels the controversy into the establishment mode of legal procedure and deals with the other participants in the process—the prosecutor, the judge—on the level of professional understanding of the rules and their respective roles. When the lawyer loses that detachment by too closely identifying with his client, a large measure of the lawyer's value is lost; indeed he then suffers some of the same disabilities as an accused acting as his own counsel.

To fulfill the role of the truly professional advocate, the lawyer must be free to bring to bear on the problems of defense the skills, experience and judgment he possesses. He can do this only if he knows all that his client knows concerning the facts. The client is not competent to evaluate the relevance or significance of facts; hence the lawyer must insist on complete and candid disclosure. Second, he must be able to conduct the case free from interference. These two factors explain the rule of leading criminal defense lawyers that they have complete disclosure of all facts and entire control of the technical and legal aspects of the litigation.

The drama of the courtroom may tend to overemphasize in our mind's eye the lawyer trying a criminal case. The defense function in a criminal case, however, is a much broader responsibility than courtroom advocacy; the duties extend far beyond the courtroom in both time and place. As in other areas of the practice of law, negotiation is an important function performed by the defense lawyer. The concept of negotiation may seem to the uninitiated out of place in the context of criminal justice; indeed some lawyers, as well as laymen, have tended to oversimplify criminal cases into the either-or, the black-or-white difference between innocence and guilt. In reality, the criminal law is an instrument whose cutting edge must be adapted to the particular facts of each case, facts which are as varied as the range of human experiences. The defense lawyer's greatest contribution often is to mitigate the harshness of the law's judgment; that takes place on several levels: prior to the indictment in the choice of the appropriate charge to be laid against the accused; in the decision about how many of overlapping offenses should be processed; and finally the recommendation for probation, to mention only a few examples. At these stages, the accused needs an advocate or counselor as much as he does in a trial.

Another function of the lawyer is as his client's "learned friend," his counsel in the literal sense. The defense lawyer often may be the only person to whom the defendant can turn in total confidence, once a proper relationship exists, to explain fully his position, which may be incriminating, even though he is in law not guilty of the crime charged. The defendant needs counsel not only to evaluate the risks and advantages of alternative courses of action, such as trial or plea, but also to provide a broad and comprehensive approach to his predicament which will take the most advantage of the protections and benefits which the law affords him.

These functions have been suggested in their ideal and abstract form. In practice they must be performed amidst the tensions that arise from the fact that the lawyer is himself a human being with frailties and is often acting for a client and his family who are distraught and bewildered. The traditional position of the American bar has been that the lawyer may apply his personal views of his client's morality only in a limited degree and only in deciding whether to accept the case in the first instance. He is never required to perform any act which violates his own conscience, but his role as advocate permits and requires that he press all points legally available, even if he must subordinate his personal evaluation of the client's conduct. His private belief that one ought to answer fully any question asked must yield to his role as counsel; as counsel he is prevented from disclosing what he has learned in confidence from his client. He may personally believe that certain rules of law which benefit his client are wrong and ought to be changed, but it is his obligation in the course of representation to invoke them on his client's behalf.

The lawyer also sometimes operates under tensions arising from the seeming conflict between his duty to his client and his duty to the court. When the lawyer's role as an officer of the court is understood in the highest sense, there can rarely be any conflict between these duties. The lawyer's duty to his client is to give him the best professional representation of which he is capable. His duty to the court is to represent the client vigorously, in a manner consistent with his position as professional officer of the court, so that the adversary process may operate. On this level his twin duties coincide rather than conflict. But, it must be recognized, on the level of everyday practice the two duties sometimes may seem to diverge. Thus the court naturally tends to adopt a perspective on a case which differs from that of either litigant. Sometimes the zealous lawyer may seem uncooperative, particularly if he lacks the skill to couch his utterances in terms which will soften aggressive advocacy. However, there are circumstances in which a lawyer must be vigorously aggressive if important rights are not to be undermined by an excess of cooperation with the court. Sometimes the tension is created because the court improperly asks him to step out of his assigned role, as when he is improperly called upon to speak his personal views of the facts or arguments, or when a judge thoughtlessly asks defense counsel questions which impinge on confidential matter acquired from the client. In such situations the strain on counsel may be great, since to seem uncooperative may itself prejudice his client's interests. Where all three professional participants—judge, prosecutor and defense counsel—are adequately skilled, these potential collisions can be dealt with tactfully but firmly.

Another source of the tension which besets the advocate in a criminal case arises from the lawyer's fiduciary position. He holds his client's information and interests in trust, and it is his obligation to act for the protection of those interests even at the expense of his own. This means that the lawyer must pursue the course which will produce the most favorable legitimate disposition of the case for his client, rather than one which will earn him the largest fee, or a course which will avoid personal discomfort, criticism or embarrassment. An advocate must scrupulously avoid the temptation to pursue a point because of its excitement, its news value, its significance in the growth of the law, or its intrinsic intellectual interest, if to pursue it is in any way inconsistent with the furtherance of his client's legitimate interests. In short, it is the client's interests, not the law's or the lawyer's personal long-range interests,which the advocate is pledged to protect. Of course, there are cases where law reform and the client's interests correspond and the lawyer is in the happy position of being able to serve both. This does not mean that the lawyer does not have a separate and important responsibility to work for law reform. The standards provide for this role for the lawyer as a member of the legal profession, but this role must be distinguished from his role as an effective advocate for a client.

It would be dangerously naive, however, if we failed to take into account the very real tensions which proper performance of these duties create for the advocate. Though law is a profession, not a business, a lawyer must earn a living, and it would be unreasonable to create standards of professional conduct which would require him to devote unlimited time to each client without regard to the realities of supporting self and family.

All of these stresses are compounded for the defense lawyer in criminal cases by the intensity with which society and the defendant view criminal proceedings and their consequences, and the need in many cases to resolve these tensions in the heat of trial without opportunity for calm meditation. The complexity of the demands which law and life place upon the trial lawyer requires that his role be approached sympathetically, and that any set of standards for the judging of his conduct be reasonable in the demands it makes upon his capacities and his humanity. On the other hand, the very existence of standards, known and accepted by the profession, will reduce the tensions by reducing the occasions for ad hoc resolution of difficult problems and the attendant risk of diluting standards with expediency. It is the aggregate of his response to these responsibilities and challenges that make the lawyer a true professional; it is as a professional subject to professional standards that he is called upon to function within the adversary system. All this dictates that the lawyer understand his role and obligations and the limits on each and that he not confuse success in the material sense with the correct and honorable performance of his duties within the law.

Over the past decade, the rules and procedures of criminal justice administration have become extremely complex. Specialized knowledge of the criminal process has become essential for the adversary system to operate effectively. Preparation of a case for court involves detailed investigation of a crime, knowledge of court procedures, use of rules of evidence, and skills in criminal advocacy. Both the state and the individual must have this expertise, particularly when an individual's freedom is at stake. Consequently, the right to the assistance of counsel in the criminal justice system is essential if the defendant is to have a fair chance of presenting a case in the adversary process.

**THE RIGHT TO COUNSEL**

One of the most critical issues in the criminal justice system has been whether an indigent defendant has the right to counsel. Can the accused who is poor and cannot afford an attorney have a fair trial without the assistance of counsel? Is counsel required at preliminary hearings? Should the convicted indigent offender be given counsel at state expense in appeals of the case? Questions such as these have constantly arisen in recent years. The federal court system has long provided counsel to the indigent defendant on the basis of the Sixth Amendment to the United States Constitution. In the federal system, counsel was assigned to the defendant who could not afford an attorney unless he or she desired to waive this right.[22] This constitutional mandate clearly applied to the federal courts, but its application to state criminal proceedings was uncertain.

In the landmark case of *Gideon v. Wainwright* in 1963,[23] the United States Supreme Court took the first major step on the issue of right to counsel by holding that state courts must provide counsel to the indigent defendant in felony prosecutions. Some ten years later, in the case of *Argersinger v.Hamlin* in 1972,[24] the court extended the obligation to provide counsel to all criminal cases where the penalty includes imprisonment, regardless of whether the offense is a felony or misdemeanor. These two major decisions relate to the Sixth Amendment right to counsel as it applies to the presentation of a defense at the trial stage of the criminal justice system.

Numerous other Supreme Court decisions since *Gideon v. Wainwright* have followed which require the states to provide counsel for indigent defendants at virtually all other stages of the criminal process, beginning with arrest and concluding with the defendant's release from the system. This section examines the right to counsel as it concerns the pre- and post-trial stages of the criminal justice process; a detailed discussion of trial proceedings in which the right to counsel applies is found in Chapter 12.

Today, the Sixth Amendment right to counsel and the Fourteenth Amendment guarantee of due process of law have been judicially interpreted together to provide the defendant with counsel by the state in all types of criminal proceedings. Counsel is required during an interrogation of an indigent accused while in the custody of the police; this has already been discussed in the *Miranda v. Arizona*[25] decision (see Chapter 7), which held that any statements made by the accused when in custody are inadmissible at trial unless the accused is informed of the right to counsel and to have an attorney appointed by the state if indigent.

The defendant who appears in a police lineup after being formally charged with a crime has a right to have counsel present,[26] this is an effort to insure the fairness of the lineup procedures. If no indictment or formal charge has been lodged, the defendant, not entitled to counsel at that stage of the proceeding[27] (see Chapter 8).

The state is also required to provide the assistance of counsel at arraignments and preliminary hearings. This has been established by judicial interpretation in the United States Supreme Court cases of *Hamilton v. Alabama* (1961)[28] and *Coleman v. Alabama* (1970).[29] The defendant has certain advantages when assistance of counsel is available in such early stages of a criminal case: the presence of counsel safeguards the interests of the accused who might consider waiving constitutional rights; the defense attorney can more intensively investigate the circumstances of the crime if brought into the case from its inception; and the suspect benefits from the early involvement of counsel in negotiations with the government regarding whether to actually charge the individual with a crime, what the charge will be, and whether plea bargaining will be a necessary part of the case.

In addition to guaranteeing the right of counsel at police interrogations, lineups, and preliminary hearings, as well as at trials, the United States Supreme Court has moved to extend the right to counsel to post-conviction and other collateral proceedings, such as probation and parole revocation, and appeal. When, for example, the court intends to revoke a defendant's probation and impose a sentence, the probationer has a right to counsel at the deferred sentence hearing.[30] Where the state provides for an appellate review of the criminal conviction, the defendant is entitled to the assistance of counsel for this initial appeal.[31] The defendant does not have the right to counsel for an appellate review beyond the original appeal or for a discretionary review to the United States Supreme Court.

In the case of *Morrissey v. Brewer* in 1972,[32] the Supreme Court established procedural due process guidelines for parole revocation hearings but declined to decide the question of right to counsel at such hearings. The *Morrissey* case was an indication of the direction the court was taking in applying due process protections to post-conviction proceedings. Then, in *Gagnon v. Scarpelli* in 1973,[33] the court held that the parolee and probationer are both to be provided with the assistance of counsel in revocation hearings on a case-by-case basis. Rather than provide an inflexible constitutional rule requiring counsel in all probation and parole revocation hearings, the court said that counsel should be made available in complex and difficult cases at the discretion of the correctional agency. (These cases are discussed further in Chapters 14 and 17.) The United States Supreme Court has also required the states to provide counsel in other quasi-criminal proceedings, such as juvenile matters [34] and mental health commitment proceedings.[35]

Areas still remain in the criminal justice system where the courts by judicial decree have not required assistance of counsel for the accused. These include (1) pre-indictment lineups, (2) booking procedures including the taking of fingerprints and other forms of identification, (3) grand jury investigations, (4) appeals beyond the first review, and (5) disciplinary proceedings in correctional institutions. Nonetheless, recent judicial decisions regarding the right to counsel for indigent criminal defendants indicate that no person can be deprived of freedom without such representation.

The right to counsel can also be spelled out in particular federal or state statutes. For example, beyond abiding by present constitutional requirements, a state may provide counsel by statute at all stages of juvenile proceedings, or when dealing with inmate prison infractions or pre-trial release hearings, or when considering temporary confinement of drug or sex offenders for psychiatric examination.

In addition to these judicial and statutory rules, various national groups have made recommendations which closely parallel the recent decisions of the United States Supreme Court. The National Advisory Commission on Criminal Justice Standards and Goals has proposed that public defense services be made available to indigents accused in all criminal cases beginning at the times of their arrests.[36] The American Bar Association's *Standards Relating to Providing Defense Services* states:

**4.1 Criminal Cases.** Counsel should be provided in all criminal proceedings for offenses punishable by loss of liberty, except those types of offenses for which such punishment is not likely to be imposed, regardless of their denomination as felonies, misdemeanors or otherwise.

**4.2 Collateral Proceedings.** Counsel should be provided in all proceedings arising from the initiation of a criminal action against the accused, including extradition, mental competency, post-conviction and other proceedings which are adversary in nature, regardless of the designation of the court in which they occur or classification of the proceedings as civil in nature.[37]

Today, the scope of representation for the indigent defendant is believed to cover virtually all areas of the criminal process, and most certainly those critical points at which a person's liberty is at stake. Table 9.1 summarizes the major U.S. Supreme Court decisions granting defendants counsel throughout the criminal justice system.

TABLE 9.1
Major United States Supreme Court Cases Granting Right to Counsel Throughout Pre-Trial, Trial, and Post-Trial Stages of Criminal Justice Process

| Case | Stage and Ruling |
| --- | --- |
| *Escobedo v. Illinois* 378 U.S. 478 (1964) | Defendant has right to counsel during the course of any police interrogation. |
| *Miranda v. Arizona* 384 U.S. 694 (1966) | Use of procedural safeguards, including right to counsel, at custodial interrogation to secure the privilege against self-incrimination. |
| *Brewer v. Williams* 430 U.S. 387 (1977) (see also *Massiah v. U.S.* 377 U.S. 201 [1961]) | Once adversary proceedings had begun against defendant, he has a right to the assistance of counsel. |
| *Hamilton v. Alabama* 368 U.S. 52 (1961) | The "arraignment" is a critical stage in the criminal process, so that denial of the right to counsel is a violation of due process of law. |
| *Coleman v. Alabama* 399 U.S. 1 (1970) | The preliminary hearing is a critical stage in a criminal prosecution requiring the state to provide the indigent defendant with counsel. |
| *Moore v. Illinois* 434 U.S. 220 (1977) | An in-court identification at a preliminary hearing after a criminal complaint has been initiated requires counsel to protect defendant's interests. |
| *United States v. Wade* 388 U.S. 218 (1967) | A defendant in a pre-trial post indictment lineup for identification purposes has the right to assistance of counsel. |

(Table 9.1
continued)

| | |
|---|---|
| *Moore v. Michigan*<br>355 U.S. 155 (1957) | Defendant has the right to counsel when submitting a guilty plea to the court. |
| *Powell v. Alabama*<br>287 U.S. 45 (1932) | Defendants, nine black boys all charged with rape of two white girls, were not accorded the right to counsel at their trial in a proper manner in a state capital case. |
| *Gideon v. Wainwright*<br>372 U.S. 335 (1963) | An indigent defendant charged in a state court with a noncapital felony has the right to the assistance of counsel under the due process clause of Fourteenth Amendment at trial. |
| *Argersinger v. Hamlin*<br>407 U.S. 25 (1972) | The court upheld the defendant's right to counsel at trial whenever a person may be imprisoned for any offense, even one day, whether classified as a misdemeanor or felony. |
| *Scott v. Illinois*<br>U.S.    (1979) | A criminal defendant charged with a statutory offense for which imprisonment upon conviction is authorized but not imposed does not have the right to appointed counsel. |
| In re Gault<br>387 U.S. 1 (1967) | Procedural due process, including the right to counsel applies to juvenile delinquency adjudication that may lead to a child's commitment to a state institution. |
| *Faretta v. California*<br>422 U.S. 806 (1975) | A defendant in a state criminal trial has a constitutional right to proceed without counsel when he voluntarily and intelligently elects to do so. |
| *Tounsend v. Burke*<br>334 U.S. 736 (1948) | A convicted offender has a right to counsel at the time of sentencing. |

(Table 9.1
continued)

| | |
|---|---|
| *Douglas v. California* 372 U.S. 353 (1963) | An indigent defendant granted a first appeal from a criminal conviction has the right to be represented by counsel on appeal. |
| *Mempa v. Rhay* 389 U.S. 128 (1967) | A convicted offender has the right to assistance of counsel at probation revocation hearings where the sentence has been deferred. |
| *Gagnon v. Scarpelli* 411 U.S. 778 (1973) | Probationers and parolees have a constitutionally limited right to counsel on a case by case basis at revocation proceedings. |

PUBLIC
DEFENDER
SERVICES

To satisfy the constitutional requirements that indigent defendants must be provided with the assistance of counsel at various stages of the criminal process, the federal government and the states have had to evaluate and expand existing criminal defense services. Prior to the mandate of *Gideon v. Wainwright*, public defender services were mainly provided by assigned counsel systems or through limited public defender programs. In 1961, for example, defender systems existed in only 3% of the counties in the United States, serving only about a quarter of the country's population.[38] The traditional reasons for the general lack of defense services for indigents have included the following: (1) until fairly recently, the laws of most jurisdictions did not require the assistance of counsel for felony offenders and others; (2) only a few attorneys were interested in criminal law practice; (3) the organized legal bar was generally indifferent to the need for criminal defense assistance; and (4) the caseloads of lawyers working in public defender agencies were staggering.

However, beginning with the *Gideon* case in 1963 and continuing through the *Argersinger* decision in 1972, the criminal justice system has been forced to increase public defender services. Today, about 650 defender systems provide indigent services in 28% of the counties in the United States, which includes two-thirds of the nation's population.[39] Figure 9.2 illustrates the distribution and growth of organized defender services during the period between 1961 and 1973.

Yet, there is still a great need to supplement programs that provide the assistance of counsel to indigent defendants. It has been estimated, for example, that approximately 4 million persons arrested each year for felonies, nontraffic misdemeanors, and juvenile offenses are financially unable to hire private attorneys. At present, it is estimated that there are approximately 2,600 full-time defenders in the United States. If private attorneys appointed by the courts would handle only 25% of the 4 million

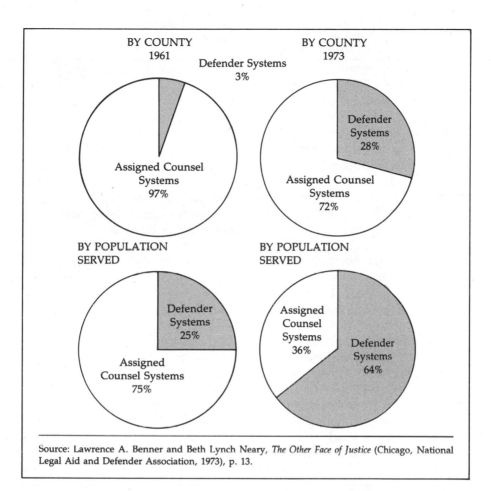

FIGURE 9.2
Growth of Defender
Services

Source: Lawrence A. Benner and Beth Lynch Neary, *The Other Face of Justice* (Chicago, National Legal Aid and Defender Association, 1973), p. 13.

indigent defendants, the National Legal Aid and Defender Association estimates that over 14,000 additional public defenders would be needed today.[40]

Programs providing assistance of counsel to indigent defendants are organized primarily in the two major categories previously mentioned: public defender systems and assigned counsel systems. In addition, other approaches to the delivery of legal services to defendants include the use of mixed systems which involve representation by both the public defender and the private bar, law school clinical programs, and prepaid legal services.[41]

Public defender systems seem to offer the most efficient and extensive representation available to the indigent. The public or private defender system involves the use of groups of lawyers working in a public agency or under private contractual agreement and spending all of their time as defense counsel to indigent defendants. Most large metropolitan communities in the country have established such defender programs. In addition, 16 states have organized indigent defense services at the state level. For example, Massachusetts approved legislation in 1960 creating the Massachusetts Defenders Committee; most legal representation furnished to indigent defendants is provided by this state-level agency. Other states which have statewide defender programs include Alaska, Florida, New Jersey, and Minnesota. The structure and operation of these statewide systems vary with each jurisdiction.

In many rural areas, individual public defenders are hired to provide indigent defense services. Generally, these defenders operate alone or with one or two other attorneys, while also maintaining private law practices. Most public defender offices, whether statewide or staffed by a few attorneys, have large caseloads, limited investigative and social service staffs, and low salaries. Despite these problems, public defender systems are preferable to other types of defense services because they focus on the criminal law alone. They can and do provide adequate legal representation, although the quality of their services are generally diminished by the ever-increasing demand for them.

In contrast to the public defender system, the assigned counsel method involves the use of private attorneys appointed by the court to represent indigent defendants. The private attorney is selected from a list of attorneys established by the court, and is reimbursed by the state for any legal services rendered to the client. The assigned counsel system, unless organized properly, suffers from such problems as unequal assignments, inadequate legal fees, and the lack of supportive or supervisory services. Nevertheless, the private bar has an important role to play in providing indigent legal services since most public defender systems are not in a position to represent all needy criminal defendants. In addition, the appointed counsel system gives attorneys the opportunity to participate in criminal defense work. While the major practical disadvantages of this system include inadequate compensation, frequent use of inexperienced attorneys, and the tendency to use the guilty plea too quickly, the assigned counsel system is simple to operate and is often used in conjunction with public defender programs.[42]

The mixed system uses both public defenders and private attorneys in an attempt to draw upon the strengths of both. In this approach, the public defender system operates simultaneously with the assigned counsel system to offer total coverage to the indigent defendant. Each system arranges to divide the courts and caseload according to their strengths and interests. Normally, the public defender agency takes on the large urban areas with their greater need for appointed counsel, while the private attorney handles those courts where public defender services do not exist. The main advantages to the mixed system generally include: (1) widespread coverage of defense needs, (2) the use of experienced attorneys, and (3) the opportunity for the defendant to have counsel early in the criminal process.

Other methods of providing counsel to the indigent include the use of law school students and the development of prepaid legal service programs (similar to comprehensive medical insurance). Most jurisdictions have a student practice rule of procedure which allows third-year law school students in clinical programs to provide supervised counsel to defendants in nonserious offenses. In *Argersinger v. Hamlin,* Justice William Brennan suggested that law students are an important resource in fulfilling constitutional defense requirements.[43]

It is possible that in the future prepaid legal service programs will offer criminal defense services to the indigent in addition to legal aid in civil matters. Federal or state governments may even legislate to support the development of prepaid defense services for persons who are unable to afford their own attorneys.

While different methods of providing counsel exist, it is becoming apparent, especially in major metropolitan areas, that the taxpayer-supported public defender system is becoming the basic type of legal representation. While it is a governmental agency and, as such, is often plagued by bureaucratic problems, the public defender program nevertheless has unique advantages over other legal service programs. It offers an agency structure comprised of qualified personnel, provides support services, and has a stable financial base of government support. The National Advisory Commission on Criminal Justice Standards and Goals has in fact recommended that a full-time publicly financed defender system be the preferred approach to delivering defender services. Its standards are presented below:

**Standard 13.1—Availability of Publicly Financed Representation in Criminal Cases.** Public representation should be made available to eligible defendants (as defined in Standard 13.2) in all criminal cases at their request, or the request of someone acting for them, beginning at the time the individual either is arrested or is requested to participate in an investigation that has focused upon him as a likely suspect. The representation should continue during trial court proceedings and through the exhaustion of all avenues of relief from conviction.

Defendants should be discouraged from conducting their own defense in criminal prosecutions. No defendant should be permitted to defend himself if there is a basis for believing that: (1) The defendant will not be able to deal effectively with the legal or factual issues likely to be raised; (2) The defendant's self-representation is likely to impede the reasonably expeditious processing of the case; or (3) The defendant's conduct is likely to be disruptive of the trial process.[44]

**Standard 13.5—Method of Delivering Defense Services.** Services of a full-time public defender organization, and a coordinated assigned counsel system involving substantial participation of the private bar, should be available in each jurisdiction to supply attorney services to indigents accused of crime. Cases should be divided between the public defender and assigned counsel in a manner that will encourage significant participation by the private bar in the criminal justice system.[45]

Standard 13.1 recommends that counsel be made available to the indigent defendant in all criminal cases, and should begin at the point of arrest. This exceeds present requirements for counsel at both the trial and arrest stages of the criminal process. *Argersinger v. Hamlin* only requires the right to counsel where there is a possibility of incarceration; in addition, this standard suggests that counsel be present at the defendant's arrest, regardless of whether or not the accused has been interrogated. In theory, public defender systems should be able to provide these services; in practice, few public defender agencies have the resources to handle the cases of all indigent criminal defendants at the arrest and trial stages.

Regarding Standard 13.5, it is generally agreed that the most effective method for delivering defense services is through an organized public defender system supplemented by the services of the private bar. The American Bar Association's *Standards Relating to Providing Defense Services* adopts the position that the public defender agency and assigned counsel system are both effective means of delivering legal services. In those states where public defender offices exist, the American Bar Association Standards recommend that the offices be staffed with full-time career personnel. Where the primary system of service is assigned counsel, the standards recommend that case assignments should be publicly distributed and that reasonable compensation should be provided for court-appointed attorneys.[46]

Despite the fact that defense services have grown in recent years, a major future concern of the adversary process will continue to be the provision of quality representation to the indigent defendant at all stages of the criminal justice system.

## SUMMARY

The judge, prosecutor, and defense attorney are the major officers of justice in the judicial system. The judge approves plea bargains, tries cases, and determines the sentence given the offender. The prosecutor, who is the people's attorney, has discretion to decide the criminal charge and disposition. The prosecutor's daily decisions have a significant impact on police and court operations.

The role of the defense attorney in the criminal justice system has grown dramatically during the past 25 years. Today, providing defense services to the indigent criminal defendant is virtually an everyday practice. Under landmark decisions of the United States Supreme Court, particularly *Gideon v. Wainwright* and *Argersinger v. Hamlin*, all defendants who may be imprisoned for any offense must be afforded counsel at trial. Methods of providing counsel include systems for assigned counsel, where an attorney is selected by the court to represent the accused, and defender programs, where public employees provide legal services. Lawyers doing criminal defense work have discovered an increasing need for their services, not only at trial, but also at the pre- and post-judicial stages of the criminal justice system.

## QUESTIONS FOR DISCUSSION

1. Under what circumstances is a prosecutor justified in exercising prosecutorial discretion? Discuss case situations where the prosecutor may exercise discretion not to charge the defendant with a crime.

2. Explain the nature and scope of the defense attorney's role in the criminal justice system today. What are some of the ways in which defense services are provided to indigent defendants?

**3.** At what stages of the criminal process does the defendant have a right to the assistance of counsel? What does the term "critical stage" of the criminal justice system mean?

**1.** American Bar Association, Special Committee on Evaluation of Ethical Standards, *Code of Professional Responsibility* (Chicago, Ill.: American Bar Assn., 1970), p. 87.

**2.** 295 U.S. 78, 55 S.Ct. 629, 79 L.Ed. 1314 (1935).

**3.** Ibid. at 88.

**4.** American Bar Association, *Standards Relating to Prosecution Function and Defense Function.* (New York: Institute of Judicial Administration, 1971) pp. 18–19. Reprinted with the permission of the American Bar Association which authored these standards and which hold the copyright.

**5.** National Advisory Commission on Criminal Justice Standards and Goals, *Courts* (Washington, D.C.: U.S. Government Printing Office, 1973), p. 439.

**6.** National Advisory Commission on Criminal Justice Standards and Goals, *Courts*, Standards 12.2 and 12.3, pp. 232, 234.

**7.** Newman Baker, "The Prosecutor-Initiation of Prosecution," *Journal of Criminal Law, Criminology and Police Science* 23:770, 771 (1933).

**8.** See generally W. Jay Merrill, Marie N. Malks, and Mark Sendrow, *Case Screening and Selected Case Processing in Prosecutors Offices* (U.S. Department of Justice, Law Enforcement Assistance Administration, National Institute of Law Enforcement and Criminal Justice, March 1973).

**9.** Frank W. Miller, *Prosecution: The Decision to Charge a Suspect With a Crime* (Boston, Mass.: Little, Brown and Co., 1970).

**10.** Charles D. Breitel, "Controls in Criminal Law Enforcement," *University of Chicago Law Review* 27:427 (1960).

**11.** Roscoe Pound, "Discretion, Dispensation and Mitigation: The Problem of the Individual Special Case," *New York University Law Review* 35:925 (1960).

**12.** American Bar Association, *Standards Relating to Prosecution Function and Defense Function*, Standard 3.8. Reprinted with the permission of the American Bar Association which authored these standards and which holds the copyright.

**13.** See generally "A Symposium on Prosecutorial Discretion," *American Criminal Law Review* 13:379 (1976).

**14.** President's Commission on Law Enforcement and Administration of Justice, *Task Force Report: The Courts* (Washington, D.C.: U.S. Government Printing Office, 1967), pp. 8–9.

**15.** American Bar Association *Standards Relating to the Prosecution Function and Defense Function*, Standard 3.8, p. 33.

**16.** See generally Note, "Pretrial Diversion from the Criminal Process," *Yale Law Journal* 83:827 (1974).

**17.** President's Commission on Law Enforcement and Administration of Justice, *The Challenge of Crime in a Free Society*, p. 150.

**18.** Ibid.

**19.** Ibid., p. 152.

**20.** See American Bar Association Special Committee on Evaluation of Ethical Standards, *Code of Professional Responsibility*, p. 81.

NOTES

21. Monroe H. Freedman, "Professional Responsibility of the Criminal Defense Lawyer: The Three Hardest Questions," *Michigan Law Review* 64:1468 (1966).

22. The Sixth Amendment provides, "In all criminal prosecutions, the accused shall enjoy the right . . . to have the Assistance of Counsel for his defense."

23. 372 U.S. 335, 83 S.Ct. 792, 9 L.Ed.2d 799 (1963).

24. 407 U.S. 25, 92 S.Ct. 2006, 32 L.Ed.2d 530 (1972).

25. 384 U.S. 436, 86 S.Ct. 1602, 16 L.Ed. 694 (1966).

26. United States v. Wade, 388 U.S. 218, 87 S.Ct. 1926, 18 L.Ed.2d 1149 (1967).

27. Kirby v. Illinois, 406 U.S. 682, 92 S.Ct. 1877, 32 L.Ed.2d 411 (1972).

28. 368 U.S. 52, 82 S.Ct. 157, 7 L.Ed.2d 114 (1961).

29. 399 U.S. 1, 90 S.Ct. 1999, 26 L.Ed.2d 387 (1970).

30. Mempa v. Rhay, 389 U.S. 128, 88 S.Ct. 254, 19 L.Ed.2d 336 (1967).

31. Douglas v. California, 372 U.S. 353, 83 S.Ct. 814, 9 L.Ed.2d 811 (1963).

32. 408 U.S. 471, 92 S.Ct. 2593, 33 L.Ed.2d 484 (1972).

33. 411 U.S. 788, 93 S.Ct. 1756, 36 L.Ed.2d 655 (1973).

34. In re Gault, 387 U.S. 1, 875 S.Ct. 1428, 18 L.Ed.2d 527 (1967).

35. Specht v. Patterson, 386 U.S. 605, 87 S.Ct. 1209, 18 L.Ed.2d 326 (1967).

36. National Advisory Commission on Criminal Justice Standards and Goals, *Courts,* Standard 13.1.

37. American Bar Association, *Standards Relating to Providing Defense Services* (New York: Institute of Judicial Administration, 1971) Standards 4.1 and 4.2. Reprinted with the permission of the American Bar Association which authored these standards and which holds the copyright.

38. See F. Brownell, *Legal Aid in the United States* (Chicago, Ill.: National Legal Aid and Defender Association, 1961).

39. Lawrence A. Benner and Beth Lynch Neary, *The Other Face of Justice, A Report of the National Defender Survey* (Chicago, Ill.: National Legal Aid and Defender Association, 1973), p. 13.

40. Ibid., p. 77.

41. Sheldon Krantz et al., *The Right to Counsel in Criminal Cases: The Mandate of Argersinger v. Hamlin* (U.S. Department of Justice, Law Enforcement Assistance Administration, National Institute of Law Enforcement and Criminal Justice, March 1976).

42. Note, "Providing Counsel for the Indigent Accused: The Criminal Justice Act," *The American Criminal Law Review* 12:794 (1975).

43. 407 U.S. 25, 92 S.Ct. 2006, 32 L.Ed.2d 530 (1972).

44. National Advisory Commission on Criminal Justice Standards and Goals, *Courts,* Standard 13.1, p. 253.

45. Ibid., Standard 13.5, p. 263.

46. See generally American Bar Association, *Standards Relating to Providing Defense Services.*

# Major Offense Bureau (MOB), Bronx County, New York

In the Bronx, New York, special prosecution efforts against habitual and violent offenders have dramatically reduced the time that potentially dangerous criminals remain free in the community awaiting trial. The average time between arrest and trial of repeat offenders has been cut from 400 to 90 days. Equally important, most of those indicted have been convicted, sentenced, and imprisoned.

These results have been achieved by creation of a Major Offense Bureau in the Bronx district attorney's office. Staffed by ten experienced assistant district attorneys, the Bureau uses an objective screening procedure to isolate those cases that deserve priority treatment. The screening mechanism—a modified version of the case weighting system developed by the Washington, D.C. Exemplary Project PROMIS (Prosecutor's Management Information System)—ranks cases according to the seriousness of the crime, the offender's criminal history, and the strength of the evidence.

Eligible cases are immediately referred to an assistant district attorney who is responsible for the case throughout the entire judicial process. Special trial sessions that hear only MOB cases virtually eliminate scheduling delays.

In its first 30 months, MOB successfully demonstrated its ability to speed up case processing while developing complete, well-prepared cases, as the following statistics show:

—99% of the indictments were voted and presented to the Supreme Court within three days of arrest compared to the usual time lapse of several weeks.
—92% of those indicted were convicted.
—94% of those convicted were sentenced to prison, compared to less than half of a group whose cases were processed traditionally.
—Sentences ranged from three to ten years.

The Bronx approach to processing serious felony cases also permits substantial economies by reducing pre-trial detention, repeated court appearances, and duplication of effort by prosecutors.

---

*From U.S. Department of Justice, LEAA, National Institute of Law Enforcement and Criminal Justice, Exemplary Projects (Washington, D.C.: LEAA, 1978), p. 11.

# 10

# Pre-Trial Procedures

CHAPTER OUTLINE

**Procedures Following Arrest**
**Bail**
**Bail Reform**
**Pre-Trial Detention**
**The Grand Jury**
**The Preliminary Hearing**
**Arraignment**
**The Plea**
Guilty plea

Plea of not guilty

Nolo contendere

**Plea Bargaining**
Role of prosecutor and defense
attorney in plea bargaining

KEY TERMS

**Guilty Plea**
**Bail**
**Plea Bargain**
**Recognizance**
**Detention**
**Manhattan Bail Project**
**No Bill**
*Santobello v. N.Y.*
**Complaint**
**Arraignment**
**Booking**
**Surety**
**Eighth Amendment**

Role of judge in plea bargaining

Plea bargaining reform

**Pre-Trial Diversion**
Diversion process

Who is diverted

Technicalities of the processing

Project services

Completion

Program goals

**Summary**
**Questions For Discussion**
**Application**

**Jail**
**Continuance**
**Trial Date**
**Federal Bail Reform Act**
**Bondsman**
**Vera Institute of Justice**
**Grand Jury**
**True Bill**
**Not Guilty**
*Brady v. U.S.*
*Bordenkircher v. Hayes*
**Diversion**

**PROCEDURES
FOLLOWING
ARREST**

In the previous chapter, the roles and functions of the major participants in the court process were discussed. This chapter deals with the procedures an individual encounters between arrest and trial.

After arrest, the accused is ordinarily taken to the police station, where the police list the possible criminal charges against the accused and obtain other information for booking purposes, such as a description of the offender and the circumstances of the offense. The defendant may then be fingerprinted, photographed, and required to participate in a lineup.

The accused who is arrested on a misdemeanor charge is ordinarily released from the police station to answer the criminal charge before the court at a later date. When arrested on a felony, the accused is usually detained by the police until arraignment at court, and the police are required to bring the accused before the court as quickly as possible. At this point, the offender enters the criminal court process.

When the accused is brought to court, a criminal complaint is initiated against the individual. The complaint is the formal written document identifying the criminal charge, the date and place of the crime's occurrence, and the circumstances of the arrest. The complaint is sworn to and signed under oath by the complainant, usually a police officer. The complaint process is normally used when the accused has committed a misdemeanor, in which case the defendant may plead guilty at the initial hearing and the case may be disposed of immediately. Where the defendant pleads not guilty to a minor offense, a date sometime in the near future is set for a trial, at which the defendant is informed of the formal charge, is provided with counsel if unable to afford a private attorney, pleads guilty or not guilty, and is generally released on bail or on his own recognizance.

Where a felony or more serious crime is involved, the formal charging process is ordinarily an *indictment* from a grand jury, or an *information* (document). An indictment is a written accusation drawn up and submitted to the grand jury by the prosecutor charging the person with a crime. The grand jury, after considering the evidence presented by the prosecutor, votes to endorse or deny the indictment. An information is a charging document which does not use the grand jury to test its sufficiency, but rather uses a preliminary hearing, or a probable cause hearing. The purpose of this hearing is to require the prosecutor to present the case so that the judge can determine whether the defendant should be held to answer for the charge in a criminal trial.

After an indictment or information in a felony offense is filed, the accused is brought before the trial court for arraignment, during which the judge informs the defendant of the charge, insures that the accused is properly represented by counsel, and determines whether the person should be released on bail or some alternative method pending a hearing or trial.

The defendant who is arraigned on an indictment or information can ordinarily plead guilty, not guilty, or *nolo contendere*, which is equivalent to a guilty plea. Where a guilty plea is entered, the defendant admits to all the elements of the crime and the court begins review of the person's background for sentencing purposes. A plea of not guilty sets the stage for a trial on the merits, or for negotiations between the prosecutor and defense attorney known as plea bargaining.

Before discussing these issues, it is important to address the question of bail, or pre-trial release, which may occur at the police station, at the initial court appearance in a misdemeanor, or at the arraignment in most felony cases.

Bail represents money or some other security provided to the court to insure the appearance of the defendant at every subsequent stage of the criminal justice process. Its purpose is to obtain the release from custody of a person charged with a crime. Once the amount of bail is set by the court, the defendant is required to pay a percentage of the entire amount in cash or security (or pay a professional bail bondsman to submit a bond) as a guarantee of the defendant's return to court. If the defendant is released on bail or by some other form of pre-trial release such as release on recognizance (ROR)—but fails to appear in court at the stipulated time, the bail deposit is forfeited. The defendant who fails to make bail is confined in jail until the court appearance.

BAIL

With few exceptions, all persons other than those accused of murder are entitled to bail that is not excessive, as stated by the Eighth Amendment of the United States Constitution. There is some controversy as to whether this means that a constitutional right to bail exists, or that the court cannot impose excessive bail resulting in the defendant's confinement. In most cases, a defendant has a right to be released on reasonable bail. Many jurisdictions also require a bail review hearing by a higher court in cases where the defendant is detained because of what might be considered excessive bail set by the initial judge.

Whether a defendant can be expected to appear at the next stage of the criminal proceedings is the key issue in determining bail. Bail cannot be used to punish an accused, nor can it be denied or revoked at the indulgence of the court. Many experts believe that money bail is one of the most unacceptable aspects of the criminal justice system. It is discriminatory because it works against the poor; it is costly because the government must pay to detain those offenders who are unable to pay bail and who could otherwise be in the community; it is believed a higher proportion of subsequent convictions are given to those kept in jail awaiting trial than to those released on bail; and the detention of individuals who cannot pay has a dehumanizing effect on them. It has become obvious that in many instances the bail system is an unsatisfactory pre-trial release procedure.[1]

Some efforts have been made to reform and even eliminate money bail. Many states now allow defendants to be released on their own recognizance and without any requirement of money bail. *Release on recognizance* (ROR) was pioneered by the Vera Institute of Justice in an experiment entitled "The Manhattan Bail Project" which began in 1961[2] with the co-

BAIL REFORM

operation of the New York City criminal courts and local law students. This project found that if the court had sufficient background information about the defendant it could make a reasonably good judgment about whether the accused would return to court. When the court's judgment was based on such information as the nature of the offense, family ties, employment record, and other factors, the project found that most defendants returned to court when placed in the community on their own personal recognizance. Their findings suggested that releasing a person on the basis of verified information more effectively guaranteed appearance in court than did money bail.

The success of ROR programs resulted in further bail reforms that culminated in the enactment of the Federal Bail Reform Act of 1966,[3] the first change in federal bail laws since 1789. This legislation sought to insure that release would be granted in all noncapital cases where there was sufficient reason to believe that the defendant would return to court.

The National Advisory Commission on Criminal Justice Standards and Goals summarized the results of ROR projects in New York, Philadelphia, and San Francisco:[4]

1. Manhattan Bail Project. The Vera Institute ROR program in New York City pioneered this form of pretrial release. A 1964 report on the Vera program provided the following figures:

   The results of the Vera Foundation's operation show that from October 16, 1961, through April 8, 1964, out of 13,000 total defendants, 3,000 fell into the excluded offense category, 10,000 were interviewed, 4,000 were recommended and 2,195 were paroled. Only 15 of these failed to show up in court, a default rate of less than 7/10 of 1%. Over the years, Vera's recommendation policy has become increasingly liberal. In the beginning, it urged release for only 28% of defendants interviewed; that figure has gradually increased to 65%. At the same time, the rate of judicial acceptance of recommendations has risen from 55% to 70%. Significantly, the District Attorney's office, which originally concurred in only about half of Vera's recommendations, today agrees with almost 80%. Since October 1963, an average of 65 defendants per week have been granted parole on Vera's recommendations.[5]

2. Philadelphia Common Pleas and Municipal Court ROR Program. The Philadelphia program, modeled on the Manhattan Bail Project, provides for release on a promise to appear at trial of selected arrested persons whose ties to the community suggest that it is reasonable to expect them to appear when directed. The program is a device to eliminate the necessity for money bail and applies to all felonies and misdemeanors.

   Arrested persons are interviewed at the police station by the staff of a pretrial services program, who obtain and verify information regarding the accused. The information sought includes residence, family ties, employment, and prior record. The interviewer submits copies of his report to the court, the district attorney, the public defender, and the ROR program agency. A point system which places values on ties to the community is applied to each accused, and from that system a recommendation is made to the court as to whether the accused qualifies for ROR. The judge at arraignment can then either accept or reject the recommendation.

The ROR investigators verify more thoroughly the information concerning defendants who are detained after arraignment. Further interviews may also be conducted. Where warranted, the interviewer may recommend that a petition be filed on behalf of the defendant requesting the court either grant ROR or reduce bail. The pre-trial services staff also follows up on persons released on ROR. Each released defendant is obligated to report by telephone to the ROR main office. ROR staff also contact defendants to remind them of their court date.

In the first year of the program ROR staff interviewed 36,252 arrested persons and initially recommended ROR for 17,175, or 47.4 percent. The court granted ROR to 13,041 of those recommended for such release and not otherwise discharged from custody.

During the same year, ROR defendants had a total of 24,790 court appearances scheduled, and only 7.4 percent failed to appear, of which 5.6 percent were willful failures.[6]

3. San Francisco Bail Project. The ROR program in San Francisco is modeled after the Vera Institute program and the results have been similar. From August 1, 1964, to July 31, 1968, 6,377 persons were released on their promise to appear. Ninety percent returned for trial and only 1 percent evaded justice altogether.[7]

Since 1966, a variety of other release alternatives have been implemented throughout the country on an experimental basis. These include refundable bail and percentage deposit bail programs, which require a deposit with the court which is returnable when the defendant appears in court; release in the custody of a third party, and the use of a stationhouse summons or citation in lieu of arrest.[8]

The criminal defendant who is not eligible for bail or ROR is subject to pre-trial detention in the local county jail. The following excerpt from the National Advisory Commission on Criminal Justice Standards and Goals, Report on Corrections, describes the problems in the pre-trial detention process.[9]

PRE-TRIAL
DETENTION

Pretrial detention today is a no man's land in both the administration and the reform of the criminal justice process. It lies at the intersection of conflicting values and concerns—the right to bail, the risk of flight, the presumption of innocence, the safety of the community. The decisionmaking process is splintered among a wide array of individuals and institutions. The management of jails and the treatment of unconvicted prisoners are the responsibility of a sheriff or correctional warden. The composition of the pretrial detainee population, and the terms and timing of their release, flow from the decisions of the police, the judge, the bondsman, the prosecutor, and the defense lawyer. The laws and rules that determine the flexibility or rigidity of the pretrial process are made by legislators, courts, and political leaders.

The fragmentation of responsibilities contributing to pretrial detention makes the plight of pretrial detainees typically worse than that of convicted prisoners. Coordinated efforts to redress the balance are required.

The current picture of detention before trial is a mass of contradictions. In terms of the number of persons affected per year, pretrial custody accounts for more incarceration in the United States than does imprisonment after sentencing.[10] In many jurisdictions, the rate of pretrial detention is rising at the same time that postconviction imprisonment is dropping. Despite the crisis in public budgets, new multimillion-dollar pretrial jails, larger than their antiquated predecessors, are being built or planned. At the same time, a decline in postsentence imprisonment is producing forecasts of or recommendations for the abandonment of some maximum security institutions for convicted offenders.

These paradoxes inevitably exact a high price in citizen disrespect for law. How else can a rational person view a system of justice that detains vast numbers of accused persons in maximum security institutions during the period of their presumed innocence, only to release most of them when they plead or are found guilty?

Excessive detention is only one aspect of a seriously flawed pretrial process. Uncontrolled release can produce a high rate of defaults in appearance for trial, thus flouting the historical purpose of bail and jeopardizing the integrity of the judicial process. In periods of rising crime and delayed court dockets, outright release facilitiates the prompt continuation of criminal careers, often rooted in addiction, which demoralize the police and endanger the community. Overwhelmed prosecutors may oppose pretrial release because detention is an incentive to a quick plea of guilty. Citizen cooperation with the police is discouraged when a seemingly guilty person whom a victim has helped arrest is promptly released on bail and returned to the streets.

The problems of excessive detention are caused or compounded by a number of widely acknowledged institutional defects in the system of pretrial justice. These include:

Excessive reliance on money bail.

Confusion of responses to crime on bail.

Substantial trial delays.

Abridgment of detainees' rights.

Overuse of the criminal process.

Haste to build large new jails for pretrial detention.

## THE GRAND JURY

The grand jury originated in the early development of English common law. According to the Magna Charta, no freeman could be seized and imprisoned unless he had been judged by his peers. In order to fairly determine who was eligible to be tried, a group of freemen were brought together to look over the facts of the particular case and determine whether the charges had some merit. Thus, the grand jury was created as a check against arbitrary prosecution by a judge who might be functioning as a puppet of the government.

The concept of the grand jury was brought to this country by early settlers and later incorporated into the Fifth Amendment of the United States Constitution which states that "no person shall be held to answer for a capital or otherwise infamous crime, unless on presentment or indictment of a grand jury."

Today, the grand jury is employed in the federal system and in about half of the states. Its functions are twofold. First, the grand jury has the power to act as an independent investigating body. In this role, it examines the possibility of criminal activity within its jurisdiction. These investigative efforts are directed toward general rather than individual criminal conduct. After an investigation is completed, a report called a *presentment* is issued. The presentment not only contains information concerning the findings of the grand jury, but also usually contains a recommendation of indictment.

The grand jury's second and most commonly known role is accusatory in nature. In this capacity, the grand jury acts as the community's conscience in determining whether the accusation of the state (the prosecution) justifies a trial. The grand jury relies on the testimony of witnesses called by the prosecution. After examining the evidence and testimony of witnesses, the grand jury decides whether probable cause exists for prosecution. If it does, an indictment or *true bill* is affirmed. If the grand jury fails to find probable cause, a *no bill* (meaning that the indictment is ignored) is passed. In some states a prosecutor can present evidence to a different grand jury if a no bill is returned; in other states this action is prohibited by statute.

A grand jury is ordinarily comprised of from 16 to 23 individuals, depending on the requirements of the jurisdiction. This group theoretically represents a county. Selection of members varies from state to state, but for the most part they are chosen at random (e.g., from voting lists). In order to qualify to serve on a grand jury, an individual must be at least 18 years of age, a United States citizen, a resident of the jurisdiction for one year or more, and possess sufficient English-speaking skills for communication.

The grand jury usually meets at the request of the prosecution. Hearings are closed and secret. The prosecuting attorney presents the charges and proceeds to call witnesses who are under oath to support the indictment. Usually, the accused is not allowed at the hearing unless asked to testify by the prosecutor or grand jury.

In recent years, the effectiveness and efficiency of the grand jury procedure has been questioned. The National Advisory Commission on Criminal Justice Standards and Goals has commented on this issue:

Empaneling and servicing a grand jury is costly in terms of space, manpower, and money. The members must be selected, notified, sworn, housed, fed and provided with a multitude of services. It is unlikely that the grand jury is effective as a buffer between the State and a person suspected of a criminal offense. The presentation of evidence is under prosecutorial control and the grand jury merely agrees to the actions of the prosecutor.[11]

Quoting from a Baltimore Court management study, the Commission further states:

The Grand Jury, which indicts almost all cases presented to it, has a negligible effect—other than delay—on the criminal process. It seems most reasonable to avoid using the Grand Jury except in cases where a community voice is needed in a troublesome or notorious case.[12]

It is generally agreed, however, that the investigative role of the grand jury is a valuable and necessary function which should not only be maintained but expanded.

**THE PRELIMINARY HEARING**

The preliminary hearing is employed in over half the states as an alternative to the grand jury. Although the purpose of preliminary and grand jury hearings are the same—to establish whether probable cause is sufficient to merit a trial—the procedures differ significantly.

The preliminary hearing is conducted before a magistrate or inferior court judge and, unlike the grand jury hearing, the proceedings are open to the public unless the defendant requests otherwise. Also present at the preliminary hearing are the prosecuting attorney, the defendant, and defendant's counsel if already retained. The prosecution presents its evidence and witnesses to the judge. The defendant or the defense counsel then has the right to cross-examine witnesses and may also challenge the prosecutor's evidence.

After hearing the evidence, the judge decides whether probable cause is sufficient to believe that the defendant committed the alleged crime. If the answer is in the affirmative, the defendant is bound over for trial and the prosecuting attorney's information (same as indictment) is filed with the Superior Court, usually within 15 days. When the judge does not find sufficient probable cause, the charges are dismissed and the defendant is released from custody.

A unique aspect of the preliminary hearing is the defendant's right to waive the proceeding. In most states, this waiver must be agreed to by the prosecutor and the judge. A waiver has advantages and disadvantages for both the prosecutor and the defendant. In most situations, a prosecutor will agree to a waiver because it avoids revealing evidence to the defense before the trial. However, if the state believes that it is necessary to obtain a record of witness testimony because of the possibility that a witness or witnesses may be unavailable for the trial or unable to clearly remember the facts, the prosecutor might override the waiver. In this situation, the record of the preliminary hearing can be used at the trial.

The defense will most likely waive the preliminary hearing for one of three reasons: (1) it has already decided to plead guilty; (2) it desires to speed up the criminal process; or (3) it hopes to avoid the negative publicity which might result from the hearing. On the other hand, the preliminary hearing is of obvious advantage to the defendant who believes that the hearing will result in a dismissal of the charges. In addition, the preliminary hearing gives the defense the opportunity to learn what evidence the prosecution has in its possession.

**ARRAIGNMENT**

An arraignment takes place after an indictment or information is filed following a grand jury or preliminary hearing. At the arraignment, the judge informs the defendant of the charges against him or her and appoints counsel if it has not yet been retained. According to the Sixth Amendment, the accused is guaranteed the right to be informed of the nature and cause of the accusation; thus, the judge at the arraignment must make sure that the defendant clearly understands the charges.

After the charges are read and explained, the defendant is asked to enter a plea. If a plea of not guilty or not guilty by reason of insanity is entered, a trial date is set. When the defendant pleads guilty or nolo contendere, a date for sentencing is arranged. The magistrate then either sets bail or releases the defendant on personal recognizance.

### The Guilty Plea

THE PLEA

More than 90% of the defendants appearing before the courts plead guilty prior to the trial stage. A guilty plea has several consequences. As the National Advisory Commission points out:

Such a plea functions not only as an admission of guilt but also as a surrender of the entire array of constitutional rights designed to protect a criminal defendant against unjustified conviction, including the right to remain silent, the right to confront witnesses against him, the right to a trial by jury, and the right to be proven guilty by proof beyond a reasonable doubt.[13]

A guilty plea signifies a surrender of several constitutional rights, including those guaranteed under the Fifth and Sixth Amendments. As a result, a judge must take certain precautions when accepting a plea of guilty. First, the judge must clearly state to the defendant the constitutional guarantees which are automatically waived by this plea. Second, the judge must feel that the facts of the case establish a basis for the plea, and that the plea is made voluntarily. Third, the defendant must be informed of the right to counsel during the pleading process. In many felony cases the judge will insist on the presence of counsel. Finally, the judge must inform the defendant of the possible sentencing outcomes, including the maximum sentence that can be imposed.

After a guilty plea has been entered, a sentencing date is arranged. In a majority of the states, a guilty plea may be withdrawn and replaced with a not guilty plea at any time prior to sentencing if good cause is shown.

### The Plea of Not Guilty

At the arraignment or prior to the trial, a not guilty plea is entered in two ways: (1) it is verbally stated by the defendant or the defense counsel; or (2) it is entered for the defendant by the court when the defendant stands mute before the bench.

Once a plea of not guilty is recorded, a trial date is set. In misdemeanor cases, trials take place in the inferior court system, while felony cases are normally transferred to the superior court. At this time, a continuance or issuance of bail is once again considered.

### The Nolo Contendere
### Plea

The plea nolo contendere, which means no contest, is essentially a plea of guilty. This plea has the same consequences as a guilty plea with one exception: it may not be held against the defendant as proof in a subsequent civil matter because technically there has been no admission of guilt.

The nolo contendere plea is utilized in those situations where the defendant is also subject to a civil suit for damages (e.g., extortion of corporation funds). This plea is acceptable in federal court cases and in about half of the states. It may only be entered at the discretion of the judge and the prosecutor, however.

## PLEA BARGAINING

One of the most common practices in the criminal justice system today is the process of *plea bargaining*. It has been estimated that more than 90% of criminal convictions result from negotiated pleas of guilty. Plea bargaining permits a defendant to plead guilty in exchange for a less serious charge or for an agreement by the prosecutor to recommend a reduced sentence to the court. A concise definition of plea bargaining is: "It is basically the exchange of prosecutorial and judicial concessions for pleas of guilty."[14]

There are normally four possible ways in which a bargain can be made between the prosecutor and the defense attorney: (1) the initial charges may be reduced to those of a lesser offense, thus automatically reducing the sentence imposed; (2) in cases where many counts are charged, the prosecutor may reduce the number of counts; (3) the prosecutor may promise to recommend a lenient sentence, such as probation; and (4) when the charge imposed has a negative label attached (e.g., child molester) the prosecutor may alter the charge to a lesser one (e.g., assault) in exchange for a plea of guilty. In a jurisdiction where it is common knowledge that sentencing disparity between judges exists, the prosecutor may even agree to arrange that the defendant appear before a lenient judge to insure the court's agreement to the bargain.

Plea bargaining is a court practice which has grown extensively in recent years. Because of overcrowded criminal court caseloads, it has become an essential yet controversial part of the administration of justice. Proponents contend that plea bargaining actually benefits both the state and the defendant in the following ways: (1) the overall financial costs of the criminal prosecution are reduced: (2) the administrative efficiency of the courts is greatly improved; (3) the prosecution is able to devote more time to cases of greater seriousness and importance; and (4) the defendant avoids possible detention and extended trial and may receive a reduced sentence.[15] Thus, those who favor plea bargaining believe it is appropriate to enter into plea discussions where the interests of the state in the effective administration of justice will be served.

Opponents of the plea bargaining process believe that the negotiated plea should be eliminated. The National Advisory Commission on Criminal Justice Standards and Goals has stated that:

As soon as possible, but in no event later than 1978, regulations between prosecutors and defendants—either personally or through their attorneys—concerning concessions to be made in return for guilty pleas should be prohibited.[16]

It has been argued that plea bargaining is basically objectionable because it encourages a defendant to waive the constitutional right to a trial. In addition, some experts suggest that sentences tend to be less severe in guilty plea situations than in actual trials, and that plea bargains result in even greater sentencing disparity. Particularly in the eyes of the general public, this allows the defendant to beat the system and further tarnishes the criminal process. Plea bargaining also raises the danger that an innocent person will be convicted of a crime if convinced that the lighter treatment from a guilty plea is preferable to the possible risk of a harsher sentence following a formal trial.

It is unlikely that plea negotiations will be eliminated or severely curtailed in the near future. Those who support their total abolition are in the minority. As a result of abuses, however, efforts are being made to improve plea bargaining operations. Such reforms include (1) the development of uniform plea practices, (2) the representation of counsel during plea negotiations, and (3) the establishment of time limits on plea negotiations.

The United States Supreme Court has reviewed the propriety of plea bargaining in several court decisions, particularly in regard to the voluntariness of guilty pleas. In *Boykin v. Alabama* (1969),[17] the court held that an affirmative action that the plea was made voluntarily must exist on the record before a trial judge may accept a guilty plea. This is essential since a guilty plea essentially constitutes a waiver of the defendant's Fifth Amendment privilege against self-incrimination and Sixth Amendment right to a jury trial. Subsequent to *Boykin*, the court ruled in the case of *Brady v. United States* (1970) that a guilty plea is not invalid merely because it is entered to avoid the possibility of the death penalty.[18] And in *Santobello v. New York* (1971),[19] which involved a guilty plea made after plea bargaining, the court held that the promise of the prosecutor must be kept and that the breaking of a plea bargaining agreement by the prosecutor required a reversal for the defendant.

The Supreme Court ruled in the 1978 case of *Bordenkircher v. Hayes* that a defendant's due process rights are not violated when a prosecutor threatens to reindict the accused on more serious charges if he does not plead guilty to the original offense. Because this case is an excellent example of the use of the prosecutor's discretion in conducting plea bargains, a summary of the case follows.

Because the plea bargaining process is largely informal, lacking in guidelines, and discretionary in nature, some effort has been made to determine what kinds of and how much information is used by the prosecutor to make plea bargaining decisions. In a recent study conducted by Stephen Lagoy, Joseph Senna, and Larry Siegel, it was found that certain information was weighed heavily in the prosecutorial decision to accept a plea negotiation.[20] Such factors as the offense; the defendant's prior

## BORDENKIRCHER V. HAYES

**Facts:** Paul Hayes, the respondent, was indicted by a Kentucky grand jury for uttering a forged instrument, punishable by a sentence of two to ten years imprisonment. Following arraignment, Hayes, his counsel and the prosecutor met to discuss a possible plea bargaining agreement. The prosecutor offered to recommend a sentence of five years' imprisonment if Hayes plead guilty. He also stated that if Hayes did not plead guilty, he would return to the grand jury and seek an indictment under the Kentucky Habitual Criminal Act, which would subject Hayes to a mandatory life sentence because of his two prior felony convictions. Hayes plead not guilty, and the prosecutor obtained an indictment charging him under the Habitual Criminal Act. A jury found Hayes guilty of the original charge of uttering a forged instrument and found that he had twice before been convicted of felonies and he was sentenced to life imprisonment. The Kentucky Court of Appeals affirmed the sentence. On habeas corpus, the federal district court dismissed the petition, but the Court of Appeals (6th Cir.) reversed, holding that the prosecutor's conduct had violated Hayes' due process rights. The U.S. Supreme Court granted certiorari to consider a constitutional question of importance in the administration of criminal justice.

The course of conduct engaged in by the prosecutor in this case, which presented the defendant with the alternatives of foregoing trial or facing charges on which he was subject to prosecution did not violate defendant's due process rights.

**Significance of the Case:** The Bordenkircher

decision further establishes the fact that the guilty plea and concomitant plea bargain are important and acceptable ingredients in the criminal justice system in this country. Properly administered, it can be a benefit to the system and defendant. Acknowledgement of this previous clandestine practice has led the court to believe in the essential need for counsel during plea negotiations. In addition, the court recognized the practice of prosecutorial discretion and its potential for individual and institutional abuse, but concluded that the prosecutor's conduct was not unlawful.

**Decision:** The question in this case was whether the due process clause of the Fourteenth Amendment was violated when the state prosecutor threatened to reindict the accused when he refused to plead guilty to the original charge of uttering a forged instrument. The Court of Appeals for the 6th Circuit overturned the defendant's conviction by holding that the substance of the plea offer itself violated the limitations imposed by the due process clause. However, the Supreme Court concluded the Appeals Court was mistaken in its ruling. It stated that in the "give and take" of plea bargaining, there is no element of punishment or retaliation so long as the accused is free to accept or reject the prosecution's offer. A rigid constitutional rule that would prohibit a prosecutor from acting forthrightly in his dealings with the defense could only invite unhealthy subterfuge that would drive the practice of plea bargaining back into the shadows from which it so recently emerged. Thus, the prosecutor's conduct in this case was appropriate.

record and age; and the type, strength, and admissibility of evidence were considered important in the plea bargaining decision. It was also discovered that the attitude of the complainant was an important factor in the decision-making process; for example, in victimless cases such as heroin possession the police attitude was most often considered, while in victim-related crimes such as rape the attitude of the victim was a primary concern.

The study also revealed that prosecutors in low-population or rural settings not only employ more information while making their decisions, but also seem more likely to accept bargains than their urban counterparts. It was suggested that "this finding tends to dispute the notion that plea bargaining is a response to overcrowding in large urban courts."[21] It appears that where caseload pressures are less there is actually a greater probability of the acceptance of a plea bargain.

### The Role of the Prosecutor and Defense Attorney in Plea Bargaining

The prosecutor in the American system of criminal justice has broad discretion in the exercise of his or her responsibilities. Such discretion includes whether to initiate a criminal prosecution, the nature of the criminal charge, the number of criminal charges, and whether to plea bargain a case and under what conditions. This discretionary power of the prosecutor was discussed in detail in Chapter 9.

In this section, our emphasis is on the role of the prosecutor in the plea bargaining decision. Plea bargaining is one of the major methods the prosecutor uses in exercising control and influence on the criminal justice system. The other two functions are the decision to initiate a charge and the ability to take the case to trial. There are very few states that have provided procedures to control the discretion of prosecutors in plea bargaining situations. Instead, the prosecutor is generally free to weigh competing alternatives and factors, such as the seriousness of the crime, the attitude of the victim, the police report regarding the incident, and applicable sentencing provisions, in making a plea bargaining decision. Some prosecutors in certain jurisdictions will place great emphasis on plea bargaining efforts. Other jurisdictions may differ in their willingness to accept plea bargaining as a form of criminal disposition. Plea bargaining occurs often in those situations where the government believes a case is weak and may be difficult to prove at trial. Consequently, bargaining permits a settlement or compromising of a weak case where the criminal trial outcome is in doubt.

The above situation describes the role of the prosecutor in relationship to individual case decisions. On a case-by-case basis, the prosecutor determines the concessions to be offered in the plea bargain and seeks to dispose of each case in a fast and efficient manner. On the broader scale, however, the role of the chief prosecutor as an administrator also has an impact on plea bargaining and leadership in the criminal justice system. While the assistant prosecutor evaluates and moves individual cases, the chief prosecutor is required to provide his office with guidelines in the plea bargaining process. In this regard, as Alschuler states, the prosecutor may be acting as an administrator.[22] Some jurisdictions have guidelines to provide consistency in plea bargaining cases. For instance, it may be required in a given office to define the kinds and types of cases and offenders that may be given a plea bargain. In other jurisdictions, approval to plea bargain may be required. Other controls might include procedures for internal review of decisions by the chief prosecutor, and the use of written memoranda to document the need and acceptability for a plea bargain in a given case. The prosecutor's role in plea bargaining is also important on a statewide or systemwide basis because it involves leadership in the criminal justice system. The most extreme example where a chief prosecutor can influence the plea negotiation process, is where efforts have been made to eliminate plea bargaining from the system. In Alaska, efforts to eliminate plea bargaining were met with resistance by assistant prosecutors and others in the system, namely judges and defense attorneys.[23] The more moderate approach by prosecutors in providing leadership in plea bargaining generally deals with the establishment of guidelines for the plea bargaining process. Such guidelines do exist, for example, in the Manhattan District Attorney's office in New York City, and include such requirements as avoiding overindictment, control over nonprovable indictments, reduction of felonies to misdemeanors, and control over bargaining with defendants.

Thus, the role of the prosecutor in plea bargaining exists on an individual case-by-case basis, as well as on an overall policy basis. In evaluating cases for plea bargaining, the strength or weakness of the government's case is generally the most important factor in the decision to bargain or establish a plea agreement. When evaluating the role of the prosecutor on a policy level, efforts have been made to provide on-line assistant prosecutors with formulas or guidelines to help them properly evaluate cases for discretionary decision making in plea bargaining.

With regard to the role of defense counsel in plea bargaining, both the U.S. Supreme Court and such organizations as the American Bar Association in its *Standards on Criminal Justice, Standards Relating to the Guilty Plea*, have established guidelines for acting on the receipt of a guilty plea.[24] No court should accept a guilty plea unless the defendant has been properly advised by counsel, and the court has determined the plea to be voluntary, that there is a factual basis for the plea, and that the court has the discretion to reject the plea if inappropriately offered. The defense attorney—a public defender or a private attorney—is required to act in an advisory role in plea negotiations. The defendant's counsel is expected to be aware of the facts of the case and of the law, and advise the defendant of the proper alternatives available in the case. It is basically the responsibility of the defense attorney to make certain that the accused understand the nature of the plea bargaining process and the guilty plea. By this is meant that the defense counsel is to explain to the defendant that he or she is waiving rights upon pleading guilty, which would be available if the defendant went to trial. In addition, the defense attorney has the duty to keep the defendant informed of developments and discussions with the prosecutor regarding plea bargaining. While doing so, the attorney for the accused cannot misrepresent evidence nor mislead his client to make any agreement that is detrimental to the accused.

When the defense attorney is representing a defendant and seeking a plea bargain, it is appropriate for the government and the prosecutor to discuss charging and sentencing concessions when the defendant pleads guilty and such actions are in the best interest of the criminal justice system. Sentencing concessions, however, are a particularly controversial issue in plea bargaining because sentencing is the court's responsibility. Theoretically, plea negotiations are not to be used to enforce prosecutorial sentencing theories, but in reality the prosecutor's recommendation regarding the sentence plays a major role in the plea bargain.

In reality, most plea negotiations occur in the chambers of the judge, or in the prosecutor's office, or in the courtroom hallway. Under these conditions, it is often difficult to assess the actual role of prosecutor and defense attorney. Even under these conditions, however, it is fundamental that a defendant should not be required to plead guilty until advised by counsel, nor should a guilty plea be made unless it is given with the consent of the accused.

### The Role of the Judge in Plea Bargaining

One of the most confusing problems in the plea bargaining process has been the proper role of the judge in this low-visibility decision-making situation. Should the judge act in a supervisory capacity over the plea bargain, or should the judicial officer enter into the negotiation process. The leading national legal organizations, the American Bar Association, as well as the National Advisory Commission on Criminal Justice Standards and Goals, are opposed to judicial participation in plea negotiations.[25] In addition, such action by a judge is prohibited by the Federal Rules of Criminal Procedure.[26] On a state-by-state basis, some jurisdictions disallow any form of judicial involvement in plea bargaining while others allow the judge to participate in plea discussions.

The American Bar Association objects generally to the judge participating in plea negotiations because of his position as chief judicial officer. A judge should not be a party to arrangements for the determination of sentence, whether as a result of a guilty plea or a finding of guilty based on proof. Reasons for such an approach include: (1) judicial participation in discussions creates the impression in the mind of the defendant that he could not receive a fair trial; (2) judicial participation in discussions lessens the objectivity of the judge to determine the voluntariness of the plea; (3) judicial participation is inconsistent with the theory behind the use of the pre-sentence investigation report; and (4) the risk of not going along with the disposition desired by the judge may seem great enough to the defendant to induce the guilty even when innocent.[27]

On the other hand, those who suggest that the judge be directly involved and participate in plea bargaining argue that such an approach would make sentencing more uniform while insuring that greater fairness and efficiency be part of the plea bargaining process.

It appears that most jurisdictions in this country have judges playing an active role in the negotiation process. Where judges simply supervise plea bargaining, they oversee the taking of the guilty plea, determine a factual basis for the plea, inform the defendant of the sentencing consequences, and control the withdrawal of the plea. In those cases in which the judge generally participates in plea bargaining, such action includes: influencing the kind and type of agreement which may be reached, encouraging prosecutors and defense attorneys to arrive at a plea agreement, expediting cases, and contributing to the efficient management of the court.

Since most authorities and the weight of the law take the position that the judge should not participate in plea discussions, the American Bar Association, Standards on Pleas of Guilty, Section 3.3 dealing with the responsibilities of the trial judge, is set out below.

Standard 3.3: Responsibilities of the Trial Judge:

A. The trial judge should not participate in plea discussions;

B. If a tentative plea agreement has been reached which contemplates entry of a plea of guilty in the expectation that other charges before that court will be dismissed, or that sentence concessions will be granted, upon request of the parties, the trial judge may permit the disclosure to him of the agreement and the reasons therefore in advance of the time for tender of the plea. He may then indicate to the prosecuting attorney and defense counsel whether he will concur in the proposed disposition, if the information in the pre-sentence report is consistent with the representations made to him. That the trial judge concurs but the final disposition does not include the charge or sentence concessions contemplated in the plea agreement, he shall state for the record what information in the pre-sentence report contributed to his decision not to grant these concessions.[28]

Although the prevailing practice seems to be that judges do not participate in plea discussions until a tentative agreement is made between the parties, it is common in many jurisdictions for judges to participate in pre-plea bargaining hearings to facilitate the disposal of criminal cases.

## Reforms in the Plea Bargaining Process

So widespread is the use of plea bargaining that it is recognized as one of the major characteristics of the criminal justice system. Despite its prevalence as we have already discussed, critics and proponents long continue to argue the merits of maintaining a plea bargaining system. Those opposed to the widespread use of plea bargaining assert that it is coercive in its inducement of guilty pleas, that it encourages the unequal exercise of prosecutorial discretion, and that it complicates the job of correctional authorities and sentencing. Others argue that it is unconstitutional, and that it results in cynicism and disrespect for the entire system.

On the other hand, proponents contend that the practice insures the flow of guilty pleas essential to administrative efficiency. It allows the system the flexibility for individualization of justice and it gives respect to the system by enhancing certainty and promptness of punishment associated with plea bargaining.

Whatever the relative merits of these arguments, plea bargaining continues to enjoy the support of the U.S. Supreme Court and such groups as the American Bar Association, American Law Institute, and other prominent organizations.[29]

In recent years, some efforts have been made to convert the practice of plea bargaining into a more visible, understandable, and fair dispositional process. On the one hand, safeguards and guidelines have been developed in many jurisdictions to prevent violations of due process and to insure that innocent defendants not plead guilty under coercion. Such safeguards include: (1) the judge questions the defendant about the facts of the guilty plea before accepting a plea; (2) the defense counsel is present and able to advise the defendant of his rights; (3) open discussions about the plea occur between prosecutor and defense attorney; (4) full and frank information regarding the offender and offense are made available at this stage of the process. In addition, judicial supervision is an effective mechanism to insure that the system of plea bargaining is undertaken in a fair manner.

Another method of reform has involved the development of specific guidelines by the Office of the Chief Prosecutor. Also, some jurisdictions have adopted the use of pre-pleading investigations which are summaries of the case before a plea rather than after the plea is given to the court. The use of the pre-pleading report helps in providing information to all the participants in the negotiations. The pre-trial settlement conference is another method used to improve the visibility and fairness in plea bargaining. In such a conference, the participants include the judge, victim, defendant, and police as well as the prosecutor and defense attorney. Generally, the defendant's guilt regarding the charge is assumed by the parties and efforts are made to contribute to a settlement of the case. If the settlement is reached and approved by the judge, the defendant enters a plea in open court. The most extreme method of reforming plea bargaining has been suggestions to abolish it completely. A ban on plea bargaining has been tried in numerous jurisdictions throughout the country. In 1975, the State of Alaska eliminated the practice of plea bargaining. In Honolulu, Hawaii, efforts were made to abolish plea bargaining. Jurisdictions in other states including Iowa, Arizona, the District of Columbia, and Delaware, also sought to limit the use of plea bargaining.[30] What this really meant was that these jurisdictions would give no consideration or concessions to the defendant in exchange for a guilty plea.

In reality, however, in these and most jurisdictions, sentence-related concessions, charge reduction concessions, and alternative methods for prosecution continued to occur in one fashion or another. In areas in which plea bargaining is reduced or abolished, the number of trials may increase, the sentence severity may change, and more questions regarding the right to a speedy trial may arise.

Thus, in view of the problems of plea bargaining and its reform, there appears to be no ideal system of adjudication and disposition in the criminal justice process. What does exist is the development of guidelines and safeguards as well as the experimental banning of plea bargaining in some jurisdictions throughout the country. Prior to the 1950s, plea bargaining or settling criminal cases was a dirty approach to case disposition. Today, efforts are being made to examine prosecutorial discretion and make plea bargaining a more visible and structured process. The application section of this chapter contains a description of how the prosecutor, defense attorney, and judge negotiate a plea bargain.

## PRE-TRIAL DIVERSION

Another important feature in the early court process is the placing of offenders into noncriminal diversion programs prior to their formal trial or conviction.

Pre-trial diversion programs were established in the late 1960s when it became apparent that a viable alternative was needed to the highly stigmatized judicial sentences. Diversion programs involve suspending formal criminal proceedings against an accused while that person participates in a community treatment program under court supervision.

Many diversion programs exist throughout the United States. These programs vary in size and emphasis, but generally possess the same goal: to constructively bypass criminal prosecution by providing a reasonable alternative in the form of treatment, counseling, or employment programs.

For example, Project DeNovo in Minneapolis, Minnesota, offers counseling, employment placement, and educational opportunities to juveniles and adult offenders, excepting those accused of violent crimes. In San Diego, California, the county probation department runs a Juvenile Narcotics Project. This program offers drug education in lieu of prosecution; it not only emphasizes drug rehabilitation and education for juvenile offenders and their parents, but also seeks to improve communication between them.

In Philadelphia, Pennsylvania, the Pre-Indictment Probation Program concentrates on diverting first offenders charged with nonviolent crimes. The offender is given a conditional probation prior to indictment with the promise that if he or she successfully completes the term of the agreement the charges and criminal record will be eliminated. The program also provides the offender with social, medical, educational, and employment services. The Baltimore Pre-Trial Intervention Project is a 90-day program specifically designed for juveniles between the ages of 15 and 17. It offers an in-house education program in addition to counseling and job placement services.

The Dade County, Florida Pre-Trial Intervention Project deals with first offenders between the ages of 17 and 25. This three- to six-month program places heavy emphasis on counseling and personal services, community health, and welfare agency services.[31]

## The Diversion Process

Many pre-trial diversion programs have similar operating processes and procedures, yet each maintains its own unique characteristics. In this section, a few of the more important components of these programs will be described. Since it would be difficult to categorize or discuss every diversion format, a typical model will be discussed in some detail.[32] Also, Figure 10.1 shows how diversion cases flow through the criminal justice process.

## Who Is Diverted

All existing diversion programs have admission criteria which control the selection of clients. Without exception, diversion priority is given to first-offender misdemeanants. Age, residency, and employment status are also considered as criteria for acceptance of diversion candidates. Typical requirements are as follows:

1. The defendants may be either male or female.

2. They should be between 17 and 22 (with variations) years of age.

3. They are either unemployed or underemployed or persons whose employment would be terminated if convicted.

FIGURE 10.1
*Flow of Pre-trial
Intervention Cases
Through the Criminal
Court

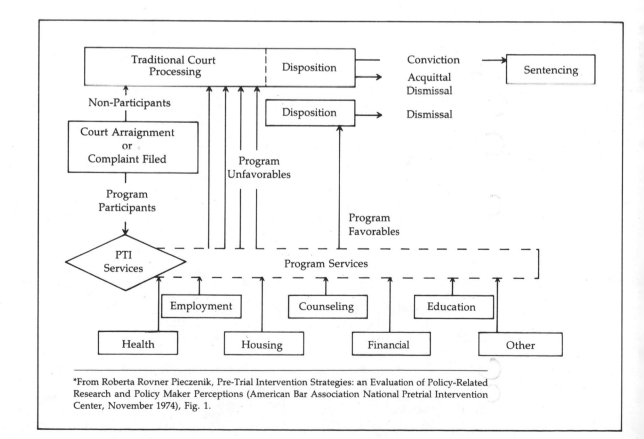

*From Roberta Rovner Pieczenik, Pre-Trial Intervention Strategies: an Evaluation of Policy-Related Research and Policy Maker Perceptions (American Bar Association National Pretrial Intervention Center, November 1974), Fig. 1.

4. They are residents of the program area and have verifiable addresses.

5. They are not identified as drug-dependent persons.

6. They cannot be charged with felonies that do not fall under the jurisdiction of the district courts.

7. They should have no more than two prior adult convictions.

### The Technicalities of the Processing

The involvement of the diversion program usually begins after the arrest
and arraignment of the individual but before trial. The selected, accused
individual is released on a continuance to the diversion program—that is,
the trial is postponed—if the relevant court personnel (judge, probation
officer, assistant DA, lawyer, arresting officer) and the program representative (usually called a screener) agree on the potential of the accused
for the program. During this initial period, the program's staff teams with
the potential client to assess the individual's suitability for the program.
Acceptance may begin with a long continuance (this time limit varies from
program to program) without entry of a plea, and upon the written waiver
by the defendant of the right to a speedy trial.

### Project Services

Services rendered by most adult pre-trial diversion programs can be
classified into three complementary units:

1. Counseling is undertaken by an *advocate* who conducts individual and
group sessions for clients throughout the initial period.

2. Employment services are executed by a *career developer* who evaluates
and implements career goals in a team effort with the client and the advocate.

3. Human services are provided, including health care, educational programs, emergency housing, and a variety of testing to assess needs and
capabilities.

### Completion

An exit disposition may be held near the end of the initial continuance,
at which the client's participation is assessed by the client's staff team.
During the evaluation, one of three things may occur:

1. Charges may be dismissed upon successful completion of the program.

2. The continuance may be extended if project members are unsure of the
client's progress.

3. The client's participation in the program may be terminated due to failure to comply with program guidelines and structures.

In the event of the third decision, the court may be notified in writing and the normal court process of trial and disposition takes place.

### Program Goals

The following have been identified to be the goals and purposes of the typical diversion program:

1. To divert selected individuals from trial to fruitful training, employment, and counseling experiences.

2. To provide the court and legal systems with much-needed resources.

3. To help the court system become more aware of its rehabilitative role.

4. To help break a beginning cycle of crime and pattern of failure.

5. To sensitize employers to offenders' needs and to help alter restrictive hiring practices.

6. To utilize existing city and state resources in a comprehensive and coordinated manner to counter fractionalized and piecemeal efforts.

7. To create effective resources where none exist.

8. To assist in the reintegration of potential offenders into the total community.

9. To train and utilize paraprofessionals in the program who have interests and abilities in the human service field, and to establish their competence and professional roles.

10. To help establish pre-trial diversion as a permanent part of the state's criminal justice system.

11. To develop and implement a system of staff selection and training, and a system of resource development which has applicability in a variety of service fields.

12. To attempt to open restricted civil service jobs to offenders.

Generally, many important decisions about what happens to a defendant occur prior to trial. Hearings such as the grand jury and preliminary hearings are held to determine if sufficient facts exist to charge the accused with a crime. If so, the defendant is arraigned; enters a plea; is informed of constitutional rights, particularly the right to the assistance of counsel; and is considered for pre-trial release. The use of money bail and other alternatives, such as release on recognizance statutes, allow most defendants to be free pending their return for trial.

SUMMARY

The issue of discretion plays a major role at this stage of the criminal process. Since only a small percentage of criminal cases eventually go to trial, many defendants agree to plea bargains or are placed in diversion programs. The criminal justice system is not able to try every defendant accused of a crime since not enough judges, prosecutors, defense attorneys, and courts exist for this purpose. As a result, subsystems such as plea bargaining and diversion are essential ingredients in the administration of our justice system.

QUESTIONS FOR DISCUSSION

1. Discuss the major differences between the grand jury vs. the information-preliminary hearing process.

2. Discuss the money bail system and the application of modern pre-trial release procedures to early court processing.

3. What are the arguments for and against plea bargaining?

4. Explain what is meant by diversion from the criminal justice system. In your opinion, is this an appropriate method of dealing with the criminal offender?

NOTES

1. The President's Crime Commission on Law Enforcement and Administration of Justice, Task Force Reports, *Courts* (Washington, D.C.: U.S. Government Printing Office, 1967), p. 38.

2. Vera Institute of Justice, *1961–1971, Programs in Criminal Justice* (New York: Vera Institute, 1972).

3. Public Law 89–465, U.S.C. 3146 (1966).

4. National Advisory Commission on Criminal Justice Standards and Goals, *Corrections* (Washington, D.C.: U.S. Government Printing Office, January, 1973), p. 101.

5. Daniel Freed and Patricia Wald, *Bail in the United States: 1964*, working paper for the National Conference on Bail and Criminal Justice (New York: Vera Institute of Justice and U.S. Department of Justice), pp. 62–63.

6. Information supplied by the Pretrial Services Division, Philadelphia Common Pleas and Municipal Court.

7. Gerald Levin, "The San Francisco Bail Project," *American Bar Association Journal* 55:135 (1969).

8. For two good examples of bail reform research, see Robert Spangenberg, William P. Homans Jr., and Franklin N. Flaschner, "Bail Reform in Massachusetts," *Massachusetts Law Quarterly* 55:135 (1967); and John Conklen and Dermot Meagher, "Percentage Deposit Bail System—An Alternative to the Professional Bondsman," *Journal of Criminal Justice* 1 (1973).

9. National Advisory Commission on Criminal Justice Standards and Goals, *Corrections*, p. 102.

10. *The 1970 National Jail Census* (Washington: Law Enforcement Assistance Administration, 1971), p. 1. shows that half of the adults and two-thirds of the juveniles confined in jails on March 15, 1970 were pre-trial detainees or other unconvicted persons.

11. National Advisory Commission on Criminal Justice Standards and Goals, *Courts* (Washington, D.C.: U.S. Govern-

ment Printing Office, January, 1973), p. 74.

**12.** Ibid.

**13.** Ibid., p. 42.

**14.** Alan Alschuler, "The Prosecutors Role in Plea Bargaining," *University of Chicago Law Review* 36:50 (1968).

**15.** For arguments favoring plea bargaining, see John Wheatley, "Plea Bargaining—A Case for Its Continuance," *Massachusetts Law Quarterly* 59:31 (1974).

**16.** National Advisory Commission on Criminal Justice Standards and Goals, *Courts* (1973), p. 46.

**17.** 395 U.S. 238, 89 S.Ct. 1709, 23 L.Ed.2d 274 (1969).

**18.** 397 U.S. 742, 90 S.Ct. 1463, 25 L.Ed.2d 747 (1970).

**19.** 404 U.S. 257, 92 S.Ct. 495, 30 L.Ed.2d 427 (1971).

**20.** Stephen P. Lagoy, Joseph J. Senna, and Larry J. Siegel, "An Empirical Study on Information Usage for Prosecutorial Decision Making in Plea Negotiations," *The American Criminal Law Review* 13.435 (1976).

**21.** Ibid., p. 462.

**22.** A. W. Alschuler, "The Prosecutor's Role in Plea Bargaining," *University of Chicago Law Review* 36:50 (1968).

**23.** National Institute of Law Enforcement and Criminal Justice, Plea Bargaining in the United States (Washington, D.C.: Georgetown University, 1978), p. 8.

**24.** See American Bar Association, Standards Relating to Pleas of Guilty (New York: Institute of Judicial Administration, 1968); also *North Carolina v. Alford* 400 U.S. 25 (1970).

**25.** American Bar Association, Standards Relating to Pleas of Guilty, 3.3; National Advisory Commission on Criminal Justice Standards and Goals, Task Force Report on Courts (Washington, D.C.: LEAA, 1973), p. 42.

**26.** Federal Rules of Criminal Procedure, Rule 11.

**27.** American Bar Association, Standards Relating to Pleas of Guilty, p. 73; see also A. Alschuler, "The Trial Judge's Role in Plea Bargaining," *Columbia Law Review* 76:1059 (1976).

**28.** American Bar Association, Standards Relating to Pleas of Guilty, Standard 3.3, p. 71.

**29.** See Ibid., also Santobello v. New York 404 U.S. 257 (1971).

**30.** National Institute of Law Enforcement, Plea Bargaining in the United States, pp. 37–40.

**31.** See generally Note, "Pretrial Diversion from the Criminal Process," *Yale Law Journal* 83:827 (1974); National Pretrial Intervention Service Center, American Bar Association, *Portfolio of Descriptive Profiles on Selected Pretrial Criminal Justice Intervention Programs* (1974); A.B.T. Associates, *Pretrial Intervention Program of the Manpower Administration*, (U.S. Department of Labor, 1971–1972).

**32.** The information in the following section was adapted from the Court Resource Program, *A Program Manual Describing the Purpose, History and Implementation of Pretrial Diversion in Boston* (Boston: Justice Resource Institute Inc., 1974); also see R. Rouner-Pieczenik, Pretrial Intervention Strategies: An Evaluation of Policy-Related Research and Policymaker Perceptions (Chicago: American Bar Association, 1974).

# Plea Bargaining

*THE QUESTION OF WHETHER OR NOT Egil Krogh would plea bargain with our office was answered sooner than I expected. He had worked with John Ehrlichman's law firm in Seattle, and Ehrlichman had brought him to Washington and to the White House. As the older man's top aide, Krogh had served ably as the White House's political link with the FBI and later with Treasury Department agencies concerned with the country's debilitating drug problems.

He was in my office now, at ease but far from cocky, bearing on his shoulders two counts of making false declarations to a grand jury. If convicted, each count could cost him five years, though Krogh knew that customarily the sentences would be allowed to run concurrently, resulting in a five-year maximum sentence. Judge Gerhard Gesell, who had heard Krogh's motion to dismiss the indictments and had denied it, had made some pointed comments which I was sure had shaken Krogh. Krogh's lawyer, Stephen Shulman, had argued that an official in Krogh's position had the authority and discretion to make false statements so as to protect classified national security information from unauthorized disclosure. Judge Gesell had emphatically rejected that argument as fundamentally incompatible with the very existence of our society.

Krogh was really in my office to see what kind of man I was. And I had allowed him and his lawyer inside for exactly the same reason. He had been nibbling at negotiating with the Plumbers Task Force for some time. Now it was time to deal. He knew that to get a lighter sentence he would have to give something to the prosecution. I knew that we needed his cooperation to obtain a full disclosure of the facts in the Fielding break-in. And we believed he could give us important information about Watergate.

Krogh had other things in his favor. He said he realized now that what he had done was unlawful, regardless of his motive, and the idea of discrediting Ellsberg was a repulsive national security goal. I believed him with all of my heart. I also believed that he was a good man who had been thrust down a crooked path. He

*From Leon Jaworski, *The Right and the Power—The Prosecution of Watergate* (New York: Gulf Publishing, 1976), pp. 31–35.

said that as a matter of principle he did not want to tell us anything to incriminate others until after he was sentenced—if we made a deal. I liked that.

I liked it. But we all knew that Judge Gesell had made it clear on various occasions when he imposed sentence in cases involving plea bargaining such as this one that he was never influenced in weighing sentence by promises of a defendant's cooperation with prosecutors. We also knew, however, that Judge Gesell would lend an ear to any man he believed had honestly repented his sins.

With all of this clear between us, I told Krogh that the proper charge against him should have been and should be conspiracy to violate Dr. Fielding's civil rights, a charge that called for a ten-year maximum sentence upon conviction. It was my feeling that if Judge Gesell believed Krogh had repented and was contrite—as I did—he would be merciful regardless of the nature of the charge.

It was judgment time. I had judged Krogh and believed him decent. He judged me and apparently believed me trustworthy and considerate of his future. He did not make a decision in a flash, but shortly thereafter he stood before Judge Gesell and pleaded guilty to the conspiracy charge. We dismissed the false declaration count in the indictment. The California indictment also was dismissed.

During his plea Krogh told the court: "My coming to this point today stems from my asking myself what ideas I wanted to stand for, what I wanted to represent to myself and to my family and to be identified with for the rest of my experience. I simply feel that what was done in the Ellsberg operation was in violation of what I perceive to be a fundamental idea in the character of this country—the paramount importance of the rights of the individual. I don't want to be associated with that violation any longer by attempting to defend it. . . ."

Judge Gesell believed him. He sentenced Krogh to a prison term of two to six years with all but six months suspended.

# PART FIVE

## The Judicial
## Process

# The Courts

THE CRIMINAL
COURT

In the previous chapters, we discussed how the accused is processed through the early stages of the criminal justice system. Attention is now focused on the central stage—the criminal court. Each of the succeeding four chapters covers such important issues as the organization of the courts, the criminal trial, sentencing and probation.

The criminal court is the arena in which many of the most important decisions in the criminal justice system are made: the setting of bail, trial, plea negotiation, and sentencing are all court-made decisions. Within the confines of the court, those accused of crime (defendants) call upon the tools of the legal system to prove their innocence; their accusors (complainants) seek redress for the wrongs allegedly done to them; and agents of the criminal justice system attempt to find, ideally, solutions which benefit the victim, the defendant, and society alike. Of course, in today's crowded court system such abstract goals are often impossible to achieve.

The court process is designed to provide an open and impartial forum for deciding the justice of a particular conflict between two or more parties. The conflict may be between criminal and victim; law enforcement agents and the violator of the law; parent and child; the federal government and the violator of governmental regulations; and so on. Regardless of the parties or issues involved, their presence in a courtroom guarantees to them that a hearing will be held which will be conducted under regulated rules of procedure, that the outcome of the hearing will be clear, and that the hearing will take place in an atmosphere of fair play and objectivity. If either party, defendant or complainant, feels that these ground rules have been violated, that party may then take the case to a higher court where the procedures of the original trial will be examined. If, upon reexamination, it is found that a violation of the rights of either the defendant or the complainant has occurred, the appellate court may deem the findings of the original trial improper and either order a new hearing or hold that some other measure must be carried out—for example, the court may dismiss the charge outright.

The court is a complex social agency with many independent but interrelated subsystems, each of which has a role in its operation: police, prosecutor, defense attorney, judge, and probation department. It is also the scene of many important elements of criminal justice decision making: detention, jury selection, trial, and sentencing.

The American court system has evolved over the years into an intricately balanced legal process which has recently come under siege due to the sheer numbers of cases it must consider and the ways in which it is forced to handle such overcrowding. Overloaded court dockets have given rise to charges of assembly-line justice in which a majority of defendants are induced to plead guilty, jury trials are rare, and the speedy trial is a highly desired but unattainable concept. Overcrowding causes conditions in which the poor languish in detention while the wealthier go free on bail, and where an innocent person may be frightened into pleading guilty and conversely a guilty person may be released because a trial has been so long delayed. Whether providing for more judges or opening new or enlarged courts will solve the problem of overcrowding remains to be seen.

Meanwhile, diversion programs, the decriminalization of certain offenses, and bail reform provide other avenues of possible relief. More efficient court management and administration in the future are also seen as easing the congestion of the courts. In this and the following chapters, the organization and process of the courts is discussed, and the major decisions made within their confines are further analyzed.

**State Court Systems**          COURT SYSTEMS

State court systems in the United States are organized in three basic *levels* of jurisdiction: appellate, general, and limited (see Figure 11.1).* Courts at each of these levels may further be classified by the *type* of cases (legal jurisdiction) they hear—civil, criminal, or a mixture of civil and criminal (see Table 11.1).

At the first level are courts of limited and special jurisdiction (hereafter referred to as "limited") where the vast majority of legal actions begin (and end) and with which the average citizen has contact. These courts constitute 77% of the total number of courts. Courts of limited jurisdiction are predominantly misdemeanant and traffic courts (over half spend a majority of their time on traffic cases). It is at this level that the greatest amount of variation in patterns of organization occur. Two states have no courts of limited jurisdiction (all actions being tried at the general jurisdiction level), a few have a single statewide system of limited courts, while the majority have several different types of limited courts covering the same geographic area. To illustrate the last situation, residents of a municipality may go to their municipal court or a justice of the peace court in a neighboring town to pay a traffic fine, to their county court for a small civil suit, a different court in their county for probate of a will, and yet another court for a divorce or juvenile proceeding.

Courts of limited jurisdiction are "limited" in one of two ways. First, they may be authorized to hear only the less serious criminal offenses—misdemeanors, municipal ordinance violations and traffic violations (83% of the courts of limited and special jurisdiction hear both lesser criminal cases and traffic cases). The extent of these limits is usually set by law as a maximum fine or sentence which the court can impose (approximately 90% have a maximum fine of $1,000 or less and either cannot sentence a person to jail or can only impose a sentence of 12 months or less).

Most limited courts also hear small civil suits when the amount of money involved is below a certain amount (usually $1,000 or less). However, the majority of limited courts spend less than 10% of their total judge-time on civil cases.

Second, these courts may be restricted to hearing only specialized types of cases, such as domestic relations courts (which hear divorce and related proceedings), juvenile courts (which hear juvenile delinquency and dependency matters) or probate courts (which hear matters relating to decedents' estates).

At the next level are the courts of general jurisdiction—also called major trial courts. Most states are divided into judicial circuits or districts for the organization of their general jurisdiction courts—with each circuit or district consisting of one or

*From U.S. Department of Justice, Law Enforcement Assistance Administration, *State Court Systems* (Washington, D.C.: U.S. Government Printing Office, 1973).

FIGURE 11.1 State Judicial System

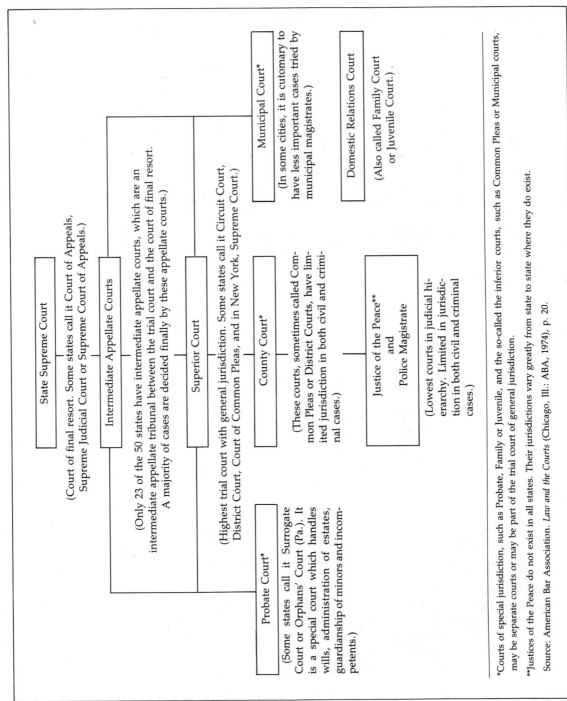

State Supreme Court

(Court of final resort. Some states call it Court of Appeals, Supreme Judicial Court or Supreme Court of Appeals.)

Intermediate Appellate Courts

(Only 23 of the 50 states have intermediate appellate courts, which are an intermediate appellate tribunal between the trial court and the court of final resort. A majority of cases are decided finally by these appellate courts.)

Superior Court

(Highest trial court with general jurisdiction. Some states call it Circuit Court, District Court, Court of Common Pleas, and in New York, Supreme Court.)

Probate Court*

(Some states call it Surrogate Court or Orphans' Court (Pa.). It is a special court which handles wills, administration of estates, guardianship of minors and incompetents.)

County Court*

(These courts, sometimes called Common Pleas or District Courts, have limited jurisdiction in both civil and criminal cases.)

Justice of the Peace**
and
Police Magistrate

(Lowest courts in judicial hierarchy. Limited in jurisdiction in both civil and criminal cases.)

Municipal Court*

(In some cities, it is customary to have less important cases tried by municipal magistrates.)

Domestic Relations Court

(Also called Family Court or Juvenile Court.)

*Courts of special jurisdiction, such as Probate, Family or Juvenile, and the so-called the inferior courts, such as Common Pleas or Municipal courts, may be separate courts or may be part of the trial court of general jurisdiction.

**Justices of the Peace do not exist in all states. Their jurisdictions vary greatly from state to state where they do exist.

Source: American Bar Association. *Law and the Courts* (Chicago, Ill.: ABA, 1974), p. 20.

358

TABLE 11.1
Number of Courts by
Type of Legal
Jurisdiction

| Level of court | Total | Civil | Type of legal jurisdiction | |
| | | | Criminal | Civil and criminal |
| --- | --- | --- | --- | --- |
| Total | 17,057 | 1,665 | 3,736 | 11,656 |
| Appellate | 206 | 26 | 7 | 173 |
| General | 3,630 | 231 | 10 | 3,389 |
| Limited and special | 13,221 | 1.408 | 3,719 | 8,094 |

more counties. Other states have general jurisdiction courts organized along county lines. Some states have more than one type of general jurisdiction court—either two circuit-type systems or a mixture of a circuit system with a county-based system.

General jurisdiction courts are unlimited in the civil, criminal, or civil and criminal cases they are authorized to hear. It is at this level that the majority of serious criminal offenses are tried—90% of all general jurisdiction courts hear felonies—however, very few are restricted to only these most serious crimes, as two-thirds hear lesser criminal cases as well.

Unlike the distribution of the workload in courts of limited jurisdiction where the majority of judge-time is spent on criminal (including traffic) cases, the civil workload in general jurisdiction courts takes up more judge-time than the criminal.

Courts of general jurisdiction and courts of limited jurisdiction together comprise the total number of courts of original jurisdiction (16,851) as distinguished from appellate jurisdiction. In most states there is some overlapping of jurisdiction between courts at the general and limited jurisdiction levels and often among courts at the same level.

In addition to hearing original actions, three-fourths of the courts of general jurisdiction hear cases on appeal from the limited courts. Such appeals may be heard on the record if one was taken in the limited court, or, as is still allowed in most states, the trial is heard anew (de novo) in the court to which it has been appealed. Appeals do not take up a significant portion of the workload in general jurisdiction courts (usually 10% or less).

Courts of appellate jurisdiction are at the top of the judicial organizational structure. They are further grouped into courts of last resort, and intermediate appellate courts (in the 23 states where they have been established). Courts of last resort have jurisdiction over final appeals from either courts of original jurisdiction or intermediate appellate courts. They also have jurisdiction of "state" issues. Where state law has expressly granted it, the courts of last resort have judicial rule-making powers and administrative authority over some or all of the courts in the state. The appellate jurisdiction of courts of intermediate appeals is usually limited by law, or at the discretion of the court of last resort, to specific types of cases (e.g., civil or criminal), cases under a certain dollar value, or cases arising in specific lower courts.

As is true in courts of general jurisdiction, appellate courts spend more time on civil cases than criminal. A small portion of their time (usually 10% or less) is spent on various original proceedings, such as writs.

The organization of the appellate courts is in many instances no less complex than that of the original trial courts. In some states, a case that has been tried in a court of limited jurisdiction may be appealed to another limited court and then to a court of general jurisdiction from where it may be appealed to an intermediate appellate court and/or a court of last resort.

Each court system authorizes a certain number of judges by law. The total number of authorized judgeship positions in the United States as of July 1, 1971 was 23,073, 75% of which were in the courts of limited jurisdiction. In appellate courts, the number of judges per court usually ranges from three to nine. However, at both the general and limited jurisdiction levels, the multiplicity of courts and their current geographic organization has resulted in a large number of one-judge courts: 60% of all general jurisdiction courts and 83% of limited jurisdiction courts operate with a single judge. The staffing situation of the limited courts is further characterized by the fact that over half (59%) of the judges in single-judge limited courts are part time. In addition, a situation where a single judge serves as judge of more than one court (i.e., is "shared") is not uncommon as 18% of the limited courts have shared judgeship positions.

Also at the limited jurisdiction level are many judges who are paid exclusively from fines collected from defendants who appear before them, or who act as judge by virtue of some other official capacity; e.g. mayor or county commissioner.

Some states have vested administrative authority in the court of last resort. One element of this authority is the power to assign judges from one court to another as the workload requires. Almost half of the courts of appellate jurisdiction, one-fourth of the courts of general jurisdiction, and one-tenth of the courts of limited jurisdiction received assistance in the form of "assigned" judges (i.e., judges from another court assigned to assist with the caseload).

Another method of obtaining additional manpower is the use of "other judicial personnel" such as commissioners, masters and referees, who perform some of the duties of a judge. The use of such personnel has not yet become widespread. It is negligible in courts of appellate jurisdiction (less than 1%) and limited jurisdiction (3%). However, 19% of the general jurisdiction courts reported employing other judicial personnel on a full-time, part-time, or special appointment basis.

In contrast to the appellate and general courts, nearly all of which have court clerks, only half (58%) of the courts of limited jurisdiction have clerks at all, and only one-fourth have clerks employed by the court on a full-time basis.

## Federal Courts

The legal basis for the federal court system is contained in Article III, Section I of the United States Constitution, which provides that "the judicial power of the United States shall be vested in one Supreme Court and in such inferior courts as Congress may from time to time ordain and establish."

Within this authority, the federal government has established a three-tiered hierarchy of court jurisdiction which, in order of ascendancy, consists of the (1) United States District Courts, (2) United States Courts of Appeals (Circuit Court), and (3) the Supreme Court (see Figure 11.2).

***District Courts.*** United States District Courts are the trial courts of the federal system. They have jurisdiction over cases involving violations of federal laws, including civil rights abuses; interstate transportation of stolen vehicles; and kidnappings. They may also hear cases on questions involving citizenship and the rights of aliens. The jurisdiction of the United States District Court will occasionally overlap with that of state courts. For example, citizens who reside in separate states and are involved in litigation of an amount in excess of $10,000 may chose to have their cases heard in either of the states or in the federal court. Finally, federal district courts hear cases in which one state sues a resident (or firm) in another state, where one state sues another, or where the federal government is a party in a suit.

FIGURE 11.2
Federal Judicial
System

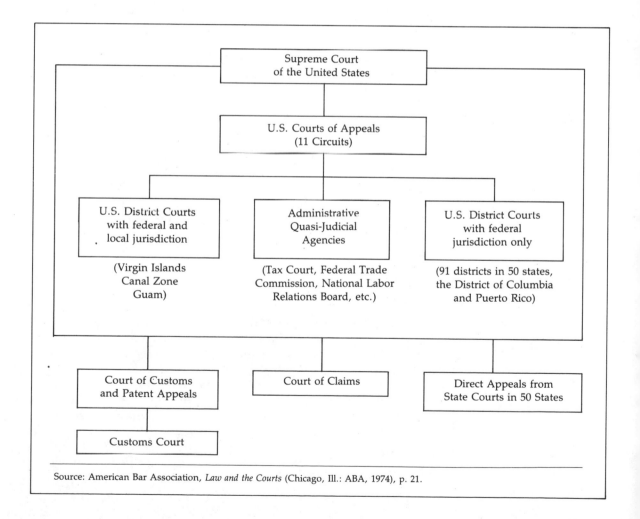

Source: American Bar Association, *Law and the Courts* (Chicago, Ill.: ABA, 1974), p. 21.

Federal district courts were organized by Congress in the Judicial Act of 1789, and today 92 independent courts are currently in operation. Originally, each state was allowed one court; as the population continued to climb, however, so did the need for courts. Now each state has from one to four district courts and the District of Columbia maintains one for itself.

In most cases, a single judge presides over trials; a defendant may request that a jury also be present. In complex civil matters, a three-judge panel may be convened.

*Federal Appeals Court.* Appeals from the district courts are heard in one of the 11 federal courts of appeals, sometimes referred to as circuit courts of appeals. This name is derived from the historical practice of having judges ride the circuit and regularly hear cases in the county seats of their various jurisdictions. Today, appellate judges are not required to travel (though some may sit in more than one court), and each federal appellate court jurisdiction contains a number of associate justices who share the caseload. Circuit court offices are usually located in major cities such as San Francisco or New York, and cases must be brought to these locations by attorneys in order to be heard.

The circuit court is empowered to review federal and state appellate court cases on substantive and procedural issues involving rights guaranteed by the Constitution. Circuit courts do not actually retry cases, nor do they determine whether the facts brought out during trial support conviction or dismissal. Instead, they analyze judicial interpretations of the law, such as the charge (or instructions) to the jury, and reflect upon the constitutional issues involved in each case they hear.

Federal appellate courts also enforce orders of federal administrative agencies such as the Food and Drug Administration, the Office of Housing and Urban Development, and others. Federal decisions in these matters are final, except when reviewed by the United States Supreme Court. Any dissatisfied litigant in a federal district court has the right to appeal the case to a circuit court.

*The United States Supreme Court.* The United States Supreme Court is the nation's highest appellate body and the court of last resort for all cases tried in the various federal and state courts. In certain rare instances, however, the Supreme Court can actually sit as a trial court—for example, in cases involving ambassadors or in suits between states.

The Supreme Court is composed of nine members appointed for lifetime terms by the President with the approval of Congress. The Court has discretion over most of the cases it will consider and may choose to hear only those it deems important, appropriate, and worthy of its attention. When the Court decides to hear a case it grants a Writ of Certiorari, requesting a transcript of the proceedings of the case for review. However, the Supreme Court must grant jurisdiction in all cases in which:

**1.** A federal court holds an act of Congress to be unconstitutional.

**2.** A United States Court of Appeals finds a state statute unconstitutional.

**3.** A state's highest court holds a federal law to be invalid.

**4.** When an individual's challenge to a state statute on constitutional grounds is upheld by a state supreme court.

When the Supreme Court rules on a case, usually by majority decision (at least five votes), its rule becomes a precedent which must be honored by all lower courts. For example, if the Court grants a particular litigant the right to counsel at a police lineup, then all similarly situated clients must be given the same right. This type of ruling is usually referred to as a landmark decision. The use of precedent in the legal system gives the Supreme Court power to influence and mold the everyday operating procedures of the police, trial courts, and corrections. In the past, this influence was not nearly as pronounced as it has been during the tenure of the last two Chief Justices, Earl Warren and Warren Burger, who greatly amplified and extended the power of the Court to interfere in criminal justice policies.

THE ROLE OF
THE JUDGE

The judge is the senior officer in a court of criminal law. His or her duties are quite varied and are actually far more extensive than the average citizen might suspect. During trials, the judge rules on the appropriateness of conduct, settles questions of evidence and procedure, and guides the questioning of witnesses. When a jury trial occurs, the judge must instruct its members on which evidence is proper to examine and which should be ignored. The judge also formally charges the jury by instructing its members on what points of law and evidence they must consider in order to reach a decision of either guilty or innocent. When a jury trial is waived, the judge must decide in the case whether to hold for complainant or defendant. Finally, in the event that a defendant is found guilty, the judge has the authority to decide upon the sentence (in some cases, this is legislatively determined). This duty includes choosing the type of sentence, its length, and—in the case of probation—the conditions under which it may be revoked. Obviously, this latter decision has a significant effect on an offender's future.

Beyond these stated duties, the trial judge has extensive control and influence over the other service agencies of the court: probation, the court clerk, the police, and the district attorney's office. Probation and the clerk may be under the judge's explicit control. In some courts, the operations, philosophy, and procedures of these agencies are within the magistrate's administrative domain. In others, for example, where a state agency controls the probation department, the attitudes of the county or district court judge still have a great deal of influence on the way in which a probation department is run and how its decisions are made.

Police and prosecutors are also directly influenced by the judge, whose sentencing discretion influences the arrest and charging processes. For example, if a judge usually chooses minimal sentences—such as a fine for a particular offense—then police may be reluctant to arrest offenders for that crime, knowing that the criminal justice procedure for that offense will basically be a waste of their time. Similarly, if a judge is known to have a liberal attitude toward police discretion, then the local department may be more inclined to engage in practices which border on entrapment, or they may become involved in cases requiring the use of easily obtained wiretaps. However, a magistrate oriented toward strict use of due process guarantees would stifle such activities by dismissing all cases involving apparent police abuses of personal freedoms. The district attorney's office may also be sensitive to judicial attitudes. The district attorney might forgo indictments in cases which the presiding magistrate expressly considers trivial or quasi-criminal and has been known to take only token action, such as the prosecution of pornographers.

Finally, the judge considers requests by police and prosecutors for leniency (or severity) in sentencing. The judge's reaction to these requests is important if police or the district attorney are to honor the bargains they may have made with defendants in order to secure information, cooperation, or guilty pleas. For example, when police tell informers that they will try to convince the judge to go easy on them in order to secure required information, communication often takes place between the police department and representatives of the court concerning the terms of the promised leniency. If a judge chooses to ignore police demands, then the department's bargaining power is severely diminished and communication within the criminal justice system is impeded.

## QUALIFICATIONS OF JUDGES

Individuals entrusted with the awesome powers of judgeship should ideally be chosen from the highest levels of the legal profession. Unfortunately, this is not always the case; many lower court and even appellate court justices are often politically connected and not necessarily prominent legal scholars. While the nation's highest federal and state courts have attracted many brilliant legal minds, such as William O. Douglas, Felix Frankfurter, Benjamin Cardozo, and Learned Hand, justices in the lower courts who actually handle the overwhelming majority of cases may merely be average or mediocre. Many municipal judges and justices of the peace do not hold law degrees and may not even be college graduates. In fact, legal scholar Roscoe Pound viewed the average judge as a victim of the legal system:

In America we take it as a matter of course that a judge should be a mere umpire, to pass upon objections and hold counsel to the rules of the game, and that the parties should fight out their own game in their own way without judicial interference . . . It leads the most conscientious judge to feel that he is merely to decide the contest, as counsel presents it according to the rules of the game, not to search independently for truth and justice.[1]

These rather negative views towards representatives of the legal system are similar to those of noted legal scholar Herman Schwartz:

Glaring down from their elevated perches, insulting, abrupt, rude, sarcastic, patronizing, intimidating, vindictive, insisting on not merely respect but almost abject servility—such judges are frequently encountered in American trial courts, particularly in the lowest criminal and juvenile courts which account for most of our criminal business. Indeed, the lower the court, the worse the behavior.[2]

Considering the less than uniform excellence of trial court justices in the United States, which qualities should actually be sought when selecting our judiciary? Opinions abound on the subject of judicial qualifications, and historically a surprising degree of unanimity on the subject exists. For example, the great philosopher Sir Francis Bacon suggested that "Judges ought to be more learned than witty; reverend than plausible; and more advised than confident. Above all things, integrity is their position and proper virtue."[3] Centuries later, Laurence M. Hyde, Jr., Dean of the National College of State Trial Judges, held a similar view: "We need judges learned in the law, as well as the mysteries of human nature. A judge must be an unusually honest man. He must be independent and believed by the community to be independent. He needs courage in much greater measure than most . . . Our list of qualifications will include patience, humility, emotional stability, compassion, toughness, energy, endurance, and good health."[4] Socrates envisioned the judge as being able "to hear courteously; to answer wisely; to consider soberly; and to decide impartially."[5] While current author and judicial scholar Leon Yankowich acknowledges that "qualities of knowledge, social idealism, courage, and integrity have always been considered the attributes of a good judge,"[6] New York Civil Court Judge Irving Younger explains succinctly: "The most important prerequisite is a vivid sense of fairness. Everything else is acquired."[7] And Attorney William Kunstler defines a good judge "as a person who understands the realities of American life and who is consciously doing something to change them."[8]

### Historical Background

[The] basic method for choosing judges in the early days of the Republic was appointive with various checks on the appointing authority provided by the legislature.* On the state level the appointment power was vested in both the executive and legislative branches. On the federal level, the power resided in the executive alone. While the appointive method continues at the federal level it enjoyed only a brief period of dominance in the states. The Jacksonian era introduced the elective method of selecting state judges.

JUDICIAL
SELECTION

---

*From Sari Escovitz with Fred Kurland and Nan Gold, *Judicial Selection and Tenure* (Chicago: American Judicature Society, 1974), pp. 3–16.

By 1846 the Union contained 29 states. Appointment by the Governor was the method for selecting some or all judges in 14 states. The legislature selected all of the judges in 12 states and some of the judges in 4 states, while 4 states also provided for popular election of some of their judges. In 1832 Mississippi became the only state to elect its entire judiciary. But Jacksonian democracy adhered to the principle of the equality of all persons in fact and testing out this principle brought political reform including popular election of judges.

New York began the trend at its constitutional convention of 1846, replacing gubernatorial and legislative appointment of judges with direct popular election. For the next century, the 19 new states entering the Union provided for an elected judiciary. Seven of the colonial states, (Connecticut, Delaware, Massachusetts, New Hampshire, New Jersey, Rhode Island, and South Carolina) totally resisted the popular trend and Maine switched to an elective process for only its probate judges. But Georgia, Maryland, Pennsylvania and Virginia left their appointive systems and joined the movement. (Virginia went back to legislative appointment of its judiciary after 14 years under an elective system.) Vermont began electing its lower court judges in 1850, but returned to legislative appointment of all judges in 1870. By the time of the Civil War, judges were elected in 24 of the 34 states. For the first time in Anglo-American history the judicial office became an integral part of the political election process.

Toward the end of the nineteenth century, the results from this experiment in participatory democracy began to emerge. They were both unexpected and un-settling. The post-Civil War increase in industrialization and urbanization nurtured political "machines" in the nation's larger cities. The Tammany Hall organization in New York epitomized the potential abuses of partisan judicial contests. Seizing control of the political processes that led to nomination, Tammany was able to run and elect its hand-picked and politically responsive slate of judicial candidates. The stranglehold of such an organization over elections was strengthened by the met-ropolitan electorate's ignorance and complacency about judicial candidates. Elec-tions often became rubber-stamp confirmations of the machine's slate, not the Jack-sonian ideal of individual and equal expression of free will through the ballot.

Dissatisfaction and resentment of political party control over judicial candidates led to a counter-reform movement. For example, the reaction of New York lawyers against the party method of nomination and election was instrumental in establish-ment of the first bar association in the nation, the Association of the Bar of the City of New York in 1870. A number of similar associations including the American Bar Association were formed during the next decade. Although the theme of "taking the judge out of politics" grew more popular, the reforms sought by the bar leaders were mostly concerned with improving the existing system of popular elections. Bar leaders attempted to control the power of the political party organization through a variety of devices such as nonpartisan ballots, separate judicial nominating con-ventions and elections and direct primaries. They also attempted to increase the influence of the legal profession on judicial selection by conducting and publishing bar association referenda with recommendations on the fitness of judicial candi-dates. These initial measures proved inadequate to break the effective control of political party leaders over elections. Although most states retained the elective system, concern over the adverse effects of political selection on the quality of judicial personnel became more pronounced with the approach of the twentieth century.

The call for a frontal attack on popular election of judges was sounded in 1906 by a young University of Nebraska law professor, Roscoe E. Pound. In an address before the American Bar Association, Pound noted that popular judicial elections were a major cause of public dissatisfaction with the administration of justice. Pound's direct assault on popular elections was continued by William Howard Taft, the ex-President of the United States and future Chief Justice of the U.S. Supreme Court. Speaking before the American Bar Association in 1913, Taft declared that even the nonpartisan judicial ballot was a failure. He asserted that such a system permitted unqualified persons who could not even muster political support to get elected to the bench through vigorous campaigns.

In that same year, the American Judicature Society was founded. Dedicated to promoting the efficient administration of justice, this organization was particularly concerned with methods for selection, tenure, and retirement of judges. As director of research for the new organization, Albert M. Kales, a law professor at Northwestern University, set out to devise a method of judicial selection that would maximize the benefits and minimize the weaknesses of both the appointment and election processes. Kales sought to preserve the informed and intelligent choice, which is the strong point of the appointive system, while retaining ultimate voter control.

The system devised by Kales and promoted by the American Judicature Society did combine appointment with election. It also added a crucial third element—a judicial nominating commission. Under the Kales Plan, an elected justice would fill judicial vacancies from a list submitted by the commission, which was expected to seek out the best available judicial talent. After serving for a period of time on the bench, these appointed judges would go before the voters on the sole question of retention. In form, this type of election is similar to a referendum, for it is noncompetitive and nonpartisan. In the event of a rejection, the resulting vacancy would be filled as before by commission nomination and appointment by the Chief Justice.

In 1926 Harold Laski, an English political scientist, proposed a variation on the Kales Plan, substituting the governor for the chief justice as the appointing authority. The Kales-Laski plan contained the basic features upon which most subsequent plans for judicial reform have been based. The three-part approach consists of: (1) a judicial nominating commission to nominate candidates for the bench; (2) an elected official (usually from the executive branch) to make appointments from the list submitted by the commission; and (3) subsequent nonpartisan and noncompetitive elections in which incumbent judges run on their records.

For nearly 25 years the plan remained dormant and most states continued to elect their judges. In 1937 the American Bar Association endorsed the Kales-Laski plan. Three years later it was voted into the constitution of Missouri and quickly became identified as the Missouri Plan. The nation's concern throughout the 1940s with international matters muted the issue of judicial reform. By midcentury, Missouri remained the only state to have adopted the plan.

In the 1950s the interest in judicial reform revived and some states instituted judicial selection plans based on the Kales-Laski model. Alaska entered the Union in 1959 as the first state to apply merit selection to all its courts. To date, 21 states (Alabama, Arizona, Alaska, Kansas, New York (New York City), Iowa, Nebraska, Colorado, Idaho, Oklahoma, Utah, Vermont, Maryland, Massachusetts, Georgia, Tennessee, Florida, Indiana, Montana, Wyoming, and Pennsylvania, plus Puerto Rico and the District of Columbia) have incorporated the merit selection plan into their court systems at some level and in varying degrees. Of these states, 11 can be considered to contain court systems in which the predominant method of judicial selection is according to merit, while 9 of the states apply the plan only to interim appointments. Five other states employ appointive systems of judicial selection that are based on the merit principle.

But the major method of judicial selection in the United States remains elective. Thirty-three states select all or most of their judges by election. (In a few cases this election is conducted by the state legislature.) Fifteen states are characterized by nonpartisan election of judges. Partisan elections remain a popular form of judicial selection, with 18 states choosing most of their judges in this way. Finally, 9 states utilize a predominantly appointive method for selecting their judiciary.

### A Summary of Judicial Selection

To summarize, there are several methods of judicial selection in use. First there is appointment to judicial office by the governor. There is also gubernatorial appointment with confirmation by (1) the state senate, (2) the governor's council, (3) an ex-officio confirming commission, (4) an executive council elected by the general assembly, or (5) a council popularly elected by the voters. Some states employ screening bodies at the very beginning of the appointive process. These screening commissions may be composed of bar association members, or political "friends" of the executive. (For some of its courts, Connecticut reverses the roles and has the governor nominate and the legislature appoint the judges.)

Under a merit selection plan, the governor appoints from a list of nominees prepared by an official, nonpartisan nominating commission. Incumbents stand for retention unopposed on a nonpartisan ballot. Clearly, the nominating commission is the key to the success of merit selection. It may be made up of only legal professionals or include laymen as well. The commissioners may themselves be elected or appointed. The commission can be created by state constitution or statute, or by executive order. It may function formally or informally. Some commissions hold open hearings and publicize judicial nominees while others make public the name of the final appointee only. Judicial offices may also be filled by election by the state legislature or appointment by another judge. Popular judicial elections can be conducted on a nonpartisan basis, or by partisan ballot following slate-making in open primaries, party conventions, or caucuses. Michigan has the unique practice of conducting nonpartisan judicial elections following partisan political nominations. Finally, judges of state courts with less than state-wide territorial jurisdiction are sometimes appointed by the mayor or local governing body or selected in a manner prescribed by local charter or ordinance.

COURT ADMINISTRATION

In 1974, Justice Warren Burger stated that "the days are . . . past when a chief judge, with the help of a secretary and the clerk of the court, can manage the increasingly complex tasks required of them to keep courts functioning effectively. We must be constantly alert to new ideas, new methods, new ways of looking at the judiciary."

The need for efficient management techniques in an ever-expanding criminal court system has led to the recognition of improved court administration as a possible device for relieving court congestion. Management goals include improving organization and scheduling of cases, devising methods to efficiently allocate court records, administering fines and monies due the court, preparing budgets, and overseeing personnel.

The federal courts have led the way in creating and organizing court administration. In 1939, Congress passed the Administrative Office Act which established the Administrative Office of the United States Courts. Its director was charged with gathering statistics on the work of the federal courts and also with preparing the judicial budget for approval by the Conference of Senior Circuit Judges. One clause of the Act created a judicial council with general supervisory responsibilities for the district and circuit courts.

Unlike the federal government, the states have experienced a slow and uneven growth in the development and application of court management principles. The first state to establish an administrative office was North Dakota in 1927. By 1972, there were 37 state court administrators and, by 1975, 46 states had established that position by legislation or constitutional provision. Those states without court administrators are Mississippi, Montana, Nevada, and New Hampshire. In New Hampshire, the Secretary of the Judicial Council serves in an administrative capacity. In the remaining 3 states, the Chief Justices of the respective state supreme courts assume administrative responsibilities.

The federal government has influenced the development of state court management by making funding available to state court systems. In addition, the federal judiciary has provided the philosophical impetus for better and more effective court management. For example, Chief Justice Warren Burger stated in 1971 at the National Conference on the Judiciary that:

The challenges of our system of justice are colossal and immediate and we must assign priorities. I would begin by giving priority to methods and machines, to procedures and techniques, to management and administration of judicial resources even over the much-needed reexamination of substantive legal issues.[9]

A court system is an extremely complex organization which is far more difficult to manage than the typical business enterprise or government agency because:

1. [T]he key people are accustomed to working as individuals and do not take kindly to regimentation.
2. [A] very high value is placed on judicial independence, and this severely limits the pressures that can be brought to bear to produce administratively desired results.
3. [P]ersons involved in the judicial performance—attorneys, jurors, witnesses, litigants—are not employed by the judiciary.
4. [P]articipants in the judicial process often have conflicting goals.[10]

Another obstacle facing court administration is the generally low profile of the courts themselves. Except in times of unusual stress, judicial performance is hidden from public view and mismanagement is rarely noted by the taxpaying public. Despite increased efforts to efficiently manage courts, successes have been few and far between. For example, an LEAA-sponsored survey of the nation's 17,057 state and local courts revealed that many have fragmented and overlapping jurisdictions, lack sufficiently trained personnel, and have no consistent pattern for handling various types of proceedings. The study concluded that:

Each court in each county in each state is different. Each has its own set of challenges. These are closely tied to the experience and temperament of the judge, the size of and quality of the bar, the people who live in the area and the kind of justice they demand.[11]

Despite the multitude of problems facing those who believe in reforming court management, some progress is being made. By order of its state supreme court, effective February 1, 1973, Florida became the first state to implement most of the American Bar Association Standards by formal court rule. Under the state constitution, the Florida supreme court exercised the power to prescribe rules of practice and procedures for all courts in the state. By 1974, 85% of the principles in the standards needing statutory implementation had been adopted in Florida.

### The Court Administrator

In many of the largest jurisdictions, court administrators have been hired to take charge of the difficult task of efficient court management. In general, the court administrator's job description would include the following: personnel, financial, and records administrator (subject to the standards of the central administrative office); governmental secretary for meetings of the judges of the court that he serves; liaison with the local government, bar, news media, and general public; and manager of physical facilities and equipment and the purchaser of outside services.

The job of the court administrator is not to usurp the judge's authority, but rather to develop the court's organizational structure so that it may be more effective. The judge remains the policymaker for the court, relying on the administrator to assist in that role to whatever degree with which the judge feels most comfortable. The administrator's job is to recommend and implement innovative ways of executing policy and help direct the court along whatever avenues seem appropriate to improving the administration of justice.

For example, in New Jersey, a state which has employed state court administrators for over 25 years, the administrator's role includes: keeping court records in order, assigning trial schedules, reviewing judges' time sheets, keeping track of overly prolonged cases, employing modern budgeting procedures, and coordinating computerized information.

Despite the apparent logic in employing court administrators as overall court managers, some courts do not respond well to centralized administrative authority. Many incentives that influence employees to respond to central executive authority in business organizations—such as increased compensation or promotion as rewards for performance, or the termination of employment as a penalty for failure—generally do not exist in the judicial system. As a result, courts have failed to make full use of business management methods and machinery.

However, Chief Justice Warren Burger's concern has done much to focus attention on the need for developing qualified court managers. With the help of such qualified personnel, modern technology and business systems can be applied to daily court operations.

### Technology and Court Management

Computers are becoming an important aid in the administration and management of courts. Rapid retrieval and organization of data can be used for such functions as:

1. Maintaining case histories and statistical reporting.

2. Monitoring and scheduling of cases.

3. Document preparation.

4. Case indexing.

5. Issuing summonses.

6. Notifying witnesses, attorneys, and others of required appearances.

Through LEAA funding, the federal government is encouraging the states to experiment with computerized information systems. In the past, the LEAA has funded a 50-state consortium for the purpose of establishing a standardized crime reporting system called SEARCH (Systems for the Electronic Analysis and Retrieval of Criminal Histories).

Other computerized research projects in the courts apply computer technology to such areas as videotaped testimonies, the development of new court reporting devices, the installation of computer-based information systems, and the use of data-processing systems to handle functions such as court docketing and jury management. In 1968, only 10 states had state-level automated information systems; today, all states employ such systems in at least one element in the field.

Two other computer systems currently in operation are PROMIS (Prosecutor's Management Information System) and COURTRAN, which is designed especially to help courts comply with the statutory time limits provision of the Speedy Trial Act of 1974. These systems monitor the flow of cases through the court, indicating problem cases and helping judges and court personnel to eliminate causes of delays. In addition, IBM has developed a basic computerized court system which includes three basic computerized files within its memory bank—case history file, name file, and court calendar file. Utilizing federal grants, Baltimore, Maryland adopted IBM's program and installed the computerized system for the recording of criminal cases, their scheduling, and their disposition. The applications section of this chapter discusses the PROMIS model and its success.

The American Bar Association Standards have classified the uses of computerized information retrieval into the following three categories:[12]

1. Judicial and administrative decision making:
   a. rules on motions
   b. assigning cases for trial

2. Information handling:
   a. making entries into official records
   b. sending out notices
   c. computerizing financial accounts

3. Monitoring and planning in court administration:
   a. analyzing case flow
   b. preparing budgets
   c. projecting future needs

The Standards stress that many essential procedures and vital decisions in a court system are made outside the direct supervision of the judges.

The computer cannot, of course, replace the judge, but may be used as an ally to help speed up the trial process by identifying backlogs and bottlenecks which can be eradicated if intelligent managerial techniques are applied. Just as an industrialist must know the type and quantity of goods on hand in a warehouse, so must an administrative judge have available information concerning those entering the judge's domain, what happened to them once they were in it, and how they have fared since leaving it.

## SUMMARY

The American court system is a very complex social institution. There is no set pattern of court organization, and court structure varies considerably between the various state jurisdictions.

Courts are organized on the federal, state, county, and local levels of government. It is a common practice for states to separately maintain felony and misdemeanant cases, as well as to operate independent trial and appellate courts. This structure is repeated on the federal level of jurisdiction. However, federal appellate courts also rule on state cases, and the United States Supreme Court is the court of last resort for all cases decided in the United States.

Directly supervising our nation's courts are the judiciary. Judges come from a variety of backgrounds and possess individual skills and qualifications.

Their functions vary according to the courts in which they sit; some rule at the trial level, while others concern themselves with appellate cases. In addition to these tasks, judges serve as decision makers in administering probation departments and in working with district attorneys and police. Some judges are appointed by the state's chief executive, the governor, while others are elected to office by popular vote.

A recent trend in the court process has been the creation of administrative bodies to oversee court operations. Within this operational sphere are court administrators, who have used sophisticated computer operations to ease the flow of cases and improve court efficiency.

**1.** What qualities should a judge have? Should the judgeship be a lifetime appointment, or should judges periodically be reviewed?

**2.** Do the pomp and formality of a courtroom impede justice by setting it apart from the common person?

**3.** What is meant when we say that the Supreme Court is the court of last resort?

**4.** Should all judges be lawyers? When can nonlegally trained people be of benefit to the court system?

QUESTIONS FOR
DISCUSSION

NOTES

**1.** Cited in William Lineberry, ed., *Justice in America: Law Order & The Courts* (New York: H.W. Wilson Co., 1972), p. 190.

**2.** John MacKenzie, *The Appearance of Justice* (New York: Charles Scribner's Sons, 1974), p. 120.

**3.** Donald Carroll, *Handbook for Judges* (Jacksonville, Fla.: H & W.B. Drew Co., 1961), p. 4.

**4.** Cited in William Swindler, ed., *Justice in the States: Addresses & Papers of the National Conference on the Judiciary* (Williamsburg, Va.: West Publishing Co., 1971), pp. 167–168.

**5.** Carroll, *Handbook for Judges*, p. 29.

**6.** Quoted in Carroll, *Handbook for Judges*, p. 10.

**7.** Donald Dale Jackson, *Judges* (New York: H. Wolff, 1974), p. vii.

**8.** Donald Jackson, *Judges*, p. 10.

**9.** Chief Justice Warren Burger, "Rx For Justice: Modernize the Courts," *Nation's Business* (September 1974), p. 62.

**10.** Cited in National Advisory Commission on Criminal Justice Standards & Goals, *Courts* (Washington, D.C.: U.S. Government Printing Office, 1973), p. 171.

**11.** Edward McConnell, "The Role of the State Administrator" in *Justice in The States, Addresses and Papers of the National Council on the Judiciary* (St. Paul, Minn.: West Publishing Co., March, 1971).

**12.** See generally American Bar Association, *Standards Relating to Court Organization*, (New York: Institute For Judicial Administration, 1973).

APPLICATION

# Computer Keeps Tabs On Criminals And Caseloads*

A computer system that can prepare court calendars, issue subpoenas and warn of possible bail jumpers will be operating in 58 cities by the end of next year.

Known as "PROMIS," an acronym for Prosecution Management Information System, the program is operating in 12 cities and will be in 9 more by December.

PROMIS can often tell why people who are arrested often don't go to jail.

"One reason prosecutions often wash out is that victims and witnesses don't turn up on trial day because they haven't even been notified," said William Hamilton, president of the Institute for Law and Social Research of Washington, D.C., and developer of the system.

"And the reason they often aren't notified is because of inadequate administrative procedures.

"PROMIS," he said, "is correcting that."

PROMIS is providing courts and prosecuting attorneys across the nation instant access to arrest and court records that formerly took days to retrieve.

It can determine whether judges in different courts are treating similar cases differently. It can consolidate all a defendant's pending cases. And it can tell what caseloads are being handled by individual prosecutors and judges.

The system can isolate and produce a printout on such items as:

—All felonies in 1975 that involved a gun charge and the defendant was arrested at a specific location.

—All cases in which "Harry Brown" was the arresting police officer and "John Smith" the defense lawyer.

—All cases in which the witness was "John Jones" and the case was dismissed or discontinued for lack of witness cooperation.

## TIGHTENS REINS ON BAIL JUMPERS

PROMIS also can tell when an arrested person has several cases pending, thus preventing him from slipping away on either low bail or his own recognizance.

*From: LEAA Newsletter, Vol. 6, No. 10, May 1977.

PROMIS is a retrieval system that contains up to 170 facts on each defendant's case and can display the information on video screens within seconds.

In addition to dramatic improvements in efficiency, PROMIS has saved cities thousands of dollars in manpower hours.

Milwaukee County District Attorney E. Michael McCann said Milwaukee County expects to save more than $600,000 a year because of PROMIS. He said the system serves both the prosecuting attorney's office and the court system.

## SPARES WITNESSES DELAY

"It prepares statistical reports, witness notices, consolidates cases against the same defendant before one judge, prepares the court calendar and increases recovery of bonds forfeited by bail jumpers," Mr. McCann said.

"The computer immediately says when a case goes off calendar at the last minute, thus enabling officials to tell witnesses not to come to court."

In Marion County, Indianapolis, where PROMIS has been operating since Jan. 1, 1976, Jim Kelley, prosecuting attorney, said the county will save about $34,000 a year in administrative and personnel costs.

Mr. Hamilton said, however, that other cities will have the same costs as before and a few may have increased expenses.

"The real value lies in the increased quality and efficiency of operating the criminal justice system," Mr. Hamilton said.

According to Mr. Hamilton, PROMIS generally costs about $100,000 a city to install and operate for one year. After that, the funding is usually taken over by local appropriations.

The Institute has published the first three of a series of 17 studies based on statistical data collected by PROMIS in the U.S. Attorney's office that handles cases in the Superior Court, Washington, D.C.

## CONFIRMS LOW CONVICTION RATE

All 17 studies reflect the disposition of about 100,000 cases entered into the PROMIS system in Washington since 1971.

Mr. Hamilton said the studies confirm a longstanding suspicion that there is little correlation between the number of reported crimes and arrests and the number of prosecutions and convictions.

He said preliminary statistics from other PROMIS cities suggest a similar pattern of relatively few convictions and incarcerations compared with the original number of crimes and arrests.

He cited the following examples for Washington, D.C.:

—Seven per cent of the arrestees over a 5½ year period accounted for 24 per cent of the caseload, because they were arrested on at least four separate occasions in that period.

—Chances of a person serving prison time after being arrested in Washington for a felony are 1 in 10. The odds of being sentenced to more than 24 months are 1 in 25.

Certain crimes have an almost negligible conviction rate. There were about 14,000 commercial burglaries reported in Washington in 1975, but only 1,472 burglary arrests and only 221 adult burglary convictions.

"Since 1930 the only dimension we have had has been police statistics, distributed through the FBI, with no indication of productiveness at the prosecution end," Mr. Hamilton said.

"Now that we can have comparable data on what happens after arrest, the country can devote resources to the neglected problems of courts and prosecutors' offices, because the data from PROMIS indicate most arrests do not result in conviction."

## HELPS MANAGEMENT

William Wessel, first assistant district attorney for New Orleans, said the most beneficial aspect of PROMIS to his staff is the management reports produced from the computer.

"This enables us to analyze the cases on the docket; what we're doing with them; and what their disposition is," Mr. Wessel said. "We can determine what impact we're having in this area and what effect our prosecutions have on the offenses committed."

Reports released to date include: "Overview and Interim Findings," "Enhancing The Policy-Making Utility of Crime Data," and "The Repeat Offender as a Priority for Prosecutors."

PROMIS is operating in Washington, D.C.; Los Angeles; Detroit; Milwaukee; New Orleans; Salt Lake City; Las Vegas; Indianapolis; Tallahassee, Fla.; Cobb County, Ga.; Kalamazoo, Mich.; the State of Rhode Island; New York City; St. Louis; San Diego; Newark; Cleveland; Louisville; Little Rock; Polk County and West Palm Beach, Fla.

Cities in the planning stage for PROMIS include: Seattle and Portland, Ore.; Buffalo; Oklahoma City; Tulsa; Albuquerque; and Des Moines.

# The Criminal Trial

CHAPTER OUTLINE

KEY TERMS

**Adjudication**
**Adversary Process**
**Jury Trial**
**Sixth Amendment**
*Apodica v. Oregon*
*Barker v. Wingo*
**Demand-waiver Role**
**Verdict**
**Challenge for Cause**
**Sentence**
*Duncan v. Louisiana*
*Baldwin v. N.Y.*
**In re Oliver**

**Six-Person Jury**
**Fourteenth Amendment**
*Faretta v. California*
**Fixed Time Rule**
**Directed Verdict**
*Williams v. Florida*
*Gideon v. Wainwright*
*Powell v. Alabama*
*Argersinger v. Hamlin*
**Waiver**
**Speedy Trial Act**
**Peremptory Challenge**
**Direct Examination**

**THE JURY TRIAL**

The adjudicatory stage of the criminal justice process begins with a hearing that seeks to determine the truth of the facts of a case before the courts. This process is usually referred to as the criminal trial.

Because criminal trials are frequently depicted on television, in motion pictures, and in fiction, and are given a great deal of coverage in the news media, many people view the criminal justice process as involving the full array of courtroom activities to determine the guilt or innocence of every person accused of a crime. In fact, the classic jury trial of a criminal case is a very uncommon occurrence. As previously mentioned, the greatest proportion of criminal offenders charged with crimes plead guilty. Others have their cases dismissed by the judge for a variety of reasons: the government may decide not to prosecute, the accused may be found to be emotionally disturbed, or the court may be willing to refrain from attaching the stigma of a criminal record to a particular defendant. Still others waive their constitutional right to a jury trial. In this situation, which occurs daily in the lower criminal courts, the judge may initiate a number of formal or informal dispositions, including dismissing the case, finding the defendant not guilty or guilty and impose a sentence, or even continuing the case indefinitely. The type of decision the judge makes often depends on the seriousness of the offense, the background and previous record of the defendant, and the judgment of the court as to whether the case can be properly dealt with in the criminal process. The *continuance*, for example, is a frequently used disposition in which the court holds a case in abeyance without a finding of guilt in order to induce the accused to improve his behavior in the community; if the defendant's behavior does improve, the case is ordinarily closed within a specific period of time. Thus, the number of actual criminal jury trials is small in comparison to all the cases processed through the criminal justice system. Since upward of 90% of all defendants plead guilty and about 5% are dealt with by other methods, it appears that fewer than 5% ever reach the trial stage. Those cases that are actually tried before a jury often involve serious crimes which require a formal inquiry into the facts to determine the guilt or innocence of the accused.

Even though proportionately few cases are actually tried by juries, the trial process remains a focal point in the criminal justice system. It symbolizes the American system of jurisprudence, in which an accused person can choose to present a defense against the government's charges. The fact that the defendant has the option of going to trial significantly affects the operation of the criminal justice system. As the National Commission on Criminal Justice Standards and Goals has stated:

Although most criminal prosecutions do not involve the adversary determination of guilt or innocence that occurs at the formal trial of a criminal case, the trial process remains a matter of vital importance to the criminal justice system. Whether or not a defendant chooses to invoke his right to trial, he has an interest in the trial process because in many cases it represents to him a legal option guaranteed by the Constitution of the United States. The opportunity to go to trial provides a valuable safeguard against abuse of informal processing and a basis for encouraging faith in the system on the part of those who acknowledge that their situation does not present any contestable issues.

Since informal disposition of a case often occurs only after the case proceeds along the formal route towards trial, procedures for formal processing at the earlier court stages may be used for a much greater number of cases than actually come to trial. Because all other means of processing cases must be evaluated as alternatives to formal trial, the attractiveness of trial is a major consideration in both prosecution and defense willingness to process a case administratively.[1]

Every trial has its constitutional issues, complex legal procedures, rules of court, and interpretations of statutes, all designed to insure that the accused will have a fair trial. This section discusses the most important constitutional rights of the accused at the trial stage of the criminal justice system and reviews the legal nature of the trial process.

**LEGAL RIGHTS DURING TRIAL**

### The Right to Jury Trial

The defendant has the right to choose whether the trial will be before a judge or a jury. Although the Sixth Amendment to the United States Constitution guarantees to the defendant the right to have a jury trial, the defendant can and often does waive this right. In fact, a substantial proportion of defendants, particularly those charged with misdemeanors, are tried before the court without a jury.

The major legal issue surrounding jury trials has been the question of whether all offenders, both misdemeanants and felons, have an absolute right to a jury trial. Because the United States Constitution is silent on this point, the Supreme Court has ruled that all defendants in felony cases have this right. In the case of *Duncan v. Louisiana* (1968),[2] the court held that the Sixth Amendment right to a jury trial was applicable to the states as well as to the federal government, and that it can be interpreted to apply to all defendants accused of serious crimes. The court in *Duncan* based its holding on the following premise:

that in the American States, as in the federal judicial system, a general grant of jury trial for serious offenses is a fundamental right, essential for preventing miscarriages of justice and for assuring that fair trials are provided for all defendants.[3]

The *Duncan* case did not settle whether all defendants charged with crimes in state courts were constitutionally entitled to jury trials. It seemed to draw the line at serious offenses only, while leaving the question of whether to grant jury trials to defendants in minor cases to the discretion of the individual states.

In 1970, in the case of *Baldwin v. New York*,[4] the United States Supreme Court departed from the distinction of serious versus minor offenses and decided that a defendant has a constitutional right to a jury trial when facing a prison sentence of six months or more, regardless of whether the crime committed was a felony or a misdemeanor. Where the possible sentence is six months or less, the accused is not entitled to a jury trial unless the state authorizes that procedure by statute.

According to the American Bar Association's *Standards Relating to Trial by Jury*, most if not all jurisdictions place some limitations upon the right to jury trial in criminal cases. Some states provide for a jury trial in all criminal cases; others provide this right to all but defendants in cases involving petty offenses such as minor gambling, traffic violations, and disorderly conduct; and still others limit jury trials in accordance with the constitutional rule of *Baldwin v. New York*.

Other important issues relate to the defendant's rights in a criminal jury trial, which include the right to a public trial, the right to a jury trial consisting of twelve people, and the right to a unanimous verdict. The Sixth Amendment guarantees the defendant the right to a public trial, which means that the general public cannot normally be excluded from criminal trials. This provision is the result of our government's distrust of secret trials and arbitrary proceedings. In the case of *In re Oliver (1948)*,[5] the United States Supreme Court held that both state and federal court systems were bound to grant public trials to criminal defendants. There are exceptions; the court may bar young people from certain sordid cases, or exclude the general public from cases involving sex crimes or where extensive publicity might result in the defendant receiving an unfair trial. Most if not all jurisdictions also exclude the general public from juvenile proceedings. Regardless of the kind of crime committed, a defendant is always permitted to have family, close associates, and legal counsel at trial.

The actual size of the jury has been a matter of great concern. Can a defendant, for instance, be tried and convicted of a crime by a jury of fewer than 12 persons? Traditionally, 12 jurors have deliberated as the triers of fact in criminal cases involving misdemeanors or felonies. However, there is no specific mention in the United States Constitution that a jury of 12 is an absolute requirement. As a result, in *Williams v. Florida*, in 1970,[6] the United States Supreme Court held that a 6-person jury in a criminal trial did not deprive a defendant of the constitutional right to a jury trial. The court made clear that the 12-person panel is not a necessary ingredient of a trial by jury, and upheld a Florida statute permitting the use of a 6-person jury in a robbery trial. The majority opinion in the *Williams* case traces the court's rationale for its decision:

We conclude, in short, as we began: the fact that a jury at common law was composed of precisely twelve is a historical accident, unnecessary to effect the purposes of the jury system and wholly without significance "except to mystics." To read the Sixth Amendment as forever codifying a feature so incidental to the real purpose of the Amendment is to ascribe a blind formalism to the Framers which would require considerably more evidence than we have been able to discover in the history and language of the Constitution or in the reasoning of our past decisions. We do not mean to intimate that legislatures can never have good reasons for concluding that the twelve man jury is preferable to the smaller jury or that such conclusions— reflected in the provisions of most States and in our federal system—are in any sense unwise. Legislatures may well have their own views about the relative value of the larger and smaller juries, and may conclude that, wholly apart from the jury's primary function, it is desirable to spread the collective responsibility for the determination of guilt among the larger group. In capital cases, for example, it appears that no State provides for less than 12 jurors—a fact that suggests implicit recognition of the value of the larger body as a means of legitimating society's decision to impose the death penalty. Our holding does no more than leave these considerations to Congress and the States, unrestrained by an interpretation of the Sixth Amendment that would forever dictate the precise number that can constitute a jury. Consistent with this holding, we conclude that petitioner's Sixth Amendment rights, as applied to the States through the Fourteenth Amendment, were not violated by Florida's decision to provide a six-man rather than a twelve-man jury. The judgment of the Florida District Court of Appeals is Affirmed.[7]

Based on this decision, many states have begun using six-person juries in misdemeanor cases, while some states such as Florida, Louisiana, and Utah even use them in felony cases (except in capital offenses). The importance of a six-person jury in the criminal justice system is that it promotes court efficiency and also helps implement the defendant's right to a speedy trial.

In addition to the erroneous belief that it was only proper to conduct criminal trials with a jury of 12 persons, tradition held that unanimity in the jurors' decision was required for jury trials. In the case of *Apodica v. Oregon* (1972),[8] the United States Supreme Court held that the Sixth and Fourteenth Amendments did not prohibit criminal convictions by less than unanimous jury verdicts in noncapital cases. In the *Apodica* case, the court upheld an Oregon statute which required only ten of twelve jurors to convict the defendant of assault with a deadly weapon, burglary, and grand larceny. It is not unusual to have such verdicts in civil matters, but much controversy remains regarding their use in the criminal process. Those in favor of less than unanimous verdicts argue, as was stated in *Apodica*, that unanimity does not materially contribute to the exercise of common sense judgment. On the other hand, some persons believe that it would be easier for the prosecutor to obtain a guilty verdict if the law required only a substantial majority to convict the defendant. Today, the unanimous verdict remains the rule in most states' jurisdictions and in the federal system.

### The Right to Counsel at Trial

Mention has already been made (Chapters 5, 8 and 10) of the defendant's right to counsel at numerous points in the criminal justice system. Through a series of leading United States Supreme Court decisions—*Powell v. Alabama* in 1932,[9] *Gideon v. Wainwright* in 1962,[10] and *Argersinger v. Hamlin* in 1972[11]—the right of a criminal defendant to have counsel in state trials has become a fundamental right in our criminal justice system. Today, state courts must provide counsel at trial to indigent defendants who face the possibility of incarceration.

It is interesting to note the historical development of the law regarding right to counsel, for it shows the gradual process of decision making in the Supreme Court, as well as reiterates the relationship between the Bill of Rights and the Fourteenth Amendment. The Bill of Rights protects citizens against federal encroachment, while the Fourteenth Amendment provides that no state shall deprive any person of life, liberty, or property without due process of law. A difficult constitutional question has been whether the Fourteenth Amendment incorporates the Bill of Rights and makes its provisions binding upon individual states. In *Powell v. Alabama*, for example, nine young black men were charged in an Alabama court with raping two young white women. They were tried and convicted without the benefit of counsel. The United States Supreme Court concluded that the presence of a defense attorney was so vital to a fair trial that the failure of the Alabama trial court to appoint counsel was a denial of due process of law under the Fourteenth Amendment of the Federal Constitution. In this instance, due process meant the right to counsel for defendants accused of committing a capital offense. Then, in the case of *Gideon v. Wainwright* some thirty years later, the United States Supreme Court was again faced with the question of whether the federal Constitution guarantees the right to counsel to a person accused of a crime in a state court. Clarence Gideon was charged with breaking and entering a pool room with the intent to commit a burglary, a felony under Florida law. He requested state-compensated counsel because he was indigent, and was then informed that counsel could be appointed by the state only when a defendant was charged with a capital offense. Gideon conducted his own defense, was found guilty, and was sentenced to prison. When he later appealed, the United States Supreme Court in a unanimous and historic decision stated that while the Sixth Amendment did not explicitly lay down a rule binding on the states, right to counsel was so fundamental and ethical to a fair trial that states were obligated to abide by it because of the Fourteenth Amendment's due process clause. Thus, the Sixth Amendment requirement regarding right to counsel in the federal court system was also binding upon the state criminal justice system.

The *Gideon* case made it clear that a person charged with a felony in a state court had an absolute constitutional right to counsel. But while some states applied the *Gideon* ruling to all criminal trials, others did not provide a defendant with an attorney in misdemeanor cases. Then, in 1972, the case of *Argersinger v. Hamlin* raised the question of whether the constitutional right to counsel also applied to misdemeanants. Argersinger was charged in Florida with carrying a concealed weapon—an offense punishable by imprisonment up to six months, a $1,000 fine, or both. Because he was indigent and could not afford a private attorney, he was tried and convicted without being represented by counsel. On appeal, the United States Supreme Court, in a momentous decision, held that no person could be imprisoned for any offense—whether classified as a petty offense, a misdemeanor, or a felony—unless offered representation by counsel at trial. The decision extended this right to virtually all defendants in state criminal prosecutions.

The majority opinions in both the *Gideon* and the *Argersinger* cases illustrate how the court reached its conclusion on the right of a defendant to have counsel at trial. In *Gideon,* the court stated:

The Sixth Amendment provides, "In all criminal prosecutions, the accused shall enjoy the right . . . to have the Assistance of Counsel for his defense." We have construed this to mean that in federal courts counsel must be provided for defendants unable to employ counsel unless the right is competently and intelligently waived. *Betts v. Brady* argued that this right is extended to indigent defendants in state courts by the Fourteenth Amendment. In response the Court stated that, while the Sixth Amendment laid down "no rule for the conduct of the States, the question recurs whether the constraint laid by the Amendment upon the national courts expresses a rule so fundamental and essential to a fair trial, and so, to due process of law, that it is made obligatory upon the States by the Fourteenth Amendment." 316. In order to decide whether the Sixth Amendment's guarantee of counsel is of this fundamental nature, the Court in *Betts* set out and considered "(r)elevant data on the subject . . . afforded by constitutional and statutory provisions subsisting in the colonies and the States prior to the inclusion of the Bill of Rights in the national Constitution, and in the constitutional legislative, and judicial history of the States to the present date 316 U.S., at 465. On the basis of this historical data the Court concluded that "appointment of counsel is not a fundamental right, essential to a fair trial." 316 U.S., at 471. It was for this reason the *Betts* Court refused to accept the contention that the Sixth Amendment's guarantee of counsel for indigent federal defendants was extended to or, in the words of that Court "made obligatory upon the States by the Fourteenth Amendment." Plainly, had the Court concluded that appointment of counsel for an indigent criminal defendant was "a fundamental right, essential to a fair trial," it would have held that the Fourteenth Amendment requires appointment of counsel in a state court, just as the Sixth Amendment requires in a federal court.

We accept *Betts v. Brady's* assumption, based as it was on our prior cases, that a provision of the Bill of Rights which is "fundamental and essential to a fair trial" is made obligatory upon the States by the Fourteenth Amendment. We think the Court in *Betts* was wrong, however, in concluding that the Sixth Amendment's guarantee of counsel is not one of these fundamental rights. Ten years before *Betts v. Brady,* this Court, after full consideration of all the historical data examined in *Betts,* had unequivocally declared that "the right to the aid of counsel is of this fundamental character." *Powell v. Alabama* 287, U.S. 45, 68 (1932). While the Court at the close of its *Powell* opinion did by its language, as this Court frequently does, limit its holding to the particular facts and circumstances of that case, its conclusions about the fundamental nature of the right to counsel are unmistakable. Several years later, in 1936, the Court reemphasized what it had said about the fundamental nature of the right to counsel in this language:

*We concluded that certain fundamental rights, safeguarded by the first eight amendments against federal action, were also safeguarded against state action by the due process of law clause of the Fourteenth Amendment, and among them the funda-*

*mental right of the accused to the aid of counsel in a criminal prosecution.* [Grosjean v. American Press Co., *297 U.S. 233, 243–244 (1936)*].

And again in 1938 this court said:

*The assistance of counsel is one of the safeguards of the Sixth Amendment deemed necessary to insure fundamental human rights of life and liberty . . . The Sixth Amendment stands as a constant admonition that if the constitutional safeguards it provides be lost, justice will not "still be done."* [Johnson v. Zerbst, *304 U.S. 458, 462 (1938). To the same effect, see* Avery v. Alabama, *308 U.S. 444 (1940), and* Smith v. O'Grady, *312 U.S. 329 (1941)*].

In light of these and many other prior decisions of this Court, it is not surprising that the *Betts* Court, when faced with the contention that "one charged with crime, who is unable to obtain counsel, must be furnished counsel by the State," conceded that "(e)xpressions in the opinions of this court lend color to the argument. . . ." 316 U.S., at 461-463. The fact is that in deciding as it did—that "appointment of counsel is not a fundamental right, essential to a fair trial"—the Court in *Betts v. Brady* made an abrupt break with its own well-considered precedents. In returning to these old precedents, sounder we believe than the new, we but restore constitutional principles established to achieve a fair system of justice. Not only these precedents but also reason and reflection require us to recognize that in our adversary system of criminal justice, any person haled into court, who is too poor to hire a lawyer, cannot be assured a fair trial unless counsel is provided for him. This seems to us to be an obvious truth. Governments, both state and federal, quite properly spend vast sums of money to establish machinery to try defendants accused of crime. Lawyers to prosecute are everywhere deemed essential to protect the public's interest in an orderly society. Similarly, there are few defendants charged with crime, few indeed, who fail to hire the best lawyers thay can get to prepare and present their defenses. That government hires lawyers to prosecute and defendants who have the money hire lawyers to defend are the strongest indications of the widespread belief that lawyers in criminal courts are necessities, not luxuries. The right of one charged with crime to counsel may not be deemed fundamental and essential to fair trials in some countries, but it is in ours. From the very beginning, our state and national constitutions and laws have laid great emphasis on procedural and substantive safeguards designed to assure fair trials before impartial tribunals in which every defendant stands equal before the law. This noble ideal cannot be realized if the poor man charged with crime has to face his accusers without a lawyer to assist him . . .

The Court in *Betts v. Brady* departed from the sound wisdom upon which the Court's holding in *Powell v. Alabama* rested. Florida, supported by two other States, has asked that *Betts v. Brady* be left intact. Twenty-two states, as friends of the Court, argue that Betts was "an anachronism when handed down" and that it should now be overruled. We agree.

The judgment is reversed and the cause is remanded to the Supreme Court of Florida for further action not inconsistent with this opinion.

Reversed.[12]

In *Argersinger,* where the emphasis was on the misdemeanant offender, the Court stated:

The assistance of counsel is often a requisite to the very existence of a fair trial
. . .

In Gideon v. Wainwright, supra (overruling Betts v. Brady, 316 U.S. 455), we dealt with a felony trial. But we did not so limit the need of the accused for a lawyer
. . .

Both *Powell* and *Gideon* involved felonies. But their rationale has relevance to any criminal trial, where an accused is deprived of his liberty. *Powell* and *Gideon* suggest that there are certain fundamental rights applicable to all such criminal prosecutions, even those, such as In re Oliver, supra, where the penalty is 60 days' imprisonment . . .

The requirement of counsel may well be necessary for a fair trial even in a petty offense prosecution. We are by no means convinced that legal and constitutional questions involved in a case that actually leads to imprisonment even for a brief period are any less complex than when a person can be sent off for six months or more . . .

Beyond the problem of trials and appeals is that of the guilty plea, a problem which looms large in misdemeanor as well as in felony cases. Counsel is needed so that the accused may know precisely what he is doing, so that he is fully aware of the prospect of going to jail or prison, and so that he is treated fairly by the prosecution.

In addition, the volume of misdemeanor cases, far greater in number than felony prosecutions, may create an obsession for speedy dispositions, regardless of the fairness of the result. The Report by the President's Commission on Law Enforcement and Administration of Justice, The Challenge of Crime in a Free Society 128 (1967), states:

*For example, until legislation last year increased the number of judges, the District of Columbia Court of General Sessions had four judges to process the preliminary stages of more than 1,500 felony cases, 7,500 serious misdemeanor cases, and 38,000 petty offenses and an equal number of traffic offenses per year. An inevitable consequence of volume that large is the almost total preoccupation in such a court with the movement of cases. The calendar is long, speed often is substituted for care, the casually arranged out-of-court compromise too often is substituted for adjudication. Inadequate attention tends to be given to the individual defendant, whether in protecting his rights, sifting the facts at trial, deciding the social risk he presents, or determining how to deal with him after conviction. The frequent result is futility and failure. As Dean Edward Barrett recently observed:*

*Wherever the visitor looks at the system, he finds great numbers of defendants being processed by harassed and overworked officials. Police have more cases than they can investigate. Prosecutors walk into courtrooms to try simple cases as they take their initial looks at the files. Defense lawyers appear having had no more than time for hasty conversations with their clients. Judges face long calendars with the certain knowledge that their calendars tomorrow and the next day will be, if anything, longer, and so there is no choice but to dispose of the cases. Suddenly it becomes clear that for most defendants in the criminal process, there is scant regard for them as individuals. They are numbers on dockets, faceless ones to be processed and sent on their way. The gap between the theory and the reality is enormous.*

*Very little such observation of the administration of criminal justice in operation is required to reach the conclusion that it suffers from basic ills.*

That picture is seen in almost every report. "The misdemeanor trial is characterized by insufficient and frequently irresponsible preparation on the part of the defense, the prosecution, and the court. Everything is rush, rush." Hellerstein, The Importance of the Misdemeanor Case on Trial and Appeal, 28 The Legal Aid Brief Case 151, 152 (1970).

There is evidence of the prejudice which results to misdemeanor defendants from this "assembly-line justice." One study concluded that "(m)isdemeanants represented by attorneys are five times as likely to emerge from police courts with all charges dismissed as are defendants who face similar charges without counsel." American Civil Liberties Union, Legal Counsel for Misdemeanants, Preliminary Report 1 (1970).

We must conclude, therefore, that the problems associated with misdemeanor and petty offenses often require the presence of counsel to insure the accused a fair trial. MR. JUSTICE POWELL suggests that these problems are raised even in situations where there is no prospect of imprisonment. Post at 48. We need not consider the requirements of the Sixth Amendment as regards the right to counsel where loss of liberty is not involved, however, for here petitioner was in fact sentenced to jail. And, as we said in Baldwin v. New York, 399 U.S. at 73, "the prospect of imprisonment for however short a time will seldom be viewed by the accused as a trivial or petty matter and may well result in quite serious repercussions affecting his career and his reputation."

We hold, therefore, that absent a knowing and intelligent waiver, no person may be imprisoned for any offense, whether classified as petty, misdemeanor, or felony, unless he was represented by counsel at his trial.[13]

## The Right to Self-Representation

Another important question regarding the right to counsel is whether criminal defendants are guaranteed the right to represent themselves; that is, to act as their own lawyers. Prior to the United States Supreme Court case of *Faretta v. California* in 1975,[14] a defendant in most state courts and in the federal system claimed the right to proceed *pro se*, or for himself, by reason of federal and state statutes and on state constitutional grounds. This permitted the defendant to choose between hiring counsel or conducting his own defense. Whether a constitutional right to represent oneself in a criminal prosecution existed remained an open question until the *Faretta* decision.

The defendant, Anthony Faretta, was charged with grand theft in Los Angeles County, California. Before the date of his trial, he requested that he be permitted to represent himself. The judge told Faretta that he believed that this would be a mistake, but accepted his waiver of counsel. The judge then held a hearing to inquire into Faretta's ability to conduct his own defense and subsequently ruled that Faretta had not made an intelligent and knowing waiver of his right to the assistance of counsel. As a result, the judge appointed a public defender to represent Faretta, who was brought to trial, found guilty, and sentenced to prison. He appealed, claiming that he had a constitutional right to self-representation.

Upon review, the United States Supreme Court recognized Faretta's pro se right on a constitutional basis, while making it conditional upon a showing that the defendant could competently, knowingly, and intelligently waive his right to counsel. The court's decision was based on the belief that the right of self-representation finds support in the structure of the Sixth Amendment, as well as in the English and Colonial jurisprudence from which the Amendment emerged.[15] Thus, in forcing Faretta to accept counsel against his will, the California trial court deprived him of his constitutional right to conduct his own defense.

It is important to recognize that the *Faretta* case dealt only with the constitutional right to self-representation. It did not provide guidelines for administering the right during the criminal process. In his dissent, Justice Harry Blackmun identified problems he believed would result from this decision:

In conclusion, I note briefly the procedural problems that, I suspect, today's decision will visit upon trial courts in the future. Although the Court indicates that a pro se defendant necessarily waives any claim he might otherwise make of ineffective assistance of counsel, the opinion leaves open a host of other procedural questions. Must every defendant be advised of his right to proceed pro se? If so, when must that notice be given? Since the right to assistance of counsel and the right to self-representation are mutually exclusive, how is the waiver of each right to be measured? If a defendant has elected to exercise his right to proceed pro se, does he still have a constitutional right to assistance of standby counsel? How soon in the criminal proceeding must a defendant decide between proceeding by counsel or pro se? Must he be allowed to switch in midtrial? May a violation of the right to self-representation ever be harmless error? Must the trial court treat the pro se defendant differently than it would professional counsel? I assume that many of these questions will be answered with finality in due course. Many of them, however, such as the standards of waiver and the treatment of the pro se defendant, will haunt the trial of every defendant who elects to exercise his right to self-representation. The procedural problems spawned by an absolute right to self-representation will far outweigh whatever tactical advantage the defendant may feel he has gained by electing to represent himself. If there is any truth to the old proverb that "one who is his own lawyer has a fool for a client," the Court by its opinion today now bestows a constitutional right on one to make a fool of himself.[16]

Today, a defendant in a criminal trial is able to waive the right to the assistance of counsel. Generally, however, the courts have encouraged defendants to accept counsel so that criminal trials may proceed in an orderly and fair manner. Where defendants ask to be permitted to represent themselves and are found competent to do so, the court normally approves their requests. The defendants in these cases are almost always cautioned by the court against self-representation. When pro se defendant's actions are disorderly and disruptive, the court can terminate their right to represent themselves.

Joint representation by counsel and defendant, in which the attorney would be retained on a standby basis, has been suggested as an alternative to the exclusive use of either representation by counsel or self-representation.[17] However, under current federal and state law, the defendant who has waived the right to counsel and is proceeding with the trial pro se is not entitled to standby counsel.

## The Right to Speedy Trial

The requirement of the right to counsel at trial in virtually all criminal cases often causes delays in the formal processing of defendants through the court system. Counsel usually seeks to safeguard the interests of the accused, and in so doing may employ a variety of legal devices—pre-trial motions, plea negotiations, trial procedures, and appeals—which require time and extend the decision-making period in a particular case. The involvement of counsel, along with inefficiencies in the court process—such as the frequent granting of continuances, poor scheduling procedures, and the abuse of time by court personnel—have made the problem of delay in criminal cases a serious practical and constitutional issue. As the American Bar Association's *Standards Relating to Speedy Trial* state, "congestion in the trial courts of this country, particularly in urban centers, is currently one of the major problems of judicial administration."[18]

The Sixth Amendment to the United States Constitution guarantees a criminal defendant the right to a speedy trial in federal prosecutions. This right has been made applicable to the states by the case of *Klopfer v. North Carolina* (1967).[19] In this case, the defendant Klopfer was charged with criminal trespass. His original trial ended in a mistrial, and the defendant sought to determine if and when the government intended to retry him. The prosecutor asked the court to take a "nolle prosequi with leave," a legal device discharging the defendant but allowing the government to prosecute him in the future. The United States Supreme Court held that the effort by the government to indefinitely postpone Klopfer's trial without reason denied him the right to a speedy trial guaranteed by the Sixth and Fourteenth Amendments.

In *Klopfer*, the United States Supreme Court emphasized the importance of the speedy trial in the criminal process by stating that this right is "as fundamental as any of the rights secured by the Sixth Amendment."[20] Its primary purposes are:

1. to improve the credibility of the trial by seeking to have witnesses available for testimony as early as possible;

2. to reduce the anxiety for the defendant in awaiting trial, as well as avoid pre-trial detention;

3. to avoid extensive pre-trial publicity and questionable conduct of public officials which would influence the defendant's right to a fair trial; and

4. to avoid any delay that can affect the defendant's ability to defend himself.

What is meant by the term speedy trial has been the subject of much litigation. First of all, the speedy trial guarantee is not initiated when the defendant is first accused of a crime. In *United States v. Marion*,[21] the Supreme Court held that the speedy trial issue only takes effect upon "either a formal indictment or information or else when the actual restraints (are) imposed by arrest and holding to answer a criminal charge."[22] In other words, the time period which determines whether the defendant received a speedy trial begins only after the defendant has been arrested or when formal charges have been made. There are, for example, no time provisions in the speedy trial guarantee covering the period during which the police must discover, investigate, or apprehend persons accused of a crime. Law enforcement officials are therefore not required to curtail criminal investigations even though they may acquire sufficient evidence to bring charges against the accused.

A second question regarding speedy trial is one of how to determine whether a delay is in violation of the constitutional requirements of the Sixth Amendment. In *Barker v. Wingo*,[23] the Supreme Court identified certain factors which are to be considered when determining if the speedy trial requirements have been complied with. These are (1) the length of the delay, (2) the reason for the delay, (3) the defendant's claim of the right to a speedy trial, and (4) prejudice toward the defendant. In *Barker*, the defendant's trial was delayed for over five years after his arrest while the government sought numerous continuances. When Willie Barker was eventually brought to trial, he was convicted and given a life sentence. The defendant did not ask for a speedy trial and did not assert that his right to a speedy trial had been violated until three years after his arrest. Based on an evaluation of the above factors in relation to his case, the Court held that Barker was not deprived of his due process right to a speedy trial. *Barker* is a significant case because it constitutionally rejects the method of measuring a speedy trial by (1) *the fixed time period rule* or (2) *the demand waiver rule*. The fixed time period rule requires that a defendant be offered a trial within a specific period of time, while the demand waiver rule restricts consideration of the issue to those cases in which the defendant has demanded a speedy trial. Instead, the Supreme Court took the approach that the speedy trial right can be determined by a test balancing the actions of the government and the accused on a case-by-case basis.

Because the numbers of persons accused of crimes continues to increase while the numbers of courtrooms and judges are limited, the government has been forced to deal with the problem of how to meet the constitutional requirement of a speedy trial. In 1967, the President's Commission on Law Enforcement and Administration of Justice suggested that nine months would be a reasonable period of time in which to litigate the typical criminal felony case through appeal. The process from arrest

FIGURE 12.1
The Litigated Case: From Arrest To Trial

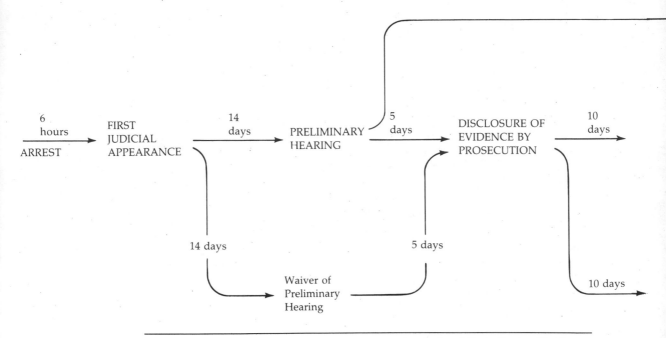

Source: National Advisory Commission on Criminal Justice Standards and Goals. Courts. Washington, D.C.: U.S. Government Printing Office, 1973, pp. xx–xxi.

through trial would involve four months, and the decision of an appeals court an additional five months.[24] Then in 1973, the National Advisory Commission on Criminal Justice Standards and Goals recommended that the period from the arrest of the defendant in a felony prosecution to the beginning of the trial generally should not be longer than 60 days, and that the period from arrest to trial in a misdemeanor prosecution should be 30 days or less.[25] Figure 12.1 summarizes the time frame suggested by the National Commission for the prompt processing of criminal cases.

Today, most states and the federal government have statutes fixing the period of time during which an accused must be brought to trial. These insure that a person's trial cannot be unduly delayed, nor can the suspect be held in custody indefinitely. The federal Congress enacted the Speedy Trial Act of 1974,[26] to guarantee the accused the right to speedy trial by establishing the following time limits: (1) an information or indictment charging a person with a crime must be filed within 30 days from the time of arrest; (2) the arraignment must be held within 10 days from the time of the information or indictment; and (3) the trial must be held within 60 days after the arraignment. This means that the accused must be brought to trial in the federal system within 100 days. Other special provisions of the Speedy Trial Act include the gradual phasing in of time standards, the use of fines against defense counsels for causing delays, and the allocation

PREPARATION FOR TRIAL

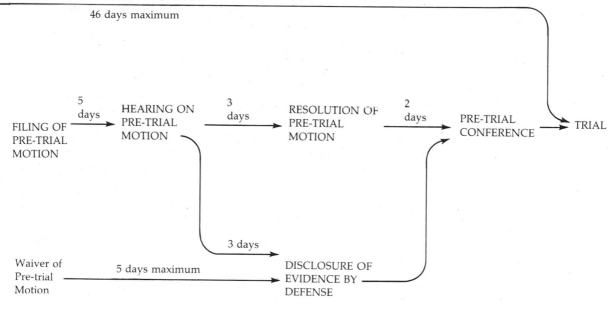

46 days maximum

FILING OF PRE-TRIAL MOTION → 5 days → HEARING ON PRE-TRIAL MOTION → 3 days → RESOLUTION OF PRE-TRIAL MOTION → 2 days → PRE-TRIAL CONFERENCE → TRIAL

3 days

Waiver of Pre-trial Motion ——— 5 days maximum ——→ DISCLOSURE OF EVIDENCE BY DEFENSE

of funds with which to plan speedy trial programs in the federal judicial districts.

In addition, many jurisdictions give trial preference to criminal matters and to cases where the defendant is in custody. This practice is one of the major recommendations of the American Bar Association's *Standards Relating to Speedy Trials:*

Priorities in scheduling criminal cases. To effectuate the right of the accused to a speedy trial and the interest of the public in prompt disposition of criminal cases, insofar as is practicable: (a) the trial of criminal cases should be given preference over civil cases; and (b) the trial of defendants in custody and defendants whose pretrial liberty is reasonably believed to present unusual risks should be given preference over other criminal cases.[27]

Although entitled to a speedy trial, the accused can waive this right either by pleading guilty or by failing to demand a prompt trial. However, if the accused makes a claim under the Sixth Amendment and it is upheld, the consequences of denying a speedy trial may involve the complete dismissal of the charges against the defendant. Although this might seem extreme, the United States Supreme Court in *Strunk v. United States,* (1973)[28] held that the restraint on the defendant's liberty, as well as his uncertainty and anxiety over his guilt or innocence, made the dismissal of the charges appropriate.

The application section of this chapter describes the one day-one trial jury system, which is another method of increasing the defendant's opportunity for a speedy trial.

THE TRIAL
PROCESS

The trial of a criminal case is a formal process conducted in a specific and orderly fashion in accordance with rules of criminal law, procedure, and evidence. Unlike what transpires in popular television programs involving lawyers, where witnesses are often asked leading and prejudicial questions, and where judges go far beyond their supervisory role, the modern criminal trial is a complicated and often time-consuming technical affair. It is a structured adversary proceeding where both the prosecution and defense follow specific procedures and argue the merits of their cases before the judge and jury. Each side seeks to present is case in the most favorable light. Where possible, the prosecutor and the defense attorney will object to evidence they consider damaging to their individual points of view. The prosecutor will use direct testimony, physical evidence, and a confession, if available, to convince the jury that the accused is guilty beyond a reasonable doubt. On the other hand, the defense attorney will rebut the government's case with his or her own evidence, make certain that the rights of the criminal defendant under the federal and state constitutions are considered during all phases of the trial, and determine whether an appeal is appropriate if the client is found guilty. From the beginning of the process to its completion, the judge promotes an orderly and fair administration of the criminal trial.

While each jurisdiction in the United States differs in its trial procedures, they all conduct criminal trials in a generally similar fashion. The basic steps of the criminal trial proceed in the following established order:

### Jury Selection
Jurors are selected randomly in both civil and criminal cases from tax assessment or voter registration lists within each court's jurisdiction. The initial list of persons chosen, which is called a *venire,* or jury array, provides the state with a group of potentially capable citizens able to serve on a jury. Many states, by rule of law, review the venire to eliminate unqualified persons and to exempt those who by reason of their professions are not allowed to be jurors; this latter group may include (but is not limited to) physicians, the clergy, doctors, and government officials. The actual jury selection process begins with those remaining on the list.

The court clerk, who handles the administrative affairs of the trial—including the processing of the complaint, evidence, and other documents—randomly selects enough names (sometimes from a box) to fill the required number of places on the jury. In most cases, the jury in a criminal trial consists of 12 persons, with 2 alternate jurors standing by to serve should one of the regular jurors be unable to complete the trial. Once the prospective jurors are chosen, the process of *voir dire* is begun, in which all persons selected are questioned by both the prosecutor and the defense to determine their appropriateness to sit on the trial. They are examined under oath by the government, the defense, and sometimes the judge about their backgrounds, occupations, residences, and possible knowledge or interest in the case. A juror who acknowledges any bias for or prejudice against the defendant—if that person is a friend or relative, for example, or has already formed an opinion about the case—is removed for "cause" and replaced with another. Thus, any prospective juror who declares the inability to be impartial and render a verdict solely on the evidence to be presented at the trial may be removed by attorneys for either the prosecution or defense. Because normally no limit is placed on the number of challenges for cause that can be exercised, it often takes considerable time to select a jury for controversial and highly publicized criminal cases.

In addition to challenges for cause, both the prosecution and the defense are allowed peremptory challenges, which allow the attorneys to excuse jurors for no particular reason or for reasons that remain undisclosed. For example, a prosecutor might not want a bartender as a juror in a drunken driving case, believing that a person with that occupation would be sympathetic to the accused. Or the defense attorney might excuse a prospective male juror because the attorney prefers to have a predominantly female jury for his client. The number of peremptory challenges permitted is limited by state statute and often varies by case and jurisdiction.

Recently, the peremptory challenge has been criticized by legal experts who question the fairness and propriety with which it has been employed.[29] Generally, the courts have left the challenge immune from judicial review while applying the nonintervention doctrine dictated by the U.S. Supreme Court case of *Swain v. Alabama.*[30] In *Swain*, the Court upheld the use of peremptory challenges in isolated cases to exclude jurors by reason of racial or other group affiliations. A recent empirical study by Hayden, Senna and Siegel regarding prosecutorial discretion in peremptory challenges found that the prosecutor may have too much power in controlling jury composition.[31] Consequently, the challenge can be used to exclude jurors by reason of economics, ethnic, or sexual affiliation.

The Sixth Amendment to the United States Constitution provides for the right to a speedy and public trial by an impartial jury. The United States Supreme Court has sought to insure compliance with this constitutional mandate of impartiality by recent decisions eliminating racial discrimination in jury selection. For instance, in *Ham v. South Carolina* in 1973,[32] the court held that the defense counsel of a black civil rights leader was entitled to question each juror on the issue of racial prejudice. And in *Taylor v. Louisiana* in 1975,[33] the Court overturned the conviction of a man by an all-male jury because a Louisiana statute allowed women but not men to exempt themselves from jury duty. These and other similar decisions have had the effect of providing safeguards against jury bias.

### Opening Statements

Once the jury has been selected and the criminal complaint has been read to the jurors by the court clerk, the prosecutor and the defense attorney may each make an opening statement about the case to the jury. The purpose of the prosecutor's statement is to introduce the judge and the jury to the particular criminal charges, to outline the facts, and to describe how the government will prove the defendant guilty beyond a reasonable doubt. The defense attorney reviews the case and indicates how the defense intends to show that the accused is innocent of the charge.

The opening statement gives the jury a concise overview of the evidence that is to follow. In the opening statement neither attorney is allowed to make prejudicial remarks or inflammatory statements or mention irrelevant facts. Both are free, however, to identify what they will eventually prove by way of evidence, which includes witnesses, physical evidence, and the use of expert testimony. As a general rule, the opening statements used in jury trials are important because they provide the finders of fact (the jury) with an initial summary of the case. They are infrequently used and less effective in bench trials, however, where juries are not employed. Most lower court judges have handled hundreds of similar cases and do not need the benefit of an opening statement.

An opening statement by a prosecutor in a case where the accused has been charged with the crime of driving under the influence of intoxicating liquor could be as follows:

"Good Morning, Mr. Foreman, ladies and gentlemen of the jury. The prosecution will offer evidence to show that on the twenty-fourth day of June, 1976, Mr. John Jones was operating a motor vehicle on a public way, Lyndale Avenue, in Minneapolis, Minnesota. When operating his motor vehicle at about 7 p.m., he was observed by Officer Smith of the Minneapolis Police Department, who was parked at the curb in a cruiser on Franklin Avenue. Officer Smith will testify that he pulled in behind Mr. Jones and observed his manner of operation, and that his operation was erratic. Mr. Jones was observed to sway from side to side as he proceeded down Lyndale Avenue. This Officer of the Minneapolis police gave chase and overtook the vehicle in question. After some scraping of fenders between the two motor vehicles, the officer succeeded in getting the car to the side of the road. He will then testify that he opened the door and Mr. Jones fell out on the street. He will testify that as he watched Mr. Jones, and with his fellow officer helped and assisted him to his feet, he had to lean Mr. Jones over the hood of the car. Otherwise, in his opinion, Mr. Jones would have fallen. He will testify that Mr. Jones had a strong odor of alcohol on his breath and slurred his words, and was completely unintelligible, and kept mumbling about onions and martinis and things of this nature. And that thereafter the officer formed an opinion that Mr. Jones was drunk and was operating the motor vehicle while under the influence of intoxicating liquor. The officer took Mr. Jones to the Bryant police station, where he was booked. Sergeant O'Brien, who booked the man, will testify how in the booking process Mr. Jones fell over a stool in the main office of the police station and had to be assisted to a cell, and how within five minutes after his arrival in that cell he fell into a sound and undisturbed sleep. And he will further testify that in his opinion Mr. Jones was drunk and under the influence of intoxicating liquor. The government will present this and all other evidence necessary to prove beyond a reasonable doubt that the defendant committed the crime of operating a motor vehicle while under the influence of intoxicating liquor."

## The Presentation of the Prosecutor's Evidence

Following the opening statement, the government begins its case by presenting evidence to the court through its witnesses. Those called as witnesses—such as police officers, victims, or expert witnesses—provide testimony via direct examination, during which the prosecutor questions the witness to reveal the facts believed pertinent to the government case. Testimony involves what the witness actually saw, heard, or touched, and does not include opinions. However, a witness's opinion can be given in certain situations, such as when describing the motion of a vehicle or indicating whether a defendant appeared to act intoxicated or insane. Witnesses may also qualify because of their professions as experts on a particular subject relevant to the case; for example, a psychiatrist may testify as to a defendant's mental capacity at the time of the crime.

After the prosecutor finishes questioning a witness, the defense cross-examines the same witness by asking questions in an attempt to clarify the defendant's role in the crime. If desired, the prosecutor may seek a redirect examination after the defense attorney has completed cross-examination; this allows the prosecutor to ask additional questions about information brought out during cross-examination. Finally, the defense attorney may then question or cross-examine the witness once again. All witnesses for the trial will be sworn in and questioned in the same basic manner.

A direct examination by the prosecutor in a case involving drunken driving could be as follows:

Question (Prosecutor): What is your name, please?

Answer (Witness): Frank Smith.

Q: Your residence address?

A: 2012 Aldrich Avenue South.

Q: Your occupation, Mr. Smith?

A: I am a police officer for the city of Minneapolis.

Q: How long have you been so employed?

A: I've been employed there for ten years.

Q: What is your rank?

A: My rank is Patrol Officer.

Q: All right, officer, directing your attention to the night of June 24, 1976, were you on duty for the Minneapolis police?

A: Yes, I was.

Q: Specifically, what was your area of responsibility that night?

A: I was in charge of a section of southwest Minneapolis, and I was on patrol in a cruiser with Patrol Officer Brown.

Q: And directing your attention to approximately 7 pm on the night of June 24, where were you, officer?

A: I was on Franklin Avenue, in the cruiser.

Q: Officer, will you tell us how long you've patrolled this road?

A: I've been patrolling it for five years at night, and prior to that I patrolled it five years during the day.

Q: During the course of your patrolling, have you had occasion to observe the street?

A: Yes, I have.

Q: Would you describe it?

A: It's paved, there are curbs, there are sidewalks, and there are street utility poles with street lights.

Q: Are these lights lit at night?

A: Yes, they are.

Q: Do you know whether or not the city of Minneapolis maintains this road?

A: Yes, it does.

Q: Have you had occasion to observe other motor vehicles on Lyndale Avenue?

A: Yes.

Q: Will you tell us on a typical evening how many motor vehicles you would estimate you observe using Lyndale Avenue?

A: Oh, I've probably observed a good 400–500 motor vehicles every night I've ever patrolled that street.

Q: Now, officer, getting back to the evening of June 24, around 7 pm, would you tell us specifically where you were on Lyndale Avenue?

A: I was parked on the north side of Franklin Avenue, right where it intersects Lyndale.

Q: Did you have occasion to come into contact with the defendant?

A: Yes, I did.

Q: Could you describe specifically how and under what conditions?

A: Well, as we were observing the street, I saw a motor vehicle approaching us on the other side of the street at a high rate of speed.

Q: Can you give us an estimate, Officer, as to the speed of that motor vehicle?

A: At that particular point I'd say he was going 50–60 miles per hour.

Q: If you know, Officer, what is the posted speed limit on Lyndale Avenue in Minneapolis?

A: The posted speed limit is 35 miles per hour.

Q: What occurred next?

A: The operator of the cruiser at my instruction turned the vehicle and we proceeded to follow the defendant's motor vehicle.

Q: And would you describe this motor vehicle to us?

A: Well, it was a 1976 Ford, color gray, Minnesota license number 146 YN.

Q: And did you observe any occupants of that car?

A: Yes, I observed a male subject and a female subject, the male subject driving and the female sitting beside him in the front seat.

Q: What happened next?

A: We gave chase, turned on our siren, put on our flashing lights and came alongside after approximately one quarter of a mile.

Q: How fast did your cruiser travel, if you know, before pulling alongside the motor vehicle?

A: We attained a speed of 70 miles per hour as we pulled alongside the Ford motor vehicle.

Q: What happened next?

A: We beckoned the car over, the car swerved, swerved a couple of more times, and finally came to a stop approximately one quarter of a mile from the place where we had originally beckoned it over.

Q: Now thinking back a little bit, Officer, would you tell us more specifically what you observed about the operation of the motor vehicle as you gave chase?

A: Yes, I observed the car to be swerving from one side of the road to the other, and going from the extreme left to the extreme right. In two instances I observed the motor vehicle hit upon and strike against the curb as it went from one side of the road to the other.

Q: All right, what happened next?

A: I got out of the motor vehicle and went over to the driver's side. I opened the door and I observed a male subject slumped over the wheel.

Q: What did you do?

A: I asked him to get out of the car.

Q: What happened?

A: The man fell out of the car.

Q: Did you have occasion to help the man up?

A: Yes. The man rose to his feet with my assistance, we leaned him up against the side of the car, and I proceeded to go to the other side to talk to the female occupant of the car.

Q: What observations, if any, did you make of the male driver at this point?

A: Well, I observed a strong odor of alcohol on his breath. I observed that he could not stand without assistance. I observed that his speech was extremely slurred, and that his eyes were glassy.

Q: And then what happened next?

A: I took a close look at the female occupant.

Q: And what did you observe about the female occupant?

A: I observed that she staggered when she attempted to walk, that she also had a strong odor of alcohol, and that she again had a very glassy look about her eyes.

Q: And at this particular point did you have any conversation with the female occupant of the car?

A: Yes, I did.

Q: And what was that conversation?

A: I asked her what her name was, where she lived, and who was the operator of the motor vehicle.

Q: Did she respond?

A: She started to say something and then she passed out.

Q: All right, what did you do next?

A: I went back to the other side of the car and asked the driver his name and address.

Q: What did he way?

A: Nothing. He passed out.

Q: What happened then?

A: We called for the paddy-wagon. When it arrived, we assisted the two individuals into the wagon and took them to the station.

Q: Now, officer, after making these observations, did you form an opinion as to the sobriety of the operator of that car?

A: Yes, I did.

Q: What is your opinion?

A: In my opinion he was drunk.

Q: Is that man in the courtroom?

A: Yes, he's the defendant in the action, Mr. Jones.

Q: And I ask further, officer, did you form an opinion as to sobriety of the woman passenger of that vehicle?

A: Yes, I did.

Q: And what was that opinion?

A: In my opinion, the woman passenger, Miss Malloy, was intoxicated.

Q: And is she in the courtroom?

A: Yes, she's the codefendant sitting right next to the gentleman in the defendants chair.

Q: What happened next, Officer?

A: The individuals were taken to the station, they were revived with coffee, they were booked, their articles of personal property were elicited from them, and we proceeded to lock them up.

Q: Officer, relating back to the scene of the crime, did you observe anything about the front seat and the ground adjacent to the motor vehicle of the defendant?

A: Well, when I opened the door, I noticed that a bottle of Canadian whiskey fell out the seat beside the driver, and that a paper cup was sitting on the dashboard of the motor vehicle.

Q: Now, officer, I show you this bottle of whiskey. And I ask you whether or not you can identify it.

A: Yes, I can.

Q: I ask you, officer, is this the same bottle that you saw fall out of the defendant's car during the night in question?

A: Yes, it is.

Q: Your Honor, the prosecution offers this bottle of whiskey into evidence.

If the court pleases, there are no further questions of this witness for the time being. The defense may cross examine. Thank you, Your Honor.

### The Motion for Directed Verdict

Once the prosecution has provided all of the government's evidence against a defendant, it will then inform the court that it rests the people's case. It is common for the defense attorney at this point to enter a motion for a directed verdict. This is a procedural device by means of which the defense attorney asks the judge to order the jury to return a verdict of not guilty. The judge must rule on the motion and will either sustain it or overrule it, depending upon whether he or she believes that the prosecution proved all the elements of the alleged crime. In essence, the defense attorney argues in the directed verdict that the prosecutor's case against the defendant is insufficient to prove guilty beyond a reasonable doubt. If the motion is sustained, the trial is terminated. If it is rejected by the court, the case continues with the defense portion of the trial.

Basically, the directed verdict is a motion to the court for a finding of not guilty on the offense charged in the indictment or complaint, when the evidence is insufficient for a conviction. In some cases, such as in jury trials, the judge may reserve decision on the motion, submit the case to the jury, and consider a decision on the motion before a jury verdict or order a verdict of guilty.

### The Presentation of Evidence by the Defense Attorney

The defense attorney has the option of presenting many, some, or no witnesses on behalf of the defendant. In addition, the defense attorney must decide if the client should take the stand and testify in his behalf.

In a criminal trial, the defendant is protected by the Fifth Amendment right to be free from self-incrimination, which means that a person cannot be forced by the State to testify against himself in a criminal trial. However, the defendant who chooses to voluntarily tell his side of the story can be subject to cross-examination by the prosecutor.

After the defense concludes its case, the government may then present rebuttal evidence. This normally involves bringing evidence forward that was not used when the prosecution initially presented its case. The defense may examine the rebuttal witnesses and introduce new witnesses in a process called a *surrebuttal*. After all the evidence has been presented to the court, the defense attorney may submit again a motion for a directed verdict. If the motion is denied, both the prosecution and the defense prepare to make closing arguments and the case on the evidence is ready for consideration by the jury.

### Closing Arguments

Closing arguments are used by the attorneys to review the facts and evidence of the case in a manner favorable to each of their positions. At this stage of the trial, both prosecution and defense are permitted to draw reasonable inferences and show how the facts prove or refute the defendant's guilt. Often, both attorneys have a free hand in arguing about the facts, issues, and evidence, including the applicable law. They cannot comment on matters not in evidence, however, nor on the defendant's failure to testify in a criminal case. Normally, the defense attorney will make a closing statement first, followed by the prosecutor. Either party can elect to forgo the right to make a final summation to the jury.

### The Instructions to the Jury

In a criminal trial, the judge will instruct, or *charge*, the jury on the principles of law that ought to guide and control their deciding the defendant's innocence or guilt. Included in the charge will be information about the elements of the alleged offense, the type of evidence needed to prove each element, and the burden of proof required to obtain a guilty verdict. Although the judge commonly provides the instructions, he may ask the prosecutor and the defense attorney to submit instructions for consideration; the judge will then use discretion in determining whether to use any of their instructions. The instructions given to the jury which cover the law applicable to the case are extremely important since they may serve as the basis for a subsequent criminal appeal.

### The Verdict

Once the charge is given to the jury, they retire to deliberate upon a verdict. As previously mentioned, the verdict in a criminal case—regardless of whether the trial involves a 6-person or a 12-person jury—is usually required to be unanimous. A review of the case by the jury may take hours or even days. The jurors are always sequestered during their deliberations and in certain lengthy, highly publicized cases are kept overnight in a hotel until the verdict is reached. In less sensational cases, the jurors may be allowed to go home but are often cautioned not to discuss the case with anyone. If a verdict cannot be reached, the trial may result in a hung jury, after which the prosecutor has to bring the defendant to trial again if the prosecution desires a conviction. If found not guilty, the defendant is released from the criminal process. On the other hand, if the defendant is convicted, the judge will normally order a pre-sentence investigation by the probation department preparatory to imposing a sentence. Prior to sentencing, the defense attorney will probably submit a motion for a new trial alleging that legal errors occurred in the trial proceedings. The judge may deny the motion and impose a sentence immediately, a practice quite familiar in most misdemeanor offenses. In felony cases, however, the judge will set a date for sentencing and the defendant will either be placed on bail or held in custody until that time.

### The Sentence

The imposition of the criminal sentence is normally the responsibility of the trial judge. In some jurisdictions, the jury may determine the sentence or be called upon to make recommendations involving leniency for certain offenses. Often, the sentencing decision is based upon information and recommendations given to the court by the probation officer after a pre-sentence investigation of the defendant. The sentence itself is determined by the statutory requirements for the particular crime as established by the legislature; in addition, the judge ordinarily has a great deal of discretion in reaching a sentencing decision. The different criminal sanctions available include fines, probation, imprisonment, and even commitment to a state hospital. The sentence that is actually imposed is a result of a combination of all the above factors.

### The Appeal

In most jurisdictions, direct criminal appeal to an appellate court exists as a matter of right. This means that the defendant has an automatic right to appeal a conviction based on errors that may have occurred during the trial proceedings. A substantial number of criminal appeals are the result of disputes over points of law, such as the introduction at the trial of illegal evidence detrimental to the defendant, or statements made during the trial which were prejudicial to the defendant. Through objections made at the pre-trial and trial stages of the criminal process the defense counsel will reserve specific legal issues on the record as the basis for appeal. A copy of the transcript of these proceedings will serve as the basis upon which the appellate court will review any errors that may have occurred during the lower court proceedings. Because an appeal is an expensive, time-consuming, and technical process involving a review of the lower court record, the research and drafting of briefs (legal explanations), and the presentation of oral arguments to the appellate court, the defendant has been granted the right to counsel at this stage of criminal process. In the United States Supreme Court case of *Douglass v. California* (1963),[34] the court held that the indigent defendant has a constitutional right to the assistance of counsel on a direct first appeal. In discretionary appeals where, for example, the defendant may appeal to the federal courts because of a constitutional violation of personal rights, the defendant must have private counsel or apply for permission to proceed in forma pauperis, meaning that the defendant may be granted counsel at public expense if the court believes the appeal has merit.

The right of appeal normally does not extend to the prosecution in a criminal case. In the United States, according to the American Bar Association, considerable differences among the states and the federal government exist as to the appropriate scope of prosecution appeals.[35] At one extreme are states which grant no right of appeal to the prosecution in criminal cases. On the other hand, some jurisdictions permit the prosecution to appeal in those instances which involve the unconstitutionality of a statute, or from pre-trial orders that terminate the government's case. However, the prosecutor cannot bring the defendant to trial again on the same charge after an acquittal or a conviction; this would violate the defendant's right to be free from double jeopardy under the Fifth Amendment to the United States Constitution. The purpose of the double jeopardy guarantee is to protect the defendant from a second prosecution for the same offense.

After an appeal has been fully heard, the appeals court renders an opinion on the merits of the case. If an error of law is found—such as an improper introduction of evidence, or an improper statement made by the prosecutor which was prejudicial to the defendant—the appeals court may reverse the decision of the trial court and order a new trial. If the lower court is upheld, the case is finished unless the defendant seeks a discretionary appeal to a higher state or federal court.

Although the steps in the criminal trial might seem totally mechanical and inflexible, informal procedures and subjective judgments affect how judicial decisions are made. Questions such as how the judge relates to the prosecutor and the defense attorney, the attitude of the jury toward the defendant, or the credibility and competency of certain witnesses all bring a human element to play in the trial process.

## STANDARDS OF PROOF

Proof beyond a reasonable doubt is the standard required to convict a defendant charged with a crime at the adjudicatory stage of the criminal process. This requirement dates back to our early American history and over the years has become the accepted measure of persuasion needed by the prosecutor to convince the judge or jury of the defendant's guilt. Many twentieth century United States Supreme Court decisions have reinforced the history of this standard by making "beyond a reasonable doubt a due process and constitutional requirement."[36] In *Brinegar v. United States* (1949),[37] for instance, the Supreme Court states:

[G]uilt in a criminal case must be proved beyond a reasonable doubt and by evidence confined to that which long experience in the common-law tradition, to some extent embodied in the Constitution, has crystallized into rules of evidence consistent with that standard. These rules are historically grounded rights of our system, developed to safeguard men from dubious and unjust convictions, with resulting forfeitures of life, liberty and property.[38]

And in the earlier case of *Davis v. United States* (1934) where a murder conviction was reversed because the judge instructed the jury to convict when the evidence was equally balanced regarding the sanity of the accused,[39] the Supreme Court held that the defendant is entitled to an acquittal where there is reasonable doubt of the capability in law of committing a crime. The Court further stated "that no man should be deprived of his life under the forms of law unless the jurors who try him are able, upon their consciences, to say that the evidence before them . . . is sufficient to show beyond a reasonable doubt the existence of every fact necessary to constitute the crime charged."[40]

The reasonable doubt standard is an essential ingredient of the criminal justice process. It is the prime instrument for reducing the risk of convictions based on factual errors.[41] The underlying premise of this standard is that it is better to release a guilty person than to convict someone who is innocent. Since the defendant is presumed innocent until proven guilty, this standard forces the prosecution to overcome this presumption with the highest standard of proof. Unlike the civil law, where a mere preponderance of the evidence is the standard, the criminal process requires proof beyond a reasonable doubt for each element of the offense. As was pointed out in the case of *In re Winship*,[42] where the reasonable doubt standard was applied to juvenile trials, "if the standard of proof for a criminal trial were a preponderance of the evidence rather than proof beyond a reasonable doubt, there would be a smaller risk of factual errors that result in freeing guilty persons, but a far greater risk of factual errors that result in convicting the innocent."[43]

## SUMMARY

The number of cases disposed of by trials is relatively small in comparison to the total number of cases that enter the criminal justice system. Nonetheless, the criminal trial provides the defendant with a very important option. Unlike other steps in the system, the American criminal trial allows the accused to assert the right to a day in court. The defendant may choose between a trial before a judge alone or a trial by jury. In either case, the purpose of the trial is to adjudicate the facts, ascertain the truth, and determine the guilt or innocence of the accused.

Criminal trials represent the adversary system at work. The state uses its authority to seek a conviction, and the defendant is protected by constitutional rights, particularly those under the Fifth and Sixth Amendments. When they involve serious crimes, criminal trials are complex legal affairs. Rules and procedures exist in each jurisdiction which have developed over many years to resolve legal issues.

An established order of steps is followed throughout a criminal trial, beginning with the reading of the complaint, proceeding through the introduction of evidence, and concluding with closing arguments and a verdict. Overall, the criminal trial is an established institution in the criminal justice system. It serves in a symbolic and pragmatic role for defendants who require a forum of last resort to adjudicate their differences with the state.

QUESTIONS FOR
DISCUSSION

1. Identify the steps involved in the criminal trial. Consider the pros and cons of a jury trial vs. a bench trial.

2. What are the legal rights of the defendant in the trial process? Trace the historical development of the right to counsel at the trial stage of the criminal justice system.

3. Discuss the significance of the following two United States Supreme Court decisions: *Gideon v. Wainwright* and *Argersinger v. Hamlin.*

4. The burden of proof in a criminal trial to show that the defendant is guilty beyond a reasonable doubt is on the government in our adversary system of criminal justice. Explain the meaning of this statement in terms of other legal standards of proof.

NOTES

1. National Advisory Commission on Criminal Justice Standards and Goals, *Courts* (Washington, D.C.: U.S. Government Printing Office, 1967), p. 66.

2. 391 U.S. 145, 88 S.Ct. 1444, 20 L.Ed.2d 491 (1968).

3. Ibid. at 157–158.

4. 399 U.S. 66, 90 S.Ct. 1914, 26 L.Ed.2d 437 (1970).

5. 333 U.S. 257, 68 S.Ct. 499, 92 L.Ed. 682 (1942).

6. 399 U.S. 78, 90 S.Ct. 1893, 26 L.Ed.2d 446 (1970).

7. Ibid. at 102–103.

8. 406 U.S. 404, 92 S.Ct. 1628, 32 L.Ed.2d 184 (1972).

9. 287 U.S. 45, 53 S.Ct. 55, 77 L.Ed. 158 (1932).

10. 372 U.S. 335, 83 S.Ct. 792, 9 L.Ed.2d 799 (1963).

11. 407 U.S. 25, 92 S.Ct. 2006, 32 L.Ed.2d 530 (1972).

12. Gideon v. Wainwright, 372 U.S. at 339–345.

13. Argersinger v. Hamlin, 407 U.S. at 32–37.

14. 422 U.S. 806, 95 S.Ct. 2525, 45 L.Ed.2d 562 (1975).

15. Ibid.

16. Ibid. at 592.

17. See Note, "Criminal Defendants At

the Bar of Their Own Defense—Faretta v. California," *The American Criminal Law Review* 60:335 (1975).

**18.** See American Bar Association, *Standards Relating to Speedy Trial* (New York: Institute of Judicial Administration, 1968), p. 1.

**19.** 386 U.S. 213, 87 S.Ct. 988, 18 L.Ed.2d 1 (1967).

**20.** Ibid. at 223.

**21.** 404 U.S. 307, 92 S.Ct. 455, 30 L.Ed.2d 468 (1971).

**22.** Ibid. at 321.

**23.** 407 U.S. 514, 92 S.Ct. 2182, 33 L.Ed.2d 101 (1972).

**24.** President's Commission on Law Enforcement and Administration of Justice, *Task Force Report: The Courts* (Washington, D.C.: U.S. Government Printing Office, 1967), pp. 86–87.

**25.** National Advisory Commission on Criminal Justice Standards and Goals, *Courts*, pp. xx–xxi.

**26.** 18 U.S.C.A. § 361 (Suppl. 1975). For a good review of this legislation, see Steinberg, "Right to Speedy Trial: The Constitutional Right and Its Applicability to the Speedy Trial Act of 1974," *Journal of Criminal Law and Criminology* 66:229 (1975).

**27.** American Bar Association, *Standards Relating to Speedy Trial, Standard 1.1.* Reprinted with the permission of the American Bar Association which authored these standards and which holds the copyright.

**28.** 412 U.S. 434, 93 S.Ct. 2260, 27 L.Ed.2d 56 (1973).

**29.** See, e.g., Note "Limiting the Peremptory Challenge: Representation of Groups on Petit Juries," Yale Law Journal, 86:1715 (1977).

**30.** 380 U.S. 202 (1964).

**31.** George Hayden, Joseph Senna, Larry Siegel, "Prosecutorial Discretion in Peremptory Challenges: An Empirical Investigation of Information Use in the Massachusetts Jury Selection Process," New England Law Review 13:768 (1978).

**32.** 409 U.S. 524, 93 S.Ct. 848, 35 L.Ed.2d 46 (1973).

**33.** 419 U.S. 522, 42 L.Ed.2d 690, 95 S.Ct. 692 (1975).

**34.** 372 U.S. 353, 83 S.Ct. 814, 9 L.Ed.2d 811 (1963).

**35.** American Bar Association, *Standards Relating to Criminal Appeals* (New York: Institute of Judicial Administration, 1970), p. 34.

**36.** See Brinegar v. United States, 338 U.S. 160, 69 S.Ct. 1302, 93 L.Ed. 1879 (1949); Speiser v. Randall, 357 U.S. 513, 78 S.Ct. 1332, 2 L.Ed.2d 1460 (1958); In re Winship, 397 U.S. 358, 90 S.Ct. 1068, 25 L.Ed.2d 368 (1970).

**37.** Brinegar v. United States, 338 U.S. 160 (1949).

**38.** Ibid. at 174.

**39.** 160 U.S. 469 (1895).

**40.** Ibid. at 484.

**41.** See In re Winship, 397 U.S. 358, 90 S.Ct. 1068, 25 L.Ed.2d 368 (1970).

**42.** Ibid.

**43.** Ibid. at 371.

# *New Jury System Praised

For 21 of 30 days of jury duty, Mark sat and waited in a court anteroom. He lost money. He was tired because he had to work nights and attend court days. And he became irritable, wondering if fulfilling a public duty was really worth it.

Each year, Mark's woes are shared with two million other Americans called for jury duty. Most say they are bored, frustrated, and suffer financial losses because of the traditional 30-day jury system in the United States.

To help overhaul what some say is an antiquated concept, LEAA is financing a new jury experiment called "One Day/One Trial."

## FULFILLS PUBLIC DUTY

Under the System, Mark—and others like him would spend only one day, or the length of one trial, (average three days) at the courthouse, and their "public duty" would be fulfilled for the year.

Wayne County, which is Michigan's Third Judicial Circuit and includes Detroit, officially adopted the One Day/One Trial jury system last year, after 18 months of preparation and testing.

Chief Judge James N. Canham, the presiding judge of the Wayne County Circuit Court, said the system is a "ray of sunshine in a very bleak picture."

## COMMUNITY ACCEPTS IT

L. M. Jacobs IV, the circuit court administrator, said since its start "the acceptance by the community, including individual citizens as well as members of the bar, is excellent."

"I think the underlying necessity for the court to consider the citizens' needs has permeated other areas of court activities and has become an important consideration in the decision to implement other administrative changes in the court," he said.

## JUROR POOLS FORMED

In the system, a juror is selected from a master list of registered voters by a computer. The

---

*From LEAA News Letter Vol. 6, No. 15, 1978, p. 1.

computer also mails a personal history questionnaire to determine if the juror is qualified and acceptable.

If the person is qualified, he or she would be either in the regular or standby juror pool. In the latter, the prospective juror would telephone and be told via a recording whether to report for duty.

On their reporting day, the jurors are shown a 16-minute slide program acquainting them with legal process and their role as jurors. Then they await assignment.

If any serve on a jury, they report to the appropriate courtroom every day until the trial is concluded and that fulfills their jury responsibility for the year.

## LARGE SAVINGS RESULT

If not accepted, they are dismissed at the end of the day and that fulfills their jury responsibility.

During its first six months of operation, the new system saved Wayne County $330,000. Annual operating costs went up because of computerization ($47,174 vs. $6,168), which meant a net savings of $288,000 for the year. Juror costs per trial decreased from $862 to $646. Jurors are paid $15 a day.

The new system has brought about much broader community representation on juries. Seven times as many citizens are summoned under the new system and 75 percent of them actually serve, compared to 45 percent under the old system.

# 13

# Sentencing

A HISTORY OF
SENTENCING

After a defendant has been found guilty by a trial court, or enters a plea of guilty, he is brought before the court for the imposition and execution of his sentence. This decision—the sentencing of the criminal offender—is one of the most critically important steps in the criminal justice system.

In the early stages of Western civilization, the primary purpose for punishing an individual for a wrongdoing was retaliation, rather than the prevention of further criminal behavior. This approach was based on the well-known principle of "lex talionis," or an eye for an eye and a tooth for a tooth. Private wars, blood feuds, and family vengeance were common during primitive times and comprised a system of justice characterized by the lack of any formally established penal code.[1] Not until the Middle Ages did sentencing become a public responsibility rather than a private matter, and all forms of capital and physical punishment were practiced for literally hundreds of state offenses. Flogging, for example, was a common punishment during the Middle Ages and continued to be sanctioned up through modern times. Imprisonment was not used extensively as a form of punishment, but rather for detaining and holding offenders who could not provide security for their releases. The death penalty, corporal punishment, and exile were the most frequently imposed societal sanctions.[2] The use of such punishments were steeped in superstition, stern religious beliefs, and tradition, and was justified by a philosophy of state retribution, vengeance, and banishment.

Many of these early forms of punishment became the basis for criminal sanctions used during the colonization of the United States. Cruel and inhuman treatments such as mutilation, whipping, and public punishment were commonly practiced by early settlers in the seventeenth and eighteenth centuries. Colonists also began to add to these the punishment of imprisonment, which had become a regular penal method in Great Britain and on the European continent during the sixteenth century. Early prison life was generally harsh, and retribution remained the primary purpose for punishing the convicted criminal. Not until the late seventeenth century, under William Penn, Governor of Pennsylvania, did some penal reform begin to take place in the United States.[3] As Sol Rubin states, "For the first time in history, imprisonment at hard labor was the prescribed punishment for the great majority of serious crimes."[4] The death penalty was used only for premeditated murder; and other sanctions such as fixed prison sentences, restitution, and fines became common sentences.

As a result of Penn's early work, methods of punishment for convicted offenders became of interest to colonists after they became independent from England. For example, an act in 1786 sought to replace the death penalty with imprisonment at hard labor for many offenses.[5] The Walnut Street Jail, which had been erected in Philadelphia in 1773, became a penitentiary for convicted offenders, and many other states built similar prisons. However, most jurisdictions did not deal humanely with inmates, and corporal punishments, including the use of shackles, irons, and collars, were used to discipline offenders.

Throughout the nineteenth century, the purpose of sentencing and imprisonment began to shift from retribution to incapacitation. The Eastern State Penitentiary and the Auburn Prison in New York epitomized the new philosophy of punishment combined with isolation from the community by employing silent confinement, tiered cellblocks, and congregate work experiences. Most early prisons were built for maximum security to prevent convicted offenders from returning to the community before completing their sentences; conditions were extremely severe, and physical punishments were commonplace when prison rules were violated. An extensive review of the history of imprisonment in America is found in Chapter 15.

One practice of the Auburn prison distinguished it from other prisons: the use of inmates to manufacture goods which could be sold to cover prison expenses. Rehabilitation of the convicted offender through prison work began to be looked upon as a new reason for sentencing. As it became apparent that retaliation and retribution were inappropriate forms of punishment in a civilized society, new and innovative practices were developed to justify the sentencing of criminals. Many people believed that punishment could be used to deter crime; imposing a sentence on the guilty offender would serve as an example for potential offenders. Deterrence thus became a viable basis for criminal punishment, but whether it has actually helped to curb criminal activities is difficult to determine. Even today, the use of the death penalty as a form of deterrence continues to be debated.

Beginning in the middle of the twentieth century and continuing up through the present, many other people have felt that rehabilitation should be the primary purpose of the criminal sentence. Rehabilitation as a sentencing goal assumes that society has a responsibility to reform and treat offenders sentenced by the courts to state care. Medium- and minimum-security institutions, probation and parole programs, community treatment centers, and the juvenile justice system all embody the idea of rehabilitation. Although seeking to reform the offender seems a sensible and humane approach to the crime problem, how to genuinely rehabilitate criminals remains an unsolved question. Much more research is needed about crime, offenders, and correctional programs if this modern goal of sentencing is to be achieved.

It is apparent that the criminal sentence has served a variety of different purposes: retribution, deterrence, and rehabilitation have all been the goal of criminal sanctions at one time or another. Law enforcement, judicial personnel, corrections, the legislature, and community groups have had and continue to have divergent views regarding the purposes of criminal sentencing. Any examination of current sentencing procedures reflects this overlap and conflict.

In effect, there is no single purpose behind the criminal sentence. Retaliation and retribution are no longer aspects of modern sentencing procedures, and the imposition of punishment today is defended on the basis of deterrence, rehabilitation, incapacitation, and reintegration of the offender into society.

Following a conviction, the court imposes a sentence on the defendant. This sentence is handed down during what is known as the post-adjudicatory or dispositional phase of the criminal proceeding. A sentence rep-

SENTENCING
DISPOSITIONS

resents the penalty or sanction for a given crime as established by the legislature, imposed by the court, and implemented by the correctional system.

Generally, four different kinds of sentences or dispositions are available to the court to impose upon the convicted offender. These are:

1. A fine.

2. A suspended sentence.

3. Probation.

4. Incarceration.

A fine is usually exacted in the case of a minor offense and may be combined with other sentencing alternatives, such as probation or confinement. A suspended sentence represents an effort by the court to refrain from enforcing a sentence, instead allowing the offender to remain in the community, often without supervision. The most common sentence is that of probation, where the offender is permitted to live in the community subject to compliance with legally imposed conditions. And finally, the sentence of total confinement or incarceration is imposed when the general public needs to be protected from further criminal activity by the defendant.

The sentence itself is generally imposed by the judge and sentencing is one of the most crucial functions of the judgeship. Sentencing authority may also be exercised by the jury, an administrative body, or a group of judges. As was previously mentioned, the length of the sentence is determined by the limits of the statute defining the particular offense. It is also determined by the discretion of the judge based upon information received about the defendant prior to the imposition of the sentence. In the case of a minor offense, the judge generally places the defendant on probation, and therefore requires only limited information in order to make such a decision. In a felony case, the court usually delays the sentence pending the completion of a pre-sentence investigation report by the probation department; this report, which is a social and personal history as well as an evaluation of the defendant, is used by the judge in making a sentencing decision. Some judges heavily weigh the pre-sentence investigation on report, while others may dismiss it completely or rely only on certain portions of it. However, such criteria as the nature of the offense and the previous record of the defendant are of prime importance to most judges in determining the type and length of a sentence to be imposed. The major dispositional choices available to the court are described as follows by the National Advisory Commission on Criminal Justice Standards and Goals *Report on Corrections:*[6]

## Sentencing to Extended
## Terms: Commentary

The traditional American approach to sentencing legislation has been to establish maximum sentences in contemplation of the most dangerous offender who might commit the offense in question. The result has been sentences authorized and imposed far in excess of what is required to satisfy both the public safety and the offender's needs. . . .

On the other hand, there are some offenders whose aggressive, repetitive, violent, or predatory behavior poses a serious threat to the community. In many instances, these offenders are not responsive to correctional programs. Public safety may require that they be incapacitated for a period of time in excess of 5 years. This standard provides that different approaches should be authorized for such offenders when there is supporting evidence.

The arguments for incapacitating the "dangerous offender" are threefold:

1. Modern American statutes contain excessively high maximum sentencing provisions largely aimed at controlling the "dangerous" offender, but unfortunately often ensnare the nondangerous offender as well, needlessly increasing the period of his incarceration.
2. Current attempts to classify the "dangerous" offender in terms of sexual crimes or by "habitual offender" laws are undeniably ineffective and have become so distorted in their application as to be meaningless.
3. Clear authority to sentence the "dangerous offender" to a long term of incapacitation may induce the legislature to agree more readily to a significantly shorter sentence for the nondangerous offender.

The concept of providing separate approaches for dangerous offenders is not new. It has been proposed by the Model Sentencing Act, the Model Penal Code, and the study draft for the revision of the Federal criminal laws. The present standard is patterned after the latter, with the exception that for a finding of dangerousness a psychiatric report indicating that the offender is "mentally abnormal" would not be required. The exception reflects the position that psychiatric "labeling" is not enlightening or conclusively reliable as to the potential or actual dangerousness of individuals. The court should base its findings on material in the pre-sentence report, which should reflect a pattern of behavior indicating the potential threat that the offender may or may not present to the public safety.

Virtually every state has a "habitual offender" law. Approximately half have special provisions dealing with sexual offenders or "sexual psychopaths." The goals of these statutes are similar and raise similar problems. They provide for extended incarceration, often life, often without eligibility for parole; they require a finding that the defendant fits within the specified category; they seek to prevent the return to the community of persons deemed especially dangerous. In the case of the sexual offender, specific psychiatric findings are required, while in the case of the recidivist, the danger is presumed from the fact of his repeated criminality.

"Sexual psychopath" laws follow a general pattern: they accept as a premise the theory that a "sexual" criminal is likely to repeat his crime unless removed from society for many years. The laws have been criticized for vagueness, overbreadth in application, and as imposing cruel and unusual punishment. Nevertheless, a majority of states now have sexual psychopath laws of one kind or another.

Both "recidivist" and "sexual psychopath" laws are aimed at the removal of potentially dangerous offenders from the society they otherwise might harass and damage. But each is grossly overbroad, poorly defined, often resulting in mismanagement and distortion of the criminal process and perpetuation of the arcane concept that the recidivist is *automatically* a danger to society, while the first offender is not. A repeater bad-check artist is hardly to be considered as dangerous to society as the professional killer who has been apprehended for the first time in his life. Within the spectrum between those two extremes lies an infinite variety of combinations of dangerousness and recidivism. . . .

### Probation: Commentary

The thrust of this report is that probation will become the standard sentence in criminal cases. Confinement will be retained chiefly for those offenders who cannot safely be returned to the community. Probation, with its emphasis on assisting the offender to adjust to the free community and supervising that process, offers greater hope for success and less chance for human misery. But probation, to meet the challenge ahead, must be carefully and fairly administered.

Probation is a sentence in itself. In the past in most jurisdictions, probation was imposed only after the court suspended the execution or imposition of sentence to confinement. It was an act of leniency moderating the harshness of confinement. It should now be recognized as a major sentencing alternative in its own right. It should be governed by the maximum terms established by the criminal code. If the offense in question provides for a five-year maximum for confinement, the same maximum should be applicable to probation. In misdemeanors, however, the maximum term generally is set so low that probation supervision would be meaningless. Thus the standard would authorize probation up to one year as a sanction for misdemeanors. As sentences of confinement can be terminated through the parole system, the court similarly should be authorized to discharge the offender from probation at any time the court determines the supervision of the probation officer is no longer necessary.

The conditions imposed are a critical factor in probation. In too many cases, courts mechanically adopt standard conditions for all probationers. Conditions should be tailored to fit the needs of the offender and society, and no condition should be imposed unless necessary for these purposes. Statutes should give the court great latitude in imposing sentence, particularly where juveniles are concerned. For most teenagers, jails are too severe and fines are usually paid by parents. Other forms of retribution, such as washing school buses, cleaning up parks, or serving as attendant in a hospital emergency room, have much more meaning. Conditions that are unrelated to any useful purpose serve mainly to provoke the probationer and make unnecessary work for the probation officer. . . .

### Fines: Commentary

The fine is as traditional a criminal sanction as imprisonment and, when mechanically applied, as counterproductive. The law of fines is as inconsistent and chaotic as that establishing prison sentences. Little guidance is given to the courts for the imposition of fines; in most jurisdictions, jail stands as the only means of collection.

Little is known about the impact of fines. However, a sanction based on the financial means of the defendant can have disparate and destructive results, particularly for the poor. In many jurisdictions, the fine is a revenue device unrelated in practice to concepts of corrections or crime reduction.

If the fine is to be an effective tool in dealing with criminal offenders, it must be employed cautiously and intelligently.

The thrust of the standard is to provide for fines the same standards as imposed for imprisonment—legislative criteria with appropriate restraints on judicial discretion. The standard lists factors that should be considered in imposing a fine.

The fine, like any other sanction, should be related to the offense and the individual offender. It should be viewed as a correctional tool and applied only where it is likely to have some beneficial effect. Imposition of fines purely for the production of revenue has little to recommend it when the goal of the criminal justice system—reduction of crime—is considered.

A fine will have little beneficial effect if it is levied on an individual who does not have the ability to pay. A large proportion of offenders confined in local jails are there for nonpayment of fines. A sentence impossible to fulfill serves neither society nor the offender. Mechanically applied, it serves merely to single out the poor for incarceration.

It is similarly inappropriate for the state to compete with the victim of an offense for the resources of the defendant. If the defendant is willing or ordered by the court to provide restitution or reparation to the victims of the offense, no additional fine should be imposed unless the defendant can meet both obligations.

The standard governmental response to nonpayment of fines is imprisonment. The Supreme Court in *Tate v. Short,* 401, U.S. 395 (1971), has recognized that this process unjustly discriminates against the poor. Likewise, it is an inefficient way to collect a debt, because imprisonment of the offender makes it impossible for him to earn the wherewithal to pay. Private creditors learned long ago that imprisonment for debt was unproductive.

Legislation should be enacted authorizing the state to utilize the same means as private creditors to recover an unpaid fine. This would include such civil remedies as garnishment, attachment, and other collection measures. The fine should become a lien on the property of the offender subject to normal foreclosure procedures. Imprisonment should be reserved only for those offenders who intentionally refuse to pay a fine or fail to exercise good faith in obtaining money with which to pay it. Courts should be specifically granted the power to impose fines to be paid in installments and to modify or revoke a fine when conditions indicate that the offender for justifiable reasons cannot meet the obligation.

Restricting the availability of the fine and the measures authorized to collect it creates the risk that the ultimate result will be imposition of incarceration on indigent offenders in lieu of imposing what the court believes to be an uncollectable fine. This may occur because all too often courts that generally utilize fines have no other alternative than imprisonment. Probation services and other community-based programs are generally not available to misdemeanor courts. The standard rejects incarceration where its imposition is based solely on the person's wealth. Imprisonment should be imposed where imprisonment serves a sentencing objective and then only when no other alternative is appropriate. A person's wealth should be an impermissible factor in sentencing.

Special provisions may be considered for the imposition of fines against corporations. The fine is perhaps more appropriate against corporations than individuals because the economic sanction relates to the purpose of most business organizations. However, for the fine to have any impact it must be substantial enough

*Omitted*

to discourage the conduct deemed criminal. Fines related not to the offense but to sales, profits, or net annual income of the corporation may be appropriate, and legislation should authorize the sentencing court to consider these factors.

## CAPTIAL PUNISHMENT AS A SENTENCE

The most severe sentence used in our nation is capital punishment, or execution. Applied extensively throughout American history, capital punishment was usually reserved for the two most serious criminal offenses: murder and rape. However, federal, state, and military courts have handed down this sentence for other crimes such as kidnapping, treason (espionage), and desertion.

Between 1930 and 1967, 3,859 alleged criminals were executed in the United States: 86.4% for murder, 11.8% for rape, and 1.8% for other offenses. Of those executed, 53.5% were black and 45.4% were white.[7] Proponents of capital punishment argue that executions serve as a strong deterrent for serious crimes and provide the only real assurance that brutal criminals can never again jeopardize society. Critics, however, have pointed to the finality and brutality of the act, and the possibility of mistakenly executing innocent persons, as viable reasons for the abolishment of capital punishment. In addition, some persons have argued that the sentence has traditionally been carried out in a racially biased manner. These charges are supported by the disproportionate numbers of blacks (53.5%) who have received the death sentence and been executed.

In recent years, the deterrent effect and the constitutionality of the death penalty have been issues of major concern to both the nation's courts and its concerned social scientists. In 1972, the United States Supreme Court in *Furman v. Georgia*[8] decided that the discretionary imposition of the death penalty was cruel and unusual punishment under the Eighth and Fourteenth Amendments of the Constitution. This case not only questioned whether capital punishment is a more effective deterrent than life imprisonment, but also challenged the very existence of the death penalty on the grounds of its brutality and finality. The Court, however, did not rule out the use of capital punishment as a penalty; rather, it objected to the arbitrary and capricious manner in which it was imposed. After *Furman*, many states changed statutes which had previously allowed jury discretion to impose the death penalty. In some states, this was accomplished by enacting statutory guidelines for jury decisions; in others, the death penalty was made mandatory for certain crimes only. Despite these changes in statutory law, no further executions were carried out while the Supreme Court pondered additional cases concerning the death penalty.

Then, in July of 1976, the Supreme Court ruled on the constitutionality of five state death penalty statutes. In the first case, *Gregg v. Georgia*,[9] the Court found valid the Georgia statute which held that a finding by the jury of at least one "aggravating circumstance" out of ten is required in pronouncing the death penalty in murder cases. In the *Gregg* case, for example, the jury imposed the death penalty after finding beyond a reasonable doubt two aggravating circumstances:

1) the offense of murder was committed while the offender was engaged in the commission of two other capital felonies; and 2) the offender committed the offense of murder for the purpose of receiving money and other financial gains (e.g., an automobile). In delivering the opinion of the court, Justice Potter Stewart stated:

The basic concern of *Furman* centered on those defendants who were being condemned to death capriciously and arbitrarily. Under the procedures before the Court in that case, sentencing authorities were not directed to give attention to the nature or circumstances of the crime committed or to the character or record of the defendant. Left unguided, juries imposed the death sentence in a way that could only be called freakish. The new Georgia sentencing procedures, by contrast, focus the jury's attention on the particularized nature of the crime and the particularized characteristics of the individual defendant. While the jury is permitted to consider any aggravating or mitigating circumstances, it must find and identify at least one statutory aggravating factor before it may impose a penalty of death. In this way the jury's discretion is channeled. No longer can a jury wantonly and freakishly impose the death sentence; it is always circumscribed by the legislative guidelines. In addition, the review function of the Supreme Court of Georgia affords additional assurance that the concerns that prompted our decision in *Furman* are not present to any significant degree in the Georgia procedure applied here.

For the reasons expressed in this opinion, we hold that the statutory system under which Gregg was sentenced to death does not violate the Constitution. Accordingly, the judgment of the Georgia Supreme Court is affirmed.[10]

The Court also upheld the constitutionality of a Texas statute on capital punishment in *Jurek v. Texas*,[11] and of a Florida statute in *Proffitt v. Florida*.[12] The statutes of these states are similar to those of Georgia in that they limit sentencing discretion by specifying not only the crimes for which capital punishment can be handed down, but also by stipulating criteria concerning the circumstances surrounding the crimes. For example, the Texas statute required that the death sentence could be imposed only if the jury in a proceeding following the verdict responded in the affirmative to two and sometimes three of the following questions:

1. whether the conduct of the defendant that caused the death of the deceased was committed deliberately and with the reasonable expectation that the death of the deceased or another would result.
2. whether there is a probability that the defendant would commit criminal acts of violence that would constitute a continuing threat to a society.
3. if raised by the evidence, whether the conduct of the defendant in killing the deceased was unreasonable in response to the provocation, if any, by the deceased.[13]

The Supreme Court, however, overruled the death penalty statutes of Louisiana in *Roberts v. Louisiana*[14] and North Carolina in *Woodson v. North Carolina*.[15] These two statutes provided for a mandatory death penalty in all first-degree murder cases. The reason surrounding the decision of the unconstitutionality of the statutes was expressed in *Woodson:*

> The history of mandatory death penalty statutes in the United States thus reveals that the practice of sentencing to death all persons convicted of a particular offense has been rejected as unduly harsh and unworkably rigid. . . . While the prevailing practice of individualizing sentencing determinations generally reflects simply enlightened policy rather than a constitutional imperative, we believe that in capital cases, the fundamental respect of humanity underlying the Eighth Amendment requires consideration of the character and record of the individual offender and the circumstances of the particular offense as a constitutionally indispensable part of the process of inflicting the penalty of death.[16]

The Supreme Court continued to deal with the death penalty and the "cruel and unusual punishment" question during the 1977–78 term, when it handed down decisions in the following major cases: *Coker v. Georgia; Gardner v. Florida;* and *Lockett v. Ohio.* In Coker, the Court ruled unconstitutional a death penalty sentence in Georgia for the crime of rape, but left unanswered the issue of imposing a death penalty to prevent and deter other types of crimes.[17] The Court overruled a death sentence penalty in Gardner because information contained in the pre-sentence report was not disclosed to the defense attorney.[18] And in *Lockett v. Ohio*, the Court declared that the imposition of a capital punishment sentence must be based on reason and not emotion. Limiting a judge's sentencing discretion to narrow circumstances of the crime and record of the offender makes it impossible to consider an individualized decision essential in capital cases.[19]

Table 13.1 summarizes the major U.S. Supreme Court decisions on capital punishment during the last decade.

Whether the death penalty is cruel and unusual punishment under the Eighth Amendment remains unclear. Although the practical effect of the *Furman* decision was to outlaw the death penalty in America, recent decisions seem to hold that a convicted offender can be sentenced to death under a fairly and properly administered capital punishment statute. Support for this position is evidenced by the fact that in January, 1977 the state of Utah executed by firing squad a convicted murderer, Gary Gilmore. This was the first execution in the United States since 1967, and none had occurred previously since 1947. Gilmore's execution was unusual in that he voluntarily sought to have the death penalty imposed on him.

The most recent execution in America was that of John Spenkelink, a convicted murderer who was put to death by the state of Florida in 1979. Today, there are about 450 death-row inmates. In addition, there has been an increase since the Furman decision in the number of persons sentenced to death each year by state courts. Consequently, as a result of recent court decisions, the go-ahead by the United States Supreme Court, and the Gilmore and Spenkelink executions, many other states where offenders are on death row may well contemplate the imposition of death sentences

| Case | Ruling |
|------|--------|
| *Furman v. Georgia* 408 U.S. 238 | Discretionary imposition of death penalty without proper guidelines against arbitrary action is cruel and unusual punishment under the Eighth and Fourteenth Amendments. |
| *Gregg v. Georgia* 428 U.S. 153 (1976) | Court upheld a Georgia death penalty statute which provided guidlines for mitigating circumstances for the implementation of the law. |
| *Proffitt v. Florida* 428 U.S. 242 (1976) *Jurek v. Texas* 428 U.S. 262 (1976) | The Court upheld Florida and Texas statutes by declaring that the death penalty was not cruel or unusual punishment where the statutes limited sentencing discretion. |
| *Woodson v. North Carolina* 428 U.S. 280 (1976) *Roberts v. Louisiana* 428 U.S. 325 (1976) | Imposition of a mandatory penalty in all first-degree murder cases is cruel and unusual punishment because of its rigidity. |
| *Roberts v. Louisiana* 431 U.S. 633 (1977) | Louisiana mandatory death penalty statute which does not allow for consideration of mitigating circumstances relevant to the offender or offense is cruel and unusual punishment and unconstitutional. |
| *Coker v. Georgia* 433 U.S. 584 (1977) | Court struck down a death penalty sentence for the crime of rape as disproportionate to the crime for which it is imposed and excessive punishment in violation of the Eighth and Fourteenth Amendments. |
| *Gardner v. Florida* 430 U.S. 349 (1977) | Court vacates a death penalty sentence where defendant was denied due process of law because a portion of the pre-sentence report contained confidential information which was not disclosed to defense counsel. |
| *Lockett v. Ohio* 438 U.S. (1978) *Bell v. Ohio* 438 U.S. (1978) | Court declared the Ohio death penalty statute unconstitutional where it narrowly limited the sentence discretion to consider the circumstances of the crime and the records and character of the offender. |

TABLE 13.1
Recent Supreme Court
Decisions Involving
Capital Punishment

in the near future. Capital punishment will continue to be a viable and controversial issue in the American justice system in the 1980s.

Considerable empirical research has been carried out on the effectiveness of capital punishment as a deterrent.* In particular, studies have tried to discover whether the mandatory death sentence serves as a more effective deterrent than life imprisonment for capital crimes such as homicide. One of the first noteworthy studies was conducted in Philadelphia in 1935 by Robert Dann.[20] He chose five highly publicized executions of convicted murderers in different years and determined the number of homicides in the 60-day period prior to and after each execution. Each 120-day period had approximately the same number of homicides, as well as the same number of days on which homicides occurred. Dann's rationale was that if capital punishment does deter crime, this deterrent effect should cause a drop in the number of homicides in the days immediately following an execution. However, his study revealed that more homicides occurred during the sixty days following an execution than prior to it, suggesting that the overall impact of executions might actually serve to increase the incidence of homicide. Dann concluded that no deterrent effect was demonstrated.

The position that capital punishment has no deterrent effect on crime was also confirmed by Karl Schuessler in 1952 after his analysis of 11 states during the years 1930 to 1949.[21] Schuessler examined annual data for homicide rates and execution risks (the numbers of executions for murder per 1,000 homicides per year) and concluded that homicide rates and executions risks move independently of each other. Extending this analysis to include the examination of European countries before and after the abolition of the death penalty, Schuessler found nothing in the data to suggest that homicide trends were influenced by the abolition of capital punishment.

One of the most noted capital punishment studies was conducted by Thorsten Sellin in 1959.[22] Contiguous states were grouped in threes wherever at least one in the group differed from the others in maximum penalties for homicide; in each set, at least one state did not provide the death penalty for the research period in question, while the other two did. Within these clusters of similar jurisdictions, the homicide rate in states with capital punishment were therefore compared with the homicide rate in states without a mandatory death penalty. Since the homicide trends in all states studied were found to be similar regardless of whether the death penalty was provided, Sellin concluded that capital punishment did not appear to have any influence on the reported rate of homicide.

Another contiguous-state analysis was carried out in 1969 by Walter Reckless, who compared nine states in which the death penalty had been abolished with nine states in which it still applied.[23] Using data from the 1967 Uniform Crime Reports, Reckless compared rates of murder, aggra-

*The authors would like to express their appreciation to Shari N. Wittenberg for helping to develop the research studies cited in the following section.

vated assault, and combined violent crimes. Reckless found that five out of seven abolition states had lower crime rates than did their contiguous death penalty states, while the remaining two states tied. Reckless concluded that the death penalty is not an effective deterrent in such capital crimes.

One of the few studies in which capital punishment was found to have a deterrent effect was conducted in 1975 by Isaac Ehrlich of the University of Chicago.[24] Using highly advanced and complex statistical techniques, Ehrlich found evidence that murder is committed as a result of the hatred produced by interpersonal conflicts, and that the likeness of a person's committing a crime is influenced by that person's perception of what can be gained by the criminal act. Thus, according to Ehrlich, the perception of execution risk (the number of people executed upon being convicted of murder) is an important determinant of whether one individual will murder another. As a result of his analysis, Ehrlich concluded that each additional execution per year in the United States would save seven or eight people from being victims of murder.

Ehrlich's research has been widely cited by death penalty advocates as empirical proof of the deterrent effect of capital punishment. Notably, his unpublished results were used in the Solicitor General's brief in the case of *Gregg v. Georgia* as new proof of the effectiveness of the death penalty. However, a subsequent analysis by William Bowers and Glenn Pierce, replicating Ehrlich's analysis but using a somewhat different statistical technique, showed that his approach merely confirms previous findings that capital punishment is no more effective a deterrent than is life imprisonment.[25]

In sum, studies that have attempted to show the actual impact of capital punishment on the murder rate indicate that the execution of convicted criminals has relatively little effect as a deterrent measure. Nevertheless, many people still hold to the efficacy of the death penalty as a crime deterrent, and recent Supreme Court decisions seem to herald a resumption of its use.

When a convicted offender is to be sentenced to prison, the statutes of a jurisdiction provide the possible penalties that may be imposed by the court. Over the years, the states have adopted a variety of sentencing approaches. Some states grant extensive discretion to the judge in fixing the punishment, while others place limits on judicial discretion by imposing minimum and maximum sentences for certain offenses. The minimum term generally refers to the earliest time at which an incarcerated offender can be considered for release, while the maximum term represents the outer limits of the sentence. A legislatively fixed minimum sentence may range from as low as 1 year up to 30 years with a 10-year minimum being common for most serious offenses. Life imprisonment, on the other hand, is the most consistent example of a maximum term.

Most states today have many variations in sentencing schemes within their own jurisdictions. As the American Bar Association found in its sur-

SENTENCING
STRUCTURES

vey on "Sentencing Computation—Laws and Practices," there is probably no area in criminal justice which is characterized by such disparity, diversity, and confusion as is the field of sentencing.[26] Difficulty exists even in finding agreement over the precise meanings of such terms as indeterminate, indefinite, determinate, and definite when they refer to types of sentences. The situation is further confused because what one state may designate as an indefinite sentence may be called a definite sentence in another state. Even though present sentencing schemes vary greatly from one jurisdiction to another, it is important to our understanding of sentencing to set forth some of the major classifications.

## The Indeterminate-Indefinite Sentence

This type of sentence normally describes a situation where there is a maximum sentence but either no term or a different minimum term which the prisoner must complete before becoming eligible to leave the institution under any circumstances. Theoretically, the true indeterminate sentence involves a term of from one day to life. Both a zero to ten or a one- to ten-year term would also fit this type of sentencing structure. Under this scheme, the actual length of time served by the inmate is controlled by the correction agency. The inmate may be released from confinement whenever the institution and parole personnel believe that he or she is ready to live in the community. The basic purpose underlying the indeterminate sentencing approach, particularly during the middle of the twentieth century, has been to individualize each sentence in the interests of rehabilitating the offender. This type of sentencing allows for flexibility not only regarding the type of sentence to be imposed, but also in the length of the sentence to be served.

Most states do not have true indeterminate criminal sentencing. Rather, they incorporate some of the basic principles of indeterminate sentencing, such as the minimum-maximum term or the use of a maximum sentence. The *Model Sentencing Act* of the National Council on Crime and Delinquency recommends that maximum sentencing procedures with no minimum be used for felonies giving parole boards much authority in determining an inmate's eligibility for release. The American Law Institutes' *Model Penal Code,* on the other hand, provides felony offenders with indeterminate sentencing consisting of maximum terms and short minimum sentences. For example, a maximum of ten years might be set for a particular offense with a minimum term not exceeding one-half of the maximum limit. Recently, the American Bar Association's *Standards Relating to Sentencing Alternatives* suggested that statutory maximum terms be used for designated offenses, and that minimum terms be left to the discretion of the court. This approach strikes a balance between the *Model Penal Code,* which calls for minimum terms, and the *Model Sentencing Act,* which supports maximum terms only.

Today, almost all states use some form of the indeterminate sentence. Critics of this approach allege that the uncertainty of the sentence works a hardship on inmates. The true indeterminate sentence would probably not be acceptable to inmates or criminal justice authorities, but the fixed maximum as established by the legislature is a judicially valid sentencing scheme.

In some jurisdictions, the indeterminate sentence is often referred to as an indefinite sentence. Where the time for release in the true indeterminate sentence is set by correctional agencies, the maximum penalty prescribed in an indefinite sentence is normally set by the legislature. This type of sentence may also have a minimum-maximum term, but the exact sentence will be set by the judge according to these outer limits. Many states have what they refer to as indeterminate sentences—where minimum and maximum terms are set—while they are really indefinite sentences. For example, the minimum term for the crime of burglary might be not less than two years or more than ten years in prison; it would be up to the judge to decide the exact sentence. The judge might sentence the offender to two to five years, with five years being less than the statutory maximum.

Excerpts from the *Model Sentencing Act* and *Model Penal Code* describing indeterminate sentencing provisions for felony offenders are found below.[27]

ADVISORY COUNCIL OF JUDGES
NATIONAL COUNCIL ON CRIME AND DELINQUENCY
MODEL SENTENCING ACT (1963)

Section 9. Sentencing for Felonies Generally. Upon a verdict or plea of guilty but before an adjudication of guilt the court may, without entering a judgment of guilt and with the consent of the defendant, defer further proceedings and place the defendant on probation upon such terms and conditions as it may require. Upon fulfillment of the terms of probation the defendant shall be discharged without court adjudication of guilt. Upon violation of the terms, the court may enter an adjudication of guilt and proceed as otherwise provided.

If a defendant is convicted of a felony and is not committed under Section 5 or 7 (or 8) the court shall a) suspend the imposition or execution of sentence with or without probation, or b) place the defendant on probation, or c) impose a fine as provided by law for the offense, with or without probation or commitment, or d) commit the defendant to the custody of (director of correction) for a term of five years or a lesser term, or to a local correctional facility for a term of one year or a lesser term. Where a sentence of fine is not otherwise authorized by law, in lieu of or in addition to any of the dispositions authorized in this paragraph, the court may impose a fine of not more than $1000. In imposing a fine the court may authorize its payment in installments. In placing a defendant on probation the court shall direct that he be placed under the supervision of (the probation agency).

AMERICAN LAW INSTITUTE
MODEL PENAL CODE
(Proposed Official Draft, 1962)

Section 6.06. Sentence of Imprisonment for Felony; Ordinary Terms. A person who has been convicted of a felony may be sentenced to imprisonment, as follows:

1. in the case of a felony of the first degree, for a term the minimum of which shall be fixed by the Court at not less than one year nor more than ten years, and the maximum of which shall be life imprisonment;
2. in the case of a felony of the second degree, for a term the minimum of which shall be fixed by the Court at not less than one year nor more than three years, and the maximum of which shall be ten years;
3. in the case of a felony of the third degree, for a term the minimum of which shall be fixed by the Court at not less than one year nor more than two years, and the maximum of which shall be five years.

In its recent study of sentencing structures, the American Bar Association found that a substantial majority of the 41 states using indeterminate sentencing had statutes that fix minimum and maximum terms but allow the judge some discretion within those limits.[28] Thus, the indeterminate sentence is the predominate form of sentence used in the criminal process. It is the heart of the treatment model of corrections. Yet, because rehabilitation of offenders has generally failed and the crime rate continues to soar, alternative sentencing schemes are being given more consideration.

**The Determinate-**
**Definite Sentence**
This type of sentence differs from the indeterminate sentence in that a single fixed term of years is specified for each crime. The fixed term for a crime is normally a maximum specified by the judge as established by the legislature. The number of years actually served under this type of sentence depends on the statutory provisions regarding the inmate's parole eligibility. If no parole provisions existed, the inmate could not be released until completing the entire sentence. In many respects, the determinate sentence is similar to what is known as a definite sentence, which also requires the judge to sentence the defendant to a fixed number of years in prison. However, as the American Bar Association's *Report on Sentencing Computation, Laws and Practice* states, "there is no such thing as a determinate or definite sentence in this country."[29] All states have parole programs which shorten the amount of time served by the defendant. Thus, in a state where parole eligibility begins at one-half of the maximum sentence, a determinate sentence of 20 years is actually a sentence of from 10 to 20 years. The determinate-definite sentence was originally developed to impose specific sentences equally on all those convicted of similar offenses.

In years past, the completely definite sentence, for example, involved a sentence of a fixed term of years in prison over which the judge had no control, being required to sentence the defendant in accordance with the penalty set by the legislature. If a defendant was convicted of second-degree murder and the statute called for a straight life sentence, the judge would be required to impose that sentence.

The definite sentence fell out of favor because those who were interested in reform rehabilitation saw it as a rigid sentence which did not consider the defendant's individual characteristics. As a result, most states eventually passed parole laws permitting early release from the definite sentence. In addition to parole laws, the states also began to change the definite sentence to a determinate sentence by making the legislatively fixed term of years equal to a maximum term, with the number of years to be actually served specified by the judge. Thus, in a state where the definite sentence as established by the legislature and imposed by the judge was 15 years, this same sentence became a determinate one of up to 15 years with the exact term being set by the judge and early release being made available under parole. This allowed more judicial flexibility in the sentencing process. For the most part, up through the early 1970s, the definite sentence had become an anachronism within the criminal justice system.

In the past few years, however, the flat-time or fixed sentence, similar to the definite sentence, has again become popular. This involves sentencing the defendant to a specific or definite number of years in prison, such as ten years for manslaughter. Ironically, flat-time sentencing was common practice in the early twentieth century but, as stated above, was eventually replaced by the indeterminate sentence and the widespread use of parole. Today, due to the increasing crime rate and the inability of the correctional system to reform the offender, the fixed or definite sentence has again come into use. In its new penal code, for instance, the state of Maine has switched from indeterminate to fixed sentences, abolished parole, and made prison rehabilitation programs voluntary. Other states such as Indiana, California, Alaska, Illinois, and Connecticut are also considering fixed sentencing laws. It may be that many experts in criminal justice have lost confidence in the ability of indeterminate sentences to rehabilitate the offender.[30]

### Mandatory Sentences

Another effort to limit judicial discretion has been the development of the mandatory sentence. Some states, for example, exclude offenders convicted of certain offenses from being placed on probation; others exclude recidivists; and still others bar certain offenders from being considered for parole. Mandatory sentencing legislation may impose minimum-maximum terms or fixed prison sentences. Crimes which often call for mandatory prison sentences include murder and multiple convictions for crimes such as rape, drug violations, and robbery. Mandatory sentencing generally limits the judge's discretionary power to impose any disposition but that which is authorized by the legislature; as a result, it destroys the idea of the individualized sentence and often impedes rehabilitation efforts by the courts. On the other hand, mandatory sentencing provides equal treatment for all offenders who commit the same crime regardless of age, sex, or other individual characteristics. One argument against mandatory sentences states that such sentencing is defective because it violates the cruel and unusual punishment clause of the Eighth Amendment to the United States Constitution.

One illustration of a mandatory sentence is the Massachusetts Gun Control Law, which requires a sentence of imprisonment for not less than one year nor more than two and one-half years for illegally carrying a firearm.[31] The unique feature of this statute is that the punishment is a mandatory sentence which must be a one-year prison sentence and which cannot be suspended by the court. Neither can the offender be considered for probation, parole, or other forms of early release until completion of the one-year sentence.

Although mandatory sentences have not traditionally been common in the penal laws of the United States, they seem to be receiving considerable attention today. The United States Congress has considered imposing mandatory sentencing provisions into revisions of the Federal Penal Code; federal and state parole boards exclude certain offenders from parole; and many state legislatures are currently studying mandatory sentences for serious drug offenses, auto theft, and the illegal possession of firearms. Twelve states have already replaced discretionary sentencing with fixed-term mandatory sentences for the sale of hard drugs, kidnaping, and arson.[32] The primary purpose behind such laws is to impose swift and certain punishment on the offender. It is difficult to say if depriving the judiciary of discretion and placing all sentencing power in the hands of the legislature will have a deterrent effect on the commission of these offenses. Only time and further research will provide the answer.

### Presumptive Sentencing

The most valid criticism of current sentencing practices in the United States, whether we are referring to an indeterminate or a mandatory sentence, comes from three major sources—the public, the convicted offender, and the criminal justice practitioner. The public is currently upset about a system of justice that imposes incarceration at one moment, and releases offenders just as quickly. A five-year sentence does not mean five years; it may mean only one year; and two years may mean only eight months of imprisonment. A review of various parole regulations often can provide the offender with release substantially earlier than the minimum sentence imposed by the court.

The offender and the criminal justice practitioner, on the other hand, are generally upset about the inequity and disparity of the sentences imposed by the court. Two and three offenders with similar convictions may receive probation from one judge, a fine from another, and a sentence of incarceration from a third. And although some differences in sentencing may be expected, the fault for extremely different sentences where circumstances are similar often lies in the broad, unfettered discretion of the sentencing judge. Such prominent critics as U.S. District Judge Marvin Frankel, Andrew von Hirsch, Allen Dershowitz, and David Fogel have identified the problems engendered by these disparate practices.[33]

We have seen in the previous section that one of the movements in the criminal justice field is the trend toward the establishment of determinate or "fixed" and mandatory sentences. Several states have already enacted such legislation and others have established study groups for this purpose. Marvin Zalman, for instance, has impressively reviewed the rise and fall of the indeterminate sentence and the current campaign for new forms of definite sentencing.[34]

But such approaches as mandatory sentences are not a panacea for crime control. Oftentimes, similar offenses are committed in different ways and each offender is different from the other. Grouping all offenders who commit a particular crime into one category can often result in hardships on defendants with particular personal characteristics. A recent critique of mandatory sentencing by the Twentieth Century Fund supports the position that it may lead to court delays, arbitrary judicial decision making, and an increase in prosecutorial discretion and overcrowded prisons.[35]

Consequently, some groups are making a case for the establishment of "presumptive sentencing." This approach would allow the legislature to set a minimum and maximum term for a particular crime, with the judge setting a fixed or determinate sentence within this range. In this situation, the legislature retains the authority to exercise policy decisions, and the judge maintains some degree of sentencing discretion. Offenders convicted under this scheme would be given a specific sentence unless mitigating or aggravating circumstances were found in the commission of the offense or regarding the offender's personal background. In other words, a judge would be permitted to sentence below or above the maximum but would be required to write an opinion justifying such action. Armed robbery in the first degree with a lower legislative limit of three years and a maximum limit of ten years, and a determinate sentence of five years would be an example of a presumptive sentencing approach. This idea has the advantage of retaining flexibility in sentencing while providing a substantial degree of certainty about the imposition of the sentence for the offender and the general public. It also seeks to eliminate the problem of widely disparate sentences for similar crimes imposed by judges with different sentencing philosophies.

In addition, the heart of the presumptive sentencing approach requires the development of objective sentencing guidelines which outline the elements of a crime and provide predetermined weights to the elements, which then leads to a selection of a most appropriate sentence. This idea is similar to the use of a point system for consideration by judges for pretrial release. The sentencing factors are designed to help the judge in choosing the correct sentence.

Thus, the important objectives of presumptive sentencing are: (1) to reduce sentencing disparity, (2) to limit judicial discretion without completely eliminating it, and (3) to impose a sentence which the offender is required to serve. Zalman points out that presumptive sentencing proposals have grown out of a climate of distrust of judicial and parole board discretion.[36] In order to restrict such discretion, legislatures are expanding their role in the sentencing process.

At this juncture, those jurisdictions experimenting with sentencing reform have primarily taken the approach of abolishing indeterminate sentences and replacing them with determinate or fixed sentences with presumptive characteristics. Such has been the case in Illinois, Indiana, California, Maine, and Minnesota. Zalman describes the range and different characteristics of these sentencing proposals. Generally speaking, they have focused on penal code reform which prescribed specific sentences for each crime.[37] But researchers such as Lagoy, Hussey, and Cramer, in a comparative assessment of determinate sentencing, suggest that uniformity, equality, and less disparity may not be easily achieved with this approach, particularly if it has a spiraling effect on sentence lengths and prison populations.[38]

Nonetheless, presumptive sentencing continues to receive national attention. Legislation of this kind has been proposed in more than a dozen states. The National Conference of Commissioners on Uniform State Laws has approved a Model Sentencing Act which includes a presumptive sentencing model.[39] And the often-proposed Federal Penal Code would establish determinate guidelines similar to the presumptive sentence.[40] Consequently, it appears that legislatures in particular will be seriously considering proposed legislation pertaining to presumptive sentencing in their criminal codes in the future.

Sentencing reform is a popular criminal justice topic today. We do know that criminal sentences should be fair and designed to deter and control crime. Which sentencing schemes of all those discussed above would achieve this purpose is unclear. However, as Leonard Orland cautions:

> The future of rehabilitation is as bright or as dismal today as it was a decade or two decades ago. It would be a profound mistake to attempt to legislate rehabilitation out of existence and to substitute a system of sentencing based upon vengeance, the consequences of which will be to substantially increase time served in U.S. prisons.[41]

A summary of the similarities and differences between the various sentencing schemes is presented in Table 13.2. In addition, the application section of this chapter describes the recently enacted sentencing models of the states of Maine, California, and Indiana.

## THE EFFECT OF GOOD TIME CREDIT ON INCARCERATION

One of the most important factors influencing decisions regarding imprisonment is the use of good time credit and meritorious behavior. An inmate can have a sentence reduced by obeying prison rules and by performing meritorious actions, such as doing exceptional work, donating blood, or attending academic or vocational school programs.

Good time credits are provided by legislation to inmates in most states and the federal system. This system was originally based on the idea that rewards would more effectively control an inmate's behavior than punishments. In addition, their use represents an early effort by reformers throughout the nineteenth and early twentieth centuries to rehabilitate and reintegrate the offender into the community prior to the completion of the entire sentence.

TABLE 13.2
Common Sentencing
Schemes

| Sentencing Scheme | Common Characteristics |
|---|---|
| Indeterminate | Minimum and maximum terms prescribed by legislature; place and length of sentence controlled by corrections and parole; judge has little discretion over time served; goal is rehabilitation; sentence to fit offender; uncertainty and disparity in sentencing is major problem. |
| Indefinite | Similar to indeterminate sentence in some states; minimum and maximum terms, or only maximum term prescribed by legislature; sentence to match offender's needs; judge has some sentencing discretion; wide disparity in sentences imposed; parole used for early release. |
| Definite | Fixed period prescribed by legislature and imposed by judge; goal to punish and deter offender from further crime; allows for same sentence to apply to all convicted of particular offenses; eliminates disparity; judge has no discretion over length of sentence, but only over choice of sentence; offender required to serve entire sentence; no parole, inflexibility and rigidity is major problem. |
| Determinate | Similar to definite sentence; has one fixed term of years set by judge; offender required to serve entire sentence where no parole exists. |
| Mandatory | Fixed term set by legislature for particular crimes; sentence must be imposed by judge; judge has no discretion in choice of sentence; goal is punishment and deterrence; contrary to individualized sentence; no sentencing disparity; no parole. |
| Presumptive | Legislatively prescribed range of sentences for given crimes; minimum and maximum terms with judge setting determinate sentence within these bounds; judge maintains some discretion; guidelines and use of mitigating and aggravating circumstances established by legislature; goal is justice, deterrence and individualization in sentencing; "just desserts." |

The statutes which control how credit against a prison sentence is given to an inmate vary from one jurisdiction to another. According to the American Bar Association's *Report on Sentencing Computation, Laws and Practices*, good time credits are deducted from both the minimum and maximum terms in 20 states, all of which have indeterminate sentencing statutes. In 23 other jurisdictions, including the District of Columbia and the federal system, credit can be deducted from the maximum term only.[42]

The amount of good time granted an inmate also varies among the jurisdictions. Some states allow good time on a flat basis per month or per year. This would mean, for example, that all eligible inmates would receive a reduction of two months per year during the periods of their incarceration. Other states grant good time at an increasing rate with each additional year served by the inmate. Thus, the offender would receive a reduction of one month for the first year of sentence, two months for the second year, three months for the third, and so on. Still other states allow good time based solely on a rate related to the length of the sentence: in a sentence of one to two years, allowable good time would be six days per month; in a sentence of four to six years, the inmate would be allowed seven days per month.

In most jurisdictions, the good time allowance is only granted while the inmate is incarcerated in a penal institution. In many cases, inmates do not receive credit for time spent in jail awaiting trial, in mental institutions pending psychiatric examinations, or while incarcerated pending an appeal. In the recent case of *McGinnis v. Royster* (1973),[43] the United States Supreme Court upheld the constitutionality of a New York correction law which did not require calculating jail detention time into good time credits when the inmate was transferred to a state prison. The Court reasoned that the purposes of pre-trial and post-trial incarceration differ, and that offenders awaiting trial in jail should not be granted good time credits because they are not yet participating in any state rehabilitation program. On the other hand, good time programs exist not only to rehabilitate offenders but to control and discipline them; why, then, should a defendant receive credit for prison time but not for the time spent in custody prior to sentencing or pending an appeal after the sentence has been imposed? This inconsistent logic has resulted in a haphazard approach to the development of statutory programs dealing with good time credit.

Another important issue concerns the forfeiture of good time credit once it has been granted to the inmate. State and federal statutes that allow for good time include provisions governing the amounts of time that may be lost, and by what methods. Ordinarily, the warden or superintendent of the institution, in conjunction with other prison officials, administers good time credit programs. For minor prison infractions, the inmate may lose a month of good time; for serious violations of rules, such as an attempted escape, an inmate may lose all credit accumulated since incarceration. Some states provide for notice, hearing, proof of violation, and appeal when deciding to take away or lessen inmate's good time credits, while others offer no procedural protections. Usually, any good time forfeited by the inmate can be restored by the same correctional authorities who removed it.

PROBLEMS IN
SENTENCING

Unlike other areas of criminal justice—such as the police and prisons, where reform efforts have been going on for over a decade—the process of sentencing has long been neglected. Up until a few years ago, few experts recognized the far-reaching impact that the sentencing process had on the offender and the criminal justice system. If a sentence was too short or if it involved probation when incarceration was appropriate, it deprived society of proper protection from criminal behavior. On the other hand, if the sentence was too harsh the defendant was unduly penalized; efforts to rehabilitate the offender were lost and criminal values were reinforced.

Serious problems were created by legislative decisions which created various sentencing structures within each state. An indeterminate sentence, for example, may lead to the establishment of irresponsible release procedures by correctional administrators; as a result, offenders may be released earlier than either the court or society anticipates. Mandatory sentences may be too rigid and promote the possibility that they will not be enforced by prosecutors and judges. It may also happen that a court will impose a sentence of confinement and the parole board will decide the actual length of time the inmate will serve. These are just some of the problems which exist in a very critical and complex sentencing process.

Generally speaking, the current problems of sentencing revolve around the following major issues: (1) sentencing discretion; (2) sentencing information; (3) sentencing structure; (4) dispositions; and (5) due process of law.

In past years, the process of sentencing and the correctional course to be taken by the defendant were largely determined by the trial. The judge imposed a sentence based on limits set by statute as well as on personal and professional inclinations. Today, although the judge still determines whether an offender will be incarcerated or placed in the community, many states now require that the place and length of confinement be set by correctional personnel. In either situation, the decision about what will actually happen to a defendant is a discretionary judgment. As a matter of fact, most sentencing laws give judges unusually broad discretion in fixing penalties for various offenses; Judge Marvin Frankel has stated that "the almost wholly unchecked and sweeping powers we give to judges in the fashioning of sentences are terrifying and intolerable for a society that professes devotion of the rule to law."[44]

One major concern regarding extreme judicial discretion is the degree to which disparity exists in the sentencing process. Different sentences are often given to offenders who are convicted of similar offenses and whose backgrounds are similar. Disparity in sentencing is particularly acute when there is basically no difference in the backgrounds and previous criminal records of offenders. It is obviously unfair for one offender with no previous criminal record who is convicted of stealing an automobile to be placed on probation, while another offender with a similar background who is convicted of the same crime is sentenced to a house of correction for one year. Nevertheless, this kind of sentencing disparity exists within courts and between jurisdictions on both federal and state levels.[45]

Of course, there are other reasons why decisions made by the trial courts result in unequal and unjustifiable sentences. These include: (1) inequitable statutes, (2) the lack of sentencing criteria, (3) unfamiliarity on the part of judges with the programs and institutions to which they sentence offenders, and (4) the lack of available sentencing alternatives. To a great degree, however, the disparity problem results from the broad discretion each judge has in sentencing offenders according to the judge's perception of the circumstances of a particular crime.

Another major problem in sentencing concerns the court's need to obtain relevant and necessary information in order to make a sentencing decision. As was previously mentioned, the pre-sentence investigation and report is the predominant means for providing this information. Yet, wide variations can be found in the manner in which these reports are used throughout the country. Some states require reports for certain classes of offenses, such as felonies; others make the report a discretionary request from the court; and still others make the pre-sentence report both mandatory and discretionary for certain types of crimes and dispositions.[46] Few states have adopted the recommendation of the President's Crime Commission that all courts should require pre-sentence reports for all offenders, whether those reports result from full field investigations by probation officers or, in the case of minor offenders, from the use of short forms.[47] Thus, many offenders are sentenced by courts who lack information necessary for making the sentencing decision.

Furthermore, the reliability and accuracy of the information used in the pre-sentence reports are often questionable. The report must not be used until the court has made a determination of the defendant's guilt, so as not to prejudice the judge or the jury during the trial; however, much of the information in the report, even when used at the sentencing stage of the criminal process, goes unchallenged and is generally not subject to cross-examination or review. Occasionally, information in a pre-sentence report is erroneous and results in an inappropriate sentencing disposition. One such example is the extreme case of *United States v. Weston*,[48] which occurred in 1971. In that case, the defendant was convicted of receiving, concealing, and transferring heroin from one jurisdiction to another. Prior to examining the pre-sentence report, the judge indicated his desire to impose a minimum sentence. Upon reviewing the report, the judge found statements indicating that the defendant was allegedly the chief supplier of heroin to the western Washington state area. The judge then imposed the maximum sentence. On appeal, the circuit court of appeals revised the case because the government could not prove the allegations made in the pre-sentence report and because the basic content of the report was not disclosed to the defense attorney.

It is therefore important that the report be compiled in a highly professional manner by probation officers, and that the defense attorney have access to the report prior to the sentencing hearing to allow him to refute any incorrect information. In addition, the pre-sentence report should not be treated as a public record but should be made available only to personnel and agencies having a professional interest in the information contained in the report.

A third problem, and one of the most fundamental issues in sentencing, is the law governing sentence structures. As was previously mentioned, most jurisdictions have penal codes which include different sentencing systems: there are indeterminate sentences which give wide discretion to the court; mandatory sentences which allow the court no discretion; and parole laws which affect the length of the sentence. In addition, the judge has to choose a disposition from a variety of options ranging from dismissal to incarceration. As the National Advisory Commission on Criminal Justice Standards and Goals has stated:

> With little guidance from the legislature or little training in sentencing techniques, the judge must select the proper sentence on the basis of his personal view of the purposes of the criminal law and the effect of a particular sentence on a particular offender.[49]

This complex situation exists because the sentencing process represents a tripartite function—namely, the involvement of the legislative, judicial, and executive branches of government.

The legislature creates the statutes which represent the sentencing policy of each jurisdiction. However, most legislatures have enacted criminal statutes in an inconsistent, haphazard, and unplanned fashion. Many statutes are enacted in response to some specific crime, while others are passed which are unrelated to the seriousness of the crime. Thus, statutory inequities develop because legislative bodies often fail to relate new criminal sanctions to existing law.

The judiciary is required to impose the sentencing decision; however, the sentencing judge often receives little guidance from the statute about what the court is expected to accomplish with a particular law. Normally, the judge's primary decision is one of whether a particular defendant will remain in the community or be placed in confinement.

The third aspect of sentencing involves the executive branch, which is ordinarily represented by a corrections agency. This agency is required to implement the sentencing decision of the court. How corrections deals with an offender may be totally contrary to what the court intended when it sentenced the offender.

As a result, the most flagrant kinds of sentencing conflict exist within the sentencing process, primarily because sentencing is a combined judicial, legislative, and executive function. To partially resolve this dilemma, the legislative system must establish more clearly defined sentencing goals and alternatives to guide decisions made by the courts and correctional agencies.[50]

A fourth area requiring further work involves the application of due process safeguards at the imposition of the sentence. Initially, it was felt that constitutional protections for the defendant extended only at the criminal trial. Of course, that is no longer true; the accused is guaranteed certain rights at pre-trial and post-trial proceedings as well. Most sentencing courts hold sentencing hearings, and all are required to provide the convicted offender with the right to counsel. At the time of sentencing, other rights such as the right to a hearing, the right to present witnesses at the sentencing hearing, the right of cross-examination, the right of review and exclusion of unsubstantiated information, and the right to a statement of reasons for the sentencing decision are all issues for which no clear-cut court ruling exists. However, based on the development of formal safeguards in other areas of criminal justice, it can be expected that the courts will begin to examine sentencing procedures more thoroughly in the near future.

SENTENCING
REFORM

In light of the serious problems associated with present sentencing practices, it is important to identify some of the major suggestions that have been made for improving the sentencing system in the United States.

For the past few years, many states and federal government have been examining their penal codes in an effort to simplify the classification of offenses, remove long maximum prison terms, and decriminalize minor offenses. This process of self-examination has occurred in many states, including such diverse jurisdictions as New York, Maine, and Florida. Other states such as Massachusetts have sought legislative approval for proposed criminal codes which would completely revise their sentencing structures. The Congress of the United States has also been involved in the process of revising the Federal Penal Code, which defines crimes and establishes punishments for federal offenses.

A great deal of work has been done by three particular groups in an attempt to establish statutory guidelines for sentencing. The American Law Institute in its *Model Penal Code* provides a constructive approach to classifying and standardizing various offenses and penalties.[51] It reduces all crimes to three grades of felony and two grades of misdemeanor and calls for shorter maximum penalties within each grade. The judge may set minimum terms of imprisonment, but correctional authorities have discretion to grant parole. Under the Code, probation can be allowed in almost all cases, and criteria are listed for the granting or withholding of probation. The *Model Penal Code* also establishes standards for dealing with the habitual offender.

The *Model Sentencing Act* of the National Council on Crime and Delinquency, published in 1963 and redrafted in 1972, is another important reference for statutory sentencing standards.[52] The Act deals with the sentencing of felony offenders, and not misdemeanants, and seeks to reduce long maximum sentences, encourage the use of probation, and provide procedural safeguards at the dispositional hearing. It establishes a 5-year maximum prison sentence for nondangerous offenders (if they are not placed on probation), and a 30-year maximum term for the habitual offender.

A third set of standards, created in 1968, is the American Bar Association's *Standards Relating to Sentencing Alternatives and Procedures*. These Standards include recommendations regarding the sentence authority, statutory structure, judicial discretion, an information base for sentencing, and the development of sentencing criteria. They establish lower and more realistic maximum terms for most offenses and recommend that mandatory and minimum sentences be abolished. The *Standards* operate under the philosophy that lengthy prison sentences are often given to offenders who do not pose a serious threat to society; as a result, they call for greater flexibility in sentencing, the extensive use of probation, partial confinement, special facilities, and fines. These *Standards,* along with the *Model Penal Code* and the *Model Sentencing Act*, are used as guidelines to assist jurisdictions in amending their sentencing codes to more closely conform with the needs of a modern criminal justice system.

In addition, certain devices have been developed in an attempt to promote greater efficiency and fairness in the sentencing decision. These include (1) sentencing institutes, (2) sentencing councils, and (3) appellate reviews of sentences.

Groups of judges meet at sentencing institutes for the purpose of discussing problems relating to sentencing. These institutes came into being through federal legislation passed by Congress in 1958, and have existed in the federal judicial system since that time. Some states such as New York, California, and Massachusetts have also been successful in developing sentencing institutes. The goals of proceedings such as these, as stated in the American Bar Association's *Standards Relating to Sentencing Alternatives and Procedures,* are "to develop criteria for the imposition of sentences, to provide a forum in which newer judges can be exposed to more experienced judges, and to expose all sentencing judges to new developments and techniques."[53]

Sentencing councils, on the other hand, are meetings of judges who sit regularly in a particular court. During a sentencing council, the judges discuss appropriate dispositions of defendants who are awaiting sentencing. The sentencing judge retains the ultimate responsibility for selecting and imposing the sentence, while the other judges act in an advisory capacity. Normally, the judges meet in groups of three to consider the sentencing alternatives in pending cases. The sentencing council has the following advantages: (1) it reveals to judges their differences in sentencing philosophies; (2) it provides an opportunity for judges to debate their differences; and (3) it provides a forum for periodic evaluation of a court's sentencing practice.

Ordinarily, the sentencing decision for a particular case is in the hands of a single judge. Although sentencing councils provide a departure from this individual approach, they are also particularly useful in that they serve to lessen the amount of disparity in sentencing practices. One major difficulty regarding the sentencing council is the fact that information gathered from other judges may impair the ability of the sentencing judge to give open-minded consideration to all arguments at the dispositional hearing. The United States District Court for the Eastern District of Michigan originally developed the idea for the sentencing council, and such councils have since been implemented in other federal as well as state court systems. Another effort at sentencing reform provides the convicted offender with an appellate review of the sentence in an attempt to prevent the excessive and arbitrary use of judicial discretion which often results in widely disparate sentences for the same offense. This device, which was established through statutory authority, allows a person sentenced to a prison term to appeal for a review of the sentence, and not for a retrial of the case. An appellate court, often sitting with three judges, reviews the petition for the change in the sentence and is empowered to reduce or increase the original sentence of the trial court.

In the past, few states allowed for appellate review of sentences. Even today, no more than one-half of the states review the merits of a sentence upon appeal. Review has been unavailable in many jurisdictions because: (1) there are fears that it might greatly increase litigation, (2) appellate judges are less able to determine appropriate sentences because they do not observe the defendants, and (3) sentencing is generally a matter of judicial discretion and not a matter of law.

On the other hand, the American Bar Association's *Standards Relating to Appellate Review of Sentences* proposes that sentence review should be available in every case in which review of a trial leading to conviction would be available.[54]

SUMMARY

The practice of sentencing can be traced back to ancient history, when retaliation and physical abuse were used to punish an offender for wrong-doing. Modern sentencing in today's criminal justice system is based on deterrence, incapacitation, and rehabilitation. Traditional dispositions include fines, probation, and incarceration, with probation being the most common choice. The death penalty continues to be the most controversial sentence, with over half of the states reinstituting capital punishment laws since the *Furman v. Georgia* decision of 1972.

One of the most significant features of the sentencing process is its tripartite structure involving the legislature, the judge, and the correctional agency. Actions of each of these agencies affect the type of sentence, the length of sentence, and the release time imposed on the offender.

While the courts today seek to fit the sentence to the individual and not to the crime, this philosophy often results in sentencing disparity. Methods for making dispositions more uniform include appellate reviews of sentences and the use of sentencing councils and institutes.

QUESTIONS FOR DISCUSSION

1. Discuss the sentencing dispositions in your jurisdiction. What are the pros and cons of each?

2. Compare the different sentencing structures. What are the similarities and differences? Why are many jurisdictions considering the passage of mandatory sentencing laws?

3. Discuss the issue of capital punishment. In your opinion, does it serve as a deterrent? What new rulings have the United States Supreme Court made on the legality of the death penalty?

4. Why does the problem of sentencing disparity exist? Do programs exist that can reduce disparate sentences? If so, what are they?

**1.** See generally Sol Rubin, *Law of Criminal Correction—Student Edition* (St. Paul, Minn.: West Publishing Co., 1973), Chapter 1.

**2.** Ibid., pp. 13–15.

**3.** See Richard R. Korn and Lloyd W. McCorkle, *Criminology and Penology* (New York: Holt, Rinehart and Winston, 1965).

**4.** Sol Rubin, *Law of Criminal Correction*, p. 17.

**5.** Ibid.

**6.** National Advisory Commission on Criminal Justice Standards and Goals, *Corrections*, (Washington, D.C.: U.S. Government Printing Office, 1973), Standards 5.3, 5.4, 5.5, pp. 155–163.

**7.** William Bowers, *Executions in America* (Lexington, Mass.: D.C. Heath & Co., 1974).

**8.** 408 U.S. 238, 92 S.Ct. 2726, 33 L.Ed.2d 346 (1972).

**9.** 428 U.S. 153, 96 S.Ct. 2909, 49 L.Ed.2d 859 (1976).

**10.** Ibid., 96 S.Ct. at 2940–2941.

**11.** 428 U.S. 262, 96 S.Ct. 2950, 49 L.Ed.2d 929 (1976).

**12.** 428 U.S. 242, 96 S.Ct. 2960, 49 L.Ed.2d 913 (1976).

**13.** *Jurek*, 96 S.Ct. at 2955.

**14.** 428 U.S. 325, 96 S.Ct. 3001, 49 L.Ed.2d 974 (1976).

**15.** 428 U.S. 280, 96 S.Ct. 2978, 49 L.Ed.2d 944 (1976).

**16.** Ibid., 96 S.Ct. at 2986, 2991.

**17.** 438 U.S. 584, 97 S.Ct. 2861, 53 L.Ed.2d 982 (1977).

**18.** 430 U.S. 349, 97 S.Ct. 1197, 51 L.Ed.2d 393 (1977).

**19.** 438 U.S. 801, 98 S.Ct. 2981, 57 L.Ed.2d 973 (1978).

**20.** Robert H. Dann, "The Deterrent Effect of Capital Punishment," *Friends Social Service Series* 29:1 (1935).

**21.** Karl F. Schuessler, "The Deterrent Influence of the Death Penalty," *The Annals* 284:54 (1952).

**22.** Thorsten Sellin, "Effect of Repeal and Reintroduction of the Death Penalty on Homicide Rates" in *The Death Penalty* Thorsten Sellin, ed., (Philadelphia: The American Law Institute, 1959).

**23.** Walter C. Reckless, "Use of the Death Penalty," *Crime and Delinquency* 15:43 (1969).

**24.** Isaac Ehrlich, "The Deterrent Effect of Capital Punishment: A Question of Life or Death," *American Economic Review* 65:397 (1975).

**25.** William J. Bowers and Glenn L. Pierce, "The Illusion of Deterrence in Isaac Ehrlich's Research on Capital Punishment," *Yale Law Journal* 85:187–208 (1975).

**26.** American Bar Association, Commission on Correctional Facilities and Services, *Sentencing Computation, Laws and Practice, A Preliminary Survey*, (Washington, D.C.: American Bar Assn., 1974), p. 1.

**27.** Model Sentencing Act, Sec. 9. Reprinted with permission of the National Council on Crime and Delinquency, from Model Sentencing Act in Crime and Delinquency, Oct. '72; Model Penal Code, Sec. 6.06. Copyright 1962 by the American Law Institute. Reprinted with the permission of the American Law Institute.

**28.** American Bar Association, Commission on Correctional Facilities and Services, *Sentencing Computation, Laws and Practice, A Preliminary Survey*, p. 8.

**29.** Ibid., p. 7.

**30.** Leonard Cargan and Mary A. Coates, "The Indeterminate Sentence and Judicial Bias," *Crime and Delinquency* 20, no. 2, (April 1974): 144–156.

31. See Massachusetts General Laws, Chap. 269 §10, Chap. 649, Acts of 1974.

32. Timothy Schellhardt, "Law and Order," *The Wall Street Journal* 24 June, 1976.

33. See generally, "A Symposium on Sentencing," Part I & II, Hofstra Law Review 7:1 (1979).

34. Marvin Zalman, "The Rise and Fall of the Indeterminate Sentence," Wayne Law Review 24:857 (1978).

35. Twentieth Century Fund, Fair and Certain Punishment—Report of Twentieth Century Fund Task Force on Criminal Sentencing (New York, 1976).

36. Zalman, "The Rise and Fall of the Indeterminate Sentence," p. 877.

37. Ibid., pp. 867–878.

38. Stephen P. Lagoy, Frederick Hussey and John Kramer, "A Comparative Assessment of Determinate Sentencing in the Four Pioneer States," Crime and Delinquency Journal 10:400 (1978).

39. National Conference of Commissioners on Uniform State Laws, Model Sentencing and Corrections Act, July, 1978.

40. See 96th Federal Congress, 1979–1980 H.R. 6233.

41. Leonard Orland, "From Vengeance to Vengeance: Sentencing Reform and the Demise of Rehabilitation," Hofstra Law Review 7:51 (1979).

42. American Bar Association, Commission on Correctional Facilities and Services, *Sentencing Computation, Laws and Practice, A Preliminary Survey*, p. 32.

43. 410 U.S. 263, 35 L.Ed.2d 282, 93 S.Ct. 1055 (1973).

44. See Marvin E. Frankel, *Criminal Sentences—Law Without Order* (New York: Hill & Wang, 1973), p. 5.

45. National Advisory Commission on Criminal Justice Standards and Goals, *Corrections*, pp. 146–147.

46. See American Bar Association, *Standards Relating to Sentencing Alternatives and Procedures* (New York: Institute of Judicial Administration, 1968), Sec. 4.1, pp. 202–203.

47. President's Commission on Law Enforcement and Administration of Justice, *The Challenge of Crime in a Free Society* (Washington, D.C.: U.S. Government Printing Office, 1967), p. 144.

48. 448 F.2d 626 (9th Cir. 1971).

49. National Advisory Commission on Criminal Justice Standards and Goals, *Corrections*, p. 146.

50. Ibid., p. 143.

51. American Law Institute, *Model Penal Code* (Proposed Official Draft, 1962).

52. National Council on Crime and Delinquency, *Model Sentencing Act*, 1963 and 1972.

53. American Bar Association, *Standards Relating to Sentencing Alternatives and Procedures*, Standard 7.2 and Commentary, p. 299.

54. See generally American Bar Association, *Standards Relating to Appellate Review of Sentences* (New York: Institute of Judicial Administration, 1968).

# New Forms of Sentencing*

## THE JUDICIAL MODEL: MAINE

On May 1, 1976, Maine became the first jurisdiction to abandon the indeterminate sentence and the parole system. Although its comprehensive criminal code revision was characterized as a harbinger of a new era in criminal sentencing, Maine's "definite" or "flat" sentence approach differs considerably from those that have appeared since.

The critical feature in Maine's new sentencing scheme is the centrality of the judiciary in the determination of sentence. The very nature of the indeterminate sentence demands that judges exercise great discretion in imposing punishments. Yet actual time served is, in turn, controlled to a considerable degree by administrative agencies such as the parole board. In contrast, determinate sentencing schemes generally focus on a legislatively oriented model in which specific sentences or sentence ranges are prescribed for each offense. Maine is unique in that its judges are empowered to impose fixed sentences limited only by statutory maxima. There is no external review. Specifically, the Maine code establishes six categories of crime and, except for murder, prescribes only the upper limit of the criminal sanction for each category. The trial court may impose imprisonment for any definite term, within this upper limit. The categories of crime established by the code and the maximum sentences permitted are illustrated in Table 13.3.

## THE LEGISLATIVE MODEL: CALIFORNIA

The California legislature's intent in revising the state's sentencing structure is not only apparent in its attempts to limit sentence discretion by law but is also clearly stated in the statute itself. Unlike the Indiana code which contains no statement of purpose, or the Maine criminal code in which the purposes of sentencing are enumerated but ambiguous (for example, both the elimination of inequalities and the encouragement of differentiation are cited), the California code states explicitly that the sole purpose of sentencing is punishment and that

---

*From Stephen P. Lagoy, Frederick A. Hussey, and John H. Kramer, "A Comparative Assessment of Determinate Sentencing in the Four Pioneer States," Crime and Delinquency (October, 1978): pp. 385–400. Footnotes omitted.

TABLE 13.3
Crime Categories and
Sentencing Ranges in Maine

| Class | Maximum Term | Fine | Example(s) |
|---|---|---|---|
| Murder | Life or any term of imprisonment that is not less than 25 years | | |
| Class A | 20 years | | Felony murder; kidnapping; rape; armed robbery |
| Class B | 10 years | Not more than $10,000 | Trafficking in narcotic drugs; robbery (unarmed); theft (in excess of $5,000) |
| Class C | 5 years | Not more than $2,500 | Manslaughter by motor vehicle; burglary (unarmed, no injury) |
| Class D | 1 year | Not more than $1,000 | Unlawful gambling |
| Class E | 6 months | Not more than $500 | Prostitution; theft (less than $500) |

the goals of the sentencing system should be the elimination of sentence disparity and the promotion of sentence uniformity. To the extent that the California code revision meets these objectives, it follows the blueprint for determinacy drafted by such notable proponents of sentencing reform as the American Friends Service Committee, Alan Dershowitz, David Fogel, and Andrew von Hirsch to a much greater degree than have sentencing statutes enacted thus far in the other states.

The California legislature established a presumptive sentencing scheme which limits prison terms to a very narrow range of possibilities. Parole discretion is abolished and judicial discretion is narrowly defined. Every felony offense falls into one of four categories for purposes of sentencing, and for each category, three possible incarcerative terms are specified. The middle term, or "presumptive" sentence, must be imposed by courts unless aggravating or mitigating circumstances are

presented and proved during a sentencing hearing. In cases involving aggravating circumstances, the court is limited to the high term prescribed by the legislature; in those involving mitigating circumstances, to the lower term. If the court determines that the higher or lower term should be imposed, the judge's factual findings and the reasons for the sentence must be stated in writing. Table 13.4 contains a summary and an illustration of these provisions.

## THE HYBRID APPROACH: INDIANA

The sentencing provisions of the Indiana code might be best described as a hybrid approach to determinate sentencing. While adopting the mechanics of presumptive sentencing (specified penalties, aggravating and mitigating factors, limited parole function), the code grants considerable judicial discretion in the determination of sentence lengths. Thus, in terms of its apportionment of sentencing

TABLE 13.4
Felony Categories and Range
of Penalties in California

| Presumptive Sentence | Range in Aggravation | Range in Mitigation | Example(s) |
|---|---|---|---|
| 6 years | +1 year | −1 year | Murder (second degree) |
| 4 years | +1 year | −1 year | Rape; sale of heroin |
| 3 years | +1 year | −1 year | Robbery (unarmed); manslaughter |
| 2 years | +1 year | −8 months | Burglary; grand theft |

authority, the code is neither "judicial" (as in Maine) nor "legislative" (as in California).

The Indiana code classifies all crime into ten categories (five classes of felonies, two classes of misdemeanors, and three classes of infractions), prescribes the appropriate range of sentences for each category, and requires the trial court to impose a fixed term at the time of sentencing. It specifies a presumptive incarcerative sentence for all felonies while allowing substantial deviations from that sentence in cases where the trial court finds aggravating or mitigating circumstances (though still requiring some period of incarceration). These provisions are summarized and illustrated in Table 13.5.

TABLE 13.5
Felony Categories and
Sentencing Ranges in Indiana

| Class | Presumptive Sentence | Range in Aggravation | Range in Mitigation | Fine | Example(s) |
|---|---|---|---|---|---|
| Murder* | 40 years | +20 years | −10 years | Not more than $10,000 | |
| Class A | 30 years | +20 years | −10 years | Not more than $10,000 | Kidnapping (for ransom); dealing in major narcotics |
| Class B | 10 years | +10 years | −4 years | Not more than $10,000 | Rape; armed robbery |
| Class C | 5 years | +3 years | −3 years | Not more than $10,000 | Robbery (unarmed); burglary |
| Class D** | 2 years | +2 years | 0 | Not more than $10,000 | Theft |

*The death sentence may be imposed in instances in which the state proves the existence of an aggravating circumstance as defined by law.

**The judge has the discretion to treat such offenses as Class A misdemeanors.

# Probation

CHAPTER OUTLINE

KEY TERMS

THE CONCEPT
OF PROBATION

Probation may take on a number of different meanings, depending on how and when the term is used and by whom. Probation can refer to a sentence; a convicted offender is placed and maintained in the community under the supervision of a duly authorized agent of the court. It can also connote a status or process; the individual on probation is subject to certain rules and conditions which must be followed in order to remain in the community. Probation can also refer to an organization; the probation department manages, supervises, and treats offenders and carries out investigations for the court. Although the term has many meanings, it usually indicates a nonpunitive form of sentencing for convicted criminal offenders and delinquent youth, which emphasizes maintenance in the community and treatment without institutionalization or other forms of punishment.

The philosophy of probation is one which believes that the average offender is not actually a dangerous criminal or a menace to society. Advocates of probation suggest that when offenders are institutionalized instead of being granted community release, the prison community becomes their new reference point, they are forced to interact with hardened criminals, and the ex-con label prohibits them from making successful adjustments to society. Probation provides offenders with the opportunity to prove themselves, gives them a second chance, and also allows them to be closely supervised by trained personnel who can help them to reestablish proper forms of behavior in the community.

In actual practice, probation usually involves the suspension of the offender's sentence (usually replacing a term in an institution, though minors can simply be placed on probation without the threat of detention) in return for the promise of good behavior in the community under the supervision of the probation department. As practiced in all 50 states and by the federal government, probation implies a contract between the court and the offender in which the former promises to hold a prison term in abeyance while the latter promises to adhere to a set of rules or conditions mandated by the court. If the rules are violated, and especially if the probationer commits another criminal offense, probation may be revoked; this means that the contract is terminated and the original sentence enforced. If an offender on probation commits a second offense which is more severe than the first, he or she may also be indicted, tried, and sentenced on that second offense. Probation may be revoked simply because the rules and conditions of probation have not been met, however; it is not necessary for an offender to commit further crime.

Each probationary sentence is for a fixed period of time, depending on the seriousness of the offense and the statutory law of the jurisdiction. Probation is considered served when the offender fulfills the conditions set by the court for that period of time; he can then live without interference from the state.

THE GRANTING
OF PROBATION

Probationary sentences may be granted by state and federal district courts and state superior (felony) courts. Probation has become an accepted and widely used sentence for adult felons and misdemeanants and juvenile delinquents.

In some states, juries may grant probation as part of their sentencing power, or they may make recommendations to judges which they will usually follow if the case meets certain legally regulated criteria (e.g., if it falls within a certain class of offenses as determined by statute).[1] While juries can recommend probation, the judge has the final say in the matter and may grant probation at his or her discretion. In nonjury trials probation is granted solely by judicial mandate.

In most jurisdictions, all juvenile offenders are eligible for probation, as are most adults. Some state statutes prohibit probation for certain types of adult offenders, usually those who have engaged in repeated and serious violent crimes such as murder or rape.

The term of a probationary sentence may extend to the limit of the suspended prison term, or the court may set a time limit which reflects the sentencing period. For misdemeanors, probation usually extends for the entire period of the jail sentence, while felonies are more likely to warrant probationary periods which are actually shorter and more limited than their prison sentences would have been. The Federal Criminal Code recommends that probation for felons last 5 years; juveniles are typically placed on probation for periods extending from 6 to 24 months. Some state court judges may also impose monetary fines when granting probation; this practice is commonly applied to white-collar crimes, where an offender may have profited from an illegal business practice.

Some judges may wish to grant an offender probation only after the offender has sampled prison life, perhaps to emphasize that the rules of probation must be kept. While probation cannot be granted after the offender has actually been incarcerated (this practice is known as parole), a judge does have a number of devices which allow institutionalization of a convicted offender for a limited period of time prior to probation. For example, when the offender is charged with a variety of offenses, the judge may impose a short jail term on one criminal count and probation on the others. In some states and in the Federal Criminal Code, a jail term can actually be a condition of probation. The Federal Probation Statute states that the court "may impose a sentence in excess of six months and provide that the defendant be confined in a jail-type institution for a period not exceeding six months and that the execution of the remainder of the sentence be suspended and the defendant placed on probation for such period and upon such terms and conditions as the court deems best."[2]

However, the granting of probation after a jail sentence is frowned upon by experts who believe that even a brief period of incarceration can mitigate the purpose of probation which is to provide the offender with nonstigmatized, community-based treatment. The National Advisory Commission on Criminal Justice Standards and Goals shares this view:

With this goal in mind, the practice of commitment to an institution for the initial period of probation (variously known as shock probation, split sentence, etc.), as the Federal and some State statutes permit, should be discontinued. This type of sentence defeats the purpose of probation, which is the earliest possible reintegration of the offender into the community. Short-term commitment subjects the probationer to the destructive effects of institutionalization, disrupts his life in the community, and stigmatizes him for having been in jail. Further, it may add to his confusion as to his status.[3]

Some states such as Illinois have disallowed by statute the practice of combining probation with jail sentences. Those who disagree with this view, however, would argue that an initial jail sentence probably makes the offender more receptive to the conditions of probation, since it amply illustrates the problems the offender will face if probation is violated.

CRITERIA FOR PROBATION

Probation is the sentence of choice in most jurisdictions. A majority of juvenile offenders found to be delinquent are granted probation, while the proportion of probation sentences given out to adults varies among jurisdictions and may depend on the quality of probation services available in the community. One study reported that probationary sentences granted in the United States ranged from 13.9% in a West Virginia jurisdiction to 78.3% in Michigan.[4]

The popularity of the probationary sentence is borne out by the findings of the first comprehensive survey of state and local probation departments in the United States.[5] The study found that 923,064 adults and 328,854 juveniles were on probation at the time of the survey. The survey also found that 86% of adult and 77% of juvenile probationers were males; half the adults were felons.

The national survey investigated the staff and workload of probation departments. It discovered that almost two million people are supervised on probation annually, that almost one million pre-sentence investigations are conducted, and that this monumental workload is borne by a total staff of under 60,000 probation officers and 20,000 volunteer workers. The average caseload at any one time was 48.

Several criteria are involved in granting probation. On one level, the statutes of many states determine the factors that should be taken into account when a judge makes a decision to grant probation.[6] In a similar vein, the Model Penal Code lists the following elements as proper criteria for the consideration of a probation sentence.[7]

1. The Court shall deal with a person who has been convicted of a crime without imposing sentence of imprisonment unless, having regard to the nature and circumstances of the crime and the history, character and condition of the defendant, it is of the opinion that his imprisonment is necessary for protection of the public because:
   a. there is undue risk that during the period of a suspended sentence or probation the defendant will commit another crime; or
   b. the defendant is in need of correctional treatment that can be provided most effectively by his commitment to an institution; or
   c. a lesser sentence will depreciate the seriousness of the defendant's crime.
2. The following grounds, while not controlling the direction of the Court, shall be accorded weight in favor of withholding sentence of imprisonment:

a. the defendant's criminal conduct neither caused nor threatened serious harm;
b. the defendant did not contemplate that his criminal conduct would cause or threaten serious harm;
c. the defendant acted under a strong provocation;
d. there were substantial grounds tending to excuse or justify the defendant's criminal conduct, though failing to establish a defense;
e. the victim of the defendant's criminal conduct induced or facilitated its commission;
f. the defendant has compensated or will compensate the victim of his criminal conduct for the damage or injury that he sustained;
g. the defendant has no history of prior delinquency or criminal activity or has led a law-abiding life for a substantial period of time before the commission of the present crime;
h. the defendant's criminal conduct was the result of circumstances unlikely to recur;
i. the character and attitudes of the defendant indicate that he is unlikely to commit another crime;
j. the defendant is particularly likely to respond affirmatively to probationary treatment;
k. the imprisonment of the defendant would entail excessive hardship to himself or his dependents.
3. When a person has been convicted of a crime and is not sentenced to imprisonment, the Court shall place him on probation if he is in need of the supervision, guidance, assistance or direction that the probation service can provide.

While these suggested criteria are often followed by judges, probation decision making is quite varied and an individual offender granted probation in one jurisdiction might not be if tried in another. In addition to being provided for by statutory mandate, probation is often granted by a discretionary decision based on the beliefs and attitudes of the presiding judge and probation staff.

## CONDITIONS OF PROBATION

A probation sentence is usually viewed as an act of clemency on the part of court, and is reflective of the rehabilitative aspects of the criminal justice system. Yet, there are two distinct sides to the probationary contract drawn up between the offender and the court; one side involves the treatment and rehabilitation of the offender through regular meetings with trained probation staff or other treatment personnel; and the other reflects the supervision and enforcement aspects of probation. Probation as practiced today often saddles the probationer with rules and conditions which may impede achievement of the stated treatment goals of the probation department by emphasizing the punitive aspects of criminal justice.

When probation is fixed as a sentence, the court sets down certain rules as conditions for qualifying for community treatment. In many jurisdictions, statutory law mandates that certain conditions be applied in every probation case; usually, the sentencing judge maintains broad discretion to add to or lessen these standard conditions on a case-by-case basis.

A presiding judge may not, of course, impose capricious or cruel conditions, such as requiring an offender to make restitution far beyond financial capacity. In one case, for example, it was held that a condition of probation which (1) had no relationship to the crime of which the offender was convicted, (2) related to conduct which was not itself criminal, and (3) required or forbade conduct which was not reasonably related to future criminality, did not serve the statutory ends of probation and was therefore invalid.[8]

Probation conditions vary from jurisdiction to jurisdiction and among age groups of offenders. A number of national sources have suggested standard conditions which reflect the conflict inherent in the control vs. treatment approach to probation. The American Bar Association's standards for probation conditions are a good example.[9]

Nature and determination of conditions.

1.  It should be a condition of every sentence to probation that the probationer lead a law-abiding life during the period of his probation. No other conditions should be required by statute; but the sentencing court should be authorized to prescribe additional conditions to fit the circumstances of each case. Development of standard conditions as a guide to sentencing courts is appropriate so long as such conditions are not routinely imposed.

2.  Conditions imposed by the court should be designed to assist the probationer in leading a law-abiding life. They should be reasonably related to his rehabilitation and not unduly restrictive of his liberty or incompatible with his freedom of religion. They should not be so vague or ambiguous as to give no real guidance.

3.  Conditions may appropriately deal with matters such as the following:
    a.  cooperating with a program of supervision;
    b.  meeting family responsibilities;
    c.  maintaining steady employment or engaging or refraining from engaging in a specific employment or occupation;
    d.  pursuing prescribed educational or vocational training;
    e.  undergoing available medical or psychiatric treatment;
    f.  maintaining residence in a prescribed area or in a special facility established for or available to persons on probation;
    g.  refraining from consorting with certain types of people or frequenting certain types of places;
    h.  making restitution of the fruits of the crime or reparation for loss or damage caused thereby.

4.  Conditions requiring payment of fines, restitution, reparation, or family support should not go beyond the probationer's ability to pay.

5.  The performance bond now authorized in some jurisdictions should not be employed as a condition of probation.

6.  Probationers should not be required to pay the costs of probation.

These conditions are not too dissimilar from those prescribed by law in each of the 50 states.

Judges may amplify or restrict these conditions as befits a particular case. The offender who has a drinking problem may be required to participate in Alcoholics Anonymous or a similar treatment program. According to a common practice in the juvenile sector, a judge may assign work projects to youthful probationers; they may help charitable organizations or even aid the victims of their crimes. Indigent adults who cannot make any financial restitution, or cannot afford to pay a fine, may also be assigned work projects. It is not unusual for juveniles involved in vandalism or other acts of willful destruction of property to be required to clean up and repair the targets of their actions.

State and federal courts have allowed probation rules which vary from these general guidelines, but which seem to uphold the purposes of the probation concept, namely, rehabilitation and protection of the public. For example, a recent survey found that state and federal courts have allowed probation conditions barring probationers from their former line of employment if their criminal behavior indicates they cannot be trusted.[10] In one case of this kind, a Puerto Rican police officer who was found guilty of beating a citizen was placed on probation by a federal court under condition that he resign from the police department during the probationary period.[11] Probationers have also been prohibited from engaging in hobbies or pastimes which might lead them astray, such as going to the race track.[12] Ironically, courts have refrained from permitting probation rules requiring a lawyer convicted of a serious crime to resign from the legal profession.[13]

Other unique probation rules have required probationers to refrain from political associations, such as being an Irish Republican Army sympathizer,[14] or taking part in political demonstrations.[15] However, courts have been reluctant to allow probation conditions which conflict with basic human rights of privacy and liberty, such as requiring that a sex offender undergo sterilization, or a child abuser to refrain from having any more children.[16] Nonetheless, the privacy issue does not extend to all areas of human endeavor; for example, a federal court found it permissible for a court to order a probationer to provide his supervisor with copies of his tax returns.[17] In general, probation rules cannot be capricious, cruel, or beyond the capacity of a normal person to comply.

THE ADMINISTRATION OF PROBATION SERVICES

Probation services are organized in a variety of different ways, depending on the state and jurisdiction in which they are located. In some states such as Massachusetts, a statewide probation service exists but actual control over departments is localized within each court jurisdiction. Other states maintain a strong statewide authority with centralized control and administration. Many states combine probation and parole services in a single unit; some states combine juvenile and adult probation departments, while others maintain these departments separately.

The typical probation department is situated in a single court district, such as a juvenile, superior, district, or municipal court. The relationship between the department and court personnel (especially the judge) is an extremely close one.

In the typical department, the chief probation officer (CPO) sets policy, supervises hiring, determines what training should be emphasized, and may personally discuss with or recommend sentencing to the judge. In state-controlled departments, some of the CPO's duties are mandated by the central office; training guidelines, for example, may be determined at the state level. If, on the other hand, the department is locally controlled, the CPO is invested with great discretion in the management of the department.

In most large probation departments, the administration also comprises one or more assistant chiefs. Sometimes, in departments of moderate size, each of these middle managers will be responsible for a particular aspect of probation services: one assistant chief will oversee training; another will supervise treatment and counseling services; and another will act as a liaison with police or other agencies. In smaller departments, the CPO and the executive officers may also maintain a caseload or investigate cases for the court. For example, the chief may handle a few of the most diffficult cases personally and concentrate on these. In larger municipal departments, however, the probation chief is a purely administrative figure.

The line staff, or the probation officers (POs), may be in direct and personal contact with the entire supervisory staff, or they may be independent from the chief and answer mainly to the assistant chiefs. Line staff perform the following major functions: (1) they supervise or monitor cases assigned to them to insure that the rules of probation are maintained; (2) they attempt to rehabilitate their cases through specialized treatment techniques; (3) they investigate the lives of convicted offenders in order to enable the court to make intelligent sentencing decisions; (4) occasionally, probation officers will collect fines due the court or oversee the collection of delinquent payments, such as child support; and (5) they will interview complainants and defendants to judge whether criminal action should be taken, whether cases can be decided informally, or whether a diversion should be advocated, and so on. This last procedure, called intake, is common in juvenile probation.

In some major cities the probation department is quite complex, controlling detention facilities, treatment programs, research, and evaluation staffs. In such a setting the CPO's role is similar to that of a director of a multiservice public facility. This CPO rarely comes into direct contact with clients, and behavior, attitudes, and values are quite different from the rural CPO who maintains a full caseload.

### State vs. Local Control of Probation

A number of reasons are advanced for probation being a local function.* First, local programs can typically develop better support from local citizenry and agencies.

---

*From President's Commission on Law Enforcement and Administration of Justice, *Task Force Report: The Courts* (Washington, D.C.: U.S. Government Printing Office, 1967) pp. 36–37.

Once the offender is adjudged and criminal or delinquent, and turned over to a state agency, there is a tendency to withdraw local services. Agencies at the same jurisdictional level tend to be united by a variety of administrative and traditional ties that do not extend to other levels. Employees of local jurisdictions usually have greater identification and ties with their communities, hence greater access to local resources.

Second, smaller operations tend to be more flexible and less bound by bureaucratic rigidity. Given aggressive leadership and community support, they may indeed outstrip the larger, more cumbersome state service. Finally, combining all local probation services in several large states, such as New York, Illinois, or California, could result in very large state operations. It would place a tremendous burden on administration. If it were weak, ineffectual, or politically determined, serious damage could result. While all of these risks prevail at lower levels of government—indeed they probably occur more frequently—the impact of any single poor leader is less widely spread.

On the other hand, state administration has some clear advantages. First there exists a greater probability that the same level of services will be extended to all areas and all clients. Uniform and equitable policies will be applied in recommendations for institutional and out-of-home placement. Wide variations in policy are manifest where administration is local. Some economies in detention and diagnostic services are possible if they are operated regionally rather than locally.

Another major advantage in the state's operation of probation services is the possibility of combining them with parole services and also better coordinating them with institution programs. Presently 30 of the 50 states combine felony probation and parole services for adults while 13 do so wholly or in part for juveniles.

The advantages of such combined services are several. A single agency is able to offer a continuity of service. Thus, the youngster placed on probation who fails and is sent to a training school can be handled by the same community agency when later released on parole. Information about the youth is readily available to the agency and important contacts with families and other significant persons can be maintained and further developed.

Combined services provide economies in the distribution of services. A single officer in a sparsely populated area of a state can service both probation and parole cases in the area. Similarly, the officer in an urban area can mobilize community resources in a given area of a city for both types of cases.

Additionally, there is a tendency for a local agency to "solve" a problem case, or one that requires a substantial investment of services or money, by commitment to the state instituion. This would be minimized if a single agency operated both programs.

The greatest resistance to combining probation and parole sevices generally stems from the fact that this inevitably means that probation services would become part of a state system and move away from local control. The opposite alternative— parole supervision services being administered by a series of local agencies—is clearly undesirable. Virtually every correctional authority contends that parole services must be centrally administered and coordinated with the institutional system, particularly in view of the increasing need to coordinate such services with various institutional and part-way programs.

A final argument for state administration of probation services is the historical fact that state agencies have generally been in the forefront of developing innovative

programs, demonstration projects, and correctional research. . . . Extensive research and demonstration are almost nonexistent at the local level.

DUTIES OF
PROBATION
OFFICERS

Staff officers in probation departments are usually charged with four primary tasks: investigation, intake, diagnosis, and treatment supervision.[18]

In the investigative stage, the officer conducts an inquiry within the
community in an effort to discover the factors related to the criminality of
the offender. The investigation is conducted primarily to gain information
for judicial sentences, but in the event the offender is placed on probation
the investigation becomes a useful testimony on which to base treatment
and supervision.

Intake is a process by which probation officers interview cases which
have been summoned to the court for initial appearances. Intake is most
common in the juvenile justice process but may also be employed in adult
misdemeanant cases. During juvenile court intake, the petitioner (e.g., the
juvenile) and the complainant (e.g., the private citizen or the police officer)
may work with the probation officer to determine an equitable solution to
the case. The PO may settle the case without further court action, recommend restitution or other compensation, initiate actions that result in
a court hearing, or recommend unofficial or informal probation.

Diagnosis is the analysis of the probationer's personality and the subsequent development of a personality profile which may be helpful in
treating the offender. Diagnosis involves the evaluation of the probationer,
using information from an initial interview (intake) or the pre-sentence
investigation, for the purpose of planning a proper treatment schedule.
The diagnosis should not merely reflect the desire or purpose of labeling
the offender neurotic or psychopathic, for example, but should "codify all
that has been learned about the individual, organized in such a way as to
provide a means for the establishment of future treatment goals."[19]

Finally, the probation officer participates in treatment supervision.
Based on knowledge of psychology, social work, or counseling and the
diagnosis of the offender, the probation officer plans a treatment schedule
which hopefully will allow the probationer to fulfill the probation contract
and make a reasonable adjustment to the community.

The treatment function is a product of both the investigative and
diagnostic aspect of probation. It is based on the PO's perceptions of the
probationer, including family problems, peer relationships, and employment background. Treatment may also involve the use of community resources. For example, a probation officer who discovers that a client has
a drinking problem may help to find a detoxification center willing to
accept the case, while a chronically underemployed offender may be given
job counseling or training. Or, in the case of juvenile delinquency, a probation officer may work with teachers and other school officials to help
a young offender stay in school. Of course, most cases do not (or cannot)
receive such individualized treatment; some treatment mechanisms merely
involve a weekly or biweekly phone call to determine whether a job is

being maintained or school attendance is satisfactory. In one large eastern probation office, for example, the senior probation administrator admitted that only 30% of their cases are actually given formal treatment supervision.

The proper diagnostic, treatment, and investigative skills needed for effective probation work are difficult to find in a single individual. Probation officers are often recruited from social work backgrounds, and the master's degree may be a prerequisite to senior advancement in most departments. Today, most jurisdictions require officers to have a background in the social sciences and to hold at least a bachelor's degree.

As the 1980s begin, it is evident that important changes are occurring in probation services. The probation concept continues to be viewed as a rehabilitory mechanism designed to give a "second chance" to worthy clients. Nonetheless, probation services are currently undergoing change and expansion, and probation officers are now engaging in new and more complex duties than ever before. In this section, a few of the more important expansions of probation service are documented.

EXPANSION OF
PROBATION
SERVICES

### Pre-Trial Programs

As mentioned in Chapter 10, the criminal justice system has witnessed the growth of many pre-trial programs designed to minimize the interface between offenders and agents of the law. These include Release on Recognizance programs (ROR) which allow suspects who lack bail money to avoid pre-trial detention in jails, and diversion programs which provide noncriminal alternatives for first time or minor criminal acts.

Though many pre-trial programs originated as federally sponsored demonstration projects, the termination of funding has led to their being implemented by local probation staffs.

An example of one of the more successful diversion programs is Hennepin County, Minnesota's *Operation De Novo*. Originally developed by the Urban Coalition of Minneapolis and sponsored by LEAA, the program has been operated by the Hennepin County Probation Department since 1975.[20]

Operation de Novo now works with both juvenile and adult offenders of both sexes, excluding only those accused of crimes of violence.[21] The staff is composed of both professionals and paraprofessionals, with substantial minority representation. Some of those hired would not meet prevailing civil service requirements. The program directors view this greater flexibility in choice of staff as contributing to the program's effectiveness.

In addition to individual counseling, clients participate in group sessions which address survival skills, personal growth, and problems related to juveniles, parents, drug dependency, and the family. Program staff work with clients to meet emergency needs, explore vocational options and set career goals, find suitable training or educational programs, and work out an acceptable restitution payment plan. In-house resources are supplemented by those available from community service agencies.

As of September, 1974, 1,600 defendants had been diverted: 84% are 18 to 25 years old, 30% are minority group members, 35% are women, and 66% of all clients are unemployed at the time of diversion. Since inception of the program, 67% of Operation de Novo clients have successfully met program goals and initial arrest charges have been dismissed. Thirty-three % have voluntarily terminated program services and returned to the courts for disposition. Only 17% of all diverted clients have been rearrested.

### Restitution

Probation officers have also been assigned to operate court-based restitution programs. The restitution concept requires defendants to either pay back the victims of crime (monetary restitution) or serve the community to compensate for their criminal acts (community service restitution). While the restitution concept also received its impetus from government funding, the termination of support has seen ongoing programs incorporated into existing court structures such as probation departments.

Ordinarily, restitution programs require offenders to pay back victims of crime (or serve the community) as a condition of probation. The process thus offers the convicted offender a chance to avoid a jail sentence or more lengthy probationary period. Restitution may also be used as a diversionary device, and offer some offenders the chance to avoid a criminal record altogether. In this instance, a judge will continue the case "without a finding" while the defendant completes the restitution order; after the probation department determines that restitution has been made, the case is dismissed.[22]

One well-known project is the Win-onus program which services Winona County, Minnesota. The program is offered to nonviolent adult misdemeanants and it is estimated that about 10% of the county's misdemeanor and traffic arrests are involved in the program. The program uses the following format: After screening and determination of eligibility for restitution by the judge, a plan is agreed to by the offender and a court service officer. The restitution plan is then presented to the judge for acceptance, rejection, or modification. If restitution is accepted, the Court Service Department monitors the order which may take the form of either monetary payments or community service. Credit for work service is given at $2.50 per hour; $10 is the equivalent to one day in jail; completing an Alcoholics Anonymous program or similar rehabilitation programs is the equivalent of $100; and a blood donation equals $15. A university-run evaluation of the program reveals a 2.7% recidivism rate as compared to 27% at the county jail. In addition, thousands of hours have been contributed to charitable organizations and thousands of dollars returned to victims.[23]

The Alternative Work Sentencing Program of the Quincy, Massachusetts, District Court (EARN-IT) services juveniles referred by the court, county probation department, and the district attorney's office.[24] This program seeks to bring the youth together with the victim of the crime in order to work out an equitable work program. The program staff also help determine the extent of the loss the victims incurred and help place the offender in paying jobs in order to earn the required restitution. Some jobs are in reality nonpaying community service placements in which youths are placed to work off court orders such as court costs, fines, and program costs at a rate of $2.30 an hour. All indications suggest that EARN-IT has been a tremendous success. In 1975, during the first year of its operation, the program returned $36,000 in restitution payments; in 1978, over $100,000 was collected to be returned to victims, the court, and the community. The success of EARN-IT has encouraged programs of a similar nature to be developed in many other areas around the country.

While the value of restitution seems evident due to its savings for the victim, defendant, criminal justice system, and community, there has been by no means unanimity concerning its effectiveness. Some critics have charged it is a "band-aid" approach to serious social problems and that it allows some criminals to simply "write a check" to avoid prosecution. On the other hand, restitution can actually be viewed as a punitive mechanism, since offenders are required to perform service tasks or pay penalties which would not otherwise be levied against them.[25]

Despite such sentiments, restitution is becoming a common practice in probation departments around the country.

### Volunteers in Probation

Since probation services are so widely used, the burden on individual probation officers is tremendous. It is not unusual for probation officers to maintain over one hundred clients. To meet this challenge, it has become commonplace for probation departments to employ paraprofessionals and volunteers in what might be considered regular-line positions. As mentioned previously, volunteers make up a significant portion of probation department staffs.

This practice is not without controversy. While volunteers and paraprofessionals can certainly make an important contribution, their employment has not always been met with enthusiasm by regular probation staff. They are sometimes viewed as a threat to job security and as an excuse for legislatures to deny budgetary increases for probation services.

Despite such fears, the volunteer concept has thrived. For example, in Travis County, Texas, 160 volunteers assist 34 regular probation officers to manage a caseload of 4,000 and provide intake and investigative functions.[26] In this program volunteers come from a variety of occupations and social circumstances. One hundred of them are women; 61 are men. About 25% are of minority extraction. Since the campus of the University of Texas is but a few blocks from the probation office, the program finds substantial volunteer support from both faculty and student body; some 27 law students assist with the completion of pre-sentence reports. Some volunteers perform specialized functions such as leadership of formal group counseling sessions or training of other volunteers in counseling procedures.

However, their principle method is to establish teams consisting of a probation officer, an assistant, and three to five volunteers who share a common responsibility for the management of an otherwise unreasonable caseload, some of which run as high as 200 cases.

Another project, the Volunteer Probation Counselor Program of Lincoln, Nebraska, matched probationers on a one-to-one basis with a group of probationers identified as "high risk." An in-house evaluation indicated that clients assigned to volunteers committed fewer additional offenses than those assigned to regular staff.[27]

## PROBATION OFFICERS' STYLES

Like the police officer (as discussed in Chapter 7), the probation officer brings a wide variety of outlooks, philosophies, and attitudes to the job. Some individual officers view themselves as law enforcement agents entrusted with protecting societal interests, while others approach their position from a social work perspective and concentrate on the needs of their clients. In his analysis of the ways in which probation officers investigated clients' backgrounds, Paul Keve identified the following styles:[28]

1. There is the probation officer who borrows the accoutrements of the constabulary; confusing his profession with the police function, as seen in his use of a police-type badge; the carrying of handcuffs, blackjack or gun; the use of a police radio in his car; the overemphasis given in his presentence reports to detailed accounts of the defendant's offense.
2. The legalistic probation officer whose presentence reports are replete with legalistic language and whose supervision of probationers finds contentment in the upholding of law for the sake of upholding law, whether or not inward improvement of the probationer is accomplished.
3. The probation officer who belongs to the world of investigators. He is an investigator in a special, narrow sense, and his reports take the safe procedure of presenting facts, facts, facts, with impressive thoroughness but with no illumination as to their meaning.
4. The probation officer who obtains reports from psychologists and psychiatrists or other clinicians, but attaches these to, or copies these verbatim into his presentence report without integrating their message with the "facts" he has uncovered in his own investigation.

Other probation officer styles include the following:

*The Rule Enforcer.* This probation officer is similar to Keve's first probation type—the pseudo-police officer. This individual views probation as a privilege, not a right. The client may be perceived as a criminal who must be watched and controlled; the client is believed to be a danger from whom society must be protected.

The rule enforcer is quick to remind clients that probation will be revoked if rules are violated. He or she may periodically make surprise checks on the client's behavior, such as call at night to see if a client is maintaining proper curfew regulations.

The rule enforcer may personally care for a client, but believes that tough treatment is actually beneficial and can put a young criminal back on the right path. Juvenile probation officers of this type may complain that parents today are too lenient with their children. The rule enforcer is primarily concerned with maintaining the best interests of the community. This type of probation officer believes that probation is a frontline deterrent to crime, and that if probation rules are violated the responsibility must rest not only with the client but also with the department for inadequately enforcing probation conditions.

Louis Tomaino has suggested that the problem inherent in this type of control is that its effectiveness, if any, may only be temporary and superficial.[29] If the probationer only obeys out of fear, the habits developed during the probationary period may quickly disappear after the probationary period has run out. Moreover, the resentment built up against the system by the insensitive treatment given the probationer may in fact contribute to further antisocial behavior. It would be wrong, however, to condemn the rule enforcer as simply having a nontreatment or antitreatment style. In fact, the style is that of the stern parent who rigidly sets standards which, it is hoped, through repetition will become behavior patterns.

*The Social Worker.* The social worker, the opposite of the rule enforcer, is concerned solely with the client, and may view the rules or conditions of probation as hindering proper treatment.

The social worker views the probationary period as a time for diagnosing, evaluating, and treating deviant members of society. This type of probation officer attempts to develop personal relationships with clients in order to present them with treatment plans which may help them to avoid future criminal behavior and make their lives more productive. Within this context, the social worker views clients as disturbed, troubled, neurotic, or in need of help and guidance rather than as hardened criminals. It is likely that this type of PO has studied the social sciences in college and may have, or is pursuing, an advanced degree in social work or counseling.

During departmental meetings, the social worker may be quick to clash with the rule enforcer. The former views the latter as a fascist or police officer, while the rule enforcer sees the social worker as a bleeding heart. A department split between these two styles may be subject to infighting, dissension, and low morale.

The problems associated with the social work style involve the quality of the PO's relationship with the client. Some clients will become disenchanted with their probation officers and seek to evade them. Since the social worker emphasizes the client's well being, this type may be more easily fooled. An experienced client may have learned to use the proper social work jargon (e.g., "I'm getting in touch with my feelings") to ensure the maximum amount of freedom during probation at the expense of real therapeutic change. In addition, the social work-oriented probation officer may neglect to consider the client while preparing a treatment model; this type may prescribe cures and dictate activities which conflict with the needs of the client. Finally, the need to achieve a therapeutic model often prohibits the social-work oriented probation officer from using the power of revocation for all but the most flagrant violations of probations' rules. The well-being of society may be sacrificed in favor of the criminal offender.

*The Civil Servant.* This type of PO exhibits little concern for client or society; instead, concentration is on the need to maintain or improve his own position within the organization. The civil servant is more concerned with rising within the probation bureaucracy than with performing the duties of the probation officer, and may be looking forward to retirement, pension, or entry into another field such as private social work. Major concerns of this type are attendance, proper report writing, and the kind of self-improvement that will result in salary increases.

In dealing with clients, the civil servant pays little attention to rules, therapy, or the like. This PO may meet with the client initially and explain the rules of probation; subsequent meetings are sporadic and may be conducted via letter or telephone. The protection of the community is minimized. "Why worry about the community," this type may reason. "If the offender is so bad, he would have been put in prison in the first place."

The civil servant is prompt at meetings, and attendance is always regular. This type avoids conflict and wonders why the social workers and rule enforcers do not have a more realistic attitude toward probation.

One danger of the civil servant style is that aspects of this lackadaisical approach to probation services may actually be transmitted to the client's behavior. Not only may the client perceive a lack of caring on the part of the supervisor, but may also perceive the rejection as typical of society's lack of interest in him. The probation officer's modest efforts may be viewed as similar to past rejections by teachers, employers, parents, and law enforcement officials. This model of probation may actually have some benefits, though; labeling and stigma are minimized since contact between PO and client is so sporadic; and, by leaving compliance with probation rules more or less up to the client, the civil servant forces rehabilitation to be self-motivated, and it is thus less likely to end after probation has been terminated.

*The Traditionalist.* The traditionalist probation officer believes that probation is a worthwhile tool for treatment and supervision, and focuses on playing it by ear. Each case is evaluated on an individual level, and some clients are more closely supervised while others receive more treatment.

The traditionalist does not claim to be a quasi-therapist or a police officer, and may be amused by the technical language of the former and the tough rhetoric of the latter. The traditionalist brand of probation is based on the body of literature on supervision, investigation, and treatment which is unique to probation services; common sense and experience are stressed. The probation department is viewed as a unique agency which can provide assistance to those offenders who want and deserve its attention. The primary interest of this type of PO lies in maintaining the integrity, reputation, and ability of the department.

In making reports and investigations, the traditionalist sticks to facts and comments in a professional rather than dogmatic manner. His report or log is viewed as being important since it can help a future probation supervisor if a client is transferred, thus maintaining the department's efficiency.

At meetings, the traditionalist might be mildly critical of the social worker, the rule enforcer, and the civil servant, viewing them as nonproductive in the probation setting. This PO may suggest, for example, that these other officers become better acquainted with the rules and goals of the department and forget their other allegiances. The traditionalist's greatest quarrel might be with the civil servant, viewed as an opportunist and a discredit to the department's goals.

In considering revoking probation, the traditionalist would be careful to ensure that clients are not giving the department a bad name in the community. If a member of his caseload is flaunting probation rules or associating with unsavory characters, the traditionalist may be quick to reprimand the client for making the department look bad. If the client's behavior does not improve, revocation will result.

The major problem associated with the traditional style is one of organizational inertia. This officer may be less likely to embrace new and innovative materials or adopt methods from other fields and disciplines than some more flexible coworkers. By upholding the standards of the department, the traditionalist may sometimes overlook the needs of the community and the client.

*The Team Player.* The team player believes that probation can be of maximum benefit if the client can become an equal partner in the treatment experience. Rules must be obeyed, since they represent a pattern of behavior that can lead to the eventual rehabilitation of the offender; however, the team player would never present probation rules as imperatives to be followed without question by clients. Rather, this type would work with the probationer in a spirit of mutual cooperation to establish a set of conditions amenable to both probationer and society.

The team player would be quick to point out that there is no one answer for every case or client. The probation officer is not a miracle worker; the team player believes that the resources of the community must be marshalled to help solve the client's special problems. Among the support services to be tapped include mental health clinics, job counseling services, drug and alcohol abuse programs and educational resources. The team player may work with the client to establish better relationships in the community, work out family problems, and mitigate problems with law enforcement agencies. For example, the team player might develop a relationship with the local police so that if a client is arrested on a minor charge the case will be referred back to the department before booking.

The team player style differs from the other probation styles in its efforts to heed the skills and personal characteristics of the offender in formulating the treatment plan. While respecting the needs of the community and the department, this officer does not neglect the fact that it is the probationer's life being dealt with, and that the client's personal values and strengths must be included within the probation strategy.

## PRE-SENTENCE INVESTIGATIONS

Another important task of probation officers is the investigation and evaluation of defendants coming before the court for sentencing. Pre-sentence investigations are reports which are used by the court in making decisions whether to grant probation, incarcerate, or use other forms of treatment. In juvenile probation services, the pre-sentence investigation can recommend outright release, the continuance of a case with no finding, probation, or placement in a youth center.

The pre-sentence investigation has a number of unique purposes:[30]

**1.** The report aids the court in determining an appropriate sentence. Information contained within the investigation helps the court decide whether there is reason to maintain the case in the community, or whether institutionalization is required.

**2.** It aids the probation officer in developing a treatment program in the event that the offender is placed on probation. The social and psychological strengths and weaknesses of the offender as revealed in the report may be taken into account in planning treatment strategy.

**3.** It develops a body of personal knowledge that can aid prison or other institutional officials in the classifying, treating, and releasing functions.

**4.** It furnishes the parole board (see Chapter 17) with information that may help them plan a proper parole program if and when the imprisoned offender is released.

**5.** It serves as a source of information for systematic research in criminal justice; for example, researchers using these reports can determine the characteristics which correlate with or predict probation success or failure.

The style and content of pre-sentence investigations may vary between jurisdictions and also among individual probation officers within the same jurisdiction. On the one hand, some departments require voluminous reports covering every aspect of the defendant's life; other departments which may be rule-oriented require that officers stick to the basic facts, such as the defendant's age, race, sex, and previous offense record. In addition, individual probation officers working within a single department may bring their personal styles to bear during pre-sentence investigation. The social worker might stress psychological data, while the rule enforcer might concentrate on the offender's prior record, the PO's perceptions of the offender, and how dangerous the offender is. These disparities are combined with the fact that each department has its own standards for pre-sentence investigations.[31]

A number of national committees and organizations have attempted to design a proper form for the pre-sentence investigation, embodying the most important sentencing information in a concise format. The model investigation form prepared by federal probation authorities is contained in the applications section of this chapter.

At the conclusion of most pre-sentence investigations, a recommendation is made to the presiding judge which reflects the department's sentencing posture on the case at hand. This is a very crucial aspect of the report because it has been estimated that the probation department's recommendation is followed in about 95% of all cases.

### Probation Recommendation Decision-Making Criteria

In Chapter 7 we discussed several factors influencing police decision making, such as the officer's environment, the offender's personality and demeanor, and situational influences. Probation officers must make critical decisions when recommending sentences to a judge, and many of these same environmental and situational factors are thought to influence their decisions.

One obvious influence on pre-sentence recommendations is the working environment of the department and the court. If close working relationships exist between the probation staff and their chief, and between the chief and the trial judge, then the decision making of junior officers will be affected. When dissonance exists within a department, either among staff members or between staff and administration, then the department's influence will probably have less effect on the kinds of recommendations POs will make. In larger departments, where the chief may be functionally separated from the staff and where close personal supervision is rare, guidance in decision making may come from middle managers (assistant chiefs) or more experienced staff.

Another factor influencing probation decision making is the probation styles employed by the individual officers. For example, the rule enforcer, viewing probation as a privilege, not a right, may be more likely to recommend prison sentences. The social worker might, on the other hand, advocate probation for the same offender the rule enforcer rejects, since this type views community supervision as a chance to rehabilitate the known offender. The civil servant may be motivated by a desire to keep caseloads to a minimum, while the traditionalist may seek to protect the good name of the department. Of course, adherence to style can produce unexpected results; for example, the social worker may become frustrated with cases that demand authoritative supervision or with cases that require close surveillance, since this PO's skills do not lie in those areas, and may consequently not recommend probation for these types of offenders.[32]

The personal and individual characteristics of offenders are also believed to significantly affect the probation officer's recommendations. Gross found that the following factors (ranked according to importance) influence probation decision making in juvenile court.[33]

1. Child's attitude
2. Family data
3. Previous delinquency
4. Present offense
5. Interview impression
6. School data
7. Psychological data
8. Psychiatric examination
9. Interest and activity
10. Religious data

Yona Cohn also studied the criteria probation officers use in making recommendations to the court. She discovered that the seriousness of the act was only of secondary importance in the decision-making process, and that such issues as the PO's perception of the offender's personality, the offender's family background, and the probability that the offender would be able to adjust to society were of primary significance. Those not recommended for probation frequently included sex deviants and persons with physical handicaps or behavioral disorders.[34] In still another study, Robert Carter found that offense, prior record, psychological and psychiatric reports, age, family status, and attitude were all considered important by probation officers.[35]

It is evident that the factors influencing recommendation decision making involve much more information than offense type and category alone. They represent the full range of information obtained by the probation officer, as well as personal and departmental influences.

## PROBATION REVOCATION

During the course of a probationary term, a violation of the rules of probation or the commitment of a new crime can result in probation being revoked, at which time the offender may be placed in an institution. Revocation is often not an easy decision, since it conflicts with the treatment philosophy of most probation departments.

When revocation is the course decided upon, the offender is given notice of the pending revocation procedure and a formal hearing is scheduled. If the charges against the probationer are upheld, the offender can then be placed in an institution to serve the remainder of the sentence. Most departments will not revoke probation unless the offender commits another crime or seriously violates the rules of the probation.

Because placing a person on probation implies that probation will continue unless the probationer commits some major violation, the defendant has been given certain procedural due process rights at this stage of the criminal process. In three significant decisions, the United States Supreme Court provided procedural safeguards to apply at revocation of probation and parole proceedings.

In *Mempa v. Rhay*, in 1967,[36] the Court unanimously held that a probationer was constitutionally entitled to counsel in a revocation of probation proceeding where the imposition of sentence had been suspended. Prior to the *Mempa* case, it was traditionally held that a probationer was not entitled to be represented or assisted by counsel at a proceeding to revoke probation.[37]

The *Mempa* case resulted in a variety of judicial interpretations. Most lower court rulings treated *Mempa* as a sentencing case and limited its application to probation revocation proceedings involving deferred sentencing, and did not apply it to cases where the probationer was sentenced at the time of the trial. Other courts, however, extended *Mempa* to mean that every probation revocation required counsel because the probation revocation hearing itself was a critical stage needing total due process protection. Thus, some jurisdictions provided counsel to indigent offenders at probation revocation hearings, while others did not.

Then, in 1972, the United States Supreme Court in the case of *Morrissey v. Brewer*[38] handed down an important decision detailing the procedural aspects required for parole revocation. Because the revocation of probation and parole were similar in nature, the standards in the *Morrissey* case affected the probation process as well. In *Morrissey*, the court required an informal inquiry to determine if there was probable cause to believe the arrested parolee had violated the conditions of parole, as well as a formal revocation hearing with minimum due process requirements. However, in the *Morrissey* case the court did not deal with the issue of right to counsel. Chief Justice Warren Burger stated, "We do not reach or decide the question whether the parolee is entitled to the assistance of retained counsel or to appointed counsel if he is indigent." Thus, the court avoided dealing with this issue until some future decision. The full details of the *Morrissey* case are found in Chapter 17.

However, the question of the right to counsel in revocation proceedings did come up again in the 1973 case of *Gagnon v. Scarpelli*.[39] In that decision, which involved a probationer, the United States Supreme Court held that both probationers and parolees have a constitutionally limited right to counsel in revocation proceedings. Because of the importance of this decision, the case is detailed on the following pages.

The *Gagnon* case can be viewed as a step forward in the constitution application of procedural safeguards to the correctional process. It should provide some control over the unlimited discretion exercised in the past by probation and parole personnel in revocation proceedings.

In practice, almost all states today provide counsel to indigent defendants at probation revocation hearings, while fewer states provide counsel at parole proceedings.[41]

Since *Gagnon*, state and federal courts have reached a number of important decisions further defining legal rights during the revocation pro-

## GAGNON V. SCARPELLI

**Facts:** Gerald Scarpelli, the petitioner, had pleaded guilty in July, 1965 to a charge of armed robbery in Wisconsin. The trial judge sentenced him to 15 years imprisonment but suspended the sentence and placed him on probation for 7 years in the custody of the Wisconsin Department of Public Welfare. At that time, Scarpelli signed an agreement specifying the terms of his probation and also signed a "Travel Permit and Agreement to Return," allowing him to reside under supervision in Illinois pursuant to an interstate compact. On August 5, 1965, he was accepted for supervision by the Adult Probation Department of Cook County, Illinois; on August 6, he was apprehended with another person in the course of burglarizing a house. Scarpelli was apprised of his constitutional rights. He admitted to the crime, but later asserted that his statement was made under duress and was a fake. On September 1, 1965, Scarpelli's probation was revoked by the Wisconsin Department of Public Welfare without a hearing, and on September 4, he was incarcerated in the Wisconsin State Reformatory to begin serving the 15 years to which he had been sentenced by the trial judge. At no time was Scarpelli given a hearing or access to counsel. Three years later, on December 16, 1968, Scarpelli applied to the Federal District Court for a writ of habeas corpus, and it was held that revocation without hearing and counsel was denial of due process. The Court of Appeals affirmed, and the United States Supreme Court granted certiorari.

**Decision:** In *Gagnon*, the Court dealt with the issue of counsel but within the framework of a probation revocation procedure. Specifically, the question was whether a previously sentenced probationer was entitled to a hearing when his probation was revoked, and whether he was entitled to be represented by appointed counsel at such hearing. The Court discussed the character of probation and parole. It indicated that both systems were intended to provide a supervised course of treatment for the offender. Under the meaning of due process, a conflict between the probationer and the probation officer had to be resolved by a hearing. The Court, however, did not overlook the fact that probationers or parolees might be at a disadvantage in presenting their version of a disputed case. This thinking provided the basis for a limited right to counsel.

The Court rejected the claim that a constitutional basis exists for providing counsel in all probation or parole revocation cases. Thus, the holding of the court of appeals that the state is under a constitutional duty to provide counsel for indigents in all cases was overruled. The Supreme Court held that the introduction of counsel into a revocation

cess. For example, in *United States v. Reed*,[42] a probation officer requested that a client's probation be revoked because he failed to maintain employment, notify him of an address change, and report as directed. However in making the revocation order, the trial judge also mentioned the defendant's failure to comply with a restitution order originally made by the sentencing court. Upon review, the appellate court found that it was improper to revoke probation on the alleged failure to make restitution since the defendant did not receive proper notice that this charge would be considered. Furthermore, in reversing the revocation order, the circuit court stressed the rehabilitory value of probation, and indicated that the accumulation of a few minor technical violations should not necessarily be grounds for revocation.[43]

In a similar vein, courts have reviewed the evidence standards permissible at a revocation hearing. For example, they have allowed reliable proceeding would change the nature of the proceeding and result in hearings less attuned to the rehabilitative needs of the probationer or parolee. Requiring counsel at all times would prolong decision making and impose greater financial costs on the state. The Court also believed that differences exist between criminal trials and probation and parole revocation hearings that allow for the imposition of a more limited right to the assistance of counsel. Thus, the Court held:

1. That due process requires that preliminary and final revocation hearings in the case of a probationer be similar to conditions for a parolee.

2. That the body conducting the hearings should decide in each individual case whether due process requires that an indigent probationer or parolee be represented by counsel. Though the state is not constitutionally obliged to provide counsel in all cases, it should do so where the indigent probationer or parolee may have difficulty in presenting his or her version of disputed facts without the examination or cross-examination of witnesses or the presentation of complicated documentary evidence. "Presumptively, counsel should be provided where, after being informed of his right, the probationer or parolee requests counsel, based on a timely and colorable claim that he has not committed the alleged violation or, if the violation is a matter of public record or uncontested, there are substantial reasons in justification or mitigation that make revocation inappropriate."

3. That any case where a request for counsel is refused, the grounds for refusal should be stated in the record.

4. That in the present case because Scarpelli made an admission which he claims was taken under duress, he should have been given counsel and the case should be reconsidered in light of the new guidelines.[40]

**Significance of the Case:** One of the most important features of the *Gagnon* case was that it equated probation revocation with parole revocation. In so doing, it concluded that a hearing was to be held as outlined in the Morrissey case (see Chapter 17), and that the need for counsel was to be decided on a case-by-case basis. *Gagnon* also apparently answered the question left undecided in *Morrissey* regarding right to counsel at parole revocation hearings. Finally, the decision in *Gagnon* was a firm denial that the United States Constitution requires counsel to be present at the probation and parole revocation hearings.

"hearsay" evidence to be considered.[44] Federal courts have also held that the "beyond a reasonable doubt" standard need not be used at a revocation hearing; proof of a violation need only "reasonably satisfy" the court.[45]

SUMMARY

Probation is the community supervision of convicted offenders by order of the court. It is a sentence reserved for those defendants whom the magistrate views as having potential for rehabilitation without needing to serve prison or jail terms. Probation is practiced in every state and by the federal government, and includes both adult and juvenile sections.

In the decision to grant probation, most judges are influenced by their own personal discretion and the pre-sentence reports of the probation staff. Once on probation, the offender must follow a set of rules or conditions, the violation of which may lead to the revocation of probation and reinstatement of a prison sentence. These rules vary from state to state but usually involve such demands as refraining from use of alcohol, curfew maintenance, and termination of past criminal associations.

Today, probation departments have instituted a number of new and innovative programs designed to bring better services to their clients. These include restitutions and diversionary programs and the use of volunteers in probation.

Probation officers are usually organized into countywide departments, though some agencies are statewide and others are combined parole-probation departments. Each department and the officers within it are believed to exhibit a unique "style" of operations—some are law-enforcement oriented, while others are social-work oriented and still others fall somewhere in between the two extremes.

In recent years, the Supreme Court has granted the probationer greater due process rights; today, when the state wishes to revoke probation, it must conduct a full hearing into the matter and also provide the probationer with the assistance of an attorney when that assistance is warranted.

## QUESTIONS FOR DISCUSSION

1. What is the purpose of probation? Identify some conditions of probation and discuss the responsibilities of the probation officer.

2. Discuss the procedures involved in probation revocation. What are the rights of the probationer?

3. Should probation be a privilege and not a right?

4. Should a convicted criminal make restitution to the victim? When is restitution inappropriate?

## NOTES

1. G. Killinger, H. Kerper, and P. Cromwell, *Probation & Parole in the Criminal Justice System* (St. Paul, Minn.: West Publishing Co., 1976), p. 35.

2. 18 U.S.C.A. § 3651 ff.

3. National Advisory Commission on Criminal Justice Standards & Goals, *Corrections* (Washington, D.C.: U.S. Government Printing Office, 1974), p. 321.

4. Killinger, Kerper, and Cromwell, *Probation & Parole in the Criminal Justice System*, p. 46.

5. U.S. Bureau of Census, State and Local Probation and Parole Systems (Washington, D.C.: U.S. Government Printing Office, 1978).

6. N.Y.P.C. § 65.00–1.

7. Model Penal Code, Proposed Official Draft, § 7.01. Copyright 1962 by the American Law Institute. Reprinted with the permission of the American Law Institute.

8. Killinger, Kerper, and Cromwell, *Probation & Parole in the Criminal Justice System.* p. 72.

9. American Bar Association, *Standards Relating to Probation* (New York: Institute of Judicial Administration, 1970) Standard 3.2. Reprinted with the permission of the American Bar Association which authored these standards and which holds the copyright.

**10.** Harvey Jaffe, "Probation With a Flair: A Look at Some Out-of-the-Ordinary Conditions," *Federal Probation* 33:29 (1979).

**11.** United States v. Villarin Gerena, 553 F.2d 675, 677 (2nd Cir., 1976).

**12.** United States v. Bishop 537 F.2d 1184 (4th Cir., 1976).

**13.** United States v. Pastore 537 F.2d 675 (2d Cir., 1976).

**14.** Malone v. United States, 502 F.2d 554 (9th Cir., 1974).

**15.** People v. Kerry, 73 Cal.Rptr. 440 (Ct.App.1968). Cert. denied 396 U.S. 1028 (1970).

**16.** State v. Lexington, 372 N.E.2d 1335 (Ohio, Ct.App., 1976).

**17.** United States v. Kahl 583 F.2d 1351 (5th Cir., 1978).

**18.** Charles Newman, "Concepts of Treatment in Probation & Parole Supervision," *Federal Probation*, 25:11 (March 1961).

**19.** Ibid.

**20.** Discussed in E. Kim Nelson, Howard Ohmart, and Nora Harlow, *Promising Strategies in Probation and Parole*, (Washington, D.C.: U.S. Government Printing Office, 1978), pp. 16–17 (herein cited as *New Strategies*).

**21.** The following description adapted from *Ibid.*, p. 17.

**22.** For a further analysis of restitution, see Larry Siegel, "Court Ordered Victim-Restitution: An Overview of Theory and Action," *New England Journal of Prison Law* 5:135–150 (1979).

**23.** Ibid., p. 142.

**24.** Descriptive materials may be obtained from the EARN-IT Program, District Court of East Norfolk, 50 Chestnut Street, Quincy, MA 02169. This program is not part of the probation department but works closely with it.

**25.** See generally Larry Siegel, "Court Ordered Victim-Restitution," p. 141.

**26.** *New Strategies*, p. 28.

**27.** Ibid., p. 29.

**28.** Paul Keve, "The Professional Character of the Presentence Report," *Federal Probation* 26:52 (June 1962).

**29.** Louis Tomaino, "The Five Faces of Probation," *Federal Probation* 39:42 (1975).

**30.** Division of Probation, "The Selective Presentence Investigation Report," *Federal Probation* 38:48 (December 1974).

**31.** See generally R. Carter, R. McGee, and E. Kim Nelson, *Corrections In America* (Philadelphia: J. B. Lippincott Co., 1975).

**32.** Richard Quincy, *Social Reality of Crime* (Boston: Little, Brown and Co., 1970), p. 171.

**33.** S. Gross, "The Prehearing Juvenile Report, Probation Officer's Conceptions" in *Probation & Parole*, R. Carter and L. Wilkins, eds. (New York: John Wiley & Sons, 1970), p. 109.

**34.** Yona Cohn, "Criteria for the Probation Officers Recommendations to the Juvenile Court Judge," *Crime & Delinquency* 9:262 (July 1963).

**35.** Robert Carter, "The Presentence Report & The Decision-Making Process" in *Probation & Parole*, R. Carter and L. Wilkins, eds. (New York: John Wiley & Sons, 1970), pp. 128–137.

**36.** 389 U.S. 128, 88 S.Ct. 254, 19 L.Ed.2d 336 (1967).

**37.** Fred Cohen, "Sentencing, Probation and the Rehabilitation Ideal: The View From Mempa v. Rhay," *Texas Law Review* 47:1 (1968).

**38.** 408 U.S. 471, 92 S.Ct. 2593, 33 L.Ed.2d 484 (1972).

**39.** 411 U.S. 778, 93 S.Ct. 1756, 36 L.Ed.2d 655 (1973).

40. Ibid. at 791.

41. Joseph J. Senna, "Right to Counsel at Adult Probation Revocation Hearings—A Survey and Analysis of Current Law: A Comment," *Criminal Law Bulletin* 10:228 (1974).

42. 573 F.2d 1020 (8th Cir., 1978).

43. Ibid., p. 1024; see also U.S. v. Dane 570 F.2d 840 (5th Cir., 1977).

44. U.S. v. Buckhalter, 588 F.2d 604 (8th Cir., 1979); U.S. v. Pattman, 535 F.2d 562 (8th Cir., 1976).

45. U. S. v. Jurgins, 465 F.Supp. 982 (W.D.Pa.1979).

# Presentence Reports: Outline, Contents, and Format of The Report*

## FACE SHEET

The current face sheet, Probation Form 2, will be used for all presentence reports. In addition to its normal use, for selective reports the face sheet may provide information in capsule form if doing so eliminates material from the body of the report. For example, there may be an additional typed entry: "Religion _____ (faith) _____ (attends)." The face sheet may contain reference to alcohol or drug involvement. The "Custody" category may inform as to whether bond was made, by whom, and the amount. . . .

## OFFENSE: OFFICIAL VERSION

The official version of the offense may be obtained from the office of the U.S. attorney. The report should contain information on codefendants, if any, the relative culpability of the defendant, and whether the codefendant has been apprehended and the disposition made in his case.

In those instances in which an adequate concise report delineating the defendant's relative culpability is available from the investigating officer the "Official Version" may simply refer the reader to that report as an attachment. In that event details of the offense need not be provided in the text.

## DEFENDANT'S VERSION OF OFFENSE

A summary of the defendant's version of the offense should be provided. Whatever the defendant says about the offense and his part in it is necessary to understand him.

## PRIOR RECORD

The prior criminal record shall be provided in detail, except that multiple prior arrests of a minor nature may be summarized e.g., "From 1968 to 1972 Mr. Jones was arrested a total of 10 times for drunkenness and minor traffic violations. The drunk arrests were resolved by referral to the county rehabilitation center, the traffic violations resulted in forfeiture of bail ranging from $25 to $50."

*From Division of Probation, "The Selective Presentence Investigation," pp. 52–53.

PROBATION FORM 2          UNITED STATES DISTRICT COURT
      FEB 65               Central District of New York

                            PRESENTENCE REPORT


NAME  John Jones                          DATE  January 4, 1974

ADDRESS                                   DOCKET NO.  74-103
      1234 Astoria Blvd.
      New York City                       OFFENSE    Theft of Mail by Postal
                                                     Employee (18 U.S.C.
LEGAL RESIDENCE                                       Sec. 1709) 2 cts.
      Same


AGE  33      DATE OF BIRTH  2-8-40         PENALTY    Ct. 2 - 5 years and/or
                      New York City                   $2,000 fine

SEX  Male        RACE Caucasian


CITIZENSHIP  U.S. (Birth)                 PLEA  Guilty on 12-16-73 to Ct. 2
                                                Ct. 1 pending

EDUCATION  10th grade                     VERDICT

MARITAL STATUS  Married                   CUSTODY  Released on own
                                                   recognizance.  No time in
                                                   custody.
DEPENDENTS  Three                         ASST. U.S. ATTY
(wife and 2 children)                               Samuel Hayman

SOC. SEC. NO.  112-03-9559
                                          DEFENSE COUNSEL  Thomas Lincoln
                                                           Federal Public
FBI NO.  256 1126                                          Defender


DETAINERS OR CHARGES PENDING:             Drug/Alcohol Involvement:
      None                                     Attributes offense to
                                               need for drinking money
CODEFENDANTS  (Disposition)
      None


=============================================================

DISPOSITION


DATE

SENTENCING JUDGE

Although the FBI record has a fairly complete coverage of arrests and convictions, the probation officer shall clear with local identification bureaus, police departments, and sheriffs' offices in those communities where the defendant has resided. Where the FBI fingerprint record does not give the disposition of a case, the probation officer shall obtain the missing information from the law enforcement office which filed the print or the court in which the case was tried.

## PERSONAL HISTORY

This topical heading is a composite of several headings used in the comprehensive report. The probation officer shall provide a history of the development and social relationships of the defendant. This section should include a reference to educational attainment, any drug or alcohol history, and employment stability. However, extraneous detail about the family is to be avoided. The officer shall bear in mind that detailed information about the family is more pertinent in understanding juvenile and youth offenders than it is in the case of the older offender. In many instances it is sufficient to provide a summary that informs the court that the family history has been explored and found to be unremarkable.

No pre-sentence investigation is complete unless the spouse, if any, has been interviewed. The report shall carry the essential details of the marriage, date, number of children, and a synopsis of the relationship.

## EVALUATIVE SUMMARY

The opening paragraph of the evaluative summary gives a concise restatement of the pertinent highlights in the body of the report. The attitude of the defendant toward his offense is significant in determining whether he should be considered for probation. Writing the evaluative summary is the most demanding task in the preparation of the report. It is here that the probation officer focuses on those factors, social and personal, that result in this defendant's presence before the court and the special assistance that will be required in this person's situation.

## RECOMMENDATION

If it is recommended that the defendant be placed on probation, the proposed plans for residence, employment, education, and medical and psychiatric treatment, if relevant should be given. The part to be played in the social adjustment of the defendant by the parental and immediate family, close friends, and other resources in the community should also be shown. If commitment is recommended, the probation officer shall indicate what special problems and needs should receive the attention of the institutional staff. Where the judge asks for sentencing alternatives, they may be included.*

---

*The selective pre-sentence investigation report . . . is presented to illustrate the outline, format, and style recommended in writing a selective presentence report. Names and dates in the report have been altered to protect the identity of the defendant.

# PART SIX

## Corrections

# An Overview of
# Correctional History
# and Institutions

KEY TERMS

Incapacitation
Custodial Convenience
The Tombs
Maximum Security Prison
Prison Farm
Halfway House
Justice Perspective
Auburn Prison
David Fogel

Andrew von Hirsch
Michel Foucault
Corrections
William Penn
David Rothman
Western Penitentiary
Eastern Penitentiary

THE CURRENT
STATE OF
CORRECTIONS

When a person is convicted for a criminal offense, state and federal governments through their sentencing authority reserve the right to institutionally confine the offender for an extended period of time. The system of corrections comprises the entire range of treatment and/or punishment options available to the government, including community treatment, jails, reformatories, and penal institutions (prisons). Probation and parole may also be considered part of corrections, but for the purposes of organization these areas are discussed separately in chapters 13 and 18.

Correctional treatment is currently practiced on federal, state, and local county levels of government. Felons may be placed in state or federal penitentiaries (prisons), which are usually isolated, fortresslike structures; misdemeanants are usually housed in county jails, sometimes called reformatories or houses of correction; and juvenile offenders have their own institutions, sometimes euphemistically called schools, camps, ranches, or homes. Typically, the latter are low- or nonsecurity facilities, often located in rural areas, which provide both confinement and rehabilitative services for young offenders.

Other types of correctional institutions currently employed are ranches and farms for adult offenders, and community correctional settings such as halfway houses. Today's correctional facilities cover a wide range of institutions, ranging from the infamous closed institutions such as Attica and San Quentin to the informal low-security Swift Trail Federal Prison Camp in Safford, Arizona, where former presidential aide John Erlichman was housed after his Watergate-related crimes.

It is one of the great tragedies of our time that correctional institutions, whatever form they may take, do not seem to correct. They are in most instances overcrowded, understaffed, outdated warehouses for the human outcasts of our society. Prisons are more suited to control, punishment, and security than to rehabilitation and treatment. It is a sad but unfortunately accurate assessment that today's correctional institution has become a revolving door, and all too many of its residents return time and again. Though no completely accurate statement of the recidivism rate is currently available, estimates range from about 50% to over 80%.[1] Regardless of which estimate is the more accurate, the results are far too high to be considered acceptable.

Despite the apparent lack of success experienced by penal institutions, great debate still ranges over the direction of their future operations. On the one hand, there are experts such as David Fogel, James Q. Wilson, and Andrew von Hirsch who maintain that prisons and jails are not really places for rehabilitation and treatment, but should be used to keep dangerous offenders apart from society and give them the "just desserts" for their crimes.[2] In this sense, prison success would be measured by such factors as physical security, length of incapacitation, reduction in the crime rate while offenders were incarcerated, and lack of recidivism.

On the other hand, there still remain penal experts who maintain that prisons can be useful places for offender rehabilitation, that beneficial programs can be devised, and that rehabilitated offenders should be released (paroled) once they satisfy prison authorities with their progress.

Currently, it seems evident that the "just dessert" incapacitation approach to penal philosophy is fast gaining recognition in American courts and correctional systems. This conclusion is supported by the facts that: (1) presumptive and mandatory sentencing structures, discussed in Chapter 13, have become increasingly popular in influential areas such as California, Massachusetts, and Illinois; (2) the number of people under lock and key has risen precipitously in the past few years; and (3) there has been general acceptance that the prison as a rehabilitation dispensing institution is a failure.[3] The popular notion therefore is to view the prison as a place of *incapacitation* in which offenders who have harmed innocent people are kept apart from society. Despite the growth of this view, there still exist many vestiges of the rehabilitation philosophy—evident in flourishing education, vocational training, and treatment programs within the institution (see Chapter 16).

In this and the following four chapters, we will explore the correctional system, beginning with the history and nature of correctional institutions. Then institutional life will be examined in some detail, and the following two chapters will view the issues of prisoners' rights and parole.

A HISTORY OF CORRECTIONS

In their earliest European form, prisons, jails, and other areas of confinement were not the places of punishment or reform they are today.[4] Instead, they served as centers for the detention of prisoners awaiting trial. Typically, jails were used to hold political prisoners who had to be confined within a secure facility while awaiting the decisions which determined their fate. In England, the Tower of London served this purpose; in France, the Bastille; and Swiss political prisoners were held in Chillion Prison.

Following confinement awaiting trial, the actual punishments were meted out—death, mutilation, branding, or flogging. Another popular treatment was banishment, and each royal house had its own favorite exile for convicted prisoners. The French sent exiles to Devil's Island or plantations in the Caribbean Islands; Russian political exiles went to Siberia; and England's American colonies and Australia were populated by many banished convicts.

The rationale behind these modes of punishment was actually more economic than punitive. It was simply too expensive to confine and feed large numbers of physically capable individuals while many citizens went hungry or lived at a bare subsistence level. Banishment to developing colonies, slavery, whipping, and mutilation made much more sense economically; they were thorough, immediate, and inexpensive (and sometimes, as in the case of banishment or slavery, actually turned a profit for the government). However, some political prisoners, many of whom were of royal blood, could not be harmed or made to suffer indignities; others had to be held for eventual ransoming during times of hostility. Consequently, their detention sometimes lasted many years and the use of the prison grew in order to house and detain political prisoners.

**Early American
Corrections:
Pennsylvania**

The American correctional system had its origin in Pennsylvania under the leadership of William Penn. At the end of the seventeenth century, Penn revised Pennsylvania's Criminal Code in such a fashion that torture and the capricious use of mutilations and physical punishments were forbidden. These devices were replaced by the penalties of imprisonment at hard labor, moderate flogging, fines, and forfeiture of property. All lands and goods belonging to felons were to be used to make restitution to the victims of crimes, with restitution being limited to twice the value of the damages. Those felons who owned no property were required by law to work in the prison workhouse until the victim was compensated.

Penn ordered that a new type of institution be built to replace the widely used public forms of punishment—stocks, pillories, the gallows, and the branding iron. Each county was instructed to "build a sufficient house, at least 20 feet square, for restraint, corrections, labor and punishment for all persons as shall be there unto committed by law."[5] These measures remained in effect until Penn's death in 1718, when the Criminal Penal Code reverted to its earlier format of open public punishment and harsh brutality.

In 1776, post-revolutionary Pennsylvania again adopted William Penn's code, and in 1787 a group of Quakers formed the Philadelphia Society for Alleviating the Miseries of Public Prisons. The aim of the society was to bring some degree of humane and orderly treatment to the growing penal system. The Quakers' influence on the Legislature resulted in the limiting of the use of the death penalty to cases involving treason, murder, rape, and arson. Their next step was to reform the existing institutional system so that it could serve as a suitable alternative to physical punishment.

The only models of custodial institutions at that time were the local county jails that Penn had established. These facilities were designed to detain offenders, to securely incarcerate convicts awaiting other punishment, or to hold those offenders who were working off their crimes. Early reports depicted the Pennsylvania jails as "scenes of promiscuous and unrestricted intercourse and of universal debauchery."[6] Men, women, and children of all ages were indiscriminately herded into one room. Liquor was often freely sold at a bar which was maintained by a guard. Under pressure from the Quakers to improve these conditions, the Pennsylvania State Legislature in 1790 called for the renovation of the prison system, which ultimately resulted in the creation of Philadelphia's Walnut Street prison. At this institution, prisoners were separated into two distinct classes: serious offenders were placed in solitary cells, where they remained in isolation and solitude and did not have the right to work; and the remaining majority of offenders were housed in large rooms, working together eight hours per day. Women had separate quarters and every inmate was forced to wear a uniform of coarse, dark material.[7]

Those quarters which contained the solitary or separate cells were called the Penitentiary House, as was already the custom in England. Each cell was eight feel long and six feet wide and had an outer wooden door and an inner one of iron.[8] Windows were wired to prevent any contraband from being passed inside. At the time, the populace viewed these cells as the harshest punishment imaginable. However, many other conditions improved—compulsory work laws were repealed, chains abolished, and flogging limited. A board of 12 unpaid managers called inspectors were appointed to make weekly visits to the penitentiary house to supervise conditions and make sure that the prisoners were being treated fairly.

The new Pennsylvania Prison System took credit for a rapid decrease in the crime rate—from 131 convictions in 1789 to 45 in 1793.[9] The prison became known as a school for reform and a place for public labor. Walnut Street prison's equitable conditions were credited with reducing escapes to *none* in the first four years of its existence (except for 14 on opening day).

### The Spread of the Penitentiary

The Pennsylvania prison system influenced similar developments in other states including New York, New Jersey, and Massachusetts.[10] In 1796, Thomas Eddy, a New York Quaker and philanthropist, aided the state in erecting the Newgate prison, which adopted many of the ideals of the Pennsylvania system.

Prisoners at Newgate were required to work and eat meals in silence. Inmates worked to support themselves and could save money over and above their maintenance expenses. All the needs of the institution, including food and clothing, were provided by the inmates. However reasonable the system seemed initially, problems were soon to follow. Fearing the unfair competition of cheap labor, the free labor market lobby forced passage of laws in 1801 requiring prison-made goods to be labeled as such and limited the production and variety of prison wares. As a result, the prison suffered severe economic setbacks.

Massachusetts entered into the era of modern corrections when it constructed the Castle Island prison in 1785. Frequent escapes resulted in the closing of the institution, and in 1804 it was replaced by the Charlestown Prison. A maximum security institution, Charlestown had a high flintstone wall that surrounded the structure, and two sides were also bordered by water. Considered impregnable by its builders, it could neither be tunneled out of nor burned down.[11] Inmates were expected to work in such occupations as blacksmith, shoemaker, stonemason, and others.

At the Charlestown prison, inmates' uniforms varied according to their classification: first offenders wore a half-red and half-blue uniform; second offenders wore a tricolored uniform of red, yellow, and blue; and third (or more) offenders wore a uniform of four colors—red, yellow, blue, and black. Lifestyle, work, and food also depended on this classification scheme: all three groups were segregated from one another; second offenders were only allowed two meals a day; and third offenders performed the most menial labor and were given the worst food.[12]

Unfortunately, the states continued to treat inmates with what seems today to be immense cruelty. In the Massachusetts state institution, the following order was given in 1811: "A gallows shall be erected in the prison yard at an elevation of 20 feet; on it certain prisoners, seven in number, shall be placed, and sit with a rope about their necks for one hour once a week, for three successive weeks; that for 60 days they wear an iron collar and chain as the warden shall direct, and that they wear a yellow cap with asses ears for 60 days; and that they eat at a table by themselves, etc. The sentence shall be read in the Hall at breakfast in presence of all the Prisoners."[13] Other punishments included wearing an iron jacket, an iron ball chained to the leg, and a diet of bread and water; until 1829, it was also the custom to brand the arms of repeaters with the initials MSP (for Massachusetts State Prison).[14]

### The Auburn System

In the early 1800s, both the Pennsylvania and the New York prison systems were experiencing difficulties maintaining the ever-increasing numbers of convicted criminals. Initially, administrators dealt with the problem by increasing the use of pardons, relaxing prison discipline, and limiting supervision.

In 1816, New York State built a new prison at Auburn, hoping to alleviate some of the overcrowding at Newgate. The Auburn Prison design became known as the tier system because cells were built vertically on five floors of the structure. It was sometimes also referred to as the congregate system, since most prisoners ate and worked in groups. Later, in 1819, construction was started on a wing of solitary cells to house unruly prisoners. Three classes of prisoners were then created: one group remained continually in solitary confinement as a result of breach of prison discipline; the second group was allowed labor as an occasional form of recreation; and the third and largest class worked and ate together during the days and only went into seclusion at night.

The philosophy of the Auburn system was crime prevention through fear of punishment and silent confinement. The worst felons were to be cut off from all contact with other prisoners, and though they were treated and fed relatively well, they had no hope of pardon to relieve their solitude or isolation. For a period of time, some of the worst convicts were forced to remain totally alone and silent during the entire day; this practice caused many prisoners to have mental breakdowns, resulting in many suicides and self-mutilations until the practice was abolished in 1823.[15]

The combination of silence and solitude as a method of punishment was not abandoned easily, however. Prison officials sought to overcome the side effects of total isolation while maintaining the penitentiary system. The solution Auburn adopted was to keep convicts in separate cells at night but allow them to work together during the days under enforced silence. Hard work and silence became the foundation of the Auburn

System wherever it was adopted. Silence was the key to prison discipline; it prohibited the formulation of escape plans, it averted plots, and riots, and it allowed prisoners to contemplate their infractions.

The concept of using harsh discipline and control in order to "retrain" the heart and soul of offenders has been the subject of an important book on penal philosophy by French sociologist Michel Foucault called *Discipline and Punish*.[16]

Foucault's thesis is that as societies evolve and become more complex, they create increasingly more elaborate mechanisms to discipline their recalcitrant members and make them "docile" enough to obey social rules. [17] In the seventeenth and eighteenth centuries, discipline was directed toward the human *body* itself, vis a vis torture. In the development of the nineteenth century prison, the object was to discipline the offender psychologically, ". . . the expiation that once rained down upon the body must be replaced by a punishment that acts in the depths of the heart."[18] We can still see the remnants of the philosophy in today's "treatment" oriented prisons.

According to historian David Rothman, regimentation became the standard mode of prison life. Convicts did not simply walk from place to place; rather, they went in close order and single file, each looking over the shoulder of the preceding person, faces inclined to the right, feet moving in unison; the lockstep prison shuffle was developed at Auburn and is still employed in some institutions today.[19]

When discipline was breached in the Auburn System, punishment was applied in the form of a rawhide whip on the inmate's back. Immediate and effective, the Auburn discipline was so successful that when 100 inmates were chosen to build the famous Sing-Sing prison in 1825, not one dared escape, though they were housed in a open field with only minimal supervision.[20]

### The New Pennsylvania System

In 1818, the state of Pennsylvania took the radical step of authorizing a prison which separated *every* inmate in single cells and did not provide them with any work to do. Classifications were abolished because each cell was intended as a mini-prison which would prevent the inmates from contaminating one another.

The new Pennsylvania state prison had an unusual architectural design. It was built in a semicircle, with the cells positioned along its circumference. Built back-to-back, some cells faced the boundary wall while others faced the internal area of the circle. Called the Western Penitentiary, each cell in it was nine by seven and had a small private exercise area in front of it about six feet long.[21]

The Pennsylvania System failed because it was simply too expensive to maintain an institution without convict labor. Inmates could not work but devised ways to talk to one another, thereby subverting the system.

Western Penitentiary was replaced in the late 1820s by a new institution located near Philadelphia, called Eastern Penitentiary.

The facade of this prison was 670 feet wide. In the center of the yard was a rotunda, or observatory, from which seven rows of cell blocks diverged like the arms of a starfish. Each cell was about 12 by 7 feet, and those on the ground floor had exercise yards. All the necessities of life could be provided in the cell and, upon entering it, the inmate remained there, isolated and silent, until the completion of the sentence.[22]

The supporters of the Eastern system believed that the penitentiary was truly a place to do penance. By totally removing the sinner from society, and allowing the prisoner a period of isolation in which to reflect alone upon the evils of crime the supporters of the Eastern system reflected the influence of religion and religious philosophy on corrections. In fact, its advocates believed that solitary confinement (with in-cell labor as a recreation) would eventually make working so attractive that upon release the inmate would be well-suited to resume a productive existence in society.

The Eastern system obviated the need for large numbers of guards or disciplinary measures. Isolated from each other, inmates could not plan escapes or collectively break rules. When discipline was a problem, however, the whip and the iron gag were used.

Many fiery debates occurred between advocates of the Pennsylvania and the Auburn systems. Those supporting the latter position boasted of its supposed advantages; their system was the cheapest and most productive way to reform prisoners. They criticized the Pennsylvania system as cruel and inhumane, suggesting that solitary confinement was both physically and mentally damaging. The Pennsylvania system devotees, on the other hand, argued that their system was quiet, efficient, humane, well ordered, and provided the ultimate correctional facility.[23] They chided the Auburn system for tempting inmates to talk by putting them together for meals and work and then punishing them when they did talk. Finally, the Auburn System was accused of becoming a breeding place for criminal associations by allowing inmates to get to know one another.

The Auburn system eventually won out and spread throughout the United States; many of its features are still used today. Its innovations include congregate working conditions, the use of solitary to punish unruly inmates, military regimentation, and discipline. In Auburn-like institutions, prisoners were marched from place to place; their time was regulated by bells telling them to wake up, sleep, and work. The system was so like the military that many of its early administrators were recruited from the armed services.

Today's larger state prisons are strikingly similar to the Auburn system. Strict silence is no longer maintained, most prisoners are not isolated in the evenings, and rehabilitation is the keynote. Yet, the military discipline and prison uniforms still exist, solitary is still used for punishment, and until the 1960s the whip was used as a disciplinary measure in some institutions.

## Post-Civil War
## Developments

Following the Civil War, radical changes shook the nation's economy, with adverse consequences for prison industries.* The major problem of the prisons was overcrowding, and the theory of the "single cell" broke down. Construction of new prisons became financially prohibitive. Labor protests against prison labor became politically more significant, and by 1870 many state legislators became seriously concerned. The problem became pressing enough to create a growing interest in the idea of the indeterminate sentence which had originated in Ireland. It was adopted as one of the cardinal principles of the newly organized National Prison Association and became the central feature of [Z.R.] Brockway's new reformatory institution at Elmira, New York. Implementation of the indeterminate sentence would require a program of activities flexible enough to select certain inmates for earlier release from prison.

The reformatory program initiated by Brockway included elementary education for illiterates, designated library hours, lectures by faculty of the local Elmira College, and a group of vocational training ships. The cost to the state of the institution's operations was to be held to a minimum. Although Brockway proclaimed Elmira to be an ideal reformatory, his actual achievements were limited. The greatest significance of his contributions was the injection of a degree of humanitarianism into the industrial prisons of that day. However, the construction of many institutions across the country that were labeled reformatories was influenced in design and programs by the Elmira model, but most of them continued to be industrially oriented.

At the beginning of the twentieth century, the political progressive movement reinforced a revived interest in prison reform. Most of the changes introduced into the prisons and reformatories included much of what Brockway and the advocates of the reformatory idea pleaded for and to some extent had put into operation. These changes brought modernized heating and toilet facilities and some other improvements in physical structures. More attention was given to health services, especially to the detection of tuberculosis. Libraries, recreation, athletics, and sports were included in the daily activities. In a few institutions a semblance of inmate participation in the formulation of minor rules and regulations appeared. Vocational training again was emphasized in word, if not in deed. However, the prison and reformatory remained primarily an industrialized facility, and the major problem continued to be the use of prison labor in an overcrowded institution.

The disruptive years of World War I brought some short-term improvements, but the prison administrators continued to be plagued with overcrowding and idleness. The pressure against prison-made goods in the open market mounted. The state-use system appeared to be the most likely resolution of the problem.

The past four decades have seen two parallel lines of action. One was essentially the continuing humanitarian effort to upgrade the standards of living for those confined in the institutions. The other was the introduction of "classification" into the administrative structure of the institution. The term was borrowed from the army psychologists who had demonstrated during World War II the usefulness of psy-

---

*From Joint Commission on Correctional Manpower and Training, *Perspectives on Correctional Manpower and Training* (Washington, D.C., 1970), p. 8.

chological tests for the measurement of human abilities, aptitudes, and personality traits. In the prisons, classification meant two things: first, it meant a differentiation of the prisoner population into custodial or security groupings, thus permitting a degree of planned custodial flexibility not possible previously; and second, it opened the gates of the prison to the teacher, psychologist, social worker, psychiatrist, and others.

Following the lead of the New Jersey and the federal prison systems, classification became the administrative device through which all such services would be coordinated into a process of individualized program planning and the professional staff would become involved in the day-to-day operations of the institution. Federal legislation of the 1930s added significance and impetus by virtually ending the sale of prison-made goods except for state use. One virtue of this development was the elimination of the economic expliotation of prisoners. In addition, increased centralization of state agencies resulted in a hesitant movement toward integration of prisons, parole, and, in a more limited way, probation, into a coordinated approach toward the correction of the convicted offender.

## CORRECTIONAL POPULATION

The precise number of people under secure correctional care is difficult to calculate since so many varieties of correctional facilities exist and so much of their population is highly transient.

County jails, which house pre-trial detainees (those who cannot make bail) and people convicted of misdemeanors and minor felonies, have recently experienced a minor upsurge in population. The 1972 Department of Justice "Survey of Inmates in Local Jails" found that approximately 141,000 people were confined in the nation's jail system; the more recent 1978 update of this survey showed that 158,394 people were jailed as of December 31, 1977. This increase was recorded despite the number of diversion and alternative programs in operation during the mid-1970s.

A strikingly different trend has been occurring in the nation's prison system. As Figure 15.1 indicates, there were approximately 180,000 people in state and federal prisons in 1939; this number declined during the war years to 133,000 in 1945, probably reflecting the large number of people in the armed services. After the war, the prison population slowly rose to 220,000 in 1961, then again started to decline to 187,614 by 1968.

A number of factors may have contributed to the trend toward a stable or actually declining correctional population. One such factor may have been the growth of alternatives to incarceration such as probation, parole, and other community-based corrections. Judges who recognized the availability of these treatment alternatives and the destructive effects of imprisonment may have refrained from the use of incarceratory sentences. In some courts, prison sentences were used only as a last resort after all other methods of treatment had failed.

In addition, it became more difficult to actually get a conviction in a court of law. Overcrowding, delays, the increase of a defendant's due process rights, and the universal availability of legal counsel may all have contributed to lower conviction rates, more dismissals, the increased use

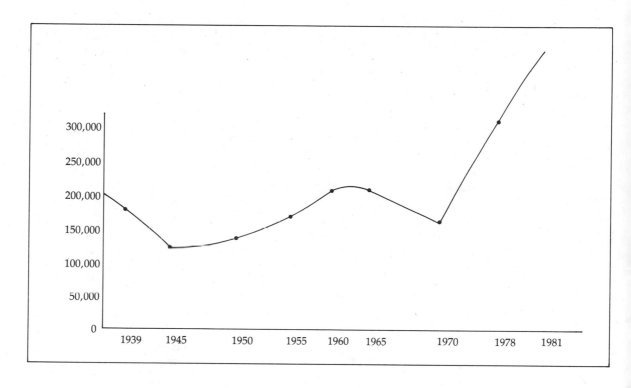

of plea bargaining, and consequently fewer attempts by prosecution to press for prison sentences.

However, in 1973, the declining trend was reversed and over the next four years, the prison population increased by 44% to 280,000 in 1976.

In the last few years, there have been about 292,000 prisoners held in custody in state and federal institutions. In addition, 7,091 prisoners throughout the United States were housed in local jails due to lack of space in state facilities.[24] While the great majority of inmates were male, there were 12,055 institutionalized women, and the rate at which female offenders have been institutionalized has been double that of males.

Finally, it is important to note that despite the general increase, 12 states managed to reduce their inmate populations. These states are led by California, which reduced its prison population by 1,465 inmates between 1976 and 1977. How may this somewhat surprising change be explained? Of course, the increase in the prison population may simply be a short-term phenomenon which will level off and quickly return to normal. Or it may portend a long-term change and toughening of the sentencing policy of the nation's judiciary. Perhaps public outcry against crime has finally altered the criminal justice system's preference for community supervision and treatment as a means of controlling offenders. Furthermore, students of crime will probably pay careful attention to the relationship between the reported crime rate and the size of the prison population. Some may go as far as to suggest that as greater numbers of dangerous offenders are incarcerated, the violent crime rate may actually decrease.

FIGURE 15.1
Population Trends in
State and Federal
Penitentiaries

If, in fact, such conclusions can be reached, a major shift in the criminal justice system's operating philosophy may occur, moving it away from rehabilitation, treatment, and community supervision toward punishment and confinement.

JAILS

The county jail (sometimes called a house of correction) is an institutional facility which is widely used in corrections. Jails have two major purposes: they detain accused offenders prior to trial (if they cannot make bail), and they serve as the principle institutions of reform and correction for offenders convicted of misdemeanors. However, the National Jail Census indicates that a great number of jailed residents are actually felony offenders; in fact, 36% of blacks and 20% of whites held in jails had been convicted of one of the seven felony FBI-index crimes.[25]

Jails were a European import and originally housed the majority of convicted offenders in the Colonies. With the development of the penitentiary and other correctional institutions, jails reverted to their more limited roles of detention centers and misdemeanant correctional facilities.

Unfortunately, jails are low-priority items in the criminal justice field. Since they are almost always administered on a county level, jail services have not been sufficiently regulated nor has a unified national policy been developed to mandate what constitutes adequate jail conditions. Many jails have consequently developed into squalid, crumbling holding pens—such as Manhattan County's now-closed jail, which was appropriately called the Tombs.

### History of Jails

Remote from public view and concern, the jail has evolved more by default than by plan.* Perpetuated without major change from the days of Alfred the Great, it has been a disgrace to every generation.

Colonists brought to the new world the concept of the jail as an instrument of confinement, coercion, and correction of those who broke the law or were merely nuisances. In the early nineteenth century, the American innovation of the state penitentiary made punitive confinement the principal response to criminal acts and removed the serious offender from the local jail. Gradually, with the building of insane asylums, orphanages, and hospitals, the jail ceased to be the repository of some social casualties.[26] But it continued to house the town's minor offenders along with the poor and the vagrant, all crowded together without regard to sex, age, and history, typically in squalor and misery.

Many European visitors came to examine and admire the new American penitentiaries. Two observers—Beaumont and Tocqueville—also saw, side by side with the new penitentiaries, jails in the old familiar form: ". . . nothing has been changed;

---

*The History of Jails; was taken from National Advisory Commission on Criminal Justice Standards and Goals, *Corrections* (Washington, D.C.: U.S. Government Printing Office, 1973), p. 273.

disorder, confusion, mixture of different ages and moral characters, all the vices of the old system still exist." In an observation that should have served as a warning, they said:

There is evidently a deficiency in a prison system which offers anomalies of this kind. These shocking contradictions proceed chiefly from the want of unison in the various parts of government in the United States.[27]

By and large, the deficiencies the two travellers found remain today, the intervening decades having brought only the deterioration of jail facilities from use and age. Changes have been limited to minor variations in the clientele. Jails became residual organizations into which were shunted the more vexing and unpalatable social problems of each locality. Thus, "the poor, the sick, the morally deviant, and the merely unaesthetic, in addition to the truly criminal—all end in jail."[28]

Although larger urban areas have built some facilities for special groups of offenders, in most parts of the country a single local institution today retains the dual purposes of custodial confinement and misdemeanant punishment. The most conspicuous additions to the jail's function have been the homeless and the drunks. Thus jails are the catchall for social and law enforcement problems.

Jails are the intake point for our entire criminal justice system. There are more jails than any other type of correctional institution. Indeed, the current trend toward the decreased use of confinement in major state institutions promises to increase the size and scope of the burden jails must bear. Perhaps this is a short-term expedient that will not become permanent. There are some faint stirrings of hope that it will not be so. For the first time since the colonial era, attention is being given to the place where social problems originate—the community—as the logical location for solving these problems.

### Current Jail Population

The 1978 National Jail Census and Survey of Inmates in Local Jails is a product of the Census Bureau in cooperation with the Law Enforcement Assistance Administration.[29] The findings of this national study gives a good indication of the nature of the jail problem today.

The national survey found that more than 158,000 persons were held in the nation's jails in February 1978, a 12% increase over the 1972 total of 141,600, according to a previous LEAA survey of local jails.

The jails generally held persons awaiting trial and those serving sentences primarily for misdemeanor convictions. Prison overcrowding prompted several states to also hold in jails persons convicted of more serious crimes.

In February 1978, there were 3,493 jails holding 158,394 persons— 89,418 white, 65,104 black, and 3,873 of other races. Of the total, 9,555 or 6%, were women. There were 3,921 jails in 1972.[30]

Who were jail inmates? The vast majority were young men in their twenties. Three of five had not completed high school, and 43% were jobless prior to admission. The median income was $3,255 per inmate during the year prior to arrest.

One in four had a record of military service, most during the Vietnam era. 16% were regular heroin users, while 10% had used heroin occasionally. Approximately one in five unconvicted inmates did not have a lawyer at the survey date. 82% of those who had counsel were represented by court-appointed lawyers, public defenders, or legal aid attorneys.

About three-fourths of the convicted inmates entered guilty pleas, of which 3 of every 10 agreed to plead guilty after plea bargaining.

Four of every 10 inmates were being held awaiting trial. Of the unconvicted, 4 of 5, or a third of all jail inmates, were in jail even though the courts had set bail.

Almost 50% of the jails, holding about 43% of the inmates, were in the South. Georgia, Nevada, Alabama, and Louisiana ranked highest in the ratio of jail inmates to total population. California, Texas, New York, and Florida had the largest totals—each with at least 10,000 in jail. California, with 26,206 inmates, held more than twice as many as each of the other three states.[31]

## Jail Conditions

Jails are the oldest and most deteriorated institutions in the criminal justice system. Since they are usually run by the county government (and controlled by a sheriff), it is difficult to encourage taxpayers to appropriate money for improved facilities. In fact, jails are usually administered under the concept of "custodial convenience" which involves giving inmates minimum standards of treatment and benefits while controlling the cost of jail operations. Jail employees are often underpaid, ill-trained, and totally lacking in professional experience.

A study of conditions in the District of Columbia Jail which was undertaken for the American Civil Liberties Union by volunteer lawyers and law students documents the results:

*The District of Columbia jail is a filthy example of man's inhumanity to man. It is a case study in cruel and unusual punishment, in the denial of due process, in the failure of justice.*

*The Jail is a century old and crumbling. It is overcrowded. It offers inferior medical attention to its inmates, when it offers any at all. It chains sick men to beds. It allows—forces—men to live in crowded cells with rodents and roaches, vomit and excreta. It is the scene of arbitrary and capricious punishment and discipline. While there is little evidence of racial discrimination (the Jail "serves" the male population of the District of Columbia and is, therefore, virtually an all-black institution), there are some categories of prisoners who receive better treatment than others.*

*The eating and living conditions would not be tolerated anywhere else. The staff seems, at best, indifferent to the horror over which it presides. This, they say, is the job society wants them to do. The facilities and amounts of time available for recreation and exercise are limited, sometimes by a guard's whim. Except for a few privileged prisoners on various details, there is no means by which an inmate may combat idleness—certainly nothing that could be called education, counseling or self-help.[32]*

The sad fact is that conditions in the D.C. jail are by no means unique.

Some jails are practically run by violent inmate cliques who terrorize other prisoners; one former IBM executive who served time in jail for writing bad checks, relates this story:

I've seen people raped, especially young kids. You can get a kid as young as . . . 16. These young boys would come in and if they were fresh and young, the guys who run the tank and lived in the first cell, they would take the kid, forcibly hold him and someone would rape him . . . Some of them go to pieces just right there and then, kids who can't hack it and are torn apart.[33]

Conditions such as these have led to a rash of suicides in many jail facilities. In addition, the generally deteriorated nature of jails have resulted in deaths by fire and other natural calamities. On December 27, 1979, eleven inmates were killed in the 156-year-old Lancaster, South Carolina jail, which did not have to comply with county fire regulations. This event prompted Allan Breed, of the National Institute of Corrections to claim, "the very nature of jails and prisons can make them death traps in the event a fire erupts."[34]

The rapid rise in the crime rate has outstripped the ability of jails to adequately contain detainees and convicts. Even in smaller population centers, jails are often old and overcrowded. Coffee County, Tennessee's 75-year-old jail in Manchester, was built for 44 inmates but has housed as many as 109 people. Because of the cramped quarters, Coffee County prisoners were thrown together with workhouse prisoners and convicted state prisoners, and felons were housed with misdemeanor offenders. Females were placed out of sight of males but their cells were within "hooting" distance of the drunk tank.[35]

Similar conditions were encountered by inmates at New York City's Manhattan House of Detention, more commonly known as the "Tombs." Containing 835 cells, with enough room for 900 inmates, the Tombs held over 1400 inmates in 1970 when inmates rioted and held hostages for four days until New York Mayor John Lindsay agreed to meet with inmate leaders. Among the grievances filed by the inmates was included:[36]

We now address ourselves to the physical brutality perpetrated by the officials of Tombs Prison against the inmates thereof. This unnecessary brutality has been largely directed against the black and Puerto Rican inmate population. We vehemently denounce this policy of inhumane treatment.

It is common practice for an inmate to be singled out by some Correction Department employee because he did not hear the officer call his name or because the officer did not like the way this or that inmate looked or because of the manner in which the inmate walked or because the officer brings the turmoil of his own personal problems to work with him, and together with other officers, beat the defenseless inmate into unconsciousness, often injuring him for life physically and mentally or both.

The attacks on the inmates are made by officers wielding blackjack, nightsticks, fists and feet. After such attacks it is the policy of the officials in collusion with any one of the institution doctors to fix up fake accident reports to cover up the mayhem that has been committed against the person of the inmate.

Yet, conditions in the Tombs did not improve, resulting in the eventual closing of the jail by court order.

The deplorable conditions of jails today is highlighted by the results of a General Accounting Office survey which reviewed conditions in 22 jails that had received federal assistance. Some of the findings include:

Seven of the 22 jails did not have operable emergency exits and at least 9 did not have fire extinguishers.

Sanitary conditions were inadequate. Elementary commodities such as soap, tooth-brushes, and clean bedding were in short supply or totally absent from the jails.

Six of the jails had cells that did not contain toilets or had toilets that were inoperable when GAO visited.

Eating facilities in 15 of the 22 jails were in the cell block in full view of the sanitary facilities.

Only 3 jails provided space where inmates could have private conversations with visitors.

Eight of the 22 jails did not have a private area to search the prisoners. In fact, in one jail, searches were done in an open corridor between the two main cell blocks.[37]

Furthermore, an LEAA survey conducted in April of 1977 reported that 361 jails have attracted the attention of the courts. Twenty-eight of these are under federal court order, 144 are under administrative review, 95 are restricted from receiving additional inmates, 87 are cited as failing to meet state standards, and 7 have been ordered closed.[38]

Jail inmates have begun to file court cases to improve jail conditions. Areas of contention include inmate safety, medical care, and treatment (see Chapter 18 for a complete discussion on legal actions by inmates). A recent survey by the National Association of Counties reveals that jail administrators have had their hands full with inmate law suits. Inmates in San Bernadino County, California, filled 1 law suit against jail officials in 1978 and 3 in 1979; in Allen County, Indiana, 9 suits were filed in 1979, none in 1978; Nassau County, New York had 7 cases filed against it in 1978, 26 in 1979. Apparently, the prisoners rights movement has begun to extend to the jail as well as the state penitentiary.[39]

**Future of Jails**
Despite all these problems and handicaps, there is still hope for the future. The federal government and American Correctional Association have co-operated to form the Commission on Accreditation for Corrections. This body has set up standards on health care, food service, treatment, and

visitation, which are contained in a *Manual of Standards For Local Detention Facilities.*[40]

An 11-state pilot project has been set up to help local facilities improve conditions so that they may be successfully "accredited" by the Commission.

Individual states have also expanded their concern. Washington passed a minimum Physical Plant and Custodial Standards Act in 1979 which forces an improvement in jail conditions. Funds were made available for areas that could not comply with conditions due to funding problems.[41] A similar program was begun in New York State in October 1979 to insure tighter admissions, food services, and sanitation standards.

The sanitation standards include cleanliness requirements, insect and rodent control, and health department inspections. The food standards mandate nutritional adequacy and require jail officials to provide food to accommodate the religious or dietary wishes of prisoners. The admissions standards also cover fingerprinting and custody of inmates' personal property. Inmates must also be told of their right to make phone calls upon their admission to a lockup under the new regulations.[42]

In an effort to improve the quality of jail personnel—who are often the lowest paid and poorest trained in the criminal justice system—the National Institute of Corrections has established a National Jail Center in Boulder, Colorado. The center is equipped to develop training materials and hold workshops for jail employees.

Whether new construction or improvement of existing jails should be encouraged is also a question for debate. New or improved facilities may mean the increased reliance on an institution which by its very nature cannot function as it should.

Rehabilitation services may be improved by providing regional educational or treatment centers to aid inmates; the use of furloughs, work-release, and other programs may also help. However, the future of the jail might be determined outside the county corrections system. Bail services must be widened and improved, improved court management must insure that speedy trials limit the duration of jail stays, and diversion programs could eliminate all sentenced offenders from jails except the most violent and dangerous. Those offenders who must be confined to protect the public can then be more easily managed in the existing facilities or in newer, smaller residential ones. Finally, if nothing else, the integration of sentenced offenders, detainees, and juvenile offenders in the same facilities must be ended. While some county jails maintain separate juvenile wings, these are often in close proximity to the adult sections and are physically their equivalent. It is difficult to maintain a separate juvenile justice system when in practice children and adults are housed in identical quarters.

The nation's closed correctional facilities are quite varied in nature and thus are physically and organizationally designed for the particular functions they serve. This section discusses individual types of correctional facilities and their functions.

CLOSED
INSTITUTIONS

**The Prison**

The Federal Bureau of Prisons, and every state government maintain closed correctional facilities, also called prisons, penitentiaries, or reformatories. Usually, prisons are organized or classified on three levels—maximum, medium, and minimum security—and each has distinct characteristics:

1. *Maximum security* prisons are probably the institution most familiar to the public, since they house the most famous criminals and are often the subject of films and stories. Famous "max-prisons" have included Sing-Sing, Joliet, Attica, Yuma, and the most fearsome of all, the now-closed federal facility on Alcatraz Island known as The Rock.

A typical maximum facility is fortresslike, surrounded by stone walls with guard towers at strategic places. These walls may be 25 feet high and sometimes inner and outer walls divide the prison into courtyards. Barbed wire or electrified fences are all designed to discourage escapes. High security, armed guards, and stone walls give the inmate the sense that the facility is impregnable, and reassure the citizen outside that convicts will be completely incapacitated.

Inmates live in interior, metal-barred cells which contain their own plumbing and sanitary facilities, and are locked securely either by key or electronic device. Cells are organized in sections called blocks, and in large prisons a number of cellblocks comprise a wing. During the evening period, each cell block is sealed off from the others, as is each wing. Thus, an inmate may be officially located in, for example, block 3 of E Wing.

Every inmate is assigned a number and uniform upon entering the prison system. Unlike the striped, easily identifiable uniforms of old, the max-inmate today wears khaki attire not unlike military fatigues. Dress codes may be strictly enforced in some institutions, but the closely-cropped scalp and other strict features are usually vestiges of the past.

During the day, the inmate is marched between activities: meals, workshops, education, and so on. Rule violators may be constantly confined to their cells, and working and other shared recreational activities are viewed as privileges.

The byword of the max-security prison is security. Guards and other correctional workers are made aware that each inmate may be a dangerous criminal or violent, and as a result the utmost in security must be maintained. In keeping with this philosophy, prisons are designed to eliminate hidden corners where people can congregate, and passages are constructed so that they can be easily blocked off to quell disturbances.

2. *Medium security* prisons may be quite similar in appearance to the max-prison; however, security and atmosphere are neither so tense nor so vigilant. Medium security prisons are also surrounded by walls, but they are not as high as those of the max-prison nor are there as many guard towers or other security precautions. For example, visitor privileges may be more extensive and skin contact allowed; in a max-prison visitors may be required to be separated from inmates by plexiglass or other barriers (so as to prohibit the passing of contraband). While most prisoners are housed in cells, individual honor rooms are used to reward those who

make exemplary rehabilitative efforts. Finally, medium security prisons promote greater treatment efforts, and the relaxed atmosphere allows freedom of movement for rehabilitation workers and other therapeutic personnel.

3. *Minimum security* prisons operate without armed guards or walls; usually, they are constructed in compounds surrounded by a cyclone-type fence.

Minimum security prisons usually house the most trustworthy and least violent offenders; white-collar criminals may be their most common occupants. A great deal of personal freedom is allowed to inmates. Instead of being marched to activities by guards, they are summoned by bells or loudspeaker announcements and assemble on their own. Work furloughs and educational releases are encouraged, and vocational training is of the highest level. Dress codes are lax, and some inmates are allowed to grow beards or mustaches or demonstrate other individualistic characteristics.

Minimum facilities may employ dormitory living or have small private rooms for inmates. Prisoners are allowed quite a bit of discretion in acquiring or owning personal possessions which might be deemed dangerous in a max-prison, such as radios.

Minimum prisons have sometimes been scoffed at for being too much like country clubs; some federal facilities catering to white-collar criminals even have tennis courts and pools. Yet they remain prisons, and the isolation and loneliness of prison life deeply affects the inmates at these facilities.

### Farms and Camps

In addition to closed institutions, prison farms and camps are used to detain offenders. This type of facility is found primarily in the South and West. Today, about 40 farms, 40 forest camps, 80 road camps, and 67 similar facilities (vocational training centers, ranches, etc.) exist in the nation. Prisoners on farms produce dairy products and grain and vegetable crops which are used in the state correctional system and other government facilities such as hospitals and schools. Forestry camp inmates maintain state parks, fight forest fires, and aid in reforestation. Ranches, primarily a western phenomenon, employ inmates in cattle raising and horse breeding, among others. Road gangs repair roads and state highways.

Community treatment in corrections has come into prominence in the last 15 years, and today more than 300 facilities exist throughout the nation. Most are of the halfway house variety. A halfway house, as the name suggests, is a facility which houses offenders just prior to their release into the community and bridges the gap between institutional living and the community. Specialized treatment may be offered, and the resident uses the experience to cushion the shock of reentering society. In some instances, a commitment to a halfway house or community correctional cen-

COMMUNITY CORRECTIONS

ter may be the sole mode of treatment; an offender may be given a probationary sentence and as a condition of probation may be assigned to a community treatment center. This practice is common in the treatment of drug addicts.

Halfway houses can look like residential homes and, in many instances were originally residences; in urban centers, older apartment buildings can be adapted for the purpose. Usually, these facilities have a central treatment theme—such as group therapy, or reality therapy—which is used to rehabilitate and reintegrate clients. Another popular approach in community-based corrections is the use of ex-offenders as staff members. These individuals have experienced making the transition between closed institution and society, and can be invaluable in helping residents overcome the many hurdles they face in proper readjustment. The application section of this chapter discusses one such program begun in Maryland.

Despite the encouraging philosophical concept presented by the halfway house, evaluation of specific programs has not led to a definitive endorsement of this type of treatment. For example, an evaluation of the first four years of the federally administered pre-release guidance centers indicated that inmates recidivated at a rate of 37%, compared to a control group's 32% rate.[43]

Evaluative studies of halfway houses for drug users reveal the same inadequate results, and similar findings have been determined for juvenile institutions. One program evaluation concluded:

[The program] . . . may be doing an excellent job of rehabilitation even though the return rate of program youth is higher than the return rate for the rest of the male population.[44]

One study of the effectiveness of a drug rehabilitation center found the following:

The program appeared to foster the addict's rejection of his environment and the destruction of what might be described as undesirable defenses. However, there was no evidence of an increased positive attitude toward socially approved goals, with the result that the addict experienced an increase in feelings of self-estrangement.[45]

The rather disappointing performance of halfway houses is reinforced by a recent survey of a federally sponsored program called the Community Treatment Centers (CTC).[46] After a careful analysis comparing CTC clients with a control group of inmates released directly into the community, the survey found, "there was no evidence indicating that overall, offenders referred to a CTC engaged in criminal activity less often or that their criminal activity was relatively less serious."[47]

There are a number of possible explanations for the apparent failure of the halfway house concept. For one thing, there has been a lack of support from community residents who fear the establishment of an institution housing "dangerous offenders" in their neighborhood. Court actions and zoning restrictions have been brought in some areas to foil efforts to create halfway houses. As a result, many halfway houses are located in decrepit neighborhoods, in the worst area of town—certainly a condition which must influence the self-attitudes and behavior of inmates. Furthermore, the climate of control exercised in most halfway houses, where rule violation can be met with a quick return to the institution, may not be one which the average inmate can distinguish from their former high-security penal institution. Thus, while the halfway house promised to be an innovative correctional response, the research conducted on halfway house effectiveness has not been encouraging.

### New Community-Based Corrections Models

A number of different community corrections strategies have been employed recently. The traditional halfway house serves as a transitional setting between institution and community for selected inmates. A more recent model is for offenders to serve their entire term within the halfway house setting. For example, Portland House, a private residential center in Minneapolis, Minnesota, operates as an alternative to county jail or state prison commitment for young adult felony offenders. Residents receive group therapy, financial, employment, education, family, and personal counseling on a regular basis. With funds withheld from their earnings at work-release employment, residents pay room and board, family and self-support, and income taxes.

Portland House appears to be successful: it is significantly cheaper to run than a state institution and the recidivism rate of clients is much lower than those who have gone through traditional correctional programs.[48]

Another innovative program is the Park Center Settlement House located in three aging two-story houses in San Diego, California. Park Center House is unique because it: (1) does not have the restrictive admission criteria found in many halfway houses, and (2) clients are admitted because they believe they are in need of the settlement house's services. The only criteria for admission are that the parolee has no other place to go and wishes to be placed there. Residents (currently 16 males and 9 females) may stay as long as they wish unless they are evicted after a formal hearing or subject to revocation and return to an institution by reason of further law violation. The average period of stay is 90 days.[49]

Still another innovative community corrections approach utilizes the concept of having parolees pay restitution to the victims of their crimes. While restitution programs are widespread and of long standing, few have utilized a live-in component in their operation. An exception, and probably one of the country's best-known programs, is operated by the Minnesota Department of Corrections. Located in Minneapolis, Restitution House was established as a program for parolees from the Minnesota prison system. The Restitution House concept is unusual in that it attempts to encourage prison inmates to volunteer for placement in the house and for payment of restitution to victims as a condition of early release from prison. It thus requires the participation and agreement of the paroling authority.

The program, based in the central-city YMCA, is similar to other work-release programs except that all participants are required to make some form of restitution. Its earlier promising performance currently is threatened by a dwindling population—a result of the reluctance of a new parole board to approve a sufficient number of cases to maintain the population (capacity 40) at a reasonable and cost-efficient level.

Earlier program managers, enthused with the apparent success of the operation, brought into being the first national conference on restitution. Subsequently, other states (e.g., Louisiana and Kentucky) have developed similar programs.[50]

## THE "JUSTICE" PERSPECTIVE

No discussion of today's correctional system would be complete without mention of the "Justice Model" of penology proposed by criminologist David Fogel in his widely read book ". . . We Are The Living Proof."[51] Fogel is perhaps the most well-known (and controversial) of those prison experts who have trumpeted the end of the "rehabilitation era" of corrections. He, along with commentators such as James Q. Wilson, Robert Martinson, and Richard McGee,[52] suggests that prisons should be used for what they are best suited—punishment and incapacitation—and not what they are unsuited for by virtue of their harsh physical conditions—rehabilitation and treatment.

A penal sanction should only mean a temporary deprivation of liberty. It is the legal cost for the violation of some laws. The prison is responsible for executing the sentence, not for rehabilitating the convict.[53]

Thus, according to Fogel, a prison sentence should merely represent the deprivation of liberty caused by violation of an existing legal rule. All the rights accorded to free citizens, consistent with the problem of maintaining order in a mass living situation, should follow the prisoner into the institution.

The prison, according to Fogel's Justice Model, is a place where formerly lawless men and women are taught the value of conducting their lives in a rational and fair model. Since inmates did not use justice in the outside world, they must be taught justice within the institution.[54] Below, some of the programs which Fogel believes can bring justice to the prison are briefly noted:

1. *Flat Sentencing and the Abolition of Parole.* In Chapter 13, we discussed the growing importance of the flat-presumptive sentencing concept. Limiting the discretion of prison authorities to release convicts is believed tantamount to restoring confidence and a sense of justice to inmates who have often been the victims of disparity in the early release process.

2. *Self-Governance.* Citing early efforts by Z. R. Brockway in Detroit and the Hatch Plan in Michigan, Fogel calls for the development of staff-inmate self-governance

councils which will cooperatively formulate policy on program planning and grievance procedures.[55]

3. *Conflict Resolution*. Inmate groups must be allowed to peacefully mediate conflict between inmates and staff, and inmates and other inmates, before violence becomes the only alternative means of resolving disputes.

4. *Legal Aid*. The justice model calls for the development of legal aid programs, and law-school run clinics, to insure that inmates can have easy access to courts. This process can develop a sense of justice in the inmate population.

5. *Administrative Due Process*. Eliminate unnecessary and arbitrary discretion, have clear rules, follow fair procedures for determining and punishing rule infractions (give inmates notice, a hearing, the chance to cross-examine witnesses, written findings, appeal). In addition, prisons should improve their medical care, diets, labor, recreational programs, and inhumane segregation units.

6. *Ombudsman*. Appoint an objective caretaker who will listen to complaints from inmates and investigate abuses within prisons. The ombudsman can also improve and clarify administrative procedures, increase access to judicial review, seek corrective legislation, and alleviate tension within the prison community.[56]

7. *Vocational and Education*. Current education and treatment programs should be dismantled and inmates offered the option of selecting programs that they feel will help them in their own self-improvement. Fogel is especially harsh on current counseling and treatment programs.

*All clinical programs can be dismantled . . . The spectacle of organizing inmates into therapy groups or caseloads is embarrassingly tragic. It is best described as a psychic lock-step. When the indomitability of the human spirit could not be crushed by our 'break the spirit' forefathers, we relinquished that task to technology of psychiatry.[57]*

8. *Make prisons smaller*. Fogel calls for an end to fortresslike prisons and argues that institutions should hold no more than 300 inmates, subdivided into living groups of 30.

There is no question that Fogel's call for stern but fair measures in penology has reached a sympathetic ear among the nation's lawyers, legislators, and prison officials. Currently, the trend has been to keep as many people out of prison as possible through community-based programs, but to punish serious offenders with longer and more certain sentences.

SUMMARY

Today's correctional institutions can trace their development from European origins. Punishment methods developed in Europe were modified and improved by American colonists, most notably William Penn. He replaced the whip and other methods of physical punishment with confinement in county institutions or penitentiaries.

Later, as needs grew larger, the newly formed states created their own large facilities. Discipline was harsh within them, and most enforced a code of total and absolute silence. The Auburn System of congregate working conditions during the day and isolation at night has been adopted in our present penal system.

The current correctional population has grown dramatically in the past few years. Though the number of inmates diminished in the late 1960s and early 1970s, most recently the number of prison and jail residents has hit an all-time high. This development may reflect a toughening of sentencing procedures nationwide.

A number of different institutions currently house convicted offenders. Jails are used for misdemeanants and minor felons. Since conditions are so poor in jails, they have become a major trouble spot for the criminal justice system.

Federal and state prisons—classified as minimum, medium, and maximum security—house most of the nation's incarcerated felons. However, their rather poor track record of success has spurred the development of new correctional models, specifically the halfway house and community correctional center. Nonetheless, the success of these institutions has been challenged by research efforts indicating that their recidivism rates are equal to those of state prisons.

A new penal model has captured the imagination of many prison officials and state policy makers. Called the Justice Model, its proponents recommend the establishment of mandatory sentences, the abolition of parole, and increased fairness within the institution.

QUESTIONS FOR DISCUSSION

**1.** Identify and define the purpose of the different correctional models.

**2.** What are the advantages and disadvantages of community-based corrections? How would you feel if a halfway house was built in your neighborhood?

**3.** Does the idea of requiring inmates to make restitution to the victims of their crime make sense? Discuss the pros and cons of a restitution-based halfway house.

NOTES

**1.** Robert Carter, Richard McGee, and E. Kim Nelson, *Corrections In America* (Philadelphia: J. B. Lippincott Co., 1975), p. 117.

**2.** See David Fogel, ". . . We Are the Living Proof . . ." (2nd ed.) (Cincinnati, Ohio: Anderson, 1978); Andrew Von Hirsch, *Doing Justice: The Choice of Punishments* (New York: Hill and Wang, 1976); R. G. Singer, *Just Desserts—Sentencing Based on Equality and Dessert* (Cambridge, Mass.: Ballinger, 1979).

**3.** The most widely cited authority on the fact is Robert Martinson. See Robert Martinson, Douglas Lipton, and Judith Wilks, *The Effectiveness of Correctional Treatment* (New York: Praeger, 1975).

**4.** Among the most helpful sources for this section are included Benedict Alper, *Prisons Inside-Out* (Cambridge, Mass.: Ballinger Publishing Co., 1974); Gustave de Beaumont and Alexis de Tocqueville, *On the Penitentiary System in the United States and Its Application In France* (Carbondale, Ill.: Southern Illinois University Press, 1964); Orlando Lewis, *The Development of American Prisons and Prison Customs 1776–1845* (Montclair, N.J.: Patterson-Smith, 1967); Leonard Orland, *Justice, Punishment & Treatment* (New York: Free Press, 1973).

5. Lewis, *Development of American Prisons & Prison Customs 1776–1845*, p. 12.

6. Ibid., p. 16.

7. Ibid., p. 17.

8. Ibid., p. 18.

9. Ibid., p. 29.

10. Ibid., p. 76.

11. Leonard Orland, *Justice, Punishment, Treatment*, p. 145.

12. Orlando Lewis, *Development of American Prisons and Prison Customs 1776–1845*, p. 71.

13. Ibid.

14. Ibid., p. 76.

15. Beaumont and de Tocqueville, *On the Penitentiary System in the United States and Its Application in France*, p. 42.

16. Michel Foucault, *Discipline and Punish* (New York: Vintage Books, Random House, 1979).

17. Ibid., p. 139.

18. Ibid., p. 16.

19. Cited in Orland, *Justice, Punishment & Treatment*, p. 152.

20. Ibid., p. 151.

21. Lewis, *Development of American Prisons and Prison Customs 1776–1845*, p. 119.

22. Orland, *Justice, Punishment & Treatment*, p. 143.

23. Ibid., p. 144.

24. Prisoners in State and Federal Institutions on December 21, 1977. National Prisoner Statistics Bulletin, April 1978. (Washington, D.C.).

25. Law Enforcement Assistance Administration, *National Jail Census* (Washington, D.C.: National Criminal Justice Information & Statistics Service, 1970).

26. For an account of this development, see David J. Rothman, *The Discovery of the Asylum: Social Order and Disorder in the New Republic* (Little, Brown and Co., 1971).

27. Gustave de Beaumont and Alexis de Tocqueville, *On the Penitentiary System of the United States and Its Application in France*, H. R. Lantz, ed. (Southern Illinois University Press, 1964), p. 49.

28. Hans W. Mattick and Alexander Aikman, "The Cloacal Region of American Corrections," *Annals of the American Academy of Political and Social Science* 381:114 (1969).

29. *National Jail Census;* National Survey of Inmates of Local Jails. Preliminary reports available from 16 National Criminal Justice Reference Service, Rockville, Maryland.

30. Survey of Local Jails was also conducted by the Census Bureau and LEAA in 1972.

31. Analysis of the Survey of Inmates of Local Jails is contained in *Jail Administration Digest.* 2:4 (1979). (Herein cited as *JAD*.)

32. *The Seeds of Anguish*, p. 1.

33. Cited in Ben Bagdikan and Leon Dash, *The Shame of the Prisons* (N.Y.: Pocket Books, 1972).

34. Cited in *J.A.D.* 3:1 (Feb. 1980).

35. *J.A.D.*, 2:5 (March 1979).

36. Taken from: American Friends Service Committee, *Struggle for Justice* (New York: Hill and Wang, 1971) pp. 1–6.

37. Cited in Sherman Day, "Community Action Needed to Upgrade Local Jails." LEAA Newsletter, V.6N.11 (1977) p. 2.

38. Ibid.

39. *J.A.D.* 3:4 (Feb. 1980).

40. The Commission is located in Rockville, Maryland.

**41.** Ronald Kespohl, "Jail Management", The *National Sheriff* (Feb.–March, 1965), p. 6.

**42.** *J.A.D.*, 2:6 (Oct. 1979).

**43.** Correctional Research Associates, *Treating Youthful Offenders in The Community*, An evaluation conducted by A. J. Reiss (Washington, D.C.: 1966).

**44.** Illinois Corrections Department, *Parole Outcome Studies: Adult Community Centers and Juvenile Halfway Houses*, (Kevin Houlihan).

**45.** Howard Kaplan and Joseph Meyerowitz, "Evaluation of a Halfway House: Integrated Community Approach in the Rehabilitation of Narcotic Addicts," *International Journal of Addictions* 4:65 (Winter 1969).

**46.** James Beck, "An Evaluation of Federal Community Treatment Centers," *Federal Probation* 43:36–40 (1979).

**47.** Ibid., p. 40.

**48.** This program is evaluated in E. Kim Nelson, Howard Ohmart, and Nora Harlow, *Promising Strategies in Probation and Parole*, (Washington, D.C.: U.S. Government Printing Office, 1978, pp. 25–26).

**49.** Ibid., p. 26.

**50.** Adapted from Ibid., p. 30. See also Steven L. Chesney, "The Assessment of Restitution in the Minnesota Probation Services," In Joe Hudson (ed.), *Restitution in Criminal Justice* (St. Paul, Minnesota, Minnesota Department of Corrections, 1975).

**51.** David Fogel, ". . . We Are the Living Proof . . ." 2nd ed., (Cincinnati, Ohio: Anderson Publishing Co., 1979).

**52.** See, for example, Richard McGee, "A New Look at Sentencing: Part II, *Federal Probation* 7–8 (1974).

**53.** Fogel, ". . . We Are the Living Proof . . .", p. 202.

**54.** Ibid., p. 207.

**55.** Ibid., p. 204.

**56.** ibid., p. 232.

**57.** Ibid., p. 262.

# Montgomery County Work Release/Pre-Release Center (PRC), Montgomery County, Maryland*

Finding a job can be a difficult and stressful situation for anyone. For the newly released offender, it could be an insurmountable obstacle to becoming a productive member of the community. The Montgomery County Work Release/Pre-Release Center helps to ease the transition from incarceration to freedom by assuring that its clients have employment, housing, and cash savings at the time of release.

Montgomery County PRC is a coeducational, residential, community-based correctional facility serving sentenced offenders within six months of their release or parole hearing, pretrial detainees, and selected probationers and parolees. The program involves extensive supervision, counseling services, social awareness instruction, and work or education release from the center.

With the assistance of a Work Release Coordinator, all PRC residents obtain jobs shortly after their arrival (unless they intend to enroll in a full-time academic or vocational training program). All employed residents—full-time or part-time—pay up to $200 a month for their room and board. Many residents also pay fines, restitution, legal fees, and family support.

Each resident's activities at the Center are prescribed by a contractual agreement developed prior to his or her arrival at PRC. A tri-phased furlough/release plan allows increasing privileges as the resident demonstrates responsible behavior through adherence to his contract and PRC rules.

PRC has had significant impact on the recidivism rates of its clients. During the three-year study period, a total of 407 residents successfully passed through the program. A one-year follow-up study showed that under 20% were rearrested subsequent to leaving the program. Less than 1% were arrested for new crimes while assigned to the Center.

PRC has also succeeded in marshalling community support in Montgomery County. The Center has gained the acceptance and support of both neighbors and local civic groups and its funding was completely assumed by the county government upon termination of its LEAA grant.

---

*From National Institute of Law Enforcement, U.S. Dept. of Justice Exemplary Projects Program (Washington, D.C.: U.S. Government Printing Office, 1979), p. 19.

# Institutional Life

PHYSICAL
CONDITIONS OF
PRISONS

This chapter will focus directly on the administration, conditions, and life in the nation's closed institution system—the medium, maximum and minimum security prisons and penitentiaries.

The physical conditions of prisons are often appalling. While some care has been taken to maintain facilities, many institutions are so old and have been in continuous use for so long that proper upkeep is impossible. A census conducted by the Federal Bureau of Prisons in 1974 revealed that of the 577 state institutions in operation, 6% were built after 1969; 41% dated from 1949–1969, 32% from 1924–1948, 11% from 1899–1923, and 6% from 1874–1898; and 24 institutions still in operation were built before 1874. The 1974 census indicated that high-security state prisons tended to be housed in the oldest institutions; 70% were built prior to 1949, and only 8 had been constructed since 1969.[1]

Today, state facilities contain approximately 120,000 cells and 2,000 other quarters. Most cells (86%) house one inmate, 13% hold two, and 1% contain three or more.

The physical amenities of individual cells also vary widely, depending on the state and the type of prison in which they are located. Most cells contain toilets and sinks, while tables, chairs, lamps, and other equipment are benefits reserved for less than one half of all inmates. Such privileges may be given as rewards to honor inmates, sometimes called trusties, who have proven receptive to treatment and cooperate with guards and other institutional personnel.

Most prisons usually have a standard set of facilities for recreation and education, which may include game rooms, a library, a barber shop, gyms, and athletic fields.

Sports are also an important part of prison life. Prison boxing teams have provided Olympic hopefuls, and have also been the training ground for some professional champions. The baseball or softball team is also extremely popular.

While prison conditions are still deficient they have come a long way from the whip, isolation, and enforced silence of the Auburn and Pennsylvania systems.

MEN IN
PRISON
"—A PROFILE"

Who is the prison inmate? What are his characteristics? Are some groups overrepresented in the prison population compared with others?

To answer these questions, the United States Department of Justice undertook a survey of the prison population of the United States. From this information, which follows, a profile of the typical male inmate can be derived.[2]

Males constitute an overwhelming majority of all inmates, outnumbering females 97% to 3%. Whites amounted to approximately 51% of the population; blacks, who make up 11% of the civilian population, are disproportionately represented in prison (47%). Other ethnic minorities such as Indians and Orientals account for the other 2% of the inmate population.

Most inmates were rather youthful, with 18 to 34 being the model age (75%). The median age (fiftieth percentile) was 27.

Prisoners sentenced to state correctional institutions had usually received less education than the general population. About 61% of inmates had terminated their education before high school graduation; only 2% had received college education.

Before arrest, the majority of inmates held full-time jobs (75%), destroying the myth that crime is a full-time profession; however, the 25% unemployment rate was still quite high. Of those who were unemployed, about 40% were looking for work; 16% were not actively job hunting; and the rest simply had no desire for employment.

Inmates' marital status also tended to differ from that of members of the general population. About half had been married, as compared to 80% of the general population over 18. About 20% were married when they began serving time, and the rest were divorced or separated. Once they began serving their sentences, the divorce rate increased another 25%.

Inmates very often had in the past, or were currently having, a drinking or drug problem; an estimated 43% claimed to have been drinking at the time they committed the offenses for which they were imprisoned. About 60% claimed to have used drugs at one time or another, though for a great majority of these individuals the drug of choice was marijuana.

About 26% stated that they were on drugs when they committed the crime of which they were accused. Clearly, the influence of alcohol and drugs is a major factor in the commission of crime. When we combine both totals, it appears that approximately 70% of incarcerated inmates claim to have been under the effects of alcohol or drugs while they were committing the criminal acts that resulted in their imprisonment.

In terms of correctional background, 70% of inmates had previously been sentenced for crimes (this includes juvenile and youth crimes). By combining their present terms with all others provides data which states that 30% were first offenders, 23% had served two terms, 19% three sentences, 12% four sentences, and 16% five or more. The median time served was 3.5 years on all sentences. Not surprisingly, 52% of repeat offenders had served time for the same offenses. The claim that corrections does not correct seems to be substantiated by this information.

In conclusion, it appears that the profile of the average prison inmate is as follows: a white male, in his twenties, underemployed, undereducated, and unmarried. He uses alcohol and drugs too often; his background is one of criminal behavior, and he repeats the same type of offense often. He may even specialize in a particular offense. *Also, he gets caught.*

Prisons in America are total institutions. Inmates locked within their walls are segregated from the outside world, kept under constant scrutiny and surveillance, and forced to obey a strict code of official rules to avoid facing formal sanctions. Their personal possessions are taken from them and they must conform to institutional dress and personal appearance norms. Many human functions are strictly curtailed—heterosexual activity, friendship, family relationships, society, education, and participation in groups become past events.

MALE INMATES'
ADJUSTMENT TO
PRISON

Inmates in large, inaccessible prisons may find themselves physically cut off from families, friends, and former associates. Visitors may find it difficult to travel great distances to visit them; mail is censored and sometimes destroyed.

The inmate may go through a variety of attitude and behavior changes, or cycles, as his sentence unfolds. During the early part of his prison stay, the inmate may become easily depressed while considering the long duration of the sentence and the loneliness and dangers of prison life. He must learn the ins and outs of survival in the institution; what persons can be befriended, what persons are best avoided? Who will grant favors, and for what repayment? The inmate may find that some prisoners have formed cliques or groups based on ethnic backgrounds or personal interests; mafialike or racial terror groups will soon be encountered and must be dealt with. He may be the victim of homosexual attacks. Most important, the new inmate must learn to deal with the guards and other correctional personnel; these relationships will determine whether the inmate does "hard time" or "easy time." Each prisoner has his own method of adaptation; he may stay alone, become friends with another inmate, join a group, or seek the advice of treatment personnel. Regardless of adaptation style, the first stage of an inmate's prison cycle is marked by a growing awareness that he can no longer depend on his traditional associates for help and support, and that for better or worse the institution is a new home which must be adjusted to.

Part of an inmate's early adjustment involves his becoming familiar with and perhaps participating in the black-market, hidden economy of the prison—the Hustle. Hustling provides inmates with a source of steady income and the satisfaction they are beating the system.[3]

Hustling involves sales of such illegal commodities as drugs (uppers, downers, pot), alcohol, weapons, or illegally obtained food and supplies. When prison officials crack down on hustled goods, it merely serves to drive the price up—giving hustlers a greater incentive to promote their black-market activities.[4]

The inmate must also learn to deal with the racial conflict which is a daily fact of life. Prisoners tend to segregate themselves and, if peace is to reign in the institution, stay out of each other's way. Often racial groupings are quite exact; for example, Hispanics will separate themselves according to their national origin (Mexico, Puerto Rico, Columbia, etc.). Since sentencing disparity is a common practice in many American courts, prisons are one area in which minorities often hold power; as sociologist James B. Jacobs observed, "Prison may be the one institution in American society that blacks control."[5]

The second phase of the institution cycle occurs toward the middle of the inmate's sentence. This is a low-energy period during which relationships are cemented and the inmate becomes a fixture within the prison community. He may find that the social support of inmate peers can make incarceration somewhat less painful than originally expected. The inmate may begin to take stock of his situation and enter into education or vocational training programs if they are available. He heeds the inmate grapevine in order to determine what the parole board considers important in their decisions to grant community release. He may become more politically aware due to the influence of other inmates, and the personal guilt he may have felt may be shifted to society at large. Why should the inmate be in prison when those equally guilty go free? He learns the importance of money and politics. Eventually, he may be called upon by new arrivals to aid them in adapting to the system.

The third and final phase of the prison cycle begins when the sentence nears its end and a release date is in sight. During this period, the inmate may be less likely to become involved in prison affairs. Inmate leaders will not call upon him when planning demonstrations, protests, escapes, or other clandestine activities since they know that he will be careful to avoid actions that may jeopardize his release. Instead of rejecting authority, the inmate may try to impress prison officials with his willingness to cooperate and demonstrate the improved extent of his rehabilitation. During this period, the inmate may also begin to feel a great deal of anxiety. He may question his ability to reenter society,[6] or fear that a major breach of prison rules by individuals or groups may result in the development of a more stringent policy by the parole board and delay his release.

During the early period of adjustment to prison social life, the prisoner may find that he must adapt to what is known as the inmate social code. These unwritten guidelines express the values, attitudes, and types of behavior which the older inmates demand of the younger. Passed on from one generation of inmates to another, the inmate social code represents the values of interpersonal relations within the prison. In a careful analysis of the components of the inmate social code, Gresham Sykes and Sheldon Messinger have identified the following as its most important principles:[7]

1. Don't interfere with inmates' interests. Within this area of the code are maxims concerning the serving of the least amount of time in the greatest possible comfort. For example, inmates are warned . . . never [to betray another] inmate to authorities; . . . [in other words,] grievances must be handled personally. Other aspects of the noninterference doctrine include "Don't be nosy," "don't have a loose lip," "keep off [the other inmates' backs,"] and "don't put [another inmate] on the spot."
2. Don't lose your head. Inmates are also cautioned to refrain from arguing, [quarreling or engaging in] other emotional displays with fellow inmates. The novice may hear such warnings as "play it cool" and "do your own time."
3. Don't exploit inmates. Prisoners are warned not to take advantage of one another—"Don't steal from cons," "don't welsh on a debt," "[b]e right."
4. Inmates are cautioned to be tough and not lose their dignity. While rule 2 forbids conflict, once it starts an inmate must be prepared to deal with it effectively and [thoroughly]. Maxims include "Don't cop out," "Don't weaken," "Be tough; be a man."
5. Don't be a sucker. Inmates are cautioned not to make fools . . . of themselves and support the guards or prison administration over the interest of the inmates— "Be sharp."

SOCIAL CODE
OF THE MALE
INMATE

Sykes and Messinger discovered that a prisoner's relationship to the inmate social code is reflected in the roles he takes on in the institution and the labels he is given by peers. A con who cooperates with authorities is labeled a "rat" or "squealer" and is treated with universal scorn and disdain; highly aggressive inmates who quarrel and fight easily are called "toughs," and a violent controlling individual may be called a "gorilla"; someone who exploits other inmates economically is a "merchant" or "peddler"; and those men who fail to live up to the maxim "be tough" are called "weak sisters." Male inmates who actively engage in homosexual liaisons are "wolves," while their passive partners are "fags."

There is also a particular term to describe someone who always sticks to the major tenets of the inmate social code: the "right guy." According to Sykes and Messigner:

A right guy is always loyal to his fellow prisoners. He never lets you down, no matter how rough things get. He keeps his promises. He's dependable and trustworthy . . . The "right guy" never interferes with inmates who are conniving against the officials. He doesn't go around looking for a fight, but he never runs away from one when he is in the right . . . he acts like a man.[8]

In a similar vein, McCorkle and Korn have suggested that the inmate social structure provides mechanisms for inmates to reject their rejectors rather than themselves.[9] The prison social system only works for the benefit of those who are willing to be acculturated within it and reject the pulls of the outside world; the adaptive inmate is thus protected and insulated from the loss of face and group memberships which incarceration has caused him.

Sociologist Clarence Schrag suggests that the inmate social code requires conforming to one of four roles: "right guys" who conform to the rules of the inmate culture; "square johns" who define their role in terms of the prison staff's rules; "con politicians" who switch allegiance back and forth as the situation dictates; "outlaws" who are in a constant state of rebellion against both codes.[10] These proposed role models have been identified in the present prison system. In a study of California prisons, inmates labeled "square johns" were found to be nonmilitant, acquiescent, and displayed allegiance to prison rules; "con politicians" also rejected militancy and disruptive behavior because it was counterproductive to their strategy of increasing personal benefits; "outlaws" engaged in violent and aggressive behavior; "right guys" organized prison unions and were outspoken in their demands for prisoners rights.[11]

## TREATMENT OF MALE INMATES WITHIN THE INSTITUTION

Almost every prison facility employs some mode of treatment for inmates. This may come in the form of individual or group therapy programs, or educational or vocational training.

Despite good intentions, rehabilitative treatment within prison walls is extremely difficult to achieve. Trained professional treatment personnel are usually high salaried and most institutions do not have sufficient budgets to adequately staff therapeutic programs. Usually, a large facility may have a single staff psychiatrist and/or a few social workers. A second problem revolves around the philosophy of "less eligibility"; this doctrine has been interpreted to mean that prisoners should always be treated less well than the most underprivileged law-abiding citizen. Translated into today's terms, less eligibility usually involves the question, "Why should correctional system inmates be treated to expensive programs denied to the average honest citizen?" Enterprising state legislators use this argument to block expenditures for prison budgets, and some prison administrators may actually agree with them.

Finally, correctional treatment is hampered by the ignorance surrounding the practical effectiveness of one type of treatment program over another. It has not yet been determined what constitutes proper treatment, and studies evaluating treatment effectiveness have suggested that few if any of the programs currently employed in prisons actually produce significant numbers of rehabilitated offenders.

This section discusses a selected number of therapeutic methods which have been employed nationally in correctional settings and attempts to identify some of their more salient features.

### Group Treatment Techniques

One of the most commonly used treatment techniques within the prison community is group counseling. It has a number of beneficial features, not the least of which is the use of nonprofessional treatment personnel as group leaders. Group counseling does not depend on or attempt to make fundamental changes in the client's personality, but instead makes use of the group to stimulate the inmate's self-awareness and his ability to deal with everyday problems within the institution. The inmate may use the group to learn to understand how others view him, and how he views himself. Or the group may be used to help the inmate solve perplexing personal problems which he alone is incapable of dealing with.

During the group process, the counselor's role is to lead the group discussion and insure that every participant has a chance to express feelings while directing the flow of the conversation in certain directions. The counselor does not, however, attempt to analyze clients or create changes in their personalities.

*Guided Group Interaction.* This program was developed while working with delinquent youth in experimental treatment programs at Highfields, New Jersey and Provo, Utah.[12] Guided group interaction makes use of a nonprofessional therapist who may often be an ex-offender. This technique uses the group process to allow individual inmates to evaluate and understand their own behavior. Its basic premise is that the streetwise peer group is less likely to be conned by individual group members than are classically trained therapists who are not used to working with this type of clientele. Since the group is a microcosm of the real world, containing winners, losers, toughs, straights, and others, successful adaptation to the group process is believed to be analogous to improving relationships with other social groups. Thus, by identifying roles and behaviors which occur within the group, and uncovering the motivations underlying them, the inmate learns to understand why he acts the way he does, and how others react to his behavior.

Graduates of guided group interaction programs often remain in the corrections field and serve as counselor leaders with new groups of inmates.

*Group Therapy.* Led by a clinically trained social worker, psychologist, or psychiatrist, group therapy uses the techniques of psychoanalysis to help inmates learn more about themselves and their relationship to others. By opening up avenues of communication, the therapist attempts to actually restructure the personality of the group and, by implication, its members. Olive Irwin has commented on how this process affects juvenile offenders:

When they learn in the group they can discover some of the truth that has been denied them about their relationship to the world, there is evident relief; their relationship to it shifts. An understanding, an unspoken, often unconscious, agreement develops in which they feel safe to risk themselves, to face their own limitations, to accept inevitable disappointments and pain. Although in the group they are provoked into conflict and confronted with their inadequacies, they are doing it themselves and the leader meets their struggle with imparted honesty."[13]

### Individual Forms of Treatment

*Reality Therapy* was developed by Dr. William Glasser, who suggests that traditional therapeutic techniques are ineffective in a nonconventional setting such as the prison. Glasser argues that human behavior, especially when it reflects emotional problems, is related to the individual's inability to satisfy the need to feel worthwhile to himself and others.[14]

In the dehumanized, alienated atmosphere of the prison, these basic needs are often violated. Glasser and his followers believe that help may be made available in the form of a relationship between the inmate and another person—the therapist—who can supply the love, encouragement, and feelings of worth which are denied the inmate when he is cut off from the rest of the world. The reality therapist focuses on the here and now rather than emphasizing childhood experiences; instead of maintaining the detachment of the Freudian analyst, the therapist becomes a friend who helps or teaches the client how to better meet his own needs. In summary, reality therapy focuses on improving the client's self-image through a close personal relationship with a concerned therapist.

*Transactional Analysis (TA)*, developed by psychiatrist Eric Berne, is another variation on traditional psychotherapy which has particular utility for the prison inmate and other offenders within the correctional system.[15]

Berne postulates that the personality of every human being contains three distinct elements: (a) the Parent (or judgmental part), which incorporates nuances, prejudices, and attitudes derived from relationships with one's parents; (b) the Child (or prejudgmental part), which encompasses recollections of childhood perceptions and feelings which are evident in demands for immediate gratification and nonrational thinking; and (c) the Adult (or rational aspect of the personality), which rejects judgmental and emotional inclinations and strives for reason and logic. Berne believes that each component is unique and separate, and that each of us maintains elements of all three in his consciousness.

Berne suggests that in some individuals one personality component becomes dominant over the others. For example, the irrational child or the judgmental parent may assert itself and block the behavior of the rational adult. When this happens, relationships may be adversely affected and one's lifestyle may be interfered with. Finally, Berne believes that people's behavior falls into set social patterns which he labels games, similar to those played by children.

The TA therapist develops in his client an awareness of these ego-states and life games; in practice, the therapist teaches TA techniques to the client. This therapy aims at developing the adult portion of the personality, while retaining the useful parts of the parent and child, such as spontaneity and caution. When its techniques are taught to the client, TA can become a permanent tool for change and free the client from becoming too dependent on the analyst.

*Behavior Therapy (BT)* is based upon the pioneering work of Dr. B. F. Skinner and his associates.[16] Skinner's basic premise is that behavior is governed by its consequences. A BT specialist does not attempt to psychoanalyze a client or deal with the unconscious motivations for feelings and attitudes; instead, he focuses directly on a certain type of behavior. BT aims at reinforcing beneficial types of behavior and extinguishing harmful ones.

The behavior therapist first identifies the particular behavior to be dealt with (e.g., drinking, aggression, or tardiness,) and then attempts to identify the reinforcers which directly influence that behavior. Reinforcers are usually of two types: one set consists of *positive* ones, and these can be characterized as rewards for performing a certain behavior; for example, money, leisure, praise, or attention. The second set is composed of negative or aversive reinforcers, and these are characterized by such acts as threats, punishment, or confinement. Behavior therapy emphasizes the gradual positive reinforcement of some types of behavior and the aversive (extinctive), reinforcement of others. For example, a reward system might be developed to encourage good work habits; every time the client did an assigned task promptly and accurately, a token would be granted which could be redeemed for some reward at the prison commissary. While slowly building up proper habits in the client, the behavior therapist hopes that the reinforced behavior will be maintained even after the rewards are withdrawn. BT has had marked success in curing some types of behavior such as bedwetting, smoking, and drinking. However, it can be a relatively expensive and long-term proposition, and its opponents have questioned both the provision of positive rewards for criminals and the excessive use of adversive conditioners, which sometimes seem cruel and unusual.

*Psychoanalysis* may use classical Freudian analytical techniques or various offshoots, such as Adlerian, Jungian, or Rogerian methods. Almost all branches stress the client's recollection of early childhood experiences which have shaped current behavior and personality. Psychoanalysis is a long involved process which may require many years' involvement and may achieve success only after great expense. While it may be a useful tool within the correctional setting, its obvious expense precludes its use in all but the most selected cases.

*Milieu Therapy* uses the social structure and processes of the institution to influence the behavior patterns of offenders. Advocates of this technique attempt to create a therapeutic community in which inmates become involved with ongoing operations and organization. By developing clients' skills within the correctional community and delegating decision-making authority to inmates, the milieu therapist tries to build responsible behavior patterns in inmates which they can carry over into the outside world. By understanding the successes and failures of interpersonal relationships within the institution, the offender can begin to learn the appropriateness of his behavior with people he will meet in working relationships on the outside.

Milieu therapy has been used primarily in minimum security institutions, halfway houses, and youth homes. It can be a useful tool for helping the inmate make the transition back into society.[17]

## VOCATIONAL AND EDUCATIONAL PROGRAMS

In addition to treatment programs stressing personal growth through individual analysis or group process, inmate rehabilitation may also be pursued within programs stressing (1) vocational training or (2) educational training and/or rehabilitation. While these two approaches may sometimes differ in style and content, they can also overlap when, for example, education is directed toward a practical area of job-related study.

The first prison treatment programs were in fact educational in nature. A prison school was opened at the Walnut Street Jail in 1784. Elementary courses were offered in New York's prison system in 1801, and in Pennsylvania's in 1844. An actual school system was established in Detroit's House of Corrections in 1870, and Elmira Reformatory opened a vocational trade school in 1876.[18]

Today, most institutions provide some type of educational program. At some prisons, inmates are given the opportunity to obtain a high school diploma through equivalency exams or general educational development (GED) certificates. Other institutions provide an actual classroom education, usually staffed by full-time certified teachers or by part-time teachers who work at an institution following a full day's teaching in a nearby public school. The number of hours devoted to educational programs and the quality and intensity of these efforts vary greatly. Some are full-time programs employing highly qualified and concerned educators, while others are part-time programs without any real goals or objectives.[19]

A recent survey of over 16 prison institutions sheds some light on the extent of educational and vocational programming. The study found that 96% of survey institutions had both basic education (basic literacy) and secondary education (high school level) programs, 83% had post-secondary education (college level), 89% had vocational (skilled job training) education, and 44% had social education (includes life-skills, consumer education, problem-solving skills). Inmate enrollment ranged from 10% in post-secondary (college level) education to 19% in vocational programs. Unfortunately, the study also found a great deal of conflict over the educational-vocational training issue. There was a lack of adequate funding in many institutions, a lack of comprehensive planning, and resistance to programs for guards and staff who view inmates as receiving benefits often unavailable to "honest" citizens.[20]

Many prison educational programs have faced problems in their inability to adequately serve the entire prison population. One difficulty often encountered is the fact that levels of education within the inmate population may range from the third grade up to college. The potential audience also includes inmates who can't read or write; in some areas, a substantial number cannot speak or understand English. Educational programs are also hampered by motivational, security, and disciplinary problems which curtail the enrollment of inmates.

The picture is not totally bleak, however. In some institutions, programs have been designed to circumvent the difficulties inherent within the prison structure. They encourage volunteers from the community and local schools to aid in tutoring willing and motivated inmates. Some prison administrators have arranged flexible schedules, and actively encourage participation in these programs. In several states such as Texas, Connecticut, and Illinois, statewide school districts serving prisons have been created.[21] The formulation of districts such as these can make available better qualified staff and provide the materials and resources necessary for meaningful educational programs.

At the Draper Correctional Center in Montgomery, Alabama, a unique approach to education using programmed learning has been utilized. Through federal grants, various self-taught programmed instruction courses have been designed for subjects such as English and reading and for various vocational objectives such as welding, sign writing, and mechanics; the study of musical instruments and foreign languages has also been encouraged. This program also uses autovisual aids and other equipment to make the courses available to all inmates.[22]

Besides encouraging elementary and high school educational development, some institutions also provide college-level instruction for inmates. College programs are presently operating or have operated in California, the District of Columbia, Florida, Illinois, Kansas, Kentucky, Maryland, Michigan, New Jersey, New York, Ohio, Oregon, Texas, and

Washington.[23] In Massachusetts, inmates at Walpole and Norfolk prisons have received counseling under the STEP Program (Student Tutor Education Project) from Brandeis University and the University of Massachusetts. Inmates have been encouraged to continue their educations and are able to earn credits towards degrees at these universities.[24]

Prison college programs are often not limited to standard subjects. At the Florida state prison at Starke, inmates have been offered college-level human relations courses taught by volunteers. The program is organized to develop self-control and discipline. Studies include discussion on topics such as "Helping the student find himself," "Finding out why he does things," and "Why other people do things they do."[25]

*Vocational Programs.* Many institutions also provide vocational training programs. In New York state, for example, more than 42 different trade and technical courses are provided in organized training shops under qualified civilian instructors. Some of these courses not only benefit the inmate, but also provide services for the institution.[26] For example, New York has trained inmates to become dental laboratory technicians; this program provides dentures for inmates and saves the state money. Another New York program trains inmates to become optical technicians and has the added benefit of providing eyeglasses for inmates. Other New York state correctional training programs include barber training, electronic computer programming, auto mechanics, auto body work, and radio and television repair. The products of most of these programs save the taxpayers money, and the programs themselves provide the inmates with practical experience.[27]

In a similar New Jersey program, inmates have been trained to be cooks, bakers, and meatcutters. This operation has employed on-the-job training and traditional text and theory curricula to train inmates in the preparation and delivery of institutional meals. Trained inmates have been able to assist the food service staff at various state-run institutions. In its first 30 months of operation, this program was able to place over 350 trained inmates in food service jobs. The inmates have also operated a full-service restaurant in Trenton on the grounds of a former school for girls, where they have provided meals for civilians working on the grounds and employees of the division of correction and parole.[28]

A program at the federal correctional institution at Danbury, Connecticut arranged for private corporations to train inmates in various skills.[29] In Massachusetts, the Massachusetts Department of Public Health has established programs to train inmates in skills and techniques which may lead to health careers.[30]

In addition to vocational training, some institutions have seen the need for vocational rehabilitation. In states such as Georgia, Tennessee, and Oklahoma, federal funds are obtained through Section 2 of the Vocational Rehabilitation Act to help special offenders. These programs locate inmates with physical disabilities involving vision, hearing, or orthopedic problems and recommend that they receive medical treatment and vocational counseling. At the Montefiore Hospital in New York, a similar program employed plastic surgeons who removed scars and facial disfigurements which might have contributed to the offenders' antisocial attitudes.[31]

Despite the promising aspects of such programs, major criticisms have been directed at vocational and educational training. It is often difficult to find skill-related, high-paying jobs upon release; equipment in prisons is often second-hand, obsolete, and hard to come by; some programs are thinly disguised excuses for prison upkeep and maintenance; and unions and other groups resent the intrusion of prison labor into their markets. These problems were reflected in a recent evaluation which found that only 66 of 1000 surveyed programs were actually effective. As McCollum has suggested:

In too many cases, these traditional training programs bear no relationship to the actual vocational interests or aptitudes of the inmate/students. If an inmate is faced with a limited number of choices, he frequently 'selects' what's available, quite apart from personal interests. Many institutions offer long waiting lists for future classes as supporting evidence of inmate interest in traditional vocational training areas. All too often, this is evidence, not of popularity or relevance of the course, but rather of the reality that there are no alternatives open to the prisoner. It is highly unlikely that the individual preferences, aspirations, and competency levels of 500 individuals, who happen to share a common address, the correctional facility, can be met by four or five or even ten vocational and industrial occupational educational areas.[32]

To supplement programs stressing rehabilitation via in-house job training or education, a number of states have attempted to implement work release or furlough programs. These allow deserving inmates to leave the institution and hold regular jobs in the community. Today, almost every state has at least one institution that maintains a furlough program.

Inmates enrolled in work release may live at the institutions at night while working in the community during the day. However, security problems (e.g., contraband may be brought in) and the usual remoteness of prisons often make this arrangement difficult. More typical is the extended work release where prisoners are allowed to remain in the community for significant periods of time. To help the client adjust, some states such as South Carolina operate community-based pre-release centers where inmates live while working. In some instances, inmates can work at their previous jobs, while in others other work is found.

Like other programs, work release has its good points and bad. Inmates are sometimes reluctantly received in the community and find that certain areas of employment are closed to them. Citizens who demand higher wages are often sensitive to prisoners "stealing" jobs. Federal Public Law 89-176, which controls the federal work release program has attempted to deal with this problem by requiring the following:

1. representatives of local union central bodies or similar labor union organizations are consulted;
2. such paid employment will not result in the displacement of employed workers, or be applied in skills, crafts, or trades in which there is a surplus of available gainful labor in the locality to impair existing contracts for services; and

**WORK RELEASE AND WORK DEVELOPMENT PROGRAMS**

3. the rates of pay and other conditions of employment will not be less than those paid or provided for work of similar nature in the locality in which the work is to be performed.[33]

On the other hand, there are many benefits to work release, which can best be summarized as follows:

The benefits of the offender on work release are readily apparent. For the misdemeanant it means continuation of family and employment ties. For the felon, it reduces the dislocating effects of release such as resuming his responsibilities immediately, with welfare aid to the family terminated all too often before he is in a position to shoulder family expenses.

Work release provides a transitional period that can reduce the floundering often experienced by the man who must accept any job in order to gain his freedom on parole. However, in many cases, the work release facility is far from his home location where the man will be released, and he will have to find new work there unless he stays where the work release facility is located.

The opportunity for gainful employment has psychological results that cannot be measured. Receiving financial support strengthens family ties. For the inmate who had steady employment before imprisonment, the job that pays a fair wage can only have a positive effect. For those who have learned a skill in the institution, work release offers an excellent opportunity to test out a new occupation. For others, the job may be a training situation in which new skills are acquired.[34]

In addition to work furlough programs, a number of state correctional departments have instituted pre- and post-release employment services. Employment program staff assess inmates' backgrounds to determine their abilities, interests, goals, and capabilities. They also consult with clients to help them create job plans essential to receiving early release (parole), and subsequently, to be successfully reintegrated within the community. Some programs maintain community correctional placements in sheltered environments which help inmates bridge the gap between institutions and the outside world: services include job placement, skill development, family counseling, and legal and medical attention.[35]

Preliminary results indicate that recidivism rates (repeat offenders) for vocational support program clients were generally better than expected. For example, Minnesota's H.I.R.E., Inc. program reported that over a nine month period, clients experienced lower recidivism rates (25.5%) than a nonparticipating control group (36.3%).[36]

Similarly, New York's Project Develop, a comprehensive employment services program for young male parolees found that participants had a parole delinquency rate of 15%, while a control group of parolees had a rate of 23%. The recidivism rate for parolees in the program was 6%, as compared with 12% for the control group.[37]

Another effort in Denver, Colorado, Employ-Ex, Inc., a program for ex-offenders, reported that the rearrest rate over one year for persons who entered the program between January and June 1975, was only 12.8%.[38]

These are but a few of the employment efforts which are being undertaken in prison systems around the country.

The conjugal visit is another mode of treatment which has received renewed emphasis from correctional administrators. During conjugal visits prisoners are able to have completely private meetings with wives or girlfriends on a regular basis. The explicit purpose of the program is to grant inmates access to normal sexual outlets and thereby counteract the pains of imprisonment.

Conjugal visitation is more frequently used in Latin American and European countries than in the United States; however, Mississippi has had such programs since 1900, and California has begun a program of family visits at its Tehachapi facility.

If properly administered, conjugal visits could provide a number of important benefits; inmate frustration levels would diminish, family ties would be strengthened, and normal sexual patterns would be continued. However, there are many problems inherent in conjugal visitation which so far have lessened their chances for implementation.

As Johns points out, conjugal visitation suffers because:

1. [such visits] can serve only the minority of inmates who have wives or other female associates. Thus, there is a question of fairness;
2. appropriate facilities are almost universally lacking;
3. administrative problems abound; security, staff abuses of power, jealousy;
4. administrative support is lacking;
5. wives may feel embarrassment at openly sexual visits; and
6. children may be born to men who cannot support them.[39]

Johns concludes that these visits should only be possible when:

1. there are facilities available which could be converted satisfactorily and not too expensively to such use;
2. administrative interest in such a program is reasonably high;
3. opposition to such programs is neither strong nor actively organized; and
4. the practical problems can be carefully recognized, planned for, and managed.[40]

THE CONJUGAL VISIT

One recent trend, though one with strong historical roots, has been the coeducational prison. Since 1973, prisons housing both men and women have proliferated throughout the United States. Examples of coed institutions include Renz Correctional Center in Cedar City, Missouri established in 1975, and the Maine Correctional Center in South Windham, Maine established in 1976.[41]

In all it is estimated that in the federal prison system, 58.1% of females and 7.5% of males are in coed prisons; the figures for the state system are much smaller—9.7% of females and .53% males.

Generally speaking, the typical coed prison is a small, low-security institution, predominantly of one sex (either mostly male or mostly female), populated by nonviolent carefully screened offenders. In most instances, males and females live in physically separate housing—either in different buildings or in separate cottages.

COEDUCATIONAL PRISONS

The value of the coed prison is still at issue. It appears to be a useful mechanism for helping both male and female offenders to avoid the social isolation and unnatural living conditions that a one-sex institution can produce. While some institutions, such as the Dwight Correctional Center in Illinois, and the Metropolitan Training Center in Circle Pines, Minnesota have been phased out, there exists the likelihood that coed corrections will continue to grow in the future.

## PRISON INDUSTRIES

Prisoners are normally expected to work within the institution as part of their treatment program. Aside from saving money for the institution, prison work programs are supposed to help inmates develop good habits and skills. Most prominent among traditional prison industries are those designed to help maintain and run the institution and provide services for other public or state facilities such as mental hospitals. These include:

1. *Food Services:* inmates are expected to prepare and supply food for the other prisoners and for the prison staff. These duties include baking bread, cooking and preparing meat and vegetables, and cleaning and maintaining kitchen facilities.

2. *Maintenance:* the building and grounds of most prisons are cared for by the inmate population. Electrical work, masonry, plumbing, and painting are all inmate activities. Of a less skilled nature are work duties such as garbage, gardening, and clean-up.

3. *Laundry:* most prisons have their own inmate-run laundries. Quite often, prison laundries will also furnish services to other state institutions.

4. *Agriculture:* in Western and Southern states, many prisons have farmed their own land. Dairy herds, crops, and poultry are all managed by inmates. Products are used in the prison and in other state institutions.

Aside from these self-help functions, prison industry has in the past spread into other areas of work. License plates, rope, hemp and burlap, work clothes, brushes, and other products have all been made by prisoners. While it is illegal to ship prison goods across state lines, these industrial items are often purchased directly by the state for its own use or for resale to private parties. Finally, prisoners have been used extensively in public work projects such as forestry services and road maintenance. Payment for these services varies widely, but in a majority of the states and the federal prison system inmates are given a nominal compensation for their labors.

## WOMEN IN PRISON

As indicated in Chapter 15, the number of women in prison, approximately 12,000, is much smaller than the number of men. Nonetheless, the female inmate has taken on great importance since the number of female inmates is increasing at a much faster rate than the number of males. A recent national survey sheds some light on women in prison, and the most important findings of the study are reported below.*

Women's prisons tend to be smaller than those housing male inmates, ranging in size from the Minnesota Property Offender Program housing 16, to the 979 in the Sybil Brand Institute in Los Angeles.

Similarly, most women's facilities are generally not the high security institutions commonly used for male inmates. Though some female institutions are strictly penal, with steel bars, concrete floors, and other security measures, the majority are nonsecure institutions similar to college dormitories and other group homes in the community. It is common for women's facilities, especially those in the community, to offer a great deal of autonomy to inmates and allow them to make decisions affecting their daily life in the institution.

Women's prisons also suffer from the same lack of adequate training, health, treatment, and educational facilities as those which house male inmates. Psychological counseling often takes the form of group sessions conducted by lay people such as correctional officers. Most trained psychologists and psychiatrists restrict themselves to such activities as intake classification, court-ordered examinations, and prescribing mood-controlling medication.

Educational programs usually offer only remedial level education, or occasional junior college classes. Of course, the rather small size of many women's prisons make large-scale educational programs difficult to maintain. In a similar vein, vocational training tends to stress what is considered to be "traditional" women's jobs: cosmetician, secretarial work, and food services. There has been relatively little effort to update the types of educational and vocational skills needed for successful readjustment upon release.

**PROFILE OF INCARCERATED WOMEN**

Incarcerated women are young—two-thirds are under 30 years of age (the median age for misdemeanants is approximately 24, for felons, 27). Blacks are overrepresented in the inmate population (50%), as are native Americans; the proportion of Hispanic women, however, appears to be similar to their representation in the general population.

The family life of incarcerated women also appears to diverge from the norm: Only one-half of incarcerated women came from two-parent homes, one-third had been on welfare as children, and over one-half (56%) have received welfare during their adult lives. Moreover, their nuclear family life seems to have been extremely fluid: although 60% have been married at least once, only 10% had actually been living with a husband prior to incarceration.

Another serious problem of women in prison is the disruption of their families—56% of incarcerated women had children living at home prior

---

*Information in this section was adapted from a recent survey, Ruth Glick and Virginia Noto, *National Study of Women's Correctional Programs* (Wash., D.C.: U.S. Gov't P.O., 1977).

to their incarceration. Who took care of the children while their mothers were incarcerated? It did not appear that children of incarcerated women were bound for foster homes. Eighty-five percent of the time, the woman's parents or other relatives took the children; however, husbands provided only 10% of all childcare arrangements. Ethnic differences in childcare were significant, with whites and Indians relying more on husbands and on nonrelatives, including agencies.

What were women incarcerated for? Misdemeanants serving one year or less had been convicted in the following proportions: 41% for property crimes (shoplifting, forgery, fraud); 20% for drug offenses; and 11% for violent crimes (usually assault, battery, or armed robbery).

Convicted felons were serving one year or more: 43% for violent crimes (murder, armed robbery); 29% for property crimes (forgery, fraud, some larceny); 22% for drug offenses.

Most unsentenced women had been charged with the following felony-type offenses: 30% for violent crimes; 22% for drug offenses; and 14% for forgery or fraud.

Nearly one-third of the women had been arrested for the first time at age 17 or younger. Another 49% were first arrested between ages 18 and 24. Almost one-third of the women had spent time in juvenile institutions.

Property offenders were most often recidivists; murderers were most likely to be first offenders. The women with the most extensive involvement with the criminal justice system were the habitual offenders—prostitutes, drug offenders, and petty thieves.

Daily life in the women's prison community is also somewhat different than that which exists in male institutions. For one thing, women usually don't present the immediate, violent physical danger to staff and fellow inmates that many male prisoners do. Nor does there exist the rigid antiauthority inmate social code found in many male institutions. Confinement for women, however, may produce severe anxiety and anger, due to separation from families and loved ones and the inability to function in normal female roles. Unlike men, who direct their anger outward, female prisoners may revert to more self-destructive acts in order to cope with their problems. Female inmates are perhaps more likely than males to mutilate their own bodies and attempt suicides.

One common practice of female inmates is self-mutilation or "carving." This ranges from simple scratches, to carving the name of their boyfriends in their bodies, to complex statement or sentences ("To mother, with hate"). A recent survey of clients in one correctional institution for adolescent girls found that 117 of 136 girls had "carved" themselves at least once and that some girls cut themselves more than 30 times.[42]

One common form of adaptation to prison employed by women is the surrogate family. This group contains masculine and feminine figures acting as fathers and mothers; some even act as children and take on the role of either brother or sister. Formalized marriages and divorces may be conducted. Sometimes multiple roles are held by one inmate, so that a "sister" in one family may "marry" and become the "wife" of another inmate. However, there exists relatively little of the physical coercion found in the male institutions, and women not wishing to participate in surrogate families are given the freedom to refuse.

Every penal institution—jail, prison, or reformatory—has a specific set of official rules which guide the prisoners' lives and dictates what they can and can't do. These rules are of great significance; a violation may result in a loss of good time which can extend the life of the sentence. Violation of prison rules may also result in harsh disciplinary measures such as solitary confinement, suspension of privileges, or transfer to a more secure facility.

PRISON RULES
AND DISCIPLINE

Today rules are more lenient than were those in the past. Conversation is no longer prohibited, and rigid military discipline is rare. Yet most institutions still abide by lengthy sets of rules, the violation of which constitutes reason for disciplinary action. The following list provides an example of one set of rules used to govern behavior in a Massachusetts reformatory:

### PUNISHABLE OFFENSES

The following are punishable offenses while in the institution:

1. Disobeying or refusing to obey an order of the Master, the Deputy Master, or any officer of the institution. If you feel an order is unreasonable, obey it and then discuss the matter with superior officers.
2. Disrespect to any officer or employee of the institution or any person visiting the institution.
3. Swearing, cursing, or using vulgar, abusive, insolent, threatening or any other improper language or gesture against another resident or officer of the institution.
4. Committing of any assault or fighting with another resident or Correctional Officer.
5. Entering a room other than your own without consent or direction of an officer.
6. Leaving your cell or place of assignment without permission.
7. Willful damage to any part of the institution.
8. Committing any mutinous act, inciting a riot or general disturbance within the institution.
9. Drugs, narcotics, weapons, items of food and or supplies not allowed, are considered contraband and will be confiscated.
10. Being intoxicated or under the influence from any kind of drugs.
11. Theft or borrowing without permission of any item from the institution, fellow residents or officers.
12. Making or having in your possession any type of dangerous weapon.
13. Possession of any monies, coin or paper, without authorization.
14. Refusal to keep your person clean and tidy in general.
15. Obtaining or attempting to obtain unauthorized medication.
16. Giving false information to an officer.

Any violation of prison rules may result in the disciplinary action being taken against the inmate. Usually, a disciplinary board will meet to hear cases referred by administrative staff. Typically, the board will consist of members of the custodial, treatment, and administrative staffs. Punishment when deemed necessary is meted out by these individuals, and it affects good time, privileges, and parole. The legal issues involved in prison discipline are discussed in Chapter 18.

PRISON
VIOLENCE

Prison violence and brutality is a sad but ever present feature of institutional life. Violence can be individualistic—inmate vs. inmate, or inmate vs. guard (and vice versa)—or collective—widescale prison riots such as the infamous Attica riot in 1971 which claimed 39 lives, and the more recent New Mexico State Prison riot of February 1980 in which the death toll was 33.[43] It is evident that prisons are highly volatile arenas ready to explode. Reports of violent deaths in prison are daily occurrences which the American citizen has more or less learned to accept.[44]

What are the causes of prison violence? While there is no single explanation for either collective or individualistic violence, a number of theories abound. One position holds that inmates themselves are often violence-prone individuals who have always used force to get their own way. In the crowded, dehumanizing world of the prison, it is not surprising that they resort to force to exert their dominance over others.[45]

A second view is that prisons convert men to violence by their inhuman conditions, including overcrowding, depersonalization, and threat of homosexual rape.[46] Social scientist Charles Silberman suggests that even in the most humane prisons, life is a constant put-down, and prison conditions are a threat to the inmates' sense of self-worth; violence is a nonsurprising consequence of these conditions.[47]

Still another view is that prison violence stems from prison mismanagement, lack of strong security, and inadequate control by prison officials.[48] This view has contributed to the escalation of solitary confinement in recent years as a means of control. In a survey of 60 prisons conducted by Robert Freeman, Simon Dinitz, and John Conrad, 19 reported that the number of inmates in solitary confinement ranged from 250 to 600.[49]

Others view the fact that few prisons have effective grievance procedures for complaints against either prison officials or other inmates as a cause of prison violence. Prisoners who complain about other inmates are viewed as "finks" and marked for death by their enemies. Similarly, complaints or law suits filed against prison administrators may result in the inmate being placed in solitary confinement—"the hole." The lack of communication is heightened by the diverse ethnic and racial backgrounds of guards and inmates. The typical inmate at Attica Prison at the time of the riot was a 25-year-old black male from New York City, while the typical guard was a middle-aged white male from upstate rural New York.[50] The frustration caused by living in a prison with a climate that promotes violence—that is, without adequate mechanisms for complaint, lack of physical security, and where the "code of silence" protects violators—is believed to promote both collective and individual violence by inmates who might otherwise be controlled.[51]

### The New Mexico Riot

All the above factors seem to have contributed to the New Mexico State Penitentiary riot of 1980. The prison was designed for 800 but actually held 1,136 prisoners; conditions of overcrowding, squalor, poor food, and lack of medical treatment abounded.[52]

The State government which had been called on to spend more for guard training, physical plant quality, and to relieve overcrowding, was reluctant to spend money on improving physical conditions.

The riot started when a guard attempted to confiscate some "home-brew" liquor from an inmate. With only 22 guards on duty, inmates quickly seized control over the entire prison. After taking the guards hostage, the inmates seized the infirmary and made free use of drugs. Rather than taking all their anger out on the hostage guards (though some guards were seriously injured), rioting inmates broke into Cell Block 4 in which "snitches" (informers) were held in protective custody; the means of execution was so brutal that they defy imagination. While inmates made demands on prison authorities for better conditions, the widespread bloodletting soon caused many inmates, fearful for their lives, to try to escape into the hands of authorities. After almost totally destroying the institution, the remaining inmates peacefully surrendered to police units without a shot being fired. The inmates' "code of silence" and fear of reprisals make prosecution of the riot's worst offenders problematic.

New Mexico is an example of how inmate rage can be turned inward against other inmates—no guards were killed during this riot. It is evident that overcrowding, lack of communication, mingling of violence-prone experienced cons with new inmates, and lack of security all contributed to the unrestrained violence. It seems equally likely that similar conditions, unless corrected, will prompt further outbreaks of prison violence in the future. In the application section of this chapter a selection from the diary of an inmate incarcerated in Walpole Prison in Massachusetts illustrates the conditions which sometimes lead to prison violence.

SUMMARY

Upon entering a major closed institution, the offender must make tremendous adjustments in order to survive. Usual behavior patterns or lifestyles are radically changed. Opportunities for personal satisfaction are reduced. Passing through a number of adjustment stages or cycles, the inmate learns to cope with the new environment.

An inmate also learns to obey the inmate social code, which dictates proper behavior and attitudes. If the code is broken, the inmate may be unfavorably labeled.

Once inside the institution, new inmates can avail themselves of a large number of treatment devices designed to help them readjust to the community. These include educational programs on the basic, high school and even college levels, as well as vocational training programs. In addition, a number of treatment programs have offered inmates individualized and group psychological counseling; work furlough, coed prisons and conjugal visits have also been employed.

Despite such measures, prisons remain forbidding structures which house desperate men and women. Violence is a byword in prisons. Women often turn their hatred inward and hurt themselves, while male inmates engage in collective and individual violence against others. The Attica and New Mexico riots are examples of the most serious collective prison violence.

QUESTIONS FOR
DISCUSSION

1. How may the prison experience be likened to living in a large university campus?

2. What steps could be taken to make prisons a more pleasant environment? *Should* these steps be taken?

3. What are the benefits and drawbacks of "coed" prisons? Of conjugal visits?

NOTES

1. United States Department of Justice, *Census of State Correctional Facilities 1974* (Washington, D.C.: U.S. Government Printing Office, 1975).

2. United States Department of Justice, *Survey of Inmates of State Correctional Facilities 1974* (Washington, D.C.: U.S. Government Printing Office, 1976).

3. Sandra Gleason, "Hustling: The 'Inside' Economy of a Prison," *Federal Probation* 42:32–39 (1978).

4. Ibid., p. 39.

5. *Newsweek*, Feb. 18, 1980, p. 75.

6. Erving Goffman, *Asylums: Essays on the Social Situation of Mental Patients & Other Inmates* (New York: Doubleday & Co., 1961), p. 70.

7. G. Sykes and S. Messinger, "The Inmate Social Code" in *The Sociology of Punishment and Corrections*, Norman Johnston et al., eds. (New York: John Wiley & Sons, 1970), pp. 401–408.

8. Sykes and Messinger, "The Inmate Social Code," p. 404.

9. L. McKorkle & R. Korn, "Resocialization Within Walls," *Annals* 293:88 (May 1954). For a similar analysis, see Donald Clemmer, *The Prison Community* (New York: Holt, Rinehart and Winston, 1958): Donald Cressey, ed., *The Prison: Studies in Institutional Organization & Change* (New York: Holt, Rinehart & Winston, 1966).

10. Clarence Schrag, "Some Foundations for a Theory of Corrections," in Donald Cressey (ed.), *The Prison: Studies in Institutional Organization and Change*, New York, Holt, Rinehart and Winston, 1961, pp. 309–357.

11. Stephen Woolpert, "Prisoners' Unions, Inmate Militancy and Correctional Policymaking," *Federal Probation* 42:4041 (1978).

12. See Lamar T. Empey and Steven Lubeck, *The Silverlake Experiment* (Chicago: Aldine Publishing Co., 1971); H. Ashley Weeks, *Youthful Offenders at Highfields* (Ann Arbor, Mich.: University of Michigan Press, 1958).

13. Olive Irwin, "Group Therapy With

Juvenile Probationers," *Federal Probation* 31:62 (September 1967).

**14.** William Glasser, *Reality Therapy* (New York: Harper & Row, 1965); for further use of this technique, see Richard Rachin, "Reality Therapy: Helping People Help Themselves," *Crime & Delinquency* 16:143 (January 1974).

**15.** Eric Berne, *Transactional Analysis in Psychotherapy* (New York: Grove Press, 1961); see also Richard Nicholson, "Transactional Analysis: A New Method For Helping Offenders," *Federal Probation* 34:29 (September, 1970).

**16.** See, for example, Gaylord Thorne et al., "Behavior Modification Techniques: New Tools For Probation Officers," *Federal Probation* 31:21 (June 1967); Ralph Schwitzgabel, *Street Corner Research* (Cambridge, Mass.: Harvard University Press, 1964); J. T. Saunders and N. D. Reppucci, "Reward & Punishment: Some Guidelines For Their Effective Application in Correctional Programs for Youthful Offenders," *Crime & Delinquency* 18:284 (June 1972).

**17.** Maxwell Jones, *Social Psychiatry in Practice* (Baltimore; Penguin Books, 1968); Loren Crabtree and James Fox, "The Overthrow of a Therapeutic Community," *International Journal of Group Psychotherapy* 22:31 (1972).

**18.** Benedict Alper, *Prisons Inside-Out* (Cambridge, Mass.: Ballinger Publishing, 1974), pp. 43–94.

**19.** Sylvia McCollum, "New Designs for Correctional Education and Training Programs," *Federal Probation* 37:6 (June 1973).

**20.** R. Bell, E. Conard, T. Laffey, J. G. Lutz, P. VanReed Miller, C. Simon, A. E. Stakelon, N. J. Wilson, *Correctional Education Programs for Inmates* (Wash., D.C.: U.S. Gov't. P.O., 1979), pp. 18–19.

**21.** Ibid., p. 10.

**22.** Albert Roberts, *Readings in Prison Education* (Springfield, Ill.: Charles C. Thomas, 1973), p. 150.

**23.** Alper, *Prisons Inside-Out*, p. 84.

**24.** Ibid.

**25.** Suzi Wilson, "Lucy Batchelor Teaches Courses to Maximum Security Group," *American Journal of Corrections* 9 (May 1969).

**26.** Roberts, *Readings in Prison Education*, p. 88.

**27.** Ibid., p. 89.

**28.** Robert Walton, "New Jersey Places over 350 Trained Cooks, Bakers, and Meatcutters on Jobs During First 30 Months of Food Training," *American Journal of Corrections* 7 (November/December, 1976).

**29.** Alper, *Prisons Inside-Out*, p. 77.

**30.** Ibid., p. 79.

**31.** Roberts, *Readings in Prison Education*, p. 194.

**32.** Cited in McCreary and McCreary, *Job Training and Placement for Offenders and Ex Offenders*, p. 10.

**33.** Ibid., p. 13.

**34.** Ibid.

**35.** M. Toborg, L. Center, R. Milkman, D. Davis, *The Transition from Prison to Employment: An Assessment of Community-Based Assistance Programs*.

**36.** _____. *Second Interim Report on the Effectiveness of H.I.R.E., Inc.* Minneapolis, Minn.: Correctional Service of Minnesota, 1973; see also _____. *H.I.R.E., Inc., Ex-Offender Employability Project, Summary Research Report No. 2, A Three-Month Follow Up of Clients Placed During the Period April 1, 1975 through February 29, 1976.* Minneapolis, Minn.: Correctional Service of Minnesota, 1976.

**37.** Leonard Witt. *Project Develop-Developing Educational-Vocational Experiences* *for Long-Term Occupational Adjustment of Parolees: Summary Report* (Albany, N.Y.: New York Division of Parole, 1968).

**38.** Employ-Ex, Inc. "Employ-Ex Annual Report", (Denver, Colo.: Employ-Ex, Inc., 1976). See also _____ "Job Development Manual," (Denver, Colo.: Employ-Ex, Inc., 1975).

**39.** Donald Johns, "Alternatives To Conjugal Visits," *Federal Probation* 35:48 (March 1971).

**40.** Ibid., p. 49.

**41.** Current information of co-ed corrections was taken from J. G. Ross, E. Hefferman, J. R. Sevick, and F. T. Johnson, *Assessment of Coeducational Corrections* (Wash., D.C.: U.S. Gov't. P.O. 1978).

**42.** R. R. Ross, H. B. McKay, W. R. T. Palmer & C. J. Kennig, "Self-Mutilation in Adolescent Female Offenders," *Canadian J. of Criminology*, Oct. 1978.

**43.** *Newsweek*, "The Killing Ground," Feb. 18, 1980.

**44.** For example, during 1979–1980, 30 inmates were believed killed in Walpole Prison in Massachusetts.

**45.** For a series of papers on the position, see A. Cohen, G. Cole and R. Baily (eds.), *Prison Violence* (Lexington, Mass.; Lexington Books, 1976).

**46.** See Hans Toch, "Social Climate and Prison Violence," *Federal Probation*, 42:21 (1978).

**47.** Charles Silberman, *Criminal Violence, Criminal Justice*, (New York: Vintage Books, 1978).

**48.** Toch, *Social Climate and Prison Violence*, p. 21.

**49.** R. Freeman, S. Dinitz & J. Conrad, "A Look at the Dangerous Offender and Society's Efforts to Control Him," *American Journal of Corrections*, Jan:30 (1977).

**50.** Claude Pepper, "Prisons in Turmoil," *Federal Probation* 36:5 (1972).

**51.** H. Toch, *Social Climate and Prison Violence*, p. 23.

**52.** Newsweek, "The Killing Ground," p. 66.

# Walpole Diary—An Account of Life in a Maximum Security Prison in Massachusetts*

**TUESDAY—MAY 1, 1979.**

It's 6:30 P.M. and the block runners (the men who clean the block, help the screws feed the men and do favors for the men in the cellblock after the block is locked in at 4:30 P.M. every day) are not out yet. The runners usually get out at 6:00 P.M. and are allowed out of their cells until 9:00 P.M. It looks like the block is locked up for the night.

There was a fist fight between two inmates on the third tier at 4:15 today. That is probably the reason/excuse they are using to keep us locked in. There is no air in this block and it is getting hot. The screws may come in and shake us down. A shakedown is when guards come to your cell, throw all your stuff around and steal something (under the guise of "contraband" that you have usually had in your possession two or three years and has survived at least 100 previous shakedowns. A shakedown is a form of harassment and makes the screws feel good because they are together in a gang and you are standing naked in the middle of them.

They feel powerful! You feel helpless, but a quiet burning rages in your stomach and at the back of your mind.

Soon you will know if there's a shakedown. For the 10,000 time today you feel angry. You feel . . . aggressive!

**WEDNESDAY—MAY 2, 1979.**

It is 9:30 A.M. We are still locked in. The screws came by and fed us in our cells. Seven packets of sugar (our daily ration) two hard boiled eggs and a pint of milk (also our daily ration).

A guard came by pouring coffee and when I put my cup to the bars he missed my cup and poured coffee on the clothes I had near the bars. Did he do it on purpose??? It's happened before. Burnt hands, spilled coffee, a part of the prison experience. Normality for an abnormal situation. Oh boy, a grapefruit half! Coffee, milk, eggs, fresh fruit, two slices of bread. Does this mean that the warden or Governor cares about me; or is it indicative that no matter how lowly

---

*This section from an inmate's diary was contributed by an inmate currently incarcerated within Walpole prison, Massachusetts. It appears courtesy of *Doing Time*, a journal put out by Family and Friends of Walpole Prison inmates.

my position, I am still a citizen of the richest and strongest (even if the power structure *is* crumbling) empire the world has seen to date?

Damn! My mousetrap is empty! I like to catch a mouse a day. Mice eat your clothes, keep you awake at night with their squeeking and scratching, defecate on your table and books and worst of all have developed a taste for legal papers and court transcripts. It's always irritating to notice a mouse has chewed up your favorite sweater or shirt, or eaten your transcripts. It's always pleasurable to gaze upon their stiff bodies when you remove them from your trap. Does that mean I'm aggressive toward mice? I'm not sure. It does mean that I harbor hostilities toward the *guards*. Mouse traps are illegal. One day a guard will come and either confiscate the trap as contraband (contraband gets thrown away in the trash, another irritation when you see your "contraband" pillow or shirt, or mop or broom dumped in the garbage,) or else ignore it and let it slide, depending whether he is a "Mike guard" (Mike is the lying pig who is the head of the guards union) or a human being.

A "Mike guard" will also write a disciplinary report on you for the trap. I'll get ten days isolation. As I've been in isolation since April 9th and won't get out until June 1st, ten days for a mouse trap sounds about right. When you are down, these people like to kick you. Five days of my isolation time is for possession of contraband coathangers, fifteen days is for possession of a contraband footlocker which I've had for seven years. The guy in the cell next to me got ten days for an alarm clock. Every man here has at least a thousand stories a day. The accumulation of these things makes us aggressive?

It's 3:30 P.M. Here comes the shakedown! These screws aren't bad. It will only take me about twenty minutes to put my ragged possessions in order. Total losses were four

boxes of rice crispies, a roll of tape and a mirror. On the plus side I killed nine large cockroaches who were agitated by the guards moving my bed around and left their living quarters in my bedboard. The "contraband" from the cells is all out on the tier now. Extra lightbulbs (smashed), toilet paper, corn flakes and other cereals, a new blanket (some guard probably decided two blankets was too many for one inmate he took a personal disliking to) and various other articles of no worth except to their former owner. All this stuff will be swept away and thrown in the trash. It wouldn't anger you so much if what they took away from you was brought to the storehouse and reissued, but to see it thrown away is infuriating. The guy next door to me had his shoes taken away as "contraband." He tried to get the guards to sign a receipt, but they wouldn't. They say "they'll be left out front to be picked up." He knows better. That's the last he'll see of them. Over the years a man gets accustomed to losing the property he has in prison. A prisoner has no property. His existence is a 'privilege' and no matter what outsiders or the man on the street may think, the inmate *knows* he owns nothing. In some prisons they don't even recognize your name. You are only a number and it is drilled into your head. Here at Walpole I am a man. In other places I've been #45921, #31830, #88918, #22968, #1164, #84961. My Walpole number is 35 thousand something. Walpole is one of the more humane prisons. As I remember my numbers which were always in the thousands, I also remember the indignities, the chains, the tear gas, the clubs, the fists, the feet and the accumulation of pin pricks to my self pride and sense of well being, which over the years have passed the million mark.

Maybe the powers that be will let us out tomorrow. They've all collected their overtime for the "shakedown." It cost the state about $100.00 worth of property (swept up in the trash), it cost the inmates about $500.00 worth of property (labelled as contraband) and it cost the taxpayers about $2,000.00 in overtime pay for the guards. (That's why guards love 'shakedowns', it not only gives them an opportunity to exert their collective power by taking things away from inmates on an arbitrary basis, it also gets them time and a half for overtime.) An example of this is when Mike got on T.V. last month and lamented the fact that after a prisoner had escaped from Walpole, not that a *search* was instituted for the missing prisoner (a search *was* instituted), but a *'shakedown'* wasn't instituted.

He didn't want a search, he wanted a 'shakedown.' (Did he think the inmate was hiding in my rice crispies?)

### THURSDAY—MAY 3, 1979.

It's Thursday and we are still locked up. The guy who got in the fight here in one block was put into two block where he was beat up by some other inmates, and now two block is locked up too.

The garbage is all over the floor. The screws haven't cleaned it up yet. No one has had a shower. One guy stepped out of his cell when they opened the door for lunch (to pass it in to him on a cardboard tray) and he walked down to the shower and took a shower. He had a visit due at 12:45. The guards told him he would have to wait until *after* his visit got here before he could take a shower. Visits are supposedly from 1:00 P.M. to 3:00 P.M., but the visitors usually do not get to the visiting room until about 1:10 and sometimes as late as 1:20. Since the inmate isn't notified and let out of his cell until about five minutes after his visit arrives, the guards were expecting him to shower and shave (the guy didn't have hot water in his cell) on his visiting time and thereby rob him of an extra ten minutes of his precious 2 hour allotment, bringing it down to about an hour and a half. It seems they (the guards) study ways to keep us on edge.

It's 2:00 P.M. and the goon squad is lugging (carrying off to block ten) guys from the third tier. Four men were taken away. I doubt if they'll let us out. The 7 A.M. to 3 P.M. shift says the 3 P.M. to 11 P.M. shift should sweep up the block since they were responsible for the shakedown and made the mess. The 3 to 11 shift says the inmates or the 7 to 3 shift should clean the block. The inmates say the guards should clean the block and put it in the same shape it was before the screws locked us up for a lousy fistfight.

Someone lit some of the trash on fire. The smoke is rising. There is no ventilation, so we will probably choke on this damn smoke all night. The guards came in with a fire extinguisher, but instead of putting out the fire they wet it down so it would smoulder and smoke. I know I should be angry with the guards, but really, I'd like to rap on the head whoever lit the fire. Their strategy of divide and conquer is working.

They cleaned out the guy's cells who they lugged this afternoon. The flats are littered with more "contraband." Two of the guards kept coughing and hacking and spitting. The smoke (four hours after the fire) was too much for them. My white lined paper has soot on it. I just blew my nose and the stuff that came out was all black. I don't smoke. I wonder what my lungs look like? Forty-five of us will be breathing this cloud for the next two or three days until it is finally absorbed into our lungs. You'd think the person who designed this place would have thought to put an exhaust pump at the top of the cell block. One more bit of madness we are subjected to.

# Parole

## THE CONCEPT
## OF PAROLE

While the previous chapter dealt with the convicted offender in an institutional setting, emphasis is now placed on the parole or community portion of the correctional process.

Parole is the planned community release and supervision of incarcerated offenders prior to the actual expiration of their prison sentences. It
is usually considered to be a way of completing a prison sentence in the
community, and is not the same as a pardon; the paroled offender can be
legally recalled to serve the remainder of a sentence in an institution if the
parole authorities deem the offender's adjustment inadequate, or if while
on parole the offender commits a further crime.

The decision to parole is determined by statutory requirement and
usually involves the completion of a minimum sentence. Parole is granted
by a state parole board, a duly constituted body of men and women whose
task it is to review inmate cases and determine whether an offender has
reached a rehabilitative level sufficient to deal with the outside world. The
board also dictates what specific parole rules a parolee must obey. (There
is also a federal parole board which services federal prisons).

Once community release has begun, the offender is supervised by a
trained staff of parole officers, who maintain the offender's place in the
community, help in the search for employment, and monitor behavior and
activities to insure that the offender conforms to the conditions of parole.

Parolees are subject to a strict standardized and/or personalized set
of rules which guide their behavior and set limits on their activities. If at
any time these rules are violated, the offender can be returned to the
institution to serve the remainder of the sentence; this is known as a
technical parole violation. The offender's parole can also be revoked by
committing a second offense while in the community, and may even be
tried and sentenced for this subsequent crime.

Today, parole is the predominant mode of release for prison inmates,
and its use may continue to grow in the future. It is currently employed
in almost every state and by the federal prison system. In some states such
as Kansas and Washington almost every inmate released from prison is
placed on some type of parole, while in other states such as Delaware and
Wyoming the number of parolees may be as low as 10%; it is estimated
that nationally about 70% of all inmates are eventually granted paroles.[1]

However, the parole concept has been heavily criticized in recent years
and some experts, as discussed later in this chapter, have called for its
abolition.

Today, parole is viewed as an act of grace on the part of the criminal
justice system. It represents an actual manifestation of the policy of returning the offender to the community. There are two conflicting sides to
parole, however; on one hand, the paroled offender is given a break and
allowed to serve part of the sentence in the community; on the other hand,
the sentiment exists that parole is a privilege and not a right and that the
parolee is in reality a dangerous criminal who must be carefully watched
and supervised. The conflict between the treatment and enforcement aspects of parole has not yet been reconciled by the criminal justice system,
and the parole process still contains elements of both orientations.

The object of the punishment of public offenders has been, and still remains to this date, a peculiar mixture of vengeance, physical restraint, deterrence, and reformation.* The earliest forms of punishment imposed by organized society upon a wrongdoer were meant to eliminate or disable him so that he would not bother society again. He was disabled or eliminated by corporal punishment, death, banishment, or transportation. Imprisonment originated as a means of holding a public offender for a short time until he was killed, banished, or released. The period of incarceration was very short and did not last beyond the sentence. Later prisons became more widely used as places of physical restraint. They were instruments of control, and accepted the inmates as they were with no attempt to change them.

With the advent of rationalism in the late eighteenth and early nineteenth centuries, sentencing structures were changed, fewer crimes required automatic death sentences, and more felons were imprisoned. Reform became fashionable, and from the ecclesiastical prison tradition of the Middle Ages the concept emerged that, perhaps, the offender might be worth saving. Prisons came to be regarded as places of contemplation, repentance, meditation, and expiation. At this point in history, two different types of prisons were built in the United States. One was modeled on Quaker concepts: this was the Eastern State Penitentiary in Pennsylvania, where the cells were arranged so that the inmate lived, worked, and was exercised and fed without seeing or talking to his fellow prisoners. This type was eventually discontinued in the United States because it was too inconvenient to manage, but was widely copied in Europe. The other type was that originally built at Auburn, New York: here the inmates were housed in single cells, but they were fed and worked together. This type of prison eventually became the model in the United States.

More and more, physical punishment gave way to imprisonment and prisons came to be regarded as places where it was hoped that the inmates could be changed, salvaged, and reformed. Punishment *per se* was repudiated and other means were sought by which the individual offender could be restored to society. Hence arose the institutions of the juvenile court, domestic relations court, probation, and parole.

Parole grew out of this change in emphasis in penal philosophy from one of punishment to one of reformation. Although the fundamental aim of penology has been the protection of society, it is now felt that the most socially economic way of protecting society is by restoring the offender to normal social functioning. However, parole, as we know it today, did not develop from any one specific source or experiment, but is an outgrowth of a number of independent measures: the conditional pardon, the apprenticeship by indenture, the transportation of criminals to colonies in America and Australia, the English and Irish experiences with the system of ticket-of-leave, and the work of American prison reformers during the nineteenth century.

A HISTORY OF
PAROLE

---

*From William Parker, *Parole (Origins, Development, Current Practices and Statutes)*, (College Park, Maryland; American Correctional Association, 1972) pp. 9–12, 17–20.

## Transportation to America

The transportation of English criminals to the American colonies began early in the seventeenth century. The precedent for this can be found in a law passed in 1597 providing for the banishment of those who appeared to be dangerous. As early as 1617, the Privy Council granted reprieves and stays of execution to persons convicted of robbery who were strong enough to be employed in the Colonies.

The London, Virginia, and Massachusetts Companies, and similar organizations supported the transportation of criminals to America. When this plan was proposed, there were acute economic conditions and widespread unemployment in England, yet the Colonies needed labor: thus the Government devised the plan to transport convicted felons to America. The King approved this proposal to grant reprieves and stays of execution to the convicted felons who were physically able to be employed in service.

English court officials compiled lists of names and the judge or frequently the mayor and recorder signed them. The lists were then presented to the Secretary of State. When a death penalty had been imposed, a stay of execution was automatically granted until the King had reviewed the judge's recommendation.

In the beginning, no specific conditions were imposed upon those receiving such pardons. However, many of those pardoned evaded transportation or returned to England prior to the expiration of their terms, and it became necessary to impose certain restrictions upon the individuals to whom these pardons were granted. About 1655 the form of pardon was amended to include specific conditions and to provide for the nullification of the pardon if the recipient failed to abide by the conditions.

When transportation was just beginning, the Government paid a fee to the contractor for each prisoner transported. However, in 1717, a new law was enacted and this procedure was discontinued. Under the new procedure the contractor or shipmaster was given "property in service" of the prisoner until the expiration of his full term. After a prisoner was delivered to the contractor or shipmaster, the Government took no interest in his welfare or behavior unless he violated the conditions of the pardon by returning to England prior to the expiration of his sentence.

When the pardoned felons arrived in the Colonies, their services were sold to the highest bidder and the shipmaster then transferred the "property in service" agreement to the new master. The felon was no longer referred to as a convicted criminal but became an indentured servant. The system of indenture dates back to the Statute of Artifices enacted in 1562, and originally it had no relation to persons convicted of crime.

Van Doren, in his biography of Benjamin Franklin, quotes the conditions imposed upon Franklin in 1718 when, at the age of twelve, he became indentured to his brother:

*. . . During which term the said apprentice his master faithfully shall or will serve, his secrets keep, his lawful demands everywhere glady do. He shall do no damage to his said master nor see it done to others, but to his power shall let or forthwith give notice to his said master of the same. The goods of his said master he shall not waste, nor the same without license of him to give or lend. Hurt to his said master he shall not do, cause or procure to be done. He shall neither buy nor sell without his master's license. Taverns, inns, or alehouses he shall not haunt. At cards*

*or dice tables or any other unlawful game he shall not play. Matrimony he shall not contract nor from the services of his master day or night absent himself but in all things as an honest faithful apprentice shall and will demean and behave himself toward said master during said term.*

This indenture bears a similarity to the procedure now followed by parole boards in this country. Like the indentured servant, a prisoner conditionally released on parole agrees in writing to accept certain conditions included on the release form, which is signed by the members of the parole board and the prisoner. Even some of the conditions imposed on conditionally released prisoners are similar to those included in the indenture agreement. . . .

## Developments in the United States

In the development of parole in the United States, there are three underlying concepts: (1) the principle of shortening the term of imprisonment as a reward for good conduct; (2) the indeterminate sentence; and (3) supervision. The first found legal recognition in the New York "good time" law of 1817. Today there is a good time law of some sort in every state, the U.S. Department of Justice, and the District of Columbia, the last one having been passed in Maryland in 1916. The indeterminate sentence was first introduced with the establishment of the Houses of Refuge for children.

In all instances, release effected under these methods of shortening the time of imprisonment was accompanied by some sort of contract between the prisoner and the releasing authority, or what we today call a parole agreement. Children released from the houses of refuge were indentured to private persons under the condition that the child would do the bidding of the master, and that the latter had the right to return the child to the institution if he was not satisfied with the child's performance. Similarly, the release of older offenders prior to the expiration of the sentence carried with it certain conditions, which included return to the institution if the conditions were violated.

The third concept of parole, supervision, was at first satisfied by the use of volunteers. The master of an indentured child from a House of Refuge was also the child's guardian and supervisor. He was in no sense forced into the contract with the institution and could terminate it at his pleasure.

Among the first volunteer parole officers were the members of prison societies. As early as 1822 the Philadelphia Society for Alleviating the Miseries of Public Prisons recognized the importance of care for discharged prisoners. In 1851 the Society appointed two agents to work with and for discharged prisoners from the Philadelphia County Prison and the Penitentiary.

It appears that supervision by a paid public employee was first provided in Massachusetts in 1845, when an agent was appointed by the state to assist released prisoners in obtaining employment, tools, clothing, transportation with the aid of public funds. Although this was not supervision in today's sense, it still provided material support for the parolee during the most critical period of his parole.

In 1865, the achievements of Sir Walter Crofton in England, Montesinos in Spain, and Obermaier in Germany were well known. Each appeared to have worked out a successful system of reformation in prison followed by conditional release. In

England and Bavaria, supervision had also been introduced, thus establishing a complete system of penal treatment. The result was the passage of the first inde- terminate sentence law in Michigan in 1869 at the instigation of Z. R. Brockway. Although this law was declared unconstitutional a year after he became Superin- tendent at the Elmira Reformatory in 1876, Brockway succeeded in having an in- determinate sentence law adopted in New York, thus establishing a complete sys- tem. It comprised not only the use of the indeterminate sentence, but also a system of grading the inmates, compulsory education, and a careful system of selection for parole. Supervision of the released prisoners was provided by volunteer citizens who were known as guardians. One of the conditions of parole was that the parolee must report to the guardian on the first of each month. Later, written reports were required and submitted to the institution after they had been countersigned by the employer and the guardian.

As early as 1839, George Combs, a Scottish philosopher, visited America to lecture; it was he who suggested the idea of a sentencing board, the indeterminate sentence, parole, and what later became the basis for the system under which modern boards of parole function. In one of his lectures, he said:

... *If the principles which I advocate shall ever be adopted, the sentence of the criminal judge, on conviction of a crime, would simply be one of finding the individual has committed a certain offense and is not fit to live in society, and therefore granting warrant for his transmission to a penitentiary to be there confined, instructed, and employed until liberated in due course of law.*

*The process of liberation would then become one of the greatest importance. There should be official inspectors of penitentiaries invested with some of the powers of a court, sitting at regular intervals and proceeding according to fixed rules. They should be authorized to receive applications for liberation at all their sessions and to grant the prayer of them on being satisfied that such a thorough change had been effected in the mental condition of the prisoner that he might safely be permitted to resume his place in society.*

*Until this conviction was produced upon examination of his disposition, of his attainment, in knowledge of his acquired skills, or some useful employment, of his habits of industry, and, in short, of his general qualifications to provide for his own support, to restrain his criminal propensities from committing abuses and to act the part of a useful citizen, he should be retained as an inmate of a penitentiary.*

Although parole was intimately tied up with the indeterminate sentence in the reformatory movement, parole legislation in the United States spread much more rapidly than indeterminate sentence legislation except as it concerned children. In fact, conditional release legislation antedates legislation on the indeterminate sen- tence for older offenders. In 1837, an act passed in Massachusetts empowered the Governor to attach conditions to the release of those who were granted pardons or remission of part of their sentences. However, the first statewide law governing parole of adults by an agency other than the Governor of the State was passed in Ohio in 1884. By 1901, twenty states had parole laws while only eleven states had indeterminate sentence laws. Today there is not a single state that does not have a parole law on its statute books. There are, though, still several states without indeterminate sentence laws.

The authority to grant parole is vested in the parole board. The American Correctional Association has suggested that state boards have four primary functions:

1. Select and place prisoners on parole.
2. Aid, supervise and provide continuing control of parolees in the community.
3. Determine when the parole function is completed and discharge from parole.
4. If violation of conditions occur, to determine whether parole revocation should take place.[2]

Organizationally, the parole board may be an independent agency or operate under the administrative control of another larger organization, usually a department of corrections. In some jurisdictions, a consolidation model is used in which the parole board is under nominal control of the corrections department but operates without direct interference under administrative fiat; today, about 20 boards are autonomous and 30 are consolidated with, or controlled by, corrections departments.

Most state boards are relatively small, usually numbering under 10 individuals. Their size, coupled with their large caseloads and the varied activities they are expected to perform, can prevent board members from becoming as well acquainted with the individual inmate as might be desired. Arguments for seating the board within a department of corrections usually cite the improved communication and availability of more intimate knowledge about offenders as justification for such an administrative setup. Vincent O'Leary and Joan Nuffield point out, however, that consolidated agencies may give more consideration to institutional needs than to those of the offender or the community:

Overcrowding, the desire to get rid of a problem case, enforcement of a relatively petty rule, or some other concern of institutional management can very easily become the basis for decision-making. Institutional decision-making also lends itself to so much formality and lack of visibility that its capacity for fairness . . . or what may be as important, the appearance of fairness . . . may be called into question.[3]

Nonetheless, O'Leary and Nuffield feel that a consolidated parole board structure may be the most appropriate type of organization, since it combines features of autonomy with the sensitivity to institutional activity that comes with being part of the correctional system:

(Consolidating) . . . promotes an increased concern for the whole correctional system and a greater sensitivity to institutional programs and at the same time that separation of parole decisions from the immediate control of an institution tends to give appropriate weight to parole decision-making consideration beyond institutional management.[4]

### The Appointments and Qualifications of Parole Board Members

How parole board members are appointed and what qualifications they must have differ among the states. A review of state and federal practices reveals that in 42 of the 52 jurisdictions, governors are the appointing authorities; in 4 jurisdictions, parole board members are chosen from civil service lists; and in the remaining 6 jurisdictions, they are appointed by a mayor (Washington, D.C.), the commissioner of correction, the President of the United States (federal) or by the governor and governor's cabinet from a prepared list.[5] Terms of appointment also tend to vary, and depending on the jurisdiction, range from a life term (4 states) to one of two years (1 state); the average term is six years (16 states).[6]

Qualifications for appointment to a parole board position also vary widely among the states. Below are listed some representative samples of statutory qualifications for parole board positions:[7]

The sample qualifications listed in Table 17.1 are typical of the various state and federal jurisdictions. Almost half of the parole boards require no particular qualifications, while the remainder seem to stress skills in the social sciences, law, law enforcement, and education.

TABLE 17.1
Qualifications and
Terms for Representative State Parole Board Members

| Jurisdiction | Qualifications | Term (Years) |
|---|---|---|
| California | Broad background in appraisal of offenders and the circumstances that bring them to prison. | 4 |
| Idaho | Experience, knowledge, and interest in sociology, rehabilitative services, psychology, and other related disciplines. | 5 |
| Massachusetts | B.A. and five years experience in parole, probation, corrections, law, law enforcement, psychology, sociology or social work. One of seven members must be an attorney, one a psychiatrist, and one a parole staff. | 5 |
| Rhode Island | One of five members must be a physician trained in psychology or neurology, one an attorney, one a professional trained in corrections or allied field; applicants must have an interest in social welfare problems. | 5 |
| South Dakota | None | 6 |
| Oregon | None | 4 |
| Texas | None | 6 |
| U.S. Board of Parole | None | 6 |

The actual parole decision is made at a parole grant hearing. At this time the full board or a selected subcommittee reviews information, may meet with the offender, and then decides whether the parole applicant has a reasonable probability of succeeding outside of prison. Candidates for parole may be chosen by statutory eligibility on the basis of time served in relation to their sentences. In most jurisdictions, the minimum sentence imposed by the judge regulates eligibility for parole; when no minimum sentence is set, parole eligibility is based on the policy of the board and/ or the corrections department. Finally, in most jurisdictions the good time an offender accumulates can serve to reduce the minimum sentence and therefore hasten eligibility for parole (see Chapter 13).

Each parole board meets in a unique way and has its own administrative setup for reviewing cases. In some, the full board meets with the applicant; in others only a few members are required. In a number of jurisdictions, a single board member can conduct a personal investigation and submit the findings to the full board for a decision.

No specific national policy exists to determine the way in which inmates are informed of the board's decision. In some jurisdictions, the inmate is informed in writing by the board at some time following the decision. A recent trend has been for the parole board to confront the offender with its decision immediately after the hearing. It is believed that this policy can promote in the offender a sense of participation in the correctional process and may also increase the offender's perceptions of its fairness. By speaking directly to the applicant, the board can also promote and emphasize the specific types of behavior and behavior changes it expects to see if the inmate is to eventually qualify for or effectively serve parole.[8]

The inmate's specific rights at a parole grant hearing also vary between jurisdictions. The inmate is permitted counsel in 21 states, or allowed to present witnesses on his or her behalf in 17; in other jurisdictions these privileges are not permitted. Because the federal courts have not yet declared that the parole applicant is entitled to any form of legal representation, the individual inmate must pay for legal services where this privilege is allowed.

In 11 parole jurisdictions the reasons for the parole decision must be given in writing, while in a few more a verbatim record of the hearing is made.

Provision of counsel is usually considered a key element in the maintenance of due process rights at any hearing within the confines of the criminal justice system. The fact that less than one half of the states allow or provide counsel, combined with the hands-off policy state and federal appellate courts maintain on the issue of parole grant hearings, seems to confirm the privileged nature of parole decision making and its immunity from the consideration of due process rights of the convicted. When state courts have made specific entries into the area of the parole hearing, they have done so in relatively limited jurisdictions and have confined their decisions to the issue of providing written reasons for denying parole. In *Monks v. New Jersey Board of Parole*,[9] for example, the court found:

The need for fairness is as urgent in the parole process as elsewhere in the law and it is evident to us that, as a general matter, the furnishing of reasons for denial would be the much fairer course; not only much fairer but much better designed towards the goal of rehabilitation. . . .

That course (granting statement of reason for denial) as a general matter would serve the acknowledged interests of procedural fairness and would also serve as a suitable and significant discipline on the Board's exercise of its wide powers. It would in no way curb the Board's discretion on the grant or denial of parole nor would it impair the scope and effect of its expertise.

We find the rule (board's rule prohibiting disclosure of reason for denial) invalid and it is now nullified. It should be replaced at an early date by a carefully prepared rule designed generally towards affording statements of reasons on parole denials, while providing for such reasonable exceptions as may be essential to rehabilitation and the sound administration of the parole system.[10]

The Supreme Court recently dealt with the issue of rights at parole grant hearings in the case of *Greenholtz vs. Inmates of the Nebraska Penal and Correction Complex*.[11] In this case, the Court held that early release vis-á-vis parole was a privilege and not a right, and that this act of "grace" did not entitle inmates to receive a full compliment of due process rights (under the Fifth and Fourteenth Amendments) at a parole hearing (for example, to have counsel or call witnesses).

Thus, the Court suggested that the right to due process is not created merely because a state provides a possibility of parole. This is only a "mere hope" and is therefore distinguishable from the revocation of parole (see this chapter for a discussion of parole revocation). This finding is similar in spirit to *Meachum v. Fano*,[12] a prison transfer case in which the Supreme Court held that an inmate could be transferred to another institution without a formal hearing because conviction extinguished the "liberty right." Thus, it has been left up to the individual states to determine inmate rights at parole hearings.

## PAROLE BOARD DISCRETION

Parole board members regularly meet together or in subgroups to review cases of inmates who have met the statutory requirements for parole and are eligible for release. In deciding whether to grant parole, the state or federal board must take into account many important factors, some of which are discussed below.

Of primary concern to the board is whether the inmate can make an adequate adjustment to the community and refrain from further criminal activity. The board must, for example, decide if it is the proper time to release the offender, or whether continued confinement will be beneficial. Those parole board members overly concerned with the protection of the community might argue that longer prison sentences help to deter crime through incapacitation and, at the same time, increase the offender's awareness that the parole agency is a no-nonsense organization whose wishes must be respected. Other board members may be more concerned with the potential harm that continuation of a prison sentence might cause the inmate; this type of member believes that prolonging the release of the offender may cause further harm by the pains of imprisonment. Regardless of their orientation, most parole board members realize that the consequences of their decision can jeopardize the state's parole program if a too-hasty release turns out to have disastrous results for the community.[13]

Parole board members may also be concerned with the inherent justice and morality of their decision: Has the offender paid the debt to society? Should consideration be given to the victims of crimes (or potential victims)? Should revenge be a motive for denying parole? The board members may also ponder the fairness of releasing one inmate into the community while retaining another who has committed the same crime and has served the same amount of time.

Another consideration influencing the board's decision may be the condition and welfare of the prisoner's family. The family of a married man left on their own while the man is imprisoned may become wards of the state, receive public welfare, and have members placed in foster homes. As a result, his incarceration becomes a triple financial burden on the state, and includes (1) the cost of imprisonment; (2) the cost of welfare and child support for his family; and (3) the lost tax dollars and revenue which would be acquired were the inmate productively employed while on parole. Furthermore, the economic, social, and psychological burdens of having a family member incarcerated may help to push other members of the family into crime. In the case of the female offender, the board may take into account the fact that she is a mother or has other dependents. These types of considerations may work against the unmarried offender who has no dependents; again, the issue of fairness is raised.

Parole board members also base their decisions on their perceptions of the values and attitudes of correctional personnel and other administrators of the criminal justice system. For example, if the parole board plans to release an inmate who has received a negative disciplinary report from prison authorities, their action may serve to notify other inmates that prison rules need not be taken seriously. A decision to parole a particular inmate thus must be balanced with the need to maintain a cordial working relationship with prison and correctional authorities. Early parole decisions may also be viewed with disappointment by judicial authorities within the state. If parole board and judicial attitudes are not similar, some judges may counteract the policies of the parole board by setting high minimum sentences where the statutory law allows them that discretion. Thus, consideration of the responses of criminal justice system personnel may influence the parole board members' decision to grant or deny parole or set specialized and stringent conditions on parolees.

The public's response to a parole grant may also influence the board's decision making. If, for example, a particularly well-known criminal such as Charles Manson or Richard Speck is up for parole, a positive finding on his behalf will receive widespread media coverage and possibly generate irate responses from the public. Conversely, in the case of public figures with well-defined sympathetic followings, such as the Berrigans and other religious and anti-Viet Nam war protestors, the board may be swayed in a positive direction.

Many other inmate-oriented factors affect the parole board's decision; the psychological growth and improvement of the inmate, the circumstances of the offense, and the parole plan (what the inmate intends to do on the outside). In 1965, the National Parole Institute attempted to identify the most important factors in deciding whether to parole an inmate. They administered a questionnaire to a national sample of parole board members and asked them to identify the five factors which influenced them most when making their decisions. Results of their study are included in Table 17.2.

As these data suggest, parole board members report that they pay the most attention to factors related to the prisoner's well-being and to the probability that the parolee would commit further crime. Of somewhat less importance are issues relating to family and criminal justice relationships.

**Parole Board Decisions**
**and the Correctional**
**System**
In many jurisdictions (about 30), the parole board is administratively a part of the state's department of corrections; in the remainder, the board may be historically and functionally tied to the prison system. Because of this connection, parole boards can be influenced by conditions within the prison and also may affect these conditions themselves.

As mentioned previously, board members may be unwilling to contradict or disregard the disciplinary reports of prison administrators. Other correctional factors influencing the board may be the conditions within the prisons themselves: if overcrowding exists, parole may be viewed as a desirable, cost-effective alternative which can ease the pressure on the prison community; conversely, empty prison cells may prompt more careful and cautious parole decision making.

Administrative bonds between parole boards and the correctional system can only help to make board members more aware of the expanding variety of programs available to prisoners both inside and outside the institution. Parole may be granted because board members believe that the single most effective treatment method rests in the outside community (e.g., a halfway house); however, if improved treatment programs can be found in the prison, parole may be denied so that inmates can avail themselves of prison-based programs.

Prison conditions can also affect parole decision making in other ways. If riots or disturbances occur, the board can systematically deny parole to present a more authoritative policy to the inmates. When inmates return to their cellblocks after being denied community release, the word may quickly spread that things are not going to be easy if violent or negative behavior continues.

Of utmost importance to most inmates is their early release. This factor, combined with the control of early release by the parole board, has the greatest impact on inmate behavior. As Carter, McGee, and Nelson suggest:

(It) is clear that parole policy affects inmate behavior, both individually and collectively, and is, in turn, affected by inmate behavior. The management and control of institutions are directly related to parole or not parole, has the coercive power of uncertainty to force institutional conformity.[14]

The inmate grapevine quickly spreads word of each parole decision. If the board seems to stress education and group counseling, then these programs are likely to be heavily attended by inmates eager to create a favorable impression; if vocational training and economic skills are stressed, then these programs may become oversubscribed.

It is evident that the outcome of board decisions and the inmates' perceptions of those decisions have a significant effect on inmates' attitudes toward the fairness of the correctional system. If minority group members see a trend for whites to be given earlier release, the repercussions may be felt throughout the prison community. All these factors must be observed by board members if equilibrium is to be maintained within the prison system.

**PAROLE PREDICTION**

Parole board members are also likely to give some attention to one or more of the numerous parole prediction devices which have been employed on a national basis. Prediction tables utilize information on past parole cases to predict the probable success of current ones. Personal information, including the offender's age, the type of offense, and the time served, is correlated with parole outcome (recidivism figures) in order to statistically derive a base expectancy rate of success for current parole cases. This number should signify the probability that an individual parolee will not recidivate.

Using a prediction device involves analysis of information about a particular parole applicant according to a formula which awards or subtracts a standard number of points depending on the particular background of the case. For example, an offender over 30 years old may receive a particular number of points, while one under 20 might receive less. A narcotics addict would lose points; so would a prior recidivist.

The most well-known parole prediction device is the U.S. Parole Commission's Salient Factor Score Index. The Salient Factor score was developed in a 2-year follow-up study of 2,500 inmates who had been released previously. Since 1974, the Salient Factor score index has been expanded to all Federal parole decision making.

The Salient Factor score uses seven elements to establish four categories of parole prognosis (very good, good, fair, poor). It is intended as a predictive aid and may be overridden by the parole board's judgment provided that they specify their reasons for ignoring the score. Scores are

TABLE 17.2
Considerations in Parole Decisions

| Considerations | A. Median percent of cases in which this consideration consciously and significantly influenced their decision | B. Percent of board members including it as one of the five most important considerations |
| --- | --- | --- |
| 1. My estimate of the chances that the prisoner would or would not commit a serious crime if paroled. | 79.4 | 92.8 |
| 2. My judgment that the prisoner would become a worse risk if confined longer. | 13.6 | 71.9 |
| 3. My judgment that the prisoner would benefit from further experience in the institution program, or at any rate, would become a better risk if confined longer. | 27.6 | 87.1 |
| 4. My judgment that the prisoner had already been punished enough to "pay" for his crime. | 13.3 | 43.2 |
| 5. What I thought the reaction of the local police might be if the prisoner were granted parole. | 3.0 | 12.2 |
| 6. What I thought the reaction of the press, radio and TV might be if the prisoner were granted parole. | 3.5 | 8.6 |
| 7. What I thought the reaction of the judge might be if the prisoner were granted parole. | 7.5 | 20.9 |
| 8. What I thought the reaction of other prisoners might be to the policy which they might ascribe to me from my decision in a particular case. | 3.7 | 12.2 |

(Table 17.2
continued)

| | | |
|---|---|---|
| 9. What I thought the reaction of prison officials might be to my decision in a particular case. | 3.1 | 5.0 |
| 10. My feelings about how my decision in this case would affect the feelings or welfare of the prisoner's relatives or dependents. | 9.2 | 33.8 |
| 11. What I thought the consequences of my decision policy might be in getting legislative support for the parole system's requests. | 0* | 7.9 |
| 12. What I thought the consequences of my decision policy might be for the governor or for other officials in the executive branch of government. | 0.4** | 8.6 |
| 13. What I thought would be the reactions of my colleagues on the parole board. | 0* | 9.4 |
| 14. The probability that the prisoner would be a misdemeanant and a burden to his parole supervisors, even if he did not commit any serious offenses on parole. | 8.9 | 35.3 |

*61 percent of the board members said this was not a consideration in any case
**49% of the board members said this was not a consideration in any case.
*58% of the board members said this was not a consideration in any case.

then cross-referenced with offense characteristic groupings, ranging from low (e.g., minor theft) to great seriousness (e.g., aggravated felony, kidnapping) in order to achieve a determination of how long an individual should serve time in prison prior to being paroled. Those with low salient factor scores (poor risks) would be required to serve quite a bit more time than those with high scores (very good risks), and those committing serious crimes serve longer than those engaging in petty offenses.[15]

A recent 6-year follow-up of the effectiveness of the salient score index revealed mixed results. During the first year of the evaluation, there was a considerable difference in the arrest rate between the four risk groups (very goods are arrested less; poor risks tend to be arrested more); however, this trend diminishes over time and by the sixth year of the follow-up study of subjects who had been out on the street, the arrest rate for all categories was quite similar.[16]

However, not all studies of parole effectiveness reach the same optimistic results. A recent six-year follow-up of 1,806 federal releasees (parolees, and those whose sentence had expired) found that 1,129 cases (62.5%) had been arrested at least once or had their parole revoked on a technical violation; in 738 cases (40.9%), more than one criminal arrest was recorded; all told, more than 2,788 separate criminal arrests were recorded.[17]

Thus, the issue of parole effectiveness remains somewhat clouded.

PAROLE RULES

Before release into the community, a parolee is supplied with a standard set of rules and conditions which must be obeyed and conformed with. As is the case with probation (see Chapter 14), the offender who violates these rules may have parole revoked and be processed back into the institution to serve the remainder of the sentence.

Parole rules may curtail or prohibit certain types of behavior while encouraging or demanding others. Some rules tend to be so overly moralistic or technical in nature that they severely inhibit the parolee's ability to adjust to society. By making life unnecessarily unpleasant without contributing to rehabilitation, parole rules reflect the punitive side of community supervision. Rules such as these can prohibit marriage, ban the use of motor vehicles or forbid the borrowing of money. Parolees must often check in and ask permission when leaving their residences, and may find that the rules bar them from associating with friends with criminal records which, in some cases, severely limits social life.

The way in which parole rules are stated, the kinds of things they forbid or encourage, and their flexibility varies between jurisdictions. Some states expressly forbid a certain type of behavior while others will require permission for it. Illustrated in the applications section of this chapter are two sets of sample parole conditions representing extremes of control—Maryland's, which are flexible, and New Mexico's, which seem to more strictly limit the parolee.[18]

Each item in the parole conditions must be obeyed lest the offender's parole be revoked for a technical violation. In addition, the parole board can impose specific conditions for a particular offender, such as demanding that the parolee receive psychiatric treatment. The difficulties and ambiguities involved in these conditions has been noted by the President's Commission, which states:

But if parole is the appropriate disposition the fact that the conditions may be less onerous than imprisonment is irrelevant in determining whether those conditions are proper. Some conditions may be too burdensome or too unrelated to the rehabilitation of the offender or the protection of the community to be justified in the particular case. Conditions may violate other important values of our system without serving any necessary correctional purpose. They may, for example, interfere with freedoms of speech, press and religion, protected by the First Amendment. And conditions may be so vague that the parolee is not adequately warned of the kind of conduct which will justify revocation.[19]

It is apparent that parole rules must undergo modernization and standardization if they are to conform with the rehabilitative or due process framework of justice desired by the majority of criminal justice experts. As they exist today, parole rules are often vestiges of prior attempts to demean and shackle offenders, both within the institution and once outside it.

Once released in the community, the offender comes under nominal control of a parole agent, who enforces parole rules, helps the inmate gain employment, and meets regularly with the parolee for reasons of treatment and rehabilitation. In general, parole officers and their supervisors may be under administrative control of the parole board, or they may comprise an autonomous branch of the department of corrections. In some states and in the federal parole service, officers have combined caseloads of probation and parole clients.

PAROLE
SUPERVISION

Supervision in probation and parole is quite similar in some respects, but differs in others. Both types of supervision attempt to help clients attain meaningful relationships in the community and use similar enforcement, counseling, and treatment skills to gain that end. However, some major differences exist between the official capacities of the two service roles.

First, parole officers deal with more difficult cases. The parolee has been institutionalized for an extended period of time; to be successful on parole, the former inmate must make an adjustment to the community which at first can seem a strange and often hostile environment. The parolee's family life has been disrupted and the person may find it difficult to resume employment. The paroled offender may have already been classified by probation officers (in a pre-sentence report) as dangerous or as a poor risk for community adjustment. Furthermore, it would be overly optimistic to presume that a prison sentence substantially improves the offender's chances for rehabilitation. To overcome these roadblocks to success, the parole officer may have to play a much greater role in directing and supervising clients' lives than is required of the probation officer. Moreover, the parole officer may have to be less flexible in accepting rule violations and need to hold the client on a tighter rein.

Secondly, the stigma of the ex-con label and former inmate status follows the parolee everywhere. The presumed dangerousness of the ex-inmate, coupled with the limitations of strict parole rules, make parole supervision more of an enforcement function than probation supervision seems to be. The parole officer is aware of the consequences which can arise if the client commits a subsequent felony offense while on parole. Such violations hurt the chances of others to gain parole and jeopardize the whole parole concept. For example, some neighborhoods have petitioned their legislative representatives to pass zoning ordinances barring halfway houses and other types of aftercare centers inhabited by parolees from their communities because they fear their clients. Parole officers sensitive to these conditions may tend to put the needs of the community ahead of the needs of the client and evolve a supervisory stance which stresses control and enforcement rather than treatment and rehabilitation.

A final difference between the two types of supervision is that parole officers may be called upon in some jurisdictions to personally arrest and take into custody parole violators; probation departments seek court orders, which are enforced by police agencies, when probation is to be revoked.

Parole supervision often begins in the institution when institutionally based agents help the inmate create a parole plan. This plan can include such activities as securing a promise of employment for the inmate, arranging for a residence, and developing community contacts. Often, the parole plan will require the inmate to spend time in a residential community treatment program such as a halfway house. The adequacy of the parole plan is an important element in the board's decision to grant community release.

Once in the community, a supervision program may develop in any number of ways. The parole officer can meet individually with the client, or they may prefer group sessions. Meetings can be weekly, biweekly, or monthly. The parole officer may check regularly with others who are in close and personal contact with the parolee, such as employers, teachers, neighbors, or family. Some agents may make unannounced spot checks to determine whether their clients are keeping regular hours, working steadily, and otherwise conforming to the parole contract.

## Supervision Styles

In previous chapters, some of the styles associated with police work and probation supervision were discussed. In principle, the various stylistic approaches of probation supervision—the rule enforcer, the social worker, the traditionalist, the civil servant, and the team player—may also be manifested by parole supervisory agents. Style can be reflected in the way in which officers conduct their supervisory activities, what parole rules they stress, and when and if they decide to alert the parole board concerning possible revocation for technical violations.

Another typology of parole supervision styles has been developed by Ohlin, Piven, and Pappenport, who have identified the following three as major parole styles: [20]

*The Punitive Officer* is the guardian of middle-class community morality; this officer attempts to coerce the offender into conformity, and stresses protection of the community and supervision of the offender.

*The Protective Agent* vacillates between protecting the offender and the community. The tools are direct assistance, lecturing, and praise and blame. Ambivalent emotionally, this type shifts back and forth in taking sides with the offender and the community.

*The Welfare Worker* has as an ultimate goal the improved welfare of the client and views this as the only genuine guarantee of improvement in the parolee. The skills which the welfare worker employs stem from an objective and theoretically based assessment of the clients' situations, needs, and capacities.

Daniel Glaser has added the following type to these three styles:[21]

*The Political Opportunist* enters into the parole field via political opportunity or achievement in other areas and uses the parole department as a steppingstone for career advancement. In spite of this, the dynamics needed for success in the political system may make this individual an attractive and effective worker.

THE LAW ENFORCEMENT DUTIES OF PAROLE AGENTS

A number of parole laws provide that officers can order a parolee to be taken into confinement, usually pending an investigation about commission of a new offense.* Clearly, this is a power that can be badly abused, and on occasion it has been. There have been instances in which parolees have been confined for extended periods of time on alleged parole violations or simply as punishment for misconduct. Consequently the parole officer's power to detain the parolee has been increasingly surrounded with procedural safeguards in many parole systems.

A more general question that has troubled parole authorities, especially those in the adult field, is the method by which essentially law enforcement functions should be carried out when serious violations of parole conditions are suspected. The predominant opinion in the parole field is that supervision staff should not assume the role of police officers. A recent survey of parole board members, for example, showed that only 27% of them believed that parole officers should be asked to arrest parole violators and only 13% believed that parole officers should be allowed to carry weapons. The task of a parole officer is generally seen as developing close working relationships with police departments rather than performing law enforcement functions directly. But this does not mean that parole officers can neglect responsibility for control and surveillance.

Programs to effect liaison with police departments have been developed in the states of New York and California. There, certain parole officers, designated as investigators, are specially trained and assigned to units responsible for liaison with police departments. They cooperate in police intelligence efforts, and they relieve parole officers of some surveillance responsibilities. Most often they undertake investigations in cases at the request of a parole officer who suspects that a parolee

---

*Taken from The President's Commission on Law Enforcement and Criminal Justice, *Task Force Report: Corrections* (Washington, D.C.: U.S. Government Printing Office, 1967), p. 69.

is involved in criminal activities. They also initiate inquiries on the basis of information from other contacts, often the police.

These efforts to achieve effective police relationships need careful study. Some observers question the practice, contending that it is not an appropriate activity for a parole agency or that it could better be handled by each parole agent in his own district. Advocates of this system contend that it creates much closer cooperation with police agencies, defines the role of the regular parole officer more clearly, and relieves him of tasks for which he has little training.

## EFFECTIVENESS OF PAROLE

Until recently, little knowledge had been accumulated on the effectiveness of parole. National record-keeping was inadequate to fully determine whether community release actually worked or whether many offenders violated parole rules or committed further offenses. Recently, however, the National Council on Crime and Delinquency has begun to collect data on a national scale from every adult parole authority. Their findings indicate that parole is actually more effective than had been believed. A followup study on a sample of over 104,000 parolees, released between 1965 and 1970, indicated that success was quite high; ranging, as Table 17.3 shows, from homicide offenders (90.1%) to motor vehicle theft violators (64.9%).[22]

In every offense category, those offenders with prior records had somewhat lower success rates than first offenders, though the differences were not enough to discourage the continued use of parole for recidivists.

To increase the effectiveness of parole, some jurisdictions have implemented experimental parole conditions such as limited caseload sizes, the use of treatment facilities, the matching of parolee and supervisor by personality, and "shock parole" (which involves immediate short-term incarcerations for violators to impress them with the seriousness of a violation). Data so far has indicated that these programs are not overly effective and may, in fact, produce a higher violation rate than traditional parole supervision. For example, limiting caseload size allows parole officers to supervise their clients more closely and allows them to more easily spot infractions.

It is probable that parole outcome will become more successful when the significant social, legal, and economic penalties levied upon those convicted of crimes are removed and when the rules of parole become more humane and ensure the basic rights of the parolee.

## REVOCATION OF PAROLE

Revocation proceedings in parole are similar in nature to those of probation. When an offender violates a condition of probation or commits a new crime, the court may revoke probation and impose a sentence of incarceration. Similarly, when a parolee violates his or her community status, the parole board has the authority to return the offender to prison.

The parole revocation process is almost always started by the parole officer who believes that the parolee has violated a parole condition, or

| Offense | Percent favorable | | | Number of cases | | |
|---------|--------|--------------|--------------|--------|--------------|--------|
|         | Priors | No priors | Com- bined | Priors | No priors | Total |
| Homicide .............................. | 87.9 | 93.3 | 90.1 | 4,738 | 3,311 | 8,049 |
| Manslaughter ........................... | 84.6 | 93.7 | 88.7 | 1,030 | 863 | 1,893 |
| Other sex offenses ....................... | 83.8 | 91.9 | 86.9 | 1,908 | 1,150 | 3,058 |
| Statutory rape .......................... | 81.8 | 89.2 | 84.4 | 572 | 306 | 878 |
| Forcible rape ........................... | 80.8 | 88.3 | 83.6 | 1,480 | 886 | 2,366 |
| Aggravated assault ....................... | 77.6 | 86.3 | 80.1 | 4,487 | 1,812 | 6,299 |
| Narcotics offenses ....................... | 75.6 | 86.3 | 77.9 | 3,916 | 1,051 | 4,967 |
| Other fraud ............................ | 75.0 | 84.2 | 78.1 | 673 | 335 | 1,008 |
| Armed robbery .......................... | 73.8 | 83.7 | 76.6 | 8,851 | 3,450 | 12,301 |
| Unarmed robbery ........................ | 71.7 | 82.8 | 74.7 | 3,450 | 1,119 | 4,169 |
| Theft or larceny ......................... | 71.4 | 79.8 | 73.7 | 7,448 | 2,755 | 10,203 |
| Burglary ............................... | 69.3 | 78.1 | 71.6 | 23,790 | 8,487 | 32,277 |
| Check fraud ............................ | 64.3 | 71.7 | 65.9 | 8,493 | 2,482 | 10,975 |
| Vehicle theft ............................ | 62.8 | 71.0 | 64.9 | 4,285 | 1,454 | 5,739 |
| Total number ........................... |  |  |  | 75,721 | 29,461 | 104,182 |

Source: Gottfredson, Don M.: M. G. Neithercutt; Joan Nuffield; and Vincent O'Leary. "Four Thousand Lifetimes: A Study of Time Served and Parole Outcomes." National Council on Crime and Delinquency. June 1973, p. 10.

Reprinted with permission of the National Council on Crime and Delinquency from *Four Thousand Lifetimes: A Study of Time Served and Parole Outcome* by Gottfredson, Neithercutt, Nuffield and O'Leary, June 1973.

when the parolee has been charged with a new crime. In the past, the statutory requirements and practices of parole agencies which applied once the parole officer initiated this process varied greatly; some states provided informal hearings to determine if reason existed to believe that the parolee violated a condition, while others held more formal revocation hearings. However, few states had established any minimum due process requirements. Parolees were often taken into custody and even returned to prison before any hearing was held on the violation of parole. This practice was not only unfair, but resulted in undue hardships on parolees and their families.

However, in 1972, the United States Supreme Court caused an uproar among parole agencies throughout the country by handing down the land-mark parole decision of *Morrissey v. Brewer*.[23] This case held that the Fourteenth Amendment requirement of due process of law actually applied to the parole revocation process. The Court's decision established specific due process guidelines which parole boards must follow before revoking an offender's parole.

Because of its impact on the parole process, the case is summarized below.

TABLE 17.3
Persons Paroled and Percent with Favorable Outcomes By Offense and Prior Record, United States, 1965–70

## MORRISSEY V. BREWER

**Facts:** The petitioner, Morrissey, was convicted of falsely drawing checks in 1967 and pursuant to his guilty plea was sentenced to not more than seven years in prison. Morrissey was released on parole from the Iowa State Prison in June, 1968. Seven months later, at the direction of his parole officer, he was arrested in his home town as a parole violator and held in the county jail. One week later, after a review of the parole officer's written report, the Iowa Board of Parole revoked Morrissey's parole and returned him to prison.

Morrissey filed a writ of habeas corpus, claiming that his parole was revoked without a hearing and that he was deprived of his due process rights.

The parole officer's report on which the Board of Parole acted shows that petitioner's parole was revoked on the basis of information that he had violated the conditions of parole by buying a car under an assumed name and operating it without permission, giving false statements to police concerning his address and insurance company after a minor accident, obtaining credit under an assumed name, and failing to report his place of residence to his parole officer. The report states that the officer

interviewed Morrissey, and that he could not explain why he did not contact his parole officer despite his effort to excuse this on the ground that he had been sick. Further, the report asserts that Morrissey admitted buying the car and obtaining credit under an assumed name, and also admitted being involved in the accident. The parole officer recommended that his parole be revoked because of "his continual violating of his parole rules."

**Decision:** The major problem of this case had to do with the constitutionality of parole revocation procedures. The Court was asked to decide whether the due process required that a state provide a parolee with a hearing and other safeguards before revoking parole.

**Significance of The Case:**

1. Though the Court decided that parole revocation does not call for the full array of rights due a defendant in a criminal proceeding, a parolee's liberty involves

In a survey of parole revocation procedures in January, 1973, the American Bar Association found that most parole boards were in compliance with the *Morrissey* requirements.[24] According to Newman, however, "the full operational significance of the Morrissey decision, particularly the requirement for a two-stage procedure involving an on-site factual determination prior to a formal hearing, remains to be assessed."[25]

Nonetheless, since the *Morrissey* decision, appellate courts have upheld the Supreme Court's basic requirement for fairness and impartiality in the revocation hearing process. For example, in *Drayton v. McCall*,[26] the U.S. Court of Appeals for the Second Circuit found that the due process clause mandates that certain procedural safeguards must be afforded to parolees before their community release may be rescinded. In reaffirming the *Morrissey* decision, the appellate court confirmed a parolee's right to a hearing before a detached and neutral hearing board, advance written notice of changes, and the right to call witnesses on behalf of the parolee. Moreover, the court expressed distress over the U.S. Parole Board's refusal of parolee Drayton's request for a lawyer to represent him at the hearing.

significant values within the protection of the Due Process Clause of the Fourteenth Amendment, and termination of that liberty requires an informal hearing to give assurance that the finding of a parole violation is based on verified facts to support the revocation.

2. Due process requires a reasonably prompt informal inquiry conducted by an impartial hearing officer near the place of the alleged parole violation or arrest to determine if there is reasonable ground to believe that the arrested parolee has violated a parole condition. The parolee should receive prior notice of the inquiry, its purpose, and the alleged violations. The parolee may present relevant information and question adverse informants. The hearing officer shall digest the evidence on probable cause and state the reasons for holding the parolee for the parole board's decision.

3. At the revocation hearing, which must be conducted reasonably soon after the parolee's arrest, minimum due process requirements are: (1) written notice of the claimed violations of parole; (2) a disclosure to the parolee of evidence against him; (3) the opportunity to be heard in person and

to present witnesses and documentary evidence; (4) the right to confront and cross-examine adverse witnesses (unless the hearing officer specifically finds good cause for not allowing confrontation); (5) a "neutral and detached" hearing body such as a traditional parole board, members of which need not be judicial officers or lawyers; and (6) a written statement by the factfinders as to the evidence relied on and reasons for revoking parole.

The *Morrissey* case imposed dual procedures upon state parole boards by which they were required to provide a preliminary inquiry at the time of the parolee's arrest, as well as a formal revocation hearing before termination of parole. The major issue left untouched by *Morrissey* was whether a parolee had the right to the assistance of counsel if indigent, and that was subsequently remedied in the case of *Gagnon v. Scarpelli* (see Chapter 14).

The principal effect of the *Morrissey* decision was to impose minimum procedural requirements on the parole revocation process.

Thus, the rights outlined in *Morrissey* have served as guidelines in subsequent parole-decision cases.

ABOLISH PAROLE?

Chapter 13 discussed the presumptive sentencing approach. Proponents of presumptive or "flat-time" sentencing have also called for abolition of parole. They believe that inmates should be sentenced by the trial judge to a fixed number of years, and thereafter, serve their total sentence in the prison setting. While parole would not be a release option, prisoners could in fact reduce their prison stay by amassing good time credit. Some states, for example California, have allowed inmates to eliminate four months of their sentence for every eight months served. Nonetheless, early release via a parole would cease to exist.

The criticism leveled against parole is threefold:[27]

1. The procedures which control the parole grant decision are vague and, heretofore, not controlled by due process considerations. Consequently, some in-

mates may be subject to the unfair denial of parole, while those who are undeserving may benefit.
2. It is beyond the capacity of parole authorities to either predict who will make a
successful adjustment on parole or to accurately monitor parolees' behavior in
the community.
3. It is unjust to decide whether to release an individual from prison based on what
we expect that person to do in the *future*. After all, we have no way of determining
that fact accurately.

Above and beyond these considerations, the parole process has been
criticized as heightening the inmate's sense of injustice and powerlessness
in the face of an omnipotent prison administration which has absolute
control over the release date. As prison expert David Fogel suggests:

Parole board decisions are also unreviewable and are not hammered out in an
adversary clash; rather they are five to fifteen minute sessions with members frequently using a combination of whim, caprice, and arbitrariness.[28]

As noted in Chapter 13, some states have already abolished parole
and revised their criminal codes to abolish the indeterminate sentence
which is the heart of the parole process. California has retained parole but
uses it as a one-year post-release supervisory authority for inmates who
have completed their prison sentences. Monitored by the Community Release Board, inmates can have up to six months of their good time revoked
for behavioral indiscretions and therefore be returned to prison; a similar
setup in Indiana grants parole authority the power to revoke all of the
inmates' good time credits and return them to prison.

It is likely that the abolition of parole would shift the locale of discretion
from the prison authorities to the district attorney (who charges the defendants and conducts plea bargains) and the judge (who sentences). Of
course the inmates' sense of frustration may still remain and sentencing
disparity will still occur. Moreover, critics allege that abolishing parole will
hurt prison discipline (except in states which maintain extremely liberal
good time allowances up to 50% of the prison sentence). And, of course,
this latter development almost seems an equivalent to the parole decision.
Despite these drawbacks, the anti-parole movement should continue in
the years ahead.

SUMMARY

Parole is the release of an offender into the community prior to the expiration of a prison sentence. Most state jurisdictions maintain an independent parole board whose members make the actual decisions to grant
parole. Their decision making is extremely discretionary and is based on
many factors such as the perception of the needs of society, the correctional
system, and the client.

Once paroled, the client is subject to control by parole officers who
ensure that the conditions set by the board (the parole rules) are main-

tained. These agents may also employ individual styles in their operations. For example, one may stress community protection and view parole as a law enforcement function, while another agent may believe in the social welfare aspects of parole and view the role as that of a treatment agent.

Parole can be revoked if the offender violates the rules of parole or commits a subsequent offense. In the past, revocation was purely an administrative function; however, recent Supreme Court decisions have granted procedural due process rights to offenders at parole revocation hearings, the most notable of which is the right to representation by an attorney. The effectiveness of parole has been questioned and some experts call for its abolition.

**1.** Define parole, including its purposes and objectives. How does it differ from probation?

**2.** What is the role of the parole board?

**3.** Identify the procedures involved in parole revocation. What are the rights of the parolee?

**4.** Should parole be abolished? How might this affect prison discipline?

QUESTIONS FOR DISCUSSION

NOTES

**1.** Bureau of Prisons, "Prisoners in State & Federal Institutions For Adult Felons," *National Prison Statistics Bulletin* 47:22–23, (April 1972).

**2.** William Parker, *Parole (Origins, Development, Current Practices & Statutes)* (College Park, Maryland: American Correctional Association, 1972) p. 23.

**3.** Vincent O'Leary and Joan Nuffield, *The Organization of Parole Systems in the United States* (Hackensack, New Jersey: National Council of Crime & Delinquency, 1972) p. XIV.

**4.** Ibid., p. xv.

**5.** Parker, *Parole,* p. 26.

**6.** O'Leary and Nuffield, *The Organization of Parole Systems in the United States,* p. xxiv.

**7.** Parker, *Parole,* pp. 57–188.

**8.** O'Leary and Nuffield, *The Organization of Parole Systems in the United States,* p. xxix.

**9.** 58 N.J. 238, 277; 277 A.2d 193 (1971).

**10.** Ibid. at 197, 199.

**11.** 99 S.Ct. 2100 (1979).

**12.** 427 U.S. 215 (1977).

**13.** National Parole Institutes, "Selection For Parole," *Parole Resource Book—Part II* (April 1966), p. 168.

**14.** Robert Carter, Richard McGee, and E. Kim Nelson, *Corrections in America* (Philadelphia: J. B. Lippincott Co., 1975), p. 206.

**15.** See Peter Hoffman and Lucille DeGostin, "Parole Decision-Making: Structuring Discretion," *Federal Probation* 38:19 (1974).

**16.** Peter Hoffman and Barbara Stone-Meierhoefer, "Post-Release Arrest Experiences of Federal Prisoners: A Six Year Follow-up," *Journal of Criminal Justice* 7:193–216 (1979).

**17.** Hoffman and Stone-Meierhoefer, "Post Release Arrest Experiences of Federal Prisoners: A Six Year Follow-up," p. 202.

**18.** Taken from Parker, *Parole,* p. 113; 139–141.

**19.** President's Commission on Law Enforcement and the Administration of Justice, *Corrections* (Washington, D.C.: U.S. Government Printing Office, 1974), p. 86.

**20.** L. Ohlin, H. Piven and D. Pappenport, "Major Dilemmas of The Social Worker in Probation and Parole," *National Probation and Parole Association Journal* 2:211 (July 1956).

**21.** Daniel Glaser, *The Effectiveness of a Prison & Parole System* (Indianapolis: Bobbs-Merrill Co., 1969), p. 293.

**22.** M. Hindelang, et al., *Sourcebook of Criminal Justice Statistics* (Washington, D.C.: U.S. Government Printing Office, 1974), p. 488.

**23.** 408 U.S. 471, 92 S.Ct. 2593, 33 L.Ed.2d 484 (1972).

**24.** American Bar Association, Commission on Correctional Facilities and Services, Resource Center on Correctional Law and Legal Issues, *Survey of Parole Revocation Procedures, State Parole Board Compliance with Morrissey v. Brewer* (Washington, D.C., January 1973).

**25.** Donald Newman, *Introduction to Criminal Justice* (New York: J. B. Lippincott Co., 1975), p. 353.

**26.** Drayton v. McCall, 584 F.2d 1208 (2d Cir. 1978).

**27.** Listed in Andrew Von Hirsch and Kathleen Hanrahan, *Abolish Parole?* (Washington, D.C.: U.S. Government Printing Office, 1978).

**28.** David Fogel, " . . . We are the Living Proof . . ." (Cincinnati, Ohio: Anderson Pub., 1979), p. 197.

# Parole Rules

## MARYLAND

*Conditions of Parole:*

1. Report to your Parole Agent as directed and follow his instructions.
2. Work regularly.
3. Get permission before:
   a. Changing your home
   b. Changing your job
   c. Leaving the State of Maryland
4. Obey all laws.
5. Notify your Parole Agent immediately if you are arrested.
6. You shall not illegally possess, use or sell any narcotic drug, "controlled dangerous substance," or related paraphernalia.
7. You shall not own, possess, use, sell or have under your control, any dangerous weapon or firearms of any description without approval of the Parole Board.

## NEW MEXICO

*Conditions of Parole:*

1. You are required to have the written permission of your parole officer before you may (a) leave the State of New Mexico or the county to which you have been paroled; (b) change your residence or employment; (c) possess or apply for a license to operate a motor vehicle of any kind; (d) get married; (e) file for a divorce.
2. If for any reason you lose your job, you will immediately report this fact to your parole officer. You will make every effort to obtain and hold a legitimate job and will cooperate with your parole officer in any effort he may make to obtain employment for you.
3. If you are arrested for any reason or on any charge, you will immediately report this fact to your parole officer.
4. You shall support your dependents, if any, to the best of your ability and fulfill all your moral and legal obligations toward them.
5. You shall abstain from the use and consumption of alcoholic beverages.
6. In general, you are not to associate with any person having a criminal record, or with any other person the Board or your parole officer forbids you to associate with. This condition may be modified by the Board or your parole officer for reasons of employment, participation in self-improvement programming, legitimate convenience in living arrangement, or for any other necessary reason deemed appropriate by your parole officer.

7. You shall comply with all municipal, county, State and Federal laws, ordinances, and orders, including laws and rules of Indian Tribal Councils.
8. You shall at all times conduct yourself in an honorable manner as a good member of the community. You will not endanger in any way the person, property, rights, dignity or morals of others.
9. If, in the opinion of the Parole Hearing Board, it would be detrimental to yourself or to the community for you to remain on parole, your parole may be revoked.
10. You shall not correspond, directly or indirectly with inmates of any prison, jail or other correctional institution. You shall not carry messages from inmates in such institutions to persons on the outside. However, communications with a relative in such an institution may be allowed when written permission of your parole officer is obtained in advance.
11. You are forbidden to own, possess, use, sell, distribute or have under your control any narcotic or other dangerous drug to include marijuana. Exceptions are drugs prescribed for your use by a physician, and the use of methadone under medical supervision.
12. You are forbidden to own, sell, use, distribute or have under your control firearms.
13. You shall permit your parole officer to visit you at your home and place of employment at any time.
14. You shall reply to any communication from a Parole Hearing Board member, parole officer, or any other accredited representative of the Adult Probation-Parole Division.
15. You are required to submit monthly written reports in accordance with instructions of your parole officer, and such other written or oral reports as may be required of you. You will be held accountable for the truthfulness of these reports, and any false reports submitted by you, either written or oral, to any official of the Adult Probation-Parole Division may result in revocation of your parole.
16. If, by the provisions of any municipal, county, State or Federal law, ordinance or order, you are required to register as a person convicted of a crime, you will register with the proper authority immediately upon your arrival in such locality.
17. If you are paroled to a detainer, you will immediately report the disposition of such to the Director, Adult Probation-Parole Division, P.O. Box 2006, Santa Fe, New Mexico 87501. Should you be released on bond, or the charges are dismissed, or you are placed on probation or suspended sentence, you will fully cooperate in such plans for your supervision as are arranged. Should the detainer result in imprisonment in another state, and your New Mexico sentence has not expired by the time of your release, you will fully cooperate in plans for your supervision for the balance of your New Mexico sentence. You would then follow, and be subject to, all provisions of this Certificate of Parole.
18. If transferred to another state for supervision, you will agree to abide by the parole conditions of that state as well as those of New Mexico, and to be subject to the Interstate Parole and Probation Compact.

# Prisoners' Rights

JUDICIAL
INVOLVEMENT IN
CORRECTIONS

The issue of prisoners' rights is relatively new to the study of criminal justice.* Prior to 1960, it was an accepted condition that upon conviction an individual forfeited all rights that were not expressly granted by statutory law or correctional policy.[1] As the National Advisory Commission on Criminal Justice Standards and Goals pointed out:

The belief was common that virtually anything could be done with an offender in the name of "corrections" or in some instances "punishment" short of extreme physical abuse. He was protected only by the restraint and responsibility of correctional administrators and their staff. Whatever comforts, services, or privileges the offender received were a matter of grace—in the law's view a privilege to be granted or withheld by the state. Inhumane conditions and practices were permitted to develop and continue in many systems.[2]

Such conditions existed primarily because state and federal courts were reluctant to intervene with an administrative branch of government, i.e., the prison. This judicial policy is referred to as the hands-off doctrine. Unless the circumstances of a case clearly indicated a serious breach of Eighth Amendment rights (protection against cruel and unusual punishment), the courts avoided dealing with correctional administrative matters.[3]

According to the National Advisory Commission, the courts used three basic justifications for their neglect of prison conditions:

1. They believed that correctional administration was a technical matter to be left to experts rather than to courts ill-equipped to make appropriate evaluations.[4]
2. Society as a whole was apathetic to the area of corrections and most individuals preferred not to associate or know about the offender.[5]
3. Most judges believed that prisoners' complaints involved privileges rather than rights. "(T)here was no special necessity to confront correctional practices, even when they infringed on basic notions of human rights and dignity protected for other groups by constitutional doctrine."[6]

The case of *Siegel v. Ragen* illustrates the hands-off doctrine.[7] In this case, the court stated that it was "prepared to protect state prisoners from death or serious bodily harm in the hands of prison authorities but (was) not prepared to establish itself as 'co-administrators' of state prisons along with the duly appointed state officials."[8] Therefore, the presiding justice ruled that such actions as placing an inmate in solitary confinement or transferring him to another prison were "strictly matters of internal administration and discipline."[9]

However, as the 1960s drew to a close, the hands-off doctrine underwent a process of erosion. Federal district courts began seriously consid-

---

*The authors wish to express their appreciation to Therese J. Libby for the development of this chapter.

ering prisoners' claims concerning conditions existing within the various state and federal institutions, and utilized their power to intervene on behalf of the inmate population. According to the National Advisory Commission, this change in attitude was:

[P]art of a sweeping concern for individual rights and administrative accountability which began with the civil rights movement and subsequently was reflected in areas such as student rights, public welfare, mental institutions, juvenile court systems and military justice. It was reinforced by vastly increased contact of middle-class systems and military justice. It was reinforced by vastly increased contact of middle-class groups with correctional agencies as by-products of other national problems (juvenile delinquency, drug abuse, and political and social dissent). The net result was a climate conducive to serious reexamination of the legal rights of offenders.[10]

Today, the Federal Civil Rights Act serves as the basis on which the courts have cautiously opened their doors to prisoners' rights cases. The Act states that:

Every person who, under color of any statute, ordinance, regulation, custom, or usage of any State or Territory subjects, or causes to be subjected, any citizen of the United States or other person within the jurisdiction thereof to the deprivation of any rights, privileges, or immunities secured by the Constitution and laws shall be liable to the party injured in an action at law, suit in equity or other proper proceeding for redress.

The role of the courts in monitoring conditions within correctional institutions is not clearcut, however. The cases of *Sostre v. Rockefeller* (1970)[11] and *Sostre v. McGinnis* (1971)[12] represent the conflicting opinions courts have had concerning the hands-off doctrine. For example, in *Sostre v. Rockefeller*, a lower federal court held that placing a prisoner in solitary confinement for over a year without first giving him the procedural safeguards of a written notice, an impartial hearing, a statement of reasons for the punishment, and the right to counsel was unconstitutional. However, on an appeal of this finding, a federal circuit court in *Sostre v. McGinnis* maintained that although minimum protection for prisoners was required by the Constitution, federal judges did not possess the expertise to decide what these requirements should be, and that courts could not actually tell administrators how to do their jobs.

It is evident from these cases that the courts are aware that they have a role in the granting of prisoners' rights, but that other elements of society and the criminal justice system must also be held accountable for improving prison conditions. For example, correctional personnel must be willing to cooperate with the court decisions, and legislatures must clarify prison policy by creating comprehensive up-to-date guidelines for the correctional system. And, finally, the individual citizen must be willing to accept and support the granting of rights and privileges to the offender.[13]

ACCESS TO
COURTS, LEGAL
SERVICES, AND
MATERIALS

Although lip service may be paid to prisoners' rights, they only become a reality when the inmate has access to the courts. Without the ability to seek judicial review of conditions causing discomfort or violating constitutional rights, the inmate must depend solely on the slow and often insensitive administrative mechanism of relief within the prison system. Therefore, the right of easy access to the courts gives the inmate hope (1) of appealing the present case, and (2) that human rights will be protected during incarceration within the institution.

In 1941, the Supreme Court in the case of *Ex Parte Clevs Hull* declared that access to the courts for an inmate was a basic constitutional right.[14] The Court stated that:

the state and its officers may not abridge or impair petitioner's right to apply to a federal court for a writ of habeas corpus. Whether a petition for writ of habeas corpus addressed to a federal court is properly drawn and what allegations it must contain are questions for that court alone to determine.[15]

Although *Ex parte Hull* granted inmates access to the courts, this right proved to be more theoretical than actual. It was not uncommon for prison officials to use harsh disciplinary actions against inmates seeking legal remedies through court action, and inmates planning an appeal often found that their legal documents had been confiscated. Inmates' access to the courts was also inhibited or curtailed because most prisons lacked legal services. Not only were professional legal services nonexistent, but in many situations the use of a jailhouse lawyer (an inmate possessing some legal skills who offers legal advice to other inmates) was restricted. Thus, the prisoner found it virtually impossible to seek relief through the courts.

In 1969, this problem was acknowledged and resolved to some extent by the United States Supreme Court in the case of *Johnson v. Avery*.[16] In this case, the Court held that unless the state could provide some reasonable alternative to inmates in the preparation of petitions for post-conviction relief, a jailhouse lawyer must be permitted to aid illiterate inmates in filing habeas corpus petitions.

Although the decision in *Johnson v. Avery* was limited to illiterate inmates filing habeas corpus petitions, the lower federal courts have expanded this right to include virtually all inmates with various legal problems. Furthermore, in the *Johnson* case the Court stated that the use of the jailhouse lawyer could only be restricted if prison officials provided a reasonable alternative for legal services. The Supreme Court, however, did not address the issue of what is a reasonable alternative. Here again, some lower federal courts have taken the initiative to decide the issue. The following case decisions exemplify this trend on the part of the lower courts to allow the use of jailhouse lawyers.

**1.** *Novak v. Beto*, 1971: Two attorneys in a prison housing 13,000 inmates do not provide a reasonable alternative to a jailhouse lawyer.

**2.** *Cross v. Powers*, 1971: Inmates have a right to the legal assistance of a jailhouse lawyer when filing civil rights actions against prison officials. (Not limited to habeas corpus.)

**3.** *Wlliams v. Dept. of Justice*, 1970: The use of a law school clinic in a prison may not be an adequate substitute to the jailhouse lawyer if there is undue delay in the preparation of the inmates' legal petitions.

Another right related to prisoners' access to the courts is the right to possess and have legal materials available so that appellate petitions can be properly filed. The case of *Gilmore v. Lynch* has dealt with this issue.[17] The court stated that the inmate's right of access to the courts "encompasses all the means a defendant or petitioner might require to get a fair hearing from the judiciary on all charges brought against him or grievances alleged by him."[18] The court maintained that having an adequate law library at the inmates' disposal was part of this right. Later, the Supreme Court in *Younger v. Gilmore*[19] affirmed this decision and reiterated that it was the responsibility of the prison officials to provide sufficient legal material to inform the prisoner of what is legally important and what is irrelevant. However, what constitutes an appropriate amount of legal material has been left to the lower courts to decide.

Substantive rights may be defined as those privileges which are given to an individual through constitutional or statutory law. Four major issues concerning substantive rights of prisoners are: (1) the freedom of the press, (2) the freedom of religion, (3) the freedom from cruel and unusual punishment, and (4) the right to medical treatment.

### Freedom of the Press and of Expression

The freedom of expression is a right guaranteed the individual through the First Amendment of the United States Constitution:

Congress shall make no law respecting an establishment of religion or prohibiting the free exercise thereof; or abridging the freedom of speech, or of the press; or the right of the people peaceably to assemble, and to petition the Government for redress of grievances.

At one time, conviction meant an offender became a "slave to the state" and lost virtually all rights. As a result, many early court decisions upheld the philosophy that a correctional agency which placed severe limitations on a prisoner's speech and expression was actually in order.[20] However, with the decay of the hands-off doctrine, many courts reconsidered this question, altering their position to maintain that prisoners possess the First Amendment right of freedom of speech. In fact, courts have consistently ruled that only when a compelling state interest exists can prisoners' First Amendment rights be modified; correctional authorities must justify the limiting of free speech by showing that granting it would threaten institutional security. The following list of cases related to prisoners' freedom of speech rights indicate current policy on the subject:

1. *Fortune Society v. McGinnis,* 1970: Prisoners have a right to receive a newsletter containing information about prison reform. No compelling state interest exists which could justify such a ban.

2. *Palmigiano v. Travisono,* 1970: The court stated the following guidelines concerning mail censorship: (1) outgoing mail cannot be read without a search warrant, (2) incoming mail excluding that from public officials and attorneys can be inspected for contraband, and (3) the only mail which may be read is that of persons not on the approved addressee list. This is for the purpose of detecting inflammatory writing and pornography.

3. *Jackson v. Godwin,* 1968: Under the equal protection clause of the Fourteenth Amendment nonsubversive black-oriented publication must be allowed in the prison in situations where white-oriented periodicals are permitted.

4. In re Van Geldern, (1971): Prison officials may refuse the entry of pornographic material into the prison.

Thus, federal and state courts have substantially increased the First Amendment rights of Freedom of Speech and Expression to prisoners. One result of this court policy has been to place the burden of proof on correctional administrators wishing to justify measures restraining unruly or recalcitrant inmates. Typically in order to restrain his speech, the institution must show that unless subject to restrictions, the inmate would have posed an actual threat to himself, his fellow inmates or members of the correctional staff.

### Procunier v. Martinez

One of the key components of the free speech issue is the inmates' right to send and receive communications with the outside world. In general, mail sent to and from attorneys, judges, and legislators is protected by the first amendment right to freedom of speech and privacy, ostensibly because of the trustworthiness of these individuals and the interest they have in communicating with inmates. However, inmates' general mail is often censored by prison authorities to make sure contraband neither leaves nor enters the institution. In *Procunier v. Martinez,*[21] the Supreme Court dealt with this issue when it reviewed a challenge to California's regulation for the censorship of prisoner correspondence. The regulation prohibited any material that tended to "agitate, unduly complain or magnify grievances," against the prison. The California law had allowed prison officials to censor letters they believed to be "lewd, obscene, or defamatory" or which expressed "inflammatory political, racial, religious, or other views." The provision had consequently been used by prison officials to censor outgoing mail critical of institutional life.

In deciding the case, the U.S. Supreme Court ruled that prison mail censorship is allowable only when (1) there exists substantial government interest in maintaining the censorship in order to further prison security and (2) the restrictions are not greater or more stringent than is demanded by security precautions. It would be difficult for prison officials to justify censoring an inmate's letters to his mother if he neither had any prior disciplinary problems at the institution, nor had there been any recent violent, or otherwise dangerous, incidents at the prison. However, it is likely that the issue of "substantial government interest" can easily be raised to justify a prison official's control over inmates' personal correspondence. Though it appears that federal and state courts have substantially increased the inmates' rights to freedom of speech, it is also true that locked within prison walls an inmate is at the mercy of institutional discretion. Nonetheless, as Justice Lewis Powell declared in *Procunier*:

. . . when a prison regulation or practice offends a fundamental constitutional guarantee, Federal Courts will discharge their duty to protect constitutional rights . . . [22]

### Corresponding With the Media

In addition to sending mail, an inmate can also express concerns about prison life by granting interviews to the press. In *Nolan v. Fitzpatrick*,[23] the First Circuit Court of Appeals upheld the right of prisoners to write to newspapers unless their letters discussed escape plans, or contained contraband or otherwise objectionable material. In the federal prison system, a "prisoner's mailbox" is now used to send unopened letters to the media.[24]

However, a setback to the inmates' right to contact the press was delivered in *Saxbe v. Washington Post Co.*[25] In this case the Supreme Court ruled that a federal prison rule forbidding individual press interviews with specific inmates was justified because there is no constitutional right to interview specific people. The Federal Bureau of Prisons successfully argued in *Saxbe* that individual interviews would enhance the reputation of particular inmates and jeopardize the federal prison authorities' desire to treat everyone equally.[26]

### Freedom of Religion

Freedom of Religion is a fundamental right guaranteed by the Constitution's First Amendment. The religious freedom clause has a dual purpose: it (a) protects one's rights to freely practice one's religion and (b) prohibits the government from being partial to any particular religious group. In light of these two clauses, several issues pertaining to religious freedom within the context of the correctional setting have been raised and brought to the attention of the courts. These include (1) religious discrimination, (2) right to hold religious services, (3) access to ministers, (4) the right to correspond with religious leaders, and (5) the right to wear religious medals.

It should be noted that religious freedom was the first area in which the courts lifted the hands-off doctrine. This action can be attributed to the growing influence of the Black Muslim movement within the prisons. With their strong organization and dedicated following, the Muslims were able to demand and finally achieve equality with the predominant religious groups. In this context, religious freedom in prison involved racial as well as religious issues. Causes such as these were somewhat stifled, however, when they demanded special dispensation to congregate for services, special diets, and so on. An inmate may hold any belief he or she chooses, but may be denied participation in some aspects of that religion. As the National Advisory Commission on Criminal Justice Standards and Goals suggests:

As in the general cases on freedom of religion, courts made a distinction between the prisoner's religious belief and his more qualified right to engage in specific religious practices. Beliefs are for the most part free from governmental intervention. But where these beliefs are reflected in actions more difficult questions arise.[27]

Some of the issues surrounding religious practices in prison, and brief examination of how some courts have handled cases concerning religious freedom, are found below:

1. *Gittlemacker v. Prasse*, 1970: The state is obligated to furnish an inmate with the opportunity to practice his religion but it is under no obligation to provide a clergyman.
2. *Coleman v. Dist. of Columbia Commissioners, 1964:* Because members of other religions have been given permission to wear religious medals, this right must be extended to Black Muslims.
3. Rowland v. Sigler, 1971: Since a medallion can be used as a weapon, prison authorities are justified in prohibiting the wearing of medallions.
4. *Long v. Parker*, 1968: Unless prison authorities can prove that security would be endangered, the Black Muslims' religious newsletter, "Mohammad Speaks," cannot be suppressed.
5. *Cruz v. Beto*, 1972: It would be discriminatory for a Buddhist prisoner to be denied a reasonable opportunity to pursue his faith as compared to more conventional religious practices of other inmates.[28]
6. *O'Malley v. Brierly*, 1973: Priests who make inflammatory statements do not have the right to hold services within an institution.[29]

## Cruel and Unusual Punishment and General Prison Conditions

The concept of cruel and unusual punishment is founded in the Eighth Amendment of the United States Constitution. The term itself has not to date been specifically defined by the United States Supreme Court. However, the Court has held that treatment constitutes cruel and unusual punishment when it:

1. Degrades the dignity of human beings.[30]
2. Is more severe than the offense for which it has been given.[31]
3. Shocks the general conscience and is fundamentally unfair.[32]

In the context of the prison setting, questions of whether the cruel and unusual punishment concept has been violated have been raised over such concerns as solitary confinement, corporal punishment, and general institutional conditions. For the most part, courts have upheld the use of solitary confinement and physical punishment but have placed restrictions on the conditions under which they can be employed. For example, the court in *Fulwood v. Clemmer* (1962)[33] held that confining an inmate for two years because he participated in an illegal religious service was cruel and unusual, since the punishment was more severe than the offense. On the question of physical abuse, in *Johnson v. Glick* (1973),[34] the court addressed the issue of what criteria must be present to constitute a violation of the protection against cruel and unusual punishment. It was stated that:

In determining whether the consitutional line has been crossed a court must look to such factors as the need for the application of force, the relationship between the need and the amount of force that was used, the extent of injury inflicted, and whether force was applied in a good faith effort to maintain or restore discipline or maliciously and sadistically for the very purpose of causing harm.[35]

One issue relating to cruel and unusual punishment concerns overall prison conditions. In 1970, the District Court of Arkansas in the case of *Holt v. Sarver*[36] looked closely at the Arkansas prison system and found the conditions so deplorable that they were constitutionally unacceptable. The court concluded:

For the ordinary convict a sentence to the Arkansas Penitentiary today amounts to a banishment from civilized society to a dark and evil world completely alien to the free world, a world that is administered by criminals under unwritten rules and customs completely foreign to free world culture.

After long and careful consideration the Court has come to the conclusion that the Fourteenth Amendment prohibits confinement under the conditions that have been described and that the Arkansas Penitentiary System as it exists today, particularly at Cummins, is unconstitutional.

Such confinement is inherently dangerous. A convict, however cooperative and inoffensive he may be, has no assurance whatever that he will not be killed, seriously injured, or sexually abused. Under the present system the State cannot protect him.

Apart from physical danger, confinement in the Penitentiary involves living under degrading and disgusting conditions. This Court has no patience with those who still say, even when they ought to know better, that to change those conditions will convert the prison into a country club; the Court has not heard any of those people volunteer to spend a few days and nights at either Tucker or Cummins incognito.

The peril and degradation to which Arkansas convicts are subjected daily are aggravated by the fact that the treatment which a convict may expect to receive depends not at all upon the gravity of his offense or the length of his term. In point of fact, a man sentenced to life imprisonment for first degree murder and who has a long criminal record may expect to fare better than a country boy with no serious record who is sentenced to a term of two years for stealing a pig.

It is one thing for the State to send a man to the Penitentiary as a punishment for crime. It is another thing for the State to delegate the governance of him to other convicts and to do nothing meaningful for his safety, well being, and possible rehabilitation. It is one thing for the State not to pay a convict for his labor; it is something else to subject him to a situation in which he has to sell his blood to obtain money to pay for his own safety, or for adequate food, or for access to needed medical attention.

However constitutionally tolerable the Arkansas system may have been in former years, it simply will not do today as the Twentieth Century goes into its eighth decade.

In recent years, courts have continued to view the issue of general prison living conditions and in some instances, have granted inmates the right to a basic standard of care and comfort. For example, the U.S. District Court for the Eastern District of Oklahoma decreed in 1977 that living and dormitory space in the prisons within its jurisdiction must be 60 and 75 square feet, respectively.[37] The court argued that while people are sent to prison *for punishment*, it does not mean that prison should be a *punishing experience*. In a similar vein, a federal circuit court declared in *Wolfish v. Levi*[38] that a prisoner's property must be accounted for, that inmates be given commissary privileges, that food packages from the outside be given to inmates, and that unmonitored calls be allowed for inmates.

In a recent decision, the U.S. Supreme Court seems to have reversed the trend for granting better living conditions to inmates. Though *Bell v. Wolfish*[39] involved a jailed inmate awaiting trial, the case should have important implications for state prisoners as well.

Louis Wolfish was incarcerated in the new Federal Metropolitan Correctional Center (MCC) in New York. This unit was designed to provide inmates with more privacy and better conditions than older jails. Though its 389 rooms were for single occupants only, the rising crime rate quickly filled the institution to overcapacity. As a result, many of the private rooms were converted to house two inmates ("double-bunking"); some inmates were forced to sleep on cots in public areas. Inmates were also prohibited from receiving packages from friends and relatives (with the exception of Christmas), were allowed reading material only if sent directly from the publisher (thereby limiting the availability of reading material), and were subject to humiliating "strip" searches after every visitation. Inmate Wolfish filed a habeas corpus petition seeking his release because of these conditions, and the suit was quickly turned into a class action on behalf of all pre-trial detainees in the jail.

After initial success for the plaintiffs in the lower courts, the U.S. Supreme Court accepted the case on appeal. They found when assessing the practices used in the jail, that "absent a showing of expressed intent to punish on the part of detention facility officials, that determination will turn on 'whether an alternative purpose . . . may rationally be (responsible for it).' "[40] In other words, if there is a legitimate purpose for the use of government restrictions, they may be considered constitutional.[41] In the present case, double-bunking was deemed an acceptable practice since it was not meant as a punishment; similarly, the restriction on reading material was upheld due to the availability of other sources of printed matter (e.g., the prison library). Moreover, the Supreme Court upheld "strip" searches and the restriction on receiving outside packages as legitimate security measures.

While *Wolfish* applies to jailed inmates awaiting trial, it may certainly affect state prisoners also, the rule of thumb being: prison conditions may be harsh as long as they are justified by expedience and security, and not motivated by punishment.

## Medical Rights

State and federal courts have usually been reluctant to take action on cases involving the medical rights of prisoners. The hands-off doctrine was almost always practiced in medical cases, probably because the courts would have had to contend with medical expertise as well as correctional experience in making their decisions.

Prior to the 1970s, the courts maintained their distance in medical rights cases through the creation of the exceptional circumstances doctrine. Using this policy, the courts would hear only those cases in which the circumstances totally disregarded human dignity, while denying hearings to other less serious cases. The cases which were allowed access to the courts usually represented a situation of total denial of medical care. The case of *Coleman v. Johnston* exemplified this trend.[42] Coleman had received bullet wounds in his leg prior to arrest and was thereafter denied treatment. As a result, the leg required amputation; on appeal, the court ruled that the inmate's complaint against the prison authorities was valid and that he was entitled to relief.

In the 1970s, the courts began to deal with the issue of what constitutes proper medical treatment for prisoners. The case of *Campbell v. Beto* exemplifies the courts' efforts in this area.[43] A prisoner with a heart condition was assigned to manual labor, thereby endangering his life; it was held that this action constituted gross negligence on the part of prison officials. The court further stated:

It is apparent that courts cannot close their judicial eyes to prison conditions which present a grave and immediate threat to the health or physical well being (of prisoners) . . . Practices which result in the deprivation of basic elements of adequate medical treatment . . . would be equally vulnerable.[44]

Moreover, the courts have begun to deal with the issue of balancing medical expertise with administrative experience and needs in deciding medical cases. The cases of *Tolbert v. Eyman* (1970)[45] and *Sawyer v. Sigler* (1970)[46] are two such examples. In the *Tolbert* case, the inmate prior to imprisonment was diagnosed as having diabetes complicated by a rare condition and was receiving effective medication. After imprisonment, treatment was discontinued despite a confirmed diagnosis by the prison doctor. This doctor indicated, however, that he would permit the inmate to receive the medication if he paid for it himself. Tolbert arranged for its arrival, but the correctional authorities refused to allow the medication into the prison for security reasons. As a result, the inmate alleged that he was nearly blind and that his legs and feet were continually swollen. Upon appeal, the court declared:

failure or refusal to provide medical care, or treatment so cursory as to amount to no treatment at all, may in the case of serious medical problems, violate the Fourteenth Amendment.

Appellee has attempted, as did the district court, to characterize Tolbert's allegations as showing only a difference of opinion between physician and patient over the proper diagnosis and treatment. Such allegations would not state a claim. However, this argument misses the thrust of Tolbert's complaint, which names as defendant not the doctors, but the warden. The argument of his claim is not that he was erroneously diagnosed by the prison doctor, but that the warden refused to allow him authorized medicine that he needed to prevent serious harm to his health. These allegations state a perfectly viable claim against the appellee.[47]

In *Sawyer v. Sigler*, the inmate was forced to take his medication in crushed pill form, causing him to become nauseous. The prison officials justified this action by claiming a legitimate compelling interest of the "prevention of abuse of drugs." The court hearing this case indicated that this form of administering medication was contrary to medical orders and the result of nausea was "sufficiently unusual, exceptional and arbitrary to constitute both cruel and inhuman punishment and is a denial of adequate medical treatment required by the Eighth and Fourteenth Amendments."[48] These two cases—*Tolbert v. Eyman* and *Sawyer v. Sigler*—are important because prior to them the distinction between the needs of medical personnel and correctional officials had never been clearly articulated.

To gain their medical rights today, prisoners have generally resorted to class actions (i.e., suits brought on the behalf of all individuals governed by similar circumstances, in this case poor medical attention). In one such case, *Newman v. Alabama* (1972),[49] the entire Alabama prison system's medical facilities were declared inadequate. The Court cited the following factors as contributing to inadequate care: insufficient physician and nurse resources; reliance on untrained inmates for paramedical work; intentional failure in treating the sick and injured; and failure to conform to proper medical standards.

In 1976, after reviewing the legal principles established over the last 20 years in cases such as *Newman v. Alabama*, the Supreme Court in *Estelle v. Gamble* clearly stated the inmate's right to have medical care:

(The) principles (behind the guarantee against cruel and unusual punishment) establish the government's obligation to provide medical care for those whom it is punishing by incarceration. An inmate must rely on prison authorities to treat his medical needs; if the authorities fail to do so, those needs will not be met.[50]

Gamble had hurt his back in a Texas prison and filed suit because he contested the type of treatment he received, and also questioned the lack of interest prison guards had shown in his case. Though the Supreme Court referred Gamble's case to a lower court to determine whether he had actually been treated in a negligent fashion, they laid down the following standard for judging future complaints:

deliberate indifference to serious medical needs of prisoners constitutes the "unnecessary and wanton infliction of pain," . . . proscribed by the Eighth Amendment. This is true whether the indifference is manifested by prison doctors in their response to the prisoner's needs or by prison guards in intentionally denying or delaying access to medical care or intentionally interfering with the treatment once prescribed.[51]

Lower courts will now decide, on a case-by-case basis, whether "deliberate indifference" actually occurred.

An inmate who breaks prison rules is subject to disciplinary measures within the institution. Discipline can range from minor penalties, such as removing television privileges, to such serious measures as the taking away of good time, solitary confinement, and transfer (see Chapter 17).

**PROCEDURAL RIGHTS OF PRISONERS**

For many years, disciplinary actions were purely administrative functions, controlled solely by the warden and other correctional personnel. Recently, however, the courts have entered into this aspect of prison life and have guaranteed to inmates certain procedural rights. This means that inmates have legal guarantees to due process and fair treatment when they are involved in any hearing or proceeding within the institution which can result in loss of liberty or privileges.

The courts used as justification for their entry into prison procedure the case of *Goldberg v. Kelley*.[52] Although this was a welfare case, it guaranteed to all citizens due process of law when the possibility existed that they might be condemned by state officials to suffer a grievous loss. The procedural rights granted inmates have varied from case to case and jurisdiction to jurisdiction; the following is a partial list of some of the principal rights.[53]

1. [The right to] notice of the nature of the complaint.
2. [The right to] a fair hearing before an impartial official or panel.
3. [The right to an] administrative review of the decision.
4. [The right to] confront witnesses.
5. [The] right to counsel or counsel substitute.

In some cases, prisoners have been granted rights in excess of these; in others, the courts have taken a more restricted view.[54]

In 1974, the Supreme Court in the case of *Wolff v. McDonnell* established the precise constitutional safeguards required at a disciplinary proceeding.[55]

At the present time, it appears that the courts are willing to hear ever-increasing numbers of cases involving prisoners' rights. The conditions under which individuals are being confined in prisons, mental health facilities, and institutions for the retarded are being challenged by the courts. One result of this trend has been a greater awareness on the part of administrators of the individual rights of confined persons. Another significant effect has been the development of guidelines by which correctional and institutional personnel can determine the constitutionality of their practices. Most important, however, is that through Court decisions such as

## WOLFF V. McDONNELL

**Facts:** In July of 1970, Robert McDonnell, on behalf of himself and other inmates of the Nebraska Penal and Correctional Complex in Lincoln, Nebraska, filed a complaint in the form of a civil rights action under 42 U.S.C. § 1983 challenging as unconstitutional several of the practices in effect at the complex. The regulations in question were that disciplinary proceedings did not comply with the due process clause of the federal Constitution; that the inmate legal assistance program did not meet constitutional standards; and that the regulations governing the inspection of inmates' mail to and from attorneys were unconstitutionally restrictive.

The United States Supreme Court granted the petition for writ of certiorari because the case involved important issues dealing with the management of a state prison.

Relief was requested by McDonnell in terms of the restoration of good time credits, the development of a plan by the prison for a hearing procedure in connection with good time, and damages for the deprivation of civil rights.

**Decision:** In a six to three decision, the Supreme Court held that the Due Process Clause of the Fourteenth Amendment provides inmates procedural protections if they are facing a loss of good time or confinement

because of an institutional disciplinary action. The court ruled that a prisoner is not completely stripped of constitutional safeguards in prison. Even though prison disciplinary proceedings do not suggest the full range of rights due a defendant in a criminal trial, such proceedings must be governed by an accommodation between prison needs and constitutional rights. Since prisoners under Nebraska law can only lose good time credits if they are guilty of serious misconduct, the procedure for determining if this occurs requires due process of law.

In accommodating the interests of the state of Nebraska with those of the inmate, the Court concluded the following with respect to what due process requires in prison disciplinary proceedings for serious violations of conduct:

1. Advance written notice of the charges must be given to the inmate no less than 24 hours before the prisoner's appearance at the disciplinary committee hearing.
2. There must be a written statement by the fact-finders as to the evidence relied upon and the reasons for the disciplinary action.
3. The inmate should be allowed to call witnesses and present documentary evidence as defense if this will not jeopardize institutional control.

*Wolff v. McDonnell* the courts have assumed responsibility for changing the American correctional system.

### Informal Complaint Mechanisms: Grievance Committees & Unions

In addition to formal complaints about prison conditions vis-à-vis law suits, prisoners today are often allowed the privilege of going before a grievance board which listens to complaints about written or unwritten policy regulations.

In 1973, the National Advisory Commission on Criminal Justice Standards and Goals observed:

4. The inmate has no constitutional right to confrontation and cross-examination in prison discipline proceedings.

5. Inmates have no right to retained or appointed counsel, although substitute counsel, such as a staff member or another inmate, may be provided in certain cases.

6. The record in this case did not show if the Adjustment Committee in the Nebraska Complex was impartial, but the inmate has the right to have an impartial group conduct disciplinary hearings.

7. In regard to regulations governing inmate mail, the Court held that the state may require that mail from an attorney to a prisoner be identified as such and that the attorney's name and address appear on the communication. In addition, as a protection against contraband, prison authorities may open mails in the inmate's presence.

In its decision, the Supreme Court rejected the state of Nebraska's assertion that disciplinary action against inmates is a matter of policy which raises no constitutional issues. At the same time, the Court could not adopt the prisoner's view that the full range of due process procedures should apply to disciplinary actions within an institutional setting. Instead, the Court addressed itself to the range of procedures applicable to a correctional institution.

**Significance of the Case:** Although the Court was faced with three major issues in this case (the adequacy of legal assistance, the confidentiality of the mail, and the loss of good time or confinement for prison infractions), primary emphasis was placed on the issue of procedural due process for prison misconduct. The *Wolff* case reaffirmed the Court's position that the hands-off doctrine of nonjudicial intervention in correctional matters no longer exists. In addition, it represented a major breakthrough in the establishment of due process guidelines in prison discipline proceedings which will affect the practices of state and federal prison systems. On the other hand, the Court recognized the violent nature of the prison setting, and did not want to restrict the ability of correctional administrators to insure the safety of their prisons. Thus, the Court sought a formula which maintained both prison security and provided constitutional safeguards. As a result, disciplinary action against an inmate for a serious infraction resulting in loss of good time credits or confinement must be accompanied by due process of law.

A formal procedure to insure that offender's grievances are fairly resolved should alleviate much of the existing tension within institutions . . . Peaceful avenues for redress of grievances are a prerequisite if violent means are to be avoided. Thus, all correctional agencies have not only a responsibility but an institutional interest in maintaining procedures that are, and appear to offenders to be, designed to resolve their complaints fairly.[56]

In many prisons, inmates grievance committees have been set up to review accusations against guards, other inmates and general prison living conditions. In some states, the committee is formed from a group of professionals, prison administration, and other interested parties, of which some are fellow inmates. For example, the New York Correctional law which established three-person committees on each penal institution mandates that at least one of them should be an inmate. Similarly, California's Ward Grievance Procedure, discussed in the applications section of this chapter, has been successful in melding inmate participation with an outside review of decisions, to provide an inmate with a sense of fair play without the necessity of court intervention.

It is believed that grievance procedures can put a damper on prison violence, as the American Correctional Association suggests.

The riots result, we believe, not from bad prison conditions or practices but from the belief of prison inmates that the only way in which they can gain public interest in improving such conditions is by rioting. Non-violent protests or requests for remedial action, prisoners believe, never accomplish anything. Riots sometimes do.[57]

While grievance mechanisms may not eliminate violence, they certainly may help to control it.

Informal grievance procedures were handed a judicial setback in the 1977 case *Jones v. North Carolina Prisoners Labor Union*.[58] The inmate union had attracted 2,000 members in four prisons throughout North Carolina. The Department of Corrections, concerned about the power of the union, passed regulations seriously curtailing the inmate organization's ability to function. The union leaders sued, stressing that other agencies, such as Alcoholics Anonymous and the Jaycees, had been given rights denied to them. The Supreme Court, however, failed to see the reasonableness of the inmates' charge. Since prison security was at stake, the court upheld the administration's right to control an organization dedicated to lobbying for prisoners' rights.

Keeping in mind recent cases such as *Jones, Bell v. Wolfish, Meachum v. Fano*, and *Greenholtz v.Inmates of Nebraska Penal Complex* (the latter two cases, discussed in the previous chapter on parole, deal with limitations set on prisoners' due process rights at transfer hearings and parole grant hearings), it appears that a trend has been set in motion to limit the rights of prisoners. The legal rules of thumb appear to be (1) prisoners have a right to personal freedom as long as they cannot be construed as interfering with prison security; and (2) prisoners have procedural rights when something is to be taken *from* them that they already have, but relatively few legal rights when they are denied special privileges that other inmates may have obtained, for example, parole or good time.

An offender loses many civil rights upon conviction, and in many states these rights are not restored even after release. The National Advisory Commission comments on this situation:

*THE LOSS OF RIGHTS OF CONVICTED OFFENDERS*

The vision of an offender leaving a correctional institution, his debt to society paid and rejoining his community, and building a new life is a false image. In many ways, the punishment an ex-convict faces is more lasting, more insidious, and more demeaning than that punishment he undergoes while incarcerated. The scar of the "offender" label can be more vicious than the physical scars sometimes inflicted in confinement.[59]

The degree to which these rights are lost varies from state to state and depends mainly on the statutory provisions, administrative rulings, and judicial decisions of a particular jurisdiction.[60] A list of rights which are now or were once lost to the convicted offender and a brief explanation of some of the most important ones are:[61]

1. **The Right to Vote:** This right has been denied on compelling state interests grounds. It was believed that the purity of the voting process must be protected against immoral and dishonest elements of society. This thinking, however, has changed in most states and today the restrictions on voting rights have been eliminated.
2. **The Right to Hold Public Office:** The denial of this right is based on the philosophy that the public must be protected.
3. **The Right to Employment:** This restriction is gradually being lifted in both private and public sectors. It is a generally held belief now that the offense must be directly related to a job in order for employment to be denied.
4. **The Right to an Occupational License:** More than 1,500 different licenses contain the requirement of "good moral character" which according to many licensing boards automatically bars ex-convicts from those fields.
5. **The Right to Serve on a Jury:** Most States maintain that the "good character" qualification excludes a convicted offender from jury duty.
6. **Right to be a Witness:** In most cases a convicted individual can serve as a witness, however, his criminal record can be used to discredit his testimony.
7. **Right to Life and Automobile Insurance:** The obtaining of insurance is often impaired if not made impossible by a criminal record.
8. **Right to Remain Married:** In a majority of states conviction is grounds for divorce.
9. **The Right to Marry and Adopt Children:** In most jurisdictions a record disqualifies an individual from adopting children; in a few states it prohibits one from marrying.
10. **All Civil Rights:** The loss of rights listed above. The individual is technically "civilly dead".

From the above list, it is evident that criminal conviction can negatively affect all aspects of an individual's life. These liabilities greatly inhibit an offender's reintegration into society. The National Advisory Commission comments that:

Some outright employment restrictions force releasees into the least remunerative jobs. Prohibiting contracts makes property holdings impossible. Being unable to vote or hold office only further aggravates the individual's alienation and isolation.[62]

In an attempt to alleviate the problems pertaining to the rights of convicted offenders, the National Advisory Commission has made the following recommendations:[63]

Retention and Restoration of Rights: Each state should enact legislation immediately to assure that no person is deprived of any license, permit, employment, office, post of trust or confidence, or political or judicial rights based solely on an accusation of criminal behavior. Also, in the implementation of Standard 16.17, Collateral Consequences of a Criminal Conviction, legislation depriving convicted persons of civil rights should be repealed. This legislation should provide further that a convicted and incarcerated person should have restored to him on release all rights not otherwise retained.

The appropriate correctional authority should:

1. With the permission of an accused person, explain to employers, families, and others the limited meaning of an arrest as it relates to the above rights.
2. Work for the repeal of all laws and regulations depriving accused or convicted persons of civil rights.
3. Provide services to accused or convicted persons to help them retain or exercise their civil rights or to obtain restoration of their rights or any other limiting civil disability that may occur.

SUMMARY

In years past, society paid little attention to the incarcerated offender. The majority of inmates confined in jails and prisons were basically deprived of the rights guaranteed them under the United States Constitution. Today, however, the judicial system is actively involved in the administration of correctional institutions. Inmates can now take their grievances to courts and seek due process and equal protection under the law. The hands-off doctrine of nonintervention by the judiciary in correctional matters no longer exists.

The courts have recognized that persons confined in correctional institutions have rights—which include access to the courts and legal counsel, the exercise of religion, the rights to correspondence and visitation, the right to adequate medical treatment, and the right to procedural due process in such areas as prison discipline, punitive isolation, and prison transfers. Administrators of correctional facilities can now make arbitrary decisions in dealing with inmates, but must recognize their basic constitutional rights. The *Wolff v. McDonald* case represents the application of procedural protections to prison discipline.

While prisoners have made advances, a number of recent cases have upheld the right of prison authorities to limit inmates' rights if they hold a justifiable belief that prison security may be breached. The policy has allowed officials to control inmate mail, visitation, and living conditions. Furthermore, courts have upheld the right of prisoners to maintain already existing conditions, but have limited their right to achieve what may be considered "privileges," for example, better living conditions.

When an offender leaves prison, the consequences of incarceration remain. The ex-offender is ordinarily subject to a variety of civil disabilities, including the loss of the right to vote, restrictive employment practices, and the inability to hold public office. Many jurisdictions today interested in a total rehabilitation program are eliminating such civil disabilities and treating ex-offenders as full fledged citizens.

**QUESTIONS FOR DISCUSSION**

1. What is meant by a hands-off policy of judicial intervention in corrections? Does it still exist? Why is the correctional field under judicial attack today?

2. Discuss the legal rights of prisoners. What nonjudicial remedies are available for the enforcement of prisoners' rights?

3. Should prisoners have unions? Should they be able to go on strike?

4. Do prisoners' rights help with their rehabilitation? Contrast prisoner rights with student rights.

**NOTES**

1. National Advisory Commission on Criminal Justice Standards and Goals, *Corrections* (Washington, D.C.: U.S. Government Printing Office, 1973), p. 18. The information in the following sections is derived from a number of sources, with special emphasis on Hazel Kerper and Janeen Kerper, *Legal Rights of the Convicted* (St. Paul, Minn.: West Publishing Co., 1974); Sheldon Krantz, *The Law of Corrections and Prisoners' Rights* (St. Paul, Minn.: West Publishing Co., 1973); John W. Palmer, *Constitutional Rights of Prisoners* (Cincinnati: The W. H. Anderson Co., 1973).

2. Ibid.

3. Hazel Kerper and Janeen Kerper, *Legal Rights of the Convicted*, p. 278.

4. National Advisory Commission, *Corrections*, p. 18.

5. Ibid.

6. Ibid.

7. 88 F.Supp. 996 (N.D.Ill.1949).

8. Ibid. at 999.

9. Ibid.

10. National Advisory Commission, *Corrections*, p. 18.

11. 312 F.Supp. 178 (S.D.N.Y.1970).

12. 442 F.2d 178 (2d Cir. 1971).

13. See National Advisory Commission, *Corrections*, pp. 20–21.

14. 312 U.S. 546, 61 S.Ct. 640, 85 L.Ed. 1034 (1941).

15. Ibid. at 549.

16. 393 U.S. 483, 89 S.Ct. 747, 21 L.Ed.2d 718 (1969).

17. 319 F.Supp. 105 (N.D.Cal.1970).

**18.** Ibid. at 110.

**19.** 404 U.S. 15, 92 S.Ct. 250, 30 L.Ed.2d 142 (1971).

**20.** National Advisory Commission, *Corrections*, p. 59.

**21.** Procunier v. Martinez 411 U.S. 396 (1974).

**22.** 40 L.Ed.2d 236.

**23.** 451 F.2d 545 (1st Cir. 1971).

**24.** Washington Post Co. v. Kleindienst, 494 F.2d 997 (D.C. Cir. 1974).

**25.** 41 L.Ed.2d 514 (1974).

**26.** Discussed in David Fogel, ". . . We are the Living Proof . . .", 2d ed. (Cincinnati, Ohio: Anderson, 1980), p. 150.

**27.** National Advisory Commission, *Corrections*, p. 64.

**28.** 92 S.Ct. 1079; 405 U.S. 319 (1972).

**29.** 477 F.2d 785 (3d Cir. 1973).

**30.** See, for example, Trop v. Dulles, 356 U.S. 86, 78 S.Ct. 590, 2d 630 (1958); see also Furman v. Georgia, 408 U.S. 238, 92 S.Ct. 2726, 33 L.Ed.2d 346 (1972).

**31.** See, for example, Weems v. United States, 217 U.S. 349, 30 S.Ct. 544, 54 L.Ed. 793 (1910).

**32.** See, for example, Lee V. Tahash, 352 F.2d 970 (8th Cir. 1965).

**33.** 206 F.Supp. 370 (D.C. Cir. 1962).

**34.** 481 F.2d 1028 (2d Cir. 1973).

**35.** Ibid. at 1033.

**36.** 309 F.Supp. 362 (E.D.Ark.1970); aff'd 442 F.2d 304 (8th Cir. 1971).

**37.** Battle v. Anderson, 447 F.Supp. 576 (1977).

**38.** Wolfish v. Levi, 573 F.2d 118.

**39.** 99 S.Ct. 1861 (1979).

**40.** Bell v. Wolfish, 99 S.Ct. 1873–1874 (1979).

**41.** See Case Comment, "Bell v. Wolfish: The Rights of Pre-Trial Detainees." *New England Journal on Prison Law* 6:134 (1979).

**42.** 247 F.2d 273 (7th Cir. 1957).

**43.** 460 F.2d 765 (5th Cir. 1972).

**44.** Ibid. at 768.

**45.** 434 F.2d 625 (9th Cir. 1970).

**46.** 320 F.Supp. 690 (D.Neb.1970).

**47.** *Tolbert,* 434 F.2d at 626.

**48.** *Sawyer,* 320 F.Supp. at 694.

**49.** 349 F.Supp. 278 (M.D.Ala.1972).

**50.** Estelle v. Gamble, 429 U.S. 97 (1976).

**51.** 97 S.Ct. 291 (1976).

**52.** 397 U.S. 254, 90 S.Ct. 1011, 25 L.Ed.2d 287 (1970).

**53.** John W. Palmer, *Constitutional Rights of Prisoners,* pp. 101–102.

**54.** Ibid.

**55.** 418 U.S. 539, 94 S.Ct. 2963, 41 L.Ed.2d 935 (1974).

**56.** National Advisory Commission on Criminal Justice Standards and Goals, *Volume on Corrections,* (Washington, D.C.: U.S. Government Printing Office, 1973), p. 57.

**57.** American Correctional Association, *Riots and Disturbances in Correctional Institutions,* (Washington, D.C., 1970), p. 66.

**58.** Jones v. North Carolina Prison's Labor Union 97 S.Ct. 2532 (1977).

**59.** National Advisory Commission, *Corrections,* p. 47.

**60.** George Killinger, Hazel Kerper and Paul Cromwell Jr., *Probation and Parole in the Criminal Justice System* (St. Paul,

Minn.: West Publishing Co., 1976), p. 125.

**61.** The following list has been adapted from George Killinger, Hazel Kerper and Paul Cromwell Jr., *Probation and Parole in the Criminal Justice System*, pp. 126–144.

**62.** National Advisory Commission, *Corrections*, p. 47.

**63.** National Advisory Commission, *Corrections*, Standard 2.10, p. 46.

# California Program Listens To Inmate Complaints*

The independent arbitrator's decision in Daniel P.'s request that he be allowed to wear long hair and a beard while a ward of the California Youth Authority was clear:

"To deny the right to wear beards appears to be inconsistent with the spirit, the procedures and the results of the school's behavior and treatment program."

So Daniel P. won his grievance, and 30 days later youths throughout the system were given the same rights.

In this and thousands of similar matters, California has provided young inmates a way to resolve conflicts ranging from personal hygiene to constitutional rights through a unique grievance procedure.

LEAA has designated the procedure as an Exemplary Project and has supported the publication of a manual to assist corrections officials in other states to develop better ways to resolve inmate complaints.

The Exemplary Projects Program is a systematic method of identifying outstanding criminal justice programs throughout the country, verifying their achievements, and publicizing them widely. The goal is to encourage widespread use of advanced criminal justice practices.

Establishing good adminstrative procedures for settling inmate grievances is one of the most important things a correctional system can do, according to LEAA officials.

The California Youth Authority procedures are based on the arbitration and mediation techniques commonly found in labor relations. One of their most important elements is a provision for an independent and unbiased review of cases about which the two sides cannot agree.

The American Arbitration Association appoints voluntary arbitrators who chair the review panels that decide unresolved conflicts. Although the arbitration panels can only advise, their actions carry important weight.

Another critical component is the joint participation of institution staff members and wards in settling all grievances. Dispute resolutions are negotiated between both sides rather than imposed.

The grievance mechanism has worked so

---

*From LEAA Newsletter, Vol. 6, No. 7, Feb. 1977.

well that Gov. Edmund G. Brown, Jr., signed the authority's procedures, including outside arbitration, into law.

The grievance procedures are even more applicable to adult institutions, said John C. Holland, the Youth Authority Ward Rights Specialist who helped develop them, because their inmates are more mature, and the longer the inmates are incarcerated the more effective is their participation.

Prisons with good ways of handling conflicts between the authorities and their wards have low potentials for violence, in the opinion of many authorities.

However, these authorities caution that conflict resolution must be effective and must, therefore, include some type of neutral arbitration.

"It takes very close monitoring to assure that the procedural requirements are met," Mr. Holland observed. "It takes an ongoing and systemwide commitment and requires constant training for wards and staff members."

The California Youth Authority's carefully drawn grievance procedure guidelines specify that there are to be no reprisals whatsoever for wards who file grievances. What protects the ward—and wins his or her support—is the formality of the process. The procedure admits no arbitrary acts. All decisions, regardless of level, must be put in writing and must include the reasons for any denials. And if the decision prescribes taking a specific remedial action, the written response must set a deadline for it to be done.

More than 7,100 grievances were filed in California between September 1973 and last February. Less than one percent had to go to arbitration. The rest were resolved through in-house negotiations or through an appeal to a higher authority.

About 40 percent of the youth authority grievance dispositions upheld the inmate in that period. An additional 20 percent upheld the inmate in part through some sort of compromise.

Jim B., who is a California ward serving a three-year term for a second-degree murder conviction, said most grievances are about prison food, health care, recreation, and clothing. Jim, who has been elected his unit's grievance clerk, added that "if you have a good grievance, it can go all the way."

# PART SEVEN

## The Nature
## and History
## of the Juvenile
## Justice Process

# The Juvenile Justice System

CHAPTER OUTLINE

KEY TERMS

Parens patriae
Juvenile Law
In re Gault
Transfer proceeding
Family Court
Right to Treatment
Nelson v. Heyne
Reform School
Children's Aid Society
Juvenile delinquency
McKeiver v. Pennsylvania
Juvenile Court

Disposition
Due process
Just Desserts
Kent v. U. S.
PINS
People v. Overton
Breed v. Jones
Adjudication
Rehabilitation
Intake
Diversion

OPPOSING
VIEWS ON
JUVENILE
JUSTICE

Independent yet interrelated with the adult criminal justice system, the juvenile justice system is primarily responsible for dealing with juvenile and youth crime, as well as with incorrigible and truant children and runaways. When the juvenile court was originally conceived at the turn of the century, its philosophy was based on the idea of *parens patriae*: the state was to act on behalf of the parent in the interests of the child. In the 1960s, however, the theme changed when the United States Supreme Court began insuring juveniles that they would be granted legal rights.

Today, the nation's juvenile justice system is in the midst of reexamining its fundamental operations and institutions. Although seven decades have passed since the first independent juvenile court was established, a comprehensive and comprehensible statement of its goals and purposes has yet to be developed. On the one hand, reformers reflecting the social welfare origins of the juvenile justice system continue to argue that the juvenile court is primarily a treatment agency which dispenses personalized, individual justice to needy children who seek the guidance and understanding of the court as a wise parent. On the other hand, those with law enforcement orientations suggest that the juvenile court's parens patriae philosophy has neglected the victims of delinquency, and that serious offenders should be punished and disciplined rather than treated and rehabilitated. A third philosophical approach to juvenile justice views court processing as having a potentially adverse effect on children, who are denied the constitutional rights afforded adult offenders. Advocates of this position believe that juvenile courts should dispense impartial justice and increase the due process rights of children who, depending on the outcomes of their trials, may be subjected to extended periods of confinement. Ideologically, persons supportive of each of these positions appear unwilling to yield to the others. Those arguing for the increase of due process rights for juveniles maintain that the substantive intent of the law implies a mandate based on duty and morality, and that the full protection of the constitution should be applied to any person who comes before its tribunals at any time. To do otherwise, they contend, would be to abrogate the equality of the law. Conflict over the proper role of the juvenile courts, and the suspected negative impact of the stigma and delinquency labeling following a juvenile court appearance, has also led some critics to advocate the total abolition of the juvenile court in favor of diversionary modes of justice.

These differing perspectives on juvenile court policy were reflected in the United States Supreme Court's reluctance to enter forcefully into the juvenile sphere until well into the 1960s. Since then, both the Warren and the Burger courts have taken a due process approach to juvenile law. Today, juveniles are accorded many due process rights similar to those of adult offenders. The United States Supreme Court has given juveniles the right to a hearing, the right to counsel, the right to cross-examination, and numerous other procedural protections.

Juvenile delinquency as it is known today did not exist in the early colonial days.* The Puritan settlers considered the young an important and vital part of the labor force. Most of their children worked by the age of 12, and many at an even younger age. Puritan children also were apprenticed and indentured, because their parents believed that it was healthy for a child to work outside the home.

The Virginia Company valued child labor and in 1619 sought to import children from London, which seized the opportunity as a way to rid its city streets, jails, and poor houses of vagrants, paupers, petty thieves, and unwanted orphans.

An English act of 1620 permitted the deportation of children with or without the child's approval, and it led to the abduction of children from every part of London. Upon arrival in the New World the children were apprenticed until they reached 21 years of age, at which age they were freed and given public land with cattle and corn. Mistreatment by masters and no guarantees that they would comply with their agreements once the children reached the end of their service were common problems.

Punishable offenses for youths in colonial days were running away from masters, incorrigibility, lying, swearing, fighting, stealing, and cheating—offenses for the most part not punishable if committed by adults.

Until the Revolution, Americans lived under English common law, which held a child accountable for its acts after the seventh birthday. Prior to that age a child was considered incapable of possessing the ability to understand the nature of criminal behavior. Judges determined culpability of children between the ages of seven and fourteen years. But the maximum sentence—death by hanging—was the same as for the adult.

Capital punishment was common for children in seventeenth-century England, where there were 33 offenses for which the sentence applied. In America it was less likely to be imposed. Instead, corporal punishment or incarceration was often used, although one eight-year old was convicted and hanged for burning a barn with "malice, revenge, craft and cunning." From the seventeenth century to the early part of the eighteenth century children were sentenced to public whippings and to long-term prison sentences. Prisons in those days held a conglomeration of men, women, and children under the same roof. Physical conditions were inhumane.

A 1748 English case typifies the thinking of that time. William York, a boy of ten, allegedly stabbed a little girl. She died and he buried her. At trial "there arose a fierce argument. . . . Could a child of that age form a criminal intention? Did he know what he was doing? If so, did he realize it was wrong?" The boy was found guilty and sentenced to death, but the judge intervened. William served a nine-year prison term and was released when he agreed to join the navy.

More humane treatment attended the beginning of the nineteenth century. The Society for the Prevention of Pauperism of New York City was established in 1817. It was one of the first groups to call attention to "those unfortunate children from 10 to 18 years of age, who from neglect of parents, from idleness and misfortune have

HISTORY OF
JUVENILE
JUSTICE SYSTEM

---

*From Law Enforcement Assistance Administration, "Juvenile Justice and Delinquency Prevention", *Two Hundred Years of American Criminal Justice, An LEAA Bicentennial Study,* (Washington, D.C.: U.S. Dept. of Justice, 1976) pp. 62–74.

. . . contravened some penal statute without reflecting on the consequences, and for hasty violations, been doomed to the penitentiary by the condemnation of the law."

The House of Refuge opened its doors in 1825 in New York City. It was one of the earliest institutional facilities for children and was funded by private donations. It admitted two types of children—those convicted of a crime and sentenced to incarceration and those who were not convicted but were destitute or neglected and who were in imminent danger of becoming delinquent.

That was the first time that children and adults were jailed separately. Superintendent Joseph Curtis designed a system of rewards and deprivations. Discipline was imposed and infractions put to a trial by a jury composed of peers, and Curtis as the judge. Whipping, solitary confinement, reduction in food supply, and the silent treatment were not uncommon. Children were placed in irons for serious offenses.

The boys made goods to be sold. The girls did domestic work and all earnings were returned to the house for upkeep. Children could be apprenticed and released in the custody of masters. All inmates were subject to recall if further character building was deemed necessary.

The house was given the right to act as a parent for neglected or criminal children. Although parents objected, they usually were unsuccessful in gaining the release of their children. Houses of refuge also were established in Boston and Philadelphia. The Boston House of Reformation was state supported. Corporal punishment was prohibited. In the privately funded Philadelphia House each child had its own small cell, lighted and ventilated and with a bed and a shelf.

## REFORM AND JUVENILE JUSTICE INSTITUTIONS

Many children remained in prisons. In 1827 the Boston Prison Discipline Society's Second Annual Report contained the following statistics:

Black children were not accepted at these houses initially, but in 1834 the New York house began making plans for the "coloured section" of its institution. Nathaniel C. Hart wrote of the necessity for facilities for blacks, describing the great increase in the number of poverty-stricken black children in the cities because of the Southern policy that forbade free blacks from continuing to "reside among them" in those states. New immigrants also were subject to discrimination. Those who arrived

TABLE 19.1
Children in Prisons in 1827

|  | Total Prisoners | Under 21 Years | Proportion |
|---|---|---|---|
| Maine | 116 | 22 | 1 to 5 |
| New Hampshire | 253 | 47 | 1 to 5 |
| Vermont | 534 | 75 | 1 to 7 |
| Connecticut | 117 | 39 | 1 to 3 |
| Virginia (Richmond) | 201 | 30 | 1 to 7 |

destitute might automatically be labeled criminals and their children incarcerated as a matter of course. In 1829, 58% of the refuge house inmates were from the immigrant population.

The report added that many of the children were under 12 years of age. During 1845, 97 children between the ages of 6 and 16 were sent to the House of Corrections in Massachusetts.

In 1847 Massachusetts opened the first state institution for the reform of juveniles. The Massachusetts State Reform School was patterned after the house of refuge. It accepted any boy under the age of 16 years convicted of an offense who was thought to be capable of change. Pupils could be bound out as servants or apprentices after they had been there for one year.

Concern for female juvenile offenders also began to grow. It was thought that reform schools for girls should be different from those for boys. The girls not only needed to have a strong mothering environment, but they also needed to be taught high moral values so that they would become good mothers. The Massachusetts State Industrial School for Girls was opened in 1856. It was the first girls reformatory and the first to adopt the cottage plan, which departed from the traditional dormitory style of institutional living. It separated children into smaller housing groups, with lesser offenders separated from repeaters.

Other institutions developed similar plans. In Chicago the cottage or family plan also was adopted. The emphasis at the Chicago school was "on creating a family life for children." The Ohio Reform School, founded in 1857, embodied all of the positive ideas of reform during the period. It followed the cottage plan and was located in the country. Prevailing theory viewed cities as evil and a cause of many juvenile problems. Cities had temptations, such as theaters and bars, that were bound to catch the interest of a child and eventually lead him or her astray. The country, on the other hand, provided hard work, close families, and few corrupting influences. In 1853 the New York Children's Aid Society was founded, providing placement services in the country rather than institutionalization. Because it was believed that the child should grow up in the country, within a family environment, many groups of children were sent West to find new lives, until it became increasingly difficult to find placement homes for these children.

The beginning of the 1860s saw yet another kind of experiment—the ship schools. Over the years it had been suggested that young male juveniles would respond positively to military life. The ship schools were supposed to provide the necessary regimentation as well as training for the merchant marine. Boys were accepted until the age of 16. On board ship they were separated into rotating work and study groups. Those on work duty spent their time in "domestic employments; in repairing sails and rigging; in going through sheet and halyard, brace and clewline, and the technical language of sailors; in short, in becoming practical seamen." These schools died a quick death because of disciplinary problems, heavy operating expenses, and the economic depressions that put adult seamen out of work.

The last of the new types of reformatories was the New York Catholic Protectory, founded in 1863. It was the largest institution of its kind at the time. An emphasis was placed on educating the children, and "benefiting the community by furnishing well-tutored and reliable youths to mechanical, agricultural, and general commercial pursuits."

Discrimination against blacks, Mexican Americans and other Spanish-speaking people, Indians, and some poor whites remained a problem in all types of reformatories and institutions across the country from their inception until the 1960s. Sexual abuse and physical attack by peers (and sometimes staff) also remained a problem, and the juvenile justice reform leaders of the 1970s are still struggling to devise means to end these evils.

The 1870s and 1880s brought a new wave of social interest in society's young criminals. The child-saving movement began. The child-savers were mostly women, well educated, politically oriented, with genteel backgrounds. By 1895 the Chicago Women's Club, one of the leaders in the child-saving movement, had a bill drafted providing for the formation of a separate court for juveniles. The bill failed, but it had aroused public interest. Illinois enacted a subsequent bill, entitled "an act to regulate the treatment and control of dependent, neglected, and delinquent children," in 1899, making the state the first to establish a separate Juvenile Court System. The city of Denver and the state of Rhode Island also passed juvenile court legislation that same year. The purpose of the juvenile court was to provide a more informal private atmosphere in which the judge could operate in a surrogate parental role—thus lessening for the child the trauma of courtroom proceedings.

## FEDERAL AND STATE EFFORTS IN THE TWENTIETH CENTURY

The first federal effort to improve child welfare and delinquency prevention was the establishment of the Children's Bureau in 1912. This was a period during which children worked under inhumane conditions in mills and factories throughout the North, South, and Midwest. Children of all races labored in sweatshops for mere pennies a day. Those conditions also prompted the passage in 1916 of the first federal child labor law, which reinforced the increasingly protective social attitudes toward children.

From 1920 to 1940 some states and manor cities constructed reformatories and other institutions for the confinement of juveniles. Although most of the institutions were built for custody and punishment, the best of them provided programs for recreation, educational programs, and follow-up family case work during incarceration and upon release. Gradually, professional counseling, education courses, psychological testing, employment, and foster family placement efforts were added to the juvenile treatment processes.

The desperate economic conditions of the Great Depression brought the first nationwide diversion program for youth. The Civilian Conservation Corps was begun in 1933 as an alternative to unemployment and rootlessness for males between the ages of 17 and 23.

Subsequent programs created to deal with the special problems of youth included the National Youth Administration during the Depression, the Congressional Interdepartmental Committee on Children and Youth in 1948, and the Midcentury White House Conference on Children and Youth in 1950.

The 1950s brought new approaches to aiding troubled juveniles. The teachings of John Dewey, Karen Horney, Carl Rogers, and Erich Fromm, among others, gained prominence. There was a greater acceptance in criminal justice work of professionals from the psychological disciplines. Several outstanding local programs were created to deal with the psychological roots of juvenile problems. Among these was the utilization of the guided group interaction therapy approach which was instituted at Highfields in New Jersey in 1950. It was a treatment approach copied across the country during the next two decades.

In 1950 the Federal Youth Correction Act established a Youth Correction Authority, as a State government unit, to improve techniques for the treatment and rehabilitation of youthful offenders. The U.S. Department of Health, Education, and Welfare was established in 1953, and included a Children's Bureau. A division of Juvenile Delinquency was established within that bureau in 1954.

During the 1960s pioneering youth programs surfaced in quantity. Front runners were Mobilization for Youth, started in 1962 in New York City, and the HARYOU-ACT, a Harlem youth involvement program begun in 1964. The VISTA (Volunteers in Service to America) program grew out of the Peace Corps concept. The Neighborhood Youth Corps, the Job Corps, Upward Bound, and various other programs were begun under the impetus of the War on Poverty. Youths were trained and paid as nonprofessional aides, community organizers, and community agency workers. Another approach involved peer counselors and workers on loan from schools and recreation centers to work with youth gangs. Storefront centers came into existence. The employment of more minority youth and those with specific language skills useful in dealing with social service clients were another innovation of the period.

During the past 75 years federal and state agencies and interested private citizens have stimulated innovations for the improvement of the corrections system for juvenile offenders. During most of the same period, however, little was known to the public about the workings of the juvenile court system. The activities of the juvenile courts remained closed—beyond public scrutiny and thus unchallenged and uncriticized.

Beginning in 1966, four landmark Supreme Court cases helped to define juvenile rights. They were *Kent v. United States,* 383 U.S. 541, (1966); *In re Gault,* 387 U.S. 1, (1967); *In re Winship,* 397 U.S. 358, (1970); *McKeiver v. Pennsylvania,* 403 U.S. 528, (1971); and *Breed v. Jones,* —— U.S. ——, 95 S.Ct. 1779 (1975). These cases and others gave juveniles the right to proper hearings, the right to counsel, the right to confront the accuser, the right to cross-examine witnesses, and the right to protection against double jeopardy. The one right denied was the right to a jury trial. These rulings ushered in a new era for juvenile justice.

Innovations in juvenile justice continued during the 1970s. In 1972 the State of Massachusetts Youth Services Department closed its juvenile reformatories and placed the children in community-based work and education programs. Other states are considering following suit.

But juvenile justice problems remain despite reform efforts. A major drawback in dealing with the juvenile problem is an overall lack of coordination and consistency in the approach to solutions. Research in evaluating the efforts also has been sorely lacking.

In the meantime, juvenile crime has continued to be a serious national problem. Between 1960 and 1973 the arrests of juveniles for acts of violence and other crimes increased by 144%. Studies showed that persons 18 years of age or younger accounted for 45% of the arrests for serious crime and 23% of arrests for violent crime. Burglaries and auto thefts were found to be committed overwhelmingly by youths. The peak age for arrests for violent crime was found to be 18 years, followed by 17, 16, and 19 years. The peak age for arrest for major property crimes was found to be 16 years, followed by 15 and 17 years.

At the same time, many juveniles were incarcerated for so-called status offenses, which are acts that would not be considered criminal if committed by an adult. These offenses include running away from home, truancy, promiscuity, curfew violation, and incorrigibility. In some states juveniles continued to be incarcerated with adult offenders. And there is no general agreement among the states on the definition of what constitutes juvenile delinquency or even on what age constitutes majority.

These conditions prompted the 1974 congressional hearings on the subject. Findings from those inquiries called attention to understaffed and overcrowded facilities, inadequate protective facilities, and a lack of technical assistance for states and cities.

The Congress pinpointed two separate but related needs—the need to protect society from juvenile crime and the need to provide the most effective management and care for juveniles in trouble. In response, the Congress enacted the Juvenile Justice and Delinquency Prevention Act of 1974.

## JUVENILE COURT JURISDICTION

The modern juvenile court is a specialized court for children.* It may be organized as an independent statewide court system, as a special session of a lower court, or even as part of a broader family court.[1] Juvenile courts are normally established by state legislation, and exercise jurisdiction over two distinct categories of juvenile offenders—delinquent and incorrigible children. Delinquent children are those who reach a jurisdictional age, which may vary from state to state, and who commit an act in violation of the penal code. Incorrigible children, on the other hand, include truants and habitually disobedient and ungovernable children. They are commonly characterized in state statutes as persons or children in need of supervision—PINS or CHINS—and their proscribed actions are in the nature of status offenses. Most states distinguish such behavior from delinquent conduct so as to lessen the effect of any stigma on the child as a result of his or her involvement with the juvenile court. In addition, juvenile courts generally have jurisdiction over situations involving conduct directed at (rather than committed by) juveniles, such as parental neglect, deprivation, abandonment, and abuse.

Today's juvenile court system embodies both rehabilitative and legalistic orientations; although the purpose of the court is therapeutic rather than punitive, children under its jurisdiction must be accorded their constitutional rights. The administrative structure of the court revolves around a diverse group of actors—a juvenile court judge, probation staff, social workers, government prosecutors, and defense attorneys. Thus, the ju-

---

*The material in the following sections of this chapter was adapted from Larry J. Siegel, Joseph J. Senna, and Therese J. Libby, "Legal Aspects of the Juvenile Justice Process: An Overview of Current Practices and Law," *New England Law Review* 12, no. 2 (March 1977): 223–264.

venile court functions in a sociolegal manner. It seeks to promote the rehabilitation of the child within a framework of procedural due process.

This dual philosophy of service and fair treatment for children has not always been the case; in fact, its development has taken place primarily in the past decade. For approximately the first 60 years of the juvenile court movement, children were accorded few constitutional protections. The juvenile court operated in an ostensibly benevolent, paternalistic, and informal manner. Children were arrested, tried, convicted, and sentenced under the banner of parens patriae—the power of the state to act in behalf of the child and provide care and protection equivalent to that of a parent.[2] Nevertheless, the application of this principle resulted in the absence of procedural formalities which, in turn, led to arbitrary treatment for many juvenile offenders. However, this philosophy has changed radically since the United States Supreme Court ruled on several occasions that children have substantial constitutional due process rights in juvenile proceedings.[3]

Juvenile court jurisdiction is established by state statute and based on several factors, the first of which is age. The states have differed in determining at what age to bring children under the jurisdiction of the juvenile court. Many state statutes include all children under 18, others set the upper limit at 17, and still others include children under 16. There are also jurisdictions which have established jurisdictional ages which vary according to the sex or geographic location of the juvenile. Recently, however, statutes employing the distinctions of sex and location as bases for differential jurisdictional ages have been held to be in violation of the equal protection and/or due process clauses of the United States Constitution.[4]

Juvenile court jurisdiction is also based on the nature of a child's actions. If an action committed by a child is a crime, this conduct normally falls into the category of delinquency. Definitions of delinquency vary from state to state, but most are based on the common element that delinquency is an intentional violation of the criminal law. On the other hand, the juvenile courts also have jurisdiction over status offenders, or children whose offenses involve some lack of parental supervision and are not the types of activity for which adults could be similarly prosecuted. Statutes attempting to define such conduct—such as the PINS and CHINS statutes—are marked by a vagueness that would most likely be impermissible in an adult criminal code. For example, terminology common to statutes of this kind includes designations such as unmanageable, unruly, and in danger of leading an idle, dissolute, lewd or immoral life. Understandably, statutory formulations such as these have been challenged as being unconstitutionally vague and indefinite.[5] However, most courts that have addressed this issue have upheld the breadth of the statutes in view of their overall concern for the welfare of the child.[6]

A juvenile court's jurisdiction is also affected by state statutes which exclude certain offenses from the court's consideration. Based on the premise that the rehabilitative resources and protective processes of the juvenile court are not appropriate in cases of serious criminal conduct, various states have excluded capital offenses, offenses punishable by death or life imprisonment, and certain other offenses from the juvenile court's jurisdiction. A more common exclusionary scheme involves transfer provisions, by means of which juvenile courts waive jurisdiction to the criminal courts.

Having once obtained jurisdiction of a child, the court ordinarily retains it until the child reaches a specified age, usually the age of majority. Court jurisdiction terminates in most states when the child is placed in a public childcare agency. Figure 19.1 describes the basic juvenile justice system.

## POLICE PROCESSING OF THE JUVENILE OFFENDER

Throughout the 1960s, many United States Supreme Court decisions significantly added to the constitutional safeguards of criminal offenders by making the provisions of the Bill of Rights applicable to the states through the due process clause of the Fourteenth Amendment. Many of these decisions affected the defendant's pre-trial rights.[7]

Children have also been granted pre-trial protections similar to those of adults. The landmark juvenile decision of *In re Gault* in 1967,[8] although specifically applicable to the trial process, served to extend constitutional guarantees of due process to juveniles at pre-adjudication proceedings.

When a juvenile is found to have engaged in delinquent or incorrigible behavior, police agencies are charged with the decision to release or detain and refer the child to juvenile court. This discretionary decision—to release or to detain—has been found to be based not only on the nature of the offense, but also on police attitudes and the social and personal conditions existing at the time of the particular arrest.[9] The following is a partial list of factors believed to be significant in police decision making regarding juvenile offenders:

1. The type and seriousness of the child's offense.

2. The ability of the parents to be of assistance in disciplining the child.

3. The history of the child's past contacts with police.

4. The degree of cooperation obtained from the child and parents.

5. Whether the child denies the allegations in the petition and insists upon a court hearing.

After processing relevant information, the police may adjust a case by simply releasing the child at the point of contact on the street, giving an official warning and releasing the offender to parents at the station house or the child's home, or referring the child to a social services program. Cases generally involving violence, victim-related crimes, or serious property offenses are most often referred to court. On the other hand, police often attempt to divert from court action minor disputes between juveniles, school and neighborhood complaints, petty shoplifting cases, runaways, and ungovernable children.

When a child is taken into custody by the police, the law of arrest requires that the police officer make a determination that probable cause

FIGURE 19.1 Juvenile Justice System

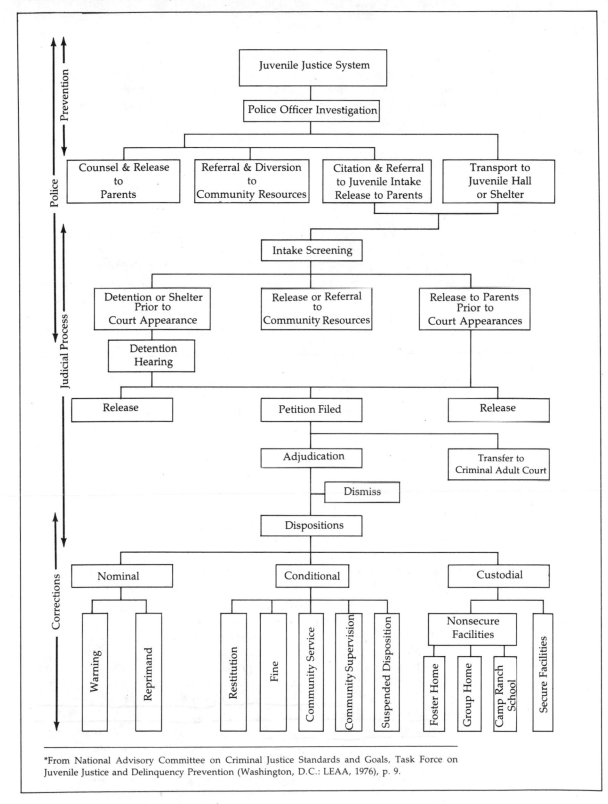

*From National Advisory Committee on Criminal Justice Standards and Goals, Task Force on Juvenile Justice and Delinquency Prevention (Washington, D.C.: LEAA, 1976), p. 9.

exists that a crime has been committed and that the child may have committed it. Most states do not have specific statutory provisions distinguishing the arrest process for children from that for adults. Some jurisdictions, however, give broad arrest powers to the police in juvenile cases by authorizing the officer to make an arrest whenever it is believed that the child's behavior falls within the jurisdiction of the juvenile court.[10] Similarly, many states give the police authority to take a child into custody if the child's welfare requires it. Because of the state's interest in the child, the police generally have more discretion in the investigatory and arrest stages of the juvenile process than they do when dealing with adult offenders. Although most juvenile arrests are warrantless, the requirements for the issuance of an arrest warrant for a juvenile are generally similar to requirements in adult cases.

Once a juvenile has been taken into custody, the child has the same Fourth Amendment right to be free from unreasonable searches and seizures as does an adult. The most common legal procedure used to exclude any incriminating evidence is for the child's attorney to make a pre-trial motion to suppress inadmissible evidence, making it inadmissible in subsequent hearings.

One of the most difficult search and seizure problems unique to juvenile law is whether a search of a child's person or possessions by a school official is constitutionally valid. In *People v. Overton* (1969).[11] the court held that a school principal had the authority to consent to the search of a student's locker, and that a subsequent police search was permissible. On the other hand, the recent case of *People v. Scott D* (1974)[12] decided that the search of a student's person by a school official acting as a governmental agent was a violation of the Fourth and Fourteenth Amendments of the Constitution. At present, the law involving searches of students and their possessions in school settings remains unclear.

Another issue related to the exclusion of evidence in juvenile matters is the use of statements made by juvenile offenders to police officers. In years past, police often questioned juveniles without the presence of their parents or an attorney. Any incriminatory statements or confessions made by juveniles could be placed in evidence at their trials. As mentioned in Chapter 8, the United States Supreme Court in *Miranda v. Arizona*,[13] in 1966, placed constitutional limitations on police interrogation procedures regarding adult offenders. The Miranda warning, which represents the adult defendant's Fifth Amendment rights against self-incrimination, has been made applicable to children. The *Gault* decision—which gave juveniles procedural safeguards similar to those awarded adults at trial proceedings, including the right to counsel, the right to confront witnesses, and the privilege against self-incrimination—has indirectly influenced and reinforced juvenile *Miranda* rights. In other words, adjudicatory rights seem to require that *Miranda* warnings be given to all juvenile offenders who are questioned in custody if the police intend to admit their statements in subsequent proceedings. Most states have since incorporated the *Miranda* decision into their juvenile statutes, and today a child's parents are usually contacted immediately after the child is taken into custody.

One of the most difficult problems involving self-incrimination is whether a juvenile can waive *Miranda* rights. This issue has resulted in considerable litigation. Some courts have concluded that it is not essential for the parent or attorney to be present for the child to effectively waive rights. The validity of the waiver in this respect is based on the totality of the circumstances of a given case. This means that the court must determine whether the child is able to make a knowing, intelligent, and voluntary waiver. On the other hand, some jurisdictions will not accept a waiver of the juvenile's *Miranda* rights unless it is made in the presence of the child's parents or attorney.

Another important issue in the early police processing of juvenile offenders is whether the constitutional safeguards established for adult offenders in lineups and other identification procedures are applicable to juvenile proceedings. As mentioned in Chapter 8, the Supreme Court in *United States v. Wade*[14] held that the accused has a right to have counsel present at post-indictment lineup procedures. The Supreme Court further clarified this issue in *Kirby v. Illinois* (1972)[15] by holding that the defendant's right to counsel at pre-trial identification proceedings attaches only after the complaint or indictment has been issued. Based on these decisions, courts have ruled that juveniles also have constitutional protection from tainted lineup and identification procedures. It has been decided that the juvenile has a right to counsel at a police lineup once charged with a delinquent act, and that if this right is violated the pre-trial identification is to be excluded.

Today, there is as much procedural protection generally given to children in juvenile courts as to adults tried in criminal courts. Figure 19.2 describes the basic similarities and differences between the juvenile and adult justice systems.

After a juvenile is formally taken into custody, either as a delinquent or as a status offender, a decision is usually made whether to release the child to the parent or guardian or detain the child in a shelter care pending trial. In the past, far too many children were routinely placed in detention while awaiting court appearances. Detention facilities were inadequate and, in many parts of the country, county jails were used to detain juvenile offenders. Although this practice continues to some degree, the emphasis in recent years has been on reducing the number of children placed in detention.

Subsequent to arrest, and after being temporarily detained by the police, the child is usually released to the parent or guardian. Most state statutes ordinarily require a hearing on the appropriateness of detention if the initial decision is to keep the child in custody. At this hearing, the child has a right to counsel and may be given other procedural due process safeguards, notably the privilege against self-incrimination and the right to confront and cross-examine witnesses.

Most state juvenile court acts provide criteria to support a decision to detain the child. This includes (1) the need to protect the child, (2) the

THE PRE-TRIAL STAGE OF JUVENILE JUSTICE

FIGURE 19.2
Similarities Between
Juvenile and Adult
Systems

1. Discretion in decision making is used by police officers, judges, and correctional personnel in both adult and juvenile systems.
2. Search and seizure law, and the applicability of the Fourth Amendment applies to juvenile and adult offenders.
3. The right to receive Miranda warnings is applicable to juveniles as well as to adults.
4. Juveniles are protected, as are adults, from prejudicial lineups or other identification procedures.
5. Procedural safeguards similar to those of adults protect juveniles when they make an admission of guilt.
6. Prosecutors and defense attorneys play an equally critical role in juvenile and adult advocacy.
7. Juveniles, like adults, have the right to counsel at most key stages of the court process.
8. Pre-trial motions are available in juvenile and criminal court proceedings.
9. Negotiations and the plea bargain exist with juvenile and adult offenders.
10. Children and adults have a right to a trial and appeal.
11. The standard of evidence in juvenile delinquency adjudications, as in adult criminal trials, is that of proof beyond a reasonable doubt.

question of whether the child presents a serious danger to the public, and (3) the likelihood of whether the juvenile will return to court for adjudication. While in adult cases the sole criterion for pre-trial release may be the offender's availability for trial, the juvenile may be detained for other reasons, including the child's own protection. Normally, the finding of the

FIGURE 19.2
continued
Differences Between
Juvenile and Adult
Systems

1. The primary purpose of juvenile procedures is protection and treatment; with adults, the aim is punishment of the guilty.
2. The jurisdiction of the juvenile court is determined chiefly by age; in the adult system, jurisdiction is determined primarily by the nature of the offense.
3. Juveniles can be held responsible for acts which would not be criminal if they were committed by an adult (status offenses).
4. Juvenile proceedings are not considered criminal, while adult proceedings are.
5. Juvenile court procedures are generally informal and private; those of adult courts are more formal and open to the public.
6. Courts cannot release identifying information to the press concerning a juvenile, but must do so in cases dealing with adults.
7. Parents are highly involved in the juvenile process; with adults, this would not be the case.
8. The standard of arrest is more stringent for adults than for juveniles.
9. As a practical matter, juveniles are released into parental custody, while adults are generally given the opportunity for bail.
10. Plea bargaining is used in most adult cases, while most juvenile cases are settled by open admission of guilt.
11. Juveniles have no constitutional right to a jury trial; adults do have this right.
12. Juvenile dispositional decisions are ordinarily based on indeterminate terms, while adult's sentences include proportionality, definiteness.
13. The procedural rights of juveniles are based on the concept of "fundamental fairness"; those of adults are based on the constitutional right to due process under the Bill of Rights and the Fourteenth Amendment.
14. Juveniles have the right to treatment under the Fourteenth Amendment; adult offenders have no such recognized right.
15. A juvenile's record is sealed when the age of majority is reached; the record of an adult is permanent.

judge that the child should be detained must be supported by factual evidence. When a valid reason for a child's detention has not appeared on the record, courts have mandated release from temporary custody.

If a child is to be detained, the question of bail arises. Federal courts have found it unnecessary to rule on the issue of constitutional right to bail since liberal statutory release provisions act as appropriate alternatives. While only a few state statutes allow release on money bail, many others have juvenile code provisions which emphasize the release of the child to the parents as an acceptable substitute. A constitutional right to bail which on its face seems to benefit a child may have unforeseen results. For example, money bail might impose serious economic strain on the child's family while simultaneously conflicting with the protective and social concerns of the juvenile court. Considerations of economic liabilities and other procedural inequities have influenced the majority of courts confronting this question to hold that juveniles do not have a right to bail.

A child may plead guilty or not guilty to a petition alleging delinquency.
Today, state jurisdictions tend to minimize the stigma associated with the use of adult criminal standards by using other terminology, such as "agree to a finding" or "deny the petition." When the child makes an admission, juvenile court acts and rules of procedure in numerous jurisdictions require the following procedural safeguards: (1) that the child know of the right to a trial; (2) that the plea or admission be made voluntarily; and (3) that the child understand the charges and consequences of the plea. The same requirements have been established in a series of cases decided by the United States Supreme Court for adult offenders.[16] Although such standards have not been established by constitutional law for juveniles, they carry equal weight in juvenile cases because the guilty plea constitutes a waiver of the juvenile's Fifth Amendment privilege against self-incrimination.

Open admission, as opposed to plea bargaining, seems to be the reason that the majority of juvenile court cases are not adjudicated. Unlike the adult system, where 70% to 90% of all charged offenders are involved in some plea bargaining, it is widely believed that little plea bargaining exists in the juvenile court. Most juvenile court legislation and rules of procedure do not provide rules governing the plea bargaining process. The parens patriae philosophy of the juvenile court, the general availability of pre-trial social services, and flexibility in the disposition of cases act to discourage the use of plea bargaining.

The practical application of plea bargaining in the juvenile court exists when the government—represented by the prosecutor, police officer, or probation officer—negotiates a guilty plea from the defense attorney in exchange for a disposition generally involving community supervision. Both parties may seek the judge's guidance in reaching an agreement and obtain judicial consent to the bargain. Efficient disposition of the case after plea bargaining is also an essential element of the process because it reduces the juvenile court caseload and enhances the rehabilitative prospects of the child.

THE INTAKE
PROCESS

As we have described, juveniles coming into contact with the police and juvenile courts generally may be categorized into two major groups: those accused of committing crimes which result in juvenile delinquency, and those who commit acts of noncriminal behavior. Police officers who confront children committing a crime or dangerous action to themselves or others, need to decide whether the situation warrants court attention or not. Such is the police role in exercising a certain amount of discretion in dealing with children. If the police officer does not initiate court action, he may provide the child with a warning, advise the parents to refer the child to a welfare agency, or refer the situation to a social agency through the police department.

When the police department believes the child needs a court referral, the police become involved in the intake division of the court. The term "intake" refers to the screening of cases by the juvenile court system. It involves the review and initial screening of a child and family by intake probation officers to determine if the child needs to be serviced by the juvenile court. In 1967, the President's Commission on Law Enforcement and Administration of Justice, Task Force Report on Juvenile Delinquency and Youth Crime, described how the intake process serves the following important functions:

Intake reduces the considerable demands on limited court resources to manageable levels; it screens out cases that are not within the court's jurisdiction; and most importantly it obtains assistance from community agencies when court authority is not necessary for referral.[17]

In addition, the intake stage is a time when the child can receive treatment in a most efficient and timely manner. It represents an opportunity to place a child in informal programs both within the court and in the community. Furthermore, the intake process is critically important because more than half of the referrals to the juvenile courts never go beyond that stage.

Juvenile court intake—which seeks to screen out cases not within the court's jurisdiction or not serious enough for court intervention—is now provided for by statute in the majority of states.[18] Also, virtually all of the model acts and standards in juvenile justice suggest the development of juvenile court intake proceedings. These include the Standard Juvenile Court Act of the National Council on Crime and Delinquency, the Uniform Juvenile Court Act of the National Conference of Commissioners on Uniform State Laws, and the Standards for Juvenile and Family Courts by the U.S. Department of Health, Education, and Welfare.[19]

Some of the reasons for the desirability of intake procedures in the juvenile court are: (1) filing a complaint against the child in a court may do more harm than good, since rehabilitation has often failed in the juvenile court system; (2) processing a child in the juvenile court labels the child a delinquent, stigmatizing the juvenile, and may reinforce antisocial behavior; (3) nonjudicial handling gives the child and the family "a second chance" and an opportunity to work with a voluntary social service agency; and (4) intake screening of children helps conserve resources which may not be available in already overburdened juvenile court systems. In addition, intake screening also provides for a wide range of nonjudicial decisions regarding the child, including the use of nonjudicial or informal probation, the provision of intake services by the intake department of the juvenile court, the additional dismissal of a complaint, and the referral to a community social service agency. Finally, intake screening has also allowed juvenile courts to enter into a consent decree with the juvenile without the filing of a petition or formal adjudication. The consent decree is basically a court order authorizing the disposition of the case without a formal finding of delinquency and based on an agreement between the intake department of the court and the juvenile who is the subject of the complaint.

Notwithstanding all the advantages of intake, there are some intake screening problems. We know that less than 50% of all juveniles who are arrested and brought to court actually proceed to trial. As a result, intake sections are constantly pressured to provide available services for the large group of children not handled by the court structure. In addition to being a link for court and community services, intake programs also need to be provided 24 hours a day in many urban courts so that dispositions can be resolved quickly on the day the child is referred to the court. Furthermore, the key to good intake service is the quality of the intake probation staff in the court. Poorly qualified personnel in intake is a serious flaw in many court systems. There are also a variety of legal problems associated with the intake process. These include whether the child has a right to counsel at this stage, whether the juvenile has a privilege against self-incrimination at intake, and to what degree the child needs to consent to nonjudicial disposition as recommended by the intake probation officer.

## JUVENILE DIVERSION

One of the most important alternatives at intake and prior to adjudication is the use of the nonjudicial disposition. As the American Bar Association's Standards Relating to Juvenile Probation Function state, "Among the wide and confusing variety of terms also used to refer to this type of intake disposition are the following: nonjudicial adjustment, handling or processing, informal disposition, adjustment, and diversion."[20] Diversion is probably the most common term used to refer to screening out children from the juvenile court without judicial determination.

Numerous national groups, commentators, lawyers, and other criminal justice experts have explored the concept of diversion since its inception in the mid-1960s. Diversion is primarily the early court process of placing offenders, both adult and juvenile, into noncriminal diversion programs prior to their formal trial or conviction (as discussed in Chapter 10). Nejelski defines diversion as "the channeling of juvenile cases to non-court institutions, in instances where these cases would ordinarily have received an adjudicatory hearing by a court."[21] The National Advisory

Commission on Criminal Justice Standards and Goals, Task Force on Courts, suggests that there is a distinction between the terms "diversion" and "screening." Diversion involves a decision to encourage an individual to participate in some specific program or activity by express or implied threat of further form of juvenile or criminal prosecution. Screening, on the other hand, involves simply abandoning efforts to apply any cohesive measures upon a defendant.[22]

Whatever formally accepted definition is used, diversion generally today refers to formally acknowledged and organized efforts to utilize alternatives to process juvenile and adult offenders outside of the justice system. As Empey states, "Diversion suggests that more first-time and petty, as well as status offenders, should be channeled away from legal processing and into community institutions.[23]

Diversion has become one of the most popular reforms in juvenile justice since it was recommended by the President's Crime Commission in 1967. Arguments for the use of diversion programs include the following: (1) it keeps the juvenile justice system operating, or it would collapse from voluminous case loads; (2) it is a preferable approach than dealing with the present inadequate juvenile justice treatment system; (3) it gives legislators and other governmental leaders the opportunity to reallocate present resources to programs that may be more successful in the treatment of juvenile offenders; and (4) the costs of diversion programs are significantly less than the per capita cost of institutionalization. As Nejelski states, "There is much that is new about juvenile diversion—new screening procedures, new programs, and new incentives from federal funding. It is the overture to the new corrections, with its emphasis on de-institutionalization and purchase of services."[24]

Many diversion programs exist throughout the United States today. Since the mid-1960s, the Law Enforcement Assistance Administration, the Youth Development and Delinquency Prevention Administration of the U.S. Department of Health, Education, and Welfare, and the Federal Office of Economic Opportunity have greatly expanded funding for diversion programs. All of the programs vary in size and emphasis, but generally possess the same goal: to constructively bypass juvenile adjudication by providing reasonable alternatives in the form of treatment, counseling, employment, or education programs.

There are police-based diversion models which include family crisis intervention projects, referral programs, and youth service bureaus. In addition, there are numerous court-based diversion models. Diversionary models in courts have been used extensively for children who are status offenders, minor first offenders, those involved in family disturbances, and those involved in such offenses as shoplifting, minor assault, and battery. Court-based diversion programs include such intervention projects as those involving employment, referral for educational programs, and the placing of juveniles who are involved with drugs in drug-related programs. Two illustrations of juvenile diversion programs, one entitled "Community Arbitration," and the other Project "New Pride" are described in the application section of this chapter.

Prior to the development of the first modern juvenile court in Illinois in 1899, juveniles were tried for violations of the law in adult criminal courts. The consequences were devastating; many children were treated as criminal offenders and often sentenced to adult prisons. Although the subsequent passage of state legislation creating juvenile courts eliminated this problem, the juvenile justice system did recognize that certain forms of conduct require children to be tried as adults. Today, most jurisdictions provide by statute for waiver, or transfer of juvenile offenders to the criminal courts.[25]

The transfer of a juvenile to the criminal court is often based on statutory criteria established by the state's Juvenile Court Act, and waiver provisions are generally quite varied among the jurisdictions. The two major criteria for waiver are the age of the child and the type of offense alleged in the petition. For example, some jurisdictions require that the child be over a certain age and be charged with a felony before being tried as an adult, while others permit waiver of jurisdiction to the criminal court if the child is above a certain age, regardless of the offense. Still other states permit waiver under any conditions, and a few states have no waiver provision. The model legislation of the Uniform Juvenile Court Act recommends transfer to the criminal court if the child is 16 or more years of age and is alleged to have committed a violation of the law; in contrast, the Department of Health, Education and Welfare Standards for Family Courts uses the age 16 but suggests that transfer be based on actions of the child which constitute a felony if committed by an adult.[26] Some jurisdictions permit waiver not only on the basis of age and type of offense, but also include consideration of the child's prior criminal record and the probability of further delinquent conduct.

Because of the nature and effect of the waiver decision on the child in terms of status and disposition, the United States Supreme Court has imposed procedural protections for juveniles in the waiver process. *Kent v. United States* in 1966,[27] the first major case before the Court on this issue, challenged the provisions of the District of Columbia Code which stated that the juvenile court could waive jurisdiction after a full investigation. The Supreme Court in *Kent* held that the waiver proceeding was a critically important stage in the juvenile process and that juveniles must be afforded minimum requirements of due process of law at such proceedings.

In reaching this decision, Justice Abraham Fortas declared:

The Juvenile Court is theoretically engaged in determining the needs of the child and of society rather than adjudicating criminal conduct. The objectives are to provide measures of guidance and rehabilitation for the child and protection for society, not to fix criminal responsibility, guilt and punishment. The State is parens patriae rather than prosecuting attorney and judge. But the admonition to function in a "parental" relationship is not an invitation to procedural arbitrariness.[28]

Consistent with this line of thought, the Supreme Court concluded that the following conditions must be observed for a valid waiver: (1) a hearing must be held on the motion of waiver; (2) the child is entitled to

THE WAIVER OF
JURISDICTION

be represented by counsel; (3) the defense attorney must be given access to all records and reports used in reaching a waiver decision; and (4) the court must provide a written statement of the reasons for the waiver decision.

As a result of the *Kent* case, many jurisdictions have established specific rules of practice for the waiver of a juvenile to the criminal court. Most jurisdictions which have waiver proceedings require the following by statute or court rule: a hearing, the presence of counsel, an investigation by the probation staff regarding whether the juvenile is amenable to treatment, evidence that reasonable ground exists to believe that the child committed the delinquent act, and a statement of reasons for the waiver.

One of the most difficult issues in the waiver process is that of deciding what standards should be used to support a waiver decision. The appendix in the *Kent* case lists eight objective criteria to be used in determing whether to transfer the child to criminal court.[29] The Uniform Juvenile Court Act and the Model Acts for Family Courts of the Department of Health, Education and Welfare provide similar criteria.[30] These conditions generally include such factors as (1) the type of offense; (2) the child's prior record; (3) the nature of past treatment efforts; (4) the availability of rehabilitative services; and (5) the reasonable likelihood of the child being rehabilitated in the juvenile court.

Another significant opinion of the United States Supreme Court on juvenile waiver proceedings was heard in the case of *Breed v. Jones* (1975),[31] which maintained that the prosecution of a juvenile as an adult in the California Superior Court, following an adjudicatory proceeding in Juvenile Court, violated the Double Jeopardy Clause of the Fifth Amendment as applied to the states through the Fourteenth Amendment. When delivering the opinion of the Court on this issue, Chief Justice Warren Burger stated:

> Although the juvenile court system had its genesis in the desire to provide a distinctive procedure and setting to deal with the problems of youth, including those manifested by antisocial conduct, our decisions in recent years have recognized that there is a gap between the originally benign conception of the system and its realities. . . . We believe it is simply too late in the day to conclude . . . that a juvenile is not put in jeopardy at a proceeding whose object is to determine whether he has committed acts that violate criminal law and whose potential consequences include both the stigma inherent in such a determination and the deprivation of liberty for many years.[32]

The Court concluded that jeopardy attaches when the juvenile court begins to hear evidence at the adjudicatory hearing; this requires that the waiver hearing take place prior to any adjudication.

## THE JUVENILE TRIAL

During the adjudicatory or trial process, often called the fact-finding hearing in juvenile proceedings, the court hears evidence on the allegations stated in the delinquency petition. In its early development, the juvenile court did not emphasize judicial rule-making similar to that of the criminal trial process. Absent were such basic requirements as the standard of proof, rules of evidence, and similar adjudicatory formalities.

Traditionally, the juvenile system was designed to diagnose and re-habilitate children appearing before the court. This was consistent with the view that the court should be social-service oriented. Proceedings were to be nonadversary, informal and noncriminal in nature. Gradually, how-ever, the juvenile court movement became the subject of much criticism. This growing dissatisfaction was based primarily on the inability of the court to rehabilitate the juvenile offender, while at the same time failing to safeguard his constitutional rights. Juvenile courts were punishing many children under the guise of being social-service agencies, arguing that constitutional protections were not necessary because the juvenile was being helped in the name of the state. Under the *parens patriae* philosophy, the adjudicatory proceeding, as well as subsequent dispositions, were seen as being in the child's best interests.[33] Thus, the philosphy of the juvenile court saw no need for legal rules and procedures, as in the criminal process, nor for the introduction of state prosecutors or defense attorneys.

These views and practices have been severely changed by the United States Supreme Court. Beginning in 1966 with *Kent v. United States*, the Supreme Court began to consider the constitutional validity of juvenile court proceedings. This study culminated in the landmark case of *In re Gault*.[34] In *Gault* the Court ruled that the concept of fundamental fairness be made applicable to juvenile delinquency proceedings.

Gerald Gault was a 15-year-old boy on probation who was committed as a delinquent child after being arrested as the result of a complaint that he had made lewd telephone calls. After hearings before a juvenile court judge, Gault was ordered committed to the State Industrial School as a juvenile delinquent until he reached his majority. The family brought a habeas corpus action in the state courts to challenge the constitutionality of the Arizona Juvenile Code on the ground that the boy was denied his procedural due process rights. The Court decided that the due process clause of the Fourteenth Amendment required that certain procedural guarantees were essential to the adjudication of delinquency cases. Justice Fortas addressed this issue in the following manner:

Due process of law is the primary and indispensable foundation of individual free-dom. It is the basic and essential term in the social compact which defines the rights of the individual and delimits the powers which the state may exercise.[35]

The Court then specified the precise nature of due process by indi-cating that a juvenile who has violated a criminal statute and who may be committed to an institution is entitled to (1) fair notice of the charges, (2) the right to representation by counsel, (3) the right to confrontation by and cross-examination of witnesses, and (4) the privilege against self-incrimi-nation.

*Gault* did not hold that the juvenile offender was entitled to all pro-cedural guarantees applicable in the case of an adult charged with a crime. The Supreme Court did not rule, for instance, on such issues as whether the juvenile had a right to a transcript of the proceedings, or the right to appellate review. Nor was it clear as to what extent the right to counsel should be provided for nondelinquent children. *Gault* specifically ruled that a juvenile is entitled to counsel in delinquency actions which may result in institutionalization. In this regard, many states have gone beyond *Gault* to provide juveniles with a right to counsel in all stages of court proceedings. However, the question of which juveniles have a right to guarantees under *Gault* has not been completely settled. Some jurisdictions specify that the right to counsel is applicable only in delinquency and status offenses, while other states go beyond *Gault* and provide counsel in neglect and dependency proceedings as well.

The *Gault* decision, particularly as it applies to the constitutional right of a juvenile to the assistance of counsel, has completely altered the juvenile justice system. Instead of dealing with children in a benign and paternalistic fashion, the court must process juvenile offenders within the framework of appropriate constitutional procedures. And, although *Gault* was technically limited to the adjudicatory stage, it has spurred further legal

## IN RE GAULT

**Facts:** Gerald Gault, 15 years of age, was taken into custody by the sheriff of Gila County, Arizona. His arrest was based on the complaint of a woman who said that he and another boy had made an obscene telephone call to her. Gerald was then under a 6-month probation as a result of being delinquent for stealing a wallet. Because of the verbal complaint, Gerald was taken to the children's home. His parents were not informed that he was being taken into custody. His mother appeared in the evening and was told by the superintendent of detention that a hearing would be held in the juvenile court the following day. On the day in question, the police officer who had taken Gerald into custody filed a petition alleging his delinquency. Gerald, his mother, and the police officer appeared before the judge in his chambers. Mrs. Cook, the complainant, was not at the hearing. Gerald was questioned about the telephone calls and was sent back to the detention home and then subsequently released a few days later.

On the day of Gerald's release, Mrs. Gault received a letter indicating that a hearing would be held on Gerald's delinquency a few days later. A hearing was held and the complainant was not present. There was no transcript or recording of the proceedings, and the juvenile officer stated that Gerald had admitted making the lewd telephone calls. Neither the boy nor his parents were advised of any right to remain silent, to be represented by counsel, or of any other constitutional rights. At the conclusion of the hearing, the juvenile court committed Gerald as a juvenile delinquent to the state industrial school in Arizona for a period of his minority.

This meant that Gerald at the age of 15 was being sent to a period of incarceration in the state school until age 21, or unless discharged sooner. Whereas an adult charged with the same crime would have received a maximum punishment of no more than a $50 fine or 2 months in prison.

**Decision in the Case:** Gerald's attorneys filed a *habeas corpus* writ, which was denied by the Superior Court of the State of Arizona, and that decision was subsequently affirmed by the Arizona Supreme Court. On appeal to the United States Supreme Court, Gerald's counsel argued that juvenile code of Arizona under which Gerald was found delinquent was invalid because it was contrary to the due process clause of the Fourteenth Amendment.

reform throughout the juvenile system. Today, the right to counsel, the privilege against self-incrimination, the right to treatment in detention and correctional facilities, and other characteristics of the adversary process are applied at all stages of the juvenile process, from investigation through adjudication to parole.[36] Because of the significance of the Gault case, it is summarized below:

After *Gault*, the Supreme Court continued its trend toward legalizing and formalizing the juvenile trial process with the decision of *In re Winship* (1970).[37] Relying on "a preponderance of the evidence" standard required by the New York Family Court Act, a judge found Winship, a 12-year-old boy, guilty of the crime of larceny. The Court, however, held in *Winship* that the standard in a criminal prosecution of proof beyond a reasonable doubt is also required in the adjudication of a delinquency petition. The *Winship* decision did not settle whether this burden of proof is also applicable to nondelinquent forms of conduct. As a result, some state statutes require proof beyond a reasonable doubt only in delinquency matters. In these jurisdictions, such standards of proof as clear and convincing evi-

In addition, Gerald was denied the following basic due process rights: (1) notice of charges with regard to the timeliness and specificity of the charges, (2) right to counsel, (3) right to confrontation and cross-examination, (4) privilege against self-incrimination, (5) right to a transcript of the trial record, and (6) right to appellate review. In deciding the case, the Supreme Court had to decide whether or not procedural due process of law within the context of fundamental fairness under the Fourteenth Amendment applied to juvenile delinquency proceedings in which a child is committed to a state industrial school.

The Court, in a far-reaching opinion written by Justice Abe Fortas, agreed that Gerald's constitutional rights were violated. Notice of charges was an essential ingredient of due process of law, as was right to counsel, right to cross-examine and to confront witnesses, and privilege against self-incrimination. The question of appellate review and a right to a transcript was not answered by the court in this case.

**Significance of the Case:** The Gault case decided that a child had procedural due process constitutional rights as listed above in delinquency adjudication proceedings based upon alleged misconduct where the consequences were that the child may be committed to a state institution. It was confined to rulings at the adjudication stage of the juvenile process.

However, this decision was not only significant because of the procedural reforms such as the right to counsel, but because of its far-reaching impact throughout the entire juvenile justice process. *Gault* instilled in juvenile proceedings the development of due process standards at the pre-trial, trial, and post-trial stages of the juvenile process. While recognizing the history and the development of the juvenile court, it sought to accommodate the motives of rehabilitation and treatment with children's rights. It recognized the principles of fundamental fairness of the law, for children as well as for adults. Judged in the context of today's juvenile justice system, *Gault* redefined the relationship between the juvenile, the parents, and the state. It remains the single most significant constitutional case in the area of juvenile justice.

dence or a preponderance of the evidence are used for incorrigibility, neglect, or dependency cases. Some jurisdictions, however, apply the reasonable doubt standard to all types of juvenile actions. In spite of various statutory differences, *Winship* does impose the constitutional requirement of proof beyond a reasonable doubt during the adjudicatory stage of a delinquency proceeding.

Although the traditional juvenile court has been severely altered by *Kent*, *Gault*, and *Winship*, the trend for increased rights for juveniles has been somewhat curtailed by the Supreme Court's decision in *McKeiver v. Pennsylvania* (1971).[38] In *McKeiver*, the Court held that trial by jury in a juvenile court's adjudicative stage is not a constitutional requirement. This decision, however, does not prevent the various states from giving the juvenile a trial by jury as a state constitutional right or by state statute. And although in the majority of states the child has no such right, a small number of jurisdictions do exist in which the child is entitled to a jury trial.

Once an adjudicatory hearing has been completed, the court is normally required to enter a judgment against the child. This may take the form of declaring the child delinquent, adjudging the child to be a ward of the court, or possibly even suspending judgment so as to avoid the stigma of a juvenile record. Sufficient facts must exist to warrant a finding; a juvenile cannot simply be declared delinquent by the court of acts alleged in the petition. Once a judgment has been entered in accordance with the appropriate state statute, the court can begin its determination of possible dispositions for the child.

## DISPOSITION AND TREATMENT

The juvenile court judge at the dispositional hearing imposes a sentence upon the juvenile offender in light of his offense, prior record, and family background. Normally, the sentence is imposed by a juvenile court judge who has broad discretionary power to decide a range of dispositions from dismissal to institutional commitment.[39] In theory, the dispositional decision is an effort by the court to serve the best interests of the child, the family, and the community. In many respects, this post-adjudicative process is the most important stage in the juvenile court system because it represents the last opportunity for the court to influence the child and control his behavior.

Most jurisdictions have statutes which require the court to proceed with disposition following adjudication of the child as a delinquent or status offender. This is done as part of the adjudicatory process or at a separate dispositional hearing.

Statutory provisions which use a two-part hearing process are preferred, since different evidentiary rules apply at both hearings. The basic purpose of having two separate hearings is to insure that only evidence appropriate to determine whether the child committed the alleged offense is considered by the court. If evidence relating to the pre-sentence report of the child is used in the adjudicatory hearing, it would normally result in a reversal of the court's delinquency finding. On the other hand, the social history report is essential for court use in the dispositional hearing. Thus, the bifurcated process seeks to insure that the adjudicatory hearing is used solely to determine the merits of the allegations, while the dispositional hearing determines whether the child is in need of rehabilitation.

In theory, the juvenile court seeks to provide a disposition which represents an individualized treatment plan for the child. This decision is normally based on the pre-sentence investigation of the probation department, reports from social agencies, and possibly a psychiatric evaluation from the juvenile court clinic. The judge generally has broad discretion in dispositional matters, but is limited by the provisions of the state's juvenile court act. The prevailing statutory model provides for the following types of alternative dispositions:

**1.** Dismissal of the petition.

**2.** Suspended judgment.

**3.** Probation.

**4.** Placement in a community treatment program.

**5.** Commitment to the state agency responsible for juvenile institutional care.

In addition, the court may place the child with parents or relatives, make dispositional arrangements with private youth-serving agencies, or order the child committed to a mental institution.

One of the most complex problems in the juvenile justice system has been the limited number of alternative dispositions available for various types of juvenile offenders. Dismissal of the case only provides the court with legal authority to relinquish control over a juvenile. This occurs if allegations in the petition have not been sustained, or where the court does not want to stigmatize the child with a juvenile court record. Similar to dismissal is suspended judgment, where the court will continue the case without any formal finding of adjudication. In some instances, the child may also be placed under court supervision for a stipulated period of time. If the child responds well to treatment, the charges are generally dismissed. On the other hand, if the delinquent or incorrigible conduct continues, the court may impose greater supervision.

The most formal dispositions used in the juvenile court include probation and commitment. Probation involves placing the child under the supervision of the probation officer for the purpose of community treatment. It is the disposition of choice in almost all juvenile court cases.[40] Conditions of probation are normally imposed on the child by either statute or court order and are of two kinds. There are general conditions, such as those which require the child to stay away from other delinquents or to obey the law. These types of conditions are often vague, but have been upheld by the courts. More specific conditions of probation include requiring the child to participate in a vocational training program, attend school regularly, obtain treatment at a child guidance clinic, or make restitution.

Once placed on probation, the child is ordinarily required to meet regularly with the probation officer for counseling and supervision and adhere to the conditions of probation established by the court. This plan may continue for a period of time, possibly six months to two years, depending upon the duration of probation as established by the statutory law. Most states allow early release from probation if the child is making a good adjustment, or may permit an extension of the probationary period. If the child complies with the court order, probation is terminated. Proceedings to revoke probation occur if the child commits a new offense. Some states provide that the child be given notice, a hearing, the right to counsel, and other due process safeguards, similar to those given adult offenders, at such proceedings.

The most severe of the statutory dispositions available to the juvenile court involves committing the child to a juvenile institution. The committed child may be sent to a state training school or private residential treatment facility. Some jurisdictions distinguish in their placement procedures between delinquent and status offenders, and prohibit the commitment of incorrigible youth to training schools for delinquent children. The reason for such an approach is generally based on the theory that only children who commit delinquent acts should be placed in state institutions.

Most state statutes vary when determining the length of the child's commitment. Traditionally, many jurisdictions would commit the child up to majority, which usually meant 21 years of age. This form of sentencing normally deprived the child of freedom for an extensive period of time—sometimes longer than an adult would be confined if sentenced for the same offense. As a result, some states have sought to circumvent this problem by passing legislation committing children for periods varying from one to three years.

Today, experts in delinquency and juvenile law are questioning the whole idea of institutionalizing juvenile offenders. Massachusetts has closed all of its state training schools, and most other states are establishing small residential facilities operated by juvenile care agencies.[41] Many large, impersonal, expensive state institutions with unqualified staff and ineffective treatment programs are being eliminated. Although some children must be confined, it is apparent that institutional training schools are being replaced by community-type programs. However, some jurisdictions are passing stricter sentencing laws resulting in children being institutionalized for longer periods. Such approaches are discussed in the following section.

## TRENDS IN JUVENILE SENTENCING

Since the inception of the juvenile court over eight decades ago, the traditional goal and philosophy has been rehabilitation and treatment of the juvenile offender at disposition. Under the rehabilitative goal, the juvenile justice system operated to provide care for children "in their best interest" but often subjected them to harsh penalties without due process of law.

In the mid-1960s, due process rights were granted to children, but the ideal of rehabilitation remained unfulfilled.

In order to achieve these traditional goals, juvenile court dispositional orders have been based on totally indeterminate sentencing terms for juvenile offenders. The indeterminate sentence is often defined as a term of incarceration with a stated minimum and maximum period, or no minimum, as described in Chpater 13. For instance, a sentence to prison for a period of from 3 to 10 years would constitute an indeterminate sentence. Based on the traditional belief that the indeterminate dispositional order should fit the child's needs, such sentencing provisions allow for individualized programs of treatment and provide for flexibility in sentencing. In some jurisdictions, the juvenile court judge could sentence the juvenile for an indeterminate period to a particular type of program. In other jurisdictions, the judge was required to send a child to a department such as a division of youth services within the given jurisdiction, and that agency would be responsible for the child's placement and treatment.

Over the past few years, juvenile justice experts and the general public have become aroused about the constantly rising juvenile crime rate, particularly with children committing serious law violations. As a result, reform groups, particularly law enforcement officials and legislators, have demanded that the juvenile justice system take a more serious stand with regard to dangerous juvenile offenders. Some state legislatures have responded by amending their juvenile codes and passing harsh laws that tighten up the juvenile justice system. For instance, in New York, children as young as 13 accused of murder may be sent to the adult courts and sentenced to terms as long as life.[42] California has lowered the age to 16 for transferring juvenile offenders to the adult court system.[43] The State of Washington has passed a determinate sentencing statute, which is discussed in detail below. Today, many jurisdictions, including the District of Columbia, Colorado, Delaware, and Florida, are passing mandatory prison sentences for juveniles convicted of serious felonies.

A second reform movement that has been going on for the past few years involves status offenders. This approach to the problem of disposition suggests that status offenders and other minor juvenile offenders be removed from the juvenile justice system and kept out of institutional programs which accept alleged juvenile delinquents. Because of the development of numerous diversion programs, as previously discussed, many children who were involved in truancy and incorrigible behavior, and who ordinarily may have been sent to a closed institution, are now being placed in community programs. Thus, dispositional orders regarding institutionalization for such children have declined and the number of children in the juvenile institutions has dropped over the past few years. In addition, the kinds of young people that are now being placed are those generally convicted of very serious juvenile crimes.

A third and probably very significant effort to reform juvenile justice and particularly the sentencing process emanates from the work of the American Bar Association and the development of its Standards for the Juvenile Justice System, in particular the volumes on Dispositions, Dispositional Procedures, Juvenile Delinquency and Sanctions, and Corrections Administration. Stanley Fisher suggests that these standards point to a shift in juvenile court philosophy from traditional rehabilitation to the concept of "just desserts."[44] This means that they recommend that juveniles be given determinate or "flat" sentences without the possibility of parole, rather than the indeterminate sentences that most juvenile offenders now receive. The Standards further recommend that punishment be classified into three major categories: nominal, conditional, and custodial sanctions. Nominal sanctions consist of reprimands, warnings, or other minor actions that do not affect the child's personal liberty. Conditional sanctions deal with such regulations as probation, restitution and counseling programs. Custodial sanctions, which are the most extreme, consider removal of the juvenile from his home into a nonsecure or secure institution. The National Advisory Committee on Criminal Justice Standards and Goals also recommend in 1976 that the dispositions available to the court for juveniles adjudicated delinquent include nominal, conditional, and custodial categories.[45]

The State of Washington has already adopted a determinate sentencing law for juvenile offenders.[46] All children convicted of juvenile delinquency are evaluated on the basis of a point system. Points are awarded to children based on their age, prior juvenile record, type of crime committed, and other factors. Minor offenders with less than so many points are handled in the community. Those committing more serious offenses are placed under probation. Children who commit the most serious offenses are subject to institutional penalties. Institutional officials, who had total discretion in the past for releasing children, now have limited discretion. As a result, juvenile offenders who commit crimes such as rape, armed robbery, or murder, are being sentenced to periods of institutionalization for two, three, and four years. This approach is different than releasing children from institutions in less than a year under the indeterminate program of sentencing when they committed a serious crime. Thus, the use of presumptive sentencing provisions or proportionality in sentencing has become a factor in juvenile justice dispositional procedures.

Although the above discussion indicates a change in traditional juvenile court sentencing, most jurisdictions continue to be preoccupied with rehabilitation as a primary dispositional goal. Goldstein, Freud, and Solnit, in their classic work entitled "Beyond the Best Interest of the Child" indicate that placements of children should be based on the "least detrimental alternative" philosophy available in order to safeguard the child's growth and development.[47] This goal exists for children involved in delinquent behavior, noncriminal behavior, and for those who may be neglected, abandoned, or abused. In reality today, most states apply custodial restrictions or institutionalization only to children who commit the most serious offenses.

In sum, rehabilitation and treatment remain the most realistic goal in the dispositional process. Proportionality in juvenile sentencing is being recognized and implemented by some jurisdictions. Whether the philosophy of "just desserts" is the answer to juvenile criminality remains unclear. Some critics suggest that the ABA Standards would "destroy the nation's juvenile court system and replace it with a junior criminal justice system."[48] There is no question that fitting the penalty to the child's behavior effects a radical change in current juvenile justice sentencing philosophy.

The post-disposition stage of the juvenile process normally involves juvenile aftercare and provisions for appeal of cases disposed of in the juvenile court. The question has been raised as to whether children committed to juvenile institutions have a constitutional or statutory right to treatment; those who support the right to treatment claim that the state must provide treatment for the juvenile offender if it intends to exercise control over him.

POST-
DISPOSITION

Once released from an institution, a juvenile may be placed on aftercare, usually involving parole under the supervision of a juvenile parole worker. The child completes the period of confinement in the community and receives assistance from the juvenile parole officer in the form of counseling, school referral, vocational training, and other services. If conditions of parole are violated, the juvenile may have parole revoked and be returned to the institution. Unlike the adult post-conviction process, where the United States Supreme Court has imposed procedural protections in revocation of probation and parole proceedings, juveniles have not yet received such due process rights.[49] State courts have also been reluctant to litigate juvenile rights in this area, and those that have have generally refused to require the whole array of rights available to adult offenders. Since the *Gault* decision, however, many states have adopted administrative regulations requiring juvenile agencies to incorporate due process procedures such as proper notice, the hearing, and the right to counsel in post-conviction proceedings.

Following the disposition of the case in the juvenile court, the child may be able to appeal the adjudication to a higher court. The provisions for such an appeal vary greatly within the jurisdictions. Many states authorize either the juvenile court or an intermediate court to review the original decision. A few states such as Massachusetts provide the child with a statutory right to appeal which results in a trial de novo, or new trial, in the Superior Court. The child may also appeal by virtue of a writ of habeas corpus, which tests the validity of the commitment.

Finally, the question exists as to whether juveniles who are committed to institutions have a right to treatment.[50] Because of the system of dealing with juvenile offenders is similar to the system of commitment for the mentally ill in that it is based on the parens patriae philosophy, juveniles have also sought a right to treatment. In light of his similarity, the case of *Martarella v. Kelly*[51] held that when juveniles judged to be "persons in need of supervision" were not furnished with adequate treatment, the failure to provide such treatment violated the Eighth and Fourteenth Amendments. In *Inmates v. Affleck* (1972),[52] the court recognized the right to treatment on statutory grounds and also required that minimum standards of treatment be implemented for juvenile offenders under institutional care. The *Inmates v. Affleck* case illustrated the horrible conditions that exist in many of our juvenile institutions. Consider the following excerpt from the appellate court record in this case:

Located on the floor above Annex C is a series of small, dimly lit, steel barred cells used for solitary confinement. Each cell is approximately eight feet by four feet, containing a metal slab bed and mattress, sink, and toilet. Boys confined there are released only to take showers, about twice a week. They get no exercise. The inmate's attorney, but not his family, is allowed to visit him there. Because windows on the wall opposite the cellblock are broken, the cells are cold. There is a small hole in the bars, through which meals, sometimes cold, are passed.[53]

Similar to *Affleck* was *Morales v. Turman*,[54] where the court specifically found that juveniles at a training school in Texas have a statutory right to treatment. In accordance with these holdings, the Court of Appeals for the

## NELSON V. HEYNE

**Facts:** In a class civil rights action on behalf of juvenile inmates of the Indiana Boys' School, a state institution, a complaint to the district court alleged that defendants' (Robert Heyne, the Commissioner of Corrections, Robert Hardin, Director of the Indiana Youth Authority, and Alfred Bennett, Superintendent of Indiana Boy's School) practices and policies at the school violated the Eight and Fourteenth Amendment rights of the juveniles under their care. Alleged practices include the use of corporal punishment, solitary confinement for periods ranging from 5 to 30 days, intramuscular injections of tranqualizing drugs, and censorship of inmate mail. The School itself was a medium security state correctional institution for boys 12–18 years of age, where about one-third were noncriminal offenders. Average length of stay at the institution was about six and one-half months, and although the School's maximum capacity was less than 300 boys, usual population was about 400. Counseling staff included 20 persons, 3 of whom were psychologists with undergraduate degrees, and one part-time psychiatrist who spent four hours per week at the institution. Medical staff included one part-time medical physician, one registered nurse, and one licensed practical nurse. The district court in this case found that it had jurisdiction over the case and thereafter held that the use of corporal punishment and the method of administering tanquilizing drugs by defendants constituted cruel and unusual punishment in violation of plaintiffs' Eighth and Fourteenth Amendment rights. In a separate judgment, the court found that the juveniles had a right to affirmative treatment, and that the school had not satisfied the minimal constitutional and statutory standards required by its rehabilitative goals. Before final relief was granted, the defendants appealed. The Seventh Circuit of the United States Court of Appeals granted review.

**Decision:** In *Nelson*, the Circuit Court dealt with the issue of a juvenile's constitutional affirmative right to treatment within a closed institution. Specifically, the questions were: (1) whether the practices alleged by defendants were violations of the cruel and unusual punishment clause of the Eighth Amendment; and (2) whether defendants had a constitutional right to rehabilitative treatment, and if so, was the treatment as provided by the school adequate? The court discussed the practices of corporal punishment in light of the cruel and unusual punishment standard suggested in *Furman v. Georgia*, 408 U.S. 238,

Seventh Circuit in *Nelson v. Heyne* (1974)[55] upheld a constitutional right to treatment for institutionalized juveniles under the Fourteenth Amendment. The *Nelson* case is significant because it was the first federal court of appeals decision to affirm a constitutional right to treatment. Although the United States Supreme Court has not yet declared that juveniles do have such a right, these recent decisions seem to indicate that juveniles do have a right, be it statutory or constitutional, to receive treatment if committed to a juvenile institution. Because of its importance, the Heyne case is described in detail below.

The termination of aftercare marks the final stage of the formal juvenile justice process.

To move from the *parens patriae* court standard adopted in Illinois in 1899 to the due process standard in *In re Gault* in 1967 has required almost three-quarters of a century. Today, courts and treatment specialists are still

FUTURE DIRECTIONS IN JUVENILE JUSTICE

279 (1971). By that standard, punishment is excessive if it is unnecessary, and is unnecessary if less severe punishment would serve the same purpose. Although the court did not find all corporal punishment to be cruel and unusual *per se*, it did find that on the basis of undisputed expert testimony, the beatings as applied were unnecessary and therefore excessive, thus violating the Eighth Amendment proscription against cruel and unusual punishment. The court next looked at the school's practice of administering tranqualizing drugs "to control excited behavior" without individual medical authorization and without first trying oral medication. Based on expert testimony at trial which established the possible serious side effects of these drugs, the court rejected the school's assertion that the use of drugs was not punishment. After stressing the need to balance the school's desire to maintain discipline with the child's right to be free from cruel and unusual punishment, the court held that the school's interest in reforming juveniles through the use of drugs in maintaining a rehabilitative atmosphere did not justify the cruel and unusual dangers resulting from poorly supervised administration of tranqualizing drugs. Turning then to the crucial holding by the District Court that incarcerated juveniles have an affirmative right to rehabilitative treatment, the Seventh Circuit noted that the Supreme Court has assumed although not explicitly stated, that the state must provide treatment for incarcerated juveniles. In light of this, the court looked at several recent cases concerning the impact of the *parens patriae* doctrine on this right, most notably the case of *Martarella v. Kelley*, 349 F.Supp. 575 (S.D.N.Y.1972), in which the court found a clear constitutional right to treatment for juveniles based on the Eighth and Fourteenth Amendments. The Seventh Circuit agreed then with the lower court that the juveniles did indeed have a constitutional as well as statutory right to rehabilitative treatment. The case was remanded to allow the lower court to determine the "minimal standards of care and treatment for juveniles" needed to provide them with their "right to 'individualized' care and treatment."

**Significance:** *Nelson v. Heyne* is significant in that it was the first federal appellate court decision affirming that juveniles have a *constitutional* as well as a statutory right to treatment. It is also the first to hold that federal judges may require standards by which to judge minimal adherence by institutions to individualized treatment.

confronting questions involving how to improve the juvenile justice system.

One of the primary legal questions involves what standard for applying rights to juvenile proceedings will be adopted by the United States Supreme Court in the future. Until now, the Court has applied the traditional due process standard of fundamental fairness in the juvenile process. Basic procedural rights such as the right to a hearing, the right to counsel, the privilege against self-incrimination, and others have been measured against the essentials of due process and fair treatment and not carved directly from the Constitution. The problem with this approach is that it does not clearly determine what rights are applicable to the juvenile process because the term due process has a convenient vagueness which makes its precise limits uncertain. For instance, is a child in the juvenile justice system entitled to all the rights that an adult has in a criminal proceeding?

Some major gaps exist in the procedural safeguards afforded children, particularly when these are compared to adult offenders. One of the major areas requiring further legal clarification is the pre-trial stage of the juvenile process. Many troublespots exist here, including detention, probable cause, waiver and other preliminary types of hearings, pre-trial disclosure of information, bail, and the right to appointed counsel throughout all of these early proceedings. In the area of adjudication, in addition to the rights established by *Gault*, the right to trial by jury for juveniles remains a controversial issue. Similarly, fair procedures at dispositions need to be further developed. Problems exist in this area concerning the legal requirement for the use of presentence investigations, the establishment of more suitable dispositions, and the need for juvenile court judges to openly state the reasons for judicial sentences.

In addition, much disparity exists in the structure of the juvenile courts and in the laws dealing with noncriminal behavior. Other problem areas include the lack of clarity regarding the rights of juveniles in school systems, particularly in search and seizures, and the uncertainty of the courts as to whether a juvenile has a constitutional right to treatment.

Apart from the legal issues, the juvenile justice system is beset by other serious problems. All we have to do is examine the following figures: More than one million children under 15 years old are not in school; the suicide rate among young people 15 to 24 years old has nearly doubled between 1968 and 1977; millions of teenagers are drug users; over 3.3 million children between ages 14 and 17 are problem drinkers; in 1978, more than three million arrests were made for juvenile crime; and more than one million children run away from home each year.[56] These statistics portray a picture of American youth not participating in traditional family, education, and community activities. Instead, we have many children involved in youthful disruptive behavior. Unfortunately, over the years, few effective prevention and rehabilitation programs have been available for juvenile offenders.

The time is ripe for an attack on these problems. The courts are clearly involved in defining the rights of all children, including juvenile offenders.

The Juvenile Justice and Delinquency Prevention Act of 1974, which established the Office of Juvenile Justice and Delinquency Prevention within the LEAA, has been given legislative responsibility to curb delinquency throughout the country.[57] Its goals for the 1980s include: (1) prevention programs for youth, (2) alternatives to juvenile incarceration, (3) ensuring compliance with the Juvenile Justice Act regarding de-institutionalization for all status offenders.[58] And, most important, the American Bar Association, in conjunction with the Institute of Judicial Administration, has completed a comprehensive set of standards for juvenile justice which can be used as a basis for making fundamental changes in the system.[59] As the United States Supreme Court stated in *McKeiver:*

The juvenile concept held high promise. We are reluctant to say that, despite disappointment of so grave dimensions, it still does not hold promise, and we are particularly reluctant to say, as do the Pennsylvania petitions here, that the system cannot accomplish its rehabilitative goals. So much depends on the availability of resources, on the interest and commitment of the public, on willingness to learn, and on understanding as to cause and effect and cure. In this field, as in so many others, one perhaps learns best by doing.[60]

SUMMARY

The juvenile justice system is concerned with delinquent children, as well as with those who are beyond the care and protection of their parents. Jurisdiction for juveniles involved in antisocial behavior exists in the juvenile or family court systems of each jurisdiction. Courts such as these belong to a system of agencies including law enforcement, child care, and institutional services.

When a child is brought to the juvenile court, the proceedings are generally nonadversarial and informal in nature. Representatives from different disciplines, such as lawyers, social workers, and psychiatrists, all play major roles in the judicial process.

In recent years, the juvenile court system has become more legalistic by virtue of United States Supreme Court decisions which have granted children procedural safeguards in these proceedings. However, neither rehabilitation programs nor the application of due process rights has stemmed the growing tide of juvenile antisocial behavior. Perhaps the answer lies outside the courthouse, in the form of job opportunities for juveniles, improved family relationships, and more effective school systems. How to cope with the needs of children in trouble remains one of the most controversial and frustrating issues in the justice system.

QUESTIONS FOR DISCUSSION

**1.** Discuss the juvenile justice system in your jurisdiction. How does it compare with the adult process? What are the similarities and differences in the two systems in terms of philosophy, services, and legal rights?

**2.** What are PINS and CHINS? How do such persons differ from delinquents?

**3.** Cite the facts, decision, and significance of the United States Supreme Court case of *In re Gault*. Discuss the impact of this case on the juvenile justice system.

NOTES

**1.** For a comprehensive view of juvenile law, see generally Joseph J. Senna and Larry J. Siegel, *Juvenile Law—Cases and Comments*, (St. Paul, Minn.: West Publishing Co., 1976).

**2.** Judge Julian Mack, a prominent pioneer juvenile court judge, summarized this philosophy eloquently in "The Chancery Procedures in Juvenile Court" in J. Adams, ed., *The Child, The Clinic and the Court* 311–12 (1927). See also J. Mack, "The Juvenile Court" in *Harvard Law Review* 23:104 (1909).

**3.** Kent v. United States, 383 U.S. 541 (1966)—(juveniles entitled to minimum procedural safeguards in the waiver proceeding): In re Gault, 387 U.S. 1 (1968)—(juveniles have the right to notice counsel, confrontation, cross-examination and privilege against self-incrimination in juvenile court proceedings): In re Winship, 397 U.S. 358 (1970)—(proof beyond a reasonable doubt necessary for conviction in juvenile proceedings): Breed v. Jones, 421 U.S. 519 (1975)—(jeopardy attaches in a juvenile court adjudicatory hearing thus barring subsequent prosecution for the same offense as an adult).

**4.** Lamb v. Brown, 456 F.2d 18 (10th Cir. 1972).

**5.** The National Council on Crime and Delinquency has launched a nationwide campaign to remove "status" offenses from the juvenile codes in all 50 states. NCCD President Milton G. Rector announced that 23% of all boys and 70% of all girls held in juvenile institutions are guilty of no crime for which an adult would be prosecuted. The most common of these status offenses are truancy, running away from home, incorrigibility, and curfew violations. *Criminal Law Reporter* 17:2095 (April 30, 1975).

**6.** See, for example, District of Columbia v. B.J.R., 332 A.2d 58 (1975).

**7.** See, for example, Mapp v. Ohio, 367 U.S. 643, 81 S.Ct. 168, 6 L.Ed.2d 1081 (1961) (extended the exclusionary rule to state court proceedings): Escobedo v. Illinois, 378 U.S. 478, 84 S.Ct. 1758, 12 L.Ed.2d 977 (1964) (held that a state must afford an accused the right to counsel in a police station); Miranda v. Arizona, 384 U.S. 436, 88 S.Ct. 1602, 16 L.Ed.2d 694 (1966) (defined a defendant's Fifth Amendment privilege against self-incrimination when taken into custody).

**8.** 387 U.S. 1, 87 S.Ct. 1428, 18 L.Ed.2d 527 (1967).

**9.** See Sullivan and Siegel, "How Police Use Information to Make Decisions," *Crime and Delinquency* (1972), pp. 253–262, for a discussion on the factors involved in Police-Decision Making.

**10.** See generally Black and Reis, "Police Control of Juveniles," *American Sociological Review* 35:63 (February 1970).

**11.** 24 N.Y.2d 522, 301 N.Y.S.2d 479, 249 N.E.2d 366 (1969).

**12.** 34 N.Y.2d 483, 358 N.Y.S.2d 403, 315 N.E.2d 466 (1974).

**13.** 384 U.S. 436, 86 S.Ct. 1602, 16 L.Ed.2d 694 (1966). *Miranda* held that an accused in police custody must be given the following warning: (1) that he has a right to remain silent; (2) that any statements made can be used against him; (3) that he has a right to counsel; and (4) that if he can't afford counsel, one will be furnished at public expense.

**14.** 388 U.S. 218, 87 S.Ct. 1926, 18 L.Ed.2d 1149 (1967). See also Gilbert v. California, 388 U.S. 263, 87 S.Ct. 1951, 18 L.Ed.2d 1178 (1967).

15. 406, U.S. 682, 92 S.Ct. 1877, 32 L.Ed.2d 411 (1972).

16. See, for example, Johnson v. Zerbst, 304 U.S. 458, 58 S.Ct. 1019, 82 L.Ed. 1461 (1938) (Plea must be made in a knowing and voluntary manner); McCarthy v. United States, 394 U.S. 459, 89 S.Ct. 1166, 22 L.Ed.2d 418 (1968)—(Defendant must know that he is simultaneously waiving several constitutional rights: (1) privilege against self-incrimination, (2) trial by jury, (3) right to confrontation); Boykin v. Alabama, 395 U.S. 238, 89 S.Ct. 1709, 23 L.Ed.2d 274, (1969) (A recorded showing of waiver of constitutional rights is required on a plea of guilty.); Brady v. United States, 397 U.S. 742, 90 S.Ct. 1463, 25 L.Ed.2d 747 (1970) (Voluntariness of guilty plea was not negated because it had been motivated by defendant's desire to avoid a harsh sentence.); Santobello v. New York, 404 U.S. 257, 92 S.Ct. 495, 30 L.Ed.2d 427 (1971) (If a guilty plea is made in exchange for a promise from the government, the promise must be honored.)

17. President's Commission on Law Enforcement and the Administration of Justice, Task Force Report: Juvenile Delinquency and Youth Crime (Washington, D.C.: U.S. Goverment Printing Office, 1967), p. 147.

18. American Bar Association, Standards Relating to Juvenile Probation Function (Cambridge, Ballinger Press, 1977), p. 23.

19. See generally National Council on Crime and Delinquency, Standard Family Court Act (New York: NCCD, 1965); National Conference of Commissioners on Uniform State Laws, Uniform Juvenile Court Act (Phil. American Law Institute, 1968), Sec. 9; William Sheridan, Model Acts for Family Courts (Washington, D.C.: Department of Health, Education, and Welfare, 1975), Sec. 13.

20. American Bar Association, Standards Relating to Juvenile Probation Function, pp. 31–53.

21. Paul Nejelski, "Diversion: The Promise and the Danger," Crime and Delinquency Journal, 22:393 (1971).

22. National Advisory Commission on Criminal Justice Standards and Goals, Task Force Report on Courts (Washington, D.C.: LEAA, 1973), p. 20.

23. LaMar T. Empey, American Delinquency—Its Meaning and Construction (Illinois: Dorsey Press, 1978), p. 532.

24. Nejelski, "Diversion: The Promise and the Danger," p. 394.

25. See generally Case Comments, "Juvenile Justice—Statutory Exclusion from the Juvenile Process of Certain Alleged Felons" in Boston University Law Review 53:212 (1973).

26. Department of Health, Education, and Welfare, Model Acts for Family Courts and State-Local Children's Programs, § 30 (1968).

27. 383 U.S. 541, 86 S.Ct. 1045, 16 L.Ed.2d 84 (1966).

28. Id. at 554–555.

29. Id. at 566–567.

30. National Conference of Commissioners On Uniform State Laws, Uniform Juvenile Court Act, 34 (1968); Department of Health, Education, and Welfare, Model Acts for Family Courts and State-Local Children's Programs, § 30 (1968).

31. 421 U.S. 519, 95 S.Ct. 1779, 44 L.Ed.2d 346 (1975).

32. Id. at 95 S.Ct. 1785.

33. See generally "The Juvenile Court and the Adversary System: Problems of Function and Form," Wisconsin Law Review 7 (1965).

34. 387 U.S. 1, 87 S.Ct. 1428, 18 L.Ed.2d 527 (1967).

35. Id. at 20.

36. See generally Popkin, Lippert, and Keiter, "Another Look at the Role of

Due Process in Juvenile Court" in *Family Law Quarterly* 6:233 (1972).

**37.** 397 U.S. 358, 25 L.Ed.2d 368, 90 S.Ct. 1068 (1970).

**38.** 403 U.S. 528, 29 L.Ed.2d 647, 91 S.Ct. 1976 (1971).

**39.** See generally Scarpitti and Stephenson, "Juvenile Court Dispositions Factors in the Decision-Making Process," *Crime & Delinquency* 17:142 (April 1971).

**40.** See President's Commission on Law Enforcement and Administration of Justice, *Task Force Report: Corrections* (1967), at 27.

**41.** See generally Bakal, *Closing Correctional Institutions: New Strategies for Youth Services* (Lexington, Mass.: Lexington Books, 1973).

**42.** "Justice, Treating Kids Like Adults," *Newsweek,* June 27, 1979, p. 54.

**43.** Ibid.

**44.** Stanley Fisher, "The Dispositional Process Under the Juvenile Justice Standards Project," *Boston University Law Review* 57:732 (1977).

**45.** National Advisory Committee on Criminal Justice Standards and Goals, Report on Task Force on Juvenile Justice and Delinquency Prevention (Washington, D.C.: LEAA, 1976), pp. 452–459.

**46.** See Michael Serrill, "Police Write a New Law on Juvenile Crime," *Police Magazine,* September 1979, p. 47.

**47.** See Joseph Goldstein, Anna Freud, and Albert Solnit, *Beyond the Best Interests of the Child* (New York: Free Press, 1973).

**48.** Stanley Fisher, "The Dispositional Process Under the Juvenile Justice Standards Project," p. 732.

**49.** See, Morrissey v. Brewer, 408 U.S. 471, 92 S.Ct. 2593, 33 L.Ed.2d 484 (1972). Upon revocation of parole a defendant is entitled to the due process rights of: (1) a hearing, (2) written notice of charges, (3) knowledge of evidence against him, (4) opportunity to present and cross-examine witnesses, and (5) written statement of reasons for parole revocation.

**50.** The basis for this right originated with such cases as Rouse v. Cameron, 363 F.2d 451 (D.C. Cir. 1966) and Wyatt v. Stickney, 325 F.Supp. 781 (1971), which dealt with the right to treatment for the mentally ill person. The *Wyatt* case was particularly important since it held that involuntary commitment without rehabilitation was a violation of due process of law.

**51.** 349 F.Supp. 575 (1972).

**52.** 346 F.Supp. 1354 (1972).

**53.** Id. at 1361.

**54.** 364 F.Supp. 166 (1973).

**55.** 491 F.2d 352 (7th Cir. 1974).

**56.** Law Enforcement Assistance Administration Newsletter, Vol. 9, No. 1, January 1980.

**57.** Juvenile Justice and Delinquency Prevention Act of 1974, 18 U.S.C.A § 5031; also, Law Enforcement Assistance Administration, History of Juvenile Justice and Delinquency Prevention Act of 1974 (Washington, D.C.: LEAA, 1979).

**58.** LEAA Newsletter, Vol. 9, No. 1, January 1980, p. 1.

**59.** Kaufman, *American Bar Association Journal* 62:730 (1975).

**60.** *McKeiver,* 403 U.S. at 547.

# *Community Arbitration Project, Anne Arundel County, Maryland and Project New Pride, Denver, Colorado.

In 1973, the juvenile intake office of Anne Arundel County, Maryland, faced heavy backlogs of relatively minor cases that impaired its ability to deal with youngsters in more serious trouble with the law. Delays in resolving cases were frequent. A child accused of a first or second misdemeanor offense typically waited four to six weeks before official action was taken on his case. By that time, the incident was no longer fresh in the youngster's mind, making it difficult to reinforce the concept of accepting responsibility for the consequence of his actions.

The offender's parents and the victim were only marginally involved as the case proceeded. Many victims were never informed of the final disposition of the case. As a result, both parents and victims felt powerless and ineffective.

Most important, case dispositions often were unsatisfactory. Because of caseload pressures, many offenses received only cursory attention.

Or cases were sent for formal adjudication—a process that may alienate the youngster and result in an unnecessary stigma. Public dissatisfaction with the county's juvenile justice system was increasing.

In 1975, the County devised an alternative to the system. The Community Arbitration Project is designed to alleviate the burden on the juvenile court while still impressing on the young offender the consequences of his or her behavior.

Under the program, juvenile misdemeanants are issued a citation which records the offense and schedules a hearing to arbitrate the case seven days later. The suspect's parents and the victim receive copies of the citation and are asked to appear at the hearing. The right to counsel is made clear to the youngster and his parents.

Although the hearing is informal, it is held in a courtroom setting to enhance the child's understanding of the meaning and importance

---

*From U.S. Department of Justice, Exemplary Projects—A Program of National Institute of Law Enforcement and Criminal Justice (Washington, D.C.: LEAA, 1979).

of the procedure. The Juvenile Intake Commissioner—an attorney with experience in juvenile cases—serves as arbitrator. The Commissioner hears the complaint and reviews the police report. If the child admits committing the offense and consents to arbitration, the Commissioner makes an informal adjustment, sentencing the child to a prescribed number of hours of community work and/or restitution, counseling, or an educational program. The case is left "open," to be closed within 90 days upon a positive report from the child's field site supervisor. If the offense is serious, if the child denies his involvement, or if the child or his parents so request, the case may be forwarded to the State's Attorney for formal adjudication.

In two years since project inception, 4,233 youths have gone through the program. Nearly half of their cases were adjudicated informally; only 8% were referred to the State's Attorney.

## *PROJECT NEW PRIDE, DENVER, COLORADO

Project New Pride is a successful attempt to help juveniles, most with lengthy records of prior arrest and conviction, to break out of what could become a lifetime pattern of crime by instilling a sense of self-pride. The project integrates education, employment, counseling, and cultural education—services which are usually highly specialized and fragmented. Intensive application of this service integration approach is the key to the success of New Pride.

The program accepts Denver County residents 14–17 years old, who have had a recent arrest or conviction for burglary, robbery, or assault related to robbery, and who have at least two prior convictions for similar offenses.

A unique feature of the program is its pioneering work with youth with learning disabilities. Tests administered to project youth in the first two years of operation showed that 71% of New Pride participants had learning disabilities. The Learning Disabilities Center has recently received a separate grant and will be able to serve an increased number of clients.

The effect on the 160 clients who have completed the New Pride program has been significant.

—— The nonstatus offense rearrest rate for New Pride clients during a 12-month period in the community was 27%. The rate for a control group was 32%.

—— 70% of clients have been placed in full or part-time jobs, and the rearrest rate for employed clients was one-third the rate for unemployed clients.

New Pride has also pointed up the potential economic advantages to the community. The cost of incarcerating a youth in Colorado is estimated at $12,000 a year. New Pride spends $4,000 per year to keep a youngster out of institutions.

Originally funded under LEAA's Impact Cities program, New Pride is now an established program of the Colorado Division of Youth Services.

# APPENDIXES

**Adjudication**–the determination of guilt or innocence; a judgement concerning criminal charges. Trial by jury is a method of adjudication; the majority of offenders charged plead guilty. Of the remainder, some cases are also adjudicated by a judge without a jury and others are dismissed.

**Adversary System**–the procedure used to determine truth in the adjudication of guilt or innocence, which puts the defense (advocate for the accused) against the prosecution (advocate for the state), with the judge acting as arbiter of the legal rules. Under the adversary system, the burden is upon the state to prove the charges beyond a reasonable doubt. This system of having the two parties "battle" or publicly debate has proved to be the most effective method of achieving the truth regarding a set of circumstances. (The *Accusatory*, or inquisitorial, *system* is used in continental Europe, under which the charge is evidence of guilt which the accused must disprove; the judge takes an active part in the proceedings.)

**Appeal**–review of lower court proceedings by a higher court. There is no constitutional right to appeal. However, the "right" to appeal is established by statute in some states and by custom in others. All states set conditions as to type of case or grounds for appeal, which appellate courts may review. Appellate courts do *not* retry the case under review. Rather, the transcript of the lower court case is read by the judges, and the lawyers for the defendant and for the state argue about the merits of the appeal—that is, the legality of lower court proceedings instead of the original testimony. Appeal is more a process for controlling police, court, and correctional practices than for rescuing innocent defendants. When appellate courts do reverse lower court judgements, it is usually because of

"prejudicial error" (deprivation of rights), and the case for retrial is remanded.

**Arraignment**–the step at which the accused is read the charges against him and is asked how he pleads. In addition, the accused is advised of his rights. Possible pleas are guilty, not guilty, nolo contendere, and not guilty by reason of insanity.

**Arrest**–the taking of a person into the custody of the law, the legal purpose of which is to restrain the accused until he can be held accountable for the offense at court proceedings. The legal requirement for an arrest is probable cause. Arrests for investigation, suspicion, or harassment are improper and of doubtful legality. The police have the responsibility to use only reasonable physical force necessary to make an arrest. The summons has been used as a substitute to arrest.

**Arrest Warrant**–a written court order issued by a magistrate authorizing and directing that an individual be taken into custody to answer criminal charges.

**Bail**–monetary amount for or condition of pre-trial release, which is normally set by a judge at the initial appearance. The purpose of bail is to ensure the return of the accused at subsequent proceedings. If he is unable to make bail, he is detained in jail.
The Eighth Amendment provides that excessive bail shall not be required.

**Booking**–an administrative record of an arrest made in police stations, involving listing offender's name, address, physical description, date of birth, employer, time of arrest, offense, name of arresting officer. Photographing and fingerprinting of the offender are also a part of booking. The Miranda Warning is given again (the first time at the scene of arrest). In addition, the accused is allowed to make a telephone call.

**Beyond A Reasonable Doubt**–the degree of proof required for conviction of a defendant in criminal proceedings: less than absolute certainty, more than high probability. If there is doubt based upon reason, the accused is entitled to the benefit of that doubt by an acquittal.

**Case Law**–law derived from the decisions of previous court decisions, as opposed to *statutory law* which is passed by legislatures.

**Complaint**–a sworn allegation made in writing to a court or judge that an individual is guilty of some designated (complained of) offense. This is often the first legal document filed regarding a criminal offense, the complaint can be "taken out" by the victim, the police officer, the District Attorney, or other interested party. Although the complaint "charges" an offense, an indictment or information may be the formal charging document.

**Common Law**–the basic legal principles which developed in England and became uniform, similar (common) law throughout the country. Judges began following previous court decisions (precedent) when new, but similar, cases arose. For various similar circumstances, specific principles were developed.

**Concurrent**–(literally, "to run together"); the condition set for serving sentences of imprisonment for multiple charges. When an accused is convicted of two or more charges, he must be sentenced on each charge. If the sentences are concurrent, they begin the same day and sentence has been completed after the longest term has been served. For example: a defendant is sentenced to three years imprisonment on a charge of assault and ten years for burglary, the

sentences to be served concurrently. After ten years in prison the sentences would be completed.

**Consecutive**–(literally, "to follow one after another"); as opposed to concurrent sentences, upon completion of one sentence the other term of incarceration begins. For example: a defendant is sentenced to three years imprisonment on a charge of assault and ten years for burglary— sentences to be served consecutively. After three years are served on the assault charge, the offender begins serving the burglary sentence. Therefore, the total term on the two charges would be thirteen years.

**Conviction**–a judgement of guilt; a verdict by a jury, a plea by a defendant, or a judgement by a court that the accused is guilty as charged.

**Crime**–an offense against the state; behavior in violation of law for which there is prescribed punishment.

**Criminal Law**–the body of law which defines criminal offenses and prescribes punishments (substantive law) and which delineates criminal procedure (procedural law).

**Criminal Justice Process**–the decision-making points from the initial investigation or arrest by police to the eventual release of the offender and his reentry into society; the various sequential criminal stages through which the offender passes.

**Criminal Justice Standards**–models, commentaries, or recommendations for the revision of Criminal Justice procedures and practices; for example, the American Law Institute's Model Penal Code, American Bar Association's *Standards for Criminal Justice*, and the recommendations of the National Advisory Commission on Criminal Justice Standards and Goals.

**Criminal Justice System**–a group of agencies and organizations—the police, courts, and corrections, as well as the legislature and appellate courts—responsible for the administration of criminal justice and crime control in our society.

**Criminology**–the study of the causes and treatment of criminal behavior, criminal law, and the administration of criminal justice.

**Defendant**–the accused in criminal proceedings; he/she has the right to be present at each stage of the criminal justice process except Grand Jury proceedings.

**Definite Sentence**–this involves "fixed" terms of incarceration, such as three years imprisonment. It is felt by many to be too restrictive for rehabilitative purposes; the advantage is that offender knows how much time he has to serve, i.e., when he will be released.

**Disposition**–for juvenile offenders the equivalent of sentencing for adult offenders. The theory is that disposition be more rehabilitative than retributive. Possible dispositions may dismiss the case, release the youth to the custody of his parents, place the offender on probation, send him to an institution or to a state correctional institution.

**District Attorney**–generally, those prosecutors representing the federal government in federal district courts or counties and districts in state courts. United States district attorneys are appointed by the President. District attorneys in counties or districts are usually elected.

**Due Process**–the basic constitutional principle based upon the concept of the primacy of the individual and the complementary concept of limitation on governmental power; a safeguard against arbitrary and unfair state procedures in judicial or administrative proceedings.

Embodied in the Due Process concept are the basic rights of a defendant in criminal proceedings and the requisites for a fair trial. These rights and requirements have been expanded by appellate court decisions and include (1) timely notice of a hearing or trial which informs the accused of the charges against him; (2) the opportunity to confront accusers, to present evidence on one's own behalf before an impartial jury or judge; (3) the presumption of innocence under which guilt must be proven by legally obtained evidence and the verdict must be supported by the evidence presented; (4) the right of an accused to be warned of his constitutional rights at the earliest stage of the criminal process; (5) protection against self-incrimination; (6) assistance of counsel at every critical stage of the criminal process; and (7) the guarantee that an individual will not be tried more than once (Double Jeopardy) for the same offense.

**Exclusionary Rule**–the principle which prohibits the use of evidence which was illegally obtained in a trial. Based on the Fourth Amendment "right of the people to be secure in their persons, houses, papers, and effects, against unreasonable searches and seizures," the rule excludes the fruits of those searches as evidence. However, the rule is not a bar to prosecution, as legally obtained evidence may be available which may be used in a trial.

**Felony**–a more serious offense which carries a penalty of incarceration in a state prison, usually for one year or more. Persons convicted of felony offenses lose certain rights such as the right to vote, hold elective office, or maintain certain licenses.

**Grand Jury**–a group (usually comprised of 23 citizens) chosen to hear testimony in secret and to issue formal criminal accusations (indictments). It also serves an investigatory function concerning possible violations of law.

**Incarceration**–the sentencing of a convicted offender to imprisonment in jail, a house of correction, or a prison.

**Indeterminate Sentence**–a term of incarceration with a stated minimum and maximum term; for example, a sentence to prison for a period of from three to ten years. Based on the belief that sentences should fit the criminal, indeterminate sentences allow "individualized" sentences and provide for sentencing flexibility. Judges can set high minimum to overcome the purpose of the indeterminate sentence.

**Index Offenses**–those crimes used by the FBI to indicate the incidence of crime in the United States and reported annually in the *Uniform Crime Report*; these crimes include: murder and non-negligent manslaughter, robbery, forcible rape, aggravated assault, burglary, larceny $50 and over, and motor vehicle theft.

**Indictment**–a written accusation returned by a grand jury charging an individual with a specified crime after determination of probable cause; the prosecutor presents enough evidence (prima facie case) to establish probable cause.

**Information**–like the indictment, a formal charging document. The prosecuting attorney makes out the *information* and files it in court. Probable cause is determined at the preliminary which, unlike grand jury proceedings, is public and attended by the accused and his attorney.

**Prison**–state or federal correctional institutions for the incarceration of felony offenders for terms of one year or more.

**Jury**–(Petit Jury) a group of citizens, twelve or less, chosen to decide questions of fact in a trial. There is no constitutional requirement that juries must contain twelve members; usually, there are twelve members in felony cases. Juries for misdemeanor cases are comprised frequently of fewer than twelve individuals.

**Juvenile Delinquent**–a youth, within the age established by statute, who has been adjudicated by a juvenile court to have committed a prohibited act or to be in need of supervision. Age limitations of "juveniles" varies among the states from 16 to 21 years of age, with the most common being 18 years.

**Juvenile Justice Process**–court proceedings for youths within the "juvenile" age group that differ from the adult criminal process. Originally, under the paternal *(parens patriae)* philosophy, juvenile procedures were informal and nonadversary, invoked *for* the juvenile offender rather than *against* him; a petition instead of a complaint is filed; courts make findings of involvement or adjudication of delinquency instead of convictions; and juvenile offenders receive dispositions instead of sentences.
Recent court decisions (Kent and Gault) have increased the adversary nature of juvenile court proceedings. However, the philosophy remains one of diminishing the stigma of delinquency and providing for the youth's well-being and rehabilitation, rather than seeking retribution.

**Initial Appearance**–the step at which the arrested suspect is brought before a magistrate for consideration of bail. The suspect must be taken for *initial appearance* within a "reasonable time" after arrest. For petty offenses this step often serves as the final criminal proceedings, either by adjudication by a judge or guilty plea.

**Interrogation**–the method of accumulating evidence in the form of information or confessions from suspects by police; questioning, which has been restricted because of concern about the use of brutal and coercive methods and interest in protecting against self-incrimination.

**Investigation**–inquiry concerning suspected criminal behavior to identify offenders or to gather further evidence to assist the prosecution of apprehended offenders.

**Jail**–usually a part of the local police station of sheriff's office; used to detain people awaiting trial, to serve as a "lock-up" for drunks and disorderly individuals and as a place of short-term confinement of offenders serving sentences of less than one year.

**House of Correction**–county correctional institution generally used for the incarceration of more serious misdemeanants, the sentences of which are usually less than one year.

**LEAA**–Law Enforcement Assistance Administration, under the United States Department of Justice, established by the Omnibus Crime Control and Safe Streets Act of 1968 to administer grants and provide guidance for crime prevention policy and programs. All jurisdictions funded by LEAA (the 50 states; Washington, D.C.; American Samoa; Guam; Puerto Rico; and the Virgin Islands) have state planning agencies (SPAs) which submit project plans to LEAA and which allocate LEAA funds.

**Miranda Warning**–the result of two supreme court decisions (*Escobedo v. Illinois* 378 US 478; and *Miranda v. Arizona* 384 US 436) which require that a police officer inform an individual under arrest of his constitutional rights. Although aimed at protecting an individual during in-custody interrogation, the warning must also be given "when the investigation shifts from the investigatory to the accusatory stage," i.e., when suspicion begins to focus on an individual.

If the police officer does not give the warning, the exclusionary rule applies and no statements or confessions made by the accused can be used as evidence at a trial.

**Misdemeanor**–a less serious offense punishable by incarceration for not more than one year in a county jail or fine or similar penalty. There is no uniform rule, as an offense may be a misdemeanor in one jurisdiction and a felony in another.

**Parole**–the release of a prisoner from imprisonment subject to conditions set by a parole board. Depending on the jurisdiction, inmates must serve a certain proportion of their sentence before becoming eligible for parole. Upon determination of the parole board, the inmate is granted parole, the conditions of which may require him to report regularly to a parole officer, to refrain from criminal conduct, to maintain and support his family, to avoid contact with other convicted criminals, to abstain from alcoholic beverages and drugs, to remain within the jurisdiction, etc.

Violations of the conditions of parole may result in revocation of parole, in which case the individual will be returned to prison.

The concept behind parole is to allow the release of the offender to community supervision, where his rehabilitation and readjustment will be facilitated.

**Plea**–an answer to formal charges by an accused. Possible pleas are guilty, not guilty, nolo contendere, not guilty by reason of insanity. A guilty plea is a confession of the offense as charged. A not guilty plea is a denial of the charge and places the burden on the prosecution to prove the elements of the offense.

**Plea Bargaining**–the discussion between the defense counsel and the prosecution by which the accused agrees to plead guilty for certain considerations. The advantage to the defendant may be in the form of a reduction of the charges, a lenient sentence, or—in the case of multiple charges—dropped charges. The advantage to the prosecution is that a conviction is obtained without the time and expense of lengthy trial proceedings.

**Preliminary Hearing**–the step at which criminal charges initiated by an "information" are tested for *probable cause;* the prosecution presents enough evidence to establish probable cause, i.e., a *prima fracie* case. The Hearing is public and may be attended by the accused and his attorney.

**Presentence Report**–an investigation performed by a probation officer attached to a trial court after the conviction of a defendant. The report contains information about the defendant's background, education, previous employment, family, his own statement concerning the offense, prior criminal record, interviews with neighbors or acquaintances, his mental and physical condition (i.e., information which would not be made record in the case of a guilty plea or which would be inadmissible as evidence at a trial but could be influential and important at the sentencing stage).

After conviction, a judge sets a date for sentencing (usually ten days to two weeks from date of conviction), during which time the presentence report is made. The report is required in felony cases in federal courts and in many states, is optional with the judge in some states, and in others is mandatory before convicted offenders can be placed on probation. In the case of juvenile offenders, the *Presentence Report* also known as a *social history report*.

**Probable Cause**–the evidentiary criterion necessary to sustain an arrest or the issuance of an arrest or search warrant; less than absolute certainty or "beyond a reasonable doubt" but greater than mere suspicion or "hunch." A set of facts, information, circumstances, or conditions which would lead a reasonable man to believe that an offense was committed and that the accused commited that offense.

An arrest made without *probable cause* may be susceptible to prosecution as an illegal arrest under "false imprisonment" statutes.

**Probation**–a sentence entailing the conditional release of a convicted offender into the community under the supervision of the court (in the form of a probation officer) subject to certain conditions for a specified time. The conditions are usually similar to those of *parole*. (NOTE: *Probation* is a sentence, an alternative to incarceration; *parole* is administrative release from incarceration.) Violation of the conditions of probation may result in revocation of probation.

**Procedural Law**–the rules which define the operation of criminal proceedings. *Procedural Law* describes the methods which must be followed in obtaining warrants, investigating offenses, affecting lawful arrests, using force, conducting trials, introducing evidence, sentencing convicted offenders, and reviewing cases by appellate courts (in general, legislatures have ignored postsentencing procedures). Given the substantive law which defines criminal offenses, procedural law delineates how the substantive offenses are to be enforced.

**Prosecutor**–a representative of the state (executive branch) in criminal proceedings; an advocate for the state's case—the charge—in the adversary trial, e.g., the Attorney General of the United States, United States attorneys, attorneys general of the states, district attorneys, and police prosecutors.

The prosecutor participates in investigations both before and after arrest, prepares legal documents, participates in obtaining arrest or search warrants, decides whether or not to charge a suspect and, if so, with which offense to charge. He/she argues the state's case at trial, advises the police, participates in plea negotiations, and makes sentencing recommendations.

**Release on
Own Recognizance**–nonmonetary condition for the pretrial release of an accused individual; an alternative to monetary bail which is granted after a determination that the individual has ties in the community, has no prior record of default, and is likely to appear at subsequent proceedings.

**Stare Decisis**–(literally, "let the decision stand"); the practice by which courts apply legal precedent to cases involving similar circumstances. For example, the court decisions *Weeks v. United States* (1914) and *Wolf v. Colorado* (1949) were at one time the precedents for use of "tainted" evidence by the prosecution in state courts. From 1949 until 1961, the Supreme Court let that practice stand. The practice was overruled by *Mapp v. Ohio* (1961), which applied the Exclusionary Rule to the states.

**Search Warrant**–a court order authorizing and directing a police officer to search designated premises for articles and property stated in the order.

**Sentence**–the criminal sanction imposed by the court upon a convicted defendant, usually in the form of a fine, incarceration, or probation. Sentencing may be carried out by a judge, jury, or sentencing council (panel of judges), depending on the statutes of the jurisdiction.

**Substantive Law**–statutes which define criminal offenses and establish punishments.

**Summons**–an alternative to arrest usually used for petty or traffic offenses; a written order notifying an individual that he has been charged with an offense. A *summons* directs him to appear in court to answer that charge. It is used primarily in instances of low risk where the person will not be required to appear at later date. The summons is advantageous to the police officer in that he is freed from the time normally spent for arrest and booking procedures; it is advantageous to the accused in that he is spared time in jail.

**Supreme Court**–the only federal court establised by the constitution (Article III). The Court has original jurisdiction—i.e., the power to try a case, to determine the facts and law concerning a particular dispute or offense—in cases involving ambassadors, public ministers, and consuls; cases in which the United States is involved; and controversies between the states. The Court has appellate jurisdiction (i.e., the right to review lower court decisions) over cases from state courts of last resort which raise substantial federal questions and over federal lower court decisions.

**Trial**–the examination of an issue before an appropriate court; in a criminal case, the issue is guilt or innocence and the criterion of proof is *beyond a reasonable doubt*; in civil proceedings the issue is liability and extent of damages and the criterion of proof is *preponderance* (greater weight or amount) *of evidence*. A trial may take place before a judge (bench trial) or before judge and jury (trial by jury).

**Venue**–(literally, "the locus of trial"); that place designated by the location of the alleged offense, the court having jurisdiction, and the community from which the jury is selected.

This legal concept, embodied in the sixth amendment, holds that criminal proceedings should be held in places in which the offense was committed (jurisdiction of the larger "district" or county.) An individual may waive this right and request a *change of venue,* usually on the basis that he feels pre-trial publicity would preclude a fair trial in that locale.

**Waiver**–the act of voluntarily relinquishing a right or advantage; often used in the context of waiving one's right to counsel (e.g., Miranda Warning) or waiving certain steps in the criminal justice process (e.g., the preliminary hearing). Essential to waiver is the voluntary consent of the individual.

**Warrant**–a written order issued by a competent magistrate authorizing a police officer or other official to perform duties relating to the administration of justice.

(The first ten Amendments, usually called the Bill of Rights, went into effect December 15, 1791.)

## Amendment I

Congress shall make no law respecting an establishment of religion, or prohibiting the free exercise thereof; or abridging the freedom of speech or of the press; or the right of the people peaceably to assemble, and to petition the government for a redress of grievances.

## Amendment II

A well-regulated militia being necessary to the security of a free state, the right of the people to keep and bear arms shall not be infringed.

## Amendment III

No soldier shall, in time of peace, be quartered in any house without the consent of the owner, nor in time of war but in a manner to be prescribed by law.

## Amendment IV

The right of the people to be secure in their persons, houses, papers, and effects, against unreasonable searches and seizures, shall not be violated, and no warrants shall issue but upon probable cause, supported by oath or affirmation, and particularly describing the place to be searched, and the persons or things to be seized.

## Amendment V

No person shall be held to answer for a capital or other infamous crime unless on a presentment or indictment of a grand jury, except in cases arising in the land or naval forces, or in the militia, when in actual service, in time of war or public danger; nor shall any person be subject for the same offence to be twice put in jeopardy of life or limb; nor shall be compelled in any criminal case to be a witness against himself, nor be deprived of life, liberty, or property, without due process of law; nor shall private property be taken for public use without just compensation.

## Amendment VI

In all criminal prosecutions, the accused shall enjoy the right to a speedy and public trial, by an impartial jury of the state and district wherein the crime shall have been committed, which district shall have been previously ascertained by law, and to be informed of the nature and cause of the accusation; to be confronted with the witnesses against him; to have compulsory process for obtaining witnesses in his favor, and to have the assistance of counsel for his defence.

## Amendment VII

In suits at common law, where the value in controversy shall exceed twenty dollars, the right of trial by jury shall be preserved, and no fact tried by a jury shall be otherwise re-examined in any court of the United States than according to the rules of the common law.

## Amendment VIII

Excessive bail shall not be required, nor excessive fines imposed, nor cruel and unusual punishments inflicted.

## Amendment IX

The enumeration in the Constitution of certain rights shall not be construed to deny or disparage others retained by the people.

## Amendment X

The powers not delegated to the United States by the Constitution, nor prohibited by it to the states, are reserved to the states respectively, or to the people.

## Amendment XIV
## (adopted 1868)

*Section 1.* All persons born or naturalized in the United States, and subject to the jurisdiction thereof, are citizens of the United States and of the state wherein they reside. No state shall make or enforce any law which shall abridge the privileges or immunities of citizens of the United States; nor shall any state deprive any person of life, liberty, or property without due process of law; nor deny to any person within its jurisdiction the equal protection of the law.

Numbers in boldface refer to pages
where definitions are given.

†